THE HISTORIANS
OF ANCIENT ROME

THE HISTORIANS
OF ANCIENT ROME

EDITED BY Ronald Mellor

ROUTLEDGE   New York & London

Published in 1998 by
Routledge
29 West 35th Street
New York, NY 10001

Published in Great Britain by
Routledge
11 New Fetter Lane
London EC4P 4EE

Library of Congress Cataloging-in-Publication Data

The historians of ancient Rome / edited by Ronald Mellor.
    p. cm.
  ISBN 0-415-91267-9 (hardcover). -- ISBN 0-415-91268-7 (pbk.)
  1. Rome--History.   I. Mellor, Ronald.
DG207.H57 1997
937--dc21   97-21974
                                            CIP

For my brother John Mellor,
like the Romans, a lover of *panem et circenses*

CONTENTS

PREFACE

This collection grew out of my frustration in trying to find translated sources for my students in Roman history or western civilization courses. Forcing undergraduates to buy several volumes each, for example, of Livy and Tacitus taxed my conscience, since even paperback books can quickly exhaust a student's budget. Since few college libraries can afford to purchase multiple copies of source material, I have tried to provide a rich selection of the most important literary sources for Roman history. I have profited from the advice of students and colleagues and, while this selection remains a personal one, I hope it will provide an adequate collection for most courses in the subject.

There has also been a growing interest in ancient history among the general population, and I hope this book will provide a handy collection of what the Romans (and a few Greeks) themselves say over six hundred years about Roman history. In my general Introduction, I have tried to sketch the development of Roman historical and biographical writing, and also to provide short introductions situating the historians in the political and literary contexts of their time. A select bibliography will direct the more intrepid reader to complete translations and modern scholarship.

My graduate students — Trevor Bond, Stephen Chappell, and Jason Moralee — served as excellent research assistants. William Germano of Routledge, who published my earlier book, *Tacitus*, encouraged me in this project and has been supportive in every way. I think Bill and I both wished to continue a commercial relationship that provides a respectable professional veneer for our many passionate conversations about opera. I am grateful to my wife Anne for many things, here specifically for her editorial revision of the Introduction.

I dedicate the book to my brother John Mellor. It is the only ploy I can think of to force him to read about the Romans whom he resembles in so many ways.

Los Angeles
April, 1997

INTRODUCTION

To be ignorant of what has happened before your birth is to remain
always a child. For what is the meaning of a man's life unless it is
intertwined with that of our ancestors by history?

(Cicero *Orator* 120)

From Legend to History

The Romans' deep devotion to their past is evident in their literature, their
political and legal institutions, their religion, and their funeral celebrations.
They were proud of their traditions—what had begun as family memories
became over the centuries a collective national mystique. Cicero provides an
important reminder that for the Romans the past was a validation of their
present greatness: it had to be preserved to give meaning to the present. Thus
the heroic legends of Rome's past were transformed from oral traditions into
written epic poems, and later the same stories, such as the exploits of Romulus, became the material of historical prose.

The Roman orator and statesman Marcus Tullius Cicero (106–43 B.C.E.)
never wrote history as such, but he wrote thoughtfully about how and why
history should be written. He said that history should be both useful and
moral: useful in keeping the statesman aware of precedents in law, foreign
policy, and military affairs; moral in providing models of conduct from
Rome's past to help its leaders act virtuously. By linking the present with the
past, history would illuminate the contemporary state of society and provide
both moral and practical guidance. Thus a Roman was encouraged to imitate
the personal and civic virtues of his ancestors in the Forum or on the battlefield. This closely intertwined code of public and private conduct was
called the *mos maiorum*—"the traditions of our ancestors"—and formed the
core of moral and political education at Rome.

Roman historical writing must, therefore, do more than tell pleasant stories; it must make moral judgments. While the Greeks used philosophy to
discuss the moral dimension of political issues, the Romans used history.
Both Sallust and Tacitus saw the problem of Rome's "decline" as a moral

question. These historians do not merely ask what occurred and how, but most importantly, why certain events came about.

History at Rome was so closely tied to public life that most historians were in fact senators, writing for other senators. As a result, Roman historical writing has a narrow focus on political and military events. Schoolteachers and the general public might look elsewhere for stories of the past: poetry, biographies, and collections of anecdotes. But if the general reading public was less interested in history than in poetry, senatorial historians cared little since their work was an extension of political life and was aimed at those who held political power in Rome.

The Beginnings of Roman Historiography

Greeks had been writing history for three centuries before the first Roman turned his hand to historical prose at the end of the third century B.C.E. But the Romans had long preserved the real or imagined achievements of their ancestors. To keep the memory of their ancestors alive, wax masks were displayed in funerals at which elaborate speeches would link the deceased with his (or her) forebears across the centuries. Such speeches, suitably embellished, were passed on from generation to generation so that the imagined past might guide the present.

Besides family records, the Romans preserved various public documents. The Twelve Tables were set up in the Forum, and the Romans displayed copies of treaties like those with Carthage that **Polybius*** transcribed. Other public decrees were also preserved, but the most important early records were the *annales Maximi* kept by the chief priest (*Pontifex Maximus*). These annual lists recorded the names of high officials, military triumphs, religious prodigies, and other important events. They were probably reliable only for the third and second century, since most earlier records would have been destroyed in the Gallic sack of the city in 390 B.C.E.

During the third century B.C.E., Rome extended its control over the Greek city-states of southern Italy and of Sicily. There the Romans ₋ncountered bilingual Greeks, including local historians like the Sicilian Greek Timaeus. Greek historical writing had begun with studies of the lands and customs of different peoples, and Greeks regarded travel and research as essential preparation for writing history. Writers like Herodotus and Thucydides were able to display sympathy with each side in their accounts of the Persian and Peloponnesian wars.

Though Greek models were available, the Roman tradition of writing history developed differently. From the beginning, Roman historical writing

*Historians in **bold-face** have selections included in this volume.

was narrower in scope and less tolerant in its attitudes. Roman historians began with an interest in the political life of Rome, and their chauvinism allowed little sympathy for Rome's opponents. It was a polemical, partisan, and moralizing history, first used against Rome's enemies and later against opposing factions in the internal struggles in Roman political life.

As in Greece, Rome's past was first treated by epic poets, though only fragments of their work survived. Naevius (270–201 B.C.E.) wrote of the First Punic War, and he included in his poem a bitter attack on an important Roman family, the Metelli. Their revenge was to send Naevius to prison, where he died. This very first Roman "historian" learned to his cost that history at Rome was an extension of political life. Naevius and other epic poets were the first written sources of Roman national history.

The first Roman to write prose history was the senator Q. Fabius Pictor who, about 200 B.C.E., wrote an account of early Roman history. He wrote in Greek, for there was as yet little written prose in Latin; Greek was the normal language for an international audience in the Hellenistic world. Syrians, Egyptians, Babylonians, Jews, and Carthaginians had all begun to use Greek for literary works and philosophical discourse. Fabius' aim was to explain Roman policy and values to the Greek world in the period when the Greeks were increasingly interested in Rome. Fabius stitched together Greek writings and Roman traditions to champion Rome's moral superiority. In the few fragments that survive, it is evident that Fabius provided a strongly nationalistic, and aristocratic, history characterized by his praise for the wisdom of the senate, especially the Fabian family, and by his scorn for the stupidity of the popular assembly.

Historians of the Roman Republic

The first historian to write in Latin was M. Porcius Cato (234–149 B.C.E.). His *Origines*, which only survives in fragments quoted by later authors, traced Rome's history from the beginning down to 149 B.C.E. Although Cato presented himself as a conservative who despised corrupting foreign influences, his history displays many characteristics of Greek historiography: interest in geography and customs, and the inclusion of speeches. He relied on Greek sources for the early books, and his treatment is much more detailed in the books covering his own lifetime. Cato viewed the Roman people as sovereign, and resented the glory that Fabius attached to Roman noble families. His partisan support of the plebeians and opposition to the Scipios set a precedent for the partisan nature of later Roman political history. Though Cato's contempt for the personality cult of the Scipios led him to omit the names of aristocratic consuls, this disdain for personal aggrandizement did not restrain him from including his own speeches in the book. Cato's main purpose in writing history was to provide political and moral instruction for Rome's future political leaders, but he also began the tradition of Roman political autobiography.

For a century after Cato there survive only fragments of those "annalistic" historians derided both now and in antiquity. With the pontifical annals as a model, these historians provided a year-by-year account of the major officials and important events, but such a structure obviously precluded treatment of longer-term political, social, or economic tendencies. They invented episodes to embellish bare names and dates, and one annalist even wrote fifteen books on the period before 389 B.C.E., of which almost nothing could have been known. The sparse record of the distant past was also expanded by the anachronistic treatment of legal and constitutional questions. The political and ideological controversies of contemporary Rome were imposed upon the shadowy past to create a nationalistic pseudohistory. During the political struggles of the first century B.C.E. the annalists turned with equal invention to contemporary history and devised fictions to attack or defend the Gracchi, to praise or damn Sulla. Valerius Antias went so far as to invent documents. This corpus of untrustworthy material was almost all that Roman historiography had achieved by the end of the republic.

Though history as yet barely existed as a literary genre, **Julius Caesar** (100–44 B.C.E.) had written his autobiographical accounts of both the Gallic and Civil Wars. These were in the form of a memoir *(commentarius)* that pretended to be a personal diary of the bare facts. Thus a *commentarius* was not a literary work in itself; Sulla called his own *commentarius* nothing more than the "raw material of history." Caesar saw an opportunity to present his own version of his wars in Gaul in the form of an unpretentious factual account. The *Gallic War* is in fact far from a general's dull reminiscences; it is a skillful work of propaganda by a literary master who was also a poet and a great orator. Caesar later ruled Rome until his assassination in 44 B.C.E.

To the Roman mind Caesar's *commentarii* were not histories. There are no reflective prefaces or background information to set the work in its historical context, nor is there any clear moral purpose. The *Gallic War* was written in a bare, precise style that brings clarity and swiftness to the narrative. Referring to himself in the third person, Caesar endows the book with an aura of plain-spoken objectivity that can deceive the unguarded reader. Here, as the Latin epigram says, "art lies in concealing artifice."

When Caesar's contemporary Cicero speculated on the theory of history, he distinguished history from poetry by its devotion to truth, yet he believed literary ability to be absolutely essential and had only contempt for the inept products of the annalists. Rhetorical training was fundamental if the historian was to make his work persuasive and affect future political life, which Cicero believed should be his goal. Here, as so often in his work,

Cicero explores the link between oratory and political action, since in republican Rome the most effective orators were in fact leading political figures. Although Cicero was Rome's greatest historical theorist, his political interests and perhaps a fear of making even more enemies kept him from doing for history what he had done for oratory and philosophy: creating a Latin genre based on Greek achievements, but with a uniquely Roman style and form.

The first surviving Roman historical monographs were written by **Sallust** (86–35 B.C.E.) after his enforced retirement from public life. That corrupt politician chronicled the decline of Roman morality while living in his notoriously luxurious villa. He presented the collapse of old Roman virtue in a state where political faction was merely a mask for personal ambition and greed. The crisis of the Republic was for Sallust a moral crisis in which the political instability resulted from the abandonment of traditional values.

Sallust employed a novelist's skill in dramatizing scenes and presenting vivid portraits of historical personalities in an acerbic, epigrammatic style. Though the later rhetorician Quintilian called Sallust the "Roman Thucydides," he also warned students against adopting his style—it was too far from Ciceronian balance and harmony. The poet Martial called Sallust the greatest Roman historian, but it was Tacitus who paid him the highest compliment of imitating both his biting style and his bleak moral vision. Augustine and other Christian writers found his views congenial, and he was much quoted and copied in medieval monasteries.

Historians of the Empire

Roman historians were typically men of wide military and political experience who held high public office and served in the senate. **Livy** (ca. 59 B.C.E.–17 C.E.) was the outstanding exception. Born in Padua in northern Italy, he received excellent rhetorical training, although he never attained that fluency in Greek which characterized the Roman intellectual elite. Since Livy held no public posts, fought no wars, and seemingly had traveled little, his history depended almost totally on what he had learned from books. Like Sallust, Livy saw Rome's decline as a moral problem, though his political attitudes were quite the reverse of his predecessor: anti-Gracchan, pro-Sullan, and unsympathetic to Julius Caesar. Livy was a Ciceronian in his approach to politics as well as in style. If not as pessimistic as Sallust or Tacitus, Livy nonetheless waxes melancholic at the cost that imperial success had exacted of the Roman people: civil war, social disorder, and finally monarchy.

Livy wrote a massive history of Rome from the founding of the city (753 B.C.E.) to his own day—more than 700 years in 142 volumes, of which only 35 books survive. For the early centuries there was little hard evidence and even in antiquity Livy's accuracy was impugned. Though we may smile at the emperor Caligula's desire to burn the history as "verbose and careless," Quintilian's comment that Livy's work was more beautiful than truthful is harsh coming from a critic who so much prized style over content. Livy disdained to go even to the Capitol to consult a document, much less travel in Italy or beyond to examine inscriptions or visit battle sites. His version, including pieces of information taken from contradictory sources, is sometimes confused, and he retains patriotic annalistic inventions while concealing Roman brutality. He is honest but uncritical, warning his readers of the unreliability of the legends of earliest Rome while accepting incredible inventions from much later periods. He personally, however, did not invent fictions and he used some excellent sources, such as Polybius. If Livy does not satisfy our own standards of history, it must be said that he took the flawed tradition of annalistic historiography and improved it enormously.

The emperor **Augustus** was enough of a politician to write an autobiography giving his version of his personal accomplishments, but that book, like the autobiographies of the emperors Tiberius, Claudius, and Hadrian, has not survived. What has survived is Augustus' summary account of his achievements—the *Res Gestae*—once displayed in Rome on bronze tablets and surviving on an inscription carved in Latin and Greek in Ankara, Turkey. Augustus wrote almost half a century after many of the events and his majestic disregard for the squabbles and constitutional niceties of the dying republic was surely (in his own mind) vindicated by the establishment of peace and prosperity. The *Res Gestae* represents the retrospective view of the emperor in his seventy-seventh year.

The other great Roman historian, and in many ways Livy's polar opposite, was **Cornelius Tacitus** (55–117 C.E.). Tacitus had a successful political career until he held the praetorship in 88. He then was absent from Rome for five years and on his return preferred research to public life until the assassination of Domitian in 96. He was consul in 97 and was on good terms with the emperors Nerva and Trajan. His strong political views were formed in the terrible years of Domitian. While some senators groveled before the tyrant, others publicly opposed the regime and were executed. Tacitus chose to withdraw into voluntary exile and to yearn nostalgically for the *libertas* of the republic. Thus his writings display bitter resentment mixed with a certain defensiveness toward the senatorial martyrs. His ambivalence toward the principate is clear and his history has a thread of self-justification. Thus he attacks the tyrants but finds the Stoic opposition too inflexible. Tacitus' work shows political ideals and a sensitive conscience that he cannot easily reconcile with political reality. Though he professes to write "without anger or favor," Tacitus' histories are great precisely because they are written with such passion.

In his *Dialogue on Orators* Tacitus asserts the need to connect literature with political reality. To do this, Tacitus said, one must write history. The greatest achievement of Roman historiography is his history of the empire from the death of Augustus to the death of Domitian. He first wrote twelve books covering the period from the civil wars of 69 to 96. Of these, which we call the *Histories,* only four books and a fragment of the fifth survive. Tacitus then wrote eighteen books (*Annales*) on the Julio-Claudians. Although these books ostensibly retain the annalistic structure and begin each year with the names of the consuls, Tacitus transformed the genre and skillfully combined biography, ethnography, and rhetorical elements in the service of history.

Tacitus was far from a mere storyteller; he wrote history to pass moral and political judgments on the past and thereby affect the future. Since no autocrat can control the future, his fear of future condemnation should restrain his present cruelties. Therefore Tacitus creates one of the most compelling psychological portraits of tyranny in historical literature. Amidst all the carnage and intrigue, the historian holds before us models of dignity, liberty, and personal courage. Economic and sociological explanations hold no interest for Tacitus, nor do the far-off provinces. He is not writing a history of the empire, but of political life and the loss of liberty. In that he has no peer. He is interested not only in what happened, but also in the effects of words and deeds on the minds and characters of the rulers and the ruled. Gibbon regarded Tacitus as the supreme "philosophical historian," and his histories examine psychological and political issues that are still very much with us.

Tacitus marked the end of serious historical writing at Rome for 250 years. As the Roman creative spirit dried up in other intellectual and literary fields, so it did in history. Serious history was regarded as too long and too complex, so the age turned to abridgments and summaries. Important work was being done in Roman history during the second and third centuries, but it was written in Greek. **Appian of Alexandria**, Cassius Dio of Bithynia, and the Syrian Herodian all wrote books on Roman history far more significant than anything being written in Latin. In the fourth century Eutropius and Festus wrote abbreviated histories of Rome. In fifteen printed pages Festus covers the period from Rome's foundation to his own time so superficially that the Punic Wars are described with the simplistic phrase "three times Africa revolted."

The single exception was a Syrian Greek, **Ammianus Marcellinus** (330–ca. 395 C.E.), who served in the emperor Julian's army. After some years of travel, Ammianus settled in Rome about 378 and began to write history. His work is a continuation of Tacitus, and the history is a masterpiece. The breadth of his interests is extraordinary: he surveys not only the political and diplomatic history of his time but, rare in any ancient historian, also the administration and the bureaucracy. His attention to detail is impressive: wherever the work can be checked against independent Greek, Latin, or Syriac sources, Ammianus is confirmed. After two centuries of barrenness in Latin literature, the work of this Syrian Greek formed part of a final florescence of pagan Latin letters. He was the last of the great Roman historians and, one might well add, the last outstanding pagan writer of classical antiquity.

Roman Biography

Though biography was one of the popular literary forms in the ancient world, it was regarded as a genre inferior to history. Ancient biography began in fourth century Greece with a moral focus on character formation. Aristotle and his followers (called "Peripatetic" philosophers) taught than an individual's character was fixed, though it might be only gradually revealed. Thus there was an emphasis on certain character-types, such as the tyrant. Biography taught moral lessons by examining the character of famous men. The great biographer Plutarch acknowledged that he was interested in the souls of men and would leave "weighty matters and great battles to be treated by others." (*Life of Alexander* I)

Roman writers did not wholly depend on Greek models of biography, since there was a native Roman tradition of funeral orations. It was only in the first century B.C.E. that Latin writers produced formal biographies, as when Brutus wrote a eulogistic life of his hero Cato the Younger (which provoked Julius Caesar to respond with a pamphlet entitled *AntiCato*). Cornelius Nepos (ca. 99–24 B.C.E.) wrote sixteen books of *Lives of Famous Men*, including not only kings and generals—both Roman and foreign—but also philosophers, poets, historians, lawgivers, and orators. The book on foreign generals (including Hannibal) survives as do lives of Cato and Atticus from the book of Roman historians. Nepos' goal was to draw moral lessons, and his limited analytical ability did not allow him much insight into historical processes. He does, however, shed some light on his own time in the life of Atticus.

Tacitus' *Life of Agricola* is a mixture of biography and history, as the author used this tribute to his father-in-law as his apprenticeship for more serious history. On the other hand, Tacitus' contemporary **Suetonius** (c. 70–140 C.E.) was neither attracted by history nor by moral biography. Like Nepos, he wrote lives of both political and literary figures, but he is best known for his *Lives of the Twelve Caesars*, which began with Julius Caesar and ended with the death of Domitian in 96. This learned author served under Trajan as imperial librarian and took a scholarly approach to biography. His lives included letters, documents, physical descriptions of the emperors, random facts, and many anecdotes that would be far too vulgar for the high-minded histories of Livy or Tacitus. Since Suetonius did not select material to support a political argument, his hodgepodge of literary, cultural, and scientific history is especially valued by modern historians.

In late antiquity thirty biographies of emperors of the second and third centuries were gathered together under the title **"Writers of Augustan History."** These lives were modeled on Suetonius and likewise contain letters, documents, and official decrees. In fact, much of this material can be shown to have been fabricated, and even the names cited are frequently bogus. Though the manuscripts attribute the lives to six different writers, most scholars now believe they are the product of a single hand, writing about 395 C.E. and showing a pagan, senatorial bias. This is literary fraud on a grand scale, but modern scholars still cannot be certain of the motives for it. Some earlier lives, for which the author presumably had more reliable sources, seem to be more trustworthy than later lives.

The Historian's Craft

Though there was little documentary evidence for the early Republic, for the later period the oral traditions could be checked against preserved treaties, census records, laws, and decrees. During the first century B.C.E., Sulla built an enormous public record office and Julius Caesar had the minutes of the senate's proceedings recorded. Yet most Roman historians had limited interest in primary documentary material and preferred to gather material from the works of other historians. On several occasions Livy alludes to documents available in Rome that he has not bothered to consult personally.

Romans regarded the practice of history as an act of literary composition rather than research. Greek historians like Herodotus, Thucydides, and Polybius regarded research with primary material as essential, but Roman historians rarely discussed research in their methodological prefaces; they expected to rewrite the data already available. Most Roman historians relied on a single source for each section of a book, though they might allude to other historians who disagreed with the principal source. (A modern analogue might be the student who writes a term paper by paraphrasing one book while adding a few quotations from other books.) Of course the Roman writer would recast the material, even speeches and documents, into his own prose. The greatest historians might impress their conception and style on the material so effectively as to change it radically, but the fact remains that there was little genuine primary research. History was, in most cases, written from other books.

How accurate, then, were the Roman historians? Cicero calls attention to the lies contained in family records and says in an essay that the first law of history is "that an author must not dare to tell anything but the truth. And the second is that he must make bold to tell the whole truth." (*De oratore* 2.15.62) This is hardly surprising. But in a private letter Cicero asks a historian friend to "celebrate my exploits with even more enthusiasm than you perhaps feel, and in this case disregard the principles of history. . . . Indulge your affection for me a trifle more than even strict truth would allow." (*Letters to Friends* 5.12) The gap between high-minded theory and actual practice was considerable in the highly politicized world of the Roman elite.

Though most Roman historians wished to avoid untruths, they did not have the critical skills to evaluate their inconsistent evidence and they made no serious distinction between primary and secondary evidence. What was essential was not truth as much as verisimilitude, since the teachers of rhetoric had emphasized the importance of probability in constructing a persuasive narrative. (In a modern American courtroom, attorneys likewise are often more concerned with presenting a *plausible* scenario than in discovering the truth.) Sometimes this is helpful to the historian, as when he rejects stories of divine intervention on the battlefield. But often an historian accepts a story, unsupported though believable, at face value, as when Livy recounts events that had occurred seven centuries earlier. For Roman historians the important issues were always political and moral ones, not the accuracy of names and dates. Thus some historians concealed the fact that the Gauls had actually captured Rome in 390 B.C.E., and Cicero arbitrarily chose one of several versions of the death of Coriolanus. (At least Livy makes clear there were several versions.) Even Tacitus, through his language, dramatic construction, and use of innuendo, created a powerful picture quite at variance with the facts that he accurately reported. Tacitus was writing a moral history to address the larger truths of tyranny and political freedom. Concern with minor details was for a pedantic antiquarian, not an historian.

The Historian as Artist

Some Hellenistic historians wished above all to entertain. This often took the form, as in the tabloid press or the Gothic novel, of shock and horror that induced a most pleasurable pity. They brought poetic devices into their histories, which Lucian condemned as artificial beauty, like dressing an athlete to look like a harlot. Quintilian described history as "a poem in prose," and Cicero called the historian an "embellisher of events" *(exornator rerum)* who would bring pleasure by depicting changes of fortune. But these are rhetoricians with an outsider's view of history. The goal of a Tacitus or an Ammianus is not to forgo literary techniques in the interest of accuracy, but to deploy his considerable stylistic and rhetorical skills to present historical truth more convincingly.

By the first century B.C.E., Roman education had become rhetorical education, and all the great Roman historians display this rhetorical training. The use of rhetoric in their histories goes far beyond the construction of speeches to the use of language, the structure of argument, and the organization of episodes. Likewise, historians could characterize by juxtaposition so that Tacitus makes Nero and his mother Agrippina resemble Tiberius and Livia, and Sallust's Catiline lies behind Tacitus' portrait of Sejanus. These portraits, together with certain formulaic scenes (death scenes, battles, trials) appealed to the reader's own rhetorical training and thus enriched the texture of the historical narrative.

Cicero says that history consists of events and speeches, and speeches were indeed used by virtually every Roman historian as they had been by their Greek predecessors. For the early republic there could have been no evidence; thus the reported speeches are wholly fictitious, although certain themes may have been transmitted through Rome's very tenacious oral tradition. In Livy's account of Rome's conquest of the East, his speeches can be checked against the Greek versions in Polybius, who was a contemporary of those events. At times Livy reliably retained the substance of the speech, but sometimes he created both the occasion and the speech. It is Tacitus who provides the only opportunity to check a literary speech against the text as delivered. A bronze tablet has fortunately preserved Claudius' speech in C.E. 48 on the admission of Gauls to the senate. It is clear that Tacitus' version (*Annals* 11.24) preserved the substance while immeasurably improving its rhetorical force.

Historians regarded speeches as a method of analysis by which the motives of a character could be made explicit. A modern historian delivers analytical judgments in his own voice, but ancient historians preferred the dramatic and rhetorical mask of a speech. In Athens or republican Rome, a speech was a political act, and Sallust so records Caesar's and Cato's proposals for the Catilinarian conspirators. But the imperial historians realized that imperial autocracy had reduced speeches to occasions for display rather than for genuine persuasion. In an autocracy, speeches, indeed words in general, are used to disguise and conceal rather than to reveal the truth. Thus Tacitus and Ammianus used speeches far less frequently and then only where a speech was actually delivered.

The use of dramatic elements goes back to the origins of ancient historiography when Herodotus divided his work into dramatic episodes, but it was the Hellenistic historians who vastly expanded the use of drama and passed these traditions on to Rome. Since history, like tragedy, intended to recount the deeds of great men (real or mythic), there is a similar preference for personalities and the human element. Livy's account of the sack of Alba Longa paints an almost cinematic picture of personal and communal destruction. But it is Tacitus who employs the full array of dramatic devices: the dramatic prologue to an episode; foreboding built up by omens as well as mood; reversals of fate and dramatic irony. His story of Germanicus' death in *The Annals* is a more effective tragedy than any written for theatrical performance in the early empire. It is no surprise that the French classical dramatists Corneille and Racine found much tragic material in the work of the Roman historians.

As a literary artist, the Roman historian exercised great care over his Latin prose, since style itself revealed the author's attitudes. Livy's literary richness is well suited to a master story-teller of heroic achievements, but Sallust and Tacitus use a leaner, harsher, and more intense Latin to uncover political realities. If Livy's congenial narrative suited the exploits of Rome's past, the contemporary history of the late republic and early empire required more biting and wittily epigrammatic prose.

Although histories were still primarily intended for the political elite, the move to a wider audience in the first century B.C.E. led to public readings by historians. Though originally intended for small private parties, these recitations later moved to the theaters and the baths with enormous audiences sometimes in attendance. Livy's fame even reached Gades (Cadiz), whence an admirer came to Rome merely to see the historian. Oral recitations afforded publicity to the historian and entertainment to his audience and were particularly appropriate in a society in which even private reading was done aloud.

Conclusion

Roman historiography grew out of the political life of the city. Save for an occasional entertaining ethnographic digression, Roman history centered its interest resolutely on the public life of the Roman people, whether in the Forum, in the senate house, on the Palatine, or on military campaigns. Since their concern was Rome, the historians rarely found it necessary to leave the city in quest of evidence. Chauvinism and a resulting xenophobia were endemic, and there was little interest in the universal history that had so inspired their Greek forerunners.

There are of course differences between the narrow vision and rigid structure of the early annalists, Tacitus' flexible use of annalistic form, and Ammianus' broad range of interests and sympathies. This is hardly surprising; from Cato the Elder to Ammianus is a longer period than from Columbus to the present day. But the continuities over five centuries are far more extraordinary: though rhetorical in expression and parochial in its scope, Roman historiography never lost its lasting concern with the moral dimensions of political issues.

This concern led Roman historians to themes of universal importance. They looked nostalgically to a lost Golden Age and repeatedly explored the decline of republican Rome. Rome had not been conquered and her empire was larger than ever, but her moral values and political institutions had eroded from within. Conquest, wealth, and perhaps civilization itself had corrupted the free Roman people and left them the subjects of a new monarchy.

Moral historiography became the conscience of the Roman people, and it is in Sallust, Livy, Tacitus, and Ammianus that we find the most cogent Roman discussions of freedom versus tyranny, the corrupting effect of individual or civic power, and the decline of political and social institutions. And these remain central issues for the historian of any age.

The genre of history occupies an important place in Latin literature, but Roman historiography is more than a literary record of the past; it is an extension of political life. Speeches were political acts in republican Rome, and Tacitus did not turn to history to escape into the past but to take a political stance in his own time. The language of history functioned as a principal mechanism of political discourse and social analysis.

From antiquity to the present day, Roman history has been read for its examples of heroic conduct. Succeeding peoples have commemorated the Romans in poetry, drama, and painting. This goes beyond nostalgia. These texts kept the dream of liberty alive to be reborn in Cola di Rienzo's medieval Roman republic (1347–1354), the Italian communes of the Renaissance, and the American and French revolutions. Tacitus believed that the function of history is to affect the future and, by that standard, Roman historiography succeeded and continues to succeed. It remains, as Cicero hoped it would be, "the witness of the past, the light of truth, the survival of memory, the teacher of life, the message of antiquity" *(On Oratory 2.9.36).*

POLYBIUS

Life

Polybius was born in the Peloponnesian city of Megalopolis about 202 B.C.E. His father, Lycortas, became the leading figure in the Achaean League—an alliance of Greek city-states—and young Polybius held military office and also served on embassies. When the Achaean League rose in revolt against Roman domination, Lycortas was killed in 168 and Polybius was one of 1,000 Achaeans taken to Rome "to stand trial." In fact they were interned as hostages in cities throughout Italy until 152, when the 300 survivors were allowed to return to Greece.

During his years in exile this young Greek transformed himself into a great historian. At a time when the Roman nobles were becoming interested in Greek culture, Polybius' intelligence, education, and political shrewdness brought him into the intellectual circle of Scipio Aemilianus, the grandson of the conqueror of Hannibal. Under Scipio's patronage Polybius was able to travel throughout Italy, as well as gain access to private libraries and archives in Rome. He abandoned an earlier plan to write a history of the Achaean League; he decided instead to demonstrate to his fellow Greeks how the small city of Rome became in little more than a century the greatest power in the Mediterranean world.

With Scipio, Polybius traveled to Spain and Gaul even before his return to Greece. He was soon recalled to Rome to assist Scipio in his negotiations with Carthage. He remained with Scipio and the Roman army throughout the Third Punic War, which ended with the final destruction of Carthage in 146. He returned to Greece to help his people adjust to Roman rule after the destruction of Corinth. Little is known of his later years, but he did visit Alexandria and met King Ptolemy; he also knew other Hellenistic kings. He accompanied his friend Scipio in the Spanish war that resulted in the siege of Numantia. Polybius' monograph on that campaign is now lost. The historian died about 120— falling from a horse in his native Greece at the age of eighty-two.

Works

Polybius had a clear idea of his historiographic goals in producing his account of Roman history. He wished to write what he called "pragmatic history," which would be, above all, politically useful. In this, his model was Thucydides. A mere factual narrative was not sufficient; the historian must evaluate causes and connections to provide a truly useful explanation of how and why events occurred. Polybius was particularly contemptuous of the Hellenistic attitude toward historical writing as entertainment, and he often attacked by name historians whose books included mythical genealogies, tragic drama, or emotional scenes.

In Polybius' view, the ideal historian should not only search for truth, but he should be exceptionally well-prepared for his task. It was Polybius who first argued passionately for the importance of archival research and set out requirements for a historian:

1) political experience, to understand the actual practice of politics;

2) geographical knowledge, preferably from personal travel;

3) he should not only rely on earlier historians, but he should personally examine archives, inscriptions, and treaties.

Polybius' initial goal was to attempt a universal history in Greek of the period from 220 to 168 B.C.E. in thirty books. Later events caused him to extend the history through the fall of Carthage and Corinth to 144 in an additional ten books. Of the forty books, only the first five are fully preserved, while the others survive in large or small excerpts. The first two books set the background from the time of the first Punic War (264–241), and the narrative begins in the third book. Since Polybius believed that Rome's strength lay in her institutions, he devoted all of his sixth book to a description and analysis of the Roman constitution and the Roman army. He looked at the Roman constitution through the lens of Aristotle's political theory and found a "mixed constitution" with elements of monarchy, aristocracy, and democracy. Though this analysis presents an incorrect picture of Roman political life, it became enormously influential in the eighteenth century and formed the basis of the "balance of powers" in the United States constitution.

Though certain philosophical ideas have been attributed to Polybius, notably that history is cyclic and thus repeats itself, he was not a deep philosophical or religious thinker. As a well-educated Greek, he was aware of Stoic ideas, but he uses notions like Tyche (Fortune) in such a loose way that it actually undermines his own rational explanations of causation.

Polybius was not without bias: his Achaean birth prejudiced him against the Macedonian kings, just as his loyalty to Scipio led him to vilify Scipio's opponents. While his psychological and political analysis never reached the level of Thucycides, it is to Polybius that we owe the creation of history-writing as a professional calling. He set standards of analysis of sources, geographical and political knowledge, and practical experience that few later historians have been able to equal.

HISTORIES*

BOOK I I–14

Introduction. Polybius argues the importance of studying the history of the Romans and provides the background to the First Punic War (264–241 B.C.E.). He reflects on the historian's duty to truth.

1. Had the praise of History been passed over by former chroniclers, it would perhaps have been incumbent upon me to urge the choice and special study of records of this sort as the readiest means men can have of correcting their knowledge of the past. But my predecessors have not been sparing in this respect. They have all begun and ended, so to speak, by enlarging on this theme: asserting again and again that the study of History is in the truest sense an education and a training for political life, and that the most instructive, or rather the only, method of learning to bear with dignity the vicissitudes of fortune is to recall the catastrophes of others. It is evident, therefore, that no one need think it his duty to repeat what has been said by many, and said well. Least of all myself, for the surprising nature of the events which I have undertaken to relate is in itself sufficient to challenge and stimulate the attention of everyone, old or young, to the study of my work. Can anyone be so indifferent or idle as not to care to know by what means, and under what kind of polity, almost the whole inhabited world was conquered and brought under the dominion of the single city of Rome, and that, too, within a period of not quite fifty-three years (219–167 B.C.E.)? Or who again can be so completely absorbed in other subjects of contemplation or study, as to think any of them superior in importance to the accurate understanding of an event for which the past affords no precedent?

2. We shall best show how marvelous and vast our subject is by comparing the most famous empires which preceded and which have been the favorite themes of historians, and measuring them with the superior greatness of Rome. There are but three that deserve even to be so compared and

---

*Polybius. 1889. *The Histories of Polybius.* Translated by Evelyn Schuckburgh.

measured, and they are these: The Persians for a certain length of time were possessed of a great empire and dominion. But every time they ventured beyond the limits of Asia, they found not only their empire, but their own existence also in danger. The Spartans, after contending for supremacy in Greece for many generations, when they did get it, held it without dispute for barely twelve years (405–394 B.C.E.). The Macedonians obtained dominion in Europe from the lands bordering on the Adriatic to the Danube—which, after all, is but a small fraction of this continent—and, by the destruction of the Persian Empire, they afterwards added to that the dominion of Asia. And yet, though they had the credit of having made themselves masters of a larger number of countries and states than any people had ever done, they still left the greater half of the inhabited world in the hands of others. They never so much as thought of attempting Sicily, Sardinia, or Libya. And as to Europe, to speak the plain truth, they never even knew of the most warlike tribes of the West. The Roman conquest, on the other hand, was not partial. Nearly the whole inhabited world was reduced by them to obedience, and they left behind them an empire not to be paralleled in the past or rivaled in the future. Students will gain from my narrative a clearer view of the whole story and of the numerous and important advantages which such an exact record of events offers.

3. My History begins in the 140th Olympiad (220–217 B.C.E.). The events from which it starts are these: In Greece, what is called the Social War—the first waged by Philip, son of Demetrius and father of Perseus, in league with the Achaeans against the Aetolians. In Asia, the war for the possession of Coele-Syria, which Antiochus and Ptolemy Philopator carried on against each other. In Italy, Libya, and their neighborhood, the conflict between Rome and Carthage, generally called the Hannibalian War. My work thus begins where that of Aratus of Sicyon leaves off. Now up to this time the world's history had been, so to speak, a series of disconnected transactions, as widely separated in their origin and results as in their localities. But from this time forth, History becomes a connected whole: the affairs of Italy and Libya are involved with those of Asia and Greece, and the tendency of all is to unity. This is why I have fixed upon this era as the starting point of my work. For it was their victory over the Carthaginians in this war and their conviction that thereby the most difficult and most essential step towards universal empire had been taken, which encouraged the Romans for the first time to stretch out their hands upon the rest and to cross with an army into Greece and Asia.

Now, had the states that were rivals for universal empire been familiarly known to us, no reference perhaps to their previous history would have been necessary to show the purpose and the forces with which they approached an undertaking of this nature and magnitude. But the fact is that the majority of the Greeks have no knowledge of the previous constitution, power, or achievements either of Rome or Carthage. I therefore concluded that it was necessary to prefix this and the next book to my History. I was anxious that no one, when fairly embarked upon my actual narrative, should feel at a loss and have to ask what were the designs entertained by the Romans or the forces and means at their disposal, that they entered upon those undertakings, which did in fact lead to their becoming masters of land and sea everywhere in our part of the world. I wished, on the contrary, that these books of mine and the prefatory sketch which they contained might make it clear that the resources they started with justified their original idea, and sufficiently explained their final success in grasping universal empire and dominion.

4. There is this analogy between the plan of my History and the marvelous spirit of the age with which I have to deal. Just as Fortune made almost all the affairs of the world incline in one direction and forced them to converge upon one and the same point, so it is my task as an historian to put before my readers a compendious view of the part played by Fortune in bringing about the general catastrophe. It was this peculiarity which originally challenged my attention and determined me on undertaking this work. And combined with this was the fact that no writer of our time has undertaken a general history. Had anyone done so, my ambition in this direction would have been much diminished. But, in point of fact, I notice that by far the greater number of historians concern themselves with isolated wars and the incidents that accompany them, while as to a general and comprehensive scheme of events, their date, origin, and catastrophe, no one as far as I know has undertaken to examine it. I thought it, therefore, distinctly my duty neither to pass by myself nor allow anyone else to pass by, without full study, a characteristic specimen of the dealings of Fortune at once brilliant and instructive in the highest degree. For fruitful as Fortune is in change, and constantly as she is producing dramas in the life of men, yet never assuredly before this did she work such a marvel or act such a drama as that which we have witnessed. And of this we cannot obtain a comprehensive view from writers of mere episodes. It would be as absurd to expect to do so as for a man to imagine that he has learnt the shape of the whole world, its entire arrangement and order, because he has visited, one after the other, the most famous cities in it or perhaps merely examined them in separate pictures. That would be indeed absurd, and it has always seemed to me that men who are persuaded that they get a competent view of universal from episodic history are very like persons who should see the limbs of some body which had once been living and beautiful, scattered and remote, and should imagine that to be quite as good as actually beholding the activity and beauty of the living creature itself. But if someone could there and then reconstruct the animal once more in the perfection of its beauty and the charm of its vitality,

and could display it to the same people, they would beyond doubt confess that they had been far from conceiving the truth and had been little better than dreamers. For indeed some idea of a whole may be got from a part, but an accurate knowledge and clear comprehension cannot. Wherefore we must conclude that episodic history contributes exceedingly little to the familiar knowledge and secure grasp of universal history, while it is only by the combination and comparison of the separate parts of the whole—by observing their likeness and their difference—that a man can attain his object: can obtain a view at once clear and complete and thus secure both the profit and the delight of History.

5. I shall adopt as the starting-point of this book the first occasion on which the Romans crossed the sea from Italy. This is just where the History of Timaeus left off, and it falls in the 129th Olympiad (264–261 B.C.E.). I shall accordingly have to describe what the state of their affairs in Italy was, how long that settlement had lasted, and on what resources they reckoned, when they resolved to invade Sicily. For this was the first place outside Italy in which they set foot. The precise cause of their thus crossing I must state without comment, for if I let one cause lead me back to another, my point of departure will always elude my grasp, and I shall never arrive at the view of my subject which I wish to present. As to dates, then, I must fix on some era agreed upon and recognized by all. And as to events, one that admits of distinctly separate treatment, even though I may be obliged to go back some short way in point of time and take a summary review of the intermediate transactions. For if the facts with which one starts are unknown, or even open to controversy, all that comes after will fail of approval and belief. But opinion being once formed on that point, and a general assent obtained, all the succeeding narrative becomes intelligible.

6. It was in the nineteenth year after the sea fight at Aegospotami and the sixteenth before the battle at Leuctra; the year in which the Spartans made what is called the Peace of Antalcidas with the king of Persia; the year in which the elder Dionysius was besieging Rhegium after beating the Italian Greeks on the River Elleporus; and in which the Gauls took Rome itself by storm and were occupying the whole of it except the Capitol (387–386 B.C.E.). With these Gauls the Romans made a treaty and settlement which they were content to accept. And having thus become beyond all expectation once more masters of their own country, they made a start in their career of expansion and in the succeeding period engaged in various wars with their neighbors. First, by dint of valor and the good fortune which attended them in the field, they mastered all the Latini; then they went to war with the Etruscans; then with the Celts; and next with the Samnites, who lived on the eastern and northern frontiers of Latium. Some time after this the Tarentines insulted the ambassadors of Rome, and, in fear of the consequences, invited and obtained the assistance of Pyrrhus. This happened in the year before the Gauls invaded Greece, some of whom perished near Delphi, while others crossed into Asia (280 B.C.E.). Then it was that the Romans—having reduced the Etruscans and Samnites to obedience, and conquered the Italian Celts in many battles—attempted for the first time the reduction of the rest of Italy. The nations for whose possessions they were about to fight they affected to regard, not in the light of foreigners, but as already for the most part belonging and pertaining to themselves. The experience gained from their contests with the Samnites and the Celts had served as a genuine training in the art of war. Accordingly, they entered upon the war with spirit, drove Pyrrhus from Italy (274 B.C.E.), and then undertook to fight with and subdue those who had taken part with him. They succeeded everywhere to a marvel and reduced to obedience all the tribes inhabiting Italy except the Celts, after which they undertook to besiege some of their own citizens, who at that time were occupying Rhegium.

7. For misfortunes befell Messene and Rhegium, the cities built on either side of the Strait, peculiar in their nature and alike in their circumstances. Not long before the period we are now describing, some Campanian mercenaries of Agathocles, having for some time cast greedy eyes upon Messene, owing to its beauty and wealth, no sooner got an opportunity than they made a treacherous attempt upon that city. They entered the town under guise of friendship, and, having once got possession of it, they drove out some of the citizens and put others to the sword. This done, they seized promiscuously the wives and children of the dispossessed citizens, each keeping those which Fortune had assigned him at the very moment of the lawless deed. All other property and the land they took possession of by a subsequent division and retained. The speed with which they became masters of a fair territory and city found ready imitators of their conduct. The people of Rhegium, when Pyrrhus was crossing to Italy, felt a double anxiety. They were dismayed at the thought of his approach, and at the same time were afraid of the Carthaginians as being masters of the sea. They accordingly asked and obtained a force from Rome to guard and support them. The garrison, four thousand in number, under the command of a Campanian named Decius Jubellius, entered the city and for a time preserved it, as well as their own faith. But at last, conceiving the idea of imitating the Mamertines and having at the same time obtained their cooperation, they broke faith with the people of Rhegium, enamored of the pleasant site of the town and the private wealth of the citizens, and seized the city after having, in imitation of the Mamertines, first driven out some of the people and put others to the sword. Now, though the Romans were much annoyed at this transaction, they could take no active steps, because they were deeply engaged in the wars I have mentioned above. But having got free from them, they invested

and besieged the troops. They presently took the place and killed the greater number in the assault—for the men resisted desperately, knowing what must follow—but took more than three hundred alive. These were sent to Rome, and there the Consuls (271 B.C.E., C. Quintus Claudus, L. Genucius Clepsina) brought them into the forum, where they were scourged and beheaded according to custom, for they wished as far as they could to vindicate their good faith in the eyes of the allies. The territory and town they at once handed over to the people of Rhegium.

8. But the Mamertines (for this was the name which the Campanians gave themselves after they became masters of Messene), as long as they enjoyed the alliance of the Roman captors of Rhegium, not only exercised absolute control over their own town and district undisturbed, but about the neighboring territory also gave no little trouble to the Carthaginians and Syracusans and levied tribute from many parts of Sicily. But when they were deprived of this support, the captors of Rhegium being now invested and besieged, they were themselves promptly forced back into the town again by the Syracusans, under circumstances which I will now detail.

Not long before this the military forces of the Syracusans had quarreled with the citizens and while stationed near Mergane elected commanders from their own body. These were Artemidorus and Hiero (275–274 B.C.E.), the latter of whom afterwards became king of Syracuse. At this time he was quite a young man but had a certain natural aptitude for kingcraft and the politic conduct of affairs. Having taken over the command and having by means of some of his connections made his way into the city, he got his political opponents into his hands but conducted the government with such mildness and in so lofty a spirit, that the Syracusans, though by no means usually acquiescing in the election of officers by the soldiers, did on this occasion unanimously approve of Hiero as their general. His first step made it evident to close observers that his hopes soared above the position of a mere general.

9. He noticed that among the Syracusans the dispatch of troops and of magistrates in command of them was always the signal for revolutionary movements of some sort or another. He knew, too, that of all the citizens, Leptines enjoyed the highest position and credit and that among the common people especially he was by far the most influential man existing. He accordingly contracted a relationship by marriage with him, that he might have a representative of his interests left at home at such times as he should be himself bound to go abroad with the troops for a campaign. After marrying the daughter of this man, his next step was in regard to the old mercenaries. He observed that they were disaffected and mutinous, and he accordingly led out an expedition, with the ostensible purpose of attacking the foreigners who were in occupation of Messene. He pitched a camp against the enemy near Centuripa and drew up his line resting on the River Cyamosorus. But the cavalry and infantry, which consisted of citizens, he kept together under his personal command at some distance, on pretense of intending to attack the enemy on another quarter. The mercenaries he thrust to the front and allowed them to be completely cut to pieces by the foreigners while he seized the moment of their rout to effect a safe retreat for himself and the citizens into Syracuse. This stroke of policy was skillful and successful. He had got rid of the mutinous and seditious element in the army; and after enlisting on his own account a sufficient body of mercenaries, he thenceforth carried on the business of the government in security. But seeing that the Mamertines were encouraged by their success to greater confidence and recklessness in their excursions, he fully armed and energetically drilled the citizen levies, led them out, and engaged the enemy on the Mylaean plain near the River Longanus. He inflicted a severe defeat upon them (268 B.C.E.), took their leaders prisoners, put a complete end to their audacious proceedings, and on his return to Syracuse was himself greeted by all the allies with the title of King.

10. Thus were the Mamertines first deprived of support from Rhegium and then subjected, from causes which I have just stated, to complete defeat on their account. Thereupon some of them betook themselves to the protection of the Carthaginians and were for putting themselves and their citadel into their hands, while others set about sending an embassy to Rome to offer a surrender of their city and to beg assistance on the ground of the ties of race which united them. The Romans were long in doubt. The inconsistency of sending such aid seemed manifest. A little while ago they had put some of their own citizens to death, with the extreme penalties of the law, for having broken faith with the people of Rhegium. And now so soon afterwards to assist the Mamertines, who had done precisely the same to Messene as well as Rhegium, involved a breach of equity very hard to justify. But while fully alive to these points, they yet saw that Carthaginian aggrandizement was not confined to Libya, but had embraced many districts in Spain as well, and that Carthage was, besides, mistress of all the islands in the Sardinian and Tyrrhenian seas. They were beginning, therefore, to be exceedingly anxious lest, if the Carthaginians became masters of Sicily also, they should find them very dangerous and formidable neighbors, surrounding them as they would on every side and occupying a position which commanded all the coasts of Italy. Now it was clear that, if the Mamertines did not obtain the assistance they asked for, the Carthaginians would very soon reduce Sicily. For should they avail themselves of the voluntary offer of Messene and become masters of it, they were certain before long to crush Syracuse also, since they were already lords of nearly the whole of the rest of Sicily. The Romans saw all this, and felt that it was absolutely necessary not to let Messene slip or allow the Carthaginians to secure what would be like a bridge to enable them to cross into Italy.

11. In spite of protracted deliberations, the conflict of motives proved too strong, after all, to allow the Senate to come to any decision, for the inconsistency of aiding the Messenians appeared to them to be evenly balanced by the advantages to be gained by doing so. The people, however, had suffered much from the previous wars and wanted some means of repairing the losses which they had sustained in every department. Besides these national advantages to be gained by the war, the military commanders suggested that individually they would get manifest and important benefits from it. They accordingly voted in favor of giving the aid. The decree having thus been passed by the people, they elected one of the consuls, Appius Claudius, to the command and sent him out with instructions to cross to Messene and relieve the Mamertines (264 B.C.E.). These latter managed, between threats and false representations, to oust the Carthaginian commander who was already in possession of the citadel. They invited Appius in and offered to deliver the city into his hands. The Carthaginians crucified their commander for what they considered to be his cowardice and folly in thus losing the citadel, stationed their fleet near Pelorus and their land forces at a place called Synes, and laid vigorous siege to Messene. Now at this juncture Hiero, thinking it a favorable opportunity for totally expelling from Sicily the foreigners who were in occupation of Messene, made a treaty with the Carthaginians. Having done this, he started from Syracuse upon an expedition against that city. He pitched his camp on the opposite side to the Carthaginians, near what was called the Chalcidian Mount, whereby the garrison were cut off from that way out as well as from the other. The Roman Consul Appius, for his part, gallantly crossed the strait by night and got into Messene (264 B.C.E.). But he found that the enemy had completely surrounded the town and were vigorously pressing on the attack, and he concluded on reflection that the siege could bring him neither credit nor security so long as the enemy commanded land as well as sea. He accordingly first endeavored to relieve the Mamertines from the contest altogether by sending embassies to both of the attacking forces. Neither of them received his proposals, and at last, from sheer necessity, he made up his mind to hazard an engagement and to begin with the Syracusans. So he led out his forces and drew them up for the fight. Nor was the Syracusan backward in accepting the challenge, but descended simultaneously to give him battle. After a prolonged struggle, Appius got the better of the enemy and chased the opposing forces right up to their entrenchments. The result of this was that Appius, after stripping the dead, retired into Messene again, while Hiero, with a foreboding of the final result, only waited for nightfall to beat a hasty retreat to Syracuse.

12. Next morning, when Appius was assured of their flight, his confidence was strengthened, and he made up his mind to attack the Carthaginians without delay. Accordingly, he issued orders to the soldiers to dispatch their preparations early and at daybreak commenced his sally. Having succeeded in engaging the enemy, he killed a large number of them and forced the rest to fly precipitately to the neighboring towns. These successes sufficed to raise the siege of Messene, and thenceforth he scoured the territory of Syracuse and her allies with impunity and laid it waste without finding anyone to dispute the possession of the open country with him, and finally he sat down before Syracuse itself and laid siege to it.

Such was the nature and motive of the first warlike expedition of the Romans beyond the shores of Italy, and this was the period at which it took place. I thought this expedition the most suitable starting point for my whole narrative and accordingly adopted it as a basis, though I have made a rapid survey of some anterior events, that in setting forth its causes no point should be left obscure. I thought it necessary, if we were to get an adequate and comprehensive view of their present supreme position, to trace clearly how and when the Romans, after the disaster which they sustained in the loss of their own city, began their upward career and how and when, once more, after possessing themselves of Italy, they conceived the idea of attempting conquests external to it. This must account in future parts of my work for my taking, when treating of the most important states, a preliminary survey of their previous history. In doing so my object will be to secure such a vantage ground as will enable us to see with clearness from what origin, at what period, and in what circumstances they severally started and arrived at their present position. This is exactly what I have just done with regard to the Romans.

13. It is time to have done with these explanations and to come to my subject, after a brief and summary statement of the events of which my introductory books are to treat. Of these, the first in order of time are those which befell the Romans and Carthaginians in their war for the possession of Sicily (264–241 B.C.E.). Next comes the Libyan or Mercenary War (240–237 B.C.E.), immediately following on which are the Carthaginian achievements in Spain (241–218 B.C.E.), first under Hamilcar and then under Hasdrubal. In the course of these events, again, occurred the first expedition of the Romans into Illyria (229–228 B.C.E.) and the Greek side of Europe and, besides that, their struggles within Italy with the Celts (225–221 B.C.E.). In Greece at the same time the war called after Cleomenes was in full action (227–221 B.C.E.). With this war I design to conclude my prefatory sketch and my second book.

To enter into minute details of these events is unnecessary and would be of no advantage to my readers. It is not part of my plan to write a history of them. My sole object is to recapitulate them in a summary manner by way of introduction to the narrative I have in hand. I will, therefore, touch lightly upon the leading events of this period in a comprehensive sketch and will endeavor to make the end of it dovetail with the commencement of my main history. In this way the narrative will acquire a continuity, and I shall be shown to have had good reason for touching on points already treated by others, while by such an arrangement the studiously inclined will find the approach to the story which has to be told made intelligible and easy for them. I shall, however, endeavor to describe with somewhat more care the first war which arose between the Romans and Carthaginians for the possession of Sicily. For it would not be easy to mention any war that lasted longer than this one nor one in which the preparations made were on a larger scale or the efforts made more sustained or the actual engagements more numerous or the reverses sustained on either side more signal. Moreover, the two states themselves were at the precise period of their history when their institutions were as yet in their original integrity, their fortunes still at a moderate level, and their forces on an equal footing. So that those who wish to gain a fair view of the national characteristics and resources of the two had better base their comparison upon this war rather than upon those which came after.

14. But it was not these considerations only which induced me to undertake the history of this war. I was influenced quite as much by the fact that Philinus and Fabius,[1] who have the reputation of writing with the most complete knowledge about it, have given us an inadequate representation of the truth. Now, judging from their lives and principles, I do not suppose that these writers have intentionally stated what was false, but I think that they are much in the same state of mind as men in love. Partisanship and complete prepossession made Philinus think that all the actions of the Carthaginians were characterized by wisdom, honor, and courage: those of the Romans by the reverse. Fabius thought the exact opposite. Now in other relations of life one would hesitate to exclude such warmth of sentiment, for a good man ought to be loyal to his friends and patriotic to his country; ought to be at one with his friends in their hatreds and likings. But directly a man assumes the moral attitude of an historian he ought to forget all considerations of that kind. There will be many occasions on which he will be bound to speak well of his enemies and even to praise them in the highest terms if the facts demand it, and, on the other hand, many occasions on which it will be his duty to criticize and denounce his own side, however dear to him, if their errors of conduct suggest that course. For as a living creature is rendered wholly useless if deprived of its eyes, so if you take truth from History, what is left is but an idle, unprofitable tale. Therefore, one must not shrink either from blaming one's friends or praising ones enemies nor be afraid of

---

[1]The Sicilian Greek Philinus was secretary of Hannibal and later wrote a pro-Carthaginian history of the Punic Wars, while the Roman annalist Fabius Pictor wrote (in Greek) a pro-Roman history. Polybius regarded them both as overly partisan.

finding fault with and commending the same persons at different times. For it is impossible that men engaged in public affairs should always be right, and unlikely that they should always be wrong. Holding ourselves, therefore, entirely aloof from the actors, we must as historians make statements and pronounce judgment in accordance with the actions themselves.

BOOK II 1–2; 7–12

Rome's first military involvement with Illyricum across the Adriatic Sea. Polybius' reflections on the rash invitations given to foreign forces.

1. In the previous book I have described how the Romans, having subdued all Italy, began to aim at foreign dominion; how they crossed to Sicily; and the reasons of the war which they entered into against the Carthaginians for the possession of that island. Next I stated at what period they began the formation of a navy and what befell both the one side and the other up to the end of the war, the consequence of which was that the Carthaginians entirely evacuated Sicily, and the Romans took possession of the whole island, except such parts as were still under the rule of Hiero. Following these events, I endeavored to describe how the mutiny of the mercenaries against Carthage, in what is called the Libyan War, burst out; the lengths to which the shocking outrages in it went; its surprises and extraordinary incidents, until its conclusion; and the final triumph of Carthage. I must now relate the events which immediately succeeded these, touching summarily upon each in accordance with my original plan.

As soon as they had brought the Libyan War to a conclusion (238 B.C.E.) the Carthaginian government collected an army and dispatched it under the command of Hamilcar to Spain. This general took over the command of the troops and with his son Hannibal, then nine years old, crossing by the Pillars of Hercules, set about recovering the Carthaginian possessions in Spain. He spent nine years in Spain (238–229 B.C.E.), and after reducing many Spanish tribes by war or diplomacy to obedience to Carthage, he died in a manner worthy of his great achievements; for he lost his life in a battle against the most warlike and powerful tribes, in which he showed a conspicuous and even reckless personal gallantry. The Carthaginians appointed his son-in-law Hasdrubal to succeed him, who was at the time in command of the fleet.

2. It was at this same period that the Romans for the first time crossed to Illyricum and that part of Europe with an army. The history of this expedition must not be treated as immaterial. It must be carefully studied by those who wish to understand clearly the story I have undertaken to tell, and to trace the progress and consolidation of the Roman Empire.

§

7. That men, in the infirmity of human nature, should fall into misfortunes which defy calculation is the fault not of the sufferers but of Fortune and of those who do the wrong. But that they should, from mere levity and with their eyes open, thrust themselves upon the most serious disasters is without dispute the fault of the victims themselves. Therefore it is that pity and sympathy and assistance await those whose failure is due to Fortune: reproach and rebuke from all men of sense await those who have only their own folly to thank for it.

§

8. To return to the Illyrians. From time immemorial they had oppressed and pillaged vessels sailing from Italy. Now while their fleet was engaged at Phoenice a considerable number of them, separating from the main body, committed acts of piracy on a number of Italian merchants (230 B.C.E.). Some they merely plundered, others they murdered, and a great many they carried off alive into captivity. Though complaints against the Illyrians had reached the Roman government in times past, they had always been neglected; but now when more and more persons approached the Senate on this subject, they appointed two ambassadors, Gaius and Lucius Coruncanius, to go to Illyricum and investigate the matter. But on the arrival of her galleys from Epirus, the enormous quantity and beauty of the spoils which they brought home (for Phoenice was by far the wealthiest city in Epirus at that time), so fired the imagination of Queen Teuta, that she was doubly eager to carry on the predatory warfare on the coasts of Greece. At the moment, however, she was stopped by the rebellion at home. But it had not taken her long to put down the revolt in Illyria, and she was engaged in besieging Issa, the last town which held out, when just at that very time the Roman ambassadors arrived. A time was fixed for their audience, and they proceeded to discuss the injuries which their citizens had sustained. Throughout the interview, however, Teuta listened with an insolent and disdainful air. When they had finished their speech, she replied that she would endeavor to take care that no injury should be inflicted on Roman citizens by Illyrian officials but that it was not the custom for the sovereigns of Illyria to hinder private persons from taking booty at sea. Angered by these words, the younger of the two ambassadors used a plainness of speech which, though thoroughly to the point, was rather ill-timed. "The Romans," he said, "O Teuta, have a most excellent custom of using the State for the punishment of private wrongs and the redress of private grievances. And we will endeavor, God willing, before long to compel you to improve the relations between the sovereign and the subject in Illyria." The queen received this plain speaking with wom-

anish passion and unreasoning anger. So enraged was she at the speech that, despite the conventions universally observed among mankind, she dispatched some men after the ambassadors as they were sailing home, to kill the one who had used this plainness. Upon this being reported at Rome the people were highly incensed at the queen's violation of the law of nations and at once set about preparations for war, enrolling legions and collecting a fleet.

9. When the season for sailing was come, Teuta sent out a larger fleet of galleys than ever against the Greek shores, some of which sailed straight to Corcyra (229 B.C.E.), while a portion of them put into the harbor of Epidamnus on the pretext of taking in victuals and water, but really to attack the town. The Epidamnians received them without suspicion and without taking any precautions. Entering the town therefore clothed merely in their tunics, as though they were only come to fetch water, but with swords concealed in the water vessels, they slew the guards stationed at the gates and in a brief space were masters of the gate-tower. Being energetically supported by a reinforcement from the ships, which came quickly up in accordance with a prearrangement, they got possession of the greater part of the walls without difficulty. But though the citizens were taken off their guard, they made a determined and desperate resistance, and the Illyrians, after maintaining their ground for some time, were eventually driven out of the town. So the Epidamnians on this occasion went near to losing their city by their carelessness; but by the courage which they displayed they saved themselves from actual damage while receiving a useful lesson for the future. The Illyrians who had engaged in this enterprise made haste to put to sea and, rejoining the advanced squadron, put in at Corcyra. There, to the terror of the inhabitants, they disembarked and set about besieging the town. Dismayed and despairing of their safety, the Corcyreans, acting in conjunction with the people of Apollonia and Epidamnus, sent off envoys to the Achaean and Aetolian leagues, begging for instant help and entreating them not to allow of their being deprived of their homes by the Illyrians. The petition was accepted, and the Achaean and Aetolian leagues combined to send aid. The ten-decked ships of war belonging to the Achaeans were manned and, having been fitted out in a few days, set sail for Corcyra in hopes of raising the siege.

10. But the Illyrians obtained a reinforcement of seven-decked ships from the Acarnanians, in virtue of their treaty with that people and, putting to sea, engaged the Achaean fleet off the islands called Paxi. The Acarnanian and Achaean ships fought without victory declaring for either and without receiving any further damage than having some of their crew wounded. But the Illyrians lashed their galleys four together and, caring nothing for any damage that might happen to them, grappled with the enemy by throwing their galleys athwart their prows and encouraging them to charge. When the enemies' prows struck them and got entangled by the lashed-together galleys getting hitched on to their forward gear, the Illyrians leaped upon the decks of the Achaean ships and captured them by the superior number of their armed men. In this way they took four triremes and sunk one quinquereme with all hands. On board this quinquereme was Margos of Caryneia, who had all his life served the Achaean league with complete integrity. The vessels engaged with the Acarnanians, seeing the triumphant success of the Illyrians and trusting to their own speed, hoisted their sails to the wind and effected their voyage home without further disaster. The Illyrians, on the other hand, filled with self-confidence by their success, continued their siege of the town in high spirits and without putting themselves to any unnecessary trouble. The Corcyreans, reduced to despair of safety by what had happened, after sustaining the siege for a short time longer, made terms with the Illyrians, consenting to receive a garrison and with it Demetrius of Pharos. After this had been settled, the Illyrian admirals put to sea again and, having arrived at Epidamnus, once more set about besieging that town.

11. In this same season one of the consuls, Gnaeus Fulvius, started from Rome with two hundred ships, and the other consul, Aulus Postumius, with the land forces (229 B.C.E.). The plan of Gnaeus was to sail direct to Corcyra, because he supposed that he should find the result of the siege still undecided. But when he found that he was too late for that, he determined nevertheless to sail to the island because he wished to know the exact facts as to what had happened there and to test the sincerity of the overtures that had been made by Demetrius. For Demetrius, being in disgrace with Teuta and afraid of what she might do to him, had been sending messages to Rome, offering to put the city and everything else of which he was in charge into their hands. Delighted at the appearance of the Romans, the Corcyreans not only surrendered the garrison to them with the consent of Demetrius, but committed themselves also unconditionally to the Roman protection, believing that this was their only security in the future against the piratical incursions of the Illyrians. So the Romans, having admitted the Corcyreans into the number of the allies of Rome, sailed for Apollonia with Demetrius to act as their guide for the rest of the campaign. At the same time the other consul, Aulus Postumius, conveyed his army across from Brundisium, consisting of twenty thousand infantry and about two thousand horsemen. This army as well as the fleet under Gnaeus Fulvius being directed upon Apollonia, which at once put itself under Roman protection, both forces were again put in motion on news being brought that Epidamnus was being besieged by the enemy. No sooner did the Illyrians learn the approach of the Romans than they hurriedly broke up the siege and fled. The Romans, taking the Epidamnians under their protection, advanced into the interior of Illyricum, subdu-

ing the Ardiaei as they went. They were met on their march by envoys from many tribes. Those of the Parthini offered an unconditional surrender, as also did those of the Atintanes. Both were accepted, and the Roman army proceeded towards Issa, which was being besieged by Illyrian troops. On their arrival, they forced the enemy to raise the siege and received the Issaeans also under their protection. Besides, as the fleet coasted along, they took certain Illyrian cities by storm, among which was Nutria, where they lost not only a large number of soldiers, but some of the military tribunes also and the quaestor. But they captured twenty of the galleys which were conveying the plunder from the country.

Of the Illyrian troops engaged in blockading Issa, those that belonged to Pharos were left unharmed, as a favor to Demetrius, while all the rest scattered and fled to Arbo. Teuta herself, with a very few attendants, escaped to Rhizon, a small town very strongly fortified and situated on the river of the same name. Having accomplished all this and having placed the greater part of Illyria under Demetrius and invested him with a wide dominion, the consuls retired to Epidamnus with their fleet and army.

12. Then Gnaeus Fulvius sailed back to Rome with the larger part of the naval and military forces, while Postumius, staying behind and collecting forty vessels and a legion from the cities in that district wintered there to guard the Ardiaei and other tribes that had committed themselves to the protection of Rome. Just before spring in the next year, Teuta sent envoys to Rome and concluded a treaty (228 B.C.E.) in virtue of which she consented to pay a fixed tribute and to abandon all Illyricum with the exception of some few districts. And what affected Greece more than anything, she agreed not to sail beyond Lissus with more than two galleys, and those unarmed. When this arrangement had been concluded, Postumius sent legates to the Aetolian and Achaean leagues, who on their arrival first explained the reasons for the war and the Roman invasion and then stated what had been accomplished in it and read the treaty which had been made with Illyrians. The envoys then returned to Corcyra after receiving the thanks of both leagues, for they had freed Greece by this treaty from a very serious cause for alarm, the fact being that the Illyrians were not the enemies of this or that people, but the common enemies of all alike.

Such were the circumstances of the first armed interference of the Romans in Illyricum and that part of Europe, and their first diplomatic relations with Greece; such, too, were the motives which suggested them. But having thus begun, the Romans immediately afterwards sent envoys to Corinth and Athens. And it was then that the Corinthians first admitted Romans to take part in the Isthmian games.

BOOK III   **I; 4; 6–17; 20–30**

The siege of Saguntum (220 B.C.E.) and causes of the Second Punic War (218–202 B.C.E.). Polybius critiques the account of Fabius Pictor, and quotes the three early treaties between Rome and Carthage.

1. I stated in my first book that my work was to start from the Social war, the Hannibalian war, and the war for the possession of Coele-Syria. In the same book I stated my reasons for devoting my first two books to a sketch of the period preceding those events. I will now, after a few prefatory remarks as to the scope of my own work, address myself to giving a complete account of these wars, the causes which led to them, and which account for the proportions to which they attained.

The one aim and object, then, of all that I have undertaken to write is to show how, when, and why all the known parts of the world fell under the dominion of Rome. Now as this great event admits of being exactly dated as to its beginning, duration, and final accomplishment, I think it will be advantageous to give, by way of preface, a summary statement of the most important phases in it between the beginning and the end. For I think I shall thus best secure to the student an adequate idea of my whole plan; for as the comprehension of the whole is a help to the understanding of details, and the knowledge of details of great service to the clear conception of the whole; believing that the best and clearest knowledge is that which is obtained from a combination of these, I will preface my whole history by a brief summary of its contents.

I have already described its scope and limits. As to its several parts, the first consists of the above mentioned wars, while the conclusion or closing scene is the fall of the Macedonian monarchy. The time included between these limits is fifty-three years; and never has an equal space embraced events of such magnitude and importance. In describing them I shall start from the 140th Olympiad (220 B.C.E.). . .

§

4. And if our judgment of individuals and constitutions, for praise or blame, could be adequately formed from a simple consideration of their successes or defeats, I must necessarily have stopped at this point, and have concluded my history as soon as I reached these last events in accordance with my original plan. For at this point the fifty-three years were coming to an end, and the progress of the Roman power had arrived at its consummation. And, besides, by this time the acknowledgment had been extorted from all that the supremacy of Rome must be accepted, and her commands obeyed. But in truth, judgments of either side founded on the bare facts of success or failure in the field are by no means final. It has often happened that what seemed the most signal successes have, from ill management, brought the most crushing disasters in their train; while not infrequently the most terrible calamities, sustained with spirit, have been turned to actual advantage. I am bound, therefore, to add to my statement of facts a discussion on the subsequent policy of the conquerors, and their administration of their universal dominion: and again on the various feelings and opinions entertained by other nations towards their rulers. And I must also describe the tastes and aims of the several nations, whether in their private lives or public policy. The present generation will learn from this whether they should shun or seek the rule of Rome; and future generations will be taught whether to praise and imitate, or to decry it. The usefulness of my history, whether for present or future, will mainly lie in this. For the end of a policy would not be, in the eyes either of the actors or their historians, simply to conquer others and bring all into subjection. Nor does any man of sense go to war with his neighbors for the mere purpose of mastering his opponents; nor go to sea for the mere sake of the voyage; nor engage in professions and trades for the sole purpose of learning them. In all these cases the objects are invariably the pleasure, honor, or profit which are the results of the several employments. Accordingly the object of this work shall be to ascertain exactly what the position of the several states was, after the universal conquest by which they fell under the power of Rome, until the commotions and disturbances which broke out at a later period. These I designed to make the starting-point of what may almost be called a new work, partly because of the greatness and surprising nature of the events themselves, but chiefly because, in the case of most of them, I was not only an eye-witness, but in some cases one of the actors, and in others the chief director.

§

6. Some historians of the Hannibalian war, when they wish to point out to us the causes of this contest between Rome and Carthage, allege first the siege of Saguntum by the Carthaginians and, secondly, their breach of treaty by crossing the river called by the natives the Ebro. But though I should call these the first actions in the war, I cannot admit them to be its causes. One might just as well say that the crossing of Alexander the Great into Asia was the *cause* of the Persian war (334 B.C.E.), and the descent of Antiochus upon Demetrias the *cause* of his war with Rome (192 B.C.E.). In neither would it be a probable or true statement. In the first case, this action of Alexander's could not be called the cause of a war, for which both he and his father Philip in his lifetime had made elaborate preparations. In the second case, we know that the Aetolian league had done the same, with a view to a war with Rome, before Antiochus came upon the scene. Such definitions are only worthy of men who cannot distinguish between a first overt act and a cause or pretext and who do not perceive that a *cause* is the first in a series of events of which such an overt act is the last. I shall therefore regard the first attempt to put into execution what had already been determined as a "beginning," but I shall look for "causes" in the motives which suggested such action and the policy which dictated it; for it is by these, and the calculations to which they give rise, that men are led to decide upon a particular line of conduct. The soundness of this method will be proven by the following considerations. The true causes and origin of the invasion of Persia by Alexander are patent to everybody. They were, first, the return march of the Greeks under Xenophon through the country from the upper Satrapies (401–400 B.C.E.), in the course of which, though throughout Asia all the populations were hostile, not a single barbarian ventured to face them. The second cause was the invasion of Asia by the Spartan king, Agesilaus, (396–394 B.C.E.) in which, though he was obliged by troubles in Greece to return in the middle of his expedition without effecting his object, he yet found no resistance of any importance or adequacy. It was these circumstances which convinced Philip of the cowardice and inefficiency of the Persians. Comparing them with his own high state of efficiency for war and with that of his Macedonian subjects, and placing before his eyes the splendor of the rewards to be gained by such a war and the popularity which it would bring him in Greece, he seized on the pretext of avenging the injuries done by Persia to Greece. He determined with great eagerness to undertake this war. He was, in fact, at the time of his death engaged in making every kind of preparation for it. Here we have the *cause* and the *pretext* of the Persian war. Alexander's expedition into Asia was the *first action* in it.

7. So, too, of the war of Antiochus with Rome. The *cause* was evidently the exasperation of the Aetolians, who, thinking that they had been slighted in a number of instances at the end of the war with Philip, not only called in the aid of Antiochus, but resolved to go to every extremity in satisfying the anger which the events of that time had aroused in them. This was the *cause.* As for the *pretext*, it was the liberation of Greece, which they went from city to city with Antiochus proclaiming, without regard to reason or truth. The *first act* in the war was the descent of Antiochus upon Demetrias.

My object in enlarging upon this distinction is not to attack the historians in question, but to rectify the ideas of the studious. A physician can do no good to the sick who does not know the causes of their ailments; nor can a statesman do any good who is unable to conceive the manner, cause, and source of the events with which he has from time to time to deal. Surely the former could not be expected to institute a suitable system of treatment for the body; nor the latter to grapple with the exigencies of the situation, without possessing this knowledge of its elements. There is nothing, therefore, which we ought to be more alive to, and to seek for, than the causes of every event which occurs. For the most important results are often produced by trifles; and it is invariably easier to apply remedial measures at the beginning, before things have got beyond the stage of conception and intention.

8. Now the Roman annalist Fabius asserts that the cause of the Hannibalian War, besides the injury inflicted upon Saguntum, was the encroaching and ambitious spirit of Hasdrubal. "Having secured great power in Spain, he returned to Libya with the design of destroying the constitution and reducing Carthage to a despotism. But the leading statesmen, getting timely warning of his intention, banded themselves together and successfully opposed him. Suspecting this, Hasdrubal retired from Libya and thenceforth governed Spain entirely at his own will without taking any account whatever of the Carthaginian Senate. This policy had had in Hannibal from his earliest youth a zealous supporter and imitator. When he succeeded to the command in Spain, he continued it. Accordingly, even in the case of this war with Rome, he was acting on his own authority and contrary to the wish of the Carthaginians, for none of the men of note in Carthage approved of his attack upon Saguntum." This is the statement of Fabius, who goes on to say that after the capture of that city an embassy arrived in Carthage from Rome demanding that Hannibal should be given up on pain of a declaration of war.

Now what answer could Fabius have given if we had put the following question to him? "What better chance or opportunity could the Carthaginians have had of combining justice and interest? According to your own account, they disliked the proceeding of Hannibal. Why did they not submit to the demands of Rome by surrendering the author of the injury and thus get rid of the common enemy of the state without the odium of doing it themselves, and secure the safety of their territory by ridding themselves of the threatened war—all of which they could have effected by merely passing a decree?" If this question were put, I say, it would admit of no answer. The fact is that, far from doing anything of the sort, they maintained the war in accordance with Hannibal's policy for seventeen years. They refused to make terms until, at the end of a most determined struggle, they found their own city and persons in imminent danger of destruction.

9. I do not allude to Fabius and his annals from any fear of their wearing such an air of probability in themselves as to gain any credit—for the fact is that his assertions are so contrary to reason, that it does not need any argument of mine to help his readers to perceive it—but I wished to warn those who take up his books not to be misled by the authority of his name, but to be guided by facts. For there is a certain class of readers in whose eyes the personality of the writer is of more account than what he says. They look to the fact that Fabius was a contemporary and a member of the Senate, and they assume without more ado that everything he says may be trusted. My view, however, is that we ought not to hold the authority of this writer lightly. Yet at the same time, we should not regard it as all-sufficient. In reading his writings we should test them by a reference to the facts themselves.

This is a digression from my immediate subject, which is the war between Carthage and Rome. The cause of this war we must reckon to be the exasperation of Hamilcar surnamed Barcas, the father of Hannibal. The result of the war in Sicily had not broken the spirit of that commander. He regarded himself as unconquered, for the troops at Eryx which he commanded were still sound and undismayed. Though he yielded so far as to make a treaty, it was a concession to the exigencies of the times brought on by the defeat of the Carthaginians at sea. But he never relaxed in his determined purpose of revenge, and had it not been for the mutiny of the mercenaries at Carthage, he would at once have sought and made another occasion for bringing about a war, as far as he was able to do so. As it was, he was preoccupied by the domestic war and had to give his attention entirely to that.

10. When the Romans, at the conclusion of this Mercenary War, proclaimed war with Carthage (238 B.C.E.), the latter at first was inclined to resist at all hazards, because the goodness of her cause gave her hopes of victory—as I have shown in my former book, without which it would be impossible to understand adequately either this or what is to follow. The Romans, however, would not listen to anything. The Carthaginians therefore yielded to the force of circumstances. Feeling bitterly aggrieved, yet being quite unable to do anything, they evacuated Sardinia and consented to pay a sum of twelve hundred talents in addition to the former indemnity paid them, on condition of avoiding the war at that time. This is the second and the most important cause of the subsequent war. For Hamilcar, having this public grievance in addition to his private feelings of anger, as soon as he had secured his country's safety by reducing the rebellious mercenaries, set at once about securing the Carthaginian power in Spain with the intention of using it as a base of operations against Rome. So I record as a third cause of the war the Carthaginian success in Spain, for it was the confidence inspired by their forces there which encouraged them to embark upon it. It would be easy to adduce other facts to show that Hamilcar, though he had been dead ten years at its commencement, largely contributed to bringing about the second Punic War, but what I am about to say will be sufficient to establish the fact.

11. When, after his final defeat by the Romans, Hannibal had at last quit his country and was staying at the court of Antiochus, the warlike attitude of the Aetolian league induced the Romans to send ambassadors to Antiochus, that they might be informed of the king's intentions. These ambassadors found that Antiochus was inclined to the Aetolian alliance and was eager for war with Rome. They accordingly paid great court to Hannibal with a view of bringing him into suspicion with the king (195 B.C.E.). And in this they

entirely succeeded. As time went on the king became ever more and more suspicious of Hannibal, until at length an opportunity occurred for an explanation of the alienation that had been thus secretly growing up between them. Hannibal then defended himself at great length, but without success, until at last he made the following statement: "When my father was about to go on his Spanish expedition (238 B.C.E.), I was nine years old. As he was offering the sacrifice to Zeus, I stood near the altar. The sacrifice successfully performed, my father poured the libation and went through the usual ritual. He than bade all the other worshippers stand a little back and, calling me to him, asked me affectionately whether I wished to go with him on his expedition. Upon my eagerly assenting and begging with boyish enthusiasm to be allowed to go, he took me by the right hand and led me up to the altar and bade me lay my hand upon the victim and swear that I would never be friends with Rome. So long, then, Antiochus, as your policy is one of hostility to Rome, you may feel quite secure of having in me a most thoroughgoing supporter. But if ever you make terms or friendship with her, then you need not wait for any slander to make you distrust me and be on your guard against me; for there is nothing in my power that I would not do against her."

12. Antiochus listened to this story and, being convinced that it was told with genuine feeling and sincerity, gave up all his suspicions. And we, too, must regard this as an unquestionable proof of the animosity of Hamilcar and of the aim of his general policy, which, indeed, is also proved by facts. For he inspired his son-in-law Hasdrubal and his son Hannibal with a bitterness of resentment against Rome which nothing could surpass. Hasdrubal, indeed, was prevented by death from showing the full extent of his purpose; but time gave Hannibal abundant opportunity to manifest the hatred of Rome which he had inherited from his father.

The most important thing, then, for statesmen to observe is the motives of those who lay aside old enmities or form new friendships and to ascertain when their consent to treaties is a mere concession to the necessities of the hour, and when it is the indication of a real consciousness of defeat. In the former case they must be on their guard against such people lying in wait for an opportunity. In the latter they may unhesitatingly impose whatever injunctions are necessary, in full reliance on the genuineness of their feelings whether as subjects or friends. So much for the causes of the war. I will now relate the first actions in it.

13. The Carthaginians were highly incensed by their loss of Sicily, but their resentment was heightened still more, as I have said, by the transaction as to Sardinia and by the addition recently made to their tribute. Accordingly, when the greater part of Spain had fallen into their power, they were on the alert to seize any opportunity that presented itself of retaliating upon Rome. At the death of Hasdrubal (221 B.C.E.), to whom they had committed the com-

mand in Spain after the death of Hamilcar (229 B.C.E.), they waited at first to ascertain the feelings of the army; but when news came from thence that the troops had elected Hannibal as commander-in-chief, a popular assembly was at once held, and the choice of the army confirmed by a unanimous vote. As soon as he had taken over the command, Hannibal set out to subdue the tribe of the Olcades. Having arrived before their most formidable city, Althaea, he pitched his camp under its walls. By a series of energetic and formidable assaults he succeeded before long in taking it. Thus the rest of the tribe were overawed into submission to Carthage. Having imposed a contribution upon the towns, and thus become possessed of a large sum of money, he went to the New Town to winter. There, by a liberal treatment of the forces under his command, giving them an installment of their pay at once and promising the rest, he established an excellent feeling towards himself in the army, as well as great hopes for the future.

14. Next summer (220 B.C.E.) he set out on another expedition against the Vaccaei, in which he took Salmantica by assault, but only succeeded in storming Arbucala, owing to the size of the town and the number and valor of its inhabitants, after a laborious siege. After this he suddenly found himself in a position of very great danger on his return march. He was set upon by the Carpesii, the strongest tribe in those parts, who were joined also by neighboring tribes, incited principally by refugees of the Olcades, but roused also to great wrath by those who escaped from Salmantica. If the Carthaginians had been compelled to give these people regular battle, there can be no doubt that they would have been defeated. As it was, Hannibal, with admirable skill and caution, slowly retreated until he had put the Tagus between himself and the enemy. Giving battle at the crossing of the stream, supported by it and the elephants, of which he had about forty, he gained, to everyone's surprise, a complete success. For when the barbarians attempted to force a crossing at several points of the river at once, the greater number of them were killed as they left the water by the elephants, who marched up and down along the brink of the river and caught them as they were coming out. Many of them also were killed in the river itself by the cavalry, because the horses were better able than the men to stand against the stream, and also because the cavalry were fighting on higher ground than the infantry which they were attacking. At length Hannibal turned the tables on the enemy and, recrossing the river, attacked and put to flight their whole army, to the number of more than a hundred thousand men. After the defeat of this host, no one south of the Ebro rashly ventured to face him except the people of Saguntum. From that town Hannibal tried his best to keep aloof because, acting on the suggestions and advice of his father Hamilcar, he did not wish to give the Romans an avowed pretext for war until he had thoroughly secured the rest of the country.

15. But the people of Saguntum kept sending ambassadors to Rome (winter of 220–219 B.C.E.), partly because they foresaw what was coming and trembled for their own existence, and partly that the Romans might be kept fully aware of the growing power of the Carthaginians in Spain. For a long time the Romans disregarded their words, but now they sent out some commissioners to see what was going on. Just at that time Hannibal had finished the conquests which he intended for that season and was going into winter quarters at the New Town again, which was in a way the chief glory and capital town of the Carthaginians in Spain. He found there the embassy from Rome, granted them an interview, and listened to the message with which they were charged. It was a strong injunction to him to leave Saguntum alone, as being under the protection of Rome, and not to cross the Ebro, in accordance with the agreement come to in the time of Hasdrubal. To this Hannibal answered with all the heat of youth, inflamed by martial ardor, recent success, and his long-standing hatred of Rome. He charged the Romans with having a short time before—when, on some political disturbances arising in the town, they had chosen to act as arbitrators—seized the opportunity to put some of the leading citizens to death. He declared that the Carthaginians would not allow the Saguntines to be thus treacherously dealt with, for it was the traditional policy of Carthage to protect all persons so wronged. At the same time he sent home for instructions as to what he was to do "in view of the fact that the Saguntines were injuring certain of their subject allies." And altogether he was in a state of unreasoning anger and violent exasperation, which prevented him from availing himself of the real causes for war and made him take refuge in pretexts which would not admit of justification, after the manner of men whose passions master all considerations of equity. How much better it would have been to demand of Rome the restoration of Sardinia and the remission of the tribute, which she had taken an unfair opportunity to impose on pain of a declaration of war. As it was, he said not a word of the real cause, but alleged the fictitious one of the matter of Saguntum. Thus he got the credit of beginning the war, not only in defiance of reason, but still more in defiance of justice. The Roman ambassadors, finding that there must undoubtedly be a war, sailed to Carthage to enter the same protest before the people there. They expected, however, that they would have to fight not in Italy, but in Spain, and that they would have Saguntum as a base of operations.

16. Wherefore the Senate, by way of preparing to undertake this business, and foreseeing that the war would be severe and protracted and at a long distance from the mother country, determined to make Illyria safe. For it happened that, just at this time (219 B.C.E.), Demetrius of Pharos was sacking and subduing to his authority the cities of Illyria which were subject to Rome, and had sailed beyond Lissus, in violation of the treaty, with fifty galleys, and had ravaged many of the Cyclades. For he had quite forgotten the former kindness done him by Rome and had conceived a contempt for its power, when he saw it threatened first by the Gauls and then by Carthage. He now rested all his hopes on the royal family of Macedonia, because he had fought on the side of Antigonus and shared with him the dangers of the war against Cleomenes. These transactions attracted the observation of the Romans, who, seeing that the royal house of Macedonia was in a flourishing condition, were very anxious to secure the country east of Italy. They felt convinced that they would have ample time to correct the rash folly of the Illyrians and rebuke and chastise the ingratitude and temerity of Demetrius. But they were deceived in their calculations. For Hannibal anticipated their measures by the capture of Saguntum. The result of this was that the war took place not in Spain, but close to Rome itself, and in various parts throughout all Italy. However, with these ideas fixed in their minds, the Romans dispatched Lucius Aemilius just before summer (219 B.C.E.) to conduct the Illyrian campaign in the first year of the 140th Olympiad.

17. But Hannibal had started from New Carthage and was leading his army straight against Saguntum. This city is situated on the seaward foot of the mountain chain on which the frontiers of Spain and Celtiberia converge, and is about seven stades from the sea. The district cultivated by its inhabitants is exceedingly productive and has a soil superior to any in all of Spain. Under the walls of this town Hannibal pitched his camp and set energetically to work on the siege, foreseeing many advantages that would accrue if he could take it. Of these, the first was that he would thereby disappoint the Romans in their expectation of making Spain the seat of war. A second was that he would thereby strike a general terror, which would render the already obedient tribes more submissive, and the still independent ones more cautious of offending him. But the greatest advantage of all was that thereby he would be able to push on his advance without leaving an enemy on his rear. Besides these advantages, he calculated that the possession of this city would secure him abundant supplies for his expedition and create an enthusiasm in the troops excited by individual acquisitions of booty, while he would conciliate the goodwill of those who remained at Carthage by the spoils which would be sent home. With these ideas he pressed on the siege with energy, sometimes setting an example to his soldiers by personally sharing in the fatigues of throwing up the siege works, and sometimes cheering on his men and recklessly exposing himself to danger. After a siege extending to the eighth month, in the course of which he endured every kind of suffering and anxiety, he finally succeeded in taking the town. An immense booty in money, slaves, and property fell into his hands, which he disposed of in accordance with his original design. The money he reserved for the needs of his projected expedition; the slaves were distributed according to merit among

his men; while the property was at once sent entire to Carthage. The result answered his expectations: the army was rendered more eager for action; the home populace more ready to grant whatever he asked; and he himself was enabled, by the possession of such abundant means, to carry out many measures that were of service to his expedition.

§

20. But when news came to Rome of the fall of Saguntum, there was indeed no debate on the question of war, as some historians assert, who even add the speeches delivered on either side. But nothing could be more ridiculous. For is it conceivable that the Romans should have, a year before, proclaimed war with the Carthaginians in the event of their entering the territory of Saguntum, and yet, when the city itself had been taken, should have debated whether they should go to war or no? Just as absurd are the wonderful statements that the senators put on mourning and that the fathers introduced their sons above twelve years old into the Senate house, who, being admitted to the debate, refrained from divulging any of its secrets even to their nearest relations. All this is as improbable as it is untrue, unless we are to believe that Fortune, among its other bounties, granted the Romans the privilege of being men of the world from their cradles. I need not waste any more words upon such compositions as those of Chaereas and Sosilus, which, in my judgment, are more like the gossip of the barber's shop and the pavement than history.

The truth is that when the Romans heard of the disaster at Saguntum, they at once elected envoys, whom they dispatched in all haste to Carthage with the offer of two alternatives. One appeared to the Carthaginians to involve disgrace as well as injury if they accepted it, while the other was the beginning of a great struggle and of great dangers. For one of these alternatives was the surrender of Hannibal and his staff to Rome; the other was war. When the Roman envoys arrived and declared their message to the Senate, the choice proposed to them between these alternatives was listened to by the Carthaginians with indignation. Still they selected the most capable of their number to state their case, which was grounded on the following pleas.

21. Passing over the treaty made with Hasdrubal as not having ever been made and, if it had, as not being binding on them because made without their consent (and on this point they quoted the precedent of the Romans themselves, who in the Sicilian war repudiated the terms agreed upon and accepted by Lutatius, as having been made without their consent)—passing over this, they pressed with all the vehemence they could, throughout the discussion, the last treaty made in the Sicilian War. They affirmed that there was no clause in it relating to Spain, but one expressly providing security for the allies of both parties to the treaty. Now, they pointed out that the Saguntines at that time were not allies of Rome and therefore were not protected by the clause. To prove their point, they read the treaty more than once aloud. On this occasion the Roman envoys contented themselves with the reply that, while Saguntum was intact, the matter in dispute admitted of pleadings and of a discussion on its merits; but that, that city having been treacherously seized, they had only two alternatives: either to deliver the persons guilty of the act and thereby make it clear that they had no share in their crime and that it was done without their consent, or, if they were not willing to do that and avowed their complicity in it, to take the consequences.

The question of treaties between Rome and Carthage was referred to in general terms in the course of this debate. But I think a more particular examination of it will be useful both to practical statesmen, who require to know the exact truth of the matter in order to avoid mistakes in any critical deliberation, and to historical students, that they may not be led astray by the ignorance or partisan bias of historians, but may have before them a conspectus, acknowledged to be accurate, of the various compacts which have been made between Rome and Carthage from the earliest times to our own day.

22. The first treaty between Rome and Carthage was made in the year of Lucius Junius Brutus and Marcus Horatius (509–508 B.C.E.), the first consuls appointed after the expulsion of the kings, by which men also the temple of Jupiter Capitolinus was consecrated. This was twenty-eight years before the invasion of Greece by Xerxes. Of this treaty I append a translation, as accurate as I could make it—for the fact is that the ancient language differs so much from that at present in use that the best scholars among the Romans themselves have great difficulty in interpreting some points in it, even after much study. The treaty is as follows:

> There shall be friendship between the Romans and their allies, and the Carthaginians and their allies, on these conditions:
>
> Neither the Romans nor their allies are to sail beyond the Fair Promontory, unless driven by stress of weather or the fear of enemies. If any one of them be driven ashore he shall not buy or take anything for himself save what is needful for the repair of his ship and the service of the gods, and he shall depart within five days.
>
> Men landing for traffic shall strike no bargain save in the presence of a herald or town clerk. Whatever is sold in the presence of these, let the price be secured to the seller on the credit of the state—that is to say, if such sale be in Libya or Sardinia.
>
> If any Roman comes to the Carthaginian province in Sicily, he shall enjoy all rights enjoyed by others. The Carthaginians shall do no injury to the people of Ardea, Antium, Laurentium, Circeii, Tarracina, nor any other people of the Latins that are subject to Rome.

From those townships even which are not subject to Rome they shall hold their hands; and if they take one, shall deliver it unharmed to the Romans. They shall build no fort in Latium; and if they enter the district in arms, they shall not stay a night therein.

23. The "Fair Promontory" here referred to is that which lies immediately to the north of Carthage. South of this the Carthaginians stipulated that the Romans should not sail with ships of war, because, as I imagine, they did not wish them to be acquainted with the coast near Byzacium, or the lesser Syrtis, which places they call Emporia, owing to the productiveness of the district. The treaty then goes on to say that if any one of them is driven thither by stress of weather or fear of an enemy, and stands in need of anything for the worship of the gods and the repair of his vessel, this and no more he may take; and all those who have come to anchor there must necessarily depart within five days. To Carthage and all the country on the Carthaginian side of the Fair Promontory in Libya, to Sardinia, and the Carthaginian province of Sicily, the treaty allows the Romans to sail for mercantile purposes; and the Carthaginians engage their public credit that such persons shall enjoy absolute security. It is clear from this treaty that the Carthaginians speak of Sardinia and Libya as belonging to them entirely; but, on the other hand, make a distinction in the case of Sicily and only stipulate for that part of it which is subject to Carthage. Similarly, the Romans also only stipulate concerning Latium. The rest of Italy they do not mention, as not being under their authority.

24. After this treaty there was a second (348 B.C.E.?), in which we find that the Carthaginians have included the Tyrians and the township of Utica in addition to their former territory. To the Fair Promontory, Mastia and Tarseium are added, as the points beyond which the Romans are not to make marauding expeditions or found a city. The treaty is as follows:

There shall be friendship between the Romans and their allies, and the Carthaginians, Tyrians, and township of Utica, on these terms: The Romans shall not maraud, nor traffic, nor found a city east of the Fair Promontory, Mastia, and Tarseium. If the Carthaginians take any city in Latium which is not subject to Rome, they may keep the prisoners and the goods, but shall deliver up the town. If the Carthaginians take any folk between whom and Rome a peace has been made in writing, though they be not subject to them, they shall not bring them into any harbors of the Romans. If such an one be so brought ashore and any Roman lay claim to him, he shall be released. In like manner shall the Romans be bound towards the Carthaginians.

If a Roman take water or provisions from any district within the juris-

*diction of Carthage, he shall not injure, while so doing, any between whom
and Carthage there is peace and friendship. Neither shall a Carthaginian in
like case. If anyone shall do so, he shall not be punished by private
vengeance, but such action shall be a public misdemeanor.*

*In Sardinia and Libya no Roman shall traffic nor found a city; he shall
do no more than take in provisions and refit his ship. If a storm drive him
upon those coasts, he shall depart within five days.*

*In the Carthaginian province of Sicily and in Carthage he may transact
business and sell whatsoever it is lawful for a citizen to do. In like manner
also may a Carthaginian at Rome.*

Once more in this treaty we may notice that the Carthaginians empha-
size the fact of their entire possession of Libya and Sardinia, and prohibit any
attempt of the Romans to land in them at all. On the other hand, in the case
of Sicily, they clearly distinguish their own province in it. So, too, the
Romans, in regard to Latium, stipulate that the Carthaginians shall do no
wrong to Ardea, Antium, Circeii, or Tarracina, all of which are on the
seaboard of Latium, to which alone the treaty refers.

25. A third treaty again was made by Rome at the time of the invasion of
Pyrrhus into Sicily (280? B.C.E.) before the Carthaginians undertook the war
for the possession of Sicily. This treaty contains the same provisions as the
two earlier treaties with these additional clauses:

*If they make a treaty of alliance with Pyrrhus, the Romans or
Carthaginians shall make it on such terms as not to preclude the one giving
aid to the other, if that one's territory is attacked.*

*If one or the other stand in need of help, the Carthaginians shall supply
the ships, whether for transport or war; but each people shall supply the pay
for its own men employed on them.*

*The Carthaginians shall also give aid by sea to the Romans if need be,
but no one shall compel the crews to disembark against their will.*

Provision was also made for swearing to these treaties. In the case of the
first, the Carthaginians were to swear by the gods of their ancestors, the
Romans by Jupiter Lapis, in accordance with an ancient custom; in the case
of the last treaty, by Mars and Quirinus. The form of swearing by Jupiter
Lapis was this. The commissioner for swearing to the treaty took a stone in
his hand and, having taken the oath in the name of his country, added these
words, "If I abide by this oath, may he bless me; but if I do otherwise in
thought or act, may all others be kept safe each in his own country, under his
own laws, in enjoyment of his own goods, household gods, and tombs—

may I alone be cast out, even as this stone is now." And having uttered these words, he throws the stone from his hand.

26. Seeing that such treaties exist and are preserved to this day, engraved on brass in the treasury of the Aediles in the temple of Jupiter Capitolinus, the historian Philinus certainly does give us some reason to be surprised at him. Not at his ignorance of their existence, for even in our own day those Romans and Carthaginians whose age placed them nearest to the times and who had the reputation of taking the greatest interest in public affairs, were unaware of it. But what is surprising is that he should have ventured on a statement exactly opposite: "That there was a treaty between Rome and Carthage, in virtue of which the Romans were bound to keep away from the whole of Sicily, the Carthaginians from the whole of Italy; and that the Romans broke the treaty and their oath when they first crossed over to Sicily." Whereas there does not exist, nor ever has existed, any such written compact at all. Yet this assertion he makes in so many words in his second book. I referred to this in the preface of my work, but reserved a more detailed discussion of it to this place. This was necessary because the assertion of Philinus has misled a considerable number of people on this point. I have nothing to say if a man chooses to attack the Romans for crossing into Sicily, on the grounds of their having taken the Mamertines into alliance at all; or in having thus acted in answer to their request, after these men's treachery to Rhegium as well as Messene. But if anyone supposes that in so crossing they broke oaths or treaties, he is manifestly ignorant of the truth.

27. At the end of the first Punic War another treaty was made, of which the chief provisions were these:

> *The Carthaginians shall evacuate Sicily and all islands lying between Italy and Sicily.*
>
> *The allies of neither of the parties to the treaty shall be attacked by the other.*
>
> *Neither party shall impose any contribution nor erect any public building or enlist soldiers in the dominions of the other nor make any compact of friendship with the allies of the other.*
>
> *The Carthaginians shall within ten years pay to the Romans two thousand two hundred talents, and a thousand on the spot; and shall restore all prisoners, without ransom, to the Romans.*

Afterwards, at the end of the Mercenary War in Africa, the Romans went so far as to pass a decree for war with Carthage, but eventually made a treaty (238 B.C.E.) to the following effect: *The Carthaginians shall evacuate Sardinia and pay an additional twelve hundred talents.* Finally, in addition to these treaties, came that negotiated with Hasdrubal (228 B.C.E.) in Spain, in which it was stipulated that *"the Carthaginians should not cross the Ebro with arms."* Such were the mutual obligations established between Rome and Carthage from the earliest times to that of Hannibal.

28. As we find, then, that the Roman invasion of Sicily was not in contravention of their oaths, so we must acknowledge in the case of the second proclamation of war, in consequence of which the treaty for the evacuation of Sardinia was made, that it is impossible to find any reasonable pretext or ground for the Roman action. The Carthaginians were beyond question compelled by the necessities of their position, contrary to all justice, to evacuate Sardinia and to pay this enormous sum of money. For as to the allegation of the Romans that the Carthaginians had during the Mercenary War been guilty of acts of hostility to ships sailing from Rome, that was barred by Rome's own act in restoring, without ransom, the Carthaginian prisoners in gratitude for similar conduct on the part of Carthage to Romans who had landed on their shores—a transaction which I have spoken of at length in my previous book. These facts established, it remains to be decided by a thorough investigation to which of the two nations the origin of the Hannibalian War is to be imputed.

29. I have explained the pleas advanced by the Carthaginians. I must now state what is alleged on the contrary by the Romans. For through it is true that in this particular interview, owing to their anger at the fall of Saguntum, they did not use these arguments, yet they were appealed to on many occasions and by many of their citizens. First, they argued that the treaty of Hasdrubal could not be ignored, as the Carthaginians had the assurance to do, for it did not contain the clause which that of Lutatius did, making its validity conditional on its ratification by the people of Rome. Hasdrubal made the agreement absolutely and authoritatively that *"the Carthaginians should not cross the Ebro in arms."* Next they alleged that the clause in the treaty respecting Sicily, which by their own admission stipulated that *"the allies of neither party should be attacked by the other,"* did not refer to then-existing allies only, as the Carthaginians interpreted it; for in that case a clause would have been added, disabling either from making new alliances in addition to those already existing, or excluding allies, taken subsequently to the making of the treaty, from its benefits. But since neither of these provisions was made, it was plain that both the then-existing allies and all those taken subsequently on either side, were entitled to reciprocal security. And this was only reasonable. For it was not likely that they would have made a treaty depriving them of the power, when opportunity offered, of taking on such friends or allies as seemed to their interest; nor, again, if they had taken any such under their protection, was it to be supposed that they would allow them to be injured by any persons whatever. But, in fact, the main thing present in the minds of both parties to the treaty was that they should mutually agree to abstain from attacking each other's allies, and on no account should they admit into alliance with themselves the allies of the other. And it was to subsequent allies that this particular clause applied: *Neither shall enlist soldiers or impose contributions on the provinces or allies of the other; and all shall be alike secure of attack from the other side.*

30. These things being so, they argued that it was beyond controversy that Saguntum had accepted the protection of Rome, several years before the time of Hannibal. The strongest proof of this, and one which would not be contested by the Carthaginians themselves, was that when political disturbances broke out at Saguntum, the people chose the Romans, not the Carthaginians, as arbitrators to settle the dispute and restore their constitution, although the latter were close at hand and were already established in Spain. I conclude, then, that if the destruction of Saguntum is to be regarded as the cause of this war, the Carthaginians must be acknowledged to be in the wrong, both in view of the treaty of Lutatius, which secured immunity from attack for the allies of both parties, and in view of the treaty of Hasdrubal, which disabled the Carthaginians from passing the Ebro with arms. If, on the other hand, the taking of Sardinia from them and imposing the heavy money fine which accompanied it are to be regarded as the causes, we must certainly acknowledge that the Carthaginians had good reason for undertaking the Hannibalian War. For as they had only yielded to the pressure of circumstances, so they seized a favorable turn in those circumstances to revenge themselves on their injurers.

BOOK VI   I; 3–9; II–18; 56–57

Polybius' analysis of the Roman constitution, which had such impact on French and American thinkers of the 18th century.

I. I am aware that some will be at a loss to account for my interrupting the course of my narrative for the sake of entering upon the following disquisition on the Roman constitution. But I think that I have already in many passages made it fully evident that this particular branch of my work was one of the necessities imposed on me by the nature of my original design; and I pointed this out with special clearness in the preface which explained the scope of my history. I there stated that the feature of my work which was at once the best in itself, and the most instructive to the students of it, was that it would enable them to know and fully realize in what manner, and under what kind of constitution, it came about that nearly the whole world fell under the power of Rome in somewhat less then fifty-three years—an event certainly without precedent. This being my settled purpose, I could see no more fitting period than the present for making a pause and examining the truth of the remarks about to be made on this constitution. In private life if you wish to satisfy yourself as to the badness or goodness of particular persons, you would not, if you wish to get a genuine test, examine their conduct at a time of uneventful repose, but in the hour of brilliant success or conspicuous reverse. For the true test of a perfect man is the power of bearing with spirit and dignity violent changes of Fortune. An examination of a constitution should be conducted in the same way. And therefore being unable to find in our day a more rapid or more signal change than that which has happened to Rome, I reserved my disquisition on its constitution for this place . . .

What is really educational and beneficial to students of history is the clear view of the causes of events and the consequent power of choosing the better policy in a particular case. Now in every practical undertaking by a state we must regard as the most powerful agent for success or failure the form of its constitution; for from this as from a fountainhead all conceptions and plans of action not only proceed, but attain their consummation . . .

3. Of the Greek republics, which have again and again risen to greatness and fallen into insignificance, it is not difficult to speak, whether we recount their past history or venture an opinion on their future. For to report what is already known is an easy task, nor is it hard to guess what is to come from our knowledge of what has been. But in regard to the Romans it is neither an easy matter to describe their present state, owing to the complexity of their constitution; nor to speak with confidence of their future, from our inadequate acquaintance with their peculiar institutions in the past whether affecting their public or their private life. It will require then no ordinary attention and study to get a clear and comprehensive conception of the distinctive features of this constitution.

Now, it is undoubtedly the case that most of those who profess to give us authoritative instruction on this subject distinguish three kinds of constitutions, which they designate *kingship, aristocracy,* and *democracy.* But in my opinion the question might fairly be put to them, whether they name these as being the *only* ones, or as the *best.* In either case I think they are wrong. For it is plain that we must regard as the *best* constitution that which partakes of all these three elements. And this is no mere assertion, but has been proved by the example of Lycurgus, who was the first to construct a constitution—that of Sparta—on this principle. Nor can we admit that these are the *only* forms, for we have had before now examples of absolute and tyrannical forms of government, which, while differing as widely as possible from kingship, appear to have some points of resemblance to it; on which account all absolute rulers falsely assume and use, as far as they can, the title of king. Again there have been many instances of oligarchic governments having in appearance some analogy to aristocracies, which are, if I may say so, as different from them as it is possible to be. The same also holds good about democracy.

4. I will illustrate the truth of what I say. We cannot hold every absolute government to be a kingship, but only that which is accepted voluntarily and is directed by an appeal to reason rather than to fear and force. Nor again is every oligarchy to be regarded as an aristocracy. The latter exists only where the power is wielded by the justest and wisest men selected on their merits. Similarly, it is not enough to constitute a democracy that the whole crowd of citizens should have the right to do whatever they wish or propose. But where reverence to the gods, succor of parents, respect to elders, and obedience to laws are traditional and habitual, in such communities, if the will of the majority prevail, we may speak of the form of government as a democracy. So then we enumerate six forms of government—the three commonly spoken of which I have just mentioned and three more allied forms. I mean *despotism, oligarchy* and *mob rule*. The first of these arises without artificial aid and in the natural order of events. Next to this, and produced from it by the aid of art and adjustment, comes *kingship;* which degenerating into the evil form allied to it, by which I mean *tyranny,* both are once more destroyed and *aristocracy* produced. Again the latter being in the course of nature perverted to *oligarchy,* and the people passionately avenging the unjust acts of their rulers, *democracy* comes into existence; which again by its violence and contempt of law becomes sheer *mob rule*. No clearer proof of the truth of what I say could be obtained than by a careful observation of the natural origin, genesis, and decadence of these several forms of government. For it is only by seeing distinctly how each of them is produced that a distinct view can also be obtained of its growth, zenith, and decadence, and the time, circumstance, and place in which each of these may be expected to recur. This method I have assumed to be especially applicable to the Roman constitution, because its origin and growth have from the first followed natural causes.

5. Now the natural laws which regulate the merging of one form of government into another are perhaps discussed with greater accuracy by Plato and some other philosophers. But their treatment, from its intricacy and exhaustiveness, is only within the capacity of a few. I will therefore endeavor to give a summary of the subject, just so far as I suppose it to fall within the scope of a practical history and the intelligence of ordinary people. For if my exposition appear in any way inadequate, owing to the general terms in which it is expressed, the details contained in what is immediately to follow will amply atone for what is left for the present unsolved.

What is the origin then of a constitution, and whence is it produced? Suppose that from floods, pestilences, failure of crops, or some such causes the race of man is reduced almost to extinction. Such things we are told have happened, and it is reasonable to think will happen again. Suppose, accordingly, all knowledge of social habits and arts to have been lost. Suppose that from the survivors, as from seeds, the race of man to have again multiplied. In that case, I presume they would, like the animals, herd together; for it is but reasonable to suppose that bodily weakness would induce them to seek those of their own kind to herd with. And in that case too, as with the animals, he who was superior to the rest in strength of body or courage of soul would lead and rule them. For what we see happen in the case of animals that are without the faculty of reason, such as bulls, goats, and cocks—among whom there can be no dispute that the strongest take the lead—that we must regard as in the truest sense the teaching of nature. Originally then, it is probable that the condition of life among men was this—herding together like animals and following the strongest and bravest as leaders. The limit of this authority would be physical strength, and the name we should give it would be despotism. But as soon as the idea of family ties and social relation has arisen amongst such agglomerations of men, then is born also the idea of kingship, and then for the first time mankind conceives the notion of goodness and justice and their reverse.

6. The way in which such conceptions originate and come into existence is this. The intercourse of the sexes is an instinct of nature, and the result is the birth of children. Now, if any one of these children who have been brought up, when arrived at maturity, is ungrateful and makes no return to those by whom he was nurtured, but on the contrary presumes to injure them by word and deed, it is plain that he will probably offend and annoy such as are present and have seen the care and trouble bestowed by the parents on the nurture and bringing up of their children. For seeing that men differ from the other animals in being the only creatures possessed of reasoning powers, it is clear that such a difference of conduct is not likely to escape their observation; but that they will remark it when it occurs and express their displeasure on the spot, because they will have an eye to the future and will reason on the likelihood of the same occurring to each of themselves. Again, if a man has been rescued or helped in an hour of danger and, instead of showing gratitude to his preserver, seeks to do him harm, it is clearly probable that the rest will be displeased and offended with him when they know it, sympathizing with their neighbor and imagining themselves in his case. Hence arises a notion in every breast of the meaning and theory of duty, which is in fact the beginning and end of justice. Similarly, again, when any one man stands out as the champion of all in a time of danger, and braves with firm courage the onslaught of the most powerful wild beasts, it is probable that such a man would meet with marks of favor and preeminence from the common people, while he who acted in a contrary way would fall under their contempt and dislike. From this, once more, it is reasonable to suppose that there would arise in the minds of the multitude a theory of the disgraceful and honorable, and of the difference between them; and that one should be sought and imitated for its advantages, the other shunned. When, therefore, the leading and most powerful man among his people ever encourages such persons in accordance with the popular sentiment, and thereby assumes in the eyes of his subject the appearance of being the distributor to each man according to his deserts, they no longer obey him and support his rule from fear of violence, but rather from conviction of its utility, however old he may be, rallying round him with one heart and soul, and fighting against all who form designs against his government. In this way he becomes a *king* instead of a *despot* by imperceptible degrees, reason having ousted brute courage and bodily strength from their supremacy.

7. This then is the natural process of formation among mankind of the notion of goodness and justice and their opposites; and this is the origin and genesis of genuine kingship. For people do not only keep up the government of such men personally, but for their descendants also for many generations, from the conviction that those who are born from and educated by men of this kind will have principles also like theirs. But if they subsequently become displeased with their descendants, they do not any longer decide their choice of rulers and kings by their physical strength or brute courage, but by the differences of their intellectual and reasoning faculties, from practical experience of the decisive importance of such a distinction.

In old times, then, those who were once thus selected and obtained this office grew old in their royal functions, making magnificent strongholds and surrounding them with walls and extending their frontiers, partly for the security of their subjects, and partly to provide them with an abundance of the necessaries of life. And while engaged in these works they were exempt from all vituperation or jealousy, because they did not make their distinctive dress, food, or drink at all conspicuous, but lived very much like the rest and joined in the everyday employments of the common people. But when their royal power became hereditary in their family, and they found every necessity for security ready to their hands, as well as more than was necessary for their personal support, then they gave the rein to their appetites; imagined that rulers must wear different clothes from those of subjects; have different and elaborate luxuries of the table; and must even seek sensual indulgence, however unlawful the source, without fear of denial. These things having given rise in the one case to jealousy and offense, in the other to outbursts of hatred and passionate resentment, the kingship became a tyranny. The first step in disintegration was taken, and plots began to be formed against the government which did not now proceed from the worst men but from the noblest, most high-minded, and most courageous, because these are the men who can least submit to the tyrannical acts of their rulers.

8. But as soon as the people got leaders, they cooperated with them against the dynasty for the reasons I have mentioned. Then *kingship* and *despotism* were alike entirely abolished, and *aristocracy* once more began to revive and start afresh. For in their immediate gratitude to those who had deposed the despots, the people employed them as leaders and entrusted their interests to them. The leaders, looking upon this charge at first as a great privilege, made the public advantage their chief concern and conducted all kinds of business, public or private, with diligence and caution. But when the sons of these men received the same position of authority from their fathers—having had no experience of misfortunes, and none at all of civil equality and freedom of speech, but having been bred up from the first under the shadow of their fathers' authority and lofty position—some of them gave themselves up with passion to avarice and unscrupulous love of money, others to drinking and the boundless debaucheries which accompany it, and others to the violation of women or the forcible appropriation of boys; and so they turned an *aristocracy* into an *oligarchy*. But it was not long before they roused in the minds of the people the same feelings as before; and their fall therefore was very like the disaster which befell the tyrants.

9. For no sooner had the knowledge of the jealousy and hatred existing in the citizens against them emboldened someone to oppose the government by word or deed, than he was sure to find the whole people ready and prepared to take his side. Having rid themselves of these rulers by assassination or exile, they do not venture to set up a king again, being still in terror of the injustice to which this led before; nor dare they entrust the common interests again to more than one, considering the recent example of their misconduct. Therefore, as the only sound hope left them is that which depends upon themselves, they are driven to take refuge in that, and so change the constitution from an oligarchy to a *democracy* and take upon themselves the superintendence and charge of the state. And as long as any survive who have had experience of oligarchic supremacy and domination, they regard their present constitution as a blessing and hold equality and freedom as of the utmost value. But as soon as a new generation has arisen, and the democracy has descended to their children's children, long association weakens their value for equality and freedom, and some seek to become more powerful than the ordinary citizens; and the most liable to this temptation are the rich. So when they begin to be fond of office and find themselves unable to obtain it by their own unassisted efforts and their own merits, they ruin their estates, while enticing and corrupting the common people in every possible way. By this means, when in their senseless mania for reputation they have made the populace ready and greedy to receive bribes, the virtue of democracy is destroyed, and it is transformed into a government of violence and the strong hand. For the mob, habituated to feed at the expense of others and to have its hopes of a livelihood in the property of its neighbors, as soon as it has got a leader sufficiently ambitious and daring, being excluded by poverty from the sweets of civil honors, produces a reign of mere violence. Then come tumultuous assemblies, massacres, banishments, and redivisions of land until, after losing all trace of civilization, it has once more found a master and a despot.

This is the regular cycle of constitutional revolutions, and the natural order in which constitutions change, are transformed, and return again to their original stage. If a man has a clear grasp of these principles, he may perhaps make a mistake as to the dates at which this or that will happen to a particular constitution; but he will rarely be entirely mistaken as to the stage of growth or decay at which it has arrived, or as to the point at which it will undergo some revolutionary change. However, it is in the case of the Roman constitution that this method of inquiry will most fully teach us its formation, its growth, and zenith, as well as the changes awaiting it in the future; for this, if any constitution ever did, owed, as I said just now, its original foundation and growth to natural causes, and to natural causes will owe its decay. My subsequent narrative will be the best illustration of what I say.

§

II. . . . I will now endeavor to describe that of Rome at the period of their disastrous defeat at Cannae (216 B.C.E.). I am fully conscious that to those who actually live under this constitution I shall appear to give an inadequate account of it by the omission of certain details. Knowing accurately every portion of it from personal experience and from having been bred up in its customs and laws from childhood, they will not be struck so much by the accuracy of the description, as annoyed by its omissions; nor will they believe that the historian has purposely omitted unimportant distinctions, but will attribute his silence upon the origin of existing institutions or other important facts to ignorance. What is told they depreciate as insignificant or beside the purpose. What is omitted they demand as vital to the question, their object being to appear to know more than the writers. But a good critic should not judge a writer by what he leaves unsaid, but from what he says. If he detects misstatement in the latter, he may then feel certain that ignorance accounts for the former; but if what he says is accurate, his omissions ought to be attributed to deliberated judgment and not to ignorance. So much for those whose criticisms are prompted by personal ambition rather than by justice. . .

Another requisite for obtaining a judicious approval for an historical disquisition is that it should be germane to the matter in hand. If this is not observed, though its style may be excellent and its matter irreproachable, it will seem out of place, and disgust rather than please. . . .

As for the Roman constitution, it had three elements, each of them possessing sovereign powers; and their respective share of power in the whole state had been regulated with such a scrupulous regard to equality and equilibrium that no one could say for certain, not even a native, whether the constitution as a whole were an aristocracy or democracy or despotism. And no wonder, for if we confine our observation to the power of the consuls, we should be inclined to regard it as despotic; if on that of the Senate, as aristocratic; and if finally one looks at the power possessed by the people, it would seem a clear case of a democracy. What the exact powers of these several parts were and still, with slight modifications, are, I will now state.

12. The consuls, before leading out the legions, remain in Rome and are supreme masters of the administration. All other magistrates except the tribunes are under them and take their orders. They introduce foreign ambassadors to the Senate; bring matters requiring deliberation before it; and see to the execution of its decrees. If, again, there are any matters of state which require the authorization of the people, it is their business to see to them, to summon the popular meetings, to bring the proposals before them, and to carry out the decrees of the majority. In the preparations for war also, and in a word in the entire administration of a campaign, they have all but absolute power. It is competent to them to impose on the allies such levies as they think good, to appoint the military tribunes, to make up the roll for soldiers and select those that are suitable. Besides, they have absolute power of inflicting punishment on all who are under their command while on active service. They have authority to expend as much of the public money as they choose, being accompanied by a quaestor who is entirely at their orders. A survey of these powers would in fact justify our describing the constitution as despotic —a clear case of royal government. Nor will it affect the truth of my description, if any of the institutions I have described are changed in our time or in that of our posterity. The same remarks apply to what follows.

13. The Senate has first of all the control of the treasury and regulates the receipts and disbursements alike. For the quaestors cannot issue any public money for the various departments of the state without a decree of the Senate, except for the service of the consuls. The Senate controls also what is by far the largest and most important expenditure, that, namely, which is made by the censors every *lustrum* for the repair or construction of public buildings. This money cannot be obtained by the censors except by the grant of the Senate. Similarly all crimes committed in Italy requiring a public investigation, such as treason, conspiracy, poisoning, or willful murder, are in the hands of the Senate. Besides, if any individual or state among the Italian allies requires a controversy to be settled, a penalty to be assessed, help or protection to be afforded—all this is the province of the Senate. Or again, outside Italy, if it is necessary to send an embassy to reconcile warring communities or to remind them of their duty or sometimes to impose requisitions upon them or to receive their submission or, finally, to proclaim war against them —this, too, is the business of the Senate. In like manner the reception to be given to foreign ambassadors in Rome and the answers to be returned to them are decided by the Senate. With such business the people have nothing to do. Consequently, if one were staying at Rome when the consuls were not in town, one would imagine the constitution to be complete aristocracy. This has been the idea entertained by many Greeks and by many kings as well, from the fact that nearly all the business they had with Rome was settled by the Senate.

14. After this, one would naturally be inclined to ask, What part is left for the people in the constitution, when the Senate has these various functions, especially the control of the receipts and expenditure of the treasury; and when the consuls, again, have absolute power over the details of military preparation and an absolute authority in the field? There is, however, a part left the people, and it is a most important one. For the people are the sole fountain of honor and of punishment; and it is by these two things and these alone that dynasties and constitutions and, in a word, human society are held together. For where the distinction between them is not sharply drawn both in theory and practice, there no undertaking can be properly administered— as indeed we might expect when good and bad are held in exactly the same honor. The people, then, are the only court to decide matters of life and death; and even in cases where the penalty is money, if the sum to be assessed is sufficiently serious, and especially when the accused have held the higher magistracies. And in regard to this arrangement there is one point deserving especial commendation and record. Men who are on trial for their lives at Rome, while sentence is in process of being voted—if even only one of the tribes whose votes are needed to ratify the sentence has not voted—have the privilege at Rome of openly departing and condemning themselves to a voluntary exile. Such men are safe at Naples or Praeneste or at Tibur, and at other towns with which this arrangement has been duly ratified on oath.

Again, it is the people who bestow offices, which are the most honorable rewards of virtue, on the deserving. They have also the absolute power of passing or repealing laws; and, most important of all, it is the people who deliberate on the question of peace or war. And when provisional terms are made for alliance, suspension of hostilities, or treaties, it is the people who ratify them or the reverse. These considerations again would lead one to say that the chief power in the state was the people's and that the constitution was a democracy.

15. Such, then, is the distribution of power between the several parts of the state. I must now show how each of these several parts can, when they choose, oppose or support each other. The consul, then, when he has started on an expedition with the powers I have described, is to all appearance absolute in the administration of the business in hand. Still he has need of the support both of people and Senate and, without them, is quite unable to bring the matter to a successful conclusion. For it is plain that he must have supplies sent to his legions from time to time; but without a decree of the Senate they can be supplied neither with corn, nor clothes, nor pay, so that all the plans of a commander must be futile if the Senate is resolved either to shrink from danger or hamper his plans. And again, whether a consul shall bring any undertaking to a conclusion or no depends entirely upon the Senate, for it has absolute authority at the end of a year to send another consul to supersede him or to continue the existing one in his command. Again, even to the successes of the generals the Senate has the power to add distinction and glory and, on the other hand, to obscure their merits and lower their credit. For these high achievements are brought in tangible form before the eyes of the citizens by what are called "triumphs." But these triumphs the commanders cannot celebrate with proper pomp or in some cases celebrate at all, unless the Senate concurs and grants the necessary money. As for the people, the consuls are preeminently obliged to court their favor, however distant from home may be the field of their operations; for it is the people, as I have said before, that ratify, or refuse to ratify, terms of peace and treaties; but most of all because when laying down their office they have to give an account of their administration before them. Therefore in no case is it safe for the consuls to neglect either the Senate or the good will of the people.

16. As for the Senate, which possesses the immense power I have described, in the first place it is obliged in public affairs to take the multitude into account and respect the wishes of the people; and it cannot put into execution the penalty for offenses against the republic, which are punishable with death, unless the people first ratify its decrees. Similarly, even in matters which directly affect the senators—for instance, in the case of a law diminishing the Senate's traditional authority or depriving senators of certain dignities and offices or even actually cutting down their property—even in such cases the people have the sole power of passing or rejecting the law. But most important of all is the fact that, if the tribunes interpose their veto, the Senate not only is unable to pass a decree, but cannot even hold a meeting at all, whether formal or informal. Now, the tribunes are always bound to carry out the decree of the people and above all things to have regard to their wishes. Therefore, for all these reasons the Senate stands in awe of the multitude and cannot neglect the feelings of the people.

17. In like manner the people, on their part, are far from being independent of the Senate and are bound to take its wishes into account both collectively and individually. For contracts, too numerous to count, are given out by the censors in all parts of Italy for the repairs or construction of public buildings. There is also the collection of revenue from many rivers, harbors, gardens, mines, and land—everything, in a word, that comes under the control of the Roman government. And in all these the people at large are engaged; so that there is scarcely a man, so to speak, who is not interested either as a contractor or as being employed in the works. For some purchase the contracts from the censors for themselves; and others go partners with them; while others again go security for these contractors or actually pledge their property to the treasury for them. Now over all these transactions the Senate has absolute control. It can grant an extension of time and, in case of unforeseen accidents, can relieve the contractors from a portion of their obligation or release them from it altogether, if they are absolutely unable to fulfill it. And there are many details in which the Senate can inflict great hardships or, on the other hand, grant great indulgences to the contractors. For in every case the appeal is to it. But the most important point of all is that the judges are taken from its members in the majority of trials, whether public or private, in which the charges are heavy. Consequently, all citizens are much at its mercy and, being alarmed at the uncertainty as to when they may need its aid, are cautious about resisting or actively opposing its will. And for a similar reason men do not rashly resist the wishes of the consuls, because one and all may become subject to their absolute authority on campaign.

18. The result of this power of the several estates for mutual help or harm is a union sufficiently firm for all emergencies, and a constitution than which it is impossible to find a better. For whenever any danger from without compels them to unite and work together, the strength which is developed by the State is so extraordinary that everything required is unfailingly carried out by the eager rivalry shown by all classes to devote their whole minds to the need of the hour and to secure that any determination come to should not fail for want of promptitude; while each individual works, privately and publicly alike, for the accomplishment of the business in hand. Accordingly, the peculiar constitution of the State makes it irresistible and certain of obtaining whatever it determines to attempt. Nay, even when these external alarms are past, and the people are enjoying their good fortune and the fruits of their victories and, as usually happens, growing corrupted by flattery and idleness, show a tendency to violence and arrogance—it is in these circumstances, more than ever, that the constitution is seen to possess within itself the power of correcting abuses. For when any one of the three classes becomes puffed up and manifests an inclination to be contentious and unduly encroaching, the mutual interdependency of all the three and the possibility of the pretensions of anyone being checked and thwarted by the others, must plainly check this tendency. And so the proper equilibrium is maintained by the impulsiveness of the one part being checked by its fear of the other. . .

§

56. Again the Roman customs and principles regarding money transactions are better than those of the Carthaginians. In the view of the latter nothing is disgraceful that makes for gain. With the former nothing is more disgraceful than to receive bribes and to make profit by improper means. For they regard wealth obtained from unlawful transactions to be as much a subject of reproach as a fair profit from the most unquestioned source is of commendation. A proof of the fact is this. The Carthaginians obtain office by open bribery, but among the Romans the penalty for it is death. With such a radical difference, therefore, between the rewards offered to virtue among the two peoples, it is natural that the ways adopted for obtaining them should be different also.

But the most important difference for the better which the Roman commonwealth appears to me to display is in their religious beliefs. For I conceive that what in other nations is looked upon as a reproach, I mean a scrupulous fear of the gods, is the very thing which keeps the Roman commonwealth together. To such an extraordinary height is this canted among them, both in private and public business, that nothing could exceed it. Many people might think this unaccountable, but in my opinion their object is to use it as a check upon the common people. If it were possible to form a state wholly of philosophers, such a custom would perhaps be unnecessary. But seeing that every multitude is fickle and full of lawless desires, unreasoning anger, and violent passion, the only resource is to keep them in check by mysterious terrors and scenic effects of this sort. Wherefore, to my mind, the ancients were not acting without purpose or at random when they brought in among the vulgar those opinions about the gods and the belief in the punishments in Hades. Much rather do I think that men nowadays are acting rashly and foolishly in rejecting them. This is the reason why, apart from anything else, Greek statesmen, if entrusted with a single talent, though protected by ten checking clerks, as many seals, and twice as many witnesses, cannot be induced to keep faith, whereas among the Romans, in their magistracies and embassies, men have the handling of a great amount of money, and yet from pure respect to their oath keep their faith intact. . . .

57. That to all things, then, which exist there is ordained decay and change I think requires no further arguments to show, for the inexorable course of nature is sufficient to convince us of it. But in all polities we observe two sources of decay existing from natural causes, the one external, the other internal and self-produced. The external admits of no certain or fixed definition, but the internal follows a definite order. What kind of polity, then, comes naturally first, and what second, I have already stated in such a way that those who are capable of taking in the whole drift of my argument can henceforth draw their own conclusions as to the future of the Roman polity. For it is quite clear in my opinion. When a commonwealth, after warding off many great dangers, has arrived at a high pitch of prosperity and undisputed power, it is evident that by the lengthened continuance of great wealth within it, the manner of life of its citizens will become more extravagant and that the rivalry for office and in other spheres of activity will become fiercer than it ought to be. And as this state of things goes on more and more, the desire of office and the shame of losing reputation, as well as the ostentation and extravagance of living, will prove the beginning of a deterioration. And of this change the people will be credited with being the authors, when they become convinced that they are being cheated by some from avarice, and are puffed up with flattery by others from love of office. For when that comes about, in their passionate resentment and acting under the dictates of anger, they will refuse to obey any longer, or to be content with having equal powers with their leaders, but will demand to have all or far the greatest themselves. And when that comes to pass, the constitution will receive a new name which sounds better than any other in the world, liberty or democracy; but, in fact, it will become that worst of all governments, mob rule.

With this description of the formation, growth, zenith, and present state of the Roman polity, and having discussed also its difference, for better and worse, from other polities, I will now at length bring my essay on it to an end.

APPIAN

Appian was born in Alexandria early in the second century C.E. He became a Roman citizen and came to Rome where he held high office at the court of Antoninus Pius (138–161 C.E.).

He wrote, in his native Greek, a history of Rome's wars, organized in twenty-four books, according to their opponents. The surviving books include the Spanish Wars, the Hannibalic Wars, and the Macedonian Wars. Appian adapted his sources without much analysis, so his history is only useful where he preserves material when other sources are lacking.

THE CIVIL WARS*

Appian's five books devoted to Rome's Civil Wars also survive. The First book is the most valuable since it remains the only surviving historical narrative to treat the era of the Gracchi, Marius, Sulla, and the Social War.

BOOK I 1–26

1. The plebeians and Senate of Rome were often at strife with each other concerning the enactment of laws, the canceling of debts, the division of

---

*Appian. 1913. *Appian's Roman History*. Book III. Translated by Horace White. Loeb Classical Library.

lands, or the election of magistrates. Internal discord did not, however, bring them to blows; they were merely dissensions and contests within the limits of the law, which they composed by making mutual concessions, and with much respect for each other. Once when the plebeians were entering on a campaign they fell into a controversy of this sort, but they did not use the weapons in their hands, but withdrew to the hill, which from that time on was called the Sacred Mount. Even then no violence was done, but they created a magistrate for their protection and called him the Tribune of the Plebs, to serve especially as a check upon the consuls, who were chosen by the Senate, so that political power should not be exclusively in their hands. From this arose still greater bitterness, and the magistrates were arrayed in stronger animosity to each other from this time on, and the Senate and plebeians took sides with them, each believing that it would prevail over the other by augmenting the power of its own magistrates. It was in the midst of contests of this kind that Marcius Coriolanus, having been banished contrary to justice, took refuge with the Volsci and levied war against his country.

2. This is the only case of armed strife that can be found in the ancient seditions, and this was caused by an exile. The sword was never carried into the assembly, and there was no civil butchery until Tiberius Gracchus, while serving as tribune and bringing forward new laws, was the first to fall a victim to internal commotion; and with him many others, who were crowded together at the Capitol round the temple, were also slain. Sedition did not end with this abominable deed. Repeatedly the parties came into open conflict, often carrying daggers; and from time to time in the temples, or the assemblies, or the forum, some tribune, or praetor, or consul, or candidate for those offices, or some person otherwise distinguished, would be slain. Unseemly violence prevailed almost constantly, together with shameful contempt for law and justice. As the evil gained in magnitude, open insurrections against the government and large warlike expeditions against their country were undertaken by exiles, or criminals, or persons contending against each other for some office or military command. There arose chiefs of factions quite frequently, aspiring to supreme power, some of them refusing to disband the troops entrusted to them by the people, others even hiring forces against each other on their own account, without public authority. Whenever either side first got possession of the city, the opposition party made war nominally against their own adversaries, but actually against their country. They assailed it like an enemy's capital, and ruthless and indiscriminate massacres of citizens were perpetrated. Some were proscribed, others banished, property was confiscated, and prisoners were even subjected to excruciating tortures.

3. No unseemly deed was left undone until, about fifty years after the death of Gracchus, Cornelius Sulla, one of these chiefs of factions, doctoring one evil with another, made himself the sole master of the state for a very long time. Such officials were formerly called dictators—an office created in the most perilous emergencies for six months only, and long since fallen into disuse. But Sulla, although nominally elected, became dictator for life by force and compulsion. Nevertheless he became satiated with power and was the first man, so far as I know, holding supreme power, who had the courage to lay it down voluntarily and to declare that he would render an account of his stewardship to any who were dissatisfied with it. And so, for a considerable period, he walked to the forum as a private citizen in the sight of all and returned home unmolested, so great was the awe of his government still remaining in the minds of the onlookers, or their amazement at his laying it down. Perhaps they were ashamed to call him to account, or entertained other good feeling toward him, or a belief that his despotism had been beneficial to the state. Thus there was a cessation of factions for a short time while Sulla lived, and a compensation for the evils which he had wrought, (4.) but after his death similar troubles broke out and continued until Gaius Caesar, who had held the command in Gaul by election for some years, when ordered by the Senate to lay down his command, excused himself on the ground that this was not the wish of the Senate, but of Pompey, his enemy, who had command of an army in Italy, and was scheming to depose him. So he sent proposals that either both should retain their armies, so that neither need fear the other's enmity, or that Pompey also should dismiss his forces and live as a private citizen under the laws in like manner with himself. Both suggestions being refused, he marched from Gaul against Pompey into Roman territory, entered Rome, and finding Pompey fled, pursued him into Thessaly, won a brilliant victory over him in a great battle, and followed him to Egypt. After Pompey had been slain by certain Egyptians Caesar set to work on Egyptian affairs and remained there until he could settle the dynasty of that country. Then he returned to Rome. Having overpowered by war his principal rival, who had been surnamed the Great on account of his brilliant military exploits, he now ruled without disguise, nobody daring any longer to dispute with him about anything, and was chosen, next after Sulla, dictator for life. Again all civil dissension ceased until Brutus and Cassius, envious of his great power and desiring to restore the government of their fathers, slew in the Senate-house one who had proved himself truly popular, and most experienced in the art of government. The people certainly mourned for him greatly. They scoured the city in pursuit of his murderers, buried him in the middle of the forum, built a temple on the site of his funeral pyre, and offer sacrifice to him as a god.

5. And now civil discord broke out again worse than ever and increased enormously. Massacres, banishments, and proscriptions of both senators and knights took place straightway, including great numbers of both classes, the

chiefs of factions surrendering their enemies to each other, and for this purpose not sparing even their friends and brothers; so much did animosity toward rivals overpower the love of kindred. So in the course of events the Roman empire was partitioned, as though it had been their private property, by these three men: Antony, Lepidus, and the one who was first called Octavius, but afterward Caesar from his relationship to the other Caesar and adoption in his will. Shortly after this division they fell to quarreling among themselves, as was natural, and Octavius, who was the superior in understanding and skill, first deprived Lepidus of Africa, which had fallen to his lot, and afterward, as the result of the battle of Actium, took from Antony all the provinces lying between Syria and the Adriatic gulf. Thereupon, while all the world was filled with astonishment at these wonderful displays of power, he sailed to Egypt and took that country, which was the oldest and at that time the strongest possession of the successors of Alexander, and the only one wanting to complete the Roman empire as it now stands. In immediate consequence of these exploits he was, while still living, the first to be regarded by the Romans as 'august,' and to be called by them "Augustus." He assumed to himself an authority like Caesar's over the country and the subject nations, and even greater than Caesar's, no longer needing any form of election, or authorization, or even the pretense of it. His government proved both lasting and masterful, and being himself successful in all things and dreaded by all, he left a lineage and succession that held the supreme power in like manner after him.

6. Thus, out of multifarious civil commotions, the Roman state passed into harmony and monarchy. To show how these things came about I have written and compiled this narrative, which is well worth the study of those who wish to know the measureless ambition of men, their dreadful lust of power, their unwearying perseverance, and the countless forms of evil. And it is especially necessary for me to describe these things beforehand since they are the preliminaries of my Egyptian history, and will end where that begins, for Egypt was seized in consequence of this last civil commotion, Cleopatra having joined forces with Antony. On account of its magnitude I have divided the work, first taking up the events that occurred from the time of Sempronius Gracchus to that of Cornelius Sulla; next, those that followed to the death of Caesar. The remaining books of the civil wars treat of those waged by the triumvirs against each other and the Roman people, up to the grand climax of these conflicts, the battle of Actium fought by Octavius Caesar against Antony and Cleopatra together, which will be the beginning of the Egyptian history.

7. The Romans, as they subdued the Italian peoples successively in war, used to seize a part of their lands and build towns there, or enroll colonists of their own to occupy those already existing, and their idea was to use these as outposts; but of the land acquired by war they assigned the cultivated part forthwith to the colonists, or sold or leased it. Since they had no leisure as yet to allot the part which then lay desolated by war (this was generally the greater part), they made proclamation that in the meantime those who were willing to work it might do so for a toll of the yearly crops, a tenth of the grain and a fifth of the fruit. From those who kept flocks was required a toll of the animals, both oxen and small cattle. They did these things in order to multiply the Italian race, which they considered the most laborious of peoples, so that they might have plenty of allies at home. But the very opposite thing happened; for the rich, getting possession of the greater part of the undistributed lands, and being emboldened by the lapse of time to believe that they would never be dispossessed, absorbing any adjacent strips and their poor neighbors' allotments, partly by purchase under persuasion and partly by force, came to cultivate vast tracts instead of single estates, using slaves as laborers and herdsmen, lest free laborers should be drawn from agriculture into the army. At the same time the ownership of slaves brought them great gain from the multitude of their progeny, who increased because they were exempt from military service. Thus certain powerful men became extremely rich and the race of slaves multiplied throughout the country, while the Italian people dwindled in numbers and strength, being oppressed by penury, taxes, and military service. If they had any respite from these evils they passed their time in idleness, because the land was held by the rich, who employed slaves instead of freemen as cultivators.

8. For these reasons the people became troubled lest they should no longer have sufficient allies of the Italian stock, and lest the government itself should be endangered by such a vast number of slaves. As they did not perceive any remedy, for it was not easy, nor in any way just, to deprive men of so many possessions they had held so long, including their own trees, buildings, and fixtures, a law was at last passed with difficulty at the instance of the tribunes, that nobody should hold more than 500 jugera of this land, or pasture on it more than 100 cattle or 500 sheep. To ensure the observance of this law it was provided also that there should be a certain number of freemen employed on the farms, whose business it should be to watch and report what was going on. Having thus comprehended all this in a law, they took an oath over and above the law, and fixed penalties for violating it, and it was supposed that the remaining land would soon be divided among the poor in small parcels. But there was not the smallest consideration shown for the law or the oaths. The few who seemed to pay some respect to them conveyed their lands to their relations fraudulently, but the greater part disregarded it altogether, (**9.**) till at length Tiberius Sempronius Gracchus, an illustrious man, eager for glory, a most powerful speaker, and for these reasons well known to all, delivered an eloquent discourse, while serving as tribune, concerning the Italian race, lamenting that a people so valiant in war, and related in blood to the Romans, were declining little by little into pauperism and paucity of numbers without any hope of remedy. He inveighed against the multitude of slaves as useless in war and never faithful to their masters, and adduced the recent calamity brought upon the masters by their slaves in Sicily, where the demands of agriculture had greatly increased the number of the latter; recalling also the war waged against them by the Romans, which was neither easy nor short, but long-protracted and full of vicissitudes and dangers. After speaking thus he again brought forward the law, providing that nobody should hold more than the 500 jugera of the public domain. But he added a provision to the former law, that the sons of the occupiers might each hold one-half of that amount, and that the remainder should be divided among the poor by three elected commissioners, who should be changed annually.

10. This was extremely disturbing to the rich because, on account of the triumvirs, they could no longer disregard the law as they had done before; nor could they buy the allotments of others, because Gracchus had provided against this by forbidding sales. They collected together in groups, and made lamentation, and accused the poor of appropriating the results of their tillage, their vineyards, and their dwellings. Some said that they had paid the price of the land to their neighbors. Were they to lose the money with the land? Others said that the graves of their ancestors were in the ground, which had been allotted to them in the division of their fathers' estates. Others said that their wives' dowries had been expended on the estates, or that the land had been given to their own daughters as dowry. Moneylenders could show loans made on this security. All kinds of wailing and expressions of indignation were heard at once. On the other side were heard the lamentations of the poor—that they were being reduced from competence to extreme penury, and from that to childlessness, because they were unable to rear their offspring. They recounted the military services they had rendered, by which this very land had been acquired, and were angry that they should be robbed of their share of the common property. They reproached the rich for employing slaves, who were always faithless and ill-disposed and for that reason unserviceable in war, instead of freemen, citizens, and soldiers. While these classes were thus lamenting and indulging in mutual accusations, a great number of others, composed of colonists, or inhabitants of the free towns, or persons otherwise interested in the lands and who were under like apprehensions, flocked in and took sides with their respective factions. Emboldened by numbers and exasperated against each other they kindled considerable disturbances, and waited eagerly for the voting on the new law, some intending to prevent its enactment by all means, and others to enact it at all costs. In addition to personal interest the spirit of rivalry spurred both

sides in the preparations they were making against each other for the appointed day.

11. What Gracchus had in his mind in proposing the measure was not money, but men. Inspired greatly by the usefulness of the work, and believing that nothing more advantageous or admirable could ever happen to Italy, he took no account of the difficulties surrounding it. When the time for voting came he advanced many other arguments at considerable length and also asked them whether it was not just to let the commons divide the common property; whether a citizen was not worthy of more consideration at all times than a slave; whether a man who served in the army was not more useful than one who did not; and whether one who had a share in the country was not more likely to be devoted to the public interests. He did not dwell long on this comparison between freemen and slaves, which he considered degrading, but proceeded at once to a review of their hopes and fears for the country, saying that the Romans possessed most of their territory by conquest, and that they had hopes of occupying the rest of the habitable world; but now the question of greatest hazard was, whether they should gain the rest by having plenty of brave men, or whether, through their weakness and mutual jealousy, their enemies should take away what they already possessed. After exaggerating the glory and riches on the one side and the danger and fear on the other, he admonished the rich to take heed, and said that for the realization of these hopes they ought to bestow this very land as a free gift, if necessary, on men who would rear children, and not, by contending about small things, overlook larger ones; especially since for any labor they had spent they were receiving ample compensation in the undisputed title to 500 jugera each of free land, in a high state of cultivation, without cost, and half as much more for each son in the case of those who had sons. After saying much more to the same purport and exciting the poor, as well as others who were moved by reason rather than by the desire for gain, he ordered the clerk to read the proposed law.

12. Marcus Octavius, however, another tribune, who had been induced by those in possession of the lands to interpose his veto (for among the Romans the negative veto always defeats an affirmative proposal), ordered the clerk to keep silence. Thereupon Gracchus reproached him severely and adjourned the comitia to the following day. Then he stationed near himself a sufficient guard, as if to force Octavius against his will, and ordered the clerk with threats to read the proposed law to the multitude. He began to read, but when Octavius again forbade he stopped. Then the tribunes fell to wrangling with each other, and a considerable tumult arose among the people. The leading citizens besought the tribunes to submit their controversy to the Senate for decision. Gracchus seized on the suggestion, believing that the law was acceptable to all well-disposed persons, and hastened to the senate-house. But, as he had only a few followers there and was upbraided by the rich, he ran back to the forum and said that he would take the vote at the comitia of the following day, both on the law and on the official rights of Octavius, to determine whether a tribune who was acting contrary to the people's interest could continue to hold office. And this Gracchus did; for when Octavius, nothing daunted, again interposed, Gracchus proposed to take the vote on him first.

When the first tribe voted to abrogate the magistracy of Octavius, Gracchus turned to him and begged him to desist from his veto. As he would not yield, he took the votes of the other tribes. There were thirty-five tribes at that time. The seventeen that voted first passionately supported the motion. If the eighteenth should do the same it would make a majority. Again did Gracchus, in the sight of the people, urgently importune Octavius in his present extreme danger not to prevent a work which was most righteous and useful to all Italy, and not to frustrate the wishes so earnestly entertained by the people, whose desires he ought rather to share in his character of tribune, and not to risk the loss of his office by public condemnation. After speaking thus he called the gods to witness that he did not willingly do any harm to his colleague. As Octavius was still unyielding he went on taking the vote. Octavius was forthwith reduced to the rank of a private citizen and slunk away unobserved. Quintus Mummius was chosen tribune in his place, and the agrarian law was enacted.

13. The first triumvirs appointed to divide the land were Gracchus himself, the proposer of the law, his brother of the same name, and his father-in-law, Appius Claudius, since the people still feared that the law might fail of execution unless Gracchus should take the lead with his whole family. Gracchus became immensely popular by reason of the law and was escorted home by the multitude as though he were the founder, not of a single city or race, but of all the nations of Italy. After this the victorious party returned to the fields from which they had come to attend to this business. The defeated ones remained in the city and talked the matter over, feeling aggrieved, and saying that as soon as Gracchus should become a private citizen he would be sorry that he had done despite to the sacred and inviolable office of tribune, and had sown in Italy so many seeds of future strife.

14. It was now summer, and the election of tribunes was imminent. As the day for voting approached it was very evident that the rich had earnestly promoted the election of those most inimical to Gracchus. The latter, fearing that evil would befall if he should not be re-elected for the following year, summoned his friends from the fields to attend the election, but as they were occupied with harvest he was obliged, when the day fixed for the voting drew near, to have recourse to the plebeians of the city. So he went around asking each one separately to elect him tribune for the ensuing year, on account of

the danger he was incurring for them. When the voting took place the first two tribes pronounced for Gracchus. The rich objected that it was not lawful for the same man to hold the office twice in succession. The tribune Rubrius, who had been chosen by lot to preside over the comitia, was in doubt about it, and Mummius, who had been chosen in place of Octavius, urged him to hand over the comitia to his charge. This he did, but the remaining tribunes contended that the presidency should be decided by lot, saying that when Rubrius, who had been chosen in that way, resigned, the casting of lots ought to be done over again by all. As there was much strife over this question, Gracchus, who was getting the worst of it, adjourned the voting to the following day. In utter despair he went about in black, though still in office, and led his son around the forum and introduced him to each man and committed him to their charge, as if he himself felt that death, at the hands of his enemies, were at hand.

15. The poor when they had time to think were moved with deep sorrow, both on their own account (for they believed that they were no longer to live in a free estate under equal laws, but would be reduced to servitude by the rich), and on account of Gracchus himself, who was in such fear and torment in their behalf. So they all accompanied him with tears to his house in the evening, and bade him be of good courage for the morrow. Gracchus cheered up, assembled his partisans before daybreak, and communicated to them a signal to be displayed if there were need for fighting. He then took possession of the temple on the Capitoline hill, where the voting was to take place, and occupied the middle of the assembly. As he was obstructed by the other tribunes and by the rich, who would not allow the votes to be taken on this question, he gave the signal. There was a sudden shout from those who knew of it, and violence followed. Some of the partisans of Gracchus took position around him like body-guards. Others, having girded up their cloaks, seized the fasces and staves in the hands of the lictors and broke them in pieces. They drove the rich out of the assembly with such disorder and wounds that the tribunes fled from their places in terror, and the priests closed the doors of the temple. Many ran away pell-mell and scattered wild rumors. Some said that Gracchus had deposed all the other tribunes, and this was believed because none of them could be seen. Others said that he had declared himself tribune for the ensuing year without an election.

16. In these circumstances the Senate assembled at the temple of Fides. It is astonishing to me that they never thought of appointing a dictator in this emergency, although they had often been protected by the government of a single ruler in such times of peril; but a resource which had been found most useful in former times was never even recollected by the people, either then or later. After reaching such decision as they did reach, they marched up to the Capitol, Cornelius Scipio Nasica, the pontifex maximus, leading the way and calling out with a loud voice, "Let those who would save our country follow me." He wound the border of his toga about his head either to induce a greater number to go with him by the singularity of his appearance, or to make for himself, as it were, a helmet as a sign of battle for those who saw it, or in order to conceal himself from the gods on account of what he was about to do. When he arrived at the temple and advanced against the partisans of Gracchus they yielded out of regard for so excellent a citizen, and because they observed the Senators following with him. The latter wresting their clubs out of the hands of the Gracchans themselves, or breaking up benches and other furniture that had been brought for the use of the assembly, began beating them, and pursued them, and drove them over the precipice. In the tumult many of the Gracchans perished, and Gracchus himself, vainly circling round the temple, was slain at the door close by the statues of the kings. All the bodies were thrown by night into the Tiber.

17. So perished on the Capitol, and while still tribune, Gracchus, the son of that Gracchus who was twice consul, and of Cornelia, daughter of that Scipio who robbed Carthage of her supremacy. He lost his life in consequence of a most excellent design too violently pursued; and this abominable crime, the first that was perpetrated in the public assembly, was seldom without parallels thereafter from time to time. On the subject of the murder of Gracchus the city was divided between sorrow and joy. Some mourned for themselves and for him, and deplored the present condition of things, believing that the commonwealth no longer existed, but had been supplanted by force and violence. Others considered that their dearest wishes were accomplished.

18. These things took place at the time when Aristonicus was contending with the Romans for the government of Asia; but after Gracchus was slain and Appius Claudius died, Fulvius Flaccus and Papirius Carbo were appointed, in conjunction with the younger Gracchus, to divide the land. As the persons in possession neglected to hand in lists of their holdings, a proclamation was issued that informers should furnish testimony against them. Immediately a great number of embarrassing lawsuits sprang up. Wherever a new field adjoining an old one had been bought, or divided among the allies, the whole district had to be carefully inquired into on account of the measurement of this one field, to discover how it had been sold and how divided. Not all owners had preserved their contracts, or their allotment titles, and even those that were found were often ambiguous. When the land was resurveyed some owners were obliged to give up their fruit-trees and farm-buildings in exchange for naked ground. Others were transferred from cultivated to uncultivated lands, or to swamps, or pools. In fact, the land having originally been so much loot, the survey had never been carefully done. As the original proclamation authorized anybody to work the undistributed land who wished to do so, many had been prompted to cultivate the parts

immediately adjoining their own, till the line of demarcation between public and private had faded from view. The progress of time also made many changes. Thus the injustice done by the rich, although great, was not easy to ascertain. So there was nothing but a general turn-about, all parties being moved out of their own places and settling down in other people's.

19. The Italian allies who complained of these disturbances, and especially of the lawsuits hastily brought against them, chose Cornelius Scipio, the destroyer of Carthage, to defend them against these grievances. As he had availed himself of their very zealous support in war he was reluctant to disregard their request. So he came into the Senate, and although, out of regard for the plebeians, he did not openly find fault with the law of Gracchus, he expatiated on its difficulties and urged that these causes should not to be decided by the triumvirs, because they did not possess the confidence of the litigants, but should be assigned to other courts. As his view seemed reasonable, they yielded to his persuasion, and the consul Tuditanus was appointed to give judgment in these cases. But when he took up the work he saw the difficulties of it, and marched against the Illyrians as a pretext for not acting as judge, and since nobody brought cases for trial before the triumvirs they remained idle. From this cause hatred and indignation arose among the people against Scipio because they saw a man, in whose favor they had often opposed the aristocracy and incurred their enmity, electing him consul twice contrary to law, now taking the side of the Italian allies against themselves. When Scipio's enemies observed this, they cried out that he was determined to abolish the law of Gracchus utterly and for that end was about to inaugurate armed strife and bloodshed.

20. When the people heard these charges they were in a state of alarm until Scipio, after placing near his couch at home one evening a tablet on which to write during the night the speech he intended to deliver before the people, was found dead in his bed without a wound. Whether this was done by Cornelia, the mother of the Gracchi (aided by her daughter, Sempronia, who though married to Scipio was both unloved and unloving because she was deformed and childless), lest the law of Gracchus should be abolished, or whether, as some think, he committed suicide because he saw plainly that he could not accomplish what he had promised, is not known. Some say that slaves under torture testified that unknown persons were introduced through the rear of the house by night who suffocated him, and that those who knew about it hesitated to tell because the people were angry with him still and rejoiced at his death. So died Scipio, and although he had been of extreme service to the Roman power he was not even honored with a public funeral; so much does the anger of the present moment outweigh gratitude for the past. And this event, sufficiently important in itself, took place as a mere incident of the sedition of Gracchus.

21. Even after these events those who were in possession of the lands postponed the division on various pretexts for a very long time. Some proposed that all the Italian allies, who made the greatest resistance to it, should be admitted to Roman citizenship so that, out of gratitude for the greater favor, they might no longer quarrel about the land. The Italians were ready to accept this, because they preferred Roman citizenship to possession of the fields. Fulvius Flaccus, who was then both consul and triumvir, exerted himself to the utmost to bring it about, but the senators were angry at the thought of making their subjects equal citizens with themselves. For this reason the attempt was abandoned, and the populace, who had been so long in the hope of acquiring land, became disheartened. While they were in this mood Gaius Gracchus, who had made himself agreeable to them as a triumvir, offered himself for the tribuneship. He was the younger brother of Tiberius Gracchus, the promoter of the law, and had been quiet for some time after his brother's death, but since many of the senators treated him scornfully he announced himself as a candidate for the office of tribune. Being elected with flying colors he began to lay plots against the Senate, and made the unprecedented suggestion that a monthly distribution of corn should be made to each citizen at the public expense. Thus he quickly got the leadership of the people by one political measure, in which he had the cooperation of Fulvius Flaccus. Directly after that he was chosen tribune for the following year, for in cases where there was not a sufficient number of candidates the law authorized the people to choose further tribunes from the whole body of citizens.

22. Thus Gaius Gracchus was tribune a second time. Having bought the plebeians, as it were, he began, by another like political maneuver, to court the equestrian order, who hold the middle place between the Senate and the plebeians. He transferred the courts of justice, which had become discredited by reason of bribery, from the senators to the knights, reproaching the former especially with the recent examples of Aurelius Cotta, Salinator, and, third in the list, Manius Aquilius (the subduer of Asia), all notorious bribe-takers, who had been acquitted by the judges, although ambassadors sent to complain of their conduct were still present, going around uttering bitter accusations against them. The Senate was extremely ashamed of these things and yielded to the law, and the people ratified it. In this way were the courts of justice transferred from the Senate to the knights. It is said that soon after the passage of this law Gracchus remarked that he had broken the power of the Senate once for all, and the saying of Gracchus received a deeper and deeper significance by the course of events. For this power of sitting in judgment on all Romans and Italians, including the senators themselves, in all matters as to property, civil rights, and banishment, exalted the knights to be rulers over them, and put senators on the level of subjects. Moreover, as the knights voted in the election to sustain the power of the tribunes, and obtained from them whatever they wanted in return, they became more and more formidable to the senators. So it shortly came about that the political mastery was turned upside down, the power being in the hands of the knights, and the honor only remaining with the Senate. The knights indeed went so far that they not only held power over the senators, but they openly flouted them beyond their right. They also became addicted to bribe-taking, and when they too had tasted these enormous gains, they indulged in them even more basely and immoderately than the senators had done. They suborned accusers against the rich and did away with prosecutions for bribe-taking altogether, partly by agreement among themselves and partly by open violence, so that the practice of this kind of investigation became entirely obsolete. Thus the judiciary law gave rise to another struggle of factions, which lasted a long time and was not less baneful than the former ones.

23. Gracchus also made long roads throughout Italy and thus put a multitude of contractors and artisans under obligations to him and made them ready to do whatever he wished. He proposed the founding of numerous colonies. He also called on the Latin allies to demand the full rights of Roman citizenship, since the Senate could not with decency refuse this privilege to men of the same race. To the other allies, who were not allowed to vote in Roman elections, he sought to give the right of suffrage, in order to have their help in the enactment of laws which he had in contemplation. The Senate was very much alarmed at this, and it ordered the consuls to give the following public notice, "Nobody who does not possess the right of suffrage shall stay in the city or approach within forty stades of it while voting is going on concerning these laws." The Senate also persuaded Livius Drusus, another tribune, to interpose his veto against the laws proposed by Gracchus, but not to tell the people his reasons for doing so; for a tribune was not required to give reasons for his veto. In order to conciliate the people they gave Drusus the privilege of founding twelve colonies, and the plebeians were so much pleased with this that they scoffed at the laws proposed by Gracchus.

24. Having lost the favor of the rabble, Gracchus sailed for Africa in company with Fulvius Flaccus, who, after his consulship, had been chosen tribune for the same reasons as Gracchus himself. It had been decided to send a colony to Africa on account of its reputed fertility, and these men had been expressly chosen the founders of it in order to get them out of the way for a while, so that the Senate might have a respite from demagogery. They marked out the city for the colony on the place where Carthage had formerly stood, disregarding the fact that Scipio, when he destroyed it, had devoted it with solemn imprecations to sheep-pasturage for ever. They assigned 6,000 colonists to this place, instead of the smaller number fixed by law, in order further to curry favor with the people thereby. When they returned to Rome they invited the 6,000 from the whole of Italy. The functionaries who were still in Africa laying out the city wrote home that wolves had pulled up and scattered the boundary marks made by Gracchus and Fulvius, and the soothsayers considered this an ill omen for the colony. So the Senate summoned the comitia, in which it was proposed to repeal the law concerning this colony. When Gracchus and Fulvius saw their failure in this matter they were furious, and declared that the Senate had lied about the wolves. The boldest of the plebeians joined them, carrying daggers, and proceeded to the Capitol, where the assembly was to be held in reference to the colony.

25. Now the people had come together already, and Fulvius had begun speaking about the business in hand, when Gracchus arrived at the Capitol attended by a body-guard of his partisans. Conscience-stricken by what he knew about the extraordinary plans on foot he turned aside from the meeting-place of the assembly, passed into the portico, and walked about waiting to see what would happen. Just then a plebeian named Antyllus, who was sacrificing in the portico, saw him in this disturbed state, laid his hand upon him, either because he had heard or suspected something, or was moved to speak to him for some other reason, and begged him to spare his country. Gracchus, still more disturbed, and startled like one detected in a crime, gave the man a sharp look. Then one of his party, although no signal had been displayed or order given, inferred merely from the angry glance that Gracchus cast upon Antyllus that the time for action had come, and thought that he should do a favor to Gracchus by striking the first blow. So he drew his dagger and slew Antyllus. A cry was raised, the dead body was seen in the midst of the crowd, and all who were outside fled from the temple in fear of a like fate. Gracchus went into the assembly desiring to exculpate himself of the deed, but nobody would so much as listen to him. All turned away from him as from one stained with blood. So both he and Flaccus were at their wits' end, and, having lost through this hasty act the chance of accomplishing what they wished, they hastened to their homes, and their partisans with them. The rest of the crowd occupied the forum after midnight as though some calamity were impending, and Opimius the consul who was staying in the city, ordered an armed force to gather in the Capitol at daybreak, and sent heralds to convoke the Senate. He took his own station in the temple of Castor and Pollux in the center of the city and there awaited events.

26. When these arrangements had been made the Senate summoned Gracchus and Flaccus from their homes to the senate-house to defend themselves. But they ran out armed toward the Aventine hill, hoping that if they could seize it first the Senate would agree to some terms with them. As they ran through the city they offered freedom to the slaves, but none listened to them. With such forces as they had, however, they occupied and fortified the temple of Diana, and sent Quintus, the son of Flaccus, to the Senate seeking to come to an arrangement and to live in harmony. The Senate replied that they should lay down their arms, come to the senate-house, and tell them what they wanted, or else send no more messengers. When they sent Quintus a second time the consul Opimius arrested him, as being no longer an ambassador after he had been warned, and at the same time sent his armed men against the Gracchans.

Gracchus fled across the river by the wooden bridge with one slave to a grove, and there, being on a the point of arrest, he presented his throat to the slave. Flaccus took refuge in the workshop of an acquaintance. As his pursuers did not know which house he was in they threatened to burn the whole row. The man who had given shelter to the suppliant hesitated to point him out, but directed another man to do so. Flaccus was seized and put to death. The heads of Gracchus and Flaccus were carried to Opimius, and he gave their weight in gold to those who brought them, but the people plundered their houses. Opimius then arrested their fellow-conspirators, cast them into prison, and ordered that they should be strangled; but he allowed Quintus, the son of Flaccus, to choose his own mode of death. After this a lustration of the city was performed for the bloodshed, and the Senate ordered the building of a temple to Concord in the forum.

SALLUST

Life

C. Sallustius Crispus (c. 86–35 B.C.E.) was born into a local aristocratic family in Sabine country northeast of Rome, and received an excellent education in Greek and Latin literature. He served as quaestor in 55 and as tribune of the people in 52. He opposed Cicero's unsuccessful defense of Milo who had killed the popular politician Clodius in a street brawl. A few years later Sallust was exiled by the Senate for immorality, but the real cause was probably his political stance. When the civil war broke out in 49, Caesar made Sallust one of his generals with the office of praetor. He then served as the first governor of the new province of Africa Nova (Numidia), but he was prosecuted for corruption soon after his return to Rome in 45. Though his Caesar protected him from trial, Sallust never again held public office and lived in a Roman villa so luxurious that it later became an imperial estate. Sallust's own version is different: that he voluntarily chose retirement from public life to achieve philosophical peace of mind.

Works

Sallust's first monograph, written about 42, concerns the conspiracy of Catiline. In it Sallust provides an unfavorable moral portrait of Catiline and his followers whose failed attempt at revolution in 63 was crushed by the consul Cicero and the Senate. His next monograph, written about 40, described the war which the Numidian king Jugurtha waged against Rome between 111 and 105 B.C.E. This subject also allowed Sallust to criticize the greed and corruption of the Roman elite and to praise the popular hero Marius. In his last years Sallust began the book he intended to be his masterpiece—The Histories, a survey of the period from 78 down to his own time. Though he completed five books taking the story down to 67, only fragments survive.

The historian adopted an archaic style of Latin, notable for its epigrams and brevity. Livy called it "hard and dry"—it was far from the Ciceronian ideal of grace and balance. Sallust's bleak interpretation of Roman history fixed the beginning of Rome's decline with the defeat of her last great enemy, Carthage, in 146 B.C.E. He believed that the social and economic changes that resulted from Rome's conquests had corrupted the Roman spirit. Despite his own hypocrisy and bias in favor of popular politicians, Sallust's interpretation had great influence and was later adopted both by Tacitus and Christian authors like Augustine.

THE CATILINARIAN CONSPIRACY*

1. It behooves all men who wish to excel the other animals to strive with might and main not to pass through life unheralded, like the beasts, which Nature has fashioned groveling and slaves to the belly. All our power, on the contrary, lies in both mind and body; we employ the mind to rule, the body rather to serve; the one we have in common with the Gods, the other with the brutes. Therefore I find it becoming, in seeking renown, that we should employ the resources of the intellect rather than those of brute strength, to the end that, since the span of life which we enjoy is short, we may make the memory of our lives as long as possible. For the renown which riches or beauty confer is fleeting and frail; mental excellence is a splendid and lasting possession.

Yet for a long time mortal men have discussed the question whether success in arms depends more on strength of body or excellence of mind; for before you begin, deliberation is necessary, when you have deliberated, prompt action. Thus each of these being incomplete in itself, requires the other's aid.

2. Accordingly in the beginning kings (for that was the first title of sovereignty among men) took different courses, some training their minds and others their bodies. Even at that time men's lives were still free from covetousness; each was quite content with his own possessions. But when Cyrus in Asia, and in Greece the Athenians and Lacedaemonians, began to subdue cities and nations, to make the lust for dominion a pretext for war, to con-

---

*Sallust. 1920. *Sallust.* Translated by J.C. Rolfe. Loeb Classical Library.

sider the greatest empire the greatest glory, then at last men learned from perilous enterprises that qualities of mind availed most in war.

Now if the mental excellence with which kings and rulers are endowed were as potent in peace as in war, human affairs would run an evener and steadier course, and you would not see power passing from hand to hand and everything in turmoil and confusion; for empire is easily retained by the qualities by which it was first won. But when sloth has usurped the place of industry, and lawlessness and insolence have superseded self-restraint and justice, the fortune of princes changes with their character. Thus the sway is always passing to the best man from the hands of his inferior.

Success in agriculture, navigation, and architecture depends invariably upon mental excellence. Yet many men, being slaves to appetite and sleep, have passed through life untaught and untrained, like mere wayfarers; in these men we see, contrary to Nature's intent, the body a source of pleasure, the soul a burden. For my own part, I consider the lives and deaths of such men as about alike, since no record is made of either. In very truth that man alone lives and makes the most of life, as it seems to me, who devotes himself to some occupation, courting the fame of a glorious deed or a noble career. But amid the wealth of opportunities Nature points out one path to one and another to another.

3. It is glorious to serve one's country by deeds; even to serve her by words is a thing not to be despised; one may become famous in peace as well as in war. Not only those who have acted, but those also who have recorded the acts of others oftentimes receive our approbation. And for myself, although I am well aware that by no means equal repute attends the narrator and the doer of deeds, yet I regard the writing of history as one of the most difficult of tasks: first, because the style and diction must be equal to the deeds recorded; and in the second place, because such criticisms as you make of others' shortcomings are thought by most men to be due to malice and envy. Furthermore, when you commemorate the distinguished merit and fame of good men, while everyone is quite ready to believe you when you tell of things which he thinks he could easily do himself, everything beyond that he regards as fictitious, if not false.

When I myself was a young man, my inclinations at first led me, like many another, into public life, and there I encountered many obstacles; for instead of modesty, incorruptibility and honesty, shamelessness, bribery and rapacity held sway. And although my soul, a stranger to evil ways, recoiled from such faults, yet amid so many vices my youthful weakness was led astray and held captive by ambition; for while I took no part in the evil practices of the others, yet the desire for preferment made me the victim of the same ill-repute and jealousy as they.

4. Accordingly, when my mind found peace after many troubles and perils and I had determined that I must pass what was left of my life aloof from public affairs, it was not my intention to waste my precious leisure in indolence and sloth, nor yet by turning to farming or the chase, to lead a life devoted to slavish employments. On the contrary, I resolved to return to a cherished purpose from which ill-starred ambition had diverted me, and write a history of the Roman people, selecting such portions as seemed to me worthy of record; and I was confirmed in this resolution by the fact that my mind was free from hope, and fear, and partisanship. I shall therefore write briefly and as truthfully as possible of the conspiracy of Catiline; for I regard that event as worthy of special notice because of the extraordinary nature of the crime and of the danger arising from it. But before beginning my narrative I must say a few words about the man's character.

5. Lucius Catiline, scion of a noble family, had great vigor both of mind and of body, but an evil and depraved nature. From youth up he reveled in civil wars, murder, pillage, and political dissension, and amid these he spent his early manhood. His body could endure hunger, cold and want of sleep to an incredible degree; his mind was reckless, cunning, treacherous, capable of any form of pretense or concealment. Covetous of others' possessions, he was prodigal of his own; he was violent in his passions. He possessed a certain amount of eloquence, but little discretion. His disordered mind ever craved the monstrous, incredible, gigantic.

After the domination of Lucius Sulla the man had been seized with a mighty desire of getting control of the government, considering little by what manner he should achieve it, provided he made himself supreme. His haughty spirit was goaded more and more every day by poverty and a sense of guilt, both of which he had augmented by the practices of which I have already spoken. He was spurred on, also, by the corruption of the public morals, which were being ruined by two great evils of an opposite character, extravagance and avarice.

Since the occasion has arisen to speak of the morals of our country, the nature of my theme seems to suggest that I go farther back and give a brief account of the institutions of our forefathers in peace and in war, how they governed the commonwealth, how great it was when they bequeathed it to us, and how by gradual changes it has ceased to be the noblest and best, and has become the worst and most vicious.

6. The city of Rome, according to my understanding, was at the outset founded and inhabited by Trojans, who were wandering about in exile under the leadership of Aeneas and had no fixed abode; they were joined by the Aborigines, a rustic folk, without laws or government, free and unrestrained. After these two peoples, different in race, unlike in speech and mode of life, were united within the same walls, they were merged into one with incredible facility, so quickly did harmony change a heterogeneous and roving band into a commonwealth. But when this new community had grown in numbers, civilization, and territory, and was beginning to seem amply rich and amply strong, then, as is usual with mortal affairs, prosperity gave birth to envy. As a result, neighboring kings and peoples made war upon them, and but few of their friends lent them aid; for the rest were smitten with fear and stood aloof from the danger. But the Romans, putting forth their whole energy at home and in the field, made all haste, got ready, encouraged one another, went to meet the foe, and defended their liberty, their country, and their parents by arms. Afterwards, when their prowess had averted the danger, they lent aid to their allies and friends, and established friendly relations rather by conferring than by accepting favors.

They had a constitution founded upon law, which was in name a monarchy; a chosen few, whose bodies were enfeebled by age but whose minds were fortified with wisdom, took counsel for the welfare of the state. These were called "Fathers,"[1] by reason either of their age or of the similarity of their duties. Later, when the rule of the kings, which at first had tended to preserve freedom and advance the state, had degenerated into a lawless tyranny, they altered their form of government and appointed two rulers with annual power, thinking that this device would prevent men's minds from growing arrogant through unlimited authority.

7. Now at that time every man began to lift his head higher and to have his talents more in readiness. For kings hold the good in greater suspicion than the wicked, and to them the merit of others is always fraught with danger; still the free state, once liberty was won, waxed incredibly strong and great in a remarkably short time, such was the thirst for glory that had filled men's minds. To begin with, as soon as the young men could endure the hardships of war, they were taught a soldier's duties in camp under a vigorous discipline, and they took more pleasure in handsome arms and war horses than in harlots and revelry. To such men consequently no labor was unfamiliar, no region too rough or too steep, no armed foe was terrible; valor was all in all. Nay, their hardest struggle for glory was with one another; each man strove to be first to strike down the foe, to scale a wall, to be seen of all while doing such a deed. This they considered riches, this fair fame and high nobility. It was praise they coveted, but they were lavish of money; their aim was unbounded renown, but only such riches as could be gained honorably. I might name the battlefields on which the Romans with a mere handful of men routed great armies of their adversaries, and the cities fortified by nature which they took by assault, were it not that such a theme would carry me too far from my subject.

---

[1] "Fathers" (*Patres*) was the term applied to the Senate.

8. But beyond question Fortune holds sway everywhere. It is she that makes all events famous or obscure according to her caprice rather than in accordance with the truth. The acts of the Athenians, in my judgment, were indeed great and glorious enough, but nevertheless somewhat less important than fame represents them. But because Athens produced writers of exceptional talent, the exploits of the men of Athens are heralded throughout the world as unsurpassed. Thus the merit of those who did the deeds is rated as high as brilliant minds have been able to exalt the deeds themselves by words of praise. But the Roman people never had that advantage, since their ablest men were always most engaged with affairs; their minds were never employed apart from their bodies; the best citizen preferred action to words, and thought that his own brave deeds should be lauded by others rather than that theirs should be recounted by him.

9. Accordingly, good morals were cultivated at home and in the field; there was the greatest harmony and little or no avarice; justice and probity prevailed among them, thanks not so much to laws as to nature. Quarrels, discord, and strife were reserved for their enemies; citizen vied with citizen only for the prize of merit. They were lavish in their offerings to the gods, frugal in the home, loyal to their friends. By practicing these two qualities, boldness in warfare and justice when peace came, they watched over themselves and their country. In proof of these statements I present this convincing evidence: firstly, in time of war punishment was more often inflicted for attacking the enemy contrary to orders, or for withdrawing too tardily when recalled from the field, than for venturing to abandon the standards or to give ground under stress; and secondly, in time of peace they ruled by kindness rather than fear, and when wronged preferred forgiveness to vengeance

10. But when our country had grown great through toil and the practice of justice, when great kings had been defeated in war, savage tribes and mighty peoples subdued by force of arms, when Rome's rival Carthage had perished root and branch, and all seas and lands were open, then Fortune began to grow cruel and to bring confusion to all our affairs. Those who had found it easy to bear hardship and dangers, anxiety and adversity, found leisure and wealth, desirable under other circumstances, a burden and a curse. Hence the lust for power first, then for money, grew upon them; these were, I may say, the root of all evils. For avarice destroyed honor, integrity, and all other noble qualities; taught in their place insolence, cruelty, to neglect the gods, to set a price on everything. Ambition drove many men to become false; to have one thought locked in the breast, another ready on the tongue; to value friendships and enmities not on their merits but by the standard of self-interest, and to show a good front rather than a good heart. At first these vices grew slowly, from time to time they were punished; finally, when the disease had spread like a deadly plague, the state was changed and a government second to none in equity and excellence became cruel and intolerable.

11. But at first men's souls were actuated less by avarice than by ambition —a fault, it is true, but not so far removed from virtue; for the noble and the base alike long for glory, honor, and power, but the former mount by the true path, whereas the latter, being destitute of noble qualities, rely upon craft and deception. Avarice implies a desire for money which no wise man covets; steeped as it were with noxious poisons, it renders the most manly body and soul effeminate; it is ever unbounded and insatiable, nor can either plenty or want make it less. But after Lucius Sulla, having gained control of the state by arms, brought everything to a bad end from a good beginning, all men began to rob and pillage. One coveted a house, another lands; the victors showed neither moderation nor restraint, but shamefully and cruelly wronged their fellow citizens. Besides all this, Lucius Sulla, in order to secure the loyalty of the army which he led into Asia, had allowed it a luxury and license foreign to the manners of our forefathers; and in the intervals of leisure those charming and voluptuous lands had easily demoralized the warlike spirit of his soldiers. There it was that an army of the Roman people first learned to indulge in women and drink; to admire statues, paintings, and vases, to steal them from private houses and public places, to pillage shrines, and to desecrate everything, both sacred and profane. These soldiers, therefore, after they had won the victory, left nothing to the defeated. In truth, prosperity tries the souls even of the wise; how then should depraved men like these make a moderate use of victory?

12. As soon as riches came to be held in honor, when glory, dominion, and power followed in their train, virtue began to lose its luster, poverty to be considered a disgrace, blamelessness to be termed malevolence. Therefore as the result of riches, luxury and greed, united with insolence, took possession of our young manhood. They pillaged, squandered; set little value on their own, coveted the goods of others; they disregarded modesty, chastity, everything human and divine; in short, they were utterly thoughtless and reckless.

It is worth your while, when you look upon houses and villas reared to the size of cities, to pay a visit to the temples of the gods built by our forefathers, most reverent of men. But they adorned the shrines of the gods with piety, their own homes with glory, while from the vanquished they took naught save the power of doing harm. The men of today, on the contrary, basest of creatures, with supreme wickedness are robbing our allies of all that those heroes in the hour of victory had left them; they act as though the one and only way to rule were to wrong.

13. Why, pray, should I speak of things which are incredible except to those who have seen them, that a host of private men have leveled mountains and built upon the seas? To such men their riches seem to me to have been but a plaything, for while they might have enjoyed them honorably, they made haste to squander them shamefully. Nay more, the passion which arose for lewdness, gluttony, and the other attendants of luxury was equally strong; men played the woman, women offered their chastity for sale; to gratify their palates they scoured land and sea; they slept before they needed sleep; they did not await the coming of hunger or thirst, of cold or of weariness, but all these things their self-indulgence anticipated. Such were the vices that incited the young men to crime, as soon as they had run through their property. Their minds, habituated to evil practices, could not easily refrain from self-indulgence, and so they abandoned themselves the more recklessly to every means of gain as well as of extravagance.

14. In a city so great and so corrupt Catiline found it a very easy matter to surround himself, as by a bodyguard, with troops of criminals and reprobates of every kind. For whatever wanton, glutton, or gamester had wasted his patrimony in play, feasting, or debauchery; anyone who had contracted an immense debt that he might buy immunity from disgrace or crime; all, furthermore, from every side who had been convicted of murder or sacrilege, or feared prosecution for their crimes; those, too, whom hand and tongue supported by perjury or the blood of their fellow citizens; finally, all who were hounded by disgrace, poverty, or an evil conscience—all these were nearest and dearest to Catiline. And if any guiltless man did chance to become his friend, daily intercourse and the allurements of vice soon made him as bad or almost as bad as the rest. But most of all Catiline sought the intimacy of the young; their minds, still pliable as they were and easily molded, were without difficulty ensnared by his wiles. For carefully noting the passion which burned in each, according to his time of life, he found harlots for some or bought dogs and horses for others; in fine, he spared neither expense nor his own decency, provided he could make them submissive and loyal to himself. I am aware that some have believed that the young men who frequented Catiline's house set but little store by their chastity; but that report became current rather for other reasons than because anyone had evidence of its truth.

15. Even in youth Catiline had many shameful intrigues—with a maiden of noble rank, with a priestess of Vesta—and other affairs equally unlawful and impious. At last he was seized with a passion for Aurelia Orestilla, in whom no good man ever commended anything save her beauty; and when she hesitated to marry him because she was afraid of his stepson, then a grown man, it is generally believed that he murdered the young man in order to make an empty house for this criminal marriage. In fact, I think that this was his special motive for hastening his plot; for his guilt-stained soul, at odds with gods and men, could find rest neither waking nor sleeping, so cruelly did conscience ravage his overwrought mind. Hence his pallid complexion,

his bloodshot eyes, his gait now fast, now slow; in short, his face and his every glance showed the madman.

16. To the young men whom he had ensnared as I have described, he taught many forms of wickedness. From their number he supplied false witnesses and forgers; he bade them make light of honor, fortune, and dangers; then, when he had sapped their good repute and modesty, he called for still greater crimes. If there was no immediate motive for wrong doing, he nevertheless waylaid and murdered innocent as well as guilty; indeed, he preferred to be needlessly vicious and cruel rather than to allow their hands and spirits to grow weak through lack of practice.

Relying upon such friends and accomplices as these, Catiline formed the plan of overthrowing the government, both because his own debt was enormous in all parts of the world and because the greater number of Sulla's veterans, who had squandered their property and now thought with longing of their former pillage and victories, were eager for civil war. There was no army in Italy; Gnaeus Pompeius was waging war in distant parts of the world; Catiline himself had high hopes as a candidate for the consulship; the senate was anything but alert; all was peaceful and quiet; this was his golden opportunity.

17. Accordingly, towards the first of June in the consulate of Lucius Caesar and Gaius Figulus, he addressed his followers at first one by one, encouraging some and sounding others. He pointed out his own resources, the unprepared condition of the state, the great prizes of conspiracy. When he had such information as he desired, he assembled all those who were most desperate and most reckless. There were present from the senatorial order Publius Lentulus Sura, Publius Autronius, Lucius Cassius Longinus, Gaius Cethegus, Publius and Servius Sulla, sons of Servius, Lucius Vargunteius, Quintus Annius, Marcus Porcius Laeca, Lucius Bestia, Quintus Curius; also of the equestrian order, Marcus Fulvius Nobilior, Lucius Statilius, Publius Gabinius Capito, Gaius Cornelius; besides these there were many men from the colonies and free towns who were of noble rank at home. There were, moreover, several nobles who had a somewhat more secret connection with the plot, men who were prompted rather by the hope of power than by want or any other exigency. The greater part of the young men also, in particular those of high position, were favorable to Catiline's project; for although in quiet times they had the means of living elegantly or luxuriously, they preferred uncertainty to certainty, war to peace. There were also at that time some who believed that Marcus Licinius Crassus was not wholly ignorant of the plot; that because his enemy Gaius Pompeius was in command of a large army, he was willing to see anyone's influence grow in opposition to the power of his rival, fully believing meanwhile that if the conspirators should be successful, he would easily be the leading man among them.

18. Now, even before that time a few men had conspired against the government, and among them was Catiline; of that affair I shall give as true an account as I am able. In the consulship of Lucius Tullus and Manius Lepidus (66 B.C.E.), the consuls elect, Publius Autronius and Publius Sulla, were arraigned under the law against bribery and paid the penalties. A little later Catiline was charged with extortion and prevented from standing for the consulship, because he had been unable to announce his candidacy within the prescribed number of days. There was at that same time a young noble called Gnaeus Piso, a man of the utmost recklessness, poor, and given to intrigue, who was being goaded on by need of funds and an evil character to overthrow the government. He revealed his plans to Catiline and Autronius; they in concert with him began, about the fifth of December, to make preparations to murder the consuls Lucius Cotta and Lucius Torquatus in the Capitol on the first of January; they then proposed that they themselves should seize the fasces and dispatch Piso with an army to take possession of the two Spanish provinces. Upon the discovery of their plot they postponed their murderous design until the fifth of February. At that time they plotted the destruction not merely of the consuls but of many of the senators, and had Catiline not been over-hasty in giving the signal to his accomplices in front of the senate-house, on that day the most dreadful crime since the founding of the city of Rome would have been perpetrated. But because the armed conspirators had not yet assembled in sufficient numbers, the affair came to naught.

19. Piso was afterwards, through the efforts of Crassus, who knew him to be a deadly enemy of Gnaeus Pompeius, sent to Hither Spain with praetorian powers, although he was only a quaestor. The senate, however, had been quite willing to give him the province, wishing to remove the shameless fellow to a distance from the seat of government. Moreover, many of the aristocracy thought they had in him a safeguard against Pompey, whose power was even then becoming formidable. Now this Piso was slain, while marching through his province, by the Spanish cavalry under his command. Some say that the barbarians could not endure his rule, unjust, insolent, and cruel; others, that the horsemen, who were old and devoted retainers of Pompey, attacked Piso at his instigation. The latter point out that the Spaniards had never before committed such a crime, but had tolerated many cruel rulers in former days. We shall not attempt to decide this question, and enough has been said about the first conspiracy.

20. When Catiline saw before him the men whom I mentioned a short time ago, although he had often had long conferences with them individually, he thought that it would be to address and encourage the entire body. Accordingly, withdrawing to a private room of the house and excluding all witnesses, he made the following speech:

"If I had not already tested your courage and loyalty, in vain would a great opportunity have presented itself; high hopes and power would have been placed in my hands to no purpose, nor would I with the aid of cowards or inconstant hearts grasp at uncertainty in place of certainty. But because I have learned in many and great emergencies that you are brave and faithful to me, my mind has had the courage to set on foot a mighty and glorious enterprise, and also because I perceive that you and I hold the same view of what is good and evil; for agreement in likes and dislikes—this, and this only, is what constitutes true friendship. As for the designs which I have formed, they have already been explained to you all individually. But my resolution is fired more and more everyday, when I consider under what conditions we shall live if we do not take steps to emancipate ourselves. For ever since the state fell under the jurisdiction and sway of a few powerful men, it is always to them that kings and potentates are tributary and peoples and nations pay taxes. All the rest of us, good and bad, nobles and commons alike, have made up the mob, without influence, without weight, and subservient to those to whom in a free state we should be an object of fear. Because of this, all influence, power, rank, and wealth are in their hands, or wherever they wish them to be; to us they have left danger, defeat, prosecutions and poverty. How long, pray, will you endure this, brave hearts? Is it not better to die valiantly, than ignominiously to lose our wretched and dishonored lives after being the sport of others' insolence? Assuredly (I swear it by the faith of gods and men!) victory is within our grasp. We are in the prime of life, we are stout of heart; to them, on the contrary, years and riches have brought utter dotage. We need only to strike; the rest will take care of itself. Pray, what man with the spirit of a man can endure that our tyrants should abound in riches to squander in building upon the sea and in leveling mountains, while we lack the means to buy the bare necessities of life? That they should join their palaces by twos or even more, while we have nowhere a hearthstone? They amass paintings, statuary and chased vases, tear down new structures and erect others, in short misuse and torment their wealth in every way; yet, with the utmost extravagance, they cannot get the upper hand of their riches. But we have destitution at home, debt without, present misery and a still more hopeless future; in short, what have we left, save only the wretched breath of life? Awake then! Lo, here, here before your eyes, is the freedom for which you have often longed, and with it riches, honor, and glory; Fortune offers all these things as prizes to the victors. The undertaking itself, the opportunity, the dangers, your need, the splendid spoils of war, speak louder than any words of mine. Use me either as your leader or as a soldier in the ranks; my soul and my body shall be at your service. These very schemes I hope to help you carry out as your consul, unless haply I delude myself and you are content to be slaves rather than to rule."

21. When these words fell upon the ears of men who had misfortune of every kind in excess, but neither means nor any honorable hope, although disorder alone seemed to them an ample reward, yet many of them called upon him to explain the conditions under which war would be waged, what the prizes of victory would be, and what resources or prospects they would have and in what quarter. Thereupon Catiline promised abolition of debts, the proscription of the rich, offices, priesthoods, plunder, and all the other spoils that war and the license of victors can offer. He added that Piso was in Hither Spain, Publius Sittius of Nuceria in Mauretania with an army, both of whom were partners in his plot; that Gaius Antonius was a candidate for the consulship, and, he hoped, would be his colleague, a man who was an intimate friend of his and was beset by every sort of necessity; consul with him, he would launch his undertaking. Thereupon he heaped maledictions upon all good citizens, lauded each of his own followers by name; he reminded one of his poverty, another of his ambition, several of their danger or disgrace, many of the victory of Sulla, which they had found a source of booty. When he saw that their spirits were all aflame, he dismissed the meeting, urging them to have his candidacy at heart.

22. It was said at the time that when Catiline, after finishing his address, compelled the participants in his crime to take an oath, he passed around bowls of human blood mixed with wine; that when after an imprecation upon traitors all had tasted it, as is usual in solemn rites, he disclosed his project; and his end in so doing was, they say, that they might be more faithful to one another because they shared the guilty knowledge of so dreadful a deed. Others thought that these and many other details were invented by men who believed that the hostility which afterwards arose against Cicero would be moderated by exaggerating the guilt of the conspirators whom he had put to death. For my own part I have too little evidence for pronouncing upon a matter of such weight.

23. Now one of the members of the conspiracy was Quintus Curius, a man of no mean birth but guilty of many shameful crimes, whom the censors had expelled from the senate because of his immorality. This man was as untrustworthy as he was reckless; he could neither keep secret what he had heard nor conceal even his own misdeeds; he was utterly regardless of what he did or said. He had an intrigue of long standing with Fulvia, a woman of quality, and when he began to lose her favor because poverty compelled him to be less lavish, he suddenly fell to boasting, began to promise her seas and mountains and sometimes to threaten his mistress with the steel if she did not bow to his will; in brief, to show much greater assurance than before. But Fulvia, when she learned the cause of her lover's overbearing conduct, had no thought of concealing such a peril to her country, but without mentioning the name of her informant she told a number of people what she had heard of Catiline's conspiracy from various sources.

It was this discovery in particular which aroused a general desire to confer the consulate upon Marcus Tullius Cicero; for before that most of the nobles were consumed with jealousy and thought the office in a way prostituted if a "new man,"[1] however excellent, should obtain it. But when danger came, jealousy and pride fell into the background.

24. Accordingly, when the elections had been held Marcus Tullius and Gaius Antonius were proclaimed consuls, and this at first filled the conspirators with consternation. And yet Catiline's frenzy did not abate. On the contrary, he increased his activity everyday, made collections of arms at strategic points in Italy, and borrowed money on his own credit or that of his friends, sending it to Fiesole to a certain Manlius, who afterwards was the first to take the field. At that time Catiline is said to have gained the support of many men of all conditions and even of some women; the latter at first had met their enormous expenses by prostitution, but later, when their time of life had set a limit to their traffic but not to their extravagance, had contracted a huge debt. Through their help Catiline believed that he could tempt the city slaves to his side and set fire to Rome; and then either attach the women's husbands to his cause or make away with them.

25. Now among these women was Sempronia, who had often committed many crimes of masculine daring. In birth and beauty, in her husband also and children, she was abundantly favored by fortune; well read in the literature of Greece and Rome, able to play the lyre and dance more skillfully than an honest woman need, and having many other accomplishments which minister to voluptuousness. But there was nothing which she held so cheap as modesty and chastity; you could not easily say whether she was less sparing of her money or her honor; her desires were so ardent that she sought men more often than she was sought by them. Even before the time of the conspiracy she had often broken her word, repudiated her debts, been privy to murder; poverty and extravagance combined had driven her headlong. Nevertheless, she was a woman of no mean endowments; she could write verses, bandy jests, and use language which was modest, or tender, or wanton; in fine, she possessed a high degree of wit and of charm.

26. After making these preparations Catiline nevertheless became a candidate for the consulship of the following year, hoping that if he should be elected he could easily do whatever he wished with Antonius. In the meantime he was not idle, but kept laying plots of all kinds against Cicero, who,

[1] The Romans called a *novus homo* (new man) a politician who was the first in his family to reach the consulship.

however, did not lack the craft and address to escape them. For immediately after the beginning of his consulate, by dint of many promises made through Fulvia, Cicero had induced Quintus Curius, the man whom I mentioned a little while ago, to reveal Catiline's designs to him. Furthermore, he had persuaded his colleague Antonius, by agreeing to make over his province to him, not to entertain schemes hostile to the public weal, and he also had surrounded himself secretly with a bodyguard of friends and dependents.

When the day of the elections came and neither Catiline's suit nor the plots which he had made against the consuls in the Campus Martius were successful, he resolved to take the field and dare the uttermost, since his covert attempts had resulted in disappointment and disgrace.

27. He therefore dispatched Gaius Manlius to Fiesole and the adjacent part of Etruria, a certain Septimius of Camerinum to the Picene district, and Gaius Julius to Apulia; others too to other places, wherever he thought that each would be serviceable to his project. Meanwhile he himself was busy at Rome with many attempts at once, laying traps for the consul, planning fires, posting armed men in commanding places. He went armed himself, bade others do the same, conjured them to be always alert and ready, kept on the move night and day, took no rest yet succumbed neither to wakefulness nor fatigue. Finally, when his manifold attempts met with no success, again in the dead of night he summoned the ringleaders of the conspiracy to the house of Marcus Porcius Laeca. There, after reproaching them bitterly for their inaction, he stated that he had sent Manlius on ahead to the force which he had prepared for war, and also other men to other important points to commence hostilities, explaining that he himself was eager to go to the front if he could first make away with Cicero, who was a serious obstacle to his plans.

28. Upon this the rest were terrified and hesitated; but Gaius Cornelius, a Roman knight, offered his services and was joined by Lucius Vargunteius, a senator. These two men determined that very night, a little later, to get access to Cicero, accompanied by a band of armed men, as if for a ceremonial call and taking him by surprise to murder the defenseless consul in his own house. When Curius learned of the great danger which threatened the consul, he hastened to report to Cicero through Fulvia the trap which was being set for him. Hence the would-be assassins were refused admission and proved to have undertaken this awful crime to no purpose.

Meanwhile Manlius in Etruria was working upon the populace, who were already ripe for revolution because of penury and resentment at their wrongs; for during Sulla's supremacy they had lost their lands and all their property. He also approached brigands of various nationalities, who were numerous in that part of the country, and some members of Sulla's colonies who had been stripped by prodigal and luxurious living of the last of their great booty.

29. When these events were reported to Cicero, he was greatly disturbed by the twofold peril, since he could no longer by his unaided efforts protect the city against these plots, nor gain any exact information as to the size and purpose of Manlius' army; he therefore formally called the attention of the senate to the matter, which had already been the subject of popular gossip. Thereupon, as is often done in a dangerous emergency, the senate voted "that the consuls should take heed that the commonwealth suffer no harm." The power which according to Roman usage is thus conferred upon a magistrate by the senate is supreme, allowing him to raise an army, wage war, exert any kind of compulsion upon allies and citizens, and exercise unlimited command and jurisdiction at home and in the field; otherwise the consul has none of these privileges except by the order of the people.

30. A few days later, in a meeting of the senate, Lucius Saenius, one its members, read a letter which he said had been brought to him from Fiesole, stating that Gaius Manlius had taken the field with a large force on the twenty-seventh day of October. At the same time, as is usual in such a crisis, omens and portents were reported by some, while others told of the holding of meetings, of the transportation of arms, and of insurrections of the slaves at Capua and in Apulia.

Thereupon by decree of the senate Quintus Marcius Rex was sent to Fiesole and Quintus Metellus Creticus to Apulia and its neighborhood. Both these generals were at the gates in command of their armies, being prevented from celebrating a triumph by the intrigues of a few men, whose habit it was to make everything, honorable and dishonorable, a matter of barter. Of the praetors, Quintus Pompeius Rufus was sent to Capua and Quintus Metellus Celer to the Picene district, with permission to raise an army suited to the emergency and the danger. The senate also voted that if anyone should give information as to the plot which had been made against the state, he should, if a slave, be rewarded with his freedom and a hundred thousand sesterces, and if a free man with immunity for complicity therein, and two hundred thousand sesterces; further, that the troops of gladiators should be quartered on Capua and the other free towns according to the resources of each place; that at Rome watch should be kept by night in all parts of the city under the direction of the minor magistrates.

31. These precautions struck the community with terror, and the aspect of the city was changed. In place of extreme gaiety and frivolity, the fruit of long-continued peace, there was sudden and general gloom. Men were uneasy and apprehensive, put little confidence in any place of security or in any human being, were neither at war nor at peace, and measured the peril each by his own fears. The women, too, whom the greatness of our country had hitherto shielded from the terrors of war, were in a pitiful state of anxiety, raised suppliant hands to heaven, bewailed the fate of their little children, asked continual questions, trembled at everything, and throwing aside haughtiness and self-indulgence, despaired of themselves and of their country.

But Catiline's pitiless spirit persisted in the same attempts, although defenses were preparing, and he himself had been arraigned by Lucius Paulus under the Plautian law. Finally, in order to conceal his designs or to clear himself, as though he had merely been the object of some private slander, he came into the senate. Then the consul Marcus Tullius, either fearing his presence or carried away by indignation, delivered a brilliant speech of great service to the state, which he later wrote out and published. When he took his seat, Catiline, prepared as he was to deny everything, with downcast eyes and pleading accents began to beg the Fathers of the Senate not to believe any unfounded charge against him; he was sprung from such a family, he said, and had so ordered his life from youth up, that he had none save the best of prospects. They must not suppose that he, a patrician, who like his forefathers had rendered great service to the Roman people, would be benefited by the overthrow of the government, while its savior was Marcus Tullius Cicero, a resident alien in the city of Rome.[1] When he would have added other insults, he was shouted down by the whole body, who called him traitor and assassin. Then in a transport of fury he cried: "Since I am brought to bay by my enemies and driven desperate, I will put out my fire by general devastation."

32. With this he rushed from the senate house and went home. There after thinking long upon the situation, since his designs upon the consul made no headway and he perceived that the city was protected against fires by watchmen, believing it best to increase the size of his army and secure many of the necessities of war before the legions were enrolled, he left for the camp of Manlius with a few followers in the dead of night. However, he instructed Cethegus, Lentulus, and the others whose reckless daring he knew to be ready for anything, to add to the strength of their cabal by whatever means they could, to bring the plots against the consul to a head, to make ready murder, arson, and the other horrors of war; as for himself, he would shortly be at the gates with a large army.

While this was going on at Rome, Gaius Manlius sent a delegation from his army to Marcius Rex with this message:

33. "We call gods and men to witness, general, that we have taken up arms, not against our fatherland nor to bring danger upon others, but to protect our own persons from outrage; for we are wretched and destitute, many of us have been driven from our country by the violence and cruelty of the moneylenders, while all have lost repute and fortune. None of us has been

---

[1] Though Marcus Tullius Cicero was born in the nearby city of Arpinum, he was from birth a Roman citizen.

allowed, in accordance with the usage of our forefathers, to enjoy the protection of the law and retain our personal liberty after being stripped of our patrimony, such was the inhumanity of the moneylenders and the praetor. Your forefathers often took pity on the Roman commons and relieved their necessities by senatorial decrees, and not long ago, within our own memory, because of the great amount of their debt, silver was paid in copper with the general consent of the nobles. Often the commons themselves, actuated by a desire to rule or incensed at the arrogance of the magistrates, have taken up arms and seceded from the patricians. But we ask neither for power nor for riches, the usual causes of wars and strife among mortals, but only for freedom, which no true man gives up except with his life. We implore you and the senate to take thought for your unhappy countrymen, to restore the bulwark of the law, of which the praetor's injustice has deprived us, and not to impose upon us the necessity of asking ourselves how we may sell our lives most dearly."

34. To this address Quintus Mucius made answer, that if they wished to ask anything of the senate, they must lay down their arms and come to Rome as suppliants; that the senate of the Roman people had always been so compassionate and merciful that no one had ever asked it for succor and been refused.

But on the way Catiline sent letters to many of the consulars and to the most prominent of the other nobles, saying that since he was beset by false accusations and unable to cope with the intrigues of his personal enemies, he bowed to fate and was on his way to exile at Massilia; not that he confessed to the dreadful crime with which he was charged, but in order that his country might be at peace and that no dissension might arise from a struggle on his part. A very different letter was read in the senate by Quintus Catulus, who said that it had been sent him in Catiline's name. The following is an exact copy of this letter:

35. "Lucius Catilina to Quintus Catulus. Your eminent loyalty, known by experience and grateful to me in my extreme peril, lends confidence to my plea. I have therefore resolved to make no defense of my unusual conduct; that I offer an explanation is due to no feeling of guilt, and I am confident that you will be able to admit its justice. Maddened by wrongs and slights, since I had been robbed of the fruits of my toil and energy and was unable to attain to a position of honor, I followed my usual custom and took up the general cause of the unfortunate; not that I could not pay my personal debts from my own estate (and the liberality of Orestilla sufficed with her own and her daughter's resources to pay off even the obligations incurred through others), but because I saw the unworthy elevated to honors, and realized that I was an outcast because of baseless suspicion. It is for this reason that, in order to preserve what prestige I have left, I have adopted measures which are honorable enough considering my situation. When I would write more, word comes that I am threatened with violence. Now I commend Orestilla to you and entrust her to your loyalty. Protect her from insult, I beseech you in the name of your own children. Farewell."

36. Catiline himself, after spending a few days with Gaius Flaminius in the vicinity of Arretium, where he supplied arms to the populace, which had already been roused to revolt, hastened to join Manlius in his camp, taking with him the fasces and the other emblems of authority. As soon as this became known at Rome, the senate pronounced Catiline and Manlius traitors and named a day before which the rest of the conspirators might lay down their arms and escape punishment, excepting those under sentence for capital offenses. It was further voted that the consuls should hold a levy and that Antonius with an army should at once pursue Catiline, while Cicero defended the capital.

At no other time has the condition of imperial Rome, as it seems to me, been more pitiable. The whole world, from the rising of the sun to its setting, subdued by her arms, rendered obedience to her; at home there was peace and an abundance of wealth, which mortal men deem the best of blessings. Yet there were citizens who from sheer perversity were bent upon their own ruin and that of their country. For in spite of the two decrees of the senate not one man of all that great number was led by the promised reward to betray the conspiracy, and not a single one deserted Catiline's camp; such was the potency of the malady which like a plague had infected the minds of many of our countrymen.

37. This insanity was not confined to those who were implicated in the plot, but the whole body of the commons through desire for change favored the designs of Catiline. In this very particular they seemed to act as the populace usually does; for in every community those who have no means envy the good, exalt the base, hate what is old and established, long for something new, and from disgust with their own lot desire a general upheaval. Amid turmoil and rebellion they maintain themselves without difficulty, since poverty is easily provided for and can suffer no loss. But the city populace in particular acted with desperation for many reasons. To begin with, all who were especially conspicuous for their shamelessness and impudence, those too who had squandered their patrimony in riotous living, finally all whom disgrace or crime had forced to leave home, had all flowed into Rome as into a cesspool. Many, too, who recalled Sulla's victory, when they saw common soldiers risen to the rank of senator, and others become so rich that they feasted and lived like kings, hoped each for himself for like fruits of victory, if he took the field. Besides this, the young men who had maintained a wretched existence by manual labor in the country, tempted by public and private doles had come to prefer idleness in the city to their hateful toil;

these, like all the others, battened on the public ills. Therefore it is not surprising that men who were beggars and without character with illimitable hopes, should respect their country as little as they did themselves. Moreover, those to whom Sulla's victory had meant the proscription of their parents, loss of property, and curtailment of their rights, looked forward in a similar spirit to the issue of a war. Finally, all who belonged to another party than that of the senate preferred to see the government overthrown rather than be out of power themselves. Such, then, was the evil which after many years had returned upon the state.

38. For after the tribunician power had been restored in the consulship of Gnaeus Pompeius and Marcus Crassus (70 B.C.E.), various young men, whose age and disposition made them aggressive, attained that high authority; they thereupon began to excite the commons by attacks upon the senate and then to inflame their passions still more by doles and promises, thus making themselves conspicuous and influential. Against these men the greater part of the nobles strove with might and main, ostensibly in behalf of the senate but really for their own aggrandizement. For, to tell the truth in a few words, all who after that time assailed the government used specious pretexts, some maintaining that they were defending the rights of the commons, others that they were upholding the prestige of the senate; but under pretense of the public welfare each in reality was working for his own advancement. Such men showed neither self-restraint nor moderation in their strife, and both parties used their victory ruthlessly.

39. When, however, Pompey had been dispatched to wage war against the pirates and against Mithridates, the power of the commons was lessened, while that of the few increased. These possessed the magistracies, the provinces and everything else; being themselves rich and secure against attack, they lived without fear and by resort to the courts terrified the others, in order that while they themselves were in office they might manage the people with less friction. But as soon as the political situation became doubtful, and offered hope of a revolution, then the old controversy aroused their passions anew. If Catiline had been victor in the first battle, or had merely held his own, beyond a doubt great bloodshed and disaster would have fallen upon the state; nor would the victors have been allowed for long to enjoy their success, but when they had been worn out and exhausted, a more powerful adversary would have wrested from them the supreme power and with it their freedom. Yet even as it was, there were many outside the ranks of the conspiracy who, when hostilities began, went to join Catiline. Among them was Fulvius, a senator's son, who was brought back and put to death by order of his father.

All this time at Rome Lentulus, following Catiline's directions, was working, personally or through others, upon those whom he thought ripe for revolution by disposition or fortune—and not merely citizens, but all sorts and conditions of men, provided only that they could be of any service in war.

40. Accordingly, he instructed one Publius Umbrenus to seek out the envoys of the Allobroges, and, if possible, entice them to an offensive alliance, thinking that they could readily be persuaded to such a course, since they were burdened with public and private debt; and besides the Gallic people are by nature prone to war. Umbrenus had carried on business with the Gauls and was personally acquainted with many of the leading men of their states; therefore as soon as he caught sight of the envoys in the Forum, he at once asked them a few questions about the condition of their country, and pretending grief at its lot, began to inquire what remedy they hoped to find for such great troubles. On learning that they had complaints to make of the avarice of the magistrates, that they reproached the senate because it rendered no aid, and looked for death as the only remedy for their wretchedness, he said: "Why, I myself, if only you will show yourselves men, will disclose a plan which will enable you to escape the great evils from which you are suffering."

When Umbrenus had said this, the Allobroges were filled with the greatest hope and begged him to take pity on them. They declared that nothing was so dangerous or difficult that they would not joyfully undertake it, provided it would relieve their country of debt. Thereupon he took them to the house of Decimus Brutus, which was not far from the Forum and not unsuitable for their plot because of the presence of Sempronia; Brutus, as it happened, was away from Rome at the time. He also sent for Gabinius, that what he was to say might have greater weight. When he arrived, Umbrenus disclosed the plot, named the participants, and, to give the envoys greater courage, included many guiltless men of all classes; then, after promising his assistance, he sent them home.

41. The Allobroges for a long time were in doubt what course to pursue. On the one hand was their debt, their love of war, and the hope of great booty in the event of victory; but on the other were the senate's greater resources, a course free from danger, and sure rewards in place of uncertain hopes. All these considerations they weighed, but in the end the fortune of the republic turned the scale. They accordingly divulged the whole affair, just as it had come to their ears, to Quintus Fabius Sanga, their nation's principal patron. Cicero, on being informed of the plan through Sanga, instructed the envoys to feign a strong interest in the conspiracy, approach the other members of it, make liberal promises, and use every effort to show the guilt of the conspirators as clearly as possible.

42. At about this same time there were disturbances in both Hither and Farther Gaul, as well as in the Picene and Bruttian districts and in Apulia; for

those whom Catiline had sent on ahead were doing everything at once, acting imprudently and almost insanely. By their meetings at night, by their transportation of arms and weapons, and by their bustle and general activity they caused more apprehension than actual danger. The praetor Quintus Metellus Celer had brought several of their number to trial by virtue of a decree of the senate, and had thrown them into prison; and in Hither Gaul his example was followed by Gaius Murena, who was governing that province as a deputy.

43. At Rome Lentulus and the other leaders of the conspiracy, having got together a great force as it appeared to them, had arranged that when Catiline arrived in the region of Fiesole with his army, Lucius Bestia, tribune of the commons, should convoke an assembly and denounce the conduct of Cicero, throwing upon that best of consuls the odium of a dangerous war. That was to be the signal for the rest of the band of conspirators to carry out their several enterprises on the following night. Now it is said that the parts assigned to them were the following: Statilius and Gabinius, with many followers, were to kindle fires at twelve important points in the city all at the same time, in order that in the ensuing confusion access might more easily be had to the consul and the others against whom their plots were directed. Cethegus was to beset Cicero's door and assault him, while to others were assigned other victims. The eldest sons of several families, the greater number of whom belonged to the nobility, were to slay their fathers. Then, when the whole city was stunned by the bloodshed and the fire, they were all to rush out and join Catiline.

During these preparations and arrangements, Cethegus constantly complained of the inaction of his associates, insisting that by indecision and delay they were wasting great opportunities; that such a crisis called for action, not deliberation, and that if a few would aid him he would himself make an attack upon the senate-house, even though the rest were faint-hearted. Being naturally aggressive, violent, and prompt to act, he set the highest value upon dispatch.

44. The Allobroges, as Cicero had recommended, were presented to the other conspirators by Gabinius. They demanded of Lentulus, Cethegus, Statilius, and also of Cassius an oath, which was to be sealed and taken to their countrymen, saying that otherwise they could not readily be induced to embark upon so serious an enterprise. The others complied without suspicion; Cassius, however, promised to come to Gaul shortly, and then left the city just before the envoys. Lentulus sent with the Allobroges a certain Titus Volturcius of Crotona, so that on their way home they might confirm the alliance by exchanging pledges of fidelity with Catiline. He gave Volturcius a letter for Catiline, of which the following is a copy: "Who I am you will learn from my messenger. See to it that you bear in mind in what peril you are, and

remember that you are a man. Consider what your plans demand; seek help from all, even the lowest." He also sent him a verbal message, inquiring what his idea was in refusing the aid of slaves, when he had been declared a rebel by the senate. The preparations which he had ordered in the city had been made; he should not himself hesitate to come nearer the walls.

45. When arrangements had been thus perfected and the night for the departure appointed, Cicero, who had been informed of everything through the envoys, ordered the praetors Lucius Valerius Flaccus and Gaius Pomptinus to lie in wait for the Allobroges and their company at the Mulvian Bridge and arrest them. He fully explained why they were sent, but left the general course of action to their discretion. The praetors, who were soldiers, quietly posted their guards, according to their orders, and secretly invested the bridge. As soon as the envoys reached the spot with Volturcius and heard a shout on both sides of them at once, the Gauls quickly saw what was going on and immediately surrendered themselves to the praetors. Volturcius at first urged on his companions, and sword in hand defended himself against superior numbers; but when he was deserted by the envoys, he at first earnestly besought Pomptinus, with whom he was acquainted, to save him, but finally, being in fear and despairing of his life, surrendered to the praetors as if to enemies.

46. When all was over, the details were quickly communicated to the consul by messengers; but he was beset at the same time by deep anxiety as well as by great joy. For while he rejoiced in the knowledge that by the disclosure of the plot his country was saved from peril, he was also troubled, and uncertain what ought to be done, when citizens of such standing were found guilty of a heinous crime. He realized that their punishment would be a load upon his own shoulders; their impunity the ruin of the state. He, therefore, steeling his resolution, ordered Lentulus, Cethegus, Statilius, and Gabinius to be brought before him, as well as a certain Caeparius of Terracina, who was making ready to go to Apulia and stir the slaves to revolt. The others came without delay; but Caeparius, who had left his home a short time before this, heard of the discovery of the plot and had made good his escape from the city. The consul himself took Lentulus by the hand, because he was praetor, and led him to the temple of Concord, bidding the rest follow under guard. Thither he summoned the senate, and when it had assembled in full numbers he led in Volturcius and the envoys. He bade the praetor Flaccus bring to the same place the portfolio, together with the letters which he had taken from the Allobroges.

47. When Volturcius was questioned about the journey and letters, and finally was asked what his design was and why he had entertained it, he at first invented another story and denied knowledge of the conspiracy. Afterwards, when invited to speak under a public pledge of pardon, he gave an

exact account of the whole affair. He declared that he had been made a member of the cabal only a few days before by Gabinius and Caeparius, and knew no more than the envoys; except that he had often heard Gabinius mention Publius Autronius, Servius Sulla, Lucius Vargunteius, and many others as being in the plot. The Gauls gave the same testimony, and when Lentulus denied his guilt they confronted him not only with his letter, but also with statements which he was in the habit of making, to the effect that in the Sibylline books the rule of Rome by three Cornelii was foretold; that there had already been Cinna and Sulla, and that he was the third who was destined to be master of the city. Furthermore, that this was the twentieth year since the burning of the Capitol, a year which because of portents the soothsayers had often declared would be stained with the blood of a civil war. Accordingly, when the letters had been read through, each man having first acknowledged his own seal, the senate voted that after Lentulus had resigned his office he and the rest should be held in free custody. As a result of this, Lentulus was delivered to Publius Lentulus Spinther, who at the time was an aedile, Cethegus to Quintus Cornificius, Statilius to Gaius Caesar, Gabinius to Marcus Crassus, and Caeparius (for he had just been caught and brought back) to a senator called Gnaeus Terentius.

48. Meanwhile, after the disclosure of the plot, the commons, who at first in their desire for a change of rulers had been only too eager for war, faced about and denounced the designs of Catiline, while they extolled Cicero to the skies, manifesting as much joy and exultation as if they had been rescued from slavery. For although they thought that other acts of war would lead to booty rather than to loss, they regarded a general conflagration as cruel, monstrous, and especially calamitous to themselves, since their sole possessions were their daily food and clothing.

On the following day one Lucius Tarquinius was brought before the senate, a man who was said to have been arrested and brought back as he was making his way to Catiline. When he said that he would give evidence about the conspiracy if the state would promise him a pardon, and when he had been invited by the consul to tell what he knew, he gave the senate practically the same testimony as Volturcius about the intended fires, the murder of loyal men, and the march of the rebels. He added that he had been sent by Marcus Crassus to advise Catiline not to be alarmed by the arrest of Lentulus, Cethegus, and the other conspirators, but to make the greater haste to come to the city, in order that he might thereby revive the spirits of the rest, and that they might the more easily be saved from their danger.

As soon, however, as Tarquinius named Crassus, a noble of great wealth and of the highest rank, some thought the charge incredible; others believed it to be true, but thought that in such a crisis so powerful a man ought to be propitiated rather than exasperated. There were many, too, who were under obligation to Crassus through private business relations. All these loudly insisted that the accusation was false, and demanded that the matter be laid before the senate. Accordingly, on the motion of Cicero, the senate in full session voted that the testimony of Tarquinius appeared to be false; that he should be kept under guard and given no further hearing until he revealed the name of the man at whose instigation he had lied about a matter of such moment. At the time some believed that this charge had been trumped up by Publius Autronius, in order that by naming Crassus and involving him in the danger he might shield the rest behind his influence. Others declared that Tarquinius had been instigated by Cicero, to prevent Crassus from taking up the cause of the wicked, after his custom, and embroiling the state. I heard Crassus himself assert afterwards that this grave insult was put upon him by Cicero.

49. But at that very time Quintus Catulus and Gaius Piso tried in vain by entreaties, influence, and bribes to induce Cicero to have a false accusation brought against Gaius Caesar, either through the Allobroges or some other witness. For both these men were bitter personal enemies of Caesar, Piso because when he was on trial for extortion Caesar had charged him with unjustly executing a native of Transpadine Gaul, while the hatred of Catulus arose from his candidacy for the pontificate, because after he had attained to ripe old age and had held the highest offices, he had been defeated by Caesar, who was by comparison a mere youth. Moreover, the opportunity for an attack upon Caesar seemed favorable, because he was heavily in debt on account of his eminent generosity in private life and lavish entertainments when in office. But when they could not persuade the consul to such an outrageous step, they took the matter into their own hands, and by circulating falsehoods which they pretended to have heard from Volturcius or the Allobroges, stirred up such hostility to Caesar that some Roman knights, who were stationed as an armed guard about the temple of Concord, carried away either by the greatness of the danger or by their own excitability, drew their swords upon Caesar as he was leaving the senate, in order to make their loyalty to their country more conspicuous.

50. While all this was going on in the senate, and rewards were being voted to the envoys of the Allobroges and to Titus Volturcius, when their information had been verified, the freedmen of Lentulus and a few of his dependents were scouring the streets and trying to rouse the artisans and slaves to rescue him, while others were seeking out the leaders of bands who were wont to cause public disturbances for hire. Cethegus, also, was sending messengers to his slaves and freedmen, a picked and trained body of men, entreating them to take a bold step, get their band together, and force their way to him with arms.

When the consul learned of these designs, stationing guards as the time and circumstances demanded and convoking the senate, he put the question what should be done with the men who had been delivered into custody, the senate having shortly before this in a full meeting resolved that they were guilty of treason to their country. On the present occasion Decimus Junius Silanus, who was consul-elect, and hence the first to be called upon for his opinion regarding those who were held in custody, as well as about Lucius Cassius, Publius Furius, Publius Umbrenus, and Titus Annius in case they should be caught, had recommended that they be put to death; later, profoundly influenced by the speech of Gaius Caesar, he said that, when a division was called for, he would give his vote for the proposal of Tiberius Nero, who had advised merely that the guards be increased and the question reopened. But Caesar, when his turn came and the consul asked him for his opinion, spoke in the following terms:

51. "Fathers of the Senate, all men who deliberate upon difficult questions ought to be free from hatred and friendship, anger and pity. When these feelings stand in the way the mind cannot easily discern the truth, and no mortal man has ever served at the same time his passions and his best interests. When you apply your intellect, it prevails; if passion possesses you, it holds sway, and the mind is impotent. I might mention many occasions Fathers of the Senate, when kings and peoples under the influence of wrath or pity have made errors of judgment; but I prefer to remind you of times when our forefathers, resisting the dictates of passion, have acted justly and in order. In the Macedonian war, which we waged with king Persius, the great and glorious community of the Rhodians, which owed its growth to the support of the Roman people, was unfaithful to us and hostile. But after the war was over and the question of the Rhodians was under discussion, our ancestors let them go unpunished for fear that someone might say that the wealth of the Rhodians, rather than resentment for the wrong they had done, had led to the declaration of war. So, too, in all the Punic wars, although the Carthaginians both in time of peace and in the course of truces had often done many abominable deeds, the Romans never retaliated when they had the opportunity, but they inquired rather what conduct would be consistent with their dignity than how far the law would allow them to go in taking vengeance on their enemies. You likewise, Fathers of the Senate, must beware of letting the guilt of Publius Lentulus and the rest have more weight with you than your own dignity, and of taking more thought for your anger than for your good name. If a punishment commensurate with their crimes can be found, I favor a departure from precedent; but if the enormity of their guilt surpasses all men's imagination, I should advise limiting ourselves to such penalties as the law has established.

"The greater number of those who have expressed their opinions before me have deplored the lot of the commonwealth in finished and noble phrases; they have dwelt upon the horrors of war, the wretched fate of the conquered, the rape of maidens and boys, children torn from their parents' arms, matrons subjected to the will of the victors, temples and homes pillaged, bloodshed and fire; in short, arms and corpses everywhere, gore and grief. But, O ye immortal gods! what was the purpose of such speeches? Was it to make you detest the conspiracy? You think that a man who has not been affected by a crime so monstrous and so cruel will be fired by a speech! Nay, not so; no mortal man thinks his own wrongs unimportant; many, indeed, are wont to resent them more than is right. But not all men, Fathers of the Senate, are allowed the same freedom of action. If the humble, who pass their lives in obscurity, commit any offense through anger, it is known to few; their fame and fortune are alike. But the actions of those who hold great power, and pass their lives in a lofty station, are known to all the world. So it comes to pass that in the highest position there is the least freedom of action. There neither partiality nor dislike is in place, and anger least of all; for what in others is called wrath, this in a ruler is termed insolence and cruelty.

"For my own part, Fathers of the Senate, I consider no tortures sufficient for the crimes of these men; but most mortals remember only that which happens last, and in the case of godless men forget their guilt and talk about the punishment they have received, if it is a little more severe than common. I have no doubt that Decimus Silanus, a gallant and brave man, was led by patriotism to say what he did say, and that in a matter of such moment he showed neither favor nor enmity; so well do I know the man's character and moderation. Yet his proposal seems to me, I will not say cruel (for what could be cruel in the case of such men?) but foreign to the customs of our country. For surely, Silanus, it was either fear or the gravity of the offense which impelled you, a consul elect, to favor a novel form of punishment. As regards fear it is needless to speak, especially since, thanks to the precautions of our distinguished consul, we have such strong guards under arms. So far as the penalty is concerned, I can say with truth that amid grief and wretchedness death is a relief from woes, not a punishment; that it puts an end to all mortal ills and leaves no room either for sorrow or for joy.

"But, by the immortal gods! why did you not, Silanus, add the recommendation that they first be scourged? Was it because the Porcian law forbids? Yes, but there are other laws too which provide that Roman citizens, even when found guilty, shall not lose their lives, but shall be permitted to go into exile. Was it because it is more grievous to be scourged than to be killed? But what punishment is rigorous or too grievous for men convicted of so great a crime? If, however, it was because scourging is the lighter punishment, what consistency is there in respecting the law in the lesser point when you have disregarded it in the greater? But, you may say, who will complain of a decree which is passed against traitors to their country? Time, I answer, the lapse of years, and Fortune, whose caprice rules the nations. Whatever befalls these prisoners will be well deserved; but you, Fathers of the Senate, are called upon to consider how your action will affect other criminals. All bad precedents have originated in cases which were good; but when the control of the government falls into the hands of men who are incompetent or bad, your new precedent is transferred from those who well deserve and merit such punishment to the undeserving and blameless.

"The Lacedaemonians, after they had conquered the Athenians, set over them thirty men to carry on their government. These men began at first by putting to death without a trial the most wicked and generally hated citizens, whereat the people rejoiced greatly and declared that it was well done. But afterwards their license gradually increased, and the tyrants slew good and bad alike at pleasure and intimidated the rest. Thus the nation was reduced to slavery and had to pay a heavy penalty for its foolish rejoicing. Within our own memory, when the conqueror Sulla ordered the execution of Damasippus and others of that kind, who had become prominent at the expense of the state, who did not commend his action? All declared that those criminal intriguers, who had vexed the country with their civil strife, deserved their fate. But that was the beginning of great bloodshed; for whenever anyone coveted a man's house in town or country, or at last even his goods or his garment, he contrived to have him enrolled among the proscribed. Thus those who had exulted in the death of Damasippus were themselves before long hurried off to execution, and the massacre did not end until Sulla glutted all his followers with riches.

"For my own part, I fear nothing of that kind for Marcus Tullius or for our times, but in a great commonwealth there are many different natures. It is possible that at another time, when someone else is consul and is likewise in command of an army, some falsehood may be believed to be true. When the consul, with this precedent before him, shall draw the sword in obedience to the senate's decree, who shall limit or restrain him?

"Our ancestors, Fathers of the Senate, were never lacking either in wisdom or courage, and yet pride did not keep them from adopting foreign institutions, provided they were honorable. They took their offensive and defensive weapons from the Samnites, the badges of their magistrates for the most part from the Etruscans. In fine, whatever they found suitable among allies or foes, they put in practice at home with the greatest enthusiasm, preferring to imitate rather than envy the successful. But in that same age, following the usage of Greece, they applied the scourge to citizens and inflicted the supreme penalty upon those found guilty. Afterwards, when the state reached maturity, and because of its large population factions prevailed; when the blameless began to be oppressed and other wrongs of that kind were perpetrated; then they devised the Porcian law and other laws, which allowed the condemned the alternative of exile. This seems to me, Fathers of the Senate, a particularly cogent reason why we should not adopt a new policy. Surely there was greater merit and wisdom in those men, who from slight resources created this mighty empire, than in us, who can barely hold what they gloriously won.

"Do I then recommend that the prisoners be allowed to depart and swell Catiline's forces? By no means! This, rather, is my advice: that their goods be confiscated and that they themselves be kept imprisoned in the strongest of the free towns; further, that no one hereafter shall refer their case to the senate or bring it before the people, under pain of being considered by the senate to have designs against the welfare of the state and the common safety."

52. After Caesar had finished speaking, the rest briefly expressed their adherence to one or another of the various proposals. But Marcus Porcius Cato[1] when called upon for his opinion, spoke to the following purport:

"My feelings are very different, Fathers of the Senate, when I turn my mind to the plot and the danger we are in, and when I reflect upon the recommendations of some of our number. The speakers appear to me to have dwelt upon the punishment of these men who have plotted warfare upon their country, parents, altars, and hearths; but the situation warns us rather to take precautions against them than to argue about what we are to do with them. For in the case of other offenses you may proceed against them after they have been committed; with this, unless you take measures to forestall it, in vain will you appeal to the laws when once it has been consummated. Once a city has been taken nothing is left to the vanquished.

"Nay, in the name of the immortal gods I call upon you, who have always valued your houses, villas, statues, and paintings more highly than your country; if you wish to retain the treasures to which you cling, of whatsoever kind they may be, if you even wish to provide peace for the enjoyment of your pleasures, wake up at last and lay hold of the reins of the state. Here is no question of revenues or the wrongs of our allies; our lives and liberties are at stake. Oftentimes, Fathers of the Senate, I have spoken at great length before this body; I have often deplored the extravagance and greed of our citizens, and in that way I have made many men my enemies. I, who had never granted to myself or to my impulses indulgence for any transgression, could not readily condone misdeeds prompted by another's passion. But although you were wont to give little weight to my words, yet the state was unshaken; its prosperity made good your neglect.

"Now, however, the question before us is not whether our morals are good or bad, nor how great or glorious the empire of the Roman people is,

---

[1] Great-grandson of the elder Marcus Porcius Cato, consul in 195 B.C.E., the opponent of Scipio.

but whether all that we have, however we regard it, is to be ours, or with our-selves is to belong to the enemy. At this point (save the mark!) someone hints at gentleness and long-suffering! But in very truth we have long since lost the true names for things. It is precisely because squandering the goods of others is called generosity, and recklessness in wrong doing is called courage, that the republic is reduced to extremities. Let these men by all means, since such is the fashion of the time, be liberal at the expense of our allies, let them be merciful to plunderers of the treasury; but let them not be prodigal of our blood, and in sparing a few scoundrels bring ruin upon all good men.

"In fine and finished phrases did Gaius Caesar a moment ago before this body speak of life and death, regarding as false, I presume, the tales which are told of the Lower World, where they say that the wicked take a different path from the good, and dwell in regions that are gloomy, desolate, unsightly, and full of fears. Therefore he recommended that the goods of the prisoners be confiscated, and that they themselves be imprisoned in the free towns, doubt-less through fear that if they remained in Rome the adherents of the plot or a hired mob would rescue them by force. As if, indeed, there were base and criminal men only in our city and not all over Italy, or as if audacity had not greatest strength where the power to resist it is weakest! Therefore, this advice is utterly futile if Caesar fears danger from the conspirators; but if amid such general fear he alone has none, I have the more reason to fear for you and for myself. Be assured, then, that when you decide the fate of Pub-lius Lentulus and the rest, you will at the same time be passing judgment on Catiline's army and all the conspirators. The more vigorous your action, the less will be their courage; but if they detect the slightest weakness on your part, they will all be here immediately, filled with reckless daring. Do not sup-pose that it was by arms that our forefathers raised our country from obscu-rity to greatness. If that were so, we should have a much fairer state than theirs, since we have a greater of number of citizens and allies than they pos-sessed, to say nothing of arms and horses. But there were other qualities which made them great, which we do not possess at all: efficiency at home, a just rule abroad, in counsel an independent spirit free from guilt or passion. In place of these we have extravagance and greed, public poverty and private opulence. We extol wealth and foster idleness. We make no distinction between good men and bad, and ambition appropriates all the prizes of merit. And no wonder! When each of you schemes for his own private inter-ests, when you are slaves to pleasure in your homes and to money or infl-uence here, the natural result is an attack upon the defenseless republic.

"But I let that pass. Citizens of the highest rank have conspired to fire their native city, they stir up to war the Gauls, bitterest enemies of the Roman people. The leader of the enemy with his army is upon us. Do you even now hesitate and doubtfully ask yourselves what is to be done with enemies taken within your walls? Have compassion upon them, I conjure you (they are but young men, led astray by ambition), and even let them go, taking their arms with them! Of a truth, if they should resort to war, that gentleness and long-suffering of yours would result in suffering. No doubt the situation is a terrible one, you say, but you are not afraid of it. Nay, but you do fear it exceedingly, though from slothfulness and weakness of spirit you hesitate, waiting one for the other, doubtless trusting to the immortal gods, who have often saved our country in moments of extreme danger. Not by vows nor womanish entreaties is the help of the gods secured; it is always through watchfulness, vigorous action, and wisdom in counsel that success comes. When you abandon yourself to cowardice and baseness, it is vain to call upon the gods; they are offended and hostile.

"In the days of our forefathers Aulus Manlius Torquatus, while warring with the Gauls, ordered the execution of his own son, because he had fought against the enemy contrary to orders, and the gallant young man paid the penalty for too great valor with his life. Do you hesitate what punishment to inflict upon the most ruthless traitors? No doubt their past lives have been such as to palliate this crime! By all means spare Lentulus because of his rank, if he ever spared his own chastity, his good name, or anyone, god or man. Pardon the youth of Cethegus, if this is not the second time that he has made war upon his country. And what shall I say of Gabinius, Statilius, and Caeparius, who would never have formed such designs against the republic if they had ever respected anything?

"Finally, Fathers of the Senate, if (Heaven help us!) there were any room for error I should be quite willing to let you learn wisdom by experience, since you scorn my advice. But as it is, we are beset on every side. Catiline with his army is at our throats; other foes are within our walls, aye, in the very heart of Rome. Neither preparations nor plans can be kept secret; therefore the more need of haste. This, then, is my recommendation: whereas our country has been subjected to the greatest peril through the abominable plot of wicked citizens, and whereas they have been proven guilty by the testimony of Titus Volturcius and the envoys of the Allobroges, and have confessed that they have planned murder, arson, and other fearful and cruel crimes against their fellow citizens and their country, let those who have confessed be treated as though they had been caught red-handed in capital offenses, and be punished after the manner of our forefathers."

53. As soon as Cato had taken his seat, all the ex-consuls, as well as a great part of the other senators, praised his proposal and lauded his courage to the skies, while they taxed one another with timorousness. Cato was hailed as great and noble, and a decree of the senate was passed in accordance with his recommendation.

For my own part, as I read and heard of the many illustrious deeds of the

Roman people at home and abroad, on land and sea, it chanced that I was
seized by a strong desire of finding out what quality in particular had been
the foundation of so great exploits. I knew that often with a handful of men
they had encountered great armies of the enemy; I was aware that with small
resources they had waged wars with mighty kings; also that they had often
experienced the cruelty of Fortune; that the Romans had been surpassed by
the Greeks in eloquence and by the Gauls in warlike glory. After long reflection I became convinced that it had all been accomplished by the eminent
merit of a few citizens; that it was due to them that poverty had triumphed
over riches, and a few over a multitude. But after the state had become
demoralized by extravagance and sloth, it was the commonwealth in its turn
that was enabled by its greatness to sustain the shortcomings of its generals
and magistrates, and for a long time, as when a mother is exhausted by child-
bearing, no one at all was produced at Rome who was great in merit. But
within my own memory there have appeared two men of towering merit,
though of diverse character, Marcus Cato and Gaius Caesar. As regards these
men, since the occasion has presented itself, it is not my intention to pass
them by in silence, or fail to give, to the best of my ability, an account of their
disposition and character.

54. In birth then, in years and in eloquence, they were about equal; in
greatness of soul they were evenly matched, and likewise in renown,
although the renown of each was different. Caesar was held great because of
his benefactions and lavish generosity, Cato for the uprightness of his life. The
former became famous for his gentleness and compassion, the austerity of
the latter had brought him prestige. Caesar gained glory by giving, helping,
and forgiving; Cato by never stooping to bribery. One was a refuge for the
unfortunate, the other a scourge for the wicked. The good nature of the one
was applauded, the steadfastness of the other. Finally, Caesar had schooled
himself to work hard and sleep little, to devote himself to the welfare of his
friends and neglect his own, to refuse nothing which was worth the giving.
He longed for great power, an army, a new war to give scope for his brilliant
merit. Cato, on the contrary, cultivated self-control, propriety, but above all
austerity. He did not vie with the rich in riches nor in intrigue with the
intriguer, but with the active in good works, with the self-restrained in moderation, with the blameless in integrity. He preferred to be, rather than to
seem, virtuous; hence the less he sought fame, the more it pursued him.

55. After the senate had adopted the recommendation of Cato, as I have
said, the consul thought it best to forestall any new movement during the
approaching night. He therefore ordered the triumvirs to make the necessary
preparations for the execution. After setting guards, he personally led Lentulus to the dungeon, while the praetors performed the same office for the
others.

In the prison, when you have gone up a little way towards the left, there is a place called the Tullianum, about twelve feet below the surface of the ground. It is enclosed on all sides by walls, and above it is a chamber with a vaulted roof of stone. Neglect, darkness, and stench make it hideous and fearsome to behold. Into this place Lentulus was let down, and then the executioners carried out their orders and strangled him. Thus that patrician, of the illustrious stock of the Cornelii, who had held consular authority at Rome, ended his life in a manner befitting his character and his crimes. Cethegus, Statilius, Gabinius, and Caeparius suffered the same punishment.

56. While this was taking place in Rome, Catiline combined the forces which he had brought with him with those which Manlius already had, and formed two legions, filling up the cohorts so far as the number of his soldiers permitted. Then distributing among them equally such volunteers or conspirators as came to the camp, he soon completed the full quota of the legions, although in the beginning he had no more than two thousand men. But only about a fourth part of the entire force was provided with regular arms. The others carried whatever weapons chance had given them; namely, javelins or lances, or in some cases pointed stakes.

When Antonius was drawing near with his army, Catiline marched through the mountains, moved his camp now towards the city and now in the direction of Gaul, and gave the enemy no opportunity for battle, hoping shortly to have a large force if the conspirators at Rome succeeded in carrying out their plans. Meanwhile he refused to enroll slaves, a great number of whom flocked to him at first, because he had confidence in the strength of the conspiracy and at the same time thought it inconsistent with his designs to appear to have given runaway slaves a share in a citizens' cause.

57. But when news reached the camp that the plot had been discovered at Rome, and that Lentulus, Cethegus, and the others whom I mentioned had been put to death, very many of those whom the hope of pillage or desire for revolution had led to take up arms began to desert. The remainder Catiline led by forced marches over rugged mountains to the neighborhood of Pistoria, intending to escape secretly by cross-roads into Transalpine Gaul. But Quintus Metellus Celer, with three legions, was on the watch in the Picene district, inferring from the difficulty of the enemy's position that he would take the very course which I have mentioned. Accordingly, when he learned through deserters in what direction Catiline was going, he quickly moved his camp and took up a position at the foot of the very mountains from which the conspirator would have to descend in his flight into Gaul. Antonius also was not far distant since he was following the fleeing rebels over more level ground with an army which, though large, was lightly equipped. Now, when Catiline perceived that he was shut in between the mountains and the forces of his enemies, that his plans in the city had failed, and that he had hope neither of escape nor reinforcements, thinking it best in such a crisis to try the fortune of battle, he decided to engage Antonius as soon as possible. Accordingly he assembled his troops and addressed them in a speech of the following purport:

58. "I am well aware, soldiers, that words do not supply valor, and that a spiritless army is not made vigorous, or a timid one stout-hearted, by a speech from its commander. Only that degree of courage which is in each man's heart either by disposition or by habit, is wont to be revealed in battle. It is vain to exhort one who is roused neither by glory nor by dangers; the fear he feels in his heart closes his ears. I have, however, called you together to offer a few words of advice, and at the same time to explain the reason for my resolution.

"You know perfectly well, soldiers, how great is the disaster that the incapacity and cowardice of Lentulus have brought upon himself and us, and how waiting for reinforcements from the city, I could not march into Gaul. At this present time, moreover, you understand as well as I do in what condition our affairs stand. Two hostile armies, one towards Rome, the other towards Gaul, block our way. We cannot remain longer where we are, however much we may desire it, because of lack of grain and other necessities. Wherever we decide to go, we must hew a path with the sword. Therefore I counsel you to be brave and ready of spirit, and when you enter the battle to remember that you carry in your own right hands riches, honor, glory; yea, even freedom and your native land. If we win, complete security will be ours, supplies will abound, free towns and colonies will open their gates; but if we yield to fear, the very reverse will be true: no place and no friend will guard the man whom arms could not protect. Moreover, soldiers, we and our opponents are not facing the same exigency. We are battling for country, for freedom, for life; theirs is a futile contest, to uphold the power of a few men. March on, therefore, with the greater courage, mindful of your former valor.

"You might have passed your life in exile and in utter infamy, at Rome some of you might look to others for aid after losing your estates; but since such conditions seemed base and intolerable to true men, you decided upon this course. If you wish to forsake it, you have need of boldness; none save the victor exchanges war for peace. To hope for safety in flight when you have turned away from the enemy the arms which should protect your body, is surely the height of madness. In battle the greatest danger always threatens those who show the greatest fear; boldness is a bulwark.

"When I think on you, my soldiers, and weigh your deeds, I have high hopes of victory. Your spirit, youth, and valor give me heart, not to mention necessity, which makes even the timid brave. In this narrow defile the superior numbers of the enemy cannot surround us. But if Fortune frowns upon your bravery, take care not to die unavenged. Do not be captured and slaughtered like cattle, but, fighting like heroes, leave the enemy a bloody and tearful victory."

59. When he had thus spoken, after a brief pause he ordered the trumpets to sound and led his army in order of battle down into the plain. Then, after sending away all the horses, in order to make the danger equal for all and thus to increase the soldiers' courage, himself on foot like the rest he drew up his army as the situation and his numbers demanded. Since, namely, the plain was shut in on the left by mountains and on the right by rough, rocky ground, he posted eight cohorts in front and held the rest in reserve in closer order. From these he took the centurions, all the picked men and reservists, as well as the best armed of the ordinary soldiers, and placed them in the front rank. He gave the charge of the right wing to Gaius Manlius, and that of the left to a man of Faesulae. He himself with his freedmen and the camp-servants took his place beside the eagle, which, it was said, had been in the army of Gaius Marius during the war with the Cimbri.

On the other side Gaius Antonius, who was ill with the gout and unable to enter the battle, entrusted his army to Marcus Petreius, his lieutenant. Petreius placed in the van the veteran cohorts which he had enrolled because of the outbreak, and behind them the rest of his army in reserve. Riding up and down upon his horse, he addressed each of his men by name, exhorted him, and begged him to remember that he was fighting against unarmed highwaymen in defense of his country, his children, his altars, and his hearth. Being a man of military experience, who had served in the army with high distinction for more than thirty years as tribune, prefect, lieutenant, or commander, he personally knew the greater number of his soldiers and their valorous deeds of arms, and by mentioning these he fired the spirits of his men.

60. When Petreius, after making all his preparations, gave the signal with the trumpet, he ordered his cohorts to advance slowly; the army of the enemy followed their example. After they had reached a point where battle could be joined by the skirmishers, the hostile armies rushed upon each other with loud shouts, then threw down their pikes and took to the sword. The veterans, recalling their old-time prowess, advanced bravely to close quarters; the enemy, not lacking in courage, stood their ground, and there was a terrific struggle. Meanwhile Catiline, with his light-armed troops, was busy in the van, aided those who were hard pressed, summoned fresh troops to replace the wounded, had an eye to everything, and at the same time fought hard himself, often striking down the foe—thus performing at once the duties of a valiant soldier and of a skillful leader.

When Petreius saw that Catiline was making so much stronger a fight than he had expected, he led his praetorian cohort against the enemy's center, threw them into confusion, and slew those who resisted in various parts of the field; then he attacked the rest on both flanks at once. Manlius and the man from Fiesole were among the first to fall, sword in hand. When Catiline saw that his army was routed and that he was left with a mere handful of men, mindful of his birth and former rank he plunged into the thickest of the enemy and there fell fighting, his body pierced through and through.

61. When the battle was ended it became evident what boldness and resolution had pervaded Catiline's army. For almost every man covered with his body, when life was gone, the position which he had taken when alive at the beginning of the conflict. A few, indeed, in the center, whom the praetorian cohort had scattered, lay a little apart from the rest, but the wounds even of these were in front. But Catiline was found far in advance of his men amid a heap of slain enemies, still breathing slightly, and showing in his face the indomitable spirit which had animated him when alive. Finally, out of the whole army not a single citizen of free birth was taken during the battle or in flight, showing that all had valued their own lives no more highly than those of their enemies.

But the army of the Roman people gained no joyful nor bloodless victory, for all the most valiant had either fallen in the fight or come off with severe wounds. Many, too, who had gone from the camp to visit the field or to pillage, on turning over the bodies of the rebels found now a friend, now a guest or kinsman; some also recognized their personal enemies. Thus the whole army was variously affected with sorrow and grief, rejoicing and lamentation.

JULIUS CAESAR

Life

Julius Caesar (100–44 B.C.E.) is one of the best known political and military figures of all antiquity—both from ancient sources and from later depictions in drama, art, and film. Though born into an aristocratic family, Caesar allied himself with the popular forces against the Senate. Since the cost of his early political career had plunged him deeply in debt, he desperately needed a provincial governorship to recoup his position. In 60, Caesar allied himself with the general Pompey and the financier Crassus to form the "First Triumvirate" to satisfy each one's goals. Caesar became consul for the year 58 and received the governorship of the Gallic provinces from 58 onward.

During his nine years in Gaul, Caesar honed his military skill and acquired a formidable reputation as a general. That reputation was greatly promoted by the dispatches he sent back to Rome, which were later collected in his Commentaries on the Gallic War. *He returned to Italy in 49 and for five years fought the senatorial forces in Greece, Egypt, Africa, and Spain. He was proclaimed perpetual dictator shortly before his assassination on the Ides of March, 44.*

Works

Caesar had a remarkable education and was a skilled poet, orator, and essayist. His commentaries were intended almost as an "anti-history," since the literary qualities of history—preface; moral purpose; literary style—are all absent. Caesar wrote in an unadorned prose style and refers to himself in the third person. The goal is to make the book appear to be a bare, unbiased, account of the events, and in this Caesar was enormously successful. The image of Caesar's decisiveness and his clemency toward defeated enemies were an important part of his public image. The Gallic War is the only surviving account of ancient military operations by a battlefield commander and Caesar's descriptions are excellent. He understandably takes great credit for successes and distances himself from any failures. There is also considerable ethnographic material on the ancient Gauls.

Caesar and his associates also recounted the battles fought in the Civil Wars. These commentaries are more openly political and they include speeches by opposing generals, even by Caesar's enemies. He created in both these commentaries an effective tool of political propaganda in his drive to take and hold power in Rome.

COMMENTARIES ON THE GALLIC WAR*

BOOK I

When the Gallic tribe called the Helvetians attempt to march westward into Gaul to secure more land, Caesar defeats them and forces them to return to their homeland in modern Switzerland. Later the German chief Ariovistus crosses the Rhine into Gaul. After their defeat by Caesar, the German forces retreat back across the Rhine.

1. All Gaul is divided into three parts, one of which the Belgae inhabit, the Aquitani another, those who in their own language are called "Celts," in ours "Gauls," the third. All these differ from each other in language, customs and laws. The river Garonne separates the Gauls from the Aquitani; the Marne and the Seine separate them from the Belgae. Of all these, the Belgae are the bravest, because they are furthest from the civilization and refinement of our Province,[1] and merchants least frequently resort to them, and import those things which tend to effeminate the mind; and they are the nearest to the Germans, who dwell beyond the Rhine, with whom they are continually waging war; for which reason the Helvetii also surpass the rest of

---

*Adapted from the translation by W. A. McDevitte, *Caesar's Commentaries on the Gallic and Civil Wars* (New York, 1869).

[1] At this time Julius Caesar was governor of both Cisalpine Gaul in northern Italy and the Province of Transalpine Gaul, which occupied the Mediterranean coast of modern France (*Provence*). Caesar only describes the three parts of Gaul unconquered by the Romans.

the Gauls in valor, as they contend with the Germans in almost daily battles, when they either repel them from their own territories, or themselves wage war on their frontiers. One part of these, which it has been said that the Gauls occupy, takes its beginning at the river Rhone; it is bounded by the river Garonne, the ocean, and the territories of the Belgae; it borders, too, on the side of the Sequani and the Helvetii, upon the river Rhine, and stretches toward the north. The Belgae rises from the extreme frontier of Gaul, extend to the lower part of the river Rhine; and look toward the north and the rising sun. Aquitania extends from the river Garonne to the Pyrenees mountains and to that part of the ocean which is near Spain: it looks between the setting of the sun, and the north star.

2. Among the Helvetii, Orgetorix was by far the most distinguished and wealthy. He, when Marcus Messala and Marcus Piso were consuls [61 B.C.E.], incited by lust of sovereignty, formed a conspiracy among the nobility, and persuaded the people to go forth from their territories with all their possessions, saying that it would be very easy, since they excelled all in valor, to acquire the supremacy of the whole of Gaul. To this he the more easily persuaded them, because the Helvetii, are confined on every side by the nature of their situation; on one side by the Rhine, a very broad and deep river, which separates the Helvetian territory from the Germans; on a second side by the Jura, a very high mountain, which is situated between the Sequani and the Helvetii; on a third by the Lake of Geneva, and by the river Rhone, which separates our Province from the Helvetii. From these circumstances it resulted, that they could range less widely, and could less easily make war upon their neighbors; for which reason men fond of war as they were, were affected with great regret. They thought that, considering the extent of their population, and their renown for warfare and bravery, they had but narrow limits, although they extended in length 240, and in breadth 180 Roman miles.

3. Induced by these considerations, and influenced by the authority of Orgetorix, they determined to provide such things as were necessary for their expedition, to buy up as great a number as possible of beasts of burden and wagons, to make their sowings as large as possible, so that on their march plenty of corn might be in store, and to establish peace and friendship with the neighboring states. They reckoned that a term of two years would be sufficient for them to execute their designs; they fix by decree their departure for the third year. Orgetorix is chosen to complete these arrangements. He took upon himself the office of ambassador to the states: on this journey he persuades Casticus, the son of Catamantaledes (one of the Sequani, whose father had possessed the sovereignty among the people for many years, and had been styled "friend" by the senate of the Roman people), to seize upon the sovereignty in his own state, which his father had held before

him, and he likewise persuades Dumnorix, an Aeduan, the brother of Divitiacus, who at that time possessed the chief authority in the state, and was exceedingly beloved by the people, to attempt the same, and gives him his daughter in marriage. He proves to them that to accomplish their attempts was a thing very easy to be done, because he himself would obtain the government of his own state; that there was no doubt that the Helvetii were the most powerful of the whole of Gaul; he assures them that he will, with his own forces and his own army, acquire the sovereignty for them. Incited by this speech, they give a pledge and oath to one another, and hope that, when they have seized the sovereignty, they will, by means of the three most powerful and valiant nations, be enabled to obtain possession of the whole of Gaul.

4. When this scheme was disclosed to the Helvetii by informers, they, according to their custom, compelled Orgetorix to plead his cause in chains; it was the law that the penalty of being burned by fire should await him if condemned. On the day appointed for the pleading of his cause, Orgetorix drew together from all quarters to the court, all his vassals to the number of ten thousand persons; and led together to the same place all his dependents and debtor-bondsmen, of whom he had a great number; by means of those he rescued himself from the necessity of pleading his cause. While the state, incensed at this act, was endeavoring to assert its right by arms, and the magistrates were mustering a large body of men from the country, Orgetorix died; and there is not wanting a suspicion, as the Helvetii think, of his having committed suicide.

5. After his death, the Helvetii nevertheless attempt to do that which they had resolved on, namely, to go forth from their territories. When they thought that they were at length prepared for this undertaking, they set fire to all their twelve towns, to their four hundred villages, and to the private dwellings that remained; they burn up all the corn, except what they intended to carry with them; that after destroying the hope of a return home, they might be the more ready for undergoing all dangers. They order everyone to carry forth from home for himself provisions for three months, ready ground. They persuade the Rauraci, and the Tulingi, and the Latobrigi, their neighbors, to adopt the same plan, and after burning down their towns and villages, to set out with them: and they admit to their party and unite to themselves as confederates the Boii, who had dwelt on the other side of the Rhine, and had crossed over into the Norican territory, and assaulted Noreia.

6. There were in all two routes, by which they could go forth from their country one through the Sequani narrow and difficult, between Mount Jura and the river Rhone (by which scarcely one wagon at a time could be led; there was, moreover, a very high mountain overhanging, so that a very few might easily intercept them; the other, through our Province, much easier and freer from obstacles, because the Rhone flows between the boundaries of the Helvetii and those of the Allobroges, who had lately been subdued, and is in some places crossed by a ford. The furthest town of the Allobroges, and the nearest to the territories of the Helvetii, is Geneva. From this town a bridge extends to the Helvetii. They thought that they should either persuade the Allobroges, because they did not seem as yet well-affected toward the Roman people, or compel them by force to allow them to pass through their territories. Having provided every thing for the expedition, they appoint a day, on which they should all meet on the bank of the Rhone. This day was the fifth before the kalends of April, in the consulship of Lucius Piso and Aulus Gabinius [B.C.E. 58].

7. When it was reported to Caesar that they were attempting to make their route through our Province he hastens to set out from the city, and, by as great marches as he can, proceeds to Further Gaul, and arrives at Geneva. He orders the whole Province to furnish as great a number of soldiers as possible, as there was in all only one legion in Further Gaul: he orders the bridge at Geneva to be broken down. When the Helvetii are apprised of his arrival they send to him, as ambassadors, the most illustrious men of their state (in which embassy Numeius and Verudoctius held the chief place), to say "that it was their intention to march through the Province without doing any harm, because they had" according to their own representations, "no other route: that they requested, they might be allowed to do so with his consent." Caesar, inasmuch as he kept in remembrance that Lucius Cassius, the consul, had been slain, and his army routed and made to pass under the yoke by the Helvetii, did not think that their request ought to be granted: nor was he of opinion that men of hostile disposition, if an opportunity of marching through the Province were given them, would abstain from outrage and mischief. Yet, in order that a period might intervene, until the soldiers whom he had ordered to be furnished should assemble, he replied to the ambassadors, that he would take time to deliberate; if they wanted any thing, they might return on the day before the Ides of April.

8. Meanwhile, with the legion which he had with him and the soldiers which had assembled from the Province, he carries along for nineteen Roman, not quite eighteen English miles a wall, to the height of sixteen feet, and a trench, from the Lake of Geneva, which flows into the river Rhone, to Mount Jura, which separates the territories of the Sequani from those of the Helvetii. When that work was finished, he distributes garrisons, and closely fortifies redoubts, in order that he may the more easily intercept them, if they should attempt to cross over against his will. When the day which he had appointed with the ambassadors came, and they returned to him; he says, that he cannot, consistently with the custom and precedent of the

Roman people, grant any one a passage through the Province; and he gives them to understand, that, if they should attempt to use violence he would oppose them. The Helvetii, disappointed in this hope, tried if they could force a passage (some by means of a bridge of boats and numerous rafts constructed for the purpose; others, by the fords of the Rhone, where the depth of the river was least, sometimes by day, but more frequently by night), but being kept at bay by the strength of our works, and by the concourse of the soldiers, and by the missiles, they desisted from this attempt.

9. There was left one way, namely through the Sequani, by which, on account of its narrowness, they could not pass without the consent of the Sequani. As they could not of themselves prevail on them, they send ambassadors to Dumnorix the Aeduan, that through his intercession, they might obtain their request from the Sequani. Dumnorix, by his popularity and liberality, had great influence among the Sequani, and was friendly to the Helvetii, because out of that state he had married the daughter of Orgetorix; and, incited by lust of sovereignty, was anxious for a revolution, and wished to have as many states as possible attached to him by his kindness toward them. He, therefore, undertakes the affair, and prevails upon the Sequani to allow the Helvetii to march through their territories, and arranges that they should give hostages to each other—the Sequani not to obstruct the Helvetii in their march—the Helvetii, to pass without mischief and outrage.

10. It is again told to Caesar, that the Helvetii intended to march through the country of the Sequani and the Aedui into the territories of the Santones, which are not far distant from those boundaries of the Tolosates, whose city, Toulouse, is a state in the Province. If this took place, he saw that it would be a great danger to the Province to have warlike men, enemies of the Roman people, bordering upon an open and very fertile tract of country. For these reasons he appointed Titus Labienus, his lieutenant, to the command of the fortification which he had made. He himself proceeds to Italy by forced marches, and there levies two legions, and leads out from winter-quarters three which were wintering around Aquileia, and with these five legions marches rapidly by the nearest route across the Alps into Further Gaul. Here the Centrones and the Graioceli and the Caturiges, having taken possession of the higher parts, attempt to obstruct the army in their march. After having routed these in several battles, he arrives in the territories of the Vocontii in the Further Province on the seventh day from Ocelum, which is the most remote town of the Hither Province; thence he leads his army into the country of the Allobroges, and from the Allobroges to the Segusiani. These people are the first beyond the Province on the opposite side of the Rhone.

11. The Helvetii had by this time led their forces over through the narrow defile and the territories of the Sequani, and had arrived at the territories

of the Aedui, and were ravaging their lands. The Aedui, as they could not defend themselves and their possessions against them, send ambassadors to Caesar to ask assistance, pleading that they had at all times so well deserved of the Roman people, that their fields ought not to have been laid waste, their children carried off into slavery, their towns stormed, almost within sight of our army. At the same time the Ambarri, the friends and kinsmen of the Aedui, apprise Caesar, that it was not easy for them, now that their fields had been devastated, to ward off the violence of the enemy from their towns: the Allobroges likewise, who had villages and possessions on the other side of the Rhone, betake themselves in flight to Caesar, and assure him that they had nothing remaining, except the soil of their land. Caesar, induced by these circumstances, decides, that he ought not to wait until the Helvetii, after destroying all the property of his allies, should arrive among the Santones.

12. There is a river called the Saone, which flows through the territories of the Aedui and Sequani into the Rhone with such incredible slowness, that it can not be determined by the eye in which direction it flows. This the Helvetii were crossing by rafts and boats joined together. When Caesar was informed by spies that the Helvetii had already conveyed three parts of their forces across that river, but that the fourth part was left behind on this side of the Saone, he set out from the camp with three legions during the third watch, and came up with that division which had not yet crossed the river. Attacking them encumbered with baggage, and not expecting him, he cut to pieces a great part of them; the rest betook themselves to flight, and concealed themselves in the nearest woods. That canton which was cut down was called the Tigurine; for the whole Helvetian state is divided into four cantons. This single canton having left their country, within the recollection of our fathers, had slain Lucius Cassius the consul, and had made his army pass under the yoke. Thus, whether by chance, or by the design of the immortal gods, that part of the Helvetian state which had brought a signal calamity upon the Roman people, was the first to pay the penalty. In this Caesar avenged not only the public but also his own personal wrongs, because the Tigurini had slain Lucius Piso the lieutenant of Cassius, the grandfather of Lucius Calpurnius Piso, his Caesar's father-in-law, in the same battle as Cassius himself.

13. This battle ended, that he might be able to come up with the remaining forces of the Helvetii, he procures a bridge to be made across the Saone, and thus leads his army over. The Helvetii, confused by his sudden arrival, when they found that he had effected in one day, what they, themselves had with the utmost difficulty accomplished in twenty namely, the crossing of the river, send ambassadors to him; at the head of which embassy was Divico, who had been commander of the Helvetii, in the war against Cassius. He thus treats with Caesar: "if the Roman people would make peace with

the Helvetii they would go to that part and there remain, where Caesar might appoint and desire them to be; but if he should persist in persecuting them with war that he ought to remember both the ancient disgrace of the Roman people and the characteristic valor of the Helvetii. As to his having attacked one canton by surprise, at a time when those who had crossed the river could not bring assistance to their friends, that he ought not on that account to ascribe very much to his own valor, or despise them; that they had so learned from their sires and ancestors, as to rely more on valor than on artifice and stratagem. Wherefore let him not bring it to pass that the place, where they were standing, should acquire a name, from the disaster of the Roman people and the destruction of their army or transmit the remembrance of such an event to posterity."

14. To these words Caesar thus replied: "on that very account he felt less hesitation, because he kept in remembrance those circumstances which the Helvetian ambassadors had mentioned, and that he felt the more indignant at them, in proportion as they had happened undeservedly to the Roman people: for if they had been conscious of having done any wrong, it would not have been difficult to be on their guard, but for that very reason had they been deceived, because neither were they aware that any offense had been given by them, on account of which they should be afraid, nor did they think that they ought to be afraid without cause. But even if he were willing to forget their former outrage, could he also lay aside the remembrance of the late wrongs, in that they had against his will attempted a route through the Province by force, in that they had molested the Aedui, the Ambarri, and the Allobroges? That as to their so insolently boasting of their victory, and as to their being astonished that they had so long committed their outrages with impunity, both these things tended to the same point; for the immortal gods are wont to allow those persons whom they wish to punish for their guilt sometimes a greater prosperity and longer impunity, in order that they may suffer the more severely from a reverse of circumstances. Although these things are so, yet, if hostages were to be given him by them in order that he may be assured these will do what they promise, and provided they will give satisfaction to the Aedui for the outrages which they had committed against them and their allies, and likewise to the Allobroges, he Caesar will make peace with them." Divico replied, that "the Helvetii had been so trained by their ancestors, that they were accustomed to receive, not to give hostages; of that fact the Roman people were witness." Having given this reply, he withdrew.

15. On the following day they move their camp from that place; Caesar does the same, and sends forward all his cavalry, to the number of four thousand (which he had drawn together from all parts of the Province and from the Aedui and their allies), to observe toward what parts the enemy are directing their march. These, having too eagerly pursued the enemy's rear, come to a battle with the cavalry of the Helvetii in a disadvantageous place, and a few of our men fall. The Helvetii, elated with this battle, because they had with five hundred horsemen repulsed so large a body of horsemen, began to face us more boldly, sometimes too from their rear to provoke our men by an attack. Caesar however restrained his men from battle, deeming it sufficient for the present to prevent the enemy from rapine, forage, and depredation. They marched for about fifteen days in such a manner that there was not more than five or six miles between the enemy's rear and our van.

16. Meanwhile, Caesar kept daily importuning the Aedui for the corn which they had promised in the name of their state; for, in consequence of the coldness (Gaul, being as before said, situated toward the north), not only was the corn in the fields not ripe, but there was not in store a sufficiently large quantity even of fodder: besides he was unable to use the corn which he had conveyed in ships up the river Saone, because the Helvetii, from whom he was unwilling to retire had diverted their march from the Saone. The Aedui kept deferring from day to day, and saying that it was being collected on the road. When he saw that he was put off too long, and that the day was close at hand on which he ought to serve out the corn to his soldiers, he called together their chiefs, of whom he had a great number in his camp, among them Divitiacus and Liscus who was invested with the chief magistracy (whom the Aedui call the Vergobretus, and who is elected annually and has power of life or death over his countrymen). He severely reprimands them, because he is not assisted by them on so urgent an occasion, when the enemy were so close at hand, and when corn could neither be bought nor taken from the fields, particularly as, in a great measure urged by their prayers, he had undertaken the war; much more bitterly, therefore does he complain of his being forsaken.

17. Then at length Liscus, moved by Caesar's speech, discloses what he had hitherto kept secret: "there are some whose influences with the people is very great, who, though private men, have more power than the magistrates themselves: that these by seditions and violent language are deterring the populace from contributing the corn which they ought to supply; by telling them that, if they cannot any longer retain the supremacy of Gaul, it were better to submit to the government of Gauls than of Romans, nor ought they to doubt that, if the Romans should overpower the Helvetii, they would wrest their freedom from the Aedui together with the remainder of Gaul. By these very men, said he, are our plans and whatever is done in the camp, disclosed to the enemy; that they could not be restrained by him: nay more, he

was well aware, that though compelled by necessity, he had disclosed the matter to Caesar, at how great a risk he had done it; and for that reason, he had been silent as long as he could."

18. Caesar perceived that by this speech of Liscus, Dumnorix, the brother of Divitiacus, was indicated; but, as he was unwilling that these matters should be discussed while so many were present, he speedily dismisses the council, but detains Liscus: he inquires from him when alone, about those things which he had said in the meeting. Liscus speaks more unreservedly and boldly. Caesar makes inquiries on the same points privately of others, and discovered that it is all true; that "Dumnorix is the person, a man of the highest daring, in great favor with the people on account of his liberality, a man eager for a revolution: that for a great many years he has been in the habit of contracting for the customs and all the other taxes of the Aedui at a small cost, because when he bids, no one dares to bid against him. By these means he has both increased his own private property, and amassed great means for giving bonuses; that he maintains constantly at his own expense and keeps about his own person a great number of cavalry, and that not only at home, but even among the neighboring states, he has great influence, and for the sake of strengthening this influence has given his mother in marriage among the Bituriges to a man the most noble and most influential there; that he has himself taken a wife from among the Helvetii, and has given his sister by the mother's side and his female relations in marriage into other states; that he favors and wishes well to the Helvetii on account of this connection; and that he hates Caesar and the Romans, on his own account, because by their arrival his power was weakened, and his brother, Divitiacus, restored to his former position of influence and dignity: that, if any thing should happen to the Romans, he entertains the highest hope of gaining the sovereignty by means of the Helvetii, but that under the government of the Roman people he despairs not only of royalty, but even of that influence which he already has." Caesar discovered too, on inquiring into the unsuccessful cavalry engagement which had taken place a few days before, that the commencement of that flight had been made by Dumnorix and his cavalry (for Dumnorix was in command of the cavalry which the Aedui had sent for aid to Caesar); that by their flight the rest of the cavalry were dismayed.

19. After learning these circumstances, since to these suspicions the most unequivocal facts were added, viz., that he had led the Helvetii through the territories of the Sequani; that he had provided that hostages should be mutually given; that he had done all these things, not only without any orders of his Caesar's and of his own state's, but even without their the Aedui knowing anything of it themselves; that he Dumnorix was reprimanded by the chief magistrate of the Aedui. Caesar considered that there was sufficient reason, why he should either punish him himself, or order the state to do so.

One thing however stood in the way of all this: that he had learned by experience his brother Divitiacus' very high regard for the Roman people, his great affection toward him, his distinguished faithfulness, justice, and moderation; for he was afraid lest by the punishment of this man, he should hurt the feelings of Divitiacus. Therefore, before he attempted any thing, he orders Divitiacus to be summoned to him, and, when the ordinary interpreters had been withdrawn, converses with him through C. Valerius Procillus, chief of the province of Gaul, an intimate friend of his, in whom he reposed the highest confidence in every thing; at the same time he reminds him of what was said about Dumnorix in the council of the Gauls, when he himself was present, and shows what each had said of him privately in his Caesar's own presence; he begs and exhorts him, that, without offense to his feelings, he may either himself pass judgment on him Dumnorix after trying the case, or else order the Aeduan state to do so.

20. Divitiacus, embracing Caesar, begins to implore him, with many tears, that "he would not pass any very severe sentence upon his brother; saying, that he knows that those charges are true, and that nobody suffered more pain on that account than he himself did; for when he himself could effect a very great deal by his influence at home and in the rest of Gaul, and Dumnorix very little on account of his youth, the latter had become powerful through his means, which power and strength he used not only to the lessening of his Divitiacus popularity, but almost to his ruin; that he, however, was influenced both by fraternal affection and by public opinion. But if any thing very severe from Caesar should befall Dumnorix, no one would think that it had been done without his consent, since he himself held such a place in Caesar's friendship: from which circumstance it would arise, that the affections of the whole of Gaul would be estranged from him." As he was with tears begging these things of Caesar in many words, Caesar takes his right hand, and, comforting him, begs him to make an end of entreating, and assures him that his regard for him is so great, that he forgives both the injuries of the republic and his private wrongs, at his desire and prayers. He summons Dumnorix to him; he brings in his brother; he points out what he censures in him; he lays before him what he of himself perceives, and what the state complains of; he warns him for the future to avoid all grounds of suspicion; he says that he pardons the past, for the sake of his brother, Divitiacus. He sets spies over Dumnorix that he may be able to know what he does, and with whom he communicates.

21. Being on the same day informed by his scouts, that the enemy had encamped at the foot of a mountain eight miles from his own camp; he sent persons to ascertain what the nature of the mountain was, and of what kind the ascent on every side. Word was brought back that it was easy. During the third watch he orders Titus Labienus, his lieutenant with praetorian powers, to ascend to the highest ridge of the mountain with two legions, and with those as guides who had examined the road; he explains what his plan is. He himself during the fourth watch, hastens to them by the same route by which the enemy had gone, and sends on all the cavalry before him. Publius Considius, who was reputed to be very experienced in military affairs, and had been in the army of Lucius Sulla, and afterward in that of Marcus Crassus, is sent forward with the scouts.

22. At day-break, when the summit of the mountain was in the possession of Titus Labienus, and he himself was not further off than a mile and half from the enemy's camp, nor, as he afterward ascertained from the captives, had either his arrival or that of Labienus been discovered; Considius, with his horse at full gallop, comes up to him says that the mountain which Caesar wished should be seized by Labienus, is in possession of the enemy; that he has discovered this by the Gallic arms and ensigns. Caesar leads off his forces to the next hill: and draws them up in battle-order. Labienus, as he had been ordered by Caesar not to come to an engagement unless Caesar's own forces were seen near the enemy's camp, that the attack upon the enemy might be made on every side at the same time, was, after having taken possession of the mountain, waiting for our men, and refraining from battle. When, at length, the day was far advanced, Caesar learned through spies, that the mountain was in possession of his own men, and that the Helvetii had moved their camp, and that Considius, struck with fear, had reported to him, as seen, that which he had not seen. On that day he follows the enemy at his usual distance, and pitches his camp three miles from theirs.

23. The next day (as there remained in all only two day's space to the time when he must serve out the corn to his army, and as he was not more than eighteen miles from Bibracte, by far the largest and best-stored town of the Aedui), he thought that he ought to provide for a supply of corn; and diverted his march from the Helvetii, and advanced rapidly to Bibracte. This circumstance is reported to the enemy by some deserters from Lucius Aemilius, a captain, of the Gallic horse. The Helvetii, either because they thought that the Romans, struck with terror, were retreating from them, the more so, as the day before, though they had seized on the higher grounds, they had not joined battle or because they flattered themselves that they might be cut off from the provisions, altering their plan and changing their route, began to pursue, and to annoy our men in the rear.

24. Caesar, when he observes this, draws off his forces to the next hill, and sent the cavalry to sustain the attack of the enemy. He himself, meanwhile, drew up on the middle of the hill a triple line of his four veteran legions in such a manner, that he placed above him on the very summit the two legions, which he had lately levied in Hither Gaul, and all the auxiliaries; and he ordered that the whole mountain should be covered with men, and that meanwhile the baggage should be brought together into one place, and the position be protected by those who were posted in the upper line. The Helvetii having followed with all their wagons, collected their baggage into one place: they themselves, after having repulsed our cavalry and formed a phalanx, advanced up to our front line in very close order.

25. Caesar, having removed out of sight first his own horse, then those of all, that he might make the danger of all equal, and do away with the hope of flight, after encouraging his men, joined battle. His soldiers hurling their javelins from the higher ground, easily broke the enemy's phalanx. That being dispersed, they made a charge on them with drawn swords. It was a great hindrance to the Gauls in fighting, that, when several of their bucklers had been by one stroke of the (Roman) javelins pierced through and pinned fast together, as the point of the iron had bent itself, they could neither pluck it out, nor, with their left hand entangled, fight with sufficient ease; so that many, after having long tossed their arm about, chose rather to cast away the buckler from their hand, and to fight with their person unprotected. At length, worn out with wounds, they began to give way, and, as there was in the neighborhood a mountain about a mile off, to betake themselves thither. When the mountain had been gained, and our men were advancing up, the Boii and Tulingi, who with about 15,000 men closed the enemy's line of march and served as a guard to their rear, having assailed our men on the exposed flank as they advanced prepared to surround them; upon seeing which, the Helvetii who had betaken themselves to the mountain, began to press on again and renew the battle. The Romans having faced about, advanced to the attack in two divisions; the first and second line, to withstand those who had been defeated and driven off the field; the third to receive those who were just arriving.

26. Thus was the contest long and vigorously carried on with doubtful success. When they could no longer withstand the ttacks of our men, the one division, as they had begun to do, betook hemselves to the mountain; the other repaired to their baggage and wagons. For during the whole of this battle, although the fight lasted from the seventh hour, i.e. noon, to eventide, no one could see an enemy with his back turned. The fight was carried on also at the baggage till late in the night, for they had set wagons in the way as a rampart, and from the higher ground kept throwing weapons upon our men, as they came on, and some from between the wagons and the wheels kept darting their lances and javelins from beneath, and wounding our men. After the fight had lasted some time, our men gained possession of their baggage and camp. There the daughter and one of the sons of Orgetorix was taken. After the battle about 130,000 men of the enemy remained alive, who marched incessantly during the whole of that night; and after a march discontinued for no part of the night, arrived in the territories of the Lingones on the fourth

day, while our men, having stopped for three days, both on account of the wounds of the soldiers and the burial of the slain, had not been able to follow them. Caesar sent letters and messengers to the Lingones with orders that they should not assist them with corn or with any thing else; for that if they should assist them, he would regard them in the same light as the Helvetii. After the three days' interval he began to follow them himself with all his forces.

27. The Helvetii, compelled by the want of everything, sent ambassadors to him about a surrender. When these had met him on the way and had thrown themselves at his feet, and speaking in suppliant tone had with tears sued for peace, and when he had ordered them to await his arrival, in the place, where they then were, they obeyed his commands. When Caesar arrived at that place, he demanded hostages, their arms, and the slaves who had deserted to them. While those things are being sought for and got together, after a night's interval, about 6,000 men of that canton which is called the Verbigene, whether terrified by fear, lest after delivering up their arms, they should suffer punishment, or else induced by the hope of safety, because they supposed that, amid so vast a multitude of those who had surrendered themselves, their flight might either be concealed or entirely overlooked, having at night-fall departed out of the camp of the Helvetii, hastened to the Rhine and the territories of the Germans.

28. But when Caesar discovered this, he commanded those through whose territory they had gone, to seek them out and to bring them back again, if they meant to be acquitted before him; and considered them, when brought back, in the light of enemies; he admitted all the rest to a surrender, upon their delivering up the hostages, arms, and deserters. He ordered the Helvetii, the Tulingi, and the Latobrigi, to return to their territories from which they had come, and as there was at home nothing whereby they might support their hunger, all the productions of the earth having been destroyed, he commanded the Allobroges to let them have a plentiful supply of corn; and ordered them to rebuild the towns and villages which they had burned. This he did, chiefly, on this account, because he was unwilling that the country, from which the Helvetii had departed, should be untenanted, lest the Germans, who dwell on the other side of the Rhine, should, on account of the excellence of the lands, cross over from their own territories into those of the Helvetii, and become borderers upon the province of Gaul and the Allobroges. He granted the petition of the Aedui, that they might settle the Boii, in their own (i. e. in the Aeduan) territories, as these were known to be of distinguished valor, to whom they gave lands, and whom they afterward admitted to the same state of rights and freedom as themselves.

29. In the camp of the Helvetii, lists were found, drawn up in Greek characters, and were brought to Caesar, in which an estimate had been drawn up, name by name, of the number which had gone forth from their country of those who were able to bear arms; and likewise the boys, the old men, and the women, separately. Of all which items the total was: Of the Helvetii 263,000; Of the Tulingi 36,000; Of the Latobrigi 14,000; Of the Rauraci 23,000; Of the Boii 32,000. The sum of all amounted to 368,000. Out of these, such as could bear arms, amounted to about 92,000. When the census of those who returned home was taken, as Caesar had commanded, the number was found to be 110,000.

30. When the war with the Helvetii was concluded, ambassadors from almost all parts of Gaul, the chiefs of states, assembled to congratulate Caesar, saying that they were well aware, that, although he had taken vengeance on the Helvetii in war, for the old wrong done by them to the Roman people, yet that circumstance had happened no less to the benefit of the land of Gaul than of the Roman people, because the Helvetii, while their affairs were most flourishing, had quitted their country with the design of making war upon the whole of Gaul, and seizing the government of it, and selecting, out of a great abundance, that spot for an abode, which they should judge to be the most convenient and most productive of all Gaul, and hold the rest of the states as tributaries. They requested that they might be allowed to proclaim an assembly of the whole of Gaul for a particular day, and to do that with Caesar's permission, stating that they had some things which, with the general consent, they wished to ask of him. This request having been granted, they appointed a day for the assembly, and ordained by an oath with each other, that no one should disclose their deliberations except those to whom this office should be assigned by the general assembly.

31. When that assembly was dismissed, the same chiefs of states, who had before been to Caesar, returned, and asked that they might be allowed to treat with him privately (in secret) concerning the safety of themselves and of all. That request having been obtained, they all threw themselves in tears at Caesar's feet, saying that they no less begged and earnestly desired that what they might say should not be disclosed, than that they might obtain those things which they wished for; inasmuch as they saw, that, if a disclosure was made, they should be put to the greatest tortures. For these Divitiacus the Aeduan spoke and told him: "That there were two parties in the whole of Gaul: that the Aedui stood at the head of one of these, the Arverni of the other. After these had been violently struggling with one another for the superiority for many years, it came to pass that the Germans were called in for hire by the Arverni and the Sequani. That about 15,000 of the Germans had at first crossed the Rhine; but after that these wild and savage men had become enamored of the lands and the refinement and the abundance of the Gauls, more were brought over, that there were now as many as 120,000 of them in Gaul. With these the Aedui and their dependents had repeatedly

struggled in arms—that they had been routed, and had sustained a great calamity—and had lost all their nobility, all their senate, all their cavalry. And that broken by such engagements and calamities, although they had formerly been very powerful in Gaul, both from their own valor and from the Roman people's hospitality and friendship, they were now compelled to give the chief nobles of their state, as hostages to the Sequani, and to bind their state by an oath, that they would neither demand hostages in return, nor supplicate aid from the Roman people, nor refuse to be forever under their sway and empire. That he was the only one out of all the state of the Aedui, who could not be prevailed upon to take the oath or to give his children as hostages. On that account he had fled from his state and had gone to the senate at Rome to beseech aid, as he alone was bound neither by oath nor hostages. But a worse thing had befallen the victorious Sequani than the vanquished Aedui, for Ariovistus the king of the Germans, had settled in their territories, and had seized upon a third of their land, which was the best in the whole of Gaul, and was now ordering them to depart from another third part, because a few months previously 24,000 men of the Harudes had come to him, for whom room and settlements must be provided. The consequence would be, that in a few years they would all be driven from the territories of Gaul, and all the Germans would cross the Rhine; for neither must the land of Gaul be compared with the land of the Germans, nor must the habit of living of the latter be put on a level with that of the former. Moreover, as for Ariovistus, no sooner did he defeat the forces of the Gauls in a battle which took place at Magetobria, than he began to lord it haughtily and cruelly, to demand as hostages the children of all the principal nobles, and wreak on them every kind of cruelty, if everything was not done at his nod or pleasure; that he was a savage, passionate, and reckless man, and that his commands could no longer be borne. Unless there was some aid in Caesar and the Roman people, the Gauls must all do the same thing that the Helvetii have done, viz. emigrate from their country, and seek another dwelling place, other settlements remote from the Germans, and try whatever fortune may fall to their lot. If these things were to be disclosed to Ariovistus, Divitiacus adds that he doubts not that he would inflict the most severe punishment on all the hostages who are in his possession, and says that Caesar could, either by his own influence and by that of his army, or by his late victory, or by name of the Roman people, intimidate him, so as to prevent a greater number of Germans being brought over the Rhine, and could protect all Gaul from the outrages of Ariovistus."

32. When this speech had been delivered by Divitiacus, all who were present began with loud lamentation to entreat assistance of Caesar. Caesar noticed that the Sequani were the only people of all who did none of those things which the others did, but, with their heads bowed down, gazed on

the earth in sadness. Wondering what was the reason of this conduct, he inquired of themselves. No reply did the Sequani make, but silently continued in the same sadness. When he had repeatedly inquired of them and could not elicit any answer at all, the same Divitiacus the Aeduan answered, that "the lot of the Sequani was more wretched and grievous than that of the rest, on this account, because they alone dare not even in secret complain or supplicate aid; and shuddered at the cruelty of Ariovistus even when absent, just as if he were present; for, to the rest, despite of everything there was an opportunity of flight given; but all tortures must be endured by the Sequani, who had admitted Ariovistus within their territories, and whose towns were all in his power."

33. Caesar, on being informed of these things, cheered the minds of the Gauls with his words, and promised that this affair should be an object of his concern, saying that he had great hopes that Ariovistus, induced both by his kindness and his power, would put an end to his oppression. After delivering this speech, he dismissed the assembly; and, besides those statements, many circumstances induced him to think that this affair ought to be considered and taken up by him; especially as he saw that the Aedui, styled as they had been repeatedly by the senate "brethren" and "kinsmen," were held in the thralldom and dominion of the Germans, and understood that their hostages were with Ariovistus and the Sequani, which in so mighty an empire as that of the Roman people he considered very disgraceful to himself and the Republic. That, moreover, the Germans should by degrees become accustomed to cross the Rhine, and that a great body of them should come into Gaul, he saw would be dangerous to the Roman people, and judged, that wild and savage men would not be likely to restrain themselves, after they had possessed themselves of all Gaul, from going forth into the province and thence marching into Italy (as the Cimbri and Teutones had done before them [101 B.C.E.]), particularly as the Rhone was the sole barrier that separated the Sequani from our province. Against which events he thought he ought to provide as speedily as possible. Moreover, Ariovistus, for his part, had assumed to himself such pride and arrogance, that he was felt to be quite insufferable.

34. He therefore determined to send ambassadors to Ariovistus to demand of him to name some intermediate spot for a conference between the two, saying that he wished to treat him on state-business and matters of the highest importance to both of them. To this embassy Ariovistus replied, that if he himself had had need of anything from Caesar, he would have gone to him; and that if Caesar wanted any thing from him he ought to come to him. That, besides, neither dare he go without an army into those parts of Gaul which Caesar had possession of, nor could he, without great expense and trouble, draw his army together to one place; that to him, moreover, it appeared strange, what business either Caesar or the Roman people at all had in his own Gaul, which he had conquered in war.

35. When these answers were reported to Caesar, he sends ambassadors to him a second time with this message. "Since, after having been treated with so much kindness by himself and the Roman people (as he had in his consulship been styled 'king and friend' by the senate), he makes this recompense to Caesar himself and the Roman people, viz. that when invited to a conference he demurs, and does not think that it concerns him to advise and inform himself about an object of mutual interest, these are the things which he requires of him; first, that he do not any more bring over any body of men across the Rhine into Gaul; in the next place, that he restore the hostages, which he has from the Aedui, and grant the Sequani permission to restore to them with his consent those hostages which they have, and that he neither provoke the Aedui by outrage nor make war upon them or their allies; if he would accordingly do this." Caesar says that "he himself and the Roman people will entertain a perpetual feeling of favor and friendship toward him; but that if he Caesar does not obtain his desires that he (forasmuch as in the consulship of Marcus Messala and Marcus Piso the senate had decreed that, whoever should have the administration of the province of Gaul should, as far as he could do so consistently with the interests of the Republic, protect the Aedui and the other friends of the Roman people), will not overlook the wrongs of the Aedui."

36. To this Ariovistus replied, that "the right of war was, that they who had conquered should govern those whom they had conquered, in what manner they pleased; that in that way the Roman people were wont to govern the nations which they had conquered, not according to the dictation of any other, but according to their own discretion. If he for his part did not dictate to the Roman people as to the manner in which they were to exercise their right, he ought not to be obstructed by the Roman people in his right; that the Aedui, inasmuch as they had tried the fortune of war and had engaged in arms and been conquered, had become tributaries to him; that Caesar was doing a great injustice, in that by his arrival he was making his revenues less valuable to him; that he should not restore their hostages to the Aedui, but should not make war wrongfully either upon them or their allies, if they abided by that which had been agreed on, and paid their tribute annually: if they did not continue to do that, the Roman people's name of 'brothers' would avail them naught. As to Caesar's threatening him, that he would not overlook the wrongs of the Aedui, he said that noone had ever entered into a contest with him Ariovistus without utter ruin to himself. That Caesar might enter the lists when he chose; he would feel what the invincible Germans, well-trained as they were beyond all others to arms, who for fourteen years had not been beneath a roof, could achieve by their valor."

37. At the same time that this message was delivered to Caesar, ambassadors came from the Aedui and the Treviri; from the Aedui to complain that the Harudes, who had lately been brought over into Gaul, were ravaging their territories; that they had not been able to purchase peace from Ariovistus, even by giving hostages: and from the Treviri, to state that a hundred cantons of the Suevi had encamped on the banks of the Rhine, and were attempting to cross it; that the brothers, Nasuas and Cimberius, headed them. Being greatly alarmed at these things, Caesar thought that he ought to use all dispatch, lest, if this new band of Suevi should unite with the old troops of Ariovistus, he Ariovistus might be less easily withstood. Having therefore, as quickly as he could, provided a supply of corn, he hastened to Ariovistus by forced marches.

38. When he had proceeded three days' journey, word was brought to him that Ariovistus was hastening with all his forces to seize on Vesontio, which is the largest town of the Sequani, and had advanced three days' journey from its territories. Caesar thought that he ought to take the greatest precautions lest this should happen, for there was in that town a most ample supply of everything which was serviceable for war; and so fortified was it by the nature of the ground, as to afford a great facility for protracting the war, inasmuch as the river Doubs almost surrounds the whole town, as though it were traced round it with a pair of compasses. A mountain of great height shuts in the remaining space, which is not more than 600 feet, where the river leaves a gap, in such a manner that the roots of that mountain extend to the river's bank on either side. A wall thrown around it makes a citadel of this mountain, and connects it with the town. Hither Caesar hastens by forced marches by night and day, and, after having seized the town, stations a garrison there.

39. While he is tarrying a few days at Vesontio, on account of corn and provisions; from the inquiries of our men and the reports of the Gauls and traders (who asserted that the Germans were men of huge stature, of incredible valor and practice in arms that oftentimes on encountering them, they could not bear even their countenance, and the fierceness of their eyes), so great a panic on a sudden seized the whole army, as to discompose the minds and spirits of all in no slight degree. This first arose from the tribunes of the soldiers, the prefects and the rest, who, having followed Caesar from the city Rome from motives of friendship, had no great experience in military affairs. And alleging, some of them one reason, some another, which they said made it necessary for them to depart, they requested that by his consent they might be allowed to withdraw; some, influenced by shame, stayed behind in order that they might avoid the suspicion of cowardice. These could neither compose their countenance, nor even sometimes check their tears: but hidden in their tents, either bewailed their fate, or deplored with their comrades the general danger. Wills were sealed universally throughout the whole camp. By the expressions and cowardice of these men, even those who possessed great experience in the camp, both soldiers and centurions, and those the decurions who were in command of the cavalry, were gradually disconcerted. Such of them as wished to be considered less alarmed, said that they did not dread the enemy, but feared the narrowness of the roads and the vastness of the forests which lay between them and Ariovistus, or else that the supplies could not be brought up readily enough. Some even declared to Caesar, that when he gave orders for the camp to be moved and the troops to advance, the soldiers would not be obedient to the command, nor advance in consequence of their fear.

40. When Caesar observed these things, having called a council, and summoned to it the centurions of all the companies, he severely reprimanded them, "particularly, for supposing that it belonged to them to inquire or conjecture, either in what direction they were marching, or with what object. That Ariovistus, during Caesar's consulship, had most anxiously sought after the friendship of the Roman people; why should any one judge that he would so rashly depart from his duty? He for his part was persuaded, that, when his demands were known and the fairness of the terms considered, he would reject neither his nor the Roman people's favor. But even if, driven on by rage and madness, he should make war upon them, that after all were they afraid of? Why should they despair either of their own valor or of his zeal? Of that enemy a trial had been made within our fathers' recollection, when, on the defeat of the Cimbri and Teutones by Gaius Marius, the army was regarded as having deserved no less praise than their commander himself. It had been made lately, too, in Italy, during the rebellion of the slaves, whom, however, the experience and training which they had received from us, assisted in some respect. From which a judgment might be formed of the advantages which resolution carries with it inasmuch as those whom for some time they had groundlessly dreaded when unarmed, they had afterward vanquished, when well armed and flushed with success. In short, that these were the same men whom the Helvetii, in frequent encounters, not only in their own territories, but also in theirs the German, have generally vanquished, and yet can not have been a match for our army. If the unsuccessful battle and flight of the Gauls disquieted any, these, if they made inquiries, might discover that, when the Gauls had been tired out by the long duration of the war, Ariovistus, after he had many months kept himself in his camp and in the marshes, and had given no opportunity for an engagement, fell suddenly upon them, by this time despairing of a battle and scattered in all directions, and was victorious more through stratagem and cunning than valor. But though there had been room for such stratagem against savage and unskilled men, not even Ariovistus himself expected that thereby our armies could be entrapped. That those who ascribed their fear to a pretense about the deficiency of supplies and the narrowness of the roads, acted presumptuously, as they seemed either to distrust their general's discharge of his duty, or to dictate to him. That these things were his concern; that the Sequani, the Leuci, and the Lingones were to furnish the corn; and that it was already ripe in the fields; that as to the road they would soon be able to judge for themselves. As to its being reported that the soldiers would not be obedient to command, or advance, he was not at all disturbed at that; for he knew, that in the case of all those whose army had not been obedient to command, either upon some mismanagement of an affair, fortune had deserted them, or, that upon some crime being discovered, covetousness had been clearly proved against them. His integrity had been seen throughout his whole life, his good fortune in the war with the Helvetii. That he would therefore instantly set about what he had intended to put off till a more distant day, and would break up his camp the next night, in the fourth watch, that he might ascertain, as soon as possible, whether a sense of honor and duty, or whether fear had more influence with them. But that, if no one else should follow, yet he would go with only the tenth legion, of which he had no misgivings, and it should be his praetorian cohort." This legion Caesar had both greatly favored, and in it, on account of its valor, placed the greatest confidence.

41. Upon the delivery of this speech, the minds of all were changed in a surprising manner, and the highest ardor and eagerness for prosecuting the war were engendered; and the tenth legion was the first to return thanks to him, through their military tribunes, for his having expressed this most favorable opinion of them; and assured him that they were quite ready to prosecute the war. Then, the other legions endeavored, through their military tribunes and the centurions of the principal companies, to excuse themselves to Caesar, saying that they had never either doubted or feared, or supposed that the determination of the conduct of the war was theirs and not their general's. Having accepted their excuse, and having had the road carefully reconnoitered by Divitiacus, because in him of all others he had the greatest faith he found that by a circuitous route of more than fifty miles he might lead his army through open parts; he then set out in the fourth watch, as he had said he would. On the seventh day, as he did not discontinue his march, he was informed by scouts that the forces of Ariovistus were only four and twenty miles distant from ours.

42. Upon being apprised of Caesar's arrival, Ariovistus sends ambassadors to him, saying that what he had before requested as to a conference, might now, as far as his permission went, take place, since Caesar had approached nearer, and he considered that he might now do it without danger. Caesar did not reject the proposal and began to think that he was now returning to a rational state of mind as he spontaneously proffered that which he had previously refused to him when requesting it; and was in great hopes that, in consideration of his own and the Roman people's great favors toward him, the issue would be that he would desist from his obstinacy upon his demands being made known. The fifth day after that was appointed as the day of conference. Meanwhile, as ambassadors were being often sent to and fro between them, Ariovistus demanded that Caesar should not bring any foot-soldier with him to the conference, saying that "he was afraid of being ensnared by him through treachery; that both should come accompanied by cavalry; that he would not come on any other condition." Caesar, as he neither wished that the conference should, by an excuse thrown in the way, be set aside, nor dare trust his life to the cavalry of the Gauls, decided that it would be most expedient to take away from the Gallic cavalry all their horses, and thereon to mount the legionary soldiers of the tenth legion, in which he placed the greatest confidence, in order that he might have a body-guard as trustworthy as possible, should there be any need for action. And when this was done, one of the soldiers of the tenth legion said, not without a touch of humor, "that Caesar did more for them than he had promised; he had promised to have the tenth legion in place of his praetorian cohort; but he now converted them into horse."

43. There was a large plain, and in it a mound of earth of considerable size. This spot was at nearly an equal distance from both camps. Thither, as had been appointed, they came for the conference. Caesar stationed the legion, which he had brought with him on horseback, 200 paces from this mound. The cavalry of Ariovistus also took their stand at an equal distance. Ariovistus then demanded that they should confer on horseback, and that, besides themselves, they should bring with them ten men each to the conference. When they were come to the place, Caesar, in the opening of his speech, detailed his own and the senate's favors toward Ariovistus, in that he had been styled king, in that he had been styled friend, by the senate, in that very considerable presents had been sent him; which circumstance he informed him had both fallen to the lot of few, and had usually been bestowed in consideration of important personal services; that he, although he had neither an introduction, nor a just ground for the request, had obtained these honors through the kindness and munificence of Caesar and the senate. He informed him too, how old and how just were the grounds of connection that existed between themselves the Romans and the Aedui, what decrees of the senate had been passed in their favor, and how frequent and how honorable; how from time immemorial the Aedui had held the supremacy of the whole of Gaul; even said Caesar before they had sought our friendship; that it was the custom of the Roman people to desire not only that its allies and friends should lose none of their property, but be advanced in influence, dignity, and honor: who then could endure that what they had

brought with them to the friendship of the Roman people should be torn from them?" He then made the same demands which he had commissioned the ambassadors to make, that Ariovistus should not make war either upon the Aedui or their allies, that he should restore the hostages; that if he could not send back to their country any part of the Germans, he should at all events suffer none of them any more to cross the Rhine.

44. Ariovistus briefly replied to the demands of Caesar; but expatiated largely on his own virtues, "that he had crossed the Rhine not of his own accord, but on being invited and sent for by the Gauls; that he had not left home and kindred without great expectations and great rewards; that he had settlements in Gaul, granted by the Gauls themselves; that the hostages had been given by their good-will; that he took by right of war the tribute which conquerors are accustomed to impose on the conquered; that he had not made war upon the Gauls, but the Gauls upon him; that all the states of Gaul came to attack him, and had encamped against him; that all their forces had been routed and beaten by him in a single battle; that if they chose to make a second trial, he was ready to encounter them again; but if they chose to enjoy peace, it was unfair to refuse the tribute, which of their own free-will they had paid up to that time. That the friendship of the Roman people ought to prove to him an ornament and a safeguard, not a detriment; and that he sought it with that expectation. But if through the Roman people the tribute was to be discontinued, and those who surrendered to be seduced from him, he would renounce the friendship of the Roman people no less heartily than he had sought it. As to his leading over a host of Germans into Gaul, that he was doing this with a view of securing himself, not of assaulting Gaul: that there was evidence of this, in that he did not come without being invited, and in that he did not make war, but merely warded it off. That he had come into Gaul before the Roman people. That never before this time did a Roman army go beyond the frontiers of the province of Gaul. What does Caesar desire? Why come into Ariovistus' domains? This was his province of Gaul, just as that is ours. As it ought not to be pardoned in him, if he were to make an attack upon our territories; so, likewise, that we were unjust, to obstruct him in his prerogative. As for Caesar's saying that the Aedui had been styled 'brethren' by the senate, he was not so uncivilized nor so ignorant of affairs, as not to know that the Aedui in the very last war with the Allobroges had neither rendered assistance to the Romans, nor received any from the Roman people in the struggles which the Aedui had been maintaining with him and with the Sequani. He must feel suspicious, that Caesar, though feigning friendship as the reason for his keeping an army in Gaul, was keeping it with the view of crushing him. And that unless he depart and withdraw his army from these parts, he shall regard him not as a friend, but as a foe; and that, even if he should put him to death, he should do what would please many of the nobles and leading men of the Roman people; he had assurance of that from themselves through their messengers, and could purchase the favor and the friendship of them all by his Caesar's death. But if he would depart and resign to him the free possession of Gaul, he would recompense him with a great reward, and would bring to a close whatever wars he wished to be carried on, without any trouble or risk to him."

45. Many things were stated by Caesar to the effect to show; "why he could not waive the business, and that neither his nor the Roman people's practice would suffer him to abandon most meritorious allies, nor did he deem that Gaul belonged to Ariovistus rather than to the Roman people; that the Arverni and the Ruteni had been subdued in war by Quintus Fabius Maximus, and that the Roman people had pardoned them and had not reduced them into a province or imposed a tribute upon them. And if the most ancient period was to be regarded, then was the sovereignty of the Roman people in Gaul most just: if the decree of the Senate was to be observed, then ought Gaul to be free, which they the Romans had conquered in war, and had permitted to enjoy its own laws."

46. While these things are being transacted in the conference it was announced to Caesar that the cavalry of Ariovistus were approaching nearer the mound, and were riding up to our men, and casting stones and weapons at them. Caesar made an end of his speech and betook himself to his men; and commanded them that they should by no means return a weapon upon the enemy. For though he saw that an engagement with the cavalry would be without any danger to his chosen legion, yet he did not think proper to engage, lest, after the enemy were routed, it might be said that they had been ensnared by him under the sanction of a conference. When it was spread abroad among the common soldiery with what haughtiness Ariovistus had behaved at the conference, and how he had ordered the Romans to quit Gaul, and how his cavalry had made an attack upon our men, and how this had broken off the conference, a much greater alacrity and eagerness for battle was infused into our army.

47. Two days after, Ariovistus sends ambassadors to Caesar, to state "that he wished to treat with him about those things which had been begun to be treated of between them, but had not been concluded;" and to beg that "he would either again appoint a day for a conference; or, if he were not willing to do that, that he would send one of his officers as an ambassador to him." There did not appear to Caesar any good reason for holding a conference; and the more so as the day before the Germans could not be restrained from casting weapons at our men. He thought he should not without great danger send to him as ambassador one of his Roman officers, and should expose him to savage men. It seemed therefore most proper to send to him C. Valerius Procillus, the son of C. Valerius Caburus, a young man of the highest courage and accomplishments (whose father had been presented with the freedom of the city by C. Valerius Flaccus), both on account of his fidelity and on account of his knowledge of the Gallic language, which Ariovistus, by long practice, now spoke fluently; and because in his case the Germans would have no motive for committing violence; and as his colleague M. Mettius, who had shared the hospitality of Ariovistus. He commissioned them to learn what Ariovistus had to say, and to report to him. But when Ariovistus saw them before him in his camp, he cried out in the presence of his army, "Why were they come to him? Was it for the purpose of acting as spies?" He stopped them when attempting to speak, and cast them into chains.

48. The same day he moved his camp forward and pitched under a hill six miles from Caesar's camp. The day following he led his forces past Caesar's camp, and encamped two miles beyond him; with this design that he might cut off Caesar from the corn and provisions, which might be conveyed to him from the Sequani and the Aedui. For five successive days from that day, Caesar drew out his forces before the camp, and put them in battle order, that, if Ariovistus should be willing to engage in battle, an opportunity might not be wanting to him. Ariovistus all this time kept his army in camp: but engaged daily in cavalry skirmishes. The method of battle in which the Germans had practiced themselves was this. There were 6,000 horsemen, and as many very active and courageous footmen, one of whom each of the horsemen selected out of the whole army for his own protection. By these footmen they were constantly accompanied in their engagements; to these the horsemen retired; these on any emergency rushed forward; if anyone, upon receiving a very severe wound, had fallen from his horse, they stood around him: if it was necessary to advance further than usual, or to retreat more rapidly, so great, from practice, was their swiftness, that, supported by the manes of the horses, they could keep pace with their speed.

49. Perceiving that Ariovistus kept himself in camp, Caesar, that he might not any longer be cut off from provisions, chose a convenient position for a camp beyond that place in which the Germans had encamped, at about 600 paces from them, and having drawn up his army in three lines, marched to that place. He ordered the first and second lines to be under arms; the third to fortify the camp. This place was distant from the enemy about 600 paces, as has been stated. Thither Ariovistus sent light troops, about 16,000 men in number, with all his cavalry; which forces were to intimidate our men, and hinder them in their fortification. Caesar nevertheless, as he had before arranged, ordered two lines to drive off the enemy: the third to execute the work. The camp being fortified, he left there two legions and a portion of the auxiliaries; and led back the other four legions into the larger camp.

50. The next day, according to his custom, Caesar led out his forces from both camps, and having advanced a little from the larger one, drew up his line of battle, and gave the enemy an opportunity of fighting. When he found that they did not even then come out from their entrenchments, he led back his army into camp about noon. Then at last Ariovistus sent part of his forces to attack the lesser camp. The battle was vigorously maintained on both sides till the evening. At sunset, after many wounds had been inflicted and received, Ariovistus led back his forces into camp. When Caesar inquired of his prisoners, wherefore Ariovistus did not come to an engagement, he discovered the reason to be that among the Germans it was the custom for their matrons to pronounce from lots and divination, whether it were expedient that the battle should be engaged in or not; that they had said, "that it was not the will of heaven that the Germans should conquer, if they engaged in battle before the new moon."

51. The day following, Caesar left what seemed sufficient as a guard for both camps; and then drew up all the auxiliaries in sight of the enemy, before the lesser camp, because he was not very powerful in the number of legionary soldiers, considering the number of the enemy; that thereby he might make use of his auxiliaries for appearance. He himself, having drawn up his army in three lines, advanced to the camp of the enemy. Then at last of necessity the Germans drew their forces out of camp, and disposed them canton by canton, at equal distances, the Harudes, Marcomanni, Tribocci, Vangiones, Nemetes, Sedusii, Suevi; and surrounded their whole army with their chariots and wagons, that no hope might be left in flight. On these they placed their women, who, with disheveled hair and in tears, entreated the soldiers, as they went forward to battle, not to deliver them into slavery to the Romans.

52. Caesar appointed over each legion a lieutenant and a questor, that everyone might have them as witnesses of his valor. He himself began the battle at the head of the right wing, because he had observed that part of the enemy to be the least strong. Accordingly our men, upon the signal being given, vigorously made an attack upon the enemy, and the enemy so suddenly and rapidly rushed forward, that there was no time for casting the javelins at them. Throwing aside therefore their javelins, they fought with swords hand to hand. But the Germans, according to their custom, rapidly forming a phalanx, sustained the attack of our swords. There were found very many of our soldiers who leaped upon the phalanx, and with their hands tore away the shields, and wounded the enemy from above. Although the army of the enemy was routed on the left wing and put to flight, they still pressed heavily on our men from the right wing, by the great number of their troops. On observing which, P. Crassus, a young man who commanded the cavalry, as he was more disengaged than those who were employed in the fight, sent the third line as a relief to our men who were in distress.

53. Thereupon the engagement was renewed, and all the enemy turned

their backs, nor did they cease to flee until they arrived at the river Rhine, about fifty miles from that place. There some few, either relying on their strength, endeavored to swim over, or, finding boats, procured their safety. Among the latter was Ariovistus, who meeting with a small vessel tied to the bank, escaped in it; our horsemen pursued and slew all the rest of them. Ariovistus had two wives, one a Suevan by nation, whom he brought with him from home; the other a Norican, the sister of King Vocion, whom he had married in Gaul, she having been sent thither for that purpose by her brother. Both perished in that flight. Of their two daughters, one was slain, the other captured. C. Valerius Procillus, as he was being dragged by his guards in the fight, bound with a triple chain, fell into the hands of Caesar himself, as he was pursuing the enemy with his cavalry. This circumstance indeed afforded Caesar no less pleasure than the victory itself; because he saw a man of the first rank in the province of Gaul, his intimate acquaintance and friend, rescued from the hand of the enemy, and restored to him, and that fortune had not diminished any of the joy and exultation of that day by his destruction. Procillus said that, in his own presence, the lots had been thrice consulted respecting him, whether he should immediately be put to death by fire, or be reserved for another time: that by the favor of the lots he was uninjured. M. Mettius, also, was found and brought back to Caesar.

54. This battle having been reported beyond the Rhine, the Suevi, who had come to the banks of that river, began to return home, when the Ubii, who dwelt nearest to the Rhine, pursuing them, while much alarmed, slew a great number of them. Caesar having concluded two very important wars in one campaign, conducted his army into winter quarters among the Sequani, a little earlier than the season of the year required. He appointed Labienus over the winter-quarters, and set out in person for Hither Gaul to hold the assizes.

BOOK VI **11-28**

Caesar provides a brief ethnographic essay on the religion, customs and political structures of the peoples of Gaul and Germany.

11. Since we have come to the place, it does not appear to be foreign to our subject to lay before the reader an account of the manners of Gaul and Germany, and wherein these nations differ from each other. In Gaul there are factions not only in all the states, and in all the cantons and their divisions, but almost in each family, and of these factions those are the leaders who are considered according to their judgment to possess the greatest influence, upon whose will and determination the management of all affairs and measures depends. And that seems to have been instituted in ancient times with this view, that no one of the common people should be in want of support against one more powerful; for, none of those leaders suffers his party to be oppressed and defrauded, and if he do otherwise, he has no influence among his party. This same policy exists throughout the whole of Gaul; for all the states are divided into two factions.

12. When Caesar arrived in Gaul, the Aedui were the leaders of one faction, the Sequani of the other. Since the latter were less powerful by themselves, inasmuch as the chief influence was from of old among the Aedui, and their dependencies were great, they had united to themselves the Germans and Ariovistus, and had brought them over to their party by great sacrifices and promises. And having fought several successful battles and slain all the nobility of the Aedui, they had so far surpassed them in power, that they brought over, from the Aedui to themselves, a large portion of their dependents and received from them the sons of their leading men as hostages, and compelled them to swear in their public character that they would enter into no design against them; and held a portion of the neighboring land, seized on by force, and possessed the sovereignty of the whole of Gaul. Divitiacus urged by this necessity, had proceeded to Rome to the senate, for the purpose of entreating assistance, and had returned without accomplishing his object. A change of affairs ensued on the arrival of Caesar, the hostages were returned to the Aedui, their old dependencies restored, and new acquired through Caesar (because those who had attached themselves to their alliance saw that they enjoyed a better state and a milder government), their other interests, their influence, their reputation were likewise increased, and in consequence, the Sequani lost the sovereignty. The Remi succeeded to their place, and, as it was perceived that they equaled the Aedui in favor with Caesar, those, who on account of their old animosities could by no means coalesce with the Aedui, consigned themselves in clientship to the Remi. The latter carefully protected them. Thus they possessed both a new and suddenly acquired influence. Affairs were then in that position that the Aedui were considered by far the leading people, and the Remi held the second post of honor.

13. Throughout all Gaul there are two orders of those men who are of any rank and dignity: for the commonality is held almost in the condition of slaves, and dares to undertake nothing of itself, and is admitted to no deliberation. The greater part, when they are pressed either by debt, or the large amount of their tributes, or the oppression of the more powerful, give themselves up in vassalage to the nobles, who possess over them the same rights without exception as masters over their slaves. But of these two orders, one is that of the Druids, the other that of the knights. The former are engaged in

things sacred, conduct the public and the private sacrifices, and interpret all matters of religion. To these a large number of the young men resort for the purpose of instruction, and they the Druids are in great honor among them. For they determine respecting almost all controversies, public and private; and if any crime has been perpetrated, if murder has been committed, if there be any dispute about an inheritance, if any about boundaries, these same persons decide it; they decree rewards and punishments; if any one, either in a private or public capacity, has not submitted to their decision, they interdict him from the sacrifices. This among them is the most heavy punishment. Those who have been thus interdicted are esteemed in the number of the impious and the criminal: all shun them, and avoid their society and conversation, lest they receive some evil from their contact; nor is justice administered to them when seeking it, nor is any dignity bestowed on them. Over all these Druids one presides, who possesses supreme authority among them. Upon his death, if any individual among the rest is pre-eminent in dignity, he succeeds; but, if there are many equal, the election is made by the suffrages of the Druids; sometimes they even contend for the presidency with arms. These assemble at a fixed period of the year in a consecrated place in the territories of the Carnutes, which is reckoned the central region of the whole of Gaul. Hither all, who have disputes, assemble from every part, and submit to their decrees and determinations. This institution is supposed to have been devised in Britain, and to have been brought over from it into Gaul; and now those who desire to gain a more accurate knowledge of that system generally proceed thither for the purpose of studying it.

14. The Druids do not go to war, nor pay tribute together with the rest; they have an exemption from military service and a dispensation in all matters. Induced by such great advantages, many embrace this profession of their own accord, and many are sent to it by their parents and relations. They are said there to learn by heart a great number of verses; accordingly some remain in the course of training twenty years. Nor do they regard it lawful to commit these to writing, though in almost all other matters, in their public and private transactions, they use Greek characters. That practice they seem to me to have adopted for two reasons; because they neither desire their doctrines to be divulged among the mass of the people, nor those who learn, to devote themselves the less to the efforts of memory, relying on writing; since it generally occurs to most men, that, in their dependence on writing, they relax their diligence in learning thoroughly, and their employment of the memory. They wish to inculcate this as one of their leading tenets, that souls do not become extinct, but pass after death from one body to another, and they think that men by this tenet are in a great degree excited to valor, the fear of death being disregarded. They likewise discuss and impart to the

youth many things respecting the stars and their motion, respecting the extent of the world and of our earth, respecting the nature of things, respecting the power and the majesty of the immortal gods.

15. The other order is that of the knights. These, when there is occasion and any war occurs (which before Caesar's arrival was for the most part wont to happen every year, as either they on their part were inflecting injuries or repelling those which others inflected on them), are all engaged in war. And those of them most distinguished by birth and resources, have the greatest number of vassals and dependents about them. They acknowledge this sort of influence and power only.

16. The nation of all the Gauls is extremely devoted to superstitious rites; and on that account they who are troubled with unusually severe diseases, and they who are engaged in battles and dangers, either sacrifice men as victims, or vow that they will sacrifice them, and employ the Druids as the performers of those sacrifices; because they think that unless the life of a man be offered for the life of a man, the mind of the immortal gods can not be rendered propitious, and they have sacrifices of that kind ordained for national purposes. Others have figures of vast size, the limbs of which formed of osiers they fill with living men, which being set on fire, the men perish enveloped in the flames. They consider that the oblation of such as have been taken in theft, or in robbery, or any other offense, is more acceptable to the immortal gods; but when a supply of that class is wanting, they have recourse to the oblation of even the innocent.

17. They worship as their divinity, Mercury in particular, and have many images of him, and regard him as the inventor of all arts, they consider him the guide of their journeys and marches, and believe him to have great influence over the acquisition of gain and mercantile transactions. Next to him they worship Apollo, and Mars, and Jupiter, and Minerva; respecting these deities they have for the most part the same belief as other nations: that Apollo averts diseases, that Minerva imparts the invention of manufactures, that Jupiter possesses the sovereignty of the heavenly powers; that Mars presides over wars. To him, when they have determined to engage in battle, they commonly vow those things which they shall take in war. When they have conquered, they sacrifice whatever captured animals may have survived the conflict, and collect the other things into one place. In many states you may see piles of these things heaped up in their consecrated spots; nor does it often happen that anyone, disregarding the sanctity of the case, dares either to secrete in his house things captured, or take away those deposited; and the most severe punishment, with torture, has been established for such a deed.

18. All the Gauls assert that they are descended from the god Dis, and say that this tradition has been handed down by the Druids. For that reason they compute the divisions of every season, not by the number of days, but of

nights; they keep birthdays and the beginnings of months and years in such an order that the day follows the night. Among the other usages of their life, they differ in this from almost all other nations, that they do not permit their children to approach them openly until they are grown up so as to be able to bear the service of war; and they regard it as indecorous for a son of boyish age to stand in public in the presence of his father.

19. Whatever sums of money the husbands have received in the name of dowry from their wives, making an estimate of it, they add the same amount out of their own estates. An account is kept of all this money conjointly, and the profits are laid by: whichever of them shall have survived the other, to that one the portion of both reverts together with the profits of the previous time. Husbands have power of life and death over their wives as well as over their children: and when the father of a family, born in a more than commonly distinguished rank, has died, his relations assemble, and, if the circumstances of his death are suspicious, hold an investigation upon the wives in the manner adopted toward slaves; and, if proof be obtained, put them to severe torture, and kill them. Their funerals, considering the state of civilization among the Gauls, are magnificent and costly; and they cast into the fire all things, including living creatures, which they suppose to have been dear to them when alive; and, a little before this period, slaves and dependents, who were ascertained to have been beloved by them, were, after the regular funeral rites were completed, burnt together with them.

20. Those states which are considered to conduct their commonwealth more judiciously, have it ordained by their laws, that, if any person shall have heard by rumor and report from his neighbors any thing concerning the commonwealth, he shall convey it to the magistrate, and not impart it to any other; because it has been discovered that inconsiderate and inexperienced men were often alarmed by false reports, and driven to some rash act, or else took hasty measures in affairs of the highest importance. The magistrates conceal those things which require to be kept unknown; and they disclose to the people whatever they determine to be expedient. It is not lawful to speak of the commonwealth, except in council.

21. The Germans differ much from these usages, for they have neither Druids to preside over sacred offices, nor do they pay great regard to sacrifices. They rank in the number of the gods those alone whom they behold, and by whose instrumentality they are obviously benefited, namely, the sun, fire, and the moon; they have not heard of the other deities even by report. Their whole life is occupied in hunting and in the pursuits of the military art; from childhood they devote themselves to fatigue and hardships. Those who have remained chaste for the longest time, receive the greatest commendation among their people; they think that by this the growth is promoted, by this the physical powers are increased and the sinews are strengthened. And to have had knowledge of a woman before the twentieth year they reckon among the most disgraceful acts; of which matter there is no concealment, because they bathe promiscuously in the rivers and only use skins or small cloaks of deer's hides, a large portion of the body being in consequence naked.

22. They do not pay much attention to agriculture, and a large portion of their food consists in milk, cheese, and flesh; nor has anyone a fixed quantity of land or his own individual limits; but the magistrates and the leading men each year apportion to the tribes and families, who have united together, as much land as, and in the place in which, they think proper, and the year after compel them to remove elsewhere. For this enactment they advance many reasons, lest seduced by long-continued custom, they may exchange their ardor in the waging of war for agriculture; lest they may be anxious to acquire extensive estates, and the more powerful drive the weaker from their possessions; lest they construct their houses with too great a desire to avoid cold and heat; lest the desire of wealth spring up, from which cause divisions and discords arise; and that they may keep the common people in a contented state of mind, when each sees his own means placed on an equality with those of the most powerful.

23. It is the greatest glory to the several states to have as wide deserts as possible around them, their frontiers having been laid waste. hey consider this the real evidence of their prowess, that their neighbors shall be driven out of their lands and abandon them, and that no one dare settle near them; at the same time they think that they shall be on that account the more secure, because they have removed the apprehension of a sudden incursion. When a state either repels war waged against it, or wages it against another, magistrates are chosen to preside over that war with such authority, that they have power of life and death. In peace there is no common magistrate, but the chiefs of provinces and cantons administer justice and determine controversies among their own people. Robberies which are committed beyond the boundaries of each state bear no infamy, and they avow that these are committed for the purpose of disciplining their youth and of preventing sloth. And when any of their chiefs has said in an assembly "that he will be their leader, let those who are willing to follow, give in their names;" they who approve of both the enterprise and the man arise and promise their assistance and are applauded by the people; such of them as have not followed him are accounted in the number of deserters and traitors, and confidence in all matters is afterward refused them. To injure guests they regard as impious; they defend from wrong those who have come to them for any purpose whatever, and esteem them inviolable; to them the houses of all are open and maintenance is freely supplied.

24. And there was formerly a time when the Gauls excelled the Germans in prowess, and waged war on them offensively, and, on account of the great number of their people and the insufficiency of their land, sent colonies over the Rhine. Accordingly, the Volcae Tectosages, seized on those parts of Germany which are the most fruitful and lie around the Hercynian forest, (which, I perceive, was known by report to Eratosthenes and some other Greeks, and which they call Orcynia), and settled there. Which nation to this time retains its position in those settlements, and has a very high character for justice and military merit; now also they continue in the same scarcity, indigence, hardihood, as the Germans, and use the same food and dress; but their proximity to the Province and knowledge of commodities from countries beyond the sea supplies to the Gauls many things tending to luxury as well as civilization. Accustomed by degrees to be overmatched and worsted in many engagements, they do not even compare themselves to the Germans in prowess.

25. The breadth of this Hercynian forest, which has been referred to above, is to a quick traveler, a journey of nine days. For it can not be otherwise computed, nor are they acquainted with the measures of roads. It begins at the frontiers of the Helvetii, Nemetes, and Rauraci, and extends in a right line along the river Danube to the territories of the Daci and the Anartes; it bends thence to the left in a different direction from the river, and owing to its extent touches the confines of many nations; nor is there any person belonging to this part of Germany who says that he either has gone to the extremity of that forest, though he had advanced a journey of sixty days, or has heard in what place it begins. It is certain that many kinds of wild beast are produced in it which have not been seen in other parts; of which the following are such as differ principally from other animals, and appear worthy of being committed to record.

26. There is an ox of the shape of a stag, between whose ears a horn rises from the middle of the forehead, higher and straighter than those horns which are known to us. From the top of this, branches, like palms, stretch out a considerable distance. The shape of the female and of the male is the same; the appearance and the size of the horns is the same.

27. There are also animals which are called elks. The shape of these, and the varied color of their skins, is much like roes, but in size they surpass them a little and are destitute of horns, and have legs without joints and ligatures; nor do they lie down for the purpose of rest, nor, if they have been thrown down by any accident, can they raise or lift themselves up. Trees serve as beds to them; they lean themselves against them, and thus reclining only slightly, they take their rest; when the huntsmen have discovered from the footsteps of these animals whither they are accustomed to betake themselves, they either undermine all the trees at the roots, or cut into them so far that the upper part of the trees may appear to be left standing. When they have leant upon them, according to their habit, they knock down by their weight the unsupported trees, and fall down themselves along with them.

28. There is a third kind, consisting of those animals which are called uri. These are a little below the elephant in size, and of the appearance, color, and shape of a bull. Their strength and speed are extraordinary; they spare neither man nor wild beast which they have espied. These the Germans take with much pains in pits and kill them. The young men harden themselves with this exercise, and practice themselves in this kind of hunting, and those who have slain the greatest number of them, having produced the horns in public, to serve as evidence, receive great praise. But not even when taken very young can they be rendered familiar to men and tamed. The size, shape, and appearance of their horns differ much from the horns of our oxen. These they anxiously seek after, and bind at the tips with silver, and use as cups at their most sumptuous entertainments.

LIVY

Life

Unlike most other Roman historians, Titus Livius (ca. 59 B.C.E.–17 C.E) never served in the Senate nor held high office. He was born in Patavium (Padua) in northern Italy—an area considered an intellectual backwater. Though Livy had excellent training in Latin literature, his Greek was faulty. The emperor Augustus became his patron, though he only half-jokingly called the historian a "Pompeian," meaning that he sympathized with the Republic overthrown by Julius Caesar. The emperor provided Livy with the leisure to compose his enormous history in 142 books. While at the court of Augustus, Livy is said to have tutored the young Claudius (emperor: 41–54 C.E) who fancied himself an historian. He died in 17 C.E.

FROM THE FOUNDING OF THE CITY*

(AB URBE CONDITA)

Livy's massive survey covered the history of Rome from 753 to 9 B.C.E. Of the 142 books only 35 have survived: 1–10; 21–45. (Summaries of all 142 books by ancient scholars have also survived.) Since the extant

* Livy. 1912–1924. Adapted from a translation by William M. Roberts. London: J. M. Dent.

books only trace the history of Rome as far as 167 B.C.E., the text is
filled with nostalgic images of Rome's glorious rise to world domination. It is difficult to imagine how Livy treated the collapse of the
Roman Republic during the first century B.C.E. His sympathies were
conservative, and he was surely outraged at much that occurred during
the revolution that brought down the Republic. He prudently refrained
from publishing his last 22 books on the rise of Octavian-Augustus
(43–9 B.C.E.) until after the emperor's death in 14 C.E. He could hardly
have publicly criticized his patron Augustus for the bloody political
murders that occurred early in his career, but Livy did believe that he
must eventually publish his own version of the events for posterity.

Livy wrote in a poetic literary style. His exciting narratives
brought history alive in much the way that modern historical novels
can do. He does resort to rhetorical character-types, so that many historical figures are one-sidedly good or evil. Likewise, the speeches are
wholly invented. In political judgment, Livy never approaches the
shrewdness of Polybius or Tacitus. Since he had no military or political experience, all he learned came from books. He is more reliable
when he depends on Polybius; less so when he turns to the jingoistic
Roman "annalists" who invented facts to serve their political purpose.
Though the early books are largely the stuff of legend, modern archae-
ologists have found much confirmation for Livy's account of the rape of
the Sabine women and the urbanization of the Forum. Livy's account
has preserved for us the Augustan age's own view of Rome's historic
past.

BOOK I 1–13; 15–49; 55–60

After a brief methodological preface, the first book traces Rome's royal
beginnings from its foundation by Romulus in 753 B.C.E. Seven kings
ruled Rome until Tarquin the Proud was overthrown in 509 B.C.E. to
establish the Roman Republic.

Preface

Whether the task I have undertaken of writing a complete history of the
Roman people from the very commencement of its existence will reward me
for the labor spent on it, I neither know for certain, nor if I did know would I
venture to say. For I see that this is an old-established and a common practice,
each fresh writer being invariably persuaded that he will either attain greater
certainty in the materials of his narrative, or surpass the rudeness of antiquity in the excellence of his style. However this may be, it will still be a great

satisfaction to me to have taken my part, too, in investing, to the utmost of my abilities, the annals of the foremost nation in the world with a deeper interest; and if in such a crowd of writers my own reputation is thrown into the shade, I would console myself with the renown and greatness of those who eclipse my fame. The subject, moreover, is one that demands immense labor. It goes back beyond 700 years and, after starting from small and humble beginnings, has grown to such dimensions that it begins to be overburdened by its greatness. I have very little doubt, too, that for the majority of my readers the earliest times and those immediately succeeding, will possess little attraction; they will hurry on to these modern days in which the might of a long paramount nation is wasting by internal decay. I, on the other hand, shall look for a further reward of my labors in being able to close my eyes to the evils which our generation has witnessed for so many years; so long, at least, as I am devoting all my thoughts to retracing those pristine records, free from all the anxiety which can disturb the historian of his own times even if it cannot warp him from the truth.

The traditions of what happened prior to the foundation of the City or whilst it was being built, are more fitted to adorn the creations of the poet than the authentic records of the historian, and I have no intention of establishing either their truth or their falsehood. This much license is conceded to the ancients, that by intermingling human actions with divine they may confer a more august dignity on the origins of states. Now, if any nation ought to be allowed to claim a sacred origin and point back to a divine paternity, that nation is Rome. For such is her renown in war that when she chooses to represent Mars as her own and her founder's father, the nations of the world accept the statement with the same equanimity with which they accept her dominion. But whatever opinions may be formed or criticisms passed upon these and similar traditions, I regard them as of small importance. The subjects to which I would ask each of my readers to devote his earnest attention are these—the life and morals of the community; the men and the qualities by which through domestic policy and foreign war dominion was won and extended. Then as the standard of morality gradually lowers, let him follow the decay of the national character, observing how at first it slowly sinks, then slips downward more and more rapidly, and finally begins to plunge into headlong ruin, until he reaches these days, in which we can bear neither our diseases nor their remedies.

There is this exceptionally beneficial and fruitful advantage to be derived from the study of the past, that you see, set in the clear light of historical truth, examples of every possible type. From these you may select for yourself and your country what to imitate, and also what, as being mischievous in its inception and disastrous in its issues, you are to avoid. Unless, however, I am misled by affection for my undertaking, there has never existed any commonwealth greater in power, with a purer morality, or more fertile in good examples; or any state in which avarice and luxury have been so late in making their inroads, or poverty and frugality so highly and continuously honored, showing so clearly that the less wealth men possessed the less they coveted. In these latter years wealth has brought avarice in its train, and the unlimited command of pleasure has created in men a passion for ruining themselves and everything else through self-indulgence and licentiousness. But criticisms which will be unwelcome, even when perhaps necessary, must not appear in the commencement at all events of this extensive work. We should much prefer to start with favorable omens, and if we could have adopted the poets' custom, it would have been much pleasanter to commence with prayers and supplications to gods and goddesses that they would grant a favorable and successful issue to the great task before us.

1. To begin with, it is generally admitted that after the capture of Troy, whilst the rest of the Trojans were massacred, against two of them—Aeneas and Antenor—the Achivi refused to exercise the rights of war, partly owing to old ties of hospitality, and partly because these men had always been in favor of making peace and surrendering Helen. Their subsequent fortunes were different. Antenor sailed into the furthest part of the Adriatic, accompanied by a number of Enetians who had been driven from Paphlagonia by a revolution, and, after losing their king Pylaemenes before Troy, were looking for a settlement and a leader. The combined force of Enetians and Trojans defeated the Euganei, who dwelt between the sea and the Alps and occupied their land. The place where they disembarked was called Troy, and the name was extended to the surrounding district; the whole nation were called Veneti. Similar misfortunes led to Aeneas becoming a wanderer, but the Fates were preparing a higher destiny for him. He first visited Macedonia, then was carried down to Sicily in quest of a settlement; from Sicily he directed his course to the Laurentian territory. Here, too, the name of Troy is found, and here the Trojans disembarked, and as their almost infinite wanderings had left them nothing but their arms and their ships, they began to plunder the neighborhood. The Aborigines, who occupied the country, with their king Latinus at their head, came hastily together from the city and the country districts to repel the inroads of the strangers by force of arms.

From this point there is a twofold tradition. According to the one, Latinus was defeated in battle, and made peace with Aeneas, and subsequently a family alliance. According to the other, whilst the two armies were standing ready to engage and waiting for the signal, Latinus advanced in front of his lines and invited the leader of the strangers to a conference. He inquired of him what manner of men they were, whence they came, what had happened to make them leave their homes, what were they in quest of when they landed in Latinus' territory. When he heard that the men were Trojans, that their leader was Aeneas, the son of Anchises and Venus, that their city had been burnt, and that the homeless exiles were now looking for a place to settle in and build a city, he was so struck with the noble bearing of the men and their leader, and their readiness to accept alike either peace or war, that he gave his right hand as a solemn pledge of friendship for the future. A formal treaty was made between the leaders and mutual greetings exchanged between the armies. Latinus received Aeneas as a guest in his house, and there, in the presence of his tutelary deities, completed the political alliance by a domestic one, and gave his daughter in marriage to Aeneas. This incident confirmed the Trojans in the hope that they had reached the end of their wanderings and won a permanent home. They built a town, which Aeneas called Lavinium after his wife. In a short time a boy was born of the new marriage, to whom his parents gave the name of Ascanius.

2. In a short time the Aborigines and Trojans became involved in war with Turnus, the king of the Rutulians. Lavinia had been betrothed to him before the arrival of Aeneas, and, furious at finding a stranger preferred to him, he declared war against both Latinus and Aeneas. Neither side could congratulate themselves on the result of the battle; the Rutulians were defeated, but the victorious Aborigines and Trojans lost their leader Latinus. Feeling their need of allies, Turnus and the Rutulians had recourse to the celebrated power of the Etruscans and Mezentius, their king, who was reigning at Caere, a wealthy city in those days. From the first he had felt anything but pleasure at the rise of the new city, and now he regarded the growth of the Trojan state as much too rapid to be safe to its neighbors, so he welcomed the proposal to join forces with the Rutulians. To keep the Aborigines from abandoning him in the face of this strong coalition and to secure their being not only under the same laws, but also the same designation, Aeneas called both nations by the common name of Latins. From that time the Aborigines were not behind the Trojans in their loyal devotion to Aeneas. So great was the power of Etruria that the renown of her people had filled not only the inland parts of Italy but also the coastal districts along the whole length of the land from the Alps to the Straits of Messina. Aeneas, however, trusting to the loyalty of the two nations who were day by day growing into one, led his forces into the field, instead of awaiting the enemy behind his walls. The battle resulted in favor of the Latins, but it was the last mortal act of Aeneas. His tomb—whatever it is lawful and right to call him—is situated on the bank of the Numicius. He is addressed as "Jupiter Indiges."

3. His son, Ascanius, was not old enough to assume the government; but his throne remained secure throughout his minority. During that interval—such was Lavinia's force of character—though a woman was regent, the Latin State, and the kingdom of his father and grandfather, were preserved unimpaired for her son. I will not discuss the question—for who could speak decisively about a matter of such extreme antiquity?—whether the man whom the Julian house claim, under the name of Iulus, as the founder of their name, was this Ascanius or an older one than he, born of Creusa, whilst Ilium was still intact, and after its fall a sharer in his father's fortunes. This Ascanius, wherever born, or of whatever mother—it is generally agreed in any case that he was the son of Aeneas—left to his mother (or his stepmother) the city of Lavinium, which was for those days a prosperous and wealthy city, with a superabundant population, and built a new city at the foot of the Alban hills, which from its position, stretching along the side of the hill, was called "Alba Longa." An interval of thirty years elapsed between the foundation of Lavinium and the colonization of Alba Longa. Such had been the growth of the Latin power, mainly through the defeat of the Etruscans, that neither at the death of Aeneas, nor during the regency of Lavinia, nor during the immature years of the reign of Ascanius, did either Mezentius and the Etruscans or any other of their neighbors venture to attack them. When terms of peace were being arranged, the river Albula, now called the Tiber, had been fixed as the boundary between the Etruscans and the Latins.

Ascanius was succeeded by his son Silvius, who by some chance had been born in the forest. He became the father of Aeneas Silvius, who in his turn had a son, Latinus Silvius. He planted a number of colonies: the colonists were called Prisci Latini. The cognomen of Silvius was common to all the remaining kings of Alba, each of whom succeeded his father. Their names are Alba, Atys, Capys, Capetus, Tiberinus, who was drowned in crossing the Albula, and his name transferred to the river, which became henceforth the famous Tiber. Then came his son Agrippa, after him his son Romulus Silvius. He was struck by lightning and left the crown to his son Aventinus, whose shrine was on the hill which bears his name and is now a part of the city of Rome. He was succeeded by Proca, who had two sons, Numitor and Amulius. To Numitor, the elder, he bequeathed the ancient throne of the Silvian house. Violence, however, proved stronger than either the father's will or the respect due to the brother's seniority; for Amulius expelled his brother and seized the crown. Adding crime to crime, he murdered his brother's sons and made the daughter, Rea Silvia, a Vestal virgin; thus, under the presence of honoring her, depriving her of all hopes of issue.

4. But the Fates had, I believe, already decreed the origin of this great city and the foundation of the mightiest empire under heaven. The Vestal was forcibly violated and gave birth to twins. She named Mars as their father, either because she really believed it, or because the fault might appear less heinous if a deity were the cause of it. But neither gods nor men sheltered her or her babes from the king's cruelty; the priestess was thrown into

prison, the boys were ordered to be thrown into the river. By a heaven-sent chance it happened that the Tiber was then overflowing its banks, and stretches of standing water prevented any approach to the main channel. Those who were carrying the children expected that this stagnant water would be sufficient to drown them, so under the impression that they were carrying out the king's orders they exposed the boys at the nearest point of the overflow, where the Ficus Ruminalis (said to have been formerly called Romularis) now stands. The locality was then a wild solitude. The tradition goes on to say that after the floating cradle in which the boys had been exposed had been left by the retreating water on dry land, a thirsty she-wolf from the surrounding hills, attracted by the crying of the children, came to them, gave them her teats to suck and was so gentle towards them that the king's flock-master found her licking the boys with her tongue. According to the story, his name was Faustulus. He took the children to his hut and gave them to his wife Larentia to bring up. Some writers think that Larentia, from her unchaste life, had got the nickname of "She-wolf" amongst the shepherds, and that this was the origin of the marvelous story. As soon as the boys, thus born and thus brought up, grew to be young men they did not neglect their pastoral duties, but their special delight was roaming through the woods on hunting expeditions. As their strength and courage were thus developed, they used not only to lie in wait for fierce beasts of prey, but they even attacked brigands when loaded with plunder. They distributed what they took amongst the shepherds, with whom, surrounded by a continually increasing body of young men, they associated themselves in their serious undertakings and in their sports and pastimes.

5. It is said that the festival of the Lupercalia, which is still observed, was even in those days celebrated on the Palatine hill. This hill was originally called Pallantium from a city of the same name in Arcadia; the name was afterwards changed to Palatium. Evander, an Arcadian, had held that territory many ages before, and had introduced an annual festival from Arcadia in which young men ran about naked for sport and wantonness, in honor of the Lycaean Pan, whom the Romans afterwards called Inuus. The existence of this festival was widely recognized, and it was while the two brothers were engaged in it that the brigands, enraged at losing their plunder, ambushed them. Romulus successfully defended himself, but Remus was taken prisoner and brought before Amulius, his captors impudently accusing him of their own crimes. The principal charge brought against them was that of invading Numitor's lands with a body of young men whom they had got together, and carrying off plunder as though in regular warfare. Remus accordingly was handed over to Numitor for punishment. Faustulus had from the beginning suspected that it was royal offspring that he was bringing up, for he was aware that the boys had been exposed at the king's command and the time at which he had taken them away exactly corresponded with that of their exposure. He had, however, refused to divulge the matter prematurely, until either a fitting opportunity occurred or necessity demanded its disclosure. The necessity came first. Alarmed for the safety of Remus he revealed the state of the case to Romulus. It so happened that Numitor also, who had Remus in his custody, on hearing that he and his brother were twins and comparing their ages and the character and bearing so unlike that of one in a servile condition, began to recall the memory of his grandchildren, and further inquiries brought him to the same conclusion as Faustulus; nothing was wanting to the recognition of Remus. So the king Amulius was being enmeshed on all sides by hostile purposes. Romulus shrunk from a direct attack with his body of shepherds, for he was no match for the king in open fight. They were instructed to approach the palace by different routes and meet there at a given time, whilst from Numitor's house Remus lent his assistance with a second band he had collected. The attack succeeded and the king was killed.

6. At the beginning of the fray, Numitor gave out that an enemy had entered the City and was attacking the palace, in order to draw off the Alban soldiery to the citadel, to defend it. When he saw the young men coming to congratulate him after the assassination, he at once called a council of his people and explained his brother's infamous conduct towards him, the story of his grandsons, their parentage and bringing up, and how he recognized them. Then he proceeded to inform them of the tyrant's death and his responsibility for it. The young men marched in order through the midst of the assembly and saluted their grandfather as king; their action was approved by the whole population, who with one voice ratified the title and sovereignty of the king. After the government of Alba was thus transferred to Numitor, Romulus and Remus were seized with the desire of building a city in the locality where they had been exposed. There was the superfluous population of the Alban and Latin towns, to these were added the shepherds: it was natural to hope that with all these Alba would be small and Lavinium small in comparison with the city which was to be founded. These pleasant anticipations were disturbed by the ancestral curse—ambition—which led to a deplorable quarrel over what was at first a trivial matter. As they were twins and no claim to precedence could be based on seniority, they decided to consult the tutelary deities of the place by means of augury as to who was to give his name to the new city, and who was to rule it after it had been founded. Romulus accordingly selected the Palatine as his station for observation, Remus the Aventine.

7. Remus is said to have been the first to receive an omen: six vultures appeared to him. The augury had just been announced to Romulus when double the number appeared to him. Each was saluted as king by his own

party. The one side based their claim on the priority of the appearance, the other on the number of the birds. Then followed an angry altercation; heated passions led to bloodshed; in the tumult Remus was killed. The more common report is that Remus contemptuously jumped over the newly raised walls and was forthwith killed by the enraged Romulus, who exclaimed, "So shall it be henceforth with every one who leaps over my walls." Romulus thus became sole ruler, and the city was called after him, its founder. His first work was to fortify the Palatine hill where he had been brought up. The worship of the other deities he conducted according to the use of Alba, but that of Hercules in accordance with the Greek rites as they had been instituted by Evander. It was into this neighborhood, according to the tradition, that Hercules, after he had killed Geryon, drove his oxen, which were of marvelous beauty. He swam across the Tiber, driving the oxen before him, and wearied with his journey, lay down in a grassy place near the river to rest himself and the oxen, who enjoyed the rich pasture. When sleep had overtaken him, as he was heavy with food and wine, a shepherd living near, called Cacus, presuming on his strength, and captivated by the beauty of the oxen, determined to secure them. If he drove them before him into the cave, their hoof-marks would have led their owner on his search for them in the same direction, so he dragged the finest of them backwards by their tails into his cave. At the first streak of dawn Hercules awoke, and on surveying his herd saw that some were missing. He proceeded towards the nearest cave, to see if any tracks pointed in that direction, but he found that every hoof-mark led from the cave and none towards it. Perplexed and bewildered he began to drive the herd away from so dangerous a neighborhood. Some of the cattle, missing those which were left behind, lowed as they often do, and an answering low sounded from the cave. Hercules turned in that direction, and as Cacus tried to prevent him by force from entering the cave, he was killed by a blow from Hercules' club, after vainly appealing for help to his comrades.

The king of the country at that time was Evander, a refugee from Peloponnesus, who ruled more by personal ascendancy than by the exercise of power. He was looked up to with reverence for his knowledge of letters—a new and marvelous thing for uncivilized men—but he was still more revered because of his mother Carmenta, who was believed to be a divine being and regarded with wonder by all as an interpreter of Fate, in the days before the arrival of the Sibyl in Italy. This Evander, alarmed by the crowd of excited shepherds standing round a stranger whom they accused of open murder, ascertained from them the nature of his act and what led to it. As he observed the bearing and stature of the man to be more than human in greatness and august dignity, he asked who he was. When he heard his name, and learnt his father and his country he said, "Hercules, son of Jupiter, hail! My mother, who speaks truth in the name of the gods, has prophesied that thou shalt join the company of the gods, and that here a shrine shall be dedicated to thee, which in ages to come the most powerful nation in all the world shall call their Ara Maxima and honor with shine own special worship." Hercules grasped Evander's right hand and said that he took the omen to himself and would fulfill the prophecy by building and consecrating the altar. Then a heifer of conspicuous beauty was taken from the herd, and the first sacrifice was offered; the Potitii and Pinarii, the two principal families in those parts, were invited by Hercules to assist in the sacrifice and at the feast which followed. It so happened that the Potitii were present at the appointed time, and the entrails were placed before them; the Pinarii arrived after these were consumed and came in for the rest of the banquet. It became a permanent institution from that time, that as long as the family of the Pinarii survived they should not eat of the entrails of the victims. The Potitii, after being instructed by Evander, presided over that rite for many ages, until they handed over this ministerial office to public servants after which the whole race of the Potitii perished. This out of all foreign rites, was the only one which Romulus adopted, as though he felt that an immortality won through courage, of which this was the memorial, would one day be his own reward.

8. After the claims of religion had been duly acknowledged, Romulus called his people to a council. As nothing could unite them into one political body but the observance of common laws and customs, he gave them a body of laws, which he thought would only be respected by a rude and uncivilized race of men if he inspired them with awe by assuming the outward symbols of power. He surrounded himself with greater state, and in particular he called into his service twelve lictors. Some think that he fixed upon this number from the number of the birds who foretold his sovereignty; but I am inclined to agree with those who think that as this class of public officers was borrowed from the same people from whom the *sella curulis* and the *toga praetexta* were adopted—their neighbors, the Etruscans—so the number itself also was taken from them. Its use amongst the Etruscans is traced to the custom of the twelve sovereign cities of Etruria, when jointly electing a king, furnishing him each with one lictor. Meantime the City was growing by the extension of its walls in various directions; an increase due rather to the anticipation of its future population than to any present overcrowding. His next care was to secure an addition to the population that the size of the City might not be a source of weakness. It had been the ancient policy of the founders of cities to get together a multitude of people of obscure and low origin and then to spread the fiction that they were the children of the soil. In accordance with this policy, Romulus opened a place of refuge on the spot where, as you go down from the Capitol, you find an enclosed space between two groves. A promiscuous crowd of freemen and slaves, eager for change, fled thither from the neighboring states. This was the first accession of strength to the nascent greatness of the city. When he was satisfied as to its strength, his next step was to provide for that strength being wisely directed. He created a hundred senators; either because that number was adequate, or because there were only a hundred heads of houses who could be created. In any case they were called the "Patres" in virtue of their rank, and their descendants were called "Patricians."

9. The Roman State had now become so strong that it was a match for any of its neighbors in war, but its greatness threatened to last for only one generation, since through the absence of women there was no hope of offspring, and there was no right of intermarriage with their neighbors. Acting on the advice of the senate, Romulus sent envoys amongst the surrounding nations to ask for alliance and the right of intermarriage on behalf of his new community. It was represented that cities, like everything else, sprung from the humblest beginnings, and those who were helped on by their own courage and the favor of heaven won for themselves great power and great renown. As to the origin of Rome, it was well known that whilst it had received divine assistance, courage and self-reliance were not wanting. There should, therefore, be no reluctance for men to mingle their blood with their fellow-men. Nowhere did the envoys meet with a favorable reception. Whilst their proposals were treated with contumely, there was at the same time a general feeling of alarm at the power so rapidly growing in their midst. Usually they were dismissed with the question, "whether they had opened an asylum for women, for nothing short of that would secure for them intermarriage on equal terms." The Roman youth could ill brook such insults, and matters began to look like an appeal to force. To secure a favorable place and time for such an attempt, Romulus, disguising his resentment, made elaborate preparations for the celebration of games in honor of "Equestrian Neptune," which he called "the Consualia." He ordered public notice of the spectacle to be given amongst the adjoining cities, and his people supported him in making the celebration as magnificent as their knowledge and resources allowed, so that expectations were raised to the highest pitch. There was a great gathering; people were eager to see the new City, all their nearest neighbors—the people of Caenina, Antemnae, and Crustumerium —were there, and the whole Sabine population came, with their wives and families. They were invited to accept hospitality at the different houses, and after examining the situation of the City, its walls and the large number of dwelling-houses it included, they were astonished at the rapidity with which the Roman State had grown.

When the hour for the games had come, and their eyes and minds were alike riveted on the spectacle before them, the preconcerted signal was given and the Roman youth dashed in all directions to carry off the maidens who were present. The larger part were carried off indiscriminately, but some particularly beautiful girls who had been marked out for the leading patricians were carried to their houses by plebeians told off for the task. One, conspicuous amongst them all for grace and beauty, is reported to have been carried off by a group led by a certain Talassius, and to the many inquiries as to whom she was intended for, the invariable answer was given, "For Talassius." Hence the use of this word in the marriage rites. Alarm and consternation broke up the games, and the parents of the maidens fled, distracted with grief, uttering bitter reproaches on the violators of the laws of hospitality and appealing to the god to whose solemn games they had come, only to be the victims of impious perfidy. The abducted maidens were quite as despondent and indignant. Romulus, however, went round in person, and pointed out to them that it was all owing to the pride of their parents in denying right of intermarriage to their neighbors. They would live in honorable wedlock, and share all their property and civil rights, and—dearest of all to human nature—would be the mothers of freemen. He begged them to lay aside their feelings of resentment and give their affections to those whom fortune had made masters of their persons. An injury had often led to reconciliation and love; they would find their husbands all the more affectionate, because each would do his utmost, so far as in him lay, to make up for the loss of parents and country. These arguments were reinforced by the endearments of their husbands, who excused their conduct by pleading the irresistible force of their passion—a plea effective beyond all others in appealing to a woman's nature.

10. The feelings of the abducted maidens were now pretty completely appeased, but not so those of their parents. They went about in mourning garb, and tried by their tearful complaints to rouse their countrymen to action. Nor did they confine their remonstrances to their own cities; they flocked from all sides to Titus Tatius, the king of the Sabines, and sent formal deputations to him, for his was the most influential name in those parts. The people of Caenina, Crustumerium, and Antemnae were the greatest sufferers; they thought Tatius and his Sabines were too slow in moving, so these three cities prepared to make war conjointly. Such, however, were the impatience and anger of the Caeninensians that even the Crustuminians and Antemnates did not display enough energy for them, so the men of Caenina made an attack upon Roman territory on their own account. Whilst they were scattered far and wide, pillaging and destroying, Romulus came upon them with an army, and after a brief encounter taught them that anger is futile without strength. He put them to a hasty flight, and following them up, killed their king and despoiled his body; then after slaying their leader took their city at the first assault. He was no less anxious to display his achievements than he had been great in performing them, so, after leading his victorious army home, he mounted to the Capitol with the spoils of his dead foe

borne before him on a frame constructed for the purpose. He hung them there on an oak, which the shepherds looked upon as a sacred tree, and at the same time marked out the site for the temple of Jupiter, and addressing the god by a new title, uttered the following invocation: "Jupiter Feretrius! these arms taken from a king, I, Romulus a king and conqueror, bring to thee, and on this domain, whose bounds I have in will and purpose traced, I dedicate a temple to receive the *spolia opima* which posterity following my example shall bear hither, taken from the kings and generals of our foes slain in battle." Such was the origin of the first temple dedicated in Rome. And the gods decreed that though its founder did not utter idle words in declaring that posterity would thither bear their spoils, still the splendor of that offering should not be dimmed by the number of those who have rivaled his achievement. For after so many years have elapsed and so many wars been waged, only twice have the *spolia opima* been offered. So seldom has Fortune granted that glory to men.

11. Whilst the Romans were thus occupied, the army of the Antemnates seized the opportunity of their territory being unoccupied and made a raid into it. Romulus hastily led his legion against this fresh foe and surprised them as they were scattered over the fields. At the very first battle-shout and charge the enemy were routed and their city captured. Whilst Romulus was exulting over this double victory, his wife, Hersilia, moved by the entreaties of the abducted maidens, implored him to pardon their parents and receive them into citizenship, for so the State would increase in unity and strength. He readily granted her request. He then advanced against the Crustuminians, who had commenced war, but their eagerness had been damped by the successive defeats of their neighbors, and they offered but slight resistance. Colonies were planted in both places; owing to the fertility of the soil of the Crustumine district, the majority gave their names for that colony. On the other hand there were numerous migrations to Rome mostly of the parents and relatives of the abducted maidens. The last of these wars was commenced by the Sabines and proved the most serious of all, for nothing was done in passion or impatience; they masked their designs till war had actually commenced. Strategy was aided by craft and deceit, as the following incident shows. Spurius Tarpeius was in command of the Roman citadel. Whilst his daughter had gone outside the fortifications to fetch water for some religious ceremonies, Tatius bribed her to admit his troops within the citadel. Once admitted, they crushed her to death beneath their shields, either that the citadel might appear to have been taken by assault, or that her example might be left as a warning that no faith should be kept with traitors. A further story runs that the Sabines were in the habit of wearing heavy gold armlets on their left arms and richly jeweled rings, and that the girl made them promise to give her "what they had on their left arms," accordingly they piled their shields upon her instead of golden gifts. Some say that in bargaining for what they had in their left hands, she expressly asked for their shields, and being suspected of wishing to betray them, fell a victim to her own bargain.

12. However this may be, the Sabines were in possession of the citadel. And they would not come down from it the next day, though the Roman army was drawn up in battle array over the whole of the ground between the Palatine and the Capitoline hill, until, exasperated at the loss of their citadel and determined to recover it, the Romans mounted to the attack. Advancing before the rest, Mettius Curtius, on the side of the Sabines, and Hostius Hostilius, on the side of the Romans, engaged in single combat. Hostius, fighting on disadvantageous ground, upheld the fortunes of Rome by his intrepid bravery, but at last he fell; the Roman line broke and fled to what was then the gate of the Palatine. Even Romulus was being swept away by the crowd of fugitives, and lifting up his hands to heaven he exclaimed: "Jupiter, it was thy omen that I obeyed when I laid here on the Palatine the earliest foundations of the City. Now the Sabines hold its citadel, having bought it by a bribe, and coming thence have seized the valley and are pressing hitherwards in battle. Do thou, Father of gods and men, drive hence our foes, banish terror from Roman hearts, and stay our shameful flight! Here do I vow a temple to thee, 'Jove the Stayer,' as a memorial for the generations to come that it is through thy present help that the City has been saved." Then, as though he had become aware that his prayer had been heard, he cried, "Back, Romans! Jupiter Optimus Maximus bids you stand and renew the battle." They stopped as though commanded by a voice from heaven—Romulus dashed up to the foremost line, just as Mettius Curtius had run down from the citadel in front of the Sabines and driven the Romans in headlong flight over the whole of the ground now occupied by the Forum. He was now not far from the gate of the Palatine, and was shouting: "We have conquered our faithless hosts, our cowardly foes; now they know that to carry off maidens is a very different thing from fighting with men." In the midst of these vaunts Romulus, with a compact body of valiant troops, charged down on him. Mettius happened to be on horseback, so he was the more easily driven back, the Romans followed in pursuit, and, inspired by the courage of their king, the rest of the Roman army routed the Sabines. Mettius, unable to control his horse, maddened by the noise of his pursuers, plunged into a morass. The danger of their general drew off the attention of the Sabines for a moment from the battle; they called out and made signals to encourage him, so, animated to fresh efforts, he succeeded in extricating himself. Thereupon the Romans and Sabines renewed the fighting in the middle of the valley, but the fortune of Rome was in the ascendant.

13. Then it was that the Sabine women, whose wrongs had led to the war, throwing off all womanish fears in their distress, went boldly into the

midst of the flying missiles with disheveled hair and rent garments. Running across the space between the two armies they tried to stop any further fighting and calm the excited passions by appealing to their fathers in the one army and their husbands in the other not to bring upon themselves a curse by staining their hands with the blood of a father-in-law or a son-in-law, nor upon their posterity the taint of parricide. "If," they cried, "you are weary of these ties of kindred, these marriage-bonds, then turn your anger upon us; it is we who are the cause of the war, it is we who have wounded and slain our husbands and fathers. Better for us to perish rather than live without one or the other of you, as widows or as orphans." The armies and their leaders were alike moved by this appeal. There was a sudden hush and silence. Then the generals advanced to arrange the terms of a treaty. It was not only peace that was made, the two nations were united into one State, the royal power was shared between them, and the seat of government for both nations was Rome. After thus doubling the City, a concession was made to the Sabines in the new appellation of Quirites, from their old capital of Cures. As a memorial of the battle, the place where Curtius got his horse out of the deep marsh on to safer ground was called the Curtian lake. The joyful peace, which put an abrupt close to such a deplorable war, made the Sabine women still dearer to their husbands and fathers, and most of all to Romulus himself. Consequently when he effected the distribution of the people into the thirty curiae, he affixed their names to the curiae. No doubt there were many more than thirty women, and tradition is silent as to whether those whose names were given to the curiae were selected on the ground of age, or on that of personal distinction—either their own or their husbands'—or merely by lot. The enrollment of the three centuries of knights took place at the same time; the Ramnenses were called after Romulus, the Titienses from T. Tatius. The origin of the Luceres and why they were so called is uncertain. Thenceforward the two kings exercised their joint sovereignty with perfect harmony.

§

15. The contagion of the war-spirit in Fidenae infected the Veientines. This people were connected by ties of blood with the Fidenates, who were also Etruscans, and an additional incentive was supplied by the mere proximity of the place, should the arms of Rome be turned against all her neighbors. They made an incursion into Roman territory, rather for the sake of plunder than as an act of regular war. After securing their booty they returned with it to Veii, without entrenching a camp or waiting for the enemy. The Romans, on the other hand, not finding the enemy on their soil, crossed the Tiber, prepared and determined to fight a decisive battle. On hearing that they had formed an entrenched camp and were preparing to advance on their city, the Veientines went out against them, preferring a combat in the open to being shut up and having to fight from houses and walls. Romulus gained the victory, not through stratagem, but through the prowess of his veteran army. He drove the routed enemy up to their walls, but in view of the strong position and fortifications of the city, he abstained from assaulting it. On his march homewards, he devastated their fields more out of revenge than for the sake of plunder. The loss thus sustained, no less than the previous defeat, broke the spirit of the Veientes, and they sent envoys to Rome to sue for peace. On condition of a cession of territory a truce was granted to them for a hundred years. These were the principal events at home and in the field that marked the reign of Romulus. Throughout— whether we consider the courage he showed in recovering his ancestral throne, or the wisdom he displayed in founding the City and adding to its strength through war and peace alike—we find nothing incompatible with the belief in his divine origin and his admission to divine immortality after death. It was, in fact, through the strength given by him that the City was powerful enough to enjoy an assured peace for forty years after his departure. He was, however, more acceptable to the populace than to the patricians, but most of all was he the idol of his soldiers. He kept a bodyguard of three hundred men round him in peace as well as in war. These he called the "Celeres."

16. After these immortal achievements, Romulus held a review of his army in the Campus Martius. A violent thunderstorm suddenly arose and enveloped the king in so dense a cloud that he was quite invisible to the assembly. From that hour Romulus was no longer seen on earth. When the fears of the Roman youth were allayed by the return of bright, calm sunshine after such fearful weather, they saw that the royal seat was vacant. Whilst they fully believed the assertion of the senators, who had been standing close to him, that he had been snatched away to heaven by a whirlwind, still, like men suddenly bereaved, fear and grief kept them for some time speechless. At length, after a few had taken the initiative, the whole of those present hailed Romulus as "a god, the son of a god, the King and Father of the City of Rome." They put up supplications for his grace and favor, and prayed that he would be propitious to his children and save and protect them. I believe, however, that even then there were some who secretly hinted that he had been torn limb from limb by the senators—a tradition to this effect, though certainly a very dim one, has filtered down to us. The other, which I follow, has been the prevailing one, due, no doubt, to the admiration felt for the man and the apprehensions excited by his disappearance. This generally accepted belief was strengthened by one man's clever device. The tradition runs that Proculus Julius, a man whose authority had weight in matters of even the gravest importance, seeing how deeply the community felt the loss of the king, and how incensed they were against the senators, came forward into

the assembly and said: "Quirites! at break of dawn, today, the Father of this City suddenly descended from heaven and appeared to me. Whilst, thrilled with awe, I stood rapt before him in deepest reverence, praying that I might be pardoned for gazing upon him, 'Go,' said he, 'tell the Romans that it is the will of heaven that my Rome should be the head of all the world. Let them henceforth cultivate the arts of war, and let them know assuredly, and hand down the knowledge to posterity, that no human might can withstand the arms of Rome.'" It is marvelous what credit was given to this man's story, and how the grief of the people and the army was soothed by the belief which had been created in the immortality of Romulus.

17. Disputes arose among the senators about the vacant throne. It was not the jealousies of individual citizens, for no one was sufficiently prominent in so young a State, but the rivalries of parties in the State that led to this strife. The Sabine families were apprehensive of losing their fair share of the sovereign power, because after the death of Tatius they had had no representative on the throne; they were anxious, therefore, that the king should be elected from amongst them. The ancient Romans could ill brook a foreign king; but amidst this diversity of political views, all were for a monarchy; they had not yet tasted the sweets of liberty. The senators began to grow apprehensive of some aggressive act on the part of the surrounding states, now that the City was without a central authority and the army without a general. They decided that there must be some head of the State, but no one could make up his mind to concede the dignity to any one else. The matter was settled by the hundred senators dividing themselves into ten "decuries," and one was chosen from each decury to exercise the supreme power. Ten therefore were in office, but only one at a time had the insignia of authority and the lictors. Their individual authority was restricted to five days, and they exercised it in rotation. This break in the monarchy lasted for a year, and it was called by the name it still bears—that of "interregnum." After a time the plebs began to murmur that their bondage was multiplied, for they had a hundred masters instead of one. It was evident that they would insist upon a king being elected and elected by them. When the senators became aware of this growing determination, they thought it better to offer spontaneously what they were bound to part with, so, as an act of grace, they committed the supreme power into the hands of the people, but in such a way that they did not give away more privilege than they retained. For they passed a decree that when the people had chosen a king, his election would only be valid after the senate had ratified it by their authority. The same procedure exists today in the passing of laws and the election of magistrates, but the power of rejection has been withdrawn; the senate give their ratification before the people proceed to vote, whilst the result of the election is still uncertain. At that time the "interrex" convened the assembly and addressed it as follows:

"Quirites! elect your king, and may heaven's blessing rest on your labors! If you elect one who shall be counted worthy to follow Romulus, the senate will ratify your choice." So gratified were the people at the proposal that, not to appear behindhand in generosity, they passed a resolution that it should be left to the senate to decree who should reign in Rome.

18. There was living, in those days, at Cures, a Sabine city, a man of renowned justice and piety—Numa Pompilius. He was as conversant as any one in that age could be with all divine and human law. His master is given as Pythagoras of Samos, as tradition speaks of no other. But this is erroneous, for it is generally agreed that it was more than a century later, in the reign of Servius Tullius, that Pythagoras gathered round him crowds of eager students, in the most distant part of Italy, in the neighborhood of Metapontum, Heraclea, and Crotona. Now, even if he had been contemporary with Numa, how could his reputation have reached the Sabines? From what places, and in what common language could he have induced any one to become his disciple? Who could have guaranteed the safety of a solitary individual traveling through so many nations differing in speech and character? I believe rather that Numa's virtues were the result of his native temperament and self-training, molded not so much by foreign influences as by the rigorous and austere discipline of the ancient Sabines, which was the purest type of any that existed in the old days. When Numa's name was mentioned, though the Roman senators saw that the balance of power would be on the side of the Sabines if the king were chosen from amongst them, still no one ventured to propose a partisan of his own, or any senator, or citizen in preference to him. Accordingly they all to a man decreed that the crown should be offered to Numa Pompilius. He was invited to Rome, and following the precedent set by Romulus, when he obtained his crown through the augury which sanctioned the founding of the City, Numa ordered that in his case also the gods should be consulted. He was solemnly conducted by an augur, who was afterwards honored by being made a State functionary for life, to the Citadel, and took his seat on a stone facing south. The augur seated himself on his left hand, with his head covered, and holding in his right hand a curved staff without any knots, which they called a "lituus." After surveying the prospect over the City and surrounding country, he offered prayers and marked out the heavenly regions by an imaginary line from east to west; the southern he defined as "the right hand," the northern as "the left hand." He then fixed upon an object, as far as he could see, as a corresponding mark, and then transferring the lituus to his left hand, he laid his right upon Numa's head and offered this prayer: "Father Jupiter, if it be heaven's will that this Numa Pompilius, whose head I hold, should be king of Rome, do thou signify it to us by sure signs within those boundaries which I have traced." Then he described

in the usual formula the augury which he desired should be sent. They were sent, and Numa being by them manifested to be king, came down from the "templum."[1]

19. Having in this way obtained the crown, Numa prepared to found, as it were, anew, by laws and customs, that City which had so recently been founded by force of arms. He saw that this was impossible whilst a state of war lasted, for war brutalized men. Thinking that the ferocity of his subjects might be mitigated by the disuse of arms, he built the temple of Janus at the foot of the Aventine as an index of peace and war, to signify when it was open that the State was under arms, and when it was shut that all the surrounding nations were at peace. Twice since Numa's reign has it been shut, once after the first Punic war in the consulship of T. Manlius, the second time, which heaven has allowed our generation to witness, after the battle of Actium, when peace on land and sea was secured by the emperor Caesar Augustus. After forming treaties of alliance with all his neighbors and closing the temple of Janus, Numa turned his attention to domestic matters. The removal of all danger from without would induce his subjects to luxuriate in idleness, as they would be no longer restrained by the fear of an enemy or by military discipline. To prevent this, he strove to inculcate in their minds the fear of the gods, regarding this as the most powerful influence which could act upon an uncivilized and, in those ages, a barbarous people. But, as this would fail to make a deep impression without some claim to supernatural wisdom, he pretended that he had nocturnal interviews with the nymph Egeria: that it was on her advice that he was instituting the ritual most acceptable to the gods and appointing for each deity his own special priests. First of all he divided the year into twelve months, corresponding to the moon's revolutions. But as the moon does not complete thirty days in each month, and so there are fewer days in the lunar year than in that measured by the course of the sun, he interpolated intercalary months and so arranged them that every twentieth year the days should coincide with the same position of the sun as when they started, the whole twenty years being thus complete. He also established a distinction between the days on which legal business could be transacted and those on which it could not, because it would sometimes be advisable that there should be no business transacted with the people.

20. Next he turned his attention to the appointment of priests. He himself, however, conducted a great many religious services, especially those

---

[1] "Templum" originally meant the section of the sky marked out for the observation of auguries, that is, omens given by the flight of birds. Later, "Templum" came to mean the place from which the priest observed and the building constructed there.

which belong to the Flamen of Jupiter. But he thought that in a warlike state there would be more kings of the type of Romulus than of Numa who would take the field in person. To guard, therefore, against the sacrificial rites which the king performed being interrupted, he appointed a Flamen as perpetual priest to Jupiter, and ordered that he should wear a distinctive dress and sit in the royal curule chair. He appointed two additional Flamens, one for Mars, the other for Quirinus, and also chose virgins as priestesses to Vesta. This order of priestesses came into existence originally in Alba and was connected with the race of the founder. He assigned them a public stipend that they might give their whole time to the temple, and made their persons sacred and inviolable by a vow of chastity and other religious sanctions. Similarly he chose twelve "Salii" for Mars Gradivus, and assigned to them the distinctive dress of an embroidered tunic and over it a brazen cuirass. They were instructed to march in solemn procession through the City, carrying the twelve shields called the "Ancilia," and singing hymns accompanied by a solemn dance in triple time. The next office to be filled was that of the Pontifex Maximus. Numa appointed the son of Marcus, one of the senators—Numa Marcius—and all the regulations bearing on religion, written out and sealed, were placed in his charge. Here was laid down with what victims, on what days, and at what temples the various sacrifices were to be offered, and from what sources the expenses connected with them were to be defrayed. He placed all other sacred functions, both public and private, under the supervision of the Pontifex, in order that there might be an authority for the people to consult, and so all trouble and confusion arising through foreign rites being adopted and their ancestral ones neglected might be avoided. Nor were his functions confined to directing the worship of the celestial gods; he was to instruct the people how to conduct funerals and appease the spirits of the departed, and what prodigies sent by lightning or in any other way were to be attended to and expiated. To elicit these signs of the divine will, he dedicated an altar to Jupiter Elicius on the Aventine, and consulted the god through auguries, as to which prodigies were to receive attention.

21. The deliberations and arrangements which these matters involved diverted the people from all thoughts of war and provided them with ample occupation. The watchful care of the gods, manifesting itself in the providential guidance of human affairs, had kindled in all hearts such a feeling of piety that the sacredness of promises and the sanctity of oaths were a controlling force for the community scarcely less effective than the fear inspired by laws and penalties. And whilst his subjects were molding their characters upon the unique example of their king, the neighboring nations, who had hitherto believed that it was a fortified camp and not a city that was placed amongst them to vex the peace of all, were now induced to respect them so highly that

they thought it sinful to injure a State so entirely devoted to the service of the gods. There was a grove through the midst of which a perennial stream flowed, issuing from a dark cave. Here Numa frequently retired unattended as if to meet the goddess, and he consecrated the grove to the Camaenae, because it was there that their meetings with his wife Egeria took place. He also instituted a yearly sacrifice to the goddess Fides and ordered that the Flamens should ride to her temple in a hooded chariot, and should perform the service with their hands covered as far as the fingers, to signify that Faith must be sheltered and that her seat is holy even when it is in men's right hands. There were many other sacrifices appointed by him and places dedicated for their performance which the pontiffs call the Argei. The greatest of all his works was the preservation of peace and the security of his realm throughout the whole of his reign. Thus by two successive kings the greatness of the State was advanced; by each in a different way, by the one through war, by the other through peace. Romulus reigned thirty-seven years, Numa forty-three. The State was strong and disciplined by the lessons of war and the arts of peace.

22. The death of Numa was followed by a second interregnum. Then Tullus Hostilius, a grandson of the Hostilius who had fought so brilliantly at the foot of the Citadel against the Sabines, was chosen king by the people, and their choice was confirmed by the senate. He was not only unlike the last king, but he was a man of more warlike spirit even than Romulus, and his ambition was kindled by his own youthful energy and by the glorious achievements of his grandfather. Convinced that the vigor of the State was becoming enfeebled through inaction, he looked all round for a pretext for getting up a war. It so happened that Roman peasants were at that time in the habit of carrying off plunder from the Alban territory, and the Albans from Roman territory. Gaius Cluilius was at the time ruling in Alba. Both parties sent envoys almost simultaneously to seek redress. Tullus had told his ambassadors to lose no time in carrying out their instructions; he was fully aware that the Albans would refuse satisfaction, and so a just ground would exist for proclaiming war. The Alban envoys proceeded in a more leisurely fashion. Tullus received them with all courtesy and entertained them sumptuously. Meantime the Romans had preferred their demands, and on the Alban governor's refusal had declared that war would begin in thirty days. When this was reported to Tullus, he granted the Albans an audience in which they were to state the object of their coming. Ignorant of all that had happened, they wasted time in explaining that it was with great reluctance that they would say anything which might displease Tullus, but they were bound by their instructions; they were come to demand redress, and if that were refused they were ordered to declare war. "Tell your king," replied Tullus, "that the king of Rome calls the gods to witness that whichever nation is the first to

dismiss with ignominy the envoys who came to seek redress, upon that nation they will visit all the sufferings of this war."

23. The Albans reported this at home. Both sides made extraordinary preparations for a war, which closely resembled a civil war between parents and children, for both were of Trojan descent, since Lavinium was an offshoot of Troy, and Alba of Lavinium, and the Romans were sprung from the stock of the kings of Alba. The outcome of the war, however, made the conflict less deplorable, as there was no regular engagement, and though one of the two cities was destroyed, the two nations were blended into one. The Albans were the first to move, and invaded the Roman territory with an immense army. They fixed their camp only five miles from the City and surrounded it with a moat; this was called for several centuries the "Cluilian Dike" from the name of the Alban general, till through lapse of time the name and the thing itself disappeared. While they were encamped Cluilius, the Alban king, died, and the Albans made Mettius Fufetius dictator. The king's death made Tullus more sanguine than ever of success. He gave out that the wrath of heaven which had fallen first of all on the head of the nation would visit the whole race of Alba with condign punishment for this unholy war. Passing the enemy's camp by a night march, he advanced upon Alban territory. This drew Mettius from his entrenchments. He marched as close to his enemy as he could, and then sent on an officer to inform Tullus that before engaging it was necessary that they should have a conference. If he granted one, then he was satisfied that the matters he would lay before him were such as concerned Rome no less than Alba. Tullus did not reject the proposal, but in case the conference should prove illusory, he led out his men in order of battle. The Albans did the same. After they had halted, confronting each other, the two commanders, with a small escort of superior officers, advanced between the lines. The Alban general, addressing Tullus, said: "I think I have heard our king Cluilius say that acts of robbery and the non-restitution of plundered property, in violation of the existing treaty, were the cause of this war, and I have no doubt that you, Tullus, allege the same pretext. But if we are to say what is true, rather than what is plausible, we must admit that it is the lust of empire which has made two kindred and neighboring peoples take up arms. Whether rightly or wrongly I do not judge; let him who began the war settle that point; I am simply placed in command by the Albans to conduct the war. But I want to give you a warning, Tullus. You know, you especially who are nearer to them, the greatness of the Etruscan State, which hems us both in; their immense strength by land, still more by sea. Now remember, when once you have given the signal to engage, our two armies will fight under their eyes, so that when we are wearied and exhausted they may attack us both, victor and vanquished alike. If then, not content with the secure freedom we now enjoy, we are determined to enter into a game of chance, where the stakes are either supremacy or slavery, let us, in heaven's name, choose some method by which, without great suffering or bloodshed on either side, it can be decided which nation is to be master of the other." Although, from natural temperament, and the certainty he felt of victory, Tullus was eager to fight, he did not disapprove of the proposal. After much consideration on both sides a method was adopted, for which Fortune herself provided the necessary means.

24. There happened to be in each of the armies a triplet of brothers, fairly matched in years and strength. It is generally agreed that they were called Horatii and Curiatii. Few incidents in antiquity have been more widely celebrated, yet in spite of its celebrity there is a discrepancy in the accounts as to which nation each belonged. There are authorities on both sides, but I find that the majority give the name of Horatii to the Romans, and my sympathies lead me to follow them. The kings suggested to them that they should each fight on behalf of their country, and where victory rested, there should be the sovereignty. They raised no objection; so the time and place were fixed. But before they engaged a treaty was concluded between the Romans and the Albans, providing that the nation whose representatives proved victorious should receive the peaceable submission of the other. This is the earliest treaty recorded, and as all treaties, however different the conditions they contain, are concluded with the same forms, I will describe the forms with which this one was concluded as handed down by tradition. The Fetial put the formal question to Tullus: "Do you, King, order me to make a treaty with the Pater Patratus of the Alban nation?" On the king replying in the affirmative, the Fetial said: "I demand of thee, King, some tufts of grass." The king replied: "Take those that are pure." The Fetial brought pure grass from the Citadel. Then he asked the king: "Do you constitute me the plenipotentiary of the People of Rome, the Quirites, sanctioning also my vessels and comrades?" To which the king replied: "So far as may be without hurt to myself and the People of Rome, the Quirites, I do." The Fetial was M. Valerius. He made Spurius Furius the Pater Patratus by touching his head and hair with the grass. Then the Pater Patratus, who is constituted for the purpose of giving the treaty the religious sanction of an oath, did so by a long formula in verse, which it is not worth while to quote. After reciting the conditions he said: "Hear, O Jupiter, hear! thou Pater Patratus of the people of Alba! Hear ye, too, people of Alba! As these conditions have been publicly rehearsed from first to last, from these tablets, in perfect good faith, and inasmuch as they have here and now been most clearly understood, so these conditions the People of Rome will not be the first to go back from. If they shall, in their national council, with false and malicious intent be the first to go back, then do thou, Jupiter, on that day, so smite the People of Rome, even as I here and now shall smite this swine, and smite them so much the more heavily, as thou

art greater in power and might." With these words he struck the swine with a flint. In similar wise the Albans recited their oath and formularies through their own dictator and their priests.

25. On the conclusion of the treaty the six combatants armed themselves. They were greeted with shouts of encouragement from their comrades, who reminded them that their fathers' gods, their fatherland, their fathers, every fellow-citizen, every fellow-soldier, were now watching their weapons and the hands that wielded them. Eager for the contest and inspired by the voices round them, they advanced into the open space between the opposing lines. The two armies were sitting in front of their respective camps, relieved from personal danger but not from anxiety, since upon the fortunes and courage of this little group hung the issue of dominion. Watchful and nervous, they gazed with feverish intensity on a spectacle by no means entertaining. The signal was given, and with uplifted swords the six youths charged like a battle-line with the courage of a mighty host. Not one of them thought of his own danger; their sole thought was for their country, whether it would be supreme or subject, their one anxiety that they were deciding its future fortunes. When, at the first encounter, the flashing swords rang on their opponents' shields, a deep shudder ran through the spectators; then a breathless silence followed, as neither side seemed to be gaining any advantage. Soon, however, they saw something more than the swift movements of limbs and the rapid play of sword and shield: blood became visible flowing from open wounds. Two of the Romans fell one on the other, breathing out their life, whilst all the three Albans were wounded. The fall of the Romans was welcomed with a burst of exultation from the Alban army; whilst the Roman legions, who had lost all hope, but not all anxiety, trembled for their solitary champion surrounded by the three Curiatii. It chanced that he was untouched, and though not a match for the three together, he was confident of victory against each separately. So, that he might encounter each singly, he took to flight, assuming that they would follow as well as their wounds would allow. He had run some distance from the spot where the combat began, when, on looking back, he saw them following at long intervals from each other, the foremost not far from him. He turned and made a desperate attack upon him, and whilst the Alban army were shouting to the other Curiatii to come to their brother's assistance, Horatius had already slain his foe and, flushed with victory, was awaiting the second encounter. Then the Romans cheered their champion with a shout such as men raise when hope succeeds to despair, and he hastened to bring the fight to a close. Before the third, who was not far away, could come up, he dispatched the second Curiatius. The survivors were now equal in point of numbers, but far from equal in either confidence or strength. The one, unscathed after his double victory, was eager for the third contest; the other, dragging himself wearily along, exhausted by his wounds and by his running, vanquished already by the previous slaughter of his brothers, was an easy conquest to his victorious foe. There was, in fact, no fighting. The Roman cried exultantly: "Two have I sacrificed to appease my brothers' shades; the third I will offer for the issue of this fight, that the Roman may rule the Alban." He thrust his sword downward into the neck of his opponent, who could no longer lift his shield, and then despoiled him as he lay. Horatius was welcomed by the Romans with shouts of triumph, all the more joyous for the fears they had felt. Both sides turned their attention to burying their dead champions, but with very different feelings, the one rejoicing in wider dominion, the other deprived of their liberty and under alien rule. The tombs stand on the spots where each fell; those of the Romans close together, in the direction of Alba; the three Alban tombs, at intervals, in the direction of Rome.

26. Before the armies separated, Mettius inquired what commands he was to receive in accordance with the terms of the treaty. Tullus ordered him to keep the Alban soldiery under arms, as he would require their services if there were war with the Veientines. Both armies then withdrew to their homes. Horatius was marching at the head of the Roman army, carrying in front of him his triple spoils. His sister, who had been betrothed to one of the Curiatii, met him outside the Capene gate. She recognized on her brother's shoulders the cloak of her betrothed, which she had made with her own hands; and bursting into tears she tore her hair and called her dead lover by name. The triumphant soldier was so enraged by his sister's outburst of grief in the midst of his own triumph and the public rejoicing that he drew his sword and stabbed the girl. "Go," he cried, in bitter reproach, "go to your betrothed with your ill-timed love, forgetful as you are of your dead brothers, of the one who still lives, and of your country! So perish every Roman woman who mourns for an enemy!" The deed horrified patricians and plebeians alike; but his recent services were a setoff to it. He was brought before the king for trial. To avoid responsibility for passing a harsh sentence, which would be repugnant to the populace, and then carrying it into execution, the king summoned an assembly of the people, and said: "I appoint two duumvirs to judge the treason of Horatius according to law." The dreadful language of the law was: "The duumvirs shall judge cases of treason; if the accused appeal from the duumvirs, the appeal shall be heard; if their sentence be confirmed, the lictor shall hang him by a rope on the fatal tree, and shall scourge him either within or without the pomoerium." The duumvirs appointed under this law did not think that by its provisions they had the power to acquit even an innocent person. Accordingly they condemned him; then one of them said: "Publius Horatius, I pronounce you guilty of treason. Lictor, bind his hands." The lictor had approached and was fastening the cord, when Horatius, at the suggestion of Tullus, who placed a merciful interpretation on the law, said, "I appeal." The appeal was accordingly brought before the people.

Their decision was mainly influenced by Publius Horatius, the father, who declared that his daughter had been justly slain; had it not been so, he would have exerted his authority as a father in punishing his son. Then he implored them not to bereave of all his children the man whom they had so lately seen surrounded with such noble offspring. Whilst saying this he embraced his son, and then, pointing to the spoils of the Curiatii suspended on the spot now called the Pila Horatia, he said: "Can you bear, Quirites, to see bound, scourged, and tortured beneath the gallows the man whom you saw, lately, coming in triumph adorned with his enemy's spoils? Why, the Albans themselves could not bear the sight of such a hideous spectacle. Go, lictor, bind those hands which when armed but a little time ago won dominion for the Roman people. Go, cover the head of the liberator of this City! Hang him on the fatal tree, scourge him within the pomoerium, if only it be amongst the trophies of his foes, or without, if only it be amongst the tombs of the Curiatii! To what place can you take this youth where the monuments of his splendid exploits will not vindicate him from such a shameful punishment?" The father's tears and the young soldier's courage ready to meet every peril were too much for the people. They acquitted him because they admired his bravery rather than because they regarded his cause as a just one. But since a murder in broad daylight demanded some expiation, the father was commanded to make an atonement for his son at the cost of the State. After offering certain expiatory sacrifices he erected a beam across the street and made the young man pass under it, as under a yoke, with his head covered. This beam exists today, having always been kept in repair by the State: it is called "The Sister's Beam." A tomb of hewn stone was constructed for Horatia on the spot where she was murdered.

27. But the peace with Alba was not a lasting one. The Alban dictator had incurred general odium through having entrusted the fortunes of the State to three soldiers, and this had an evil effect upon his weak character. As straightforward counsels had turned out so unfortunate, he tried to recover the popular favor by resorting to crooked ones, and as he had previously made peace his aim in war, so now he sought the occasion of war in peace. He recognized that his State possessed more courage than strength, he therefore incited other nations to declare war openly and formally, whilst he kept for his own people an opening for treachery under the mask of an alliance. The people of Fidenae, where a Roman colony existed, were induced to go to war by a compact on the part of the Albans to desert to them; the Veientines were taken into the plot. When Fidenae had broken out into open revolt, Tullus summoned Mettius and his army from Alba and marched against the enemy. After crossing the Anio he encamped at the junction of

that river with the Tiber. The army of the Veientines had crossed the Tiber at a spot between his camp and Fidenae. In the battle they formed the right wing near the river, the Fidenates were on the left nearer the mountains. Tullus formed his troops in front of the Veientines, and stationed the Albans against the legion of the Fidenates. The Alban general showed as little courage as fidelity; afraid either to keep his ground or to openly desert, he drew away gradually towards the mountains. When he thought he had retired far enough, he halted his entire army, and still irresolute, he began to form his men for attack, by way of gaining time, intending to throw his strength on the winning side. Those Romans who had been stationed next to the Albans were astounded to find that their allies had withdrawn and left their flank exposed, when a horseman rode up at full speed and reported to the king that the Albans were leaving the field. In this critical situation, Tullus vowed to found a college of twelve Salii and to build temples to Pallor and Pavor. Then, reprimanding the horseman loud enough for the enemy to hear, he ordered him to rejoin the fighting line, adding that there was no occasion for alarm, as it was by his orders that the Alban army was making a circuit that they might fall on the unprotected rear of the Fidenates. At the same time he ordered the cavalry to raise their spears; this action hid the retreating Alban army from a large part of the Roman infantry. Those who had seen them, thinking that what the king had said was actually the case, fought all the more keenly. It was now the enemies' turn to be alarmed; they had heard clearly the words of the king, and, moreover, a large part of the Fidenates who had formerly joined the Roman colonists understood Latin. Fearing to be cut off from their town by a sudden charge of the Albans from the hills, they retreated. Tullus pressed the attack, and after routing the Fidenates, returned to attack the Veientines with greater confidence, as they were already demoralized by the panic of their allies. They did not wait for the charge, but their flight was checked by the river in their rear. When they reached it, some, flinging away their arms, rushed blindly into the water, others, hesitating whether to fight or fly, were overtaken and slain. Never had the Romans fought in a bloodier battle.

28. Then the Alban army, who had been watching the fight, marched down into the plain. Mettius congratulated Tullus on his victory, Tullus replied in a friendly tone, and as a mark of goodwill, ordered the Albans to form their camp contiguous to that of the Romans, and made preparations for a "lustral sacrifice" on the morrow. As soon as it was light, and all the preparations were made, he gave the customary order for both armies to muster on parade. The heralds began at the furthest part of the camp, where the Albans were, and summoned them first of all; they, attracted by the novelty of hearing the Roman addressing his troops, took up their position close round him. Secret instructions had been given for the Roman legion to stand fully armed behind them, and the centurions were in readiness to execute instantly the orders they received. Tullus commenced as follows: "Romans! if in any war that you have ever waged there has been reason for you to thank, first, the immortal gods, and then your own personal courage, such was certainly the case in yesterday's battle. For whilst you had to contend with an open enemy, you had a still more serious and dangerous conflict to maintain against the treachery and perfidy of your allies. For I must undeceive you—it was by no command of mine that the Albans withdrew to the mountains. What you heard was not a real order but a pretended one, which I used as an artifice to prevent your knowing that you were deserted, and so losing heart for the battle, and also to fill the enemy with alarm and a desire to flee by making them think that they were being surrounded. The guilt which I am denouncing does not involve all the Albans; they only followed their general, just as you would have done had I wanted to lead my army away from the field. It is Mettius who is the leader of this march, Mettius who engineered this war, Mettius who broke the treaty between Rome and Alba. Others may venture on similar practices, if I do not make this man a signal lesson to all the world." The armed centurions closed round Mettius, and the king proceeded: "I shall take a course which will bring good fortune and happiness to the Roman people and myself, and to you, Albans; it is my intention to transfer the entire Alban population to Rome, to give the rights of citizenship to the plebeians, and enroll the nobles in the senate, and to make one City, one State. As formerly the Alban State was broken up into two nations, so now let it once more become one." The Alban soldiery listened to these words with conflicting feelings, but unarmed as they were and hemmed in by armed men, a common fear kept them silent. Then Tullus said: "Mettius Fufetius! if you could have learnt to keep your word and respect treaties, I would have given you that instruction in your lifetime, but now, since your character is past cure, do at least teach mankind by your punishment to hold those things as sacred which have been outraged by you. As yesterday your interest was divided between the Fidenates and the Romans, so now you shall give up your body to be divided and dismembered." Thereupon two four-horse chariots were brought up, and Mettius was bound at full length to each, the horses were driven in opposite directions, carrying off parts of the body in each chariot, where the limbs had been secured by the cords. All present averted their eyes from the horrible spectacle. This is the first and last instance amongst the Romans of a punishment so regardless of humanity. Amongst other things which are the glory of Rome is this, that no nation has ever been contented with milder punishments.

29. Meanwhile the cavalry had been sent on in advance to conduct the population to Rome; they were followed by the legions, who were marched thither to destroy the city. When they entered the gates there was not that noise and panic which are usually found in captured cities, where, after the gates have been shattered or the walls leveled by the battering-ram or the citadel stormed, the shouts of the enemy and the rushing of the soldiers through the streets throw everything into universal confusion with fire and sword. Here, on the contrary, gloomy silence and a grief beyond words so petrified the minds of all, that, forgetting in their terror what to leave behind, what to take with them, incapable of thinking for themselves and asking one another's advice, at one moment they would stand on their thresholds, at another wander aimlessly through their houses, which they were seeing then for the last time. But now they were roused by the shouts of the cavalry ordering their instant departure, now by the crash of the houses undergoing demolition, heard in the furthest corners of the city, and the dust, rising in different places, which covered everything like a cloud. Seizing hastily what they could carry, they went out of the city, and left behind their hearths and household gods and the homes in which they had been born and brought up. Soon an unbroken line of emigrants filled the streets, and as they recognized one another the sense of their common misery led to fresh outbursts of tears. Cries of grief, especially from the women, began to make themselves heard, as they walked past the venerable temples and saw them occupied by troops, and felt that they were leaving their gods as prisoners in an enemy's hands. When the Albans had left their city the Romans leveled to the ground all the public and private edifices in every direction, and a single hour gave over to destruction and ruin the work of those four centuries during which Alba had stood. The temples of the gods, however, were spared, in accordance with the king's proclamation.

30. The fall of Alba led to the growth of Rome. The number of the citizens was doubled, the Caelian hill was included in the city, and that it might become more populated, Tullus chose it for the site of his palace, and for the future lived there. He nominated Alban nobles to the senate that this order of the State might also be augmented. Amongst them were the Tullii, the Servilii, the Quinctii, the Geganii, the Curiatii, and the Cloelii. To provide a consecrated building for the increased number of senators he built the senate-house, which down to the time of our fathers went by the name of the Curia Hostilia. To secure an accession of military strength of all ranks from the new population, he formed ten troops of knights from the Albans; from the same source he brought up the old legions to their full strength and enrolled new ones. Impelled by the confidence in his strength which these measures inspired, Tullus proclaimed war against the Sabines, a nation at that time second only to the Etruscans in numbers and military strength. Each side had inflicted injuries on the other and refused all redress. Tullus complained that Roman traders had been arrested in open market at the shrine of Feronia; the Sabines' grievance was that some of their people had

previously sought refuge in the Asylum and been kept in Rome. These were the ostensible grounds of the war. The Sabines were far from forgetting that a portion of their strength had been transferred to Rome by Tatius, and that the Roman State had lately been aggrandized by the inclusion of the population of Alba; they, therefore, on their side began to look round for outside help. Their nearest neighbor was Etruria, and, of the Etruscans, the nearest to them were the Veientines. Their past defeats were still rankling in their memories, and the Sabines, urging them to revolt, attracted many volunteers; others of the poorest and homeless classes were paid to join them. No assistance was given by the State. With the Veientines—it is not so surprising that the other cities rendered no assistance—the truce with Rome was still held to be binding. Whilst preparations were being made on both sides with the utmost energy, and it seemed as though success depended upon which side was the first to take the offensive, Tullus opened the campaign by invading the Sabine territory. A severe action was fought at the Silva Malitiosa. Whilst the Romans were strong in their infantry, their main strength was in their lately increased cavalry force. A sudden charge of horse threw the Sabine ranks into confusion, they could neither offer a steady resistance nor effect their flight without great slaughter.

31. This victory threw great luster upon the reign of Tullus, and upon the whole State, and added considerably to its strength. At this time it was reported to the king and the senate that there had been a shower of stones on the Alban Mount. As the thing seemed hardly credible, men were sent to inspect the prodigy, and whilst they were watching, a heavy shower of stones fell from the sky, just like hailstones heaped together by the wind. They fancied, too, that they heard a very loud voice from the grove on the summit, bidding the Albans celebrate their sacred rites after the manner of their fathers. These solemnities they had consigned to oblivion, as though they had abandoned their gods when they abandoned their country and had either adopted Roman rites, or, as sometimes happens, embittered against Fortune, had given up the service of the gods. In consequence of this prodigy, the Romans, too, kept up a public religious observance for nine days, either—as tradition asserts—owing to the voice from the Alban Mount, or because of the warning of the soothsayers. In either case, however, it became permanently established whenever the same prodigy was reported; a nine days' solemnity was observed. Not long after a pestilence caused great distress, and made men indisposed for the hardships of military service. The warlike king, however, allowed no respite from arms; he thought, too, that it was more healthy for the soldiery in the field than at home. At last he himself was seized with a lingering illness, and that fierce and restless spirit became so broken through bodily weakness, that he who had once thought nothing less fitting for a king than devotion to sacred things, now suddenly became a

prey to every sort of religious terror, and filled the City with religious observances. There was a general desire to recall the condition of things which existed under Numa, for men felt that the only help that was left against sickness was to obtain the forgiveness of the gods and be at peace with heaven. Tradition records that the king, whilst examining the commentaries of Numa, found there a description of certain secret sacrificial rites paid to Jupiter Elicius: he withdrew into privacy whilst occupied with these rites, but their performance was marred by omissions or mistakes. Not only was no sign from heaven vouchsafed to him, but the anger of Jupiter was roused by the false worship rendered to him, and he burnt up the king and his house by a stroke of lightning. Tullus had achieved great renown in war, and reigned for two-and-thirty years.

32. On the death of Tullus, the government, in accordance with the original constitution, again devolved on the senate. They appointed an interrex to conduct the election. The people chose Ancus Martius as king, the senate confirmed the choice. His mother was Numa's daughter. At the outset of his reign—remembering what made his grandfather glorious, and recognizing that the late reign, so splendid in all other respects, had, on one side, been most unfortunate through the neglect of religion or the improper performance of its rites—he determined to go back to the earliest source and conduct the state offices of religion as they had been organized by Numa. He gave the Pontifex instructions to copy them out from the king's commentaries and set them forth in some public place. The neighboring states and his own people, who were yearning for peace, were led to hope that the king would follow his grandfather in disposition and policy. In this state of affairs, the Latins, with whom a treaty had been made in the reign of Tullus, recovered their confidence, and made an incursion into Roman territory. On the Romans seeking redress, they gave a haughty refusal, thinking that the king of Rome was going to pass his reign amongst chapels and altars. In the temperament of Ancus there was a touch of Romulus as well as Numa. He realized that the great necessity of Numa's reign was peace, especially amongst a young and aggressive nation, but he saw, too, that it would be difficult for him to preserve the peace which had fallen to his lot unimpaired. His patience was being put to the proof, and not only put to the proof but despised; the times demanded a Tullus rather than a Numa. Numa had instituted religious observances for times of peace, he would hand down the ceremonies appropriate to a state of war. In order, therefore, that wars might be not only conducted but also proclaimed with some formality, he wrote down the law, as taken from the ancient nation of the Aequicoli, under which the Fetials act down to this day when seeking redress for injuries. The procedure is as follows:

The ambassador binds his head in a woolen fillet. When he has reached the frontiers of the nation from whom satisfaction is demanded, he says, "Hear, O Jupiter! Hear, ye confines"—naming the particular nation whose they are—"Hear, O Justice! I am the public herald of the Roman People. Rightly and duly authorized do I come; let confidence be placed in my words." Then he recites the terms of the demands, and calls Jupiter to witness: "If I am demanding the surrender of those men or those goods, contrary to justice and religion, suffer me nevermore to enjoy my native land." He repeats these words as he crosses the frontier, he repeats them to whoever happens to be the first person he meets, he repeats them as he enters the gates and again on entering the forum, with some slight changes in the wording of the formula. If what he demands are not surrendered at the expiration of thirty-three days—for that is the fixed period of grace—he declares war in the following terms: "Hear, O Jupiter, and thou Janus Quirinus, and all ye heavenly gods, and ye, gods of earth and of the lower world, hear me! I call you to witness that this people"—mentioning it by name—"is unjust and does not fulfill its sacred obligations. But about these matters we must consult the elders in our own land in what way we may obtain our rights."

With these words the ambassador returned to Rome for consultation. The king forthwith consulted the senate in words to the following effect: "Concerning the matters, suits, and causes, whereof the Pater Patratus of the Roman People and Quirites hath complained to the Pater Patratus of the Prisci Latini, and to the people of the Prisci Latini, which matters they were bound severally to surrender, discharge, and make good, whereas they have done none of these things—say, what is your opinion?" He whose opinion was first asked, replied, "I am of opinion that they ought to be recovered by a just and righteous war, wherefore I give my consent and vote for it." Then the others were asked in order, and when the majority of those present declared themselves of the same opinion, war was agreed upon. It was customary for the Fetial to carry to the enemies' frontiers a blood-smeared spear tipped with iron or burnt at the end, and, in the presence of at least three adults, to say, "Inasmuch as the peoples of the Prisci Latini have been guilty of wrong against the People of Rome and the Quirites, and inasmuch as the People of Rome and the Quirites have ordered that there be war with the Prisci Latini, and the Senate of the People of Rome and the Quirites have determined and decreed that there shall be war with the Prisci Latini, therefore I and the People of Rome, declare and make war upon the peoples of the Prisci Latini." With these words he hurled his spear into their territory. This was the way in which at that time satisfaction was demanded from the Latins and war declared, and posterity adopted the custom.

33. After handing over the care of the various sacrificial rites to the Flamens and other priests, and calling up a fresh army, Ancus advanced against Politorium, a city belonging to the Latins. He took it by assault, and following the custom of the earlier kings who had enlarged the State by receiving its enemies into Roman citizenship, he transferred the whole of the population to Rome. The Palatine had been settled by the earliest Romans, the Sabines had occupied the Capitoline hill with the Citadel, on one side of the Palatine, and the Albans the Caelian hill, on the other, so the Aventine was assigned to the newcomers. Not long afterwards there was a further addition to the number of citizens through the capture of Tellenae and Ficana. Politorium after its evacuation was seized by the Latins and was again recovered; and this was the reason why the Romans razed the city, to prevent its being a perpetual refuge for the enemy. At last the whole war was concentrated round Medullia, and fighting went on for some time there with doubtful result. The city was strongly fortified and its strength was increased by the presence of a large garrison. The Latin army was encamped in the open and had had several engagements with the Romans. At last Ancus made a supreme effort with the whole of his force and won a pitched battle, after which he returned with immense booty to Rome, and many thousands of Latins were admitted into citizenship. In order to connect the Aventine with the Palatine, the district round the altar of Venus Murcia was assigned to them. The Janiculum also was brought into the city boundaries, not because the space was wanted, but to prevent such a strong position from being occupied by an enemy. It was decided to connect this hill with the City, not only by carrying the City wall round it, but also by a bridge, for the convenience of traffic. This was the first bridge thrown over the Tiber, and was known as the Pons Sublicius. The Fossa Quiritium also was the work of King Ancus, and afforded no inconsiderable protection to the lower and therefore more accessible parts of the City. Amidst this vast population, now that the State had become so enormously increased, the sense of right and wrong was obscured, and secret crimes were committed. To overawe the growing lawlessness a prison was built in the heart of the City, overlooking the Forum. The additions made by this king were not confined to the City. The Mesian Forest was taken from the Veientines, and the Roman dominion extended to the sea; at the mouth of the Tiber the city of Ostia was built; salt-pits were constructed on both sides of the river, and the temple of Jupiter Feretrius was enlarged in consequence of the brilliant successes in the war.

34. During the reign of Ancus a wealthy and ambitious man named Lucumo removed to Rome, mainly with the hope and desire of winning high distinction, for which no opportunity had existed in Tarquinii, since there also he was an alien. He was the son of Demaratus a Corinthian who had been driven from home by a revolution, and who happened to settle in Tarquinii. There he married and had two sons, their names were Lucumo and Arruns. Arruns died before his father, leaving his wife with child; Lucumo survived his father and inherited all his property. For Demaratus died shortly

after Arruns, and being unaware of the condition of his daughter-in-law, had made no provision in his will for a grandchild. The boy, thus excluded from any share of his grandfather's property, was called, in consequence of his poverty, Egerius. Lucumo, on the other hand, heir to all the property, became elated by his wealth, and his ambition was stimulated by his marriage with Tanaquil. This woman was descended from one of the foremost families in the State, and could not bear the thought of her position by marriage being inferior to the one she claimed by birth. The Etruscans looked down upon Lucumo as the son of a foreign refugee; she could not brook this indignity, and forgetting all ties of patriotism if only she could see her husband honored, resolved to emigrate from Tarquinii. Rome seemed the most suitable place for her purpose. She felt that among a young nation where all nobility is a thing of recent growth and won by personal merit, there would be room for a man of courage and energy. She remembered that the Sabine Tatius had reigned there, that Numa had been summoned from Cures to fill the throne, that Ancus himself was sprung from a Sabine mother, and could not trace his nobility beyond Numa. Her husband's ambition and the fact that Tarquinii was his native country only on the mother's side, made him give a ready ear to her proposals. They accordingly packed up their goods and removed to Rome.

They had got as far as the Janiculum when a hovering eagle swooped gently down and took off his cap as he was sitting by his wife's side in the carriage, then circling round the vehicle with loud cries, as though commissioned by heaven for this service, replaced it carefully upon his head and soared away. It is said that Tanaquil, who, like most Etruscans, was expert in interpreting celestial prodigies, was delighted at the omen. She threw her arms round her husband and bade him look for a high and majestic destiny, for such was the import of the eagle's appearance, of the particular part of the sky where it appeared, and of the deity who sent it. The omen was directed to the crown and summit of his person, the bird had raised aloft an adornment put on by human hands, to replace it as the gift of heaven. Full of these hopes and surmises they entered the City, and after procuring a domicile there, they announced his name as Lucius Tarquinius Priscus. The fact of his being a stranger, and a wealthy one, brought him into notice, and he increased the advantage which Fortune gave him by his courteous demeanor, his lavish hospitality, and the many acts of kindness by which he won all whom it was in his power to win, until his reputation even reached the palace. Once introduced to the king's notice, he soon succeeded by adroit complaisance in getting on to such familiar terms that he was consulted in matters of state, as much as in private matters, whether they referred to either peace or war. At last, after passing every test of character and ability, he was actually appointed by the king's will guardian to his children.

35. Ancus reigned twenty-four years, unsurpassed by any of his predecessors in ability and reputation, both in the field and at home. His sons had now almost reached manhood. Tarquin was all the more anxious for the election of the new king to be held as soon as possible. At the time fixed for it he sent the boys out of the way on a hunting expedition. He is said to have been the first who canvassed for the crown and delivered a set speech to secure the interest of the plebs. In it he asserted that he was not making an unheard-of request, he was not the first foreigner who aspired to the Roman throne; were this so, any one might feel surprise and indignation. But he was the third. Tatius was not only a foreigner, but was made king after he had been their enemy; Numa, an entire stranger to the City, had been called to the throne without any seeking it on his part. As to himself, as soon as he was his own master, he had removed to Rome with his wife and his whole fortune; he had lived at Rome for a larger part of the period during which men discharge the functions of citizenship than he had passed in his old country; he had learnt the laws of Rome, the ceremonial rites of Rome, both civil and military, under Ancus himself, a very sufficient teacher; he had been second to none in duty and service towards the king; he had not yielded to the king himself in generous treatment of others. Whilst he was stating these facts, which were certainly true, the Roman people with enthusiastic unanimity elected him king. Though in all other respects an excellent man, his ambition, which impelled him to seek the crown, followed him on to the throne; with the design of strengthening himself quite as much as of increasing the State, he made a hundred new senators. These were afterwards called "the Lesser Houses" and formed a body of uncompromising supporters of the king, through whose kindness they had entered the senate. The first war he engaged in was with the Latins. He took the town of Apiolae by storm, and carried off a greater amount of plunder than could have been expected from the slight interest shown in the war. After this had been brought in wagons to Rome, he celebrated the Games with greater splendor and on a larger scale than his predecessors. Then for the first time a space was marked for what is now the "Circus Maximus." Spots were allotted to the patricians and knights where they could each build for themselves stands—called "Decks"—from which to view the Games. These stands were raised on wooden props, branching out at the top, twelve feet high. The contests were horse-racing and boxing, the horses and boxers mostly brought from Etruria. They were at first celebrated on occasions of especial solemnity; subsequently they became an annual fixture, and were called indifferently the "Roman" or the "Great Games." This king also divided the ground round the Forum into building sites; arcades and shops were put up.

36. He was also making preparations for surrounding the City with a stone wall when his designs were interrupted by a war with the Sabines. So sudden was the outbreak that the enemy were crossing the Anio before a Roman army could meet and stop them. There was great alarm in Rome. The first battle was indecisive, and there was great slaughter on both sides. The enemies' return to their camp allowed time for the Romans to make preparations for a fresh campaign. Tarquin thought his army was weakest in cavalry and decided to double the centuries, which Romulus had formed, of the Ramnes, Titienses, and Luceres, and to distinguish them by his own name. Now as Romulus had acted under the sanction of the auspices, Attus Navius, a celebrated augur at that time, insisted that no change could be made, nothing new introduced, unless the birds gave a favorable omen. The king's anger was roused, and in mockery of the augur's skill he is reported to have said, "Come, you diviner, find out by your augury whether what I am now contemplating can be done." Attus, after consulting the omens, declared that it could. "Well," the king replied, "I had it in my mind that you should cut a whetstone with a razor. Take these, and perform the feat which your birds portend can be done." It is said that without the slightest hesitation he cut it through. There used to be a statue of Attus, representing him with his head covered, in the Comitium, on the steps to the left of the senate-house, where the incident occurred. The whetstone also, it is recorded, was placed there to be a memorial of the marvel for future generations. At all events, auguries and the college of augurs were held in such honor that nothing was undertaken in peace or war without their sanction; the assembly of the curies, the assembly of the centuries, matters of the highest importance, were suspended or broken up if the omen of the birds was unfavorable. Even on that occasion Tarquin was deterred from making changes in the names or numbers of the centuries of knights; he merely doubled the number of men in each, so that the three centuries contained eighteen hundred men. Those who were added to the centuries bore the same designation, only they were called the "Second" knights, and the centuries being thus doubled are now called the "Six Centuries."

37. After this division of the forces was augmented there was a second collision with the Sabines, in which the increased strength of the Roman army was aided by an artifice. Men were secretly sent to set fire to a vast quantity of logs lying on the banks of the Anio, and float them down the river on rafts. The wind fanned the flames, and as the logs drove against the piles and stuck there they set the bridge on fire. This incident, occurring during the battle, created a panic among the Sabines and led to their rout, and at the same time prevented their flight; many after escaping from the enemy perished in the river. Their shields floated down the Tiber as far as the City, and being recognized, made it clear that there had been a victory almost before it could be announced. In that battle the cavalry especially distinguished themselves. They were posted on each wing, and when the infantry

in the center were being forced back, it is said that they made such a desperate charge from both sides that they not only arrested the Sabine legions as they were pressing on the retreating Romans, but immediately put them to flight. The Sabines, in wild disorder, made for the hills, a few gained them, by far the greater number, as was stated above, were driven by the cavalry into the river. Tarquin determined to follow them up before they could recover from their panic. He sent the prisoners and booty to Rome; the spoils of the enemy had been devoted to Vulcan, they were accordingly collected into an enormous pile and burnt; then he proceeded forthwith to lead his army into the Sabine territory. In spite of their recent defeat and the hopelessness of repairing it, the Sabines met him with a hastily raised body of militia, as there was no time for concerting a plan of operations. They were again defeated, and as they were now brought to the verge of ruin, sought for peace.

38. Collatia and all the territory on this side of it was taken from the Sabines; Egerius, the king's nephew, was left to hold it. I understand that the procedure on the surrender of Collatia was as follows: The king asked, "Have you been sent as envoys and commissioners by the people of Collatia to make the surrender of yourselves and the people of Collatia?" "We have." "And is the people of Collatia an independent people?" "It is." "Do you surrender into my power and that of the People of Rome yourselves, and the people of Collatia, your city, lands, water, boundaries, temples, sacred vessels, all things divine and human?" "We do surrender them." "Then I accept them." After bringing the Sabine war to a conclusion Tarquin returned in triumph to Rome. Then he made war on the Prisci Latini. No general engagement took place, he attacked each of their towns in succession and subjugated the whole nation. The towns of Corniculum, Old Ficulea, Cameria, Crustumerium, Ameriola, Medullia, Nomentum, were all taken from the Prisci Latini or those who had gone over to them. Then peace was made. Works of peace were now commenced with greater energy even than had been displayed in war, so that the people enjoyed no more quiet at home than they had had in the field. He made preparations for completing the work, which had been interrupted by the Sabine war, of enclosing the City in those parts where no fortification yet existed with a stone wall. The low-lying parts of the City round the Forum, and the other valleys between the hills, where the water could not escape, were drained by conduits which emptied into the Tiber. He built up with masonry a level space on the Capitol as a site for the temple of Jupiter which he had vowed during the Sabine war, and the magnitude of the work revealed his prophetic anticipation of the future greatness of the place.

39. At that time an incident took place as marvelous in the appearance as it proved in the result. It is said that whilst a boy named Servius Tullius was asleep, his head was enveloped in flames, before the eyes of many who were

present. The cry which broke out at such a marvelous sight aroused the royal family, and when one of the domestics was bringing water to quench the flames the queen stopped him, and after calming the excitement forbade the boy to be disturbed until he awoke of his own accord. Presently he did so, and the flames disappeared. Then Tanaquil took her husband aside and said to him, "Do you see this boy, whom we are bringing up in such a humble style? You may be certain that he will one day be a light to us in trouble and perplexity, and a protection to our tottering house. Let us henceforth bring up with all care and indulgence one who will be the source of measureless glory to the State and to ourselves." From this time the boy began to be treated as their child and trained in those accomplishments by which characters are stimulated to the pursuit of a great destiny. The task was an easy one, for it was carrying out the will of the gods. The youth turned out to be of a truly kingly disposition, and when search was made for a son-in-law to Tarquinius, none of the Roman youths could be compared with him in any respect, so the king betrothed his daughter to him. The bestowal of this great honor upon him, whatever the reason for it, forbids our believing that he was the son of a slave, and, in his boyhood, a slave himself. I am more inclined to the opinion of those who say that in the capture of Corniculum, Servius Tullius, the leading man of that city, was killed, and his wife, who was about to become a mother, was recognized amongst the other captive women, and in consequence of her high rank was exempted from servitude by the Roman queen, and gave birth to a son in the house of Priscus Tarquinius. This kind treatment strengthened the intimacy between the women, and the boy, brought up as he was from infancy in the royal household, was held in affection and honor. It was the fate of his mother, who fell into the hands of the enemy when her native city was taken, that made people think he was the son of a slave.

40. When Tarquin had been about thirty-eight years on the throne, Servius Tullius was held in by far the highest esteem of any one, not only with the king but also with the patricians and the commons. The two sons of Ancus had always felt most keenly their being deprived of their father's throne through the treachery of their guardian; its occupation by a foreigner who was not even of Italian, much less Roman descent, increased their indignation, when they saw that not even after the death of Tarquin would the crown revert to them, but would suddenly descend to a slave—that crown which Romulus, the offspring of a god, and himself a god, had worn whilst he was on earth, now to be the possession of a slave-born slave a hundred years later! They felt that it would be a disgrace to the whole Roman nation, and especially to their house, if, while the male issue of Ancus was still alive, the sovereignty of Rome should be open not only to foreigners but even to slaves. They determined, therefore, to repel that insult by the sword. But it

was on Tarquin rather than on Servius that they sought to avenge their wrongs; if the king were left alive he would be able to deal more summary vengeance than an ordinary citizen, and in the event of Servius being killed, the king would certainly make any one else whom he chose for a son-in-law heir to the crown. These considerations decided them to form a plot against the king's life. Two shepherds, perfect desperadoes, were selected for the deed. They appeared in the vestibule of the palace, each with his usual implement, and by pretending to have a violent and outrageous quarrel, they attracted the attention of all the royal guards. Then, as they both began to appeal to the king, and their clamor had penetrated within the palace, they were summoned before the king. At first they tried, by shouting each against the other, to see who could make the most noise, until, after being repressed by the lictor and ordered to speak in turn, they became quiet, and one of the two began to state his case. Whilst the king's attention was absorbed in listening to him, the other swung aloft his ax and drove it into the king's head, and leaving the weapon in the wound both dashed out of the palace.

41. Whilst the bystanders were supporting the dying Tarquin in their arms, the lictors caught the fugitives. The shouting drew a crowd together, wondering what had happened. In the midst of the confusion, Tanaquil ordered the palace to be cleared and the doors closed; she then carefully prepared medicaments for dressing the wound, should there be hopes of life; at the same time she decided on other precautions, should the case prove hopeless, and hastily summoned Servius. She showed him her husband at the point of death, and taking his hand, implored him not to leave his father-in-law's death unavenged, nor to allow his mother-in-law to become the sport of her enemies. "The throne is yours, Servius," she said, "if you are a man; it does not belong to those who have, through the hands of others, wrought this worst of crimes. Up! follow the guidance of the gods who presaged the exaltation of that head round which divine fire once played! Let that heaven-sent flame now inspire you. Rouse yourself in earnest! We, too, though foreigners, have reigned. Bethink yourself not whence you sprang, but who you are. If in this sudden emergency you are slow to resolve, then follow my counsels." As the clamor and impatience of the populace could hardly be restrained, Tanaquil went to a window in the upper part of the palace looking out on the Via Nova—the king used to live by the temple of Jupiter Stator—and addressed the people. She bade them hope for the best; the king had been stunned by a sudden blow, but the weapon had not penetrated to any depth, he had already recovered consciousness, the blood had been washed off and the wound examined, all the symptoms were favorable, she was sure they would soon see him again, meantime it was his order that the people should recognize the authority of Servius Tullius, who would administer justice and discharge the other functions of royalty. Servius appeared in his trabea attended by the lictors, and after taking his seat in the royal chair decided some cases and adjourned others under presence of consulting the king. So for several days after Tarquin's death Servius continued to strengthen his position by giving out that he was exercising a delegated authority. At length the sounds of mourning arose in the palace and divulged the fact of the king's death. Protected by a strong bodyguard Servius was the first who ascended the throne without being elected by the people, though without opposition from the senate. When the sons of Ancus heard that the instruments of their crime had been arrested, that the king was still alive, and that Servius was so powerful, they went into exile at Suessa Pometia.

42. Servius consolidated his power quite as much by his private as by his public measures. To guard against the children of Tarquin treating him as those of Ancus had treated Tarquin, he married his two daughters to the scions of the royal house, Lucius and Arruns Tarquin. Human counsels could not arrest the inevitable course of destiny, nor could Servius prevent the jealousy aroused by his ascending the throne from making his family the scene of disloyalty and hatred. The truce with the Veientines had now expired, and the resumption of war with them and other Etruscan cities came most opportunely to help in maintaining tranquillity at home. In this war the courage and good fortune of Tullius were conspicuous, and he returned to Rome, after defeating an immense force of the enemy, feeling quite secure on the throne, and assured of the goodwill of both patricians and commons. Then he set himself to by far the greatest of all works in times of peace. Just as Numa had been the author of religious laws and institutions, so posterity extols Servius as the founder of those divisions and classes in the State by which a clear distinction is drawn between the various grades of dignity and fortune. He instituted the census, a most beneficial institution in what was to be a great empire, in order that by its means the various duties of peace and war might be assigned, not as heretofore, indiscriminately, but in proportion to the amount of property each man possessed. From it he drew up the classes and centuries and the following distribution of them, adapted for either peace or war.[1]

43. Those whose property amounted to, or exceeded, 100,000 lbs. weight of copper were formed into eighty centuries, forty of juniors and forty of seniors. These were called the First Class. The seniors were to defend the City, the juniors to serve in the field. The armor which they were to provide themselves with comprised helmet, round shield, greaves, and coat of mail, all of brass; these were to protect the person. Their offensive weapons were

---

[1] Modern scholars agree that Livy here describes the centuriate classes as they appeared in the fourth or third centuries B.C.E. The actual role of Servius Tullius in its creation is speculation.

spear and sword. To this class were joined two centuries of carpenters whose duty it was to work the engines of war; they were without arms. The Second Class consisted of those whose property amounted to between 75,000 and 100,000 lbs. weight of copper; they were formed, seniors and juniors together, into twenty centuries. Their regulation arms were the same as those of the First Class, except that they had an oblong wooden shield instead of the round brazen one and no coat of mail. The Third Class he formed of those whose property fell as low as 50,000 lbs.; these also consisted of twenty centuries, similarly divided into seniors and juniors. The only difference in the armor was that they did not wear greaves. In the Fourth Class were those whose property did not fall below 25,000 lbs. They also formed twenty centuries; their only arms were a spear and a javelin. The Fifth Class was larger it formed thirty centuries. They carried slings and stones, and they included the supernumeraries, the horn-blowers, and the trumpeters, who formed three centuries. This Fifth Class was assessed at 11,000 lbs. The rest of the population whose property fell below this were formed into one century and were exempt from military service.

After thus regulating the equipment and distribution of the infantry, he rearranged the cavalry. He enrolled from amongst the principal men of the State twelve centuries. In the same way he made six other centuries (though only three had been formed by Romulus) under the same names under which the first had been inaugurated. For the purchase of the horse, 10,000 lbs. were assigned them from the public treasury; whilst for its keep certain widows were assessed to pay 2,000 lbs. each, annually. The burden of all these expenses was shifted from the poor on to the rich. Then additional privileges were conferred. The former kings had maintained the constitution as handed down by Romulus, viz., manhood suffrage in which all alike possessed the same weight and enjoyed the same rights. Servius introduced a graduation; so that whilst no one was ostensibly deprived of his vote, all the voting power was in the hands of the principal men of the State. The knights were first summoned to record their vote, then the eighty centuries of the infantry of the First Class; if their votes were divided, which seldom happened, it was arranged for the Second Class to be summoned; very seldom did the voting extend to the lowest Class. Nor need it occasion any surprise, that the arrangement which now exists since the completion of the thirty-five tribes, their number being doubled by the centuries of juniors and seniors, does not agree with the total as instituted by Servius Tullius. For, after dividing the City with its districts and the hills which were inhabited into four parts, he called these divisions "tribes," I think from the tribute they paid, for he also introduced the practice of collecting it at an equal rate according to the assessment. These tribes had nothing to do with the distribution and number of the centuries.

44. The work of the census was accelerated by an enactment in which Servius announced imprisonment and even capital punishment against those who evaded assessment. On its completion he issued an order that all the citizens of Rome, knights and infantry alike, should appear in the Campus Martius, each in their centuries. After the whole army had been drawn up there, he purified it by the triple sacrifice of a swine, a sheep, and an ox. This was called "a closed lustrum," because with it the census was completed. Eighty thousand citizens are said to have been included in that census. Fabius Pictor, the oldest of our historians, states that this was the number of those who could bear arms. To contain that population it was obvious that the City would have to be enlarged. He added to it the two hills—the Quirinal and the Viminal—and then made a further addition by including the Esquiline, and to give it more importance he lived there himself. He surrounded the City with a mound and moats and wall; in this way he extended the "pomoerium." Looking only to the etymology of the word, they explain "pomoerium" as "postmoerium"; but it is rather a "circamoerium." For the space which the Etruscans of old, when founding their cities, consecrated in accordance with auguries and marked off by boundary stones at intervals on each side, as the part where the wall was to be carried, was to be kept vacant so that no buildings might connect with the wall on the inside (whilst now they generally touch), and on the outside some ground might remain virgin soil untouched by cultivation. This space, which it was forbidden either to build upon or to plough, and which could not be said to be behind the wall any more than the wall could be said to be behind it, the Romans called the "pomoerium." As the City grew, these sacred boundary stones were always moved forward as far as the walls were advanced.

45. After the State was augmented by the expansion of the City and all domestic arrangements adapted to the requirements of both peace and war, Servius endeavored to extend his dominion by statecraft, instead of aggrandizing it by arms, and at the same time made an addition to the adornment of the City. The temple of Diana of Ephesus was famous at that time, and it was reported to have been built by the co-operation of the states of Asia. Servius had been careful to form ties of hospitality and friendship with the chiefs of the Latin nation, and he used to speak in the highest praise of that co-operation and the common recognition of the same deity. By constantly dwelling on this theme he at length induced the Latin tribes to join with the people of Rome in building a temple to Diana in Rome. Their doing so was an admission of the predominance of Rome; a question which had so often been disputed by arms. Though the Latins, after their many unfortunate experiences in war, had as a nation laid aside all thoughts of success, there was amongst the Sabines one man who believed that an opportunity presented itself of recovering the supremacy through his own individual cunning. The story runs that a man of substance belonging to that nation had a heifer of marvelous size and beauty. The marvel was attested in after ages by the horns which were fastened up in the vestibule of the temple of Diana. The creature was looked upon as—what it really was—a prodigy, and the soothsayers predicted that, whoever sacrificed it to Diana, the state of which he was a citizen should be the seat of empire. This prophecy had reached the ears of the official in charge of the temple of Diana. When the first day on which the sacrifice could properly be offered arrived, the Sabine drove the heifer to Rome, took it to the temple, and placed it in front of the altar. The official in charge was a Roman, and, struck by the size of the victim, which was well known by report, he recalled the prophecy and addressing the Sabine, said, "Why, pray, are you, stranger, preparing to offer a polluted sacrifice to Diana? Go and bathe yourself first in running water. The Tiber is flowing down there at the bottom of the valley." Filled with misgivings, and anxious for everything to be done properly that the prediction might be fulfilled, the stranger promptly went down to the Tiber. Meanwhile the Roman sacrificed the heifer to Diana. This was a cause of intense gratification to the king and to his people.

46. Servius was now confirmed on the throne by long possession. It had, however, come to his ears that the young Tarquin was giving out that he was reigning without the assent of the people. He first secured the goodwill of the plebs by assigning to each householder a slice of the land which had been taken from the enemy. Then he was emboldened to put to them the question whether it was their will and resolve that he should reign. He was acclaimed as king by a unanimous vote such as no king before him had obtained. This action in no degree damped Tarquin's hopes of making his way to the throne, rather the reverse. He was a bold and aspiring youth, and his wife Tullia stimulated his restless ambition. He had seen that the granting of land to the commons was in defiance of the opinion of the senate, and he seized the opportunity it afforded him of traducing Servius and strengthening his own faction in that assembly. So it came about that the Roman palace afforded an instance of the crime which tragic poets have depicted, with the result that the loathing felt for kings hastened the advent of liberty, and the crown won by villainy was the last that was worn.

This Lucius Tarquinius—whether he was the son or the grandson of King Priscus Tarquinius is not clear; if I should give him as the son I should have the preponderance of authorities—had a brother, Arruns Tarquinius, a youth of gentle character. The two Tullias, the king's daughters, had, as I have already stated, married these two brothers; and they themselves were of utterly unlike dispositions. It was, I believe, the good fortune of Rome which intervened to prevent two violent natures from being joined in marriage, in order that the reign of Servius Tullius might last long enough to allow the

State to settle into its new constitution. The high-spirited one of the two, Tullias was annoyed that there was nothing in her husband for her to work on in the direction of either greed or ambition. All her affections were transferred to the other Tarquin; he was her admiration, he, she said, was a man, he was really of royal blood. She despised her sister, because having a man for her husband she was not animated by the spirit of a woman. Likeness of character soon drew them together, as evil usually consorts best with evil. But it was the woman who was the originator of all the mischief. She constantly held clandestine interviews with her sister's husband, to whom she unsparingly vilified alike her husband and her sister, asserting that it would have been better for her to have remained unmarried and he a bachelor, rather than for them each to be thus unequally mated, and fret in idleness through the poltroonery of others. Had heaven given her the husband she deserved, she would soon have seen the sovereignty which her father wielded established in her own house. She rapidly infected the young man with her own recklessness. Lucius Tarquin and the younger Tullia, by a double murder, cleared from their houses the obstacles to a fresh marriage; their nuptials were solemnized with the tacit acquiescence rather than the approbation of Servius.

47. From that time the old age of Tullius became more embittered, his reign more unhappy. The woman began to look forward from one crime to another; she allowed her husband no rest day or night, for fear lest the past murders should prove fruitless. What she wanted, she said, was not a man who was only her husband in name, or with whom she was to live in uncomplaining servitude; the man she needed was one who deemed himself worthy of a throne, who remembered that he was the son of Priscus Tarquinius, who preferred to wear a crown rather than live in hopes of it. "If you are the man to whom I thought I was married, then I call you my husband and my king; but if not, I have changed my condition for the worse, since you are not only a coward but a criminal to boot. Why do you not prepare yourself for action? You are not, like your father, a native of Corinth or Tarquinii, nor is it a foreign crown you have to win. Your father's household gods, your father's image, the royal palace, the kingly throne within it, the very name of Tarquin, all declare you king. If you have not courage enough for this, why do you excite vain hopes in the State? Why do you allow yourself to be looked up to as a youth of kingly stock? Make your way back to Tarquinii or Corinth, sink back to the position whence you sprung; you have your brother's nature rather than your father's." With taunts like these she egged him on. She, too, was perpetually haunted by the thought that whilst Tanaquil, a woman of alien descent, had shown such spirit as to give the crown to her husband and her son-in-law in succession, she herself, though of royal descent, had no power either in giving it or taking it away. Infected by

the woman's madness Tarquin began to go about and interview the nobles, mainly those of the Lesser Houses; he reminded them of the favor his father had shown them, and asked them to prove their gratitude; he won over the younger men with presents. By making magnificent promises as to what he would do, and by bringing charges against the king, his cause became stronger amongst all ranks.

At last, when he thought the time for action had arrived, he appeared suddenly in the Forum with a body of armed men. A general panic ensued, during which he seated himself in the royal chair in the senate-house and ordered the Fathers to be summoned by the crier "into the presence of King Tarquin." They hastily assembled, some already prepared for what was coming; others, apprehensive lest their absence should arouse suspicion, and dismayed by the extraordinary nature of the incident, were convinced that the fate of Servius was sealed. Tarquin went back to the king's birth, protested that he was a slave and the son of a slave, and after his (the speaker's) father had been foully murdered, seized the throne, as a woman's gift, without any interrex being appointed as heretofore, without any assembly being convened, without any vote of the people being taken or any confirmation of it by the Fathers. Such was his origin, such was his right to the crown. His sympathies were with the dregs of society from which he had sprung, and through jealousy of the ranks to which he did not belong, he had taken the land from the foremost men in the State and divided it amongst the vilest; he had shifted on to them the whole of the burdens which had formerly been borne in common by all; he had instituted the census that the fortunes of the wealthy might be held up to envy, and be an easily available source from which to shower doles, whenever he pleased, upon the neediest.

48. Servius had been summoned by a breathless messenger, and arrived on the scene while Tarquin was speaking. As soon as he reached the vestibule, he exclaimed in loud tones, "What is the meaning of this, Tarquin? How dared you, with such insolence, convene the senate or sit in that chair whilst I am alive?" Tarquin replied fiercely that he was occupying his father's seat, that a king's son was a much more legitimate heir to the throne than a slave, and that he, Servius, in playing his reckless game, had insulted his masters long enough. Shouts arose from their respective partisans, the people made a rush to the senate-house, and it was evident that he who won the fight would reign. Then Tarquin, forced by sheer necessity into proceeding to the last extremity, seized Servius round the waist, and being a much younger and stronger man, carried him out of the senate-house and flung him down the steps into the Forum below. He then returned to call the senate to order. The officers and attendants of the king fled. The king himself, half dead from the violence, was put to death by those whom Tarquin had sent in pursuit of him. It is the current belief that this was done at Tullia's suggestion, for it is quite in keeping with the rest of her wickedness. At all events, it is generally agreed that she drove down to the Forum in a two-wheeled car, and, unabashed by the presence of the crowd, called her husband out of the senate-house and was the first to salute him as king. He told her to make her way out of the tumult, and when on her return she had got as far as the top of the Cyprius Vicus, where the temple of Diana lately stood, and was turning to the right on the Urbius Clivus, to get to the Esquiline, the driver stopped horror-struck and pulled up, and pointed out to his mistress the corpse of the murdered Servius. Then, the tradition runs, a foul and unnatural crime was committed, the memory of which the place still bears, for they call it the Vicus Sceleratus—the "street of crime." It is said that Tullia, goaded to madness by the avenging spirits of her sister and her husband, drove right over her father's body, and carried back some of her father's blood with which the car and she herself were defiled to her own and her husband's household gods, through whose anger a reign which began in wickedness was soon brought to a close by a like cause. Servius Tullius reigned forty-four years, and even a wise and good successor would have found it difficult to fill the throne as he had done. The glory of his reign was all the greater because with him perished all just and lawful kingship in Rome. Gentle and moderate as his sway had been, he had nevertheless, according to some authorities, formed the intention of laying it down, because it was vested in a single person, but this purpose of giving freedom to the State was cut short by that domestic crime.

49. Lucius Tarquinius now began his reign. His conduct procured for him the nickname of "Superbus," for he deprived his father-in-law of burial, on the plea that Romulus was not buried, and he slew the leading nobles whom he suspected of being partisans of Servius. Conscious that the precedent which he had set, of winning a throne by violence, might be used against himself, he surrounded himself with a guard. For he had nothing whatever by which to make good his claim to the crown except actual violence; he was reigning without either being elected by the people, or confirmed by the senate. As, moreover, he had no hope of winning the affections of the citizens, he had to maintain his dominion by fear. To make himself more dreaded, he conducted the trials in capital cases without any assessors, and under this presence he was able to put to death, banish, or fine not only those whom he suspected or disliked, but also those from whom his only object was to extort money. His main object was so to reduce the number of senators, by refusing to fill up any vacancies, that the dignity of the order itself might be lowered through the smallness of its numbers, and less indignation felt at all public business being taken out of its hands. He was the first of the kings to break through the traditional custom of consulting the senate on all questions, the first to conduct the government on the advice of his palace favorites. War, peace, treaties, alliances were made or broken off by him, just as he thought good, without any authority from either people or senate. He made a special point of securing the Latin nation, that through his power and influence abroad he might be safer amongst his subjects at home; he not only formed ties of hospitality with their chief men, but established family connections. He gave his daughter in marriage to Octavius Mamilius of Tusculum, who was quite the foremost man of the Latin race, descended, if we are to believe traditions, from Ulysses and the goddess Circe; through that connection he gained many of his son-in-law's relations and friends.

§

55. After the acquisition of Gabii, Tarquin made peace with the Aequi and renewed the treaty with the Etruscans. Then he turned his attention to the business of the City. The first thing was the temple of Jupiter on the Tarpeian Mount, which he was anxious to leave behind as a memorial of his reign and name; both the Tarquins were concerned in it, the father had vowed it, the son completed it. That the whole of the area which the temple of Jupiter was to occupy might be wholly devoted to that deity, he decided to deconsecrate the fanes and chapels, some of which had been originally vowed by King Tatius at the crisis of his battle with Romulus, and subsequently consecrated and inaugurated. Tradition records that at the commencement of this work the gods sent a divine intimation of the future vastness of the empire, for whilst the omens were favorable for the deconsecration of all the other shrines, they were unfavorable for that of the shrine of Terminus. This was interpreted to mean that as the abode of Terminus was not moved and he alone of all the deities was not called forth from his consecrated borders, so all would be firm and immovable in the future empire. This augury of lasting dominion was followed by a prodigy which portended the greatness of the empire. It is said that whilst they were digging the foundations of the temple, a human head came to light with the face perfect; this appearance unmistakably portended that the spot would be the stronghold of empire and the head of all the world. This was the interpretation given by the soothsayers in the City, as well as by those who had been called into council from Etruria. The king's designs were now much more extensive; so much so that his share of the spoils of Pometia, which had been set apart to complete the work, now hardly met the cost of the foundations. This makes me inclined to trust Fabius—who, moreover is the older authority—when he says that the amount was only forty talents, rather than Piso, who states that forty thousand pounds of silver were set apart for that object. For not only is such a sum more than could be expected from the spoils of any single city at that time, but it would more than suffice for the foundations of the most magnificent building of the present day.

56. Determined to finish his temple, he sent for workmen from all parts of Etruria, and not only used the public treasury to defray the cost, but also compelled the plebeians to take their share of the work. This was in addition to their military service, and was anything but a light burden. Still they felt it less of a hardship to build the temples of the gods with their own hands, than they did afterwards when they were transferred to other tasks less imposing, but involving greater toil—the construction of the Decks in the Circus and that of the Cloaca Maxima, a subterranean tunnel to receive all the sewage of the City. The magnificence of these two works could hardly be equaled by anything in the present day. When the plebeians were no longer required for these works, he considered that such a multitude of unemployed would prove a burden to the State, and as he wished the frontiers of the empire to be more widely colonized, he sent colonists to Signia and Circeii to serve as a protection to the City by land and sea. While he was carrying out these undertakings a frightful portent appeared; a snake gliding out of a wooden column created confusion and panic in the palace. The king himself was not so much terrified as filled with anxious forebodings. The Etruscan soothsayers were only employed to interpret prodigies which affected the State; but this one concerned him and his house personally, so he decided to send to the world-famed oracle of Delphi. Fearing to entrust the oracular response to any one else, he sent two of his sons to Greece, through lands at that time unknown and over seas still less known. Titus and Arruns started on their journey. They had as a traveling companion L. Junius Brutus, the son of the king's sister, Tarquinia, a young man of a very different character from that which he had assumed. When he heard of the massacre of the chiefs of the State, amongst them his own brother, by his uncle's orders, he determined that his intelligence should give the king no cause for alarm nor his fortune any provocation to his avarice, and that as the laws afforded no protection, he would seek safety in obscurity and neglect. Accordingly he carefully kept up the appearance and conduct of an idiot, leaving the king to do what he liked with his person and property, and did not even protest against his nickname of "Brutus"; for under the protection of that nickname the soul which was one day to liberate Rome was awaiting its destined hour. The story runs that when brought to Delphi by the Tarquins, more as a butt for their sport than as a companion, he had with him a golden staff enclosed in a hollow one of corner wood, which he offered to Apollo as a mystical emblem of his own character. After executing their father's commission the young men were desirous of ascertaining to which of them the kingdom of Rome would come. A voice came from the lowest depths of the cavern: "Whichever of you, young men, shall be the first to kiss his mother, he shall hold supreme sway in Rome." Sextus had remained behind in Rome, and to keep him in ignorance of this oracle and so deprive him of any chance of coming to the throne, the two Tarquins insisted upon absolute silence being kept on the subject. They drew lots to decide which of them should be the first to kiss his mother on their return to Rome. Brutus, thinking that the oracular utterance had another meaning, pretended to stumble, and as he fell kissed the ground, for the earth is of course the common mother of us all. Then they returned to Rome, where preparations were being energetically pushed forward for a war with the Rutulians.

57. This people, who were at that time in possession of Ardea, were, considering the nature of their country and the age in which they lived, exceptionally wealthy. This circumstance really originated the war, for the Roman king was anxious to repair his own fortune, which had been exhausted by the magnificent scale of his public works, and also to conciliate his subjects by a distribution of the spoils of war. His tyranny had already produced disaffection, but what moved their special resentment was the way they had been so long kept by the king at manual and even servile labor. An attempt was made to take Ardea by assault; when that failed recourse was had to a regular investment to starve the enemy out. When troops are stationary, as is the case in a protracted more than in an active campaign, furloughs are easily granted, more so to the men of rank, however, than to the common soldiers. The royal princes sometimes spent their leisure hours in feasting and entertainments, and at a wine party given by Sextus Tarquinius at which Collatinus, the son of Egerius, was present, the conversation happened to turn upon their wives, and each began to speak of his own in terms of extraordinarily high praise. As the dispute became warm, Collatinus said that there was no need of words, it could in a few hours be ascertained how far his Lucretia was superior to all the rest. "Why do we not," he exclaimed, "if we have any youthful vigor about us, mount our horses and pay our wives a visit and find out their characters on the spot? What we see of the behavior of each on the unexpected arrival of her husband, let that be the surest test." They were heated with wine, and all shouted: "Good! Come on!" Setting spur to their horses they galloped off to Rome, where they arrived as darkness was beginning to close in. Thence they proceeded to Collatia, where they found Lucretia very differently employed from the king's daughters-in-law, whom they had seen passing their time in feasting and luxury with their acquaintances. She was sitting at her wool work in the hall, late at night, with her maids busy round her. The palm in this competition of wifely virtue was awarded to Lucretia. She welcomed the arrival of her husband and the Tarquins, whilst her victorious spouse courteously invited the royal princes to remain as his guests. Sextus Tarquin, inflamed by the beauty and exemplary purity of Lucretia, formed the vile project of effecting her dishonor. After their youthful frolic they returned for the time to camp.

58. A few days afterwards Sextus Tarquin went, unknown to Collatinus,

with one companion to Collatia. He was hospitably received by the household, who suspected nothing, and after supper was conducted to the bedroom set apart for guests. When all around seemed safe and everybody fast asleep, he went in the frenzy of his passion with a naked sword to the sleeping Lucretia, and placing his left hand on her breast, said, "Silence, Lucretia! I am Sextus Tarquin, and I have a sword in my hand; if you utter a word, you shall die." When the woman, terrified out of her sleep, saw that no help was near, and instant death threatening her, Tarquin began to confess his passion, pleaded, used threats as well as entreaties, and employed every argument likely to influence a female heart. When he saw that she was inflexible and not moved even by the fear of death, he threatened to disgrace her, declaring that he would lay the naked corpse of the slave by her dead body, so that it might be said that she had been slain in foul adultery. By this awful threat, his lust triumphed over her inflexible chastity, and Tarquin went off exulting in having successfully attacked her honor. Lucretia, overwhelmed with grief at such a frightful outrage, sent a messenger to her father at Rome and to her husband at Ardea, asking them to come to her, each accompanied by one faithful friend; it was necessary to act, and to act promptly; a horrible thing had happened. Spurius Lucretius came with Publius Valerius, the son of Volesus; Collatinus with Lucius Junius Brutus, with whom he happened to be returning to Rome when he was met by his wife's messenger. They found Lucretia sitting in her room prostrate with grief. As they entered, she burst into tears, and to her husband's inquiry whether all was well, replied, "No! what can be well with a woman when her honor is lost? The marks of a stranger, Collatinus, are in your bed. But it is only the body that has been violated, the soul is pure; death shall bear witness to that. But pledge me your solemn word that the adulterer shall not go unpunished. It is Sextus Tarquin, who, coming as an enemy instead of a guest, forced from me last night by brutal violence a pleasure fatal to me, and, if you are men, fatal to him." They all successively pledged their word, and tried to console the distracted woman by turning the guilt from the victim of the outrage to the perpetrator, and urging that it is the mind that sins, not the body, and where there has been no consent there is no guilt. "It is for you," she said, "to see that he gets his deserts; although I acquit myself of the sin, I do not free myself from the penalty; no unchaste woman shall henceforth live and plead Lucretia's example." She had a knife concealed in her dress which she plunged into her heart, and fell dying on the floor. Her father and husband raised the death-cry.

59. Whilst they were absorbed in grief, Brutus drew the knife from Lucretia's wound, and holding it, dripping with blood, in front of him, said, "By this blood—most pure before the outrage wrought by the king's son—I swear, and you, O gods, I call to witness that I will drive hence Lucius Tarquinius Superbus, together with his cursed wife and his whole brood, with fire and sword and every means in my power, and I will not suffer them or any one else to reign in Rome." Then he handed the knife to Collatinus and then to Lucretius and Valerius, who were all astounded at the marvel of the thing, wondering whence Brutus had acquired this new character. They swore as they were directed; all their grief changed to wrath, and they followed the lead of Brutus, who summoned them to abolish the monarchy forthwith. They carried the body of Lucretia from her home down to the Forum, where, owing to the unheard-of atrocity of the crime, they at once collected a crowd. Each had his own complaint to make of the wickedness and violence of the royal house. Whilst all were moved by the father's deep distress, Brutus bade them stop their tears and idle laments, and urged them to act as men and Romans and take up arms against their insolent foes. All the high-spirited amongst the younger men came forward as armed volunteers, the rest followed their example. A portion of this body was left to hold Collatia, and guards were stationed at the gates to prevent any news of the movement from reaching the king; the rest marched in arms to Rome with Brutus in command. On their arrival, the sight of so many men in arms spread panic and confusion wherever they marched, but when again the people saw that the foremost men of the State were leading the way, they realized that whatever the movement was it was a serious one. The terrible occurrence created no less excitement in Rome than it had done in Collatia; there was a rush from all quarters of the City to the Forum. When they had gathered there, the herald summoned them to attend the "Tribune of the Celeres"; this was the office which Brutus happened at the time to be holding. He made a speech quite out of keeping with the character and temper he had up to that day assumed. He dwelt upon the brutality and licentiousness of Sextus Tarquin, the infamous outrage on Lucretia and her pitiful death, the bereavement sustained by her father, Tricipitinus, to whom the cause of his daughter's death was more shameful and distressing than the actual death itself. Then he dwelt on the tyranny of the king, the toils and sufferings of the plebeians kept underground clearing out ditches and sewers—Roman men, conquerors of all the surrounding nations, turned from warriors into artisans and stonemasons! He reminded them of the shameful murder of Servius Tullius and his daughter driving in her accursed chariot over her father's body, and solemnly invoked the gods as the avengers of murdered parents. By enumerating these and, I believe, other still more atrocious incidents which his keen sense of the present injustice suggested, but which it is not easy to give in detail, he goaded on the incensed multitude to strip the king of his sovereignty and pronounce a sentence of banishment against Tarquin with his wife and children. With a picked body of the "Juniors," who volunteered to follow him, he went off to the camp at Ardea to incite the army against the king, leaving the command in the City to Lucretius, who had previously been made Prefect of the City by the king. During the commotion Tullia fled from the palace amidst the execrations of all whom she met, men and women alike invoking against her father's avenging spirit.

60. When the news of these proceedings reached the camp, the king, alarmed at the turn affairs were taking, hurried to Rome to quell the outbreak. Brutus, who was on the same road had become aware of his approach, and to avoid meeting him took another route, so that he reached Ardea and Tarquin Rome almost at the same time, though by different ways. Tarquin found the gates shut, and a decree of banishment passed against him; the Liberator of the City received a joyous welcome in the camp, and the king's sons were expelled from it. Two of them followed their father into exile amongst the Etruscans in Caere. Sextus Tarquin proceeded to Gabii, which he looked upon as his kingdom, but was killed in revenge for the old feuds he had kindled by his rapine and murders. Lucius Tarquinius Superbus reigned twenty-five years. The whole duration of the regal government from the foundation of the City to its liberation was two hundred and forty-four years. Two consuls were then elected in the assembly of centuries by the prefect of the City, in accordance with the regulations of Servius Tullius. They were Lucius Junius Brutus and Lucius Tarquinius Collatinus.

BOOK II 1–14

The Tarquins take refuge with Lars Porsinna, king of Clusium, who threatens the new republic until the heroism of Mucius Scaevola persuades him to withdraw.

1. It is of a Rome henceforth free that I am to write the history—her civil administration and the conduct of her wars, her annually elected magistrates, the authority of her laws supreme over all her citizens. The tyranny of the last king made this liberty all the more welcome, for such had been the rule of the former kings that they might not undeservedly be counted as founders of parts, at all events, of the city; for the additions they made were required as abodes for the increased population which they themselves had augmented. There is no question that the Brutus who won such glory through the expulsion of Superbus would have inflicted the gravest injury on the State had he wrested the sovereignty from any of the former kings, through desire of a liberty for which the people were not ripe. What would have been the result if that horde of shepherds and immigrants, fugitives from their own cities, who had secured liberty, or at all events impunity, in the shelter of an inviolable sanctuary,—if, I say, they had been freed from the restraining power of kings and, agitated by democratic storms, had begun to

foment quarrels with the patricians in a City where they were aliens before sufficient time had elapsed for either family ties or a growing love for the very soil to effect a union of hearts? The infant State would have been torn to pieces by internal dissension. As it was, however, the moderate and tranquilizing authority of the kings had so fostered it that it was at last able to bring forth the fair fruits of liberty in the maturity of its strength. But the origin of liberty may be referred to this time rather because the consular authority was limited to one year than because there was any weakening of the authority which the kings had possessed. The first consuls retained all the old jurisdiction and insignia of office, one only, however, had the *fasces,* to prevent the fear which might have been inspired by the sight of both with those dread symbols. Through the concession of his colleague, Brutus had them first, and he was not less zealous in guarding the public liberty than he had been in achieving it. His first act was to secure the people, who were now jealous of their newly-recovered liberty, from being influenced by any entreaties or bribes from the king. He therefore made them take an oath that they would not suffer any man to reign in Rome. The senate had been thinned by the murderous cruelty of Tarquin, and Brutus' next care was to strengthen its influence by selecting some of the leading men of equestrian rank to fill the vacancies; by this means he brought it up to the old number of three hundred. The new members were known as "conscripti," the old ones retained their designation of "patres." This measure had a wonderful effect in promoting harmony in the State and bringing the patricians and plebeians together.

2. He next gave his attention to the affairs of religion. Certain public functions had hitherto been executed by the kings in person; with the view of supplying their place a "king for sacrifices" was created, and lest he should become king in anything more than name, and so threaten that liberty which was their first care, his office was made subordinate to the Pontifex Maximus. I think that they went to unreasonable lengths in devising safeguards for their liberty, in all, even the smallest points. The second consul—L. Tarquinius Collatinus—bore an unpopular name—this was his sole offense—and men said that the Tarquins had been too long in power. They began with Priscus; then Servius Tullius reigned, and Superbus Tarquinius, who even after this interruption had not lost sight of the throne which another filled, regained it by crime and violence as the hereditary possession of his house. And now that he was expelled, their power was being wielded by Collatinus; the Tarquins did not know how to live in a private station, the very name was a danger to liberty. What were at first whispered hints became the common talk of the City, and as the people were becoming suspicious and alarmed, Brutus summoned an assembly. He first of all rehearsed the people's oath, that they would suffer no man to reign or to live in Rome by whom the public liberty might be imperiled. This was to be guarded with the utmost care, no means of doing so were to be neglected. Personal regard made him reluctant to speak, nor would he have spoken had not his affection for the commonwealth compelled him. The Roman people did consider that their freedom was not yet fully won; the royal race, the royal name, was still there, not only amongst the citizens but in the government; in that fact lay an injury, an obstacle to full liberty. Turning to his brother consul: "These apprehensions it is for you, L. Tarquinius, to banish of your own free will. We have not forgotten, I assure you, that you expelled the king's family, complete your good work, remove their very name. Your fellow-citizens will, on my authority, not only hand over your property, but if you need anything, they will add to it with lavish generosity. Go, as our friend, relieve the commonwealth from a, perhaps groundless, fear: men are persuaded that only with the family will the tyranny of the Tarquins depart." At first the consul was struck dumb with astonishment at this extraordinary request; then, when he was beginning to speak, the foremost men in the commonwealth gathered round him and repeatedly urged the same plea, but with little success. It was not till Spurius Lucretius, his superior in age and rank, and also his father-in-law, began to use every method of entreaty and persuasion that he yielded to the universal wish. The consul, fearing lest after his year of office had expired and he returned to private life, the same demand should be made upon him, accompanied with loss of property and the ignominy of banishment, formally laid down the consulship, and after transferring all his effects to Lanuvium, withdrew from the State. A decree of the senate empowered Brutus to propose to the people a measure exiling all the members of the house of Tarquin. He conducted the election of a new consul, and the centuries elected as his colleague Publius Valerius, who had acted with him in the expulsion of the royal family.

3. Though no one doubted that war with the Tarquins was imminent, it did not come as soon as was universally expected. What was not expected, however, was that through intrigue and treachery the new-won liberty was almost lost. There were some young men of high birth in Rome who during the late reign had done pretty much what they pleased, and being boon companions of the young Tarquins were accustomed to live in royal fashion. Now that all were equal before the law, they missed their former license and complained that the liberty which others enjoyed had become slavery for them; as long as there was a king, there was a person from whom they could get what they wanted, whether lawful or not, there was room for personal influence and kindness, he could show severity or indulgence, could discriminate between his friends and his enemies. But the law was a thing, deaf and inexorable, more favorable to the weak than to the powerful, showing no indulgence or forgiveness to those who transgressed; human nature being

what it was, it was a dangerous plan to trust solely to one's innocence. When they had worked themselves into a state of disaffection, envoys from the royal family arrived, bringing a demand for the restoration of their property without any allusion to their possible return. An audience was granted them by the senate, and the matter was discussed for some days; fears were expressed that the non-surrender would be taken as a pretext for war, while if surrendered it might provide the means of war. The envoys, meantime, were engaged on another task: whilst ostensibly seeking only the surrender of the property they were secretly hatching schemes for regaining the crown. Whilst canvassing the young nobility in favor of their apparent object, they sounded them as to their other proposals, and meeting with a favorable reception, they brought letters addressed to them by the Tarquins and discussed plans for admitting them secretly at night into the City.

4. The project was at first entrusted to the brothers Vitellii and Aquilii. The sister of the Vitellii was married to the consul Brutus, and there were grown-up children from this marriage—Titus and Tiberius. Their uncles took them into the conspiracy, there were others besides, whose names have been lost. In the meantime the opinion that the property ought to be restored was adopted by the majority of the senate, and this enabled the envoys to prolong their stay, as the consuls required time to provide vehicles for conveying the goods. They employed their time in consultations with the conspirators and they insisted on getting a letter which they were to give to the Tarquins, for without such a guarantee, they argued, how could they be sure that their envoys had not brought back empty promises in a matter of such vast importance? A letter was accordingly given as a pledge of good faith, and this it was that led to the discovery of the plot. The day previous to the departure of the envoys they happened to be dining at the house of the Vitellii. After all who were not in the secret had left, the conspirators discussed many details respecting their projected treason, which were overheard by one of the slaves who had previously suspected that something was afoot, but was waiting for the moment when the letter should be given, as its seizure would be a complete proof of the plot. When he found that it had been given, he disclosed the affair to the consuls. They at once proceeded to arrest the envoys and the conspirators, and crushed the whole plot without exciting any alarm. Their first care was to secure the letter before it was destroyed. The traitors were forthwith thrown into prison; there was some hesitation in dealing with the envoys, and although they had evidently been guilty of a hostile act, the rights of international law were accorded them.

5. The question of the restoration of the property was referred anew to the senate, who yielding to their feelings of resentment prohibited its restoration, and forbade its being brought into the treasury; it was given as plunder to the plebs, that their share in this spoliation might destroy for ever

any prospect of peaceable relations with the Tarquins. The land of the Tarquins, which lay between the City and the Tiber, was henceforth sacred to Mars and known as the Campus Martius. There happened, it is said, to be a crop of corn there which was ripe for the harvest, and as it would have been sacrilege to consume what was growing on the Campus, a large body of men were sent to cut it. They carried it, straw and all, in baskets to the Tiber and threw it into the river. It was the height of the summer and the stream was low, consequently the corn stuck in the shallows, and heaps of it were covered with mud; gradually as the debris which the river brought down collected there, an island was formed. I believe that it was subsequently raised and strengthened so that the surface might be high enough above the water and firm enough to carry temples and colonnades. After the royal property had been disposed of, the traitors were sentenced and executed. Their punishment created a great sensation owing to the fact that the consular office imposed upon a father the duty of inflicting punishment on his own children; he who ought not to have witnessed it was destined to be the one to see it duly carried out. Youths belonging to the noblest families were standing tied to the post, but all eyes were turned to the consul's children, the others were unnoticed. Men did not grieve more for their punishment than for the crime which had incurred it—that they should have conceived the idea, in that year above all, of betraying to one, who had been a ruthless tyrant and was now an exile and an enemy, a newly liberated country, their father who had liberated it, the consulship which had originated in the Junian house, the senate, the plebs, all that Rome possessed of human or divine. The consuls took their seats, the lictors were told off to inflict the penalty; they scourged their bared backs with rods and then beheaded them. During the whole time, the father's countenance betrayed his feelings, but the father's stern resolution was still more apparent as he superintended the public execution. After the guilty had paid the penalty, a notable example of a different nature was provided to act as a deterrent of crime, the informer was assigned a sum of money from the treasury and he was given his liberty and the rights of citizenship. He is said to have been the first to be made free by the "vindicta." Some suppose this designation to have been derived from him, his name being Vindicius. After him it was the rule that those who were made free in this way were considered to be admitted to the citizenship.

6. A detailed report of these matters reached Tarquin. He was not only furious at the failure of plans from which he had hoped so much, but he was filled with rage at finding the way blocked against secret intrigues; and consequently determined upon open war. He visited the cities of Etruria and appealed for help; in particular, he implored the people of Veii and Tarquinii not to allow one to perish before their eyes who was of the same blood with them, and from being a powerful monarch was now, with his children, home-

less and destitute. Others, he said, had been invited from abroad to reign in Rome; he, the king, whilst extending the rule of Rome by a successful war, had been driven out by the infamous conspiracy of his nearest kinsmen. They had no single person amongst them deemed worthy to reign, so they had distributed the kingly authority amongst themselves, and had given his property as plunder to the people, that all might be involved in the crime. He wanted to recover his country and his throne and punish his ungrateful subjects. The Veientines must help him and furnish him with resources, they must set about avenging their own wrongs also, their legions so often cut to pieces, their territory torn from them. This appeal decided the Veientines, they one and all loudly demanded that their former humiliations should be wiped out and their losses made good, now that they had a Roman to lead them. The people of Tarquinii were won over by the name and nationality of the exile; they were proud of having a countryman as king in Rome. So two armies from these cities followed Tarquin to recover his crown and chastise the Romans. When they had entered the Roman territory the consuls advanced against them; Valerius with the infantry in phalanx formation, Brutus reconnoitering in advance with the cavalry. Similarly the enemy's cavalry was in front of his main body, Arruns Tarquin, the king's son, in command; the king himself followed with the legionaries. Whilst still at a distance Arruns distinguished the consul by his escort of lictors; as they drew nearer he clearly recognized Brutus by his features, and in a transport of rage exclaimed, "That is the man who drove us from our country; see him proudly advancing, adorned with our insignia! Ye gods, avengers of kings, aid me!" With these words, he dug spurs into his horse and rode straight at the consul. Brutus saw that he was making for him. It was a point of honor in those days for the leaders to engage in single combat, so he eagerly accepted the challenge, and they charged with such fury, neither of them thinking of protecting himself, if only he could wound his foe, that each drove his spear at the same moment through the other's shield, and they fell dying from their horses, with the spears sticking in them. The rest of the cavalry at once engaged, and not long after the infantry came up. The battle raged with varying fortune, the two armies being fairly matched; the right wing of each was victorious, the left defeated. The Veientines, accustomed to defeat at the hands of the Romans, were scattered in flight, but the Tarquinians, a new foe, not only held their ground, but forced the Romans to give way.

7. After the battle had gone in this way, so great a panic seized Tarquin and the Etruscans that the two armies of Veii and Tarquinii, on the approach of night, despairing of success, left the field and departed for their homes. The story of the battle was enriched by marvels. In the silence of the next night a great voice is said to have come from the forest of Arsia, believed to be the voice of Silvanus, which spoke thus: "The fallen of the Tusci are one

more than those of their foe; the Roman is conqueror." At all events the Romans left the field as victors; the Etruscans regarded themselves as vanquished, for when daylight appeared not a single enemy was in sight. P. Valerius, the consul, collected the spoils and returned in triumph to Rome. He celebrated his colleague's obsequies with all the pomp possible in those days, but far greater honor was done to the dead by the universal mourning, which was rendered specially noteworthy by the fact that the matrons were a whole year in mourning for him, because he had been such a determined avenger of violated chastity. After this the surviving consul, who had been in such favor with the multitude, found himself—such is its fickleness—not only unpopular but an object of suspicion, and that of a very grave character. It was rumored that he was aiming at monarchy, for he had held no election to fill Brutus' place, and he was building a house on the top of the Velia, an impregnable fortress was being constructed on that high and strong position. The consul felt hurt at finding these rumors so widely believed, and summoned the people to an assembly. As he entered the "fasces" were lowered, to the great delight of the multitude, who understood that it was to them that they were lowered as an open avowal that the dignity and might of the people were greater than those of the consul. Then, after securing silence, he began to eulogize the good fortune of his colleague who had met his death, as a liberator of his country, possessing the highest honor it could bestow, fighting for the commonwealth, whilst his glory was as yet undimmed by jealousy and distrust. Whereas he himself had outlived his glory and fallen on days of suspicion and opprobrium; from being a liberator of his country he had sunk to the level of the Aquilii and Vitellii. "Will you," he cried, "never deem any man's merit so assured that it cannot be tainted by suspicion? Am I, the most determined foe to kings to dread the suspicion of desiring to be one myself? Even if I were dwelling in the Citadel on the Capitol, am I to believe it possible that I should be feared by my fellow-citizens? Does my reputation amongst you hang on so slight a thread? Does your confidence rest upon such a weak foundation that it is of greater moment where I am than who I am? The house of Publius Valerius shall be no check upon your freedom, your Velia shall be safe. I will not only move my house to level ground, but I will move it to the bottom of the hill that you may dwell above the citizen whom you suspect. Let those dwell on the Velia who are regarded as truer friends of liberty than Publius Valerius." All the materials were forthwith carried below the Velia and his house was built at the very bottom of the hill where now stands the temple of Vica Pota.

8. Laws were passed which not only cleared the consul from suspicion but produced such a reaction that he won the people's affections, hence his sobriquet of Publicola. The most popular of these laws were those which granted a right of appeal from the magistrate to the people and devoted to

the gods the person and property of any one who entertained projects of becoming king. Valerius secured the passing of these laws while still sole consul, that the people might feel grateful solely to him; afterwards he held the elections for the appointment of a colleague. The consul elected was Sp. Lucretius. But he had not, owing to his great age, strength enough to discharge the duties of his office, and within a few days he died. M. Horatius Pulvillus was elected in his place. In some ancient authors I find no mention of Lucretius, Horatius being named immediately after Brutus; as he did nothing of any note during his office, I suppose, his memory has perished. The temple of Jupiter on the Capitol had not yet been dedicated, and the consuls drew lots to decide which should dedicate it. The lot fell to Horatius. Publicola set out for the Veientine war. His friends showed unseemly annoyance at the dedication of so illustrious a shrine being assigned to Horatius, and tried every means of preventing it. When all else failed, they tried to alarm the consul, whilst he was actually holding the door-post during the dedicatory prayer, by a wicked message that his son was dead, and he could not dedicate a temple while death was in his house. As to whether he disbelieved the message, or whether his conduct simply showed extraordinary self-control, there is no definite tradition, and it is not easy to decide from the records. He only allowed the message to interrupt him so far that he gave orders for the body to be burnt; then, with his hand still on the door-post, he finished the prayer and dedicated the temple. These were the principal incidents at home and in the field during the first year after the expulsion of the royal family. The consuls elected for the next year were P. Valerius, for the second time, and T. Lucretius.

9. The Tarquins had now taken refuge with Porsena, the king of Clusium, whom they sought to influence by entreaty mixed with warnings. At one time they entreated him not to allow men of Etruscan race, of the same blood as himself, to wander as penniless exiles; at another they would warn him not to let the new fashion of expelling kings go unpunished. Liberty, they urged, possessed fascination enough in itself; unless kings defend their authority with as much energy as their subjects show in quest of liberty, all things come to a dead level, there will be no one thing pre-eminent or superior to all else in the State; there will soon be an end of kingly power, which is the most beautiful thing, whether amongst gods or amongst mortal men. Porsena considered that the presence of an Etruscan upon the Roman throne would be an honor to his nation; accordingly he advanced with an army against Rome. Never before had the senate been in such a state of alarm, so great at that time was the power of Clusium and the reputation of Porsena. They feared not only the enemy but even their own fellow-citizens, lest the plebs, overcome by their fears, should admit the Tarquins into the City, and accept peace even though it meant slavery. Many concessions were made at that time to the plebs by the senate. Their first care was to lay in a stock of corn, and commissioners were dispatched to Vulsi and Cumae to collect supplies. The sale of salt, hitherto in the hands of private individuals who had raised the price to a high figure, was now wholly transferred to the State. The plebs were exempted from the payment of harbor-dues and the war-tax, so that they might fall on the rich, who could bear the burden; the poor were held to pay sufficient to the State if they brought up their children. This generous action of the senate maintained the harmony of the commonwealth through the subsequent stress of siege and famine so completely that the name of king was not more abhorrent to the highest than it was to the lowest, nor did any demagogue ever succeed in becoming so popular in after times as the senate was then by its beneficent legislation.

10. On the appearance of the enemy the country people fled into the City as best they could. The weak places in the defenses were occupied by military posts; elsewhere the walls and the Tiber were deemed sufficient protection. The enemy would have forced their way over the Sublician bridge had it not been for one man, Horatius Cocles. The good fortune of Rome provided him as her bulwark on that memorable day. He happened to be on guard at the bridge when he saw the Janiculum taken by a sudden assault and the enemy rushing down from it to the river, whilst his own men, a panic-stricken mob, were deserting their posts and throwing away their arms. He reproached them one after another for their cowardice, tried to stop them, appealed to them in heaven's name to stand, declared that it was in vain for them to seek safety in flight whilst leaving the bridge open behind them, there would very soon be more of the enemy on the Palatine and the Capitol than there were on the Janiculum. So he shouted to them to break down the bridge by sword or fire, or by whatever means they could, he would meet the enemies' attack so far as one man could keep them at bay. He advanced to the head of the bridge. Amongst the fugitives, whose backs alone were visible to the enemy, he was conspicuous as he fronted them armed for fight at close quarters. The enemy were astounded at his preternatural courage. Two men were kept by a sense of shame from deserting him—Sp. Lartius and T. Herminius—both of them men of high birth and renowned courage. With them he sustained the first tempestuous shock and wild confused onset, for a brief interval. Then, whilst only a small portion of the bridge remained and those who were cutting it down called upon them to retire, he insisted upon these, too, retreating. Looking round with eyes dark with menace upon the Etruscan chiefs, he challenged them to single combat, and reproached them all with being the slaves of tyrant kings, and whilst unmindful of their own liberty coming to attack that of others. For some time they hesitated, each looking round upon the others to begin. At length shame roused them to action, and raising a shout they hurled their javelins from all sides on their solitary

foe. He caught them on his outstretched shield, and with unshaken resolution kept his place on the bridge with firmly planted foot. They were just attempting to dislodge him by a charge when the crash of the broken bridge and the shout which the Romans raised at seeing the work completed stayed the attack by filling them with sudden panic. Then Cocles said, "Tiberinus, holy father, I pray thee to receive into thy propitious stream these arms and this thy warrior." So, fully armed, he leaped into the Tiber, and though many missiles fell over him he swam across in safety to his friends: an act of daring more famous than credible with posterity. The State showed its gratitude for such courage; his statue was set up in the Comitium, and as much land given to him as he could drive the plough round in one day. Besides this public honor, the citizens individually showed their feeling; for, in spite of the great scarcity, each, in proportion to his means, sacrificed what he could from his own store as a gift to Cocles.

11. Repulsed in his first attempt, Porsena changed his plans from assault to blockade. After placing a detachment to hold the Janiculum he fixed his camp on the plain between that hill and the Tiber, and sent everywhere for boats, partly to intercept any attempt to get corn into Rome and partly to carry his troops across to different spots for plunder, as opportunity might serve. In a short time he made the whole of the district round Rome so insecure that not only were all the crops removed from the fields but even the cattle were all driven into the City, nor did any one venture to take them outside the gates. The impunity with which the Etruscans committed their depredations was due to strategy on the part of the Romans more than to fear. For the consul Valerius, determined to get an opportunity of attacking them when they were scattered in large numbers over the fields, allowed small forages to pass unnoticed, whilst he was reserving himself for vengeance on a larger scale. So to draw on the pillagers, he gave orders to a considerable body of his men to drive cattle out of the Esquiline gate, which was the furthest from the enemy, in the expectation that they would gain intelligence of it through the slaves who were deserting, owing to the scarcity produced by the blockade. The information was duly conveyed, and in consequence they crossed the river in larger numbers than usual in the hope of securing the whole lot. P. Valerius ordered T. Herminius with a small body of troops to take up a concealed position at a distance of two miles on the Gabian road, whilst Sp. Lartius with some light-armed infantry was to post himself at the Colline gate until the enemy had passed him and then to intercept their retreat to the river. The other consul, T. Lucretius, with a few maniples made a sortie from the Naevian gate; Valerius himself led some picked cohorts from the Caelian hill, and these were the first to attract the enemy's notice. When Herminius became aware that fighting was begun, he rose from ambush and took the enemy who were engaged with Valerius in rear.

Answering cheers arose right and left, from the Colline and the Naevian gates and the pillagers, hemmed in, unequal to the fight, and with every way of escape blocked, were cut to pieces. That put an end to these irregular and scattered excursions on the part of the Etruscans.

12. The blockade, however, continued, and with it a growing scarcity of corn at famine prices. Porsena still cherished hopes of capturing the City by keeping up the investment. There was a young noble, C. Mucius, who regarded it as a disgrace that whilst Rome in the days of servitude under her kings had never been blockaded in any war or by any foe, she should now, in the day of her freedom, be besieged by those very Etruscans whose armies she had often routed. Thinking that this disgrace ought to be avenged by some great deed of daring, he determined in the first instance to penetrate into the enemy's camp on his own responsibility. On second thoughts, however, he became apprehensive that if he went without orders from the consuls, or unknown to any one, and happened to be arrested by the Roman outposts, he might be brought back as a deserter, a charge which the condition of the City at the time would make only too probable. So he went to the senate. "I wish," he said, "Fathers, to swim the Tiber, and, if I can, enter the enemy's camp, not as a pillager nor to inflict retaliation for their pillagings. I am purposing, with heaven's help, a greater deed." The senate gave their approval. Concealing a sword in his robe, he started. When he reached the camp he took his stand in the densest part of the crowd near the royal tribunal. It happened to be the soldiers' pay-day, and a secretary, sitting by the king and dressed almost exactly like him, was busily engaged, as the soldiers kept coming to him incessantly. Afraid to ask which of the two was the king, lest his ignorance should betray him, Mucius struck as fortune directed the blow and killed the secretary instead of the king. He tried to force his way back with his blood-stained dagger through the dismayed crowd, but the shouting caused a rush to be made to the spot; he was seized and dragged back by the king's bodyguard to the royal tribunal. Here, alone and helpless, and in the utmost peril, he was still able to inspire more fear than he felt. "I am a citizen of Rome," he said, "men call me C. Mucius. As an enemy I wished to kill an enemy, and I have as much courage to meet death as I had to inflict it. It is the Roman nature to act bravely and to suffer bravely. I am not alone in having made this resolve against you, behind me there is a long list of those who aspire to the same distinction. If then it is your pleasure, make up your mind for a struggle in which you will every hour have to fight for your life and find an armed foe on the threshold of your royal tent. This is the war which we the youth of Rome, declare against you. You have no serried ranks, no pitched battle to fear, the matter will be settled between you alone and each one of us singly." The king, furious with anger, and at the same time terrified at the unknown danger, threatened that if he did not promptly explain

the nature of the plot which he was darkly hinting at he should be roasted alive. "Look," Mucius cried, "and learn how lightly those regard their bodies who have some great glory in view." Then he plunged his right hand into a fire burning on the altar. Whilst he kept it roasting there as if he were devoid of all sensation, the king, astounded at his preternatural conduct, sprang from his seat and ordered the youth to be removed from the altar. "Go," he said, "you have been a worse enemy to yourself than to me. I would invoke blessings on your courage if it were displayed on behalf of my country; as it is, I send you away exempt from all rights of war, unhurt, and safe." Then Mucius, reciprocating, as it were, this generous treatment, said, "Since you honor courage, know that what you could not gain by threats you have obtained by kindness. Three hundred of us, the foremost amongst the Roman youth, have sworn to attack you in this way. The lot fell to me first, the rest, in the order of their lot, will come each in his turn, till fortune shall give us a favorable chance against you."

13. Mucius was accordingly dismissed; afterwards he received the sobriquet of Scaevola, from the loss of his right hand. Envoys from Porsena followed him to Rome. The king's narrow escape from the first of many attempts; which was owing solely to the mistake of his assailant, and the prospect of having to meet as many attacks as there were conspirators, so unnerved him that he made proposals of peace to Rome. One for the restoration of the Tarquins was put forward, more because he could not well refuse their request than because he had any hope of its being granted. The demand for the restitution of their territory to the Veientines, and that for the surrender of hostages as a condition of the withdrawal of the detachment from the Janiculum, were felt by the Romans to be inevitable, and on their being accepted and peace concluded, Porsena moved his troops from the Janiculum and evacuated the Roman territory. As a recognition of his courage the senate gave C. Mucius a piece of land across the river, which was afterwards known as the Mucian Meadows. The honor thus paid to courage incited even women to do glorious things for the State. The Etruscan camp was situated not far from the river, and the maiden Cloelia, one of the hostages, escaped, unobserved, through the guards and at the head of her sister hostages swam across the river amidst a shower of javelins and restored them all safe to their relatives. When the news of this incident reached him, the king was at first exceedingly angry and sent to demand the surrender of Cloelia; the others he did not care about. Afterwards his feelings changed to admiration; he said that the exploit surpassed those of Cocles and Mucius, and announced that whilst on the one hand he should consider the treaty broken if she were not surrendered, he would on the other hand, if she were surrendered, send her back to her people unhurt. Both sides behaved honorably; the Romans surrendered her as a pledge of loyalty to the terms of the treaty; the Etruscan

king showed that with him courage was not only safe but honored, and after eulogizing the girl's conduct, told her that he would make her a present of half the remaining hostages, she was to choose whom she would. It is said that after all had been brought before her, she chose the boys of tender age; a choice in keeping with maidenly modesty, and one approved by the hostages themselves, since they felt that the age which was most liable to ill-treatment should have the preference in being rescued from hostile hands. After peace was thus re-established, the Romans rewarded the unprecedented courage shown by a woman by an unprecedented honor, namely an equestrian statue. On the highest part of the Sacred Way a statue was erected representing the maiden sitting on horseback.

14. Quite inconsistent with this peaceful withdrawal from the City on the part of the Etruscan king is the custom which, with other formalities, has been handed down from antiquity to our own age of "selling the goods of King Porsena." This custom must either have been introduced during the war and kept up after peace was made, or else it must have a less bellicose origin than would be implied by the description of the goods sold as "taken from the enemy." The most probable tradition is that Porsena, knowing the City to be without food owing to the long investment, made the Romans a present of his richly-stored camp, in which provisions had been collected from the neighboring fertile fields of Etruria. Then, to prevent the people seizing them indiscriminately as spoils of war, they were regularly sold, under the description of "the goods of Porsena," a description indicating rather the gratitude of the people than an auction of the king's personal property, which had never been at the disposal of the Romans. To prevent his expedition from appearing entirely fruitless, Porsena, after bringing the war with Rome to a close, sent his son Aruns with a part of his force to attack Aricia. At first the Aricians were dismayed by the unexpected movement, but the succors which in response to their request were sent from the Latin towns and from Cumae so far encouraged them that they ventured to offer battle. At the commencement of the action the Etruscans attacked with such vigor that they routed the Aricians at the first charge. The Cuman cohorts made a strategic flank movement, and when the enemy had pressed forward in disordered pursuit, they wheeled round and attacked them in the rear. Thus the Etruscans, now all but victorious, were hemmed in and cut to pieces. A very small remnant, after losing their general, made for Rome, as there was no nearer place of safety. Without arms, and in the guise of suppliants, they were kindly received and distributed amongst different houses. After recovering from their wounds, some left for their homes, to tell of the kind hospitality they had received; many remained behind out of affection for their hosts and the City. A district was assigned to them to dwell in, which subsequently bore the designation of "the Tuscan quarter."

BOOK II 31–40

Tension between the senators and the people led to the 'plebeian sol-
diers' withdrawal from the city in 494 B.C.E. Then the proud aristo-
cratic hero Gnaeus Marcius Coriolanus, after a conflict with the ple-
beian tribunes, defected to the enemy.

31. Whilst these events were occurring amongst the Volscians, the Dictator, after entering the Sabine territory, where the most serious part of the
war lay, defeated and routed the enemy and chased them out of their camp.
A cavalry charge had broken the enemy's center which, owing to the excessive lengthening of the wings, was weakened by an insufficient depth of files,
and while thus disordered the infantry charged them. In the same charge the
camp was captured and the war brought to a close. Since the battle at Lake
Regillus no more brilliant action had been fought in those years. The Dictator rode in triumph into the City. In addition to the customary distinctions, a
place was assigned in the Circus Maximus to him and to his posterity, from
which to view the Games, and the sella curulis was placed there. After the
subjugation of the Volscians, the territory of Velitrae was annexed and a
body of Roman citizens was sent out to colonize it. Some time later, an
engagement took place with the Aequi. The consul was reluctant to fight as
he would have to attack on unfavorable ground, but his soldiers forced him
into action. They accused him of protracting the war in order that the Dictator's term of office might expire before they returned home, in which case
his promises would fall to the ground, as those of the consul had previously
done. They compelled him to march his army up the mountain at all hazards;
but owing to the cowardice of the enemy this unwise step resulted in success.
They were so astounded at the daring of the Romans that before they came
within range of their weapons they abandoned their camp, which was in a
very strong position, and dashed down into the valley in the rear. So the victors gained a bloodless victory and ample spoil.

Whilst these three wars were thus brought to a successful issue, the
course which domestic affairs were taking continued to be a source of anxiety to both the patricians and the plebeians. The money-lenders possessed
such influence and had taken such skillful precautions that they rendered the
commons and even the Dictator himself powerless. After the consul Vetusius
had returned, Valerius introduced, as the very first business of the senate, the
treatment of the men who had been marching to victory, and moved a resolution as to what decision they ought to come to with regard to the debtors.
His motion was denied, on which he said, "I am not acceptable as an advocate of concord. Depend upon it, you will very soon wish that the Roman
plebs had champions like me. As far as I am concerned, I will no longer

encourage my fellow-citizens in vain hopes nor will I be Dictator in vain. Internal dissensions and foreign wars have made this office necessary to the commonwealth; peace has now been secured abroad, at home it is made impossible. I would rather be involved in the revolution as a private citizen than as Dictator." So saying, he left the House and resigned his dictatorship. The reason was quite clear to the plebs; he had resigned office because he was indignant at the way they were treated. The non-fulfillment of his pledge was not due to him, they considered that he had practically kept his word, and on his way home they followed him with approving cheers.

32. The senate now began to feel apprehensive lest on the disbandment of the army there should be a recurrence of the secret conclaves and conspiracies. Although the Dictator had actually conducted the enrollment, the soldiers had sworn obedience to the consuls. Regarding them as still bound by their oath, the senate ordered the legions to be marched out of the City on the pretext that war had been recommenced by the Aequi. This step brought the revolution to a head. It is said that the first idea was to put the consuls to death that the men might be discharged from their oath; then, on learning that no religious obligation could be dissolved by a crime, they decided, at the instigation of a certain Sicinius, to ignore the consuls and withdraw to the Sacred Mount, which lay on the other side of the Anio, three miles from the City. This is a more generally accepted tradition than the one adopted by Piso that the secession was made to the Aventine. There, without any commander in a regularly entrenched camp, taking nothing with them but the necessaries of life, they quietly maintained themselves for some days, neither receiving nor giving any provocation. A great panic seized the City, mutual distrust led to a state of universal suspense. Those plebeians who had been left by their comrades in the City feared violence from the patricians; the patricians feared the plebeians who still remained in the City, and could not make up their minds whether they would rather have them go or stay. "How long," it was asked, "would the multitude who had seceded remain quiet? What would happen if a foreign war broke out in the meantime?" They felt that all their hopes rested on concord amongst the citizens, and that this must be restored at any cost.

The senate decided, therefore, to send as their spokesman Menenius Agrippa, an eloquent man, and acceptable to the plebs as being himself of plebeian origin. He was admitted into the camp, and it is reported that he simply told them the following fable in primitive and uncouth fashion. "In the days when all the parts of the human body were not as now agreeing together, but each member took its own course and spoke its own speech, the other members, indignant at seeing that everything acquired by their care and labor and ministry went to the belly, whilst it, undisturbed in the middle of them all, did nothing but enjoy the pleasures provided for it, entered into a conspiracy; the hands were not to bring food to the mouth, the mouth was not to accept it when offered, the teeth were not to masticate it. Whilst, in their resentment, they were anxious to coerce the belly by starving it, the members themselves wasted away, and the whole body was reduced to the last stage of exhaustion. Then it became evident that the belly rendered no idle service, and the nourishment it received was no greater than that which it bestowed by returning to all parts of the body this blood by which we live and are strong, equally distributed into the veins, after being matured by the digestion of the food." By using this comparison, and showing how the internal disaffection amongst the parts of the body resembled the animosity of the plebeians against the patricians, he succeeded in winning over his audience.

33. Negotiations were then entered upon for a reconciliation. An agreement was arrived at, the terms being that the plebs should have its own magistrates, whose persons were to be inviolable, and who should have the right of affording protection against the consuls. And further, no patrician should be allowed to hold that office. Two "tribunes of the plebs" were elected, C. Licinius and L. Albinus. These chose three colleagues. It is generally agreed that Sicinius, the instigator of the secession, was amongst them, but who the other two were is not settled. Some say that only two tribunes were created on the Sacred Hill and that it was there that the *lex sacrata* was passed. During the secession of the plebs Sp. Cassius and Postumius Cominius entered on their consulship. In their year of office a treaty was concluded with the Latin towns, and one of the consuls remained in Rome for the purpose. The other was sent to the Volscian war. He routed a force of Volscians from Antium, and pursued them to Longula, which he gained possession of. Then he advanced to Polusca, also belonging to the Volscians, which he captured, after which he attacked Corioli in great force.

Amongst the most distinguished of the young soldiers in the camp at that time was Cnaeus Marcius, a young man prompt in counsel and action, who afterwards received the epithet of Coriolanus. During the progress of the siege, while the Roman army was devoting its whole attention to the townspeople whom it had shut up within their walls, and not in the least apprehending any danger from hostile movements without, it was suddenly attacked by Volscian legions who had marched from Antium. At the same moment a sortie was made from the town. Marcius happened to be on guard, and with a picked body of men not only repelled the sortie but made a bold dash through the open gate, and after cutting down many in the part of the city nearest to him, seized some fire and hurled it on the buildings which abutted on the walls. The shouts of the townsmen mingled with the shrieks of the terrified women and children encouraged the Romans and dismayed the Volscians, who thought that the city which they had come to assist was already captured. So the troops from Antium were routed and Corioli taken. The renown which Marcius won so completely eclipsed that of the consul, that, had not the treaty with the Latins—which owing to his colleague's absence had been concluded by Sp. Cassius alone—been inscribed on a brazen column, and so permanently recorded, all memory of Postumius Cominius having carried on a war with the Volscians would have perished. In the same year Agrippa Menenius died, a man who all through his life was equally beloved by the patricians and the plebeians, and made himself still more endeared to the plebeians after their secession. Yet he, the negotiator and arbitrator of the reconciliation, who acted as the ambassador of the patricians to the plebs, and brought them back to the City, did not possess money enough to defray the cost of his funeral. He was interred by the plebeians, each man contributing a sextans towards the expense.

34. The new consuls were T. Geganius and P. Minucius. In this year, whilst all abroad was undisturbed by war and the civic dissensions at home were healed, the commonwealth was attacked by another much more serious evil: first, dearness of food, owing to the fields remaining uncultivated during the secession, and following on this a famine such as visits a besieged city. It would have led to the perishing of the slaves in any case, and probably the plebeians would have died, had not the consuls provided for the emergency by sending men in various directions to buy corn. They penetrated not only along the coast to the right of Ostia into Etruria, but also along the sea to the left past the Volscian country as far as Cumae. Their search extended even as far as Sicily; to such an extent did the hostility of their neighbors compel them to seek distant help. When corn had been bought at Cumae, the ships were detained by the tyrant Aristodemus, in lieu of the property of Tarquin, to whom he was heir. Amongst the Volscians and in the Pomptine district it was even impossible to purchase corn, the corn merchants were in danger of being attacked by the population. Some corn came from Etruria up the Tiber; this served for the support of the plebeians. They would have been harassed by a war, doubly unwelcome when provisions were so scarce, if the Volscians, who were already on the march, had not been attacked by a frightful pestilence. This disaster cowed the enemy so effectively that even when it had abated its violence they remained to some extent in a state of terror; the Romans increased the number of colonists at Velitrae and sent a new colony to Norba, up in the mountains, to serve as a stronghold in the Pomptine district.

During the consulship of M. Minucius and Sempronius (492–491 B.C.E.), a large quantity of corn was brought from Sicily, and the question was discussed in the senate at what price it should be given to the plebs. Many were of opinion that the moment had come for putting pressure on the plebeians, and recovering the rights which had been wrested from the senate through the secession and the violence which accompanied it. Foremost among these was Marcius Coriolanus, a determined foe to the tribunitian power. "If," he argued, "they want their corn at the old price, let them restore to the senate its old powers. Why, then, do I, after being sent under the yoke, ransomed as it were from brigands, see plebeian magistrates, why do I see a Sicinius in power? Am I to endure these indignities a moment longer than I can help? Am I, who could not put up with a Tarquin as king, to put up with a Sicinius? Let him secede now! Let him call out his plebeians, the way lies open to the Sacred Hill and to other hills. Let them carry off the corn from our fields as they did two years ago; let them enjoy the scarcity which in their madness they have produced! I will venture to say that after they have been tamed by these sufferings, they will rather work as laborers themselves in the fields than prevent their being cultivated by an armed secession." It is not so easy to say whether they ought to have done this as it is to express one's belief that it could have been done, and the senators might have made it a condition of lowering the price of the corn that they should abrogate the tribunitian power and all the legal restrictions imposed upon them against their will.

35. The senate considered these sentiments too bitter, the plebeians in their exasperation almost flew to arms. Famine, they said, was being used as a weapon against them, as though they were enemies; they were being cheated out of food and sustenance; the foreign corn, which fortune had unexpectedly given them as their sole means of support, was to be snatched from their mouths unless their tribunes were given up in chains to Cn. Marcius, unless he could work his will on the backs of the Roman plebeians. In him a new executioner had sprung up, who ordered them either to die or live as slaves. He would have been attacked on leaving the Senate-house had not the tribunes most opportunely fixed a day for his impeachment. This allayed the excitement, every man saw himself a judge with the power of life and death over his enemy. At first Marcius treated the threats of the tribunes with contempt; they had the right of protecting not of punishing, they were the tribunes of the plebs not of the patricians. But the anger of the plebeians was so thoroughly roused that the patricians could only save themselves by the punishment of one of their order. They resisted, however, in spite of the odium: they incurred, and exercised all the powers they possessed both collectively and individually. At first they attempted to thwart proceedings by posting pickets of their clients to deter individuals from frequenting meetings and conclaves. Then they proceeded in a body—you might suppose that every patrician was impeached—and implored the plebeians, if they refused to acquit a man who was innocent, at least to give up to them, as guilty, one citizen, one senator. As he did not put in an appearance on the day of trial, their resentment remained unabated, and he was condemned in his absence. He went into exile amongst the Volscians, uttering threats against his country, and even then entertaining hostile designs against it. The Volscians welcomed his arrival, and he became more popular as his resentment against his countrymen became more bitter, and his complaints and threats were more frequently heard. He enjoyed the hospitality of Attius Tullius, who was by far the most important man at that time amongst the Volscians and a life-long enemy of the Romans. Impelled each by similar motives, the one by old-standing hatred, the other by newly-provoked resentment, they formed joint plans for war with Rome. They were under the impression that the people could not easily be induced, after so many defeats, to take up arms again, and that after their losses in their numerous wars and recently through the pestilence, their spirits were broken. The hostility had now had time to die down; it was necessary, therefore, to adopt some artifice by which fresh irritation might be produced.

36. It so happened that preparations were being made for a repetition of the "Great Games." The reason for their repetition was that early in the morning, prior to the commencement of the Games, a householder after flogging his slave had driven him through the middle of the Circus Maximus. Then the Games commenced as though the incident had no religious significance. Not long afterwards, Titus Latinius, a member of the plebs, had a dream. Jupiter appeared to him and said that the dancer who commenced the Games was displeasing to him, adding that unless those Games were repeated with due magnificence, disaster would overtake the City, and he was to go and report this to the consuls. Though he was by no means free from religious scruples, still his fears gave way before his awe of the magistrates, lest he should become an object of public ridicule. This hesitation cost him dear, for within a few days he lost his son. That he might have no doubt as to the cause of this sudden calamity, the same form again appeared to the distressed father in his sleep, and demanded of him whether he had been sufficiently repaid for his neglect of the divine will, for a more terrible recompense was impending if he did not speedily go and inform the consuls. Though the matter was becoming more urgent, he still delayed, and while thus procrastinating he was attacked by a serious illness in the form of sudden paralysis. Now the divine wrath thoroughly alarmed him, and wearied out by his past misfortune and the one from which he was suffering he called his relations together and explained what he had seen and heard, the repeated appearance of Jupiter in his sleep, the threatening wrath of heaven brought home to him by his calamities. On the strong advice of all present he was carried in a litter to the consuls in the Forum, and from there by the consuls' order into the Senate-house. After repeating the same story to the senators, to the intense surprise of all, another marvel occurred. The tradition runs that he who had been carried into the Senate-house paralyzed in every limb, returned home, after performing his duty, on his own feet.

37. The senate decreed that the Games should be celebrated on the most splendid scale. At the suggestion of Attius Tullius, a large number of Volscians came to them. In accordance with a previous arrangement with Marcius, Tullius came to the consuls, before the proceedings commenced, and said that there were certain matters touching the State which he wished to discuss privately with them. When all the bystanders had been removed, he began: "It is with great reluctance that I say anything to the disparagement of my people. I do not come, however, to charge them with having actually committed any offense, but to take precautions against their committing one. The character of our citizens is more fickle than I should wish; we have experienced this in many defeats, for we owe our present security not to our own deserts but to your forbearance. Here at this moment are a great multitude of Volscians, the Games are going on, the whole City will be intent on the spectacle. I remember what an outrage was committed by the young Sabines on a similar occasion, I shudder lest any ill-advised and reckless incident should occur. For our sakes, and yours, consuls, I thought it right to give you this warning. As far as I am concerned, it is my intention to start at once for home, lest, if I stay, I should be involved in some mischief either of speech or act." With these words he departed. These vague hints, uttered apparently on good authority, were laid by the consuls before the senate. As generally happens, the authority rather than the facts of the case induced them to take even excessive precautions. A decree was passed that the Volscians should leave the City, criers were sent round ordering them all to depart before nightfall. Their first feeling was one of panic as they ran off to their respective lodgings to take away their effects, but when they had started a feeling of indignation arose at their being driven away from the Games, from a festival which was in a manner a meeting of gods and men, as though they were under the curse of heaven and unfit for human society.

38. As they were going along in an almost continuous stream, Tullius, who had gone on in advance, waited for them at the Ferentine Fountain. Accosting their chief men as they came up in tones of complaint and indignation, he led them, eagerly listening to words which accorded with their own angry feelings, and through them the multitude, down to the plain which stretched below the road. There he began a speech: "Even though you should forget the wrongs that Rome has inflicted and the defeats which the Volscian nation has suffered, though you should forget everything else, with what temper, I should like to know, do you brook this insult of yesterday, when they commenced their Games by treating us with ignominy? Have you not felt that they have won a triumph over you today, that as you departed you were a spectacle to the townsfolk, to the strangers, to all those neighboring populations; that your wives, your children, were paraded as a gazing-stock before men's eyes? What do you suppose were the thoughts of those who heard the voice of the criers, those who watched us depart, those who met this ignominious cavalcade? What could they have thought but that there was some awful guilt cleaving to us, so that if we had been present at the Games we should have profaned them and made an expiation necessary, and that this was the reason why we were driven away from the abodes of these good and religious people and from all intercourse and association with them? Does it not occur to you that we owe our lives to the haste with which we departed, if we may call it a departure and not a flight? And do you count this City as anything else than the City of your enemies, where, had you lingered a single day, you would all have been put to death? War has been declared against you—to the great misery of those who have declared it, if you are really men." So they dispersed to their homes, with their feelings of resentment embittered by this harangue. They so worked upon the feelings of their fellow-countrymen, each in his own city, that the whole Volscian nation revolted.

39. By the unanimous vote of the states, the conduct of the war was entrusted to Attius Tullius and Cn. Marcius, the Roman exile, on whom their hopes chiefly rested. He fully justified their expectations, so that it became quite evident that the strength of Rome lay in her generals rather than in her army. He first marched against Cerceii, expelled the Roman colony and handed it over to the Volscians as a free city. Then he took Satricum, Longula, Polusca, and Corioli, towns which the Romans had recently acquired. Marching across country into the Latin road, he recovered Lavinium, and then, in succession, Corbio, Vetellia, Trebium Labici, and Pedum. Finally, he advanced from Pedum against the City. He entrenched his camp at the Cluilian Dykes, about five miles distant, and from there he ravaged the Roman territory. The raiding parties were accompanied by men whose business it was to see that the lands of the patricians were not touched; a measure due either to his rage being especially directed against the plebeians, or to his hope that dissensions might arise between them and the patricians. These certainly would have arisen—to such a pitch were the tribunes exciting the plebs by their attacks on the chief men of the State—had not the fear of the enemy outside—the strongest bond of union—brought men together in spite of their mutual suspicions and aversion. On one point they disagreed; the senate and the consuls placed their hopes solely in arms, the plebeians preferred anything to war. Sp. Nautius and Sex. Furius were now consuls. Whilst they were reviewing the legions and manning the walls and stationing troops m various places, an enormous crowd gathered together. At first they alarmed the consuls by seditious shouts, and at last they compelled them to convene the senate and submit a motion for sending ambassadors to Cn. Marcius. As the courage of the plebeians was evidently giving way, the senate accepted the motion, and a deputation was sent to Marcius with proposals for peace. They brought back the stern reply: If the territory were restored to the Volscians, the question of peace could be discussed; but if they wished to enjoy the spoils of war at their ease, he had not forgotten the wrongs inflicted by his countrymen nor the kindness shown by those who were now his hosts, and would strive to make it clear that his spirit had been roused, not broken, by his exile. The same envoys were sent on a second mission, but were not admitted into the camp. According to the tradition, the priests also in their robes went as suppliants to the enemies' camp, but they had no more influence with him than the previous deputation.

40. Then the matrons went in a body to Veturia, the mother of Coriolanus, and Volumnia his wife. Whether this was in consequence of a decree of the senate, or simply the prompting of womanly fear, I am unable to ascertain, but at all events they succeeded in inducing the aged Veturia to go with Volumnia and her two little sons to the enemies' camp. As men were powerless to protect the City by their arms, the women sought to do so by their tears and prayers. On their arrival at the camp a message was sent to Coriolanus that a large body of women were present. He had remained unmoved by the majesty of the State in the persons of its ambassadors, and by the appeal made to his eyes and mind in the persons of its priests; he was still more obdurate to the tears of the women. Then one of his friends, who had recognized Veturia, standing between her daughter-in-law and her grandsons, and conspicuous amongst them all in the greatness of her grief, said to him, "Unless my eyes deceive me, your mother and wife and children are here." Coriolanus, almost like one demented, sprung from his seat to embrace his mother. She, changing her tone from entreaty to anger, said, "Before I admit your embrace suffer me to know whether it is to an enemy or a son that I have come, whether it is as your prisoner or as your mother that I am in your camp. Has a long life and an unhappy old age brought me to this, that I have to see you an exile and from that an enemy? Had you the heart to ravage this land, which has borne and nourished you? However hostile and menacing the spirit in which you came, did not your anger subside as you entered its borders? Did you not say to yourself when your eye rested on Rome, 'Within those walls are my home, my household gods, my mother, my wife, my children?' Must it then be that, had I remained childless, no attack would have been made on Rome; had I never had a son, I should have ended my days a free woman in a free country? But there is nothing which I can suffer now that will not bring more disgrace to you than wretchedness to me; whatever unhappiness awaits me it will not be for long. Look to these, whom, if you persist in your present course, an untimely death awaits, or a long life of bondage." When she ceased, his wife and children embraced him, and all the women wept and bewailed their own and their country's fate. At last his resolution gave way. He embraced his family and dismissed them, and

moved his camp away from the City. After withdrawing his legions from the Roman territory, he is said to have fallen a victim to the resentment which his action aroused, but as to the time and circumstances of his death the traditions vary. I find in Fabius, who is by far the oldest authority, that he lived to be an old man; he relates a saying of his, which he often uttered in his later years, that it is not till a man is old that he feels the full misery of exile. The Roman husbands did not grudge their wives the glory they had won, so completely were their lives free from the spirit of detraction and envy. A temple was built and dedicated to Fortuna Muliebris, to serve as a memorial of their deed. Subsequently the combined forces of the Volscians and Aequi re-entered the Roman territory. The Aequi, however, refused any longer to accept the generalship of Attius Tullius, a quarrel arose as to which nation should furnish the commander of the combined army, and this resulted in a bloody battle. Here the good fortune of Rome destroyed the two armies of her enemies in a conflict no less ruinous than obstinate. The new consuls were T. Sicinius and C. Aquilius. To Sicinius was assigned the campaign against the Volscians, to Aquilius that against the Hernici, for they also were in arms. In that year the Hernici were subjugated, the campaign against the Volscians ended indecisively.

BOOK III 33–37; 44–49; 56–58

In 451 B.C.E. the consuls were replaced by ten magistrates (decemvirs) appointed to compile a written law code. The decemvirs' tyrannical actions, especially those of Appius Claudius, led to their fall.

33. For the second time—in the 301st year from the foundation of Rome (452 B.C.E.)—was the form of government changed; the supreme authority was transferred from consuls to decemvirs, just as it had previously passed from kings to consuls. The change was the less noteworthy owing to its short duration, for the happy beginnings of that government developed into too luxuriant a growth; hence its early failure and the return to the old practice of entrusting to two men the name and authority of consul. The decemvirs were Appius Claudius, T. Genucius, P. Sestius, L. Veturius, C. Julius, A. Manlius, P. Sulpicius, P. Curiatius, T. Romilius, and Sp. Postumius. As Claudius and Genucius were the consuls designate, they received the honor in place of the honor of which they were deprived. Sestius, one of the consuls the year before, was honored because he had, against his colleague, brought that subject before the senate. Next to them were placed the three commissioners who had gone to Athens, as a reward for their undertaking so distant an embassy, and also because it was thought that those who were familiar with the laws of foreign States would be useful in the compilation of new ones. It is said that in the final voting for the four required to complete the number, the electors chose aged men, to prevent any violent opposition to the decisions of the others. The presidency of the whole body was, in accordance with the wishes of the plebs, entrusted to Appius. He had assumed such a new character that from being a stern and bitter enemy of the people he suddenly appeared as their advocate, and trimmed his sails to catch every breath of popular favor. They administered justice each in turn, the one who was presiding judge for the day was attended by the twelve lictors, the others had only a single usher each. Notwithstanding the singular harmony which prevailed amongst them—a harmony which under other circumstances might be dangerous to individuals—the most perfect equity was shown to others. It will be sufficient to adduce a single instance as proof of the moderation with which they acted. A dead body had been discovered and dug up in the house of Sestius, a member of a patrician family. It was brought into the Assembly. As it was clear that an atrocious crime had been committed, Caius Julius, a decemvir, indicted Sestius, and appeared before the people to prosecute in person, though he had the right to act as sole judge in the case. He waived his right in order that the liberties of the people might gain what he surrendered of his power.

34. Whilst highest and lowest alike were enjoying their prompt and impartial administration of justice, as though delivered by an oracle, they were at the same time devoting their attention to the framing of the laws. These eagerly looked for laws were at length inscribed on ten tables which were exhibited in an Assembly specially convened for the purpose. After a prayer that their work might bring welfare and happiness to the State, to them and to their children, the decemvirs bade them go and read the laws which were exhibited. "As far as the wisdom and foresight of ten men admitted, they had established equal laws for all, for highest and lowest alike; there was, however, more weight in the intelligence and advice of many men. They should turn over each separate item in their minds, discuss them in conversations with each other, and bring forward for public debate what appeared to them superfluous or defective in each enactment. The future laws for Rome should be such as would appear to have been no less unanimously proposed by the people themselves than ratified by them on the proposal of others." When it appeared that they had been sufficiently amended in accordance with the expression of public opinion on each head, the Laws of the Ten Tables were passed by the Assembly of Centuries. Even in the mass of legislation today, where laws are piled one upon another in a confused heap, they still form the source of all public and private jurisprudence. After their ratification, the remark was generally made that two tables were still wanting; if they were added, the body, as it might be called, of Roman

law would be complete. As the day for the elections approached, this impression created a desire to appoint decemvirs for a second year. The plebeians had learnt to detest the name of "consul" as much as that of "king," and now as the decemvirs allowed an appeal from one of their body to another, they no longer required the aid of their tribunes.

35. But after notice had been given that the election of decemvirs would be held on the third market day, such eagerness to be amongst those elected displayed itself, that even the foremost men of the State began an individual canvass as humble suitors for an office which they had previously with all their might opposed, seeking it at the hands of that very plebs with which they had hitherto been in conflict. I think they feared that if they did not fill posts of such great authority, they would be open to men who were not worthy of them. Appius Claudius was keenly alive to the chance that he might not be re-elected, in spite of his age and the honors he had enjoyed. You could hardly tell whether to consider him as a decemvir or a candidate. Sometimes he was more like one who sought office than one who actually held it; he abused the nobility, and extolled all the candidates who had neither birth nor personal weight to recommend them; he used to bustle about the Forum surrounded by ex-tribunes of the Duellius and Scilius stamp and through them made overtures to the plebeians, until even his colleagues, who till then had been wholly devoted to him, began to watch him, wondering what he meant. They were convinced that there was no sincerity about it, it was certain that so haughty a man would not exhibit such affability for nothing. They regarded this demeaning of himself and hobnobbing with private individuals as the action of a man who was not so keen to resign office as to discover some way of prolonging it. Not venturing to thwart his aims openly, they tried to moderate his violence by humoring him. As he was the youngest member of their body, they unanimously conferred on him the office of presiding over the elections. By this artifice they hoped to prevent him from getting himself elected; a thing which no one except the tribunes of the plebs had ever done, setting thereby the worst of precedents. However, he gave out that, if all went well, he should hold the elections, and he seized upon what should have been an impediment as a good opportunity for effecting his purpose. By forming a coalition he secured the rejection of the two Quinctii—Capitolinus and Cincinnatus—his own uncle, C. Claudius, one of the firmest supporters of the nobility, and other citizens of the same rank. He procured the election of men who were very far from being their equals either socially or politically, himself amongst the first, a step which respectable men disapproved of, all the more because no one had supposed that he would have the audacity to take it. With him were elected M. Cornelius Maluginensis, M. Sergius, L. Minucius, Q. Fabius Vibulanus, Q. Poetilius, T. Antonius Merenda, K. Duillius, Sp. Oppius Cornicen, and Manlius Rabuleius.

36. This was the end of Appius' assumption of a part foreign to his nature. From that time his conduct was in accordance with his natural disposition, and he began to mold his new colleagues, even before they entered on office, into the lines of his own character. They held private meetings daily; then, armed with plans hatched in absolute secrecy for exercising unbridled power, they no longer troubled to dissemble their tyranny, but made themselves difficult of access, harsh and stern to those to whom they granted interviews. So matters went on till the middle of May. At that period, May 15, was the proper time for magistrates to take up their office. At the outset, the first day of their government was marked by a demonstration which aroused great fears. For, whereas the previous decemvirs had observed the rule of only one having the "fasces" at a time and making this emblem of royalty go to each in turn, now all the Ten suddenly appeared, each with his twelve lictors. The Forum was filled with one hundred and twenty lictors, and they bore the axes tied up in the "fasces." The decemvirs explained it by saying that as they were invested with absolute power of life and death, there was no reason for the axes being removed. They presented the appearance of ten kings, and manifold fears were entertained not only by the lowest classes but even by the foremost of the senators. They felt that a pretext for commencing bloodshed was being sought for, so that if any one uttered, either in the senate or amongst the people, a single word which reminded them of liberty, the rods and axes would instantly be made ready for him, to intimidate the rest. For not only was there no protection in the people now that the right of appeal to them was withdrawn, but the decemvirs had mutually agreed not to interfere with each other's sentences, whereas the previous decemvirs had allowed their judicial decisions to be revised on appeal to a colleague, and certain matters which they considered to be within the jurisdiction of the people they had referred to them. For some time they inspired equal terror in all, gradually it rested wholly on the plebs. The patricians were unmolested; it was the men in humble life for whom they reserved their wanton and cruel treatment. They were solely swayed by personal motives, not by the justice of a cause, since influence had with them the force of equity. They drew up their judgments at home and pronounced them in the Forum; if any one appealed to a colleague, he left the presence of the one to whom he had appealed bitterly regretting that he had not abided by the first sentence. A belief, not traceable to any authoritative source, had got abroad that their conspiracy against law and justice was not for the present only, a secret and sworn agreement existed amongst them not to hold any elections, but to keep their power, now they had once obtained it, by making the decemvirate perpetual.

37. The plebeians now began to study the faces of the patricians, to catch haply some gleam of liberty from the men from whom they had dreaded slavery and through that dread had brought the commonwealth into its present condition. The leaders of the senate hated the decemvirs, and hated the plebs; they did not approve of what was going on, but they thought that the plebeians deserved all that they got, and refused to help men who by rushing too eagerly after liberty had fallen into slavery. They even increased the wrongs they suffered, that through their disgust and impatience at the present conditions they might begin to long for the former state of things and the two consuls as of old. The greater part of the year had now elapsed; two tables had been added to the ten of the previous year; if these additional laws were passed by the "Comitia Centuriata" there was no reason why the decemvirate should be any longer considered necessary. Men were wondering how soon notice would be given of the election of consuls; the sole anxiety of the plebeians was as to the method by which they could re-establish that bulwark of their liberties, the power of the tribunes, which was now suspended. Meantime nothing was said about any elections. At first the decemvirs had bid for popularity by appearing before the plebs, surrounded by ex-tribunes, but now they were accompanied by an escort of young patricians, who crowded round the tribunals, maltreated the plebeians and plundered their property, and being the stronger, succeeded in getting whatever they had taken a fancy to. They did not stop short of personal violence, some were scourged, others beheaded, and that this brutality might not be gratuitous, the punishment of the owner was followed by a grant of his effects. Corrupted by such bribes, the young nobility not only declined to oppose the lawlessness of the decemvirs, but they openly showed that they preferred their own freedom from all restraints to the general liberty.

§

44. This was followed by a second atrocity, the result of brutal lust, which occurred in the City and led to consequences no less tragic than the outrage and death of Lucretia, which had brought about the expulsion of the royal family. Not only was the end of the decemvirs the same as that of the kings, but the cause of their losing their power was the same in each case. Ap. Claudius had conceived a guilty passion for a girl of plebeian birth. The girl's father, L. Verginius, held a high rank in the army on Algidus; he was a man of exemplary character both at home and in the field. His wife had been brought up on equally high principles, and their children were being brought up in the same way. He had betrothed his daughter to L. Icilius, who had been tribune, an active and energetic man whose courage had been proved in his battles for the plebs. This girl, now in the bloom of her youth and beauty, excited Appius' passions, and he tried to prevail on her by presents and promises. When he found that her virtue was proof against all temptation, he had recourse to unscrupulous and brutal violence. He commissioned a client, M. Claudius, to claim the girl as his slave, and to bar any claim on the part of her friends to retain possession of her till the case was tried, as he thought that the father's absence afforded a good opportunity for this illegal action. As the girl was going to her school in the Forum—the schools were held in booths there—the decemvir's pander laid his hand upon her, declaring that she was the daughter of a slave of his, and a slave herself. He then ordered her to follow him, and threatened, if she hesitated, to carry her off by force. While the girl was stupefied with terror, her maid's shrieks, invoking "the protection of the Quirites," drew a crowd together. The names of her father Verginius and her betrothed lover, Icilius, were held in universal respect. Regard for them brought their friends, feelings of indignation brought the crowd to the maiden's support. She was now safe from violence; the man who claimed her said that he was proceeding according to law, not by violence, there was no need for any excited gathering. He cited the girl into court. Her supporters advised her to follow him; they came before the tribunal of Appius. The claimant rehearsed a story already perfectly familiar to the judge as he was the author of the plot, how the girl had been born in his house, stolen from there, transferred to the house of Verginius and fathered on him; these allegations would be supported by definite evidence, and he would prove them to the satisfaction of Verginius himself, who was really most concerned, as an injury had been done to him. Meanwhile, he urged, it was only right that a slave girl should follow her master. The girl's advocates contended that Verginius was absent on the service of the State, he would be present in two days' time if information were sent to him, and it was contrary to equity that in his absence he should incur risk with regard to his children. They demanded that he should adjourn the whole of the proceedings till the father's arrival, and in accordance with the law which he himself had enacted, grant the custody of the girl to those who asserted her freedom, and not suffer a maiden of ripe age to incur danger to her reputation before her liberty was imperiled.

45. Before giving judgment, Appius showed how liberty was upheld by that very law to which the friends of Verginia had appealed in support of their demand. But, he went on to say, it guaranteed liberty only so far as its provisions were strictly adhered to as regarded both persons and cases. For where personal freedom is the matter of claim, that provision holds good, because any one can lawfully plead, but in the case of one who is still in her father's power, there is none but her father to whom her master need renounce possession. His decision, therefore, was that the father should be summoned, and in the meanwhile the man who claimed her should not forego his right to take the girl and give security to produce her on the arrival of her reputed father. The injustice of this sentence called forth many murmurs, but no one ventured an open protest, until P. Numitorius, the girl's grandfather, and Icilius, her betrothed, appeared on the scene. The intervention of Icilius seemed to offer the best chance of thwarting Appius, and the crowd made way for him. The lictor said that judgment had been given, and as Icilius continued loudly protesting he attempted to remove him. Such rank injustice would have fired even a gentle temper. He exclaimed, "I am, at your orders, Appius, to be removed at the point of the sword, that you may stifle all comment on what you want to keep concealed. I am going to marry this maiden, and I am determined to have a chaste wife. Summon all the lictors of all your colleagues, give orders for the axes and rods to be in readiness—the betrothed of Icilius shall not remain outside her father's house. Even if you have deprived us of the two bulwarks of our liberty—the aid of our tribunes and the right of appeal to the Roman plebs—that has given you no right to our wives and children, the victims of your lust. Vent your cruelty upon our backs and necks; let female honor at least be safe. If violence is offered to this girl, I shall invoke the aid of the Quirites here for my betrothed, Verginius that of the soldiers for his only daughter; we shall all invoke the aid of gods and men, and you shall not carry out that judgment except at the cost of our lives. Reflect, Appius, I demand of you, whither you are going! When Verginius has come, he must decide what action to take about his daughter; if he submits to this man's claim, he must look out another husband for her. Meantime I will vindicate her liberty at the price of my life, sooner than sacrifice my honor."

46. The people were excited and a conflict appeared imminent. The lictors had closed round Icilius, but matters had not got beyond threats on both sides when Appius declared that it was not the defense of Verginia that was Icilius' main object; a restless intriguer, even yet breathing the spirit of the tribuneship, was looking out for a chance of creating sedition. He would not, however, afford him material for it that day, but that he might know that it was not to his insolence that he was making a concession, but to the absent Verginius, to the name of father, and to liberty, he would not adjudicate on that day, or issue any decree. He would ask M. Claudius to forego his right, and allow the girl to be in the custody of her friends till the morrow. If the father did not then appear, he warned Icilius and men of his stamp that neither as legislator would he be disloyal to his own law, nor as decemvir would he lack firmness to execute it. He certainly would not call upon the lictors of his colleagues to repress the ringleaders of sedition, he should be content with his own. The time for perpetrating this illegality was thus postponed, and after the girl's supporters had withdrawn, it was decided as the very first thing to be done that the brother of Icilius and one of Numitor's sons, both active youths, should make their way straight to the gate and summon Verginius from the camp with all possible speed. They knew that the girl's safety turned upon her protector against lawlessness being present in time.

They started on their mission, and riding at full speed brought the news to the father. While the claimant of the girl was pressing Icilius to enter his plea and name his sureties, and Icilius kept asserting that this very thing was being arranged, purposely spinning out the time to allow of his messengers getting first to the camp, the crowd everywhere held up their hands to show that every one of them was ready to be security for him. With tears in his eyes, he said, "It is most kind of you. Tomorrow I may need your help, now I have sufficient securities." So Verginia was bailed on the security of her relatives. Appius remained for some time on the bench, to avoid the appearance of having taken his seat for that one case only. When he found that owing to the universal interest in this one case no other suitors appeared, he withdrew to his home and wrote to his colleagues in camp not to grant leave of absence to Verginius, and actually to keep him under arrest. This wicked advice came too late, as it deserved to do; Verginius had already obtained leave, and started in the first watch. The letter ordering his detention was delivered the next morning, and was therefore useless.

47. In the City, the citizens were standing in the Forum in the early dawn, on the tiptoe of expectation. Verginius, in mourning garb, brought his daughter, similarly attired, and accompanied by a number of matrons, into the Forum. An immense body of sympathizers stood round him. He went amongst the people, took them by the hand and appealed to them to help him, not out of compassion only but because they owed it to him; he was at the front day by day, in defense of their children and their wives; of no man could they recount more numerous deeds of endurance and of daring than of him. What good was it all, he asked, if while the City was safe, their children were exposed to what would be their worst fate if it were actually captured? Men gathered round him, whilst he spoke as though he were addressing the Assembly. Icilius followed in the same strain. The women who accompanied him made a profounder impression by their silent weeping than any words could have made. Unmoved by all this—it was really madness rather than love that had clouded his judgment—Appius mounted the tribunal. The claimant began by a brief protest against the proceedings of the previous day; judgment, he said, had not been given owing to the partiality of the judge. But before he could proceed with his claim or any opportunity was given to Verginius of replying, Appius intervened. It is possible that the ancient writers may have correctly stated some ground which he alleged for his decision, but I do not find one anywhere that would justify such an iniquitous decision. The one thing which can be propounded as being generally admitted is the judgment itself. His decision was that the girl was a slave. At first all were stupefied with amazement at this atrocity, and for a few moments there was a dead silence. Then, as M. Claudius approached the matrons standing round the girl, to seize her amidst their outcries and tears,

Verginius, pointing with outstretched arm to Appius, cried, "It is to Icilius and not to you, Appius, that I have betrothed my daughter; I have brought her up for wedlock, not for outrage. Are you determined to satisfy your brutal lusts like cattle and wild beasts? Whether these people will put up with this, I know not, but I hope that those who possess arms will refuse to do so." Whilst the man who claimed the maiden was being pushed back by the group of women and her supporters who stood round, the crier called for silence.

48. The decemvir, utterly abandoned to his passion, addressed the crowd and told them that he had ascertained not only through the insolent abuse of Icilius on the previous day and the violent behavior of Verginius, which the Roman people could testify to, but mainly from certain definite information received, that all through the night meetings had been held in the City to organize a seditious movement. Forewarned of the likelihood of disturbance, he had come down into the Forum with an armed escort, not to injure peaceable citizens, but to uphold the authority of the government by putting down the disturbers of public tranquillity. "It will therefore," he proceeded, "be better for you to keep quiet. Go, lictor, remove the crowd and clear a way for the master to take possession of his slave." When, in a transport of rage, he had thundered out these words, the people fell back and left the deserted girl a prey to injustice. Verginius, seeing no prospect of help anywhere, turned to the tribunal. "Pardon me, Appius, I pray you, if I have spoken disrespectfully to you, pardon a father's grief. Allow me to question the nurse here, in the maiden's presence, as to what are the real facts of the case, that if I have been falsely called her father, I may leave her with the greater resignation." Permission being granted, he took the girl and her nurse aside to the booths near the temple of Venus Cloacina, now known as the "New Booths," and there, snatching up a butcher's knife, he plunged it into her breast, saying, "In this the only way in which I can, I vindicate, my child, thy freedom." Then, looking towards the tribunal, "By this blood, Appius, I devote thy head to the infernal gods." Alarmed at the outcry which arose at this terrible deed, the decemvir ordered Verginius to be arrested. Brandishing the knife, he cleared the way before him, until, protected by a crowd of sympathizers, he reached the city gate. Icilius and Numitorius took up the lifeless body and showed it to the people; they deplored the villainy of Appius, the ill-starred beauty of the girl, the terrible compulsion under which the father had acted. The matrons, who followed with angry cries, asked, "Was this the condition on which they were to rear children, was this the reward of modesty and purity?" with other manifestations of that womanly grief, which, owing to their keener sensibility, is more demonstrative, and so expresses itself in more moving and pitiful fashion. The men, and especially Icilius, talked of nothing but the abolition of the tribunitian power and the right of appeal and loudly expressed their indignation at the condition of public affairs.

49. The people were excited partly by the atrocity of the deed, partly by the opportunity now offered of recovering their liberties. Appius first ordered Icilius to be summoned before him, then, on his refusal to come, to be arrested. As the lictors were not able to get near him, Appius himself with a body of young patricians forced his way through the crowd and ordered him to be taken to prison. By this time Icilius was not only surrounded by the people, but the people's leaders were there—L. Valerius and M. Horatius. They drove back the lictors and said, if they were going to proceed by law, they would undertake the defense of Icilius against one who was only a private citizen, but if they were going to attempt force, they would be no unequal match for him. A furious scuffle began, the decemvir's lictors attacked Valerius and Horatius; their "fasces" were broken up by the people; Appius mounted the platform, Horatius and Valerius followed him; the Assembly listened to them, Appius was shouted down. Valerius, assuming the tone of authority, ordered the lictors to cease attendance on one who held no official position, on which Appius, thoroughly cowed, and fearing for his life, muffled his head with his toga and retreated into a house near the Forum, without his adversaries perceiving his flight. Sp. Oppius burst into the Forum from the other side to support his colleague, and saw that their authority was overcome by main force. Uncertain what to do and distracted by the conflicting advice given him on all sides, he gave orders for the senate to be summoned. As a great number of the senators were thought to disapprove of the conduct of the decemvirs, the people hoped that their power would be put an end to through the action of the senate, and consequently became quiet. The senate decided that nothing should be done to irritate the plebs, and, what was of much more importance, that every precaution should be taken to prevent the arrival of Verginius from creating a commotion in the army.

§

56. The power of the tribunes and the liberties of the plebs were now on a secure basis. The next step was taken by the tribunes, who thought the time had come when they might safely proceed against individuals. They selected Verginius to take up the first prosecution, which was that of Appius. When the day had been fixed, and Appius had come down to the Forum with a bodyguard of young patricians, the sight of him and his satellites reminded all present of the power he had used so vilely. Verginius began: "Oratory was invented for doubtful cases. I will not, therefore, waste time by a long indictment before you of the man from whose cruelty you have vindicated yourselves by force of arms, nor will I allow him to add to his other crimes an impudent defense. So I will pass over, Appius Claudius, all the wicked and impious things that you had the audacity to do, one after another, for the last two years. One charge only will I bring against you, that contrary to law you have adjudged a free person to be a slave, and unless you name an umpire before whom you can prove your innocence, I shall order you to be taken to prison." Appius had nothing to hope for in the protection of the tribunes or the verdict of the people. Nevertheless he called upon the tribunes, and when none intervened to stay proceedings and he was seized by the apparitor, he said, "I appeal." This single word, the protection of liberty, uttered by those lips which had so lately judicially deprived a person of her freedom, produced a general silence. Then the people remarked to one another that there were gods after all who did not neglect the affairs of men; arrogance and cruelty were visited by punishments which, though lingering, were not light; that man was appealing who had taken away the power of appeal; that man was imploring the protection of the people who had trampled underfoot all their rights; he was losing his own liberty and being carried off to prison who had sentenced a free person to slavery. Amidst the murmur of the Assembly the voice of Appius himself was heard imploring "the protection of the Roman people."

He began by enumerating the services of his ancestors to the State, both at home and in the field; his own unfortunate devotion to the plebs, which had led him to resign his consulship in order to enact equal laws for all, giving thereby the greatest offense to the patricians; his laws which were still in force, though their author was being carried to prison. As to his own personal conduct and his good and evil deeds, however, he would bring them to the test when he had the opportunity of pleading his cause. For the present he claimed the common right of a Roman citizen to be allowed to plead on the appointed day and submit himself to the judgment of the Roman people. He was not so apprehensive of the general feeling against him as to abandon all hope in the impartiality and sympathy of his fellow-citizens. If he was to be taken to prison before his case was heard, he would once more appeal to the tribunes, and warn them not to copy the example of those whom they hated. If they admitted that they were bound by the same agreement to abolish the right of appeal which they accused the decemvirs of having formed, then he would appeal to the people and invoke the laws which both consuls and tribunes had enacted that very year to protect that right. For if before the case is heard and judgment given there is no power of appeal, who would appeal? What plebeian, even the humblest, would find protection in the laws, if Appius Claudius could not? His case would show whether it was tyranny or freedom that was conferred by the new laws, and whether the right of challenge and appeal against the injustice of magistrates was only displayed in empty words or was actually granted.

57. Verginius replied. Appius Claudius, he said, alone was outside the laws, outside all the bonds that held States or even human society together. Let men cast their eyes on that tribunal, the fortress of all villainies, where that perpetual decemvir, surrounded by hangmen not lictors, in contempt of gods and men alike, wreaked his vengeance on the goods, the backs, and the lives of the citizens, threatening all indiscriminately with the rods and axes, and then when his mind was diverted from rapine and murder to lust, tore a free-born maiden from her father's arms, before the eyes of Rome, and gave her to a client, the minister of his intrigues—that tribunal where by a cruel decree and infamous judgment he armed the father's hand against the daughter, where he ordered those who took up the maiden's lifeless body— her betrothed lover and her grandfather—to be thrown into prison, moved less by her death than by the check to his criminal gratification. For him as much as for others was that prison built which he used to call "the domicile of the Roman plebs." Let him appeal again and again, he (the speaker) would always refer him to an umpire on the charge of having sentenced a free person to slavery. If he would not go before an umpire he should order him to be imprisoned as though found guilty. He was accordingly thrown into prison, and though no one actually opposed this step, there was a general feeling of anxiety, since even the plebeians themselves thought it an excessive use of their liberty to inflict punishment on so great a man. The tribune adjourned the day of trial. During these proceedings ambassadors came from the Latins and Hernicans to offer their congratulations on the restoration of harmony between the patricians and the plebs. As a memorial of it, they brought an offering to Jupiter Optimus Maximus, in the shape of a golden crown. It was not a large one, as they were not wealthy States; their religious observances were characterized by devotion rather than magnificence. They also brought information that the Aequi and Volscians were devoting all their energies to preparing for war. The consuls were thereupon ordered to arrange their respective commands. The Sabines fell to Horatius, the Aequi to Valerius. They proclaimed a levy for these wars, and so favorable was the attitude of the plebs that not only did the men liable for service promptly give in their names, but a large part of the levy consisted of men who had served their time and came forward as volunteers. In this way the army was strengthened not only in numbers but in the quality of the soldiers, as veterans took their places in the ranks. Before they left the City, the laws of the decemvirs, known as the "Twelve Tables," were engraved in brass and publicly exhibited; some writers assert that the aediles discharged this task under orders from the tribunes.

58. C. Claudius, through detestation of the crimes committed by the decemvirs, and the anger which he, more than any one, felt at the tyrannical conduct of his nephew, had retired to Regillum, his ancestral home. Though advanced in years, he now returned to the City, to deprecate the dangers threatening the man whose vicious practices had driven him into retirement. Going down to the Forum in mourning garb, accompanied by the members of his house and by his clients, he appealed to the citizens individually, and implored them not to stain the house of the Claudii with such an indelible disgrace as to deem them worthy of bonds and imprisonment. To think that a man whose image would be held in highest honor by posterity, the framer of their laws and the founder of Roman jurisprudence, should be lying manacled amongst nocturnal thieves and robbers! Let them turn their thoughts for a moment from feelings of exasperation to calm examination and reflection, and forgive one man at the intercession of so many of the Claudii, rather than through their hatred of one man despise the prayers of many. So far he himself would go for the honor of his family and his name, but he was not reconciled to the man whose distressed condition he was anxious to relieve. By courage their liberties had been recovered, by clemency the harmony of the orders in the State could be strengthened. Some were moved, but it was more by the affection he showed for his nephew than by any regard for the man for whom he was pleading. But Verginius begged them with tears to keep their compassion for him and his daughter, and not to listen to the prayers of the Claudii, who had assumed sovereign power over the plebs, but to the three tribunes, kinsmen of Verginia, who, after being elected to protect the plebeians, were now seeking their protection. This appeal was felt to have more justice in it. All hope being now cut off, Appius put an end to his life before the day of trial came.

Soon after Sp. Oppius was arraigned by P. Numitorius. He was only less detested than Appius, because he had been in the City when his colleague pronounced the iniquitous judgment. More indignation, however, was aroused by an atrocity which Oppius had committed than by his not having prevented one. A witness was produced, who after reckoning up twenty-seven years of service, and eight occasions on which he had been decorated for conspicuous bravery, appeared before the people wearing all his decorations. Tearing open his dress he exhibited his back lacerated with stripes. He asked for nothing but a proof on Oppius' part of any single charge against him; if such proof were forthcoming, Oppius, though now only a private citizen, might repeat all his cruelty towards him. Oppius was taken to prison and there, before the day of trial, he put an end to his life. His property and that of Claudius were confiscated by the tribunes. Their colleagues changed their domicile by going into exile; their property also was confiscated. M. Claudius, who had been the claimant of Verginia, was tried and condemned;

Verginius himself, however, refused to press for the extreme penalty, so he was allowed to go into exile to Tibur. Verginia was more fortunate after her death than in her lifetime; her shade, after wandering through so many houses in quest of expiatory penalties, at length found rest, not one guilty person being now left.

BOOK V 34–49

The Gallic invasion of Italy in 390 B.C.E. led to the ignominious capture of Rome and the destruction of much of the city.

34. About the passage of the Gauls into Italy we have received the following account. Whilst Tarquinius Priscus was king of Rome, the supreme power amongst the Celts, who formed a third part of the whole of Gaul, was in the hands of the Bituriges; they used to furnish the king for the whole Celtic race. Ambigatus was king at that time, a man eminent for his own personal courage and prosperity as much as for those of his dominions. During his sway the harvests were so abundant and the population increased so rapidly in Gaul that the government of such vast numbers seemed almost impossible. He was now an old man, and anxious to relieve his realm from the burden of over-population. With this view he signified his intention of sending his sister's sons Bellovesus and Segovesus, both enterprising young men, to settle in whatever locality the gods should by augury assign to them. They were to invite as many as wished to accompany them, sufficient to prevent any nation from repelling their approach. When the auspices were taken, the Hercynian forest was assigned to Segovesus; to Bellovesus the gods gave the far pleasanter way into Italy. He invited the surplus population of several tribes—the Bituriges, the Averni, the Senones, the Aedui, the Ambarri, the Carnutes, and the Aulerci. Starting with an enormous force of horse and foot, he came to the Tricastini. Beyond stretched the barrier of the Alps, and I am not at all surprised that they appeared insurmountable, for they had never yet been surmounted by any route, as far at least as unbroken memory reaches, unless you choose to believe the fables about Hercules. Whilst the mountain heights kept the Gauls fenced in as it were there, and they were looking everywhere to see by what path they could cross the peaks which reached to heaven and so enter a new world, they were also prevented from advancing by a sense of religious obligation, for news came that some strangers in quest of territory were being attacked by the Salyi. These were Massilians who had sailed from Phocaea. The Gauls, looking upon this as an omen of their own fortunes, went to their assistance and enabled them to fortify the spot where they had first landed, without any interference from the Salyi. After crossing the Alps by the passes of the Taurini and the valley of the Douro, they defeated the Tuscans in battle not far from the Ticinus, and when they learnt that the country in which they had settled belonged to the Insubres, a name also borne by a canton of the Haedui, they accepted the omen of the place and built a city which they called Mediolanum.

35. Subsequently another body, consisting of the Cenomani, under the leadership of Elitovius, followed the track of the former and crossed the Alps by the same pass, with the goodwill of Bellovesus. They had their settlements where the cities of Brixia and Verona now stand. The Libui came next and the Saluvii; they settled near the ancient tribe of the Ligurian Laevi, who lived about the Ticinus. Then the Boii and Lingones crossed the Pennine Alps, and as all the country between the Po and the Alps was occupied, they crossed the Po on rafts and expelled not only the Etruscans but the Umbrians as well. They remained, however, north of the Apennines. Then the Senones, the last to come, occupied the country from the Utis to the Aesis. It was this last tribe, I find, that came to Clusium, and from there to Rome; but it is uncertain whether they came alone or helped by contingents from all the Cisalpine peoples. The people of Clusium were appalled by this strange war, when they saw the numbers, the extraordinary appearance of the men, and the kind of weapons they used, and heard that the legions of Etruria had been often routed by them on both sides of the Po. Although they had no claim on Rome, either on the ground of alliance or friendly relations, unless it was that they had not defended their kinsmen at Veii against the Romans, they nevertheless sent ambassadors to ask the senate for assistance. Active assistance they did not obtain. The three sons of M. Fabius Ambustus were sent as ambassadors to negotiate with the Gauls and warn them not to attack those from whom they had suffered no injury, who were allies and friends of Rome, and who, if circumstances compelled them, must be defended by the armed force of Rome. They preferred that actual war should be avoided, and that they should make acquaintance with the Gauls, who were strangers to them, in peace rather than in arms.

36. A peaceable enough mission, had it not contained envoys of a violent temper, more like Gauls than Romans. After they had delivered their instructions in the council of the Gauls, the following reply was given: "Although we are hearing the name of Romans for the first time, we believe nevertheless that you are brave men, since the Clusines are imploring your assistance in their time of danger. Since you prefer to protect your allies against us by negotiation rather than by armed force, we on our side do not reject the peace you offer, on condition that the Clusines cede to us Gauls, who are in need of land, a portion of that territory which they possess to a greater extent than they can cultivate. On any other conditions peace cannot be granted. We wish to receive their reply in your presence, and if territory is refused us we shall fight, whilst you are still here, that you may report to those at home how far the Gauls surpass all other men in courage." The Romans asked them what right they had to demand, under threat of war, territory from those who were its owners, and what business the Gauls had in Etruria. The haughty answer was returned that they carried their right in their weapons, and that everything belonged to the brave. Passions were kindled on both sides; they flew to arms and joined battle. Thereupon, contrary to the law of nations, the envoys seized their weapons, for the Fates were already urging Rome to its ruin. The fact of three of the noblest and bravest Romans fighting in the front line of the Etruscan army could not be concealed, so conspicuous was the valor of the strangers. And what was more, Q. Fabius rode forward at a Gallic chieftain, who was impetuously charging right at the Etruscan standards, ran his spear through his side and slew him. Whilst he was in the act of despoiling the body the Gauls recognized him, and the word was passed through the whole army that it was a Roman ambassador. Forgetting their rage against the Clusines, and breathing threats against the Romans, they sounded the retreat.

Some were for an instant advance on Rome. The older men thought that ambassadors should first be sent to Rome to make a formal complaint and demand the surrender of the Fabii as satisfaction for the violation of the law of nations. After the ambassadors had stated their case, the senate, whilst disapproving of the conduct of the Fabii, and recognizing the justice of the demand which the barbarians made, were prevented by political interests from placing their convictions on record in the form of a decree in the case of men of such high rank. In order, therefore, that the blame for any defeat which might be incurred in a war with the Gauls might not rest on them alone, they referred the consideration of the Gauls' demands to the people. Here personal popularity and influence had so much more weight that the very men whose punishment was under discussion were elected consular tribunes for the next year. The Gauls regarded this procedure as it deserved to be regarded, namely, as an act of hostility, and after openly threatening war, returned to their people. The other consular tribunes elected with the Fabii were Q. Sulpicius Longus, Q. Servilius—for the fourth time—and P. Cornelius Maluginensis.

37. To such an extent does Fortune blind men's eyes when she will not have her threatened blows parried, that though such a weight of disaster was hanging over the State, no special steps were taken to avert it. In the wars against Fidenae and Veii and other neighboring States, a Dictator had on many occasions been nominated as a last resource. But now when an enemy, never seen or even heard of before, was rousing up war from ocean and the furthest corners of the world, no recourse was had to a Dictator, no extraordinary efforts were made. Those men through whose recklessness the war had been brought about were in supreme commands as tribunes, and the levy they raised was not larger than had been usual in ordinary campaigns, they even made light of the resorts as to the seriousness of the war. Meantime the Gauls learnt that their embassy had been treated with contempt, and that honors had actually been conferred upon men who had violated the law of nations. Burning with rage—as a nation they cannot control their passions—they seized their standards and hurriedly set out on their march. At the sound of their tumult as they swept by, the affrighted cities flew to arms and the country folk took to flight. Horses and men, spread far and wide, covered an immense tract of country; wherever they went they made it understood by loud shouts that they were going to Rome. But though they were preceded by rumors and by messages from Clusium, and then from one town after another, it was the swiftness of their approach that created most alarm in Rome. An army hastily raised by a levy en masse marched out to meet them. The two forces met hardly eleven miles from Rome, at a spot where the Alia, flowing in a very deep channel from the Crustuminian mountains, joins the river Tiber a little below the road to Crustumerium. The whole country in front and around was now swarming with the enemy, who, being as a nation given to wild outbreaks, had by their hideous howls and discordant clamor filled everything with dreadful noise.

38. The consular tribunes had secured no position for their camp, had constructed no entrenchments behind which to retire, and had shown as much disregard of the gods as of the enemy, for they formed their order of battle without having obtained favorable auspices. They extended their line on either wing to prevent their being outflanked, but even so they could not make their front equal to the enemy's, whilst by thus thinning their line they weakened the center so that it could hardly keep in touch. On their right was a small eminence which they decided to hold with reserves, and this disposition, though it was the beginning of the panic and flight, proved to be the only means of safety to the fugitives. For Brennus, the Gallic chieftain, fearing some ruse in the scanty numbers of the enemy, and thinking that the rising ground was occupied in order that the reserves might attack the flank and rear of the Gauls while their front was engaged with the legions, directed his attack upon the reserves, feeling quite certain that if he drove them from their position, his overwhelming numbers would give him an easy victory on the level ground. So not only Fortune but tactics also were on the side of the barbarians. In the other army there was nothing to remind one of Romans either amongst the generals or the private soldiers. They were terrified, and all they thought about was flight, and so utterly had they lost their heads that a far greater number fled to Veii, a hostile city, though the Tiber lay in their way, than by the direct road to Rome, to their wives and children. For a short time the reserves were protected by their position. In the rest of the army, no sooner was the battle-shout heard on their flank by those nearest to the reserves, and then by those at the other end of the line heard in their rear, than they fled, whole and unhurt, almost before they had seen their untried foe, without any attempt to fight or even to give back the battle-shout. None were slain while actually fighting; they were cut down from behind whilst hindering one another's flight in a confused, struggling mass. Along the bank of the Tiber, whither the whole of the left wing had fled, after throwing away their arms, there was great slaughter. Many who were unable to swim or were hampered by the weight of their cuirasses and other armor were sucked down by the current. The greater number, however, reached Veii in safety, yet not only were no troops sent from there to defend the City, but not even was a messenger dispatched to report the defeat to Rome. All the men on the right wing, which had been stationed some distance from the river, and nearer to the foot of the hill, made for Rome and took refuge in the Citadel without even closing the City gates.

39. The Gauls for their part were almost dumb with astonishment at so sudden and extraordinary a victory. At first they did not dare to move from the spot, as though puzzled by what had happened, then they began to fear a surprise, at last they began to despoil the dead, and, as their custom is, to pile up the arms in heaps. Finally, as no hostile movement was anywhere visible, they commenced their march and reached Rome shortly before sunset. The cavalry, who had ridden on in front, reported that the gates were not shut, there were no pickets on guard in front of them, no troops on the walls. This second surprise, as extraordinary as the previous one, held them back, and fearing a nocturnal conflict in the streets of an unknown City, they halted and bivouacked between Rome and the Anio. Reconnoitering parties were sent out to examine the circuit of the walls and the other gates, and to ascertain what plans their enemies were forming in their desperate plight. As for the Romans, since the greater number had fled from the field in the direction of Veii instead of Rome, it was universally believed that the only survivors were those who had found refuge in Rome, and the mourning for all who were lost, whether living or dead, filled the whole City with the cries of lamentation. But the sounds of private grief were stifled by the general terror when it was announced that the enemy were at hand. Presently the yells and wild war-whoops of the squadrons were heard as they rode round the walls. All the time until the next day's dawn the citizens were in such a state of suspense that they expected from moment to moment an attack on the City. They expected it first when the enemy approached the walls, for they would have remained at the Alia had not this been their object; then just before sunset they thought the enemy would attack because there was not much daylight left; and then when night was fallen they imagined that the attack was delayed till then to create all the greater terror. Finally, the approach of the

next day deprived them of their senses; the entrance of the enemy's standards within the gates was the dreadful climax to fears that had known no
respite.

But all through that night and the following day the citizens afforded an
utter contrast to those who had fled in such terror at the Alia. Realizing the
hopelessness of attempting any defense of the City with the small numbers
that were left, they decided that the men of military age and the able-bodied
amongst the senators should, with their wives and children, withdraw into
the Citadel and the Capitol, and after getting in stores of arms and provisions, should from that fortified position defend their gods, themselves, and
the great name of Rome. The Flamen and priestesses of Vesta were to carry
the sacred things of the State far away from the bloodshed and the fire, and
their sacred cult should not be abandoned as long as a single person survived
to observe it. If only the Citadel and the Capitol, the abode of gods; if only
the senate, the guiding mind of the national policy; if only the men of military age survived the impending ruin of the City, then the loss of the crowd
of old men left behind in the City could be easily borne; in any case, they
were certain to perish. To reconcile the aged plebeians to their fate, the men
who had been consuls and enjoyed triumphs gave out that they would meet
their fate side by side with them, and not burden the scanty force of fighting
men with bodies too weak to carry arms or defend their country.

40. Thus they sought to comfort one another—these aged men doomed
to death. Then they turned with words of encouragement to the younger
men on their way to the Citadel and Capitol, and solemnly commended to
their strength and courage all that was left of the fortunes of a City which for
360 years had been victorious in all its wars. As those who were carrying with
them all hope and succor finally separated from those who had resolved not
to survive the fall of the City the misery of the scene was heightened by the
distress of the women. Their tears, their distracted running about as they followed first their husbands then their sons, their imploring appeals to them
not to leave them to their fate, made up a picture in which no element of
human misery was wanting. A great many of them actually followed their
sons into the Capitol, none forbidding or inviting them, for though to diminish the number of non-combatants would have helped the besieged, it was
too inhuman a step to take. Another crowd, mainly of plebeians, for whom
there was not room on so small a hill or food enough in the scanty store of
corn, poured out of the City in one continuous line and made for the Janiculum. From there they dispersed, some over the country, others towards the
neighboring cities, without any leader or concerted action, each following his
own aims, his own ideas, and all despairing of the public safety. While all this
was going on, the Flamen of Quirinus and the Vestal virgins, without giving
a thought to their own property, were deliberating as to which of the sacred

things they ought to take with them, and which to leave behind, since they had not strength enough to carry all, and also what place would be the safest for their custody. They thought best to conceal what they could not take in earthen jars and bury them under the chapel next to the Flamen's house, where spitting is now forbidden. The rest they divided amongst them and carried off, taking the road which leads by the Pons Sublicius to the Janiculum. Whilst ascending that hill they were seen by L. Albinius, a Roman plebeian who with the rest of the crowd who were unfit for war was leaving the City. Even in that critical hour the distinction between sacred and profane was not forgotten. He had his wife and children with him in a wagon, and it seemed to him an act of impiety for him and his family to be seen in a vehicle whilst the national priests should be trudging along on foot, bearing the sacred vessels of Rome. He ordered his wife and children to get down, put the virgins and their sacred burden in the wagon, and drove them to Caere, their destination.

41. After all the arrangements that circumstances permitted had been made for the defense of the Capitol, the old men returned to their respective homes and, fully prepared to die, awaited the coming of the enemy. Those who had filled curule offices resolved to meet their fate wearing the insignia of their former rank and honor and distinctions. They put on the splendid dress which they wore when conducting the chariots of the gods or riding in triumph through the City, and thus arrayed, they seated themselves in their ivory chairs in front of their houses. Some writers record that, led by M. Fabius, the Pontifex Maximus, they recited the solemn formula in which they devoted themselves to death for their country and the Quirites. As the Gauls were refreshed by a night's rest after a battle which had at no point been seriously contested, and as they were not now taking the City by assault or storm, their entrance the next day was not marked by any signs of excitement or anger. Passing the Colline gate, which was standing open, they came to the Forum and gazed round at the temples and at the Citadel, which alone wore any appearance of war. They left there a small body to guard against any attack from the Citadel or Capitol whilst they were scattered, and then they dispersed in quest of plunder through streets in which they did not meet a soul. Some poured in a body into all the houses near, others made for the most distant ones, expecting to find them untouched and full of spoils. Appalled by the very desolation of the place and dreading lest some stratagem should surprise the stragglers, they returned to the neighborhood of the Forum in close order. The houses of the plebeians were barricaded, the halls of the patricians stood open, but they felt greater hesitation about entering the open houses than those which were closed. They gazed with feelings of real veneration upon the men who were seated in the porticoes of their mansions, not only because of the superhuman magnificence of their apparel and their whole bearing and demeanor, but also because of the majestic expression of their countenances, wearing the very aspect of gods. So they stood, gazing at them as if they were statues, till, as it is asserted, one of the patricians, M. Papirius, roused the passion of a Gaul, who began to stroke his beard—which in those days was universally worn long—by smiting him on the head with his ivory staff. He was the first to be killed, the others were butchered in their chairs. After this slaughter of the magnates, no living being was thenceforth spared; the houses were rifled, and then set on fire.

42. Now—whether it was that the Gauls were not all animated by a passion for the destruction of the City, or whether their chiefs had decided on the one hand to present the spectacle of a few fires as a means of intimidating the besieged into surrender from a desire to save their homes, and on the other, by abstaining from a universal conflagration, hold what remained of the City as a pledge by which to weaken their enemies' determination—certain it is that the fires were far from being so indiscriminate or so extensive as might be expected on the first day of a captured city. As the Romans beheld from the Citadel the City filled with the enemy who were running about in all the streets, while some new disaster was constantly occurring, first in one quarter then in another, they could no longer control their eyes and ears, let alone their thoughts and feelings. In whatever direction their attention was drawn by the shouts of the enemy, the shrieks of the women and boys, the roar of the flames, and the crash of houses falling in, thither they turned their eyes and minds as though set by Fortune to be spectators of their country's fall, powerless to protect anything left of all they possessed beyond their lives. Above all others who have ever stood a siege were they to be pitied, cut off as they were from the land of their birth and seeing all that had been theirs in the possession of the enemy. The day which had been spent in such misery was succeeded by a night not one whit more restful, this again by a day of anguish, there was not a single hour free from the sight of some ever fresh calamity. And yet, though, weighed down and overwhelmed with so many misfortunes, they had watched everything laid low in flame and ruin, they did not for a moment relax their determination to defend by their courage the one spot still left to freedom, the hill which they held, however small and poor it might be. At length, as this state of things went on day by day, they became as it were hardened to misery, and turned their thoughts from the circumstances round them to their arms and the sword in their right hand, which they gazed upon as the only things left to give them hope.

43. For some days the Gauls had been making useless war merely upon the houses of the City. Now that they saw nothing surviving amidst the ashes and ruin of the captured City except an armed foe whom all these disasters had failed to appall, and who would entertain no thought of surrender unless force were employed, they determined as a last resort to make an assault on

the Citadel. At daybreak the signal was given and the whole of their number formed up in the Forum. Raising their battle-shout and locking their shields together over their heads, they advanced. The Romans awaited the attack without excitement or fear, the detachments were strengthened to guard all the approaches, and in whatever direction they saw the enemy advancing, there they posted a picked body of men and allowed the enemy to climb up, for the steeper the ground they got on to, the easier they thought it would be to fling them down the slope. About midway up the hill the Gauls halted; then from the higher ground, which of itself almost hurled them against the enemy, the Romans charged, and routed the Gauls with such loss and over-throw that they never again attempted that mode of fighting either with detachments or in full strength. All hope, therefore, of forcing a passage by direct assault being laid aside, they made preparations for a blockade. Up to that time they had never thought of one; all the corn in the City had been destroyed in the conflagrations, whilst that in the fields around had been hastily carried off to Veii since the occupation of the City. So the Gauls decided to divide their forces; one division was to invest the Citadel, the other to forage amongst the neighboring States so that they could supply corn to those who were keeping up the investment. It was Fortune herself who led the Gauls after they left the City to Ardea, that they might have some experi-ence of Roman courage. Camillus was living there as an exile, grieving more over his country's fortunes than his own, eating his heart out in reproaches to gods and men, asking in indignant wonder where the men were with whom he had taken Veii and Falerii; men whose valor in all their wars was greater even than their success. Suddenly he heard that the Gallic army was approaching, and that the Ardeates were engaged in anxious deliberation about it. He had generally avoided the council meetings, but now, seized with an inspiration nothing short of divine, he hastened to the assembled councilors and addressed them as follows:

44. "Men of Ardea! friends of old, and now my fellow-citizens—for this your kindness has granted, this my fortunes have compelled—let none of you imagine that I have come here in forgetfulness of my position. The force of circumstances and the common danger constrain every man to contribute what help he can to meet the crisis. When shall I ever be able to show my gratitude for all the obligations you have conferred if I fail in my duty now? When shall I ever be of any use to you if not in war? It was by that that I held my position in my native City as having never known defeat; in times of peace my ungrateful countrymen banished me. Now the chance is offered to you, men of Ardea, of proving your gratitude for all the kindness that Rome has shown you—you have not forgotten how great it is, nor need I bring it up against those who so well remember it—the chance of winning for your city a vast reputation for war at the expense of our common foe. Those who are coming here in loose and disorderly fashion are a race to whom nature has given bodies and minds distinguished by bulk rather than by resolution and endurance. It is for this reason that they bring into every battle a terrifying appearance rather than real force. Take the disaster of Rome as a proof. They captured the City because it lay open to them; a small force repelled them from the Citadel and Capitol. Already the irksomeness of an investment has proved too much for them, they are giving it up and wandering through the fields in straggling parties. When they are gorged with food and the wine they drink so greedily, they throw themselves down like wild beasts, on the approach of night, in all directions by the streams, without entrenching themselves, or setting any outposts or pickets on guard. And now after their success they are more careless than ever. If it is your intention to defend your walls and not to allow all this country to become a second Gaul, seize your arms and muster in force by the first watch and follow me to what will be a massacre, not a battle. If I do not deliver them, whilst enchained by sleep, into your hands to be slaughtered like cattle, I am ready to accept the same fate in Ardea which I met with in Rome."

45. Friends and foes were alike persuaded that nowhere else was there at that time so great a master of war. After the council broke up they refreshed themselves and waited eagerly for the signal to be given. When it was given in the silence of the night they were at the gates ready for Camillus. After marching no great distance from the city they came upon the camp of the Gauls, unprotected, as he had said, and carelessly open on every side. They raised a tremendous shout and rushed in; there was no battle, it was everywhere sheer massacre; the Gauls, defenseless and dissolved in sleep, were butchered as they lay. Those in the furthest part of the camp, however, startled from their lairs, and not knowing whence or what the attack was, fled in terror, and some actually rushed, unawares, amongst their assailants. A considerable number were carried into the neighborhood of Antium, where they were surrounded by the townsmen. A similar slaughter of Etruscans took place in the district of Veii. So far were these people from feeling sympathy with a City which for almost four centuries had been their neighbor, and was now crushed by an enemy never seen or heard of before, that they chose that time for making forays into Roman territory, and after loading themselves with plunder, intended to attack Veii, the bulwark and only surviving hope of the Roman name. The Roman soldiers at Veii had seen them dispersed through the fields, and afterwards, with their forces collected, driving their booty in front of them. Their first feelings were those of despair, then indignation and rage took possession of them. "Are even the Etruscans," they exclaimed, "from whom we have diverted the arms of Gaul on to ourselves, to find amusement in our disasters?" With difficulty they restrained themselves from attacking them. Caedicius, a centurion whom they had placed in command, induced them to defer operations till nightfall. The only thing lacking was a commander like Camillus, in all other respects the ordering of the attack and the success achieved were the same as if he had been present. Not content with this, they made some prisoners who had survived the night's massacre act as guides, and, led by them, surprised another body of Tuscans at the salt works and inflicted a still greater loss upon them. Exultant at this double victory they returned to Veii.

46. During these days there was little going on in Rome; the investment was maintained for the most part with great slackness; both sides were keeping quiet, the Gauls being mainly intent on preventing any of the enemy from slipping through their lines. Suddenly a Roman warrior drew upon himself the admiration of foes and friends alike. The Fabian house had an annual sacrifice on the Quirinal, and C. Fabius Dorsuo, wearing his toga in the "Gabine cincture," and bearing in his hands the sacred vessels, came down from the Capitol, passed through the middle of the hostile pickets, unmoved by either challenge or threat, and reached the Quirinal. There he duly performed all the solemn rites and returned with the same composed expression and gait, feeling sure of the divine blessing, since not even the fear of death had made him neglect the worship of the gods; finally he re-entered the Capitol and rejoined his comrades. Either the Gauls were stupefied at his extraordinary boldness, or else they were restrained by religious feelings, for as a nation they are by no means inattentive to the claims of religion. At Veii there was a steady accession of strength as well as courage. Not only were the Romans who had been dispersed by the defeat and the capture of the City gathering there, but volunteers from Latium also flocked to the place that they might be in for a share of the booty. The time now seemed ripe for the recovery of their native City out of the hands of the enemy. But though the body was strong it lacked a head. The very place reminded men of Camillus, the majority of the soldiers had fought successfully under his auspices and leadership, and Caedicius declared that he would give neither gods nor men any pretext for terminating his command; he would rather himself, remembering his subordinate rank, ask for a commander-in-chief. It was decided by general consent that Camillus should be invited from Ardea, but the senate was to be consulted first; to such an extent was everything regulated by reverence for law; the proper distinctions of things were observed, even though the things themselves were almost lost. Frightful risk would have to be incurred in passing through the enemies' outposts. Pontius Cominius, a fine soldier, offered himself for the task. Supporting himself on a cork float, he was carried down the Tiber to the City. Selecting the nearest way from the bank of the river, he scaled a precipitous rock which, owing to its steepness, the enemy had left unguarded, and found his way into the Capitol. On being brought before the supreme magistrates he delivered his instructions from the army. After receiving the decree of the senate, which was to the effect that after being recalled from exile by the comitia curiata, Camillus should be forthwith nominated Dictator by order of the people, and the soldiers should have the commander they wanted, the messenger returned by the same route and made the best of his way to Veii. A deputation was sent to Ardea to conduct Camillus to Veii. The law was passed in the comitia curiata annulling his banishment and nominating him Dictator, and it is, I think, more likely that he did not start from Ardea until he learnt that this law had been passed, because he could not change his domicile without the sanction of the people, nor could he take the auspices in the name of the army until he had been duly nominated Dictator.

47. While these proceedings were taking place at Veii, the Citadel and Capitol of Rome were in imminent danger. The Gauls had either noticed the footprints left by the messenger from Veii, or had themselves discovered a comparatively easy ascent up the cliff to the temple of Carmentis. Choosing a night when there was a faint glimmer of light, they sent an unarmed man in advance to try the road; then handing one another their arms where the path was difficult, and supporting each other or dragging each other up as the ground required, they finally reached the summit. So silent had their movements been that not only were they unnoticed by the sentinels, but they did not even wake the dogs, an animal peculiarly sensitive to nocturnal sounds. But they did not escape the notice of the geese, which were sacred to Juno and had been left untouched in spite of the extremely scanty supply of food. This proved the safety of the garrison, for their clamor and the noise of their wings aroused M. Manlius, the distinguished soldier, who had been consul three years before. He snatched up his weapons and ran to call the rest to arms, and while the rest hung back he struck with the boss of his shield a Gaul who had got a foothold on the summit and knocked him down. He fell on those behind and upset them, and Manlius slew others who had laid aside their weapons and were clinging to the rocks with their hands. By this time others had joined him, and they began to dislodge the enemy with volleys of stones and javelins till the whole body fell helplessly down to the bottom. When the uproar had died away, the remainder of the night was given to sleep, as far as was possible under such disturbing circumstances, whilst their peril, though past, still made them anxious.

At daybreak the soldiers were summoned by sound of trumpet to a council in the presence of the tribunes, when the due rewards for good conduct and for bad would be awarded. First, Manlius was commended for his bravery, and rewarded not by the tribunes alone but by the soldiers as a body, for every man brought to him at his quarters, which were in the Citadel, half a pound of meal and a quarter of a pint of wine. This does not sound much, but the scarcity made it an overwhelming proof of the affection felt for him, since each stinted himself of food and contributed in honor of that one man what had to be taken from his necessaries of life. Next, the sentinels who had been on duty at the spot where the enemy had climbed up without their noticing it were called forward. Q. Sulpicius, the consular tribune, declared that he should punish them all by martial law. He was, however, deterred from this course by the shouts of the soldiers, who all agreed in throwing the blame upon one man. As there was no doubt of his guilt, he was amidst general approval flung from the top of the cliff. A stricter watch was now kept on both sides; by the Gauls because it had become known that messengers were passing between Rome and Veii; by the Romans, who had not forgotten the danger they were in that night.

48. But the greatest of all the evils arising from the siege and the war was the famine which began to afflict both armies, whilst the Gauls were also visited with pestilence. They had their camp on low-lying ground between the hills, which had been scorched by the fires and was full of malaria, and the least breath of wind raised not dust only but ashes. Accustomed as a nation to wet and cold, they could not stand this at all, and tortured as they were by heat and suffocation, disease became rife among them, and they died off like sheep. They soon grew weary of burying their dead singly, so they piled the bodies into heaps and burned them indiscriminately, and made the locality notorious; it was afterwards known as the Busta Gallica. Subsequently a truce was made with the Romans, and with the sanction of the commanders, the soldiers held conversations with each other. The Gauls were continually bringing up the famine and calling upon them to yield to necessity and surrender. To remove this impression it is said that bread was thrown in many places from the Capitol into the enemies' pickets. But soon the famine could neither be concealed nor endured any longer. So, at the very time that the Dictator was raising his own levy at Ardea, and ordering his Master of the Horse, L. Valerius, to withdraw his army from Veii, and making preparations for a sufficient force with which to attack the enemy on equal terms, the army of the Capitol, worn out with incessant duty, but still superior to all human ills, had nature not made famine alone insuperable by them, were day by day eagerly watching for signs of any help from the Dictator. At last not only food but hope failed them. Whenever the sentinels went on duty, their feeble frames almost crushed by the weight of their armor, the army insisted that they should either surrender or purchase their ransom on the best terms they could, for the Gauls were throwing out unmistakable hints that they could be induced to abandon the siege for a moderate consideration. A meeting of the senate was now held, and the consular tribunes were empowered to make terms. A conference took place between Q. Sulpicius, the consular tribune, and Brennus, the Gallic chieftain, and an agreement was arrived at by which 1000 lbs. of gold was fixed as the ransom of a people destined ere long to rule the world. This humiliation was great enough as it was, but it was aggravated by the despicable meanness of the Gauls, who produced unjust weights, and when the tribune protested, the insolent Gaul threw his sword into the scale, with an exclamation intolerable to Roman ears: *Vae Victis*—"Woe to the vanquished!"

49. But gods and men alike prevented the Romans from living as a ransomed people. By a dispensation of Fortune it came about that before the infamous ransom was completed and all the gold weighed out, whilst the dispute was still going on, the Dictator appeared on the scene and ordered the gold to be carried away and the Gauls to move off. As they declined to do so, and protested that a definite compact had been made, he informed them that when he was once appointed Dictator no compact was valid which was made by an inferior magistrate without his sanction. He then warned the Gauls to prepare for battle, and ordered his men to pile their baggage into a heap, get their weapons ready, and win their country back by steel, not by gold. They must keep before their eyes the temples of the gods, their wives and children, and their country's soil, disfigured by the ravages of war—everything, in a word, which it was their duty to defend, to recover or to avenge. He then drew up his men in the best formation that the nature of the ground, naturally uneven and now half burnt, admitted, and made every provision that his military skill suggested for securing the advantage of position and movement for his men. The Gauls, alarmed at the turn things had taken, seized their weapons and rushed upon the Romans with more rage than method. Fortune had now turned, divine aid and human skill were on the side of Rome. At the very first encounter the Gauls were routed as easily as they had conquered at the Alia. In a second and more sustained battle at the eighth milestone on the road to Gabii, where they had rallied from their flight, they were again defeated under the generalship and auspices of Camillus. Here the carnage was complete; the camp was taken, and not a single man was left to carry tidings of the disaster. After thus recovering his country from the enemy, the Dictator returned in triumph to the City, and amongst the homely jests which soldiers are wont to bandy, he was called in no idle words of praise, "A Romulus," "The Father of his country," "The Second Founder of the City." He had saved his country in war, and now that peace was restored, he proved, beyond all doubt, to be its savior again, when he prevented the migration to Veii. The tribunes of the plebs were urging this course more strongly than ever now that the City was burnt, and the plebs were themselves more in favor of it. This movement and the pressing appeal which the senate made to him not to abandon the republic while the position of affairs was so doubtful, determined him not to lay down his dictatorship after his triumph.

BOOK XXI 1–48; 52–63

After Hannibal's successful siege of Saguntum in Spain, Rome declared war on Carthage in 218 B.C.E. Hannibal marched across southern Gaul, and brought his army and its Gallic allies through the Alps into Italy. He defeated the Roman armies at the Trebia River in northern Italy.

1. I consider myself at liberty to commence what is only a section of my history with a prefatory remark such as most writers have placed at the very beginning of their works, namely, that the war I am about to describe is the most memorable of any that have ever been waged, I mean the war which the Carthaginians, under Hannibal's leadership, waged with Rome. No states, no nations ever met in arms greater in strength or richer in resources; these Powers themselves had never before been in so high a state of efficiency or better prepared to stand the strain of a long war; they were no strangers to each other's tactics after their experience in the first Punic War; and so variable were the fortunes and so doubtful the issue of the war that those who were ultimately victorious were in the earlier stages brought nearest to ruin. And yet, great as was their strength, the hatred they felt towards each other was almost greater. The Romans were furious with indignation because the vanquished had dared to take the offensive against their conquerors; the Carthaginians bitterly resented what they regarded as the tyrannical and rapacious conduct of Rome. The prime author of the war was Hamilcar. There was a story widely current that when, after bringing the African War to a close, he was offering sacrifices before transporting his army to Spain, the boy Hannibal, nine years old, was coaxing his father to take him with him, and his father led him up to the altar and made him swear with his hand laid on the victim that as soon as he possibly could he would show himself the enemy of Rome. The loss of Sicily and Sardinia vexed the proud spirit of the man, for he felt that the cession of Sicily had been made hastily in a spirit of despair, and that Sardinia had been filched by the Romans during the troubles in Africa, who, not content with seizing it, had imposed an indemnity as well.

2. Smarting under these wrongs, he made it quite clear from his conduct of the African War which followed immediately upon the conclusion of peace with Rome, and from the way in which he strengthened and extended the rule of Carthage during the nine years' war with Spain, that he was meditating a far greater war than any he was actually engaged in, and that had he lived longer it would have been under his command that the Carthaginians effected the invasion of Italy, which they actually carried out under Hannibal. The death of Hamilcar, occurring as it did most opportunely, and the tender years of Hannibal delayed the war. Hasdrubal, coming between father and son, held the supreme power for eight years. He is said to have become a favorite of Hamilcar's owing to his personal beauty as a boy; afterwards he displayed talents of a very different order, and became his son-in-law. Through this connection he was placed in power by the influence of the Barcine party, which was unduly preponderant with the soldiers and the common people, but his elevation was utterly against the wishes of the nobles. Trusting to policy rather than to arms, he did more to extend the empire of Carthage by forming connections with the petty chieftains and winning over new tribes by making friends of their leading men than by force of arms or by war. But peace brought him no security. A barbarian whose master he had put to death murdered him in broad daylight, and when seized by the bystanders he looked as happy as though he had escaped. Even when put to the torture, his delight at the success of his attempt mastered his pain and his face wore a smiling expression. Owing to the marvelous tact he had shown in winning over the tribes and incorporating them into his dominions, the Romans had renewed the treaty with Hasdrubal. Under its terms, the River Ebro was to form the boundary between the two empires, and Saguntum, occupying an intermediate position between them, was to be a free city.

3. There was no hesitation shown in filling his place. The soldiers led the way by bringing the young Hannibal forthwith to the palace and proclaiming him their commander-in-chief amidst universal applause. Their action was followed by the plebs. Whilst little more than a boy, Hasdrubal had written to invite Hannibal to come to him in Spain, and the matter had actually been discussed in the senate. The Barcines wanted Hannibal to become familiar with military service; Hanno, the leader of the opposite party, resisted this. "Hasdrubal's request," he said, "appears a reasonable one, and yet I do not think we ought to grant it." This paradoxical utterance aroused the attention of the whole senate. He continued: "The youthful beauty which Hasdrubal surrendered to Hannibal's father he considers he has a fair claim to ask for in return from the son. It ill becomes us, however, to habituate our youths to the lust of our commanders, by way of military training. Are we afraid that it will be too long before Hamilcar's son surveys the extravagant power and the pageant of royalty which his father assumed, and that there will be undue delay in our becoming the slaves of the despot to whose son-in-law our armies have been bequeathed as though they were his patrimony? I, for my part, consider that this youth ought to be kept at home and taught to live in obedience to the laws and the magistrates on an equality with his fellow-citizens; if not, this small fire will some day or other kindle a vast conflagration."

4. Hanno's proposal received but slight support, though almost all the best men in the council were with him, but as usual, numbers carried the day against reason. No sooner had Hannibal landed in Spain than he became a

favorite with the whole army. The veterans thought they saw Hamilcar restored to them as he was in his youth; they saw the same determined expression the same piercing eyes, the same cast of features. He soon showed, however, that it was not his father's memory that helped him most to win the affections of the army. Never was there a character more capable of the two tasks so opposed to each other of commanding and obeying; you could not easily make out whether the army or its general were more attached to him. Whenever courage and resolution were needed Hasdrubal never cared to entrust the command to any one else; and there was no leader in whom the soldiers placed more confidence or under whom they showed more daring. He was fearless in exposing himself to danger and perfectly self-possessed in the presence of danger. No amount of exertion could cause him either bodily or mental fatigue; he was equally indifferent to heat and cold; his eating and drinking were measured by the needs of nature, not by appetite; his hours of sleep were not determined by day or night, whatever time was not taken up with active duties was given to sleep and rest, but that rest was not wooed on a soft couch or in silence, men often saw him lying on the ground amongst the sentinels and outposts, wrapped in his military cloak. His dress was in no way superior to that of his comrades; what did make him conspicuous were his arms and horses. He was by far the foremost both of the cavalry and the infantry, the first to enter the fight and the last to leave the field. But these great merits were matched by great vices—inhuman cruelty, a perfidy worse than Punic, an utter absence of truthfulness, reverence, fear of the gods, respect for oaths, sense of religion. Such was his character, a compound of virtues and vices. For three years he served under Hasdrubal, and during the whole time he never lost an opportunity of gaining by practice or observation the experience necessary for one who was to be a great leader of men.

5. From the day when he was proclaimed commander-in-chief, he seemed to regard Italy as his assigned field of action, and war with Rome as a duty imposed upon him. Feeling that he ought not to delay operations, lest some accident should overtake him as in the case of his father and afterwards of Hasdrubal, he decided to attack the Saguntines. As an attack on them would inevitably set the arms of Rome in motion, he began by invading the Olcades, a tribe who were within the boundaries but not under the dominion of Carthage. He wished to make it appear that Saguntum was not his immediate object, but that he was drawn into a war with her by the force of circumstances, by the conquest, that is, of all her neighbors and the annexation of their territory. Cartala, a wealthy city and the capital of the tribe, was taken by storm and sacked; the smaller cities, fearing a similar fate, capitulated and agreed to pay an indemnity. His victorious army enriched with plunder was marched into winter quarters in New Carthage. Here, by a lavish distribution of the spoils and the punctual discharge of all arrears of pay, he secured the allegiance of his own people and of the allied contingents.

At the beginning of spring he extended his operations to the Vaccaei, and two of their cities, Arbocala and Hermandica, were taken by assault. Arbocala held out for a considerable time, owing to the courage and numbers of its defenders; the fugitives from Hermandica joined hands with those of the Olcades who had abandoned their country—this tribe had been subjugated the previous year—and together they stirred up the Carpetani to war. Not far from the Tagus an attack was made upon Hannibal as he was returning from his expedition against the Vaccaei, and his army, laden as it was with plunder, was thrown into some confusion. Hannibal declined battle and fixed his camp by the side of the river; as soon as there was quiet and silence amongst the enemy, he forded the stream. His entrenchments had been carried just far enough to allow room for the enemy to cross over, and he decided to attack them during their passage of the river. He instructed his cavalry to wait until they had actually entered the water and then to attack them; his forty elephants he stationed on the bank. The Carpetani together with the contingents of the Olcades and Vaccaei numbered altogether 100,000 men, an irresistible force had they been fighting on level ground. Their innate fearlessness, the confidence inspired by their numbers, their belief that the enemy's retreat was due to fear, all made them look on victory as certain, and the river as the only obstacle to it. Without any word of command having been given, they raised a universal shout and plunged, each man straight in front of him, into the river. A huge force of cavalry descended from the opposite bank, and the two bodies met in mid-stream. The struggle was anything but an equal one. The infantry, feeling their footing insecure, even where the river was fordable, could have been ridden down even by unarmed horsemen, whereas the cavalry, with their bodies and weapons free and their horses steady even in the midst of the current, could fight at close quarters or not, as they chose. A large proportion were swept down the river, some were carried by cross currents to the other side where the enemy were, and were trampled to death by the elephants. Those in the rear thought it safest to return to their own side, and began to collect together as well as their fears allowed them, but before they had time to recover themselves Hannibal entered the river with his infantry in battle order and drove them in flight from the bank. He followed up his victory by laying waste their fields, and in a few days was able to receive the submission of the Carpetani. There was no part of the country beyond the Ebro which did not now belong to the Carthaginians, with the exception of Saguntum.

6. War had not been formally declared against this city, but there were already grounds for war. The seeds of quarrel were being sown amongst her neighbors, especially amongst the Turdetani. When the man who had sown

the seed showed himself ready to aid and abet the quarrel, and his object plainly was not to refer the question to arbitration, but to appeal to force, the Saguntines sent a deputation to Rome to beg for help in a war which was inevitably approaching. The consuls for the time being were P. Cornelius Scipio and Tiberius Sempronius Longus. After introducing the envoys they invited the senate to declare its opinion as to what policy should be adopted. It was decided that commissioners should be sent to Spain to investigate the circumstances, and if they considered it necessary they were to warn Hannibal not to interfere with the Saguntines, who were allies of Rome; then they were to cross over to Africa and lay before the Carthaginian council the complaints which they had made. But before the commission was dispatched news came that the siege of Saguntum had, to every one's surprise, actually commenced. The whole position of affairs required to be reconsidered by the senate; some were for assigning Spain and Africa as separate fields of action for the two consuls, and thought that the war ought to be prosecuted by land and sea; others were for confining the war solely to Hannibal in Spain; others again were of opinion that such an immense task ought not to be entered upon hastily, and that they ought to await the return of the commission from Spain. This latter view seemed the safest and was adopted, and the commissioners, P. Valerius Flaccus and Q. Baebius Tamphilus, were dispatched without further delay to Hannibal. If he refused to abandon hostilities they were to proceed to Carthage to demand the surrender of the general to answer for his breach of treaty.

7. During these proceedings in Rome the siege of Saguntum was being pressed with the utmost vigor. That city was by far the most wealthy of all beyond the Ebro; it was situated about a mile from the sea. It is said to have been founded by settlers from the island of Zacynthus, with an admixture of Rutulians from Ardea. In a short time, however, it had attained to great prosperity, partly through its land and sea-borne commerce, partly through the rapid increase of its population, and also through the maintenance of a high standard of political integrity which led it to act with a loyalty towards its allies that brought about its ruin. After carrying his ravages everywhere throughout the territory, Hannibal attacked the city from three separate points. There was an angle of the fortifications which looked down on a more open and level descent than the rest of the ground surrounding the city, and here he decided to bring up his vineae to allow the battering rams to be placed against the walls. But although the ground to a considerable distance from the walls was sufficiently level to admit of the vineae being brought up, they found when they had succeeded in doing this that they made no progress. A huge tower overlooked the place, and the wall, being here more open to attack, had been carried to a greater height than the rest of the fortifications. As the position was one of especial danger, so the resistance offered

by a picked body of defenders was of the most resolute character. At first they confined themselves to keeping the enemy back by the discharge of missiles and making it impossible for them to continue their operations in safety. As time went on, however, their weapons no longer flashed on the walls or from the tower, they ventured on a sortie and attacked the outposts and siege works of the enemy. In these irregular encounters the Carthaginians lost nearly as many men as the Saguntines. Hannibal himself, approaching the wall somewhat incautiously, fell with a severe wound in his thigh from a javelin, and such was the confusion and dismay that ensued that the vineae and siege works were all but abandoned.

8. For a few days, until the general's wound was healed, there was a blockade rather than an active siege, and during this interval, though there was a respite from fighting, the construction of siege works and approaches went on uninterruptedly. When the fighting was resumed it was fiercer than ever. In spite of the difficulties of the ground the vineae were advanced and the battering rams placed against the walls. The Carthaginians had the superiority in numbers—there were said to have been 150,000 fighting men—whilst the defenders, obliged to keep watch and ward everywhere, were dissipating their strength and finding their numbers unequal to the task. The walls were now being pounded by the rams, and in many places had been shaken down. One part where a continuous fall had taken place laid the city open; three towers in succession, and the whole of the wall between them fell with a tremendous crash. The Carthaginians looked upon the town as already captured after that fall, and both sides rushed through the breach as though the wall had only served to protect them from each other. There was nothing of the desultory fighting which goes on when cities are stormed, as each side gets an opportunity of attacking the other. The two bodies of combatants confronted one another in the space between the ruined wall and the houses of the city in as regular formation as though they had been in an open field. On the one side there was the courage of hope, on the other the courage of despair. The Carthaginians believed that with a little effort on their part the city would be theirs; the Saguntines opposed their bodies as a shield for their fatherland now stripped of its walls; not a man relaxed his foothold for fear of letting an enemy in through the spot which he had left open. So the hotter and closer the fighting became the greater grew the number of wounded, for no missile fell ineffectively amongst the crowded ranks. The missile used by the Saguntines was the phalarica, a javelin with a shaft smooth and round up to the head, which, as in the pilum, was an iron point of square section. The shaft was wrapped in tow and then smeared with pitch; the iron head was three feet long and capable of penetrating armor and body alike. Even if it only stuck in the shield and did not reach the body it was a most formidable weapon, for when it was discharged with the tow set on fire the flame was fanned to a fiercer heat by its passage through the air, and it forced the soldier to throw away his shield and left him defenseless against the sword thrusts which followed.

9. The conflict had now gone on for a considerable time without any advantage to either side; the courage of the Saguntines was rising as they found themselves keeping up an unhoped-for resistance, whilst the Carthaginians, unable to conquer, were beginning to look upon themselves as defeated. Suddenly the defenders, raising their battle-shout, forced the enemy back to the debris of the ruined wall; there, stumbling and in disorder, they were forced still further back and finally driven in rout and flight to their camp. Meantime it was announced that envoys had arrived from Rome. Hannibal sent messengers down to the harbor to meet them and inform them that it would be unsafe for them to advance any further through so many wild tribes now in arms, and also that Hannibal in the present critical position of affairs had no time to receive embassies. It was quite certain that if they were not admitted they would go to Carthage. He therefore forestalled them by sending messengers with a letter addressed to the heads of the Barcine party, to warn his supporters and prevent the other side from making any concessions to Rome.

10. The result was that, beyond being received and heard by the Carthaginian senate, the embassy found its mission a failure. Hanno alone, against the whole senate, spoke in favor of observing the treaty, and his speech was listened to in silence out of respect to his personal authority, not because his hearers approved of his sentiments. He appealed to them in the name of the gods, who are the witnesses and arbiters of treaties, not to provoke a war with Rome in addition to the one with Saguntum. "I urged you," he said, "and warned you not to send Hamilcar's son to the army. That man's spirit, that man's offspring cannot rest; as long as any single representative of the blood and name of Barca survives our treaty with Rome will never remain unimperilled. You have sent to the army, as though supplying fuel to the fire, a young man who is consumed with a passion for sovereign power, and who recognizes that the only way to it lies in passing his life surrounded by armed legions and perpetually stirring up fresh wars. It is you, therefore, who have fed this fire which is now scorching you. Your armies are investing Saguntum, which by the terms of the treaty they are forbidden to approach; before long the legions of Rome will invest Carthage, led by the same generals under the same divine guidance under which they avenged our breach of treaty obligations in the late war. Are you strangers to the enemy, to yourselves, to the fortunes of each nation? That worthy commander of yours refused to allow ambassadors who came from allies, on behalf of allies, to enter his camp, and set at naught the law of nations. Those men, repulsed from a place to which even an enemy's envoys are not refused access, have

come to us; they ask for the satisfaction which the treaty prescribes; they demand the surrender of the guilty party in order that the State may clear itself from all taint of guilt. The slower they are to take action, the longer they are in commencing war, so much the more persistence and determination, I fear, will they show when war has begun. Remember the Aegates and Eryx, and all you had to go through for four-and-twenty years. This boy was not commanding then, but his father, Hamilcar—a second Mars as his friends would have us believe. But we broke the treaty then as we are breaking it now; we did not keep our hands off Tarentum or, which is the same thing, off Italy then any more than we are keeping our hands off Saguntum now, and so gods and men combined to defeat us, and the question in dispute, namely, which nation had broken the treaty, was settled by the issue of the war, which, like an impartial judge, left the victory on the side which was in the right. It is against Carthage that Hannibal is now bringing up his vineae and towers, it is Carthage whose walls he is shaking with his battering rams. The ruins of Saguntum—would that I might prove a false prophet—will fall on our heads, and the war which was begun with Saguntum will have to be carried on with Rome.

"'Shall we then surrender Hannibal?' some one will say. I am quite aware that as regards him my advice will have little weight, owing to my differences with his father, but whilst I was glad to hear of Hamilcar's death, for if he were alive we should already be involved in war with Rome, I feel nothing but loathing and detestation for this youth, the mad firebrand who is kindling this war. Not only do I hold that he ought to be surrendered as an atonement for the broken treaty, but even if no demand for his surrender were made I consider that he ought to be deported to the farthest corner of the earth, exiled to some spot from which no tidings of him, no mention of his name, could reach us, and where it would be impossible for him to disturb the welfare and tranquillity of our State. This then is what I propose: 'That a commission be at once dispatched to Rome to inform the senate of our compliance with their demands, and a second to Hannibal ordering him to withdraw his army from Saguntum and then surrendering him to the Romans in accordance with the terms of the treaty, and I also propose that a third body of commissioners be sent to make reparation to the Saguntines.'"

11. When Hanno sat down no one deemed it necessary to make any reply, so completely was the senate, as a body, on the side of Hannibal. They accused Hanno of speaking in a tone of more uncompromising hostility than Flaccus Valerius, the Roman envoy, had assumed. The reply which it was decided to make to the Roman demands was that the war was started by the Saguntines not by Hannibal, and that the Roman people would commit an act of injustice if they took the part of the Saguntines against their ancient allies, the Carthaginians. Whilst the Romans were wasting time in dispatch-

ing commissioners, things were quiet round Saguntum. Hannibal's men were worn out with the fighting and the labors of the siege, and after placing detachments on guard over the vineae and other military engines, he gave his army a few days' rest. He employed this interval in stimulating the courage of his men by exasperating them against the enemy, and firing them by the prospect of rewards. After he had given out in the presence of his assembled troops that the plunder of the city would go to them, they were all in such a state of excitement that had the signal been given then and there it seemed impossible for anything to withstand them. As for the Saguntines, though they had a respite from fighting for some days, neither meeting attacks nor making any, they worked at their defenses so continuously by day and night that they completed a fresh wall at the place where the fall of the former wall had laid the town open.

The assault was recommenced with greater vigor than ever. In every direction confused shouts and clamor resounded, so that it was difficult to ascertain where to render assistance most promptly or where it was most needed. Hannibal was present in person to encourage his men, who were bringing up a tower on rollers which overtopped all the fortifications of the city. Catapults and ballistae had been put in position on each of the stories, and after it had been brought up to the walls it swept them clear of the defenders. Seizing his opportunity, Hannibal told off about 500 African troops to undermine the wall with pick-axes, an easy task, as the stones were not fixed with cement but with layers of mud between the courses in the ancient fashion of construction. More of it consequently fell than had been dug away, and through the gaping ruin the columns of armed warriors marched into the city. They seized some high ground, and after massing their catapults and ballistae there they enclosed it with a wall so as to have a fortified position actually within the city which could dominate it like a citadel. The Saguntines on their side carried an inside wall round the portion of the city not yet captured. Both sides kept up their fortifying and fighting with the utmost energy, but by having to defend the interior portion of the city the Saguntines were continually reducing its dimensions. In addition to this there was a growing scarcity of everything as the siege was prolonged, and the anticipations of outside help were becoming fainter; the Romans, their one hope, were so far away, whilst all immediately round them was in the hands of the enemy. For a few days their drooping spirits were revived by the sudden departure of Hannibal on an expedition against the Oretani and the Carpetani. The rigorous way in which troops were being levied in these two tribes had created great excitement, and they had kept the officers who were superintending the levy practically prisoners. A general revolt was feared, but the unexpected swiftness of Hannibal's movements took them by surprise and they abandoned their hostile attitude.

12. The attack on Saguntum was not slackened; Maharbal, the son of Himilco, whom Hannibal had left in command, carried on operations with such energy that the general's absence was not felt by either friends or foes. He fought several successful actions, and with the aid of three battering rams brought down a considerable portion of the wall, and on Hannibal's return showed him the place all strewn with the newly-fallen wall. The army was at once led to an assault on the citadel; a desperate fight began, with heavy losses on both sides, and a part of the citadel was captured. Attempts were now made in the direction of peace, though with but faint hopes of success. Two men undertook the task, Alco, a Saguntine, and Alorcus, a Spaniard. Alco, thinking that his prayers might have some effect, crossed over without the knowledge of the Saguntines to Hannibal at night. When he found that he gained nothing by his tears, and that the conditions offered were such as a victor exasperated by resistance would insist upon, harsh and severe, he laid aside the character of a pleader and remained with the enemy as a deserter, alleging that any one who advocated peace on such terms would be put to death. The conditions were that restitution should be made to the Turdetani, all the gold and silver should be delivered up, and the inhabitants should depart with one garment each and take up their abode wherever the Carthaginians should order them. As Alco insisted that the Saguntines would not accept peace on these terms, Alorcus, convinced, as he said, that when everything else has gone courage also goes, undertook to mediate a peace on those conditions. At that time he was one of Hannibal's soldiers, but he was recognized as a guest friend by the city of Saguntum. He started on his mission, gave up his weapon openly to the guard, crossed the lines, and was at his request conducted to the praetor of Saguntum. A crowd, drawn from all classes of society, soon gathered, and after a way had been cleared through the press, Alorcus was admitted to an audience of the senate. He addressed them in the following terms:

13. "If your fellow-townsman, Alco, had shown the same courage in bringing back to you the terms on which Hannibal will grant peace that he showed in going to Hannibal to beg for peace, this journey of mine would have been unnecessary. I have not come to you either as an advocate for Hannibal or as a deserter. But as he has remained with the enemy either through your fault or his own—his own if his fears were only feigned, yours if those who report what is true have to answer for their lives—I have come to you out of regard to the old ties of hospitality which have so long subsisted between us, that you may not be left in ignorance of the fact that there do exist terms on which you can secure peace and the safety of your lives. Now, that it is for your sake alone and not on behalf of any one else that I say what I am saying before you is proved by the fact that as long as you had the strength to maintain a successful resistance, and as long as you had any hopes of help from Rome, I never breathed a word about making peace. But now that you have no longer anything to hope for from Rome, now that neither your arms nor your walls suffice to protect you, I bring you a peace forced upon you by necessity rather than recommended by the fairness of its conditions. But the hopes, faint as they are, of peace rest upon your accepting as conquered men the terms which Hannibal as conqueror imposes and not looking upon what is taken from you as a positive loss, since everything is at the victor's mercy, but regarding what is left to you as a free gift from him. The city, most of which he has laid in ruins, the whole of which he has all but captured, he takes from you; your fields and lands he leaves you; and he will assign you a site where you can build a new town. He orders all the gold and silver, both that belonging to the State and that owned by private individuals, to be brought to him; your persons and those of your wives and children he preserves inviolate on condition that you consent to leave Saguntum with only two garments apiece and without arms. These are the demands of your victorious enemy, and heavy and bitter as they are, your miserable plight urges you to accept them. I am not without hope that when everything has passed into his power he will relax some of these conditions, but I consider that even as they are you ought to submit to them rather than permit yourselves to be butchered and your wives and children seized and carried off before your eyes."

14. A large crowd had gradually collected to listen to the speaker, and the popular Assembly had become mingled with the senate, when without a moment's warning the leading citizens withdrew before any reply was given. They collected all the gold and silver from public and private sources and brought it into the forum, where a fire had already been kindled, and flung it into the flames, and most of them thereupon leaped into the fire themselves. The terror and confusion which this occasioned throughout the city was heightened by the noise of a tumult in the direction of the citadel. A tower after much battering had fallen, and through the breach created by its fall a Carthaginian cohort advanced to the attack and signaled to their commander that the customary outposts and guards had disappeared and the city was unprotected. Hannibal thought that he ought to seize the opportunity and act promptly. Attacking it with his full strength, he took the place in a moment. Orders had been given that all the adult males were to be put to death; a cruel order, but under the circumstances inevitable, for whom would it have been possible to spare when they either shut themselves up with their wives and children and burnt their houses over their heads, or if they fought, would not cease fighting till they were killed?

15. An enormous amount of booty was found in the captured city. Although most of it had been deliberately destroyed by the owners, and the enraged soldiers had observed hardly any distinctions of age in the universal slaughter, whilst all the prisoners that were taken were assigned to them, still, it is certain that a considerable sum was realized by the sale of the goods that were seized, and much valuable furniture and apparel was sent to Carthage. Some writers assert that Saguntum was taken in the eighth month of the siege, and that Hannibal led his force from there to New Carthage for the winter, his arrival in Italy occurring five months later. In this case it is impossible for P. Cornelius and Ti. Sempronius to have been the consuls to whom the Saguntine envoys were sent at the beginning of the siege and who afterwards, whilst still in office, fought with Hannibal, one of them at the Ticinus, both shortly afterwards at the Trebia. Either all the incidents occurred within a much shorter period or else it was the capture of Saguntum, not the beginning of the siege, which occurred when those two entered upon office. For the battle of the Trebia cannot have fallen so late as the year when Cn. Servilius and C. Flaminius were in office, because C. Flaminius entered upon his consulship at Ariminum, his election taking place under the consul Tiberius Sempronius, who came to Rome after the battle of the Trebia to hold the consular elections, and, after they were over, returned to his army in winter quarters.

16. The commissioners who had been sent to Carthage, on their return to Rome, reported that everything breathed a hostile spirit. Almost on the very day they returned the news arrived of the fall of Saguntum, and such was the distress of the senate at the cruel fate of their allies, such was their feeling of shame at not having sent help to them, such their exasperation against the Carthaginians and their alarm for the safety of the State—for it seemed as though the enemy were already at their gates—that they were in no mood for deliberating, shaken as they were by so many conflicting emotions. There were sufficient grounds for alarm. Never had they met a more active or a more warlike enemy, and never had the Roman republic been so lacking in energy or so unprepared for war. The operations against the Sardinians, Corsicans, and Histrians, as well as those against the Illyrians, had been more of an annoyance than a training for the soldiers of Rome; whilst with the Gauls there had been desultory fighting rather than regular warfare. But the Carthaginians, a veteran enemy which for three-and-twenty years had seen hard and rough service amongst the Spanish tribes, and had always been victorious, trained under a general of exceptional ability, were now crossing the Ebro fresh from the sack of a most wealthy city, and were bringing with them all those Spanish tribes, eager for the fray. They would rouse the various Gaulish tribes, who were always ready to take up arms; there would be the whole world to fight against; the battleground would be Italy; the struggle would take place before the walls of Rome.

17. The seat of the campaigns had already been decided; the consuls were now ordered to draw lots. Spain fell to Cornelius, Africa to Sempronius.

It was resolved that six legions should be raised for that year, the allies were to furnish such contingents as the consuls should deem necessary, and as large a fleet as possible was to be fitted out; 24,000 Roman infantry were called up and 1,800 cavalry; the allies contributed 40,000 infantry and 4,400 cavalry, and a fleet of 220 ships of war and 20 light galleys was launched. The question was then formally submitted to the Assembly, Was it their will and pleasure that war should be declared against the people of Carthage? When this was decided, a special service of intercession was conducted; the procession marched through the streets of the city offering prayers at the various temples that the gods would grant a happy and prosperous issue to the war which the people of Rome had now ordered. The forces were divided between the consuls in the following way: To Sempronius two legions were assigned, each consisting of 4,000 infantry and 300 cavalry, and 16,000 infantry and 1,800 cavalry from the allied contingents. He was also provided with 160 warships and 12 light galleys. With this combined land and sea force he was sent to Sicily, with instructions to cross over to Africa if the other consul succeeded in preventing the Carthaginian from invading Italy. Cornelius, on the other hand, was provided with a smaller force, as L. Manlius, the praetor, was himself being dispatched to Gaul with a fairly strong detachment. Cornelius was weakest in his ships; he had only 60 warships, for it was never supposed that the enemy would come by sea or use his navy for offensive purposes. His land force was made up of two Roman legions, with their complement of cavalry, and 14,000 infantry from the allies with 1,600 cavalry. The province of Gaul was held by two Roman legions and 10,000 allied infantry with 600 Roman and 1,000 allied cavalry. This force was ultimately employed in the Punic War.

18. When these preparations were completed, the formalities necessary before entering upon war required that a commission should be dispatched to Carthage. Those selected were men of age and experience — Q. Fabius, M. Livius, L. Aemilius, C. Licinius, and Q. Baebius. They were instructed to inquire whether it was with the sanction of the government that Hannibal had attacked Saguntum, and if, as seemed most probable, the Carthaginians should admit that it was so and proceed to defend their action, then the Roman envoys were to formally declare war upon Carthage. As soon as they had arrived in Carthage they appeared before the senate. Q. Fabius had, in accordance with his instructions, simply put the question as to the responsibility of the government, when one of the members present said: "The language of your previous deputation was peremptory enough when you demanded the surrender of Hannibal on the assumption that he was attacking Saguntum on his own authority, but your language now, so far at least, is less provocative, though in effect more overbearing. For on that occasion it was Hannibal whose action you denounced and whose surrender you demanded, now you are seeking to extort from us a confession of guilt and insist upon obtaining instant satisfaction, as from men who admit they are in the wrong. I do not, however, consider that the question is whether the attack on Saguntum was an act of public policy or only that of a private citizen, but whether it was justified by circumstances or not. It is for us to inquire and take proceedings against a citizen when he has done anything on his own authority; the only point for you to discuss is whether his action was compatible with the terms of the treaty. Now, as you wish us to draw a distinction between what our generals do with the sanction of the State and what they do on their own initiative, you must remember that the treaty with us was made by your consul, C. Lutatius, and whilst it contained provisions guarding the interests of the allies of both nations, there was no such provision for the Saguntines, for they were not your allies at the time. But, you will say, by the treaty concluded with Hasdrubal, the Saguntines are exempted from attack. I shall meet that with your own arguments. You told us that you refused to be bound by the treaty which your consul, C. Lutatius, concluded with us, because it did not receive the authorization of either the senate or the Assembly. A fresh treaty was accordingly made by your government. Now, if no treaties have any binding force for you unless they have been made with the authority of your senate or by order of your Assembly, we, on our side, cannot possibly be bound by Hasdrubal's treaty, which he made without our knowledge. Drop all allusions to Saguntum and the Ebro, and speak out plainly what has long been secretly hatching in your minds." Then the Roman, gathering up his toga, said, "Here we bring you war and peace, take which you please." He was met by a defiant shout bidding him give whichever he preferred, and when, letting the folds of his toga fall, he said that he gave them war, they replied that they accepted war and would carry it on in the same spirit in which they accepted it.

19. This straightforward question and threat of war seemed to be more consonant with the dignity of Rome than a wordy argument about treaties; it seemed so previous to the destruction of Saguntum, and still more so afterwards. For had it been a matter for argument, what ground was there for comparing Hasdrubal's treaty with the earlier one of Lutatius? In the latter it was expressly stated that it would only be of force if the people approved it, whereas in Hasdrubal's treaty there was no such saving clause. Besides, his treaty had been silently observed for many years during his lifetime, and was so generally approved that, even after its author's death, none of its articles were altered. But even if they took their stand upon the earlier treaty—that of Lutatius—the Saguntines were sufficiently safeguarded by the allies of both parties being exempted from hostile treatment, for nothing was said about "the allies for the time being" or anything to exclude "any who should be hereafter taken into alliance." And since it was open to both parties to

form fresh alliances, who would think it a fair arrangement that none should be received into alliance whatever their merits, or that when they had been received they should not be loyally protected, on the understanding that the allies of the Carthaginians should not be induced to revolt, or if they deserted their allies on their own accord were not to be received into alliance by the others?

The Roman envoys in accordance with their instructions went on to Spain for the purpose of visiting the different tribes and drawing them into alliance with Rome, or at least detaching them from the Carthaginians. The first they came to were the Borgusii, who were tired of Punic domination and gave them a favorable reception, and their success here excited a desire for change amongst many of the tribes beyond the Ebro. They came next to the Volciani, and the response they met with became widely known throughout Spain and determined the rest of the tribes against an alliance with Rome. This answer was given by the senior member of their national council in the following terms: "Are you not ashamed, Romans, to ask us to form friendship with you in preference to the Carthaginians, seeing how those who have done so have suffered more through you, their allies, cruelly deserting them than through any injury inflicted on them by the Carthaginians? I advise you to look for allies where the fall of Saguntum has never been heard of; the nations of Spain see in the ruins of Saguntum a sad and emphatic warning against putting any trust in alliances with Rome." They were then peremptorily ordered to quit the territory of the Volciani, and from that time none of the councils throughout Spain gave them a more favorable reply. After this fruitless mission in Spain they crossed over into Gaul.

20. Here a strange and appalling sight met their eyes: the men attended the council fully armed, such was the custom of the country. When the Romans, after extolling the renown and courage of the Roman people and the greatness of their dominion, asked the Gauls not to allow the Carthaginian invaders a passage through their fields and cities, such interruption and laughter broke out that the younger men were with difficulty kept quiet by the magistrates and senior members of the council. They thought it a most stupid and impudent demand to make, that the Gauls, in order to prevent the war from spreading into Italy, should turn it against themselves and expose their own lands to be ravaged instead of other people's. After quiet was restored the envoys were informed that the Romans had rendered them no service, nor had the Carthaginians done them any injury to make them take up arms either on behalf of the Romans or against the Carthaginians. On the other hand, they heard that men of their race were being expelled from Italy, and made to pay tribute to Rome, and subjected to every other indignity. Their experience was the same in all the other councils of Gaul, nowhere did they hear a kindly or even a tolerably peaceable word till they reached Massilia. There all the facts which their allies had carefully and honestly collected were laid before them; they were informed that the interest of the Gauls had already been secured by Hannibal, but even he would not find them very tractable, with their wild and untamable nature, unless the chiefs were also won over with gold, a thing which as a nation they were most eager to procure. After thus traversing Spain and the tribes of Gaul the envoys returned to Rome not long after the consuls had left for their respective commands. They found the whole City in a state of excitement; definite news had been received that the Carthaginians had crossed the Ebro, and every one was looking forward to war.

21. After the capture of Saguntum, Hannibal withdrew into winter quarters at New Carthage. Information reached him there of the proceedings at Rome and Carthage, and he learnt that he was not only the general who was to conduct the war, but also the sole person who was responsible for its outbreak. As further delay would be most inexpedient, he sold and distributed the rest of the plunder, and calling together those of his soldiers who were of Spanish blood, he addressed them as follows: "I think, soldiers, that you yourselves recognize that now that we have reduced all the tribes in Spain we shall either have to bring our campaigns to an end and disband our armies or else we must transfer our wars to other lands. If we seek to win plunder and glory from other nations, then these tribes will enjoy not only the blessings of peace, but also the fruits of victory. Since, therefore, there await us campaigns far from home, and it is uncertain when you will again see your homes and all that is dear to you, I grant a furlough to every one who wishes to visit his friends. You must reassemble at the commencement of spring, so that we may, with the kindly help of the gods, enter upon a war which will bring us immense plunder and cover us with glory." They all welcomed the opportunity, so spontaneously offered, of visiting their homes after so long an absence, and in view of a still longer absence in the future. The winter's rest, coming after their past exertions, and soon to be followed by greater ones, restored their faculties of mind and body and strengthened them for fresh trials of endurance.

In the early days of spring they reassembled according to orders. After reviewing the whole of the native contingents, Hannibal left for Gades, where he discharged his vows to Hercules, and bound himself by fresh obligations to that deity in case his enterprise should succeed. As Africa would be open to attack from the side of Sicily during his land march through Spain and the two Gauls into Italy, he decided to secure that country with a strong garrison. To supply their place he requisitioned troops from Africa, a light-armed force consisting mainly of slingers. By thus transferring Africans to Spain and Spaniards to Africa, the soldiers of each nationality would be expected to render more efficient service, as being practically under recipro-cal obligations. The force he dispatched to Africa consisted of 13,850 Spanish infantry furnished with ox-hide bucklers, and 870 Balearic slingers, with a composite body of 1,200 cavalry drawn from numerous tribes. This force was destined partly for the defense of Carthage, partly to hold the African terri-tory. At the same time recruiting officers were sent to various communities; some 4,000 men of good family were called up who were under orders to be conveyed to Carthage to strengthen its defense, and also to serve as hostages for the loyalty of their people.

22. Spain also had to be provided for, all the more so as Hannibal was fully aware that Roman commissioners had been going all about the country to win over the leading men of the various tribes. He placed it in charge of his energetic and able brother, Hasdrubal, and assigned him an army mainly composed of African troops—11,850 native infantry, 300 Ligurians, and 500 Balearics. In addition to this body of infantry there were 450 Libyphoenician cavalry—these are a mixed race of Punic and aboriginal African descent—some 1,800 Numidians and Moors, dwellers on the shore of the Mediter-ranean, and a small mounted contingent of 300 Ilergetes raised in Spain. Finally, that his land force might be complete in all its parts, there were twenty-one elephants. The protection of the coast required a fleet, and as it was natural to suppose that the Romans would again make use of that arm in which they had been victorious before, Hasdrubal had assigned to him a fleet of 57 warships, including 50 quinqueremes, 2 quadriremes, and 5 triremes, but only 32 quinqueremes and the 5 triremes were ready for sea. From Gades he returned to the winter quarters of his army at New Carthage, and from New Carthage he commenced his march on Italy. Passing by the city of Onusa, he marched along the coast to the Ebro. The story runs that whilst halting there he saw in a dream a youth of god-like appearance who said that he had been sent by Jupiter to act as guide to Hannibal on his march to Italy. He was accordingly to follow him and not to lose sight of him or let his eyes wander. At first, filled with awe, he followed him without glancing round him or looking back, but as instinctive curiosity impelled him to wonder what it was that he was forbidden to gaze at behind him, he could no longer command his eyes. He saw behind him a serpent of vast and marvelous bulk, and as it moved along trees and bushes crashed down everywhere before it, whilst in its wake there rolled a thunder-storm. He asked what the mon-strous portent meant, and was told that it was the devastation of Italy; he was to go forward without further question and allow his destiny to remain hidden.

23. Gladdened by this vision he proceeded to cross the Ebro, with his army in three divisions, after sending men on in advance to secure by bribes the good-will of the Gauls dwelling about his crossing-place, and also to

reconnoiter the passes of the Alps. He brought 90,000 infantry and 12,000 cavalry over the Ebro. His next step was to reduce to submission the Ilergetes, the Bargusii, and the Ausetani, and also the district of Lacetania, which lies at the foot of the Pyrenees. He placed Hanno in charge of the whole coast-line to secure the passes which connect Spain with Gaul, and furnished him with an army of 10,000 infantry to hold the district, and 1,000 cavalry. When his army commenced the passage of the Pyrenees and the barbarians found that there was truth in the rumor that they were being led against Rome, 3,000 of the Carpetani deserted. It was understood that they were induced to desert not so much by the prospect of the war as by the length of the march and the impossibility of crossing the Alps. As it would have been hazardous to recall them, or to attempt to detain them by force, in case the quick passions of the rest of the army should be roused, Hannibal sent back to their homes more than 7,000 men who, he had personally discovered, were getting tired of the campaign, and at the same time he gave out that the Carpetani had also been sent back by him.

24. Then, to prevent his men from being demoralized by further delay and inactivity, he crossed the Pyrenees with the remainder of his force and fixed his camp at the town of Iliberri. The Gauls were told that it was against Italy that war was being made, but as they had heard that the Spaniards beyond the Pyrenees had been subjugated by force of arms, and strong garrisons placed in their towns, several tribes, fearing for their liberty, were roused to arms and mustered at Ruscino. On receiving the announcement of this movement, Hannibal, fearing delay more than hostilities, sent spokesmen to their chiefs to say that he was anxious for a conference with them, and either they might come nearer to Iliberri, or he would approach Ruscino to facilitate their meeting, for he would gladly receive them in his camp or would himself go to them without loss of time. He had come into Gaul as a friend not a foe, and unless the Gauls compelled him he would not draw his sword till he reached Italy. This was the proposal made through the envoys, but when the Gauls had, without any hesitation, moved their camp up to Iliberri, they were effectively secured by bribes and allowed the army a free and unmolested passage through their territory under the very walls of Ruscino.

25. No intelligence, meanwhile, had reached Rome beyond the fact reported by the Massilian envoys, namely that Hannibal had crossed the Ebro. No sooner was this known than the Boii, who had been tampering with the Insubres, rose in revolt, just as though he had already crossed the Alps, not so much in consequence of their old standing enmity against Rome as of her recent aggressions. Bodies of colonists were being settled on Gaulish territory in the valley of the Po, at Placentia and Cremona, and intense irritation was produced. Seizing their arms they made an attack on the land,

which was being actually surveyed at the time, and created such terror and confusion that not only the agricultural population, but even the three Roman commissioners who were engaged in marking out the holdings, fled to Mutina, not feeling themselves safe behind the walls of Placentia. The commissioners were C. Lutatius, C. Servilius, and M. Annius. There is no doubt as to the name Lutatius, but instead of Annius and Servilius some annalists have Manlius Acilius and C. Herennius, whilst others give P. Cornelius Asina and C. Papirius Maso. There is also doubt as to whether it was the envoys who had been sent to the Boii to remonstrate with them that were maltreated, or the commissioners upon whom an attack was made whilst surveying the ground. The Gauls invested Mutina, but as they were strangers to the art of conducting sieges, and far too indolent to set about the construction of military works, they contented themselves with blockading the town without inflicting any injury on the walls. At last they pretended that they were ready to discuss terms of peace, and the envoys were invited by the Gaulish chieftains to a conference. Here they were arrested, in direct violation not only of international law but of the safe-conduct which had been granted for the occasion. Having made them prisoners the Gauls declared that they would not release them until their hostages were restored to them.

When news came that the envoys were prisoners and Mutina and its garrison in jeopardy, L. Manlius, the praetor, burning with anger, led his army in separate divisions to Mutina. Most of the country was uncultivated at that time and the road went through a forest. He advanced without throwing out scouting parties and fell into an ambush, out of which, after sustaining considerable loss, he made his way with difficulty on to more open ground. Here he entrenched himself, and as the Gauls felt it would be hopeless to attack him there, the courage of his men revived, though it was tolerably certain that as many as 500 had fallen. They recommenced their march, and as long as they were going through open country there was no enemy in view; when they re-entered the forest their rear was attacked and great confusion and panic created. They lost 700 men and six standards. When they at last got out of the trackless and entangled forest there was an end to the terrifying tactics of the Gauls and the wild alarm of the Romans. There was no difficulty in repelling attacks when they reached the open country and made their way to Tannetum, a place near the Po. Here they hastily entrenched themselves, and, helped by the windings of the river and assisted by the Brixian Gauls, they held their ground against an enemy whose numbers were daily increasing.

26. When the intelligence of this sudden outbreak reached Rome and the senate became aware that they had a Gaulish war to face in addition to the war with Carthage, they ordered C. Atilius, the praetor, to go to the relief of Manlius with a Roman legion and 5,000 men who had been recently enlisted by the consul from among the allies. As the enemy, afraid to meet these reinforcements, had retired, Atilius reached Tannetum without any fighting. After raising a fresh legion in place of the one which had been sent away with the praetor, P. Cornelius Scipio set sail with sixty warships and coasted along by the shores of Etruria and Liguria, and from there past the mountains of the Salyes until he reached Marseilles. Here he disembarked his troops at the first mouth of the Rhone to which he came—the river flows into the sea through several mouths—and formed his entrenched camp, hardly able yet to believe that Hannibal had surmounted the obstacle of the Pyrenees. When, however, he understood that he was already contemplating crossing the Rhone, feeling uncertain as to where he would meet him and anxious to give his men time to recover from the effects of the voyage, he sent forward a picked force of 300 cavalry accompanied by Massilian guides and friendly Gauls to explore the country in all directions and if possible to discover the enemy.

Hannibal had overcome the opposition of the native tribes by either fear or bribes and had now reached the territory of the Volcae. They were a powerful tribe, inhabiting the country on both sides of the Rhone, but distrusting their ability to stop Hannibal on the side of the river nearest to him, they determined to make the river a barrier and transported nearly all the population to the other side, on which they prepared to offer armed resistance. The rest of the river population and those of the Volcae even, who still remained in their homes, were induced by presents to collect boats from all sides and to help in constructing others, and their efforts were stimulated by the desire to get rid as soon as possible of the burdensome presence of such a vast host of men. So an enormous number of boats and vessels of every kind, such as they used in their journeys up and down the river, was got together; new ones were made by the Gauls by hollowing out the trunks of trees, then the soldiers themselves, seeing the abundance of timber and how easily they were made, took to fashioning uncouth canoes, quite content if only they would float and carry burdens and serve to transport themselves and their belongings.

27. Everything was now ready for the crossing, but the whole of the opposite bank was held by mounted and unmounted men prepared to dispute the passage. In order to dislodge them Hannibal sent Hanno, the son of Bomilcar, with a division, consisting mainly of Spaniards, a day's march up the river. He was to seize the first chance of crossing without being observed, and then lead his men by a circuitous route behind the enemy and at the right moment attack them in the rear. The Gauls who were taken as guides informed Hanno that about 25 miles up-stream a small island divided the river in two, and the channel was of less depth in consequence. When they

reached the spot they hastily cut down the timber and constructed rafts on which men and horses and other burdens could be ferried across. The Spaniards had no trouble; they threw their clothes on to skins and placing their leather shields on the top they rested on these and so swam across. The rest of the army was ferried over on rafts, and after making a camp near the river they took a day's rest after their labors of boat-making and the nocturnal passage, their general in the meantime waiting anxiously for an opportunity of putting his plan into execution. The next day they set out on their march, and lighting a fire on some rising ground they signaled by the column of smoke that they had crossed the river and were not very far away. As soon as Hannibal received the signal he seized the occasion and at once gave the order to cross the river. The infantry had prepared rafts and boats, the cavalry mostly barges on account of the horses. A line of large boats was moored across the river a short distance up-stream to break the force of the current, and consequently the men in the smaller boats crossed over in smooth water. Most of the horses were towed astern and swam over, others were carried in barges, ready saddled and bridled so as to be available for the cavalry the moment they landed.

28. The Gauls flocked together on the bank with their customary whoops and war songs, waving their shields over their heads and brandishing their javelins. They were somewhat dismayed when they saw what was going on in front of them; the enormous number of large and small boats, the roar of the river, the confused shouts of the soldiers and boatmen, some of whom were trying to force their way against the current, whilst others on the bank were cheering their comrades who were crossing. Whilst they were watching all this movement with sinking hearts, still more alarming shouts were heard behind them; Hanno had captured their camp. Soon he appeared on the scene, and they were now confronted by danger from opposite quarters —the host of armed men landing from the boats and the sudden attack which was being made on their rear. For a time the Gauls endeavored to maintain the conflict in both directions, but finding themselves losing ground they forced their way through where there seemed to be least resistance and dispersed to their various villages. Hannibal brought over the rest of his force undisturbed, and, without troubling himself any further about the Gauls, formed his camp.

In the transport of the elephants I believe different plans were adopted; at all events, the accounts of what took place vary considerably. Some say that after they had all been collected on the bank the worst-tempered beast amongst them was teased by his driver, and when he ran away from it into the water the elephant followed him and drew the whole herd after it, and as they got out of their depth they were carried by the current to the opposite bank. The more general account, however, is that they were transported on rafts; as this method would have appeared the safest beforehand so it is most probable that it was the one adopted. They pushed out into the river a raft 200 feet long and 50 feet broad, and to prevent it from being carried downstream, one end was secured by several stout hawsers to the bank. It was covered with earth like a bridge in order that the animals, taking it for solid ground, would not be afraid to venture on it. A second raft, of the same breadth but only 100 feet long and capable of crossing the river, was made fast to the former. The elephants led by the females were driven along the fixed raft, as if along a road, until they came on to the smaller one. As soon as they were safely on this it was cast off and towed by light boats to the other side of the river. When the first lot were landed others were brought over in the same way. They showed no fear whilst they were being driven along the fixed raft; their fright began when they were being carried into mid-channel on the other raft which had been cast loose. They crowded together, those on the outside backing away from the water, and showed considerable alarm until their very fears at the sight of the water made them quiet. Some in their excitement fell overboard and threw their drivers, but their mere weight kept them steady, and as they felt their way into shallow water they succeeded in getting safely to land.

29. While the elephants were being ferried across, Hannibal sent 500 Numidian horse towards the Romans to ascertain their numbers and their intentions. This troop of horse encountered the 300 Roman cavalry who, as I have already stated, had been sent forward from the mouth of the Rhone. It was a much more severe fight than might have been expected from the number of combatants. Not only were there many wounded but each side lost about the same number of killed, and the Romans, who were at last completely exhausted, owed their victory to a panic among the Numidians and their consequent flight. Of the victors as many as 160 fell, not all Romans, some were Gauls; whilst the vanquished lost more than 200. This action with which the war commenced was an omen of its final result, but though it portended the final victory of Rome it showed that the victory would not be attained without much bloodshed and repeated defeats. The forces drew off from the field and returned to their respective commanders. Scipio found himself unable to form any definite plans beyond what were suggested to him by the movements of the enemy. Hannibal was undecided whether to resume his march to Italy or to engage the Romans, the first army to oppose him. He was dissuaded from the latter course by the arrival of envoys from the Boii and their chief, Magalus. They came to assure Hannibal of their readiness to act as guides and take their share in the dangers of the expedition, and they gave it as their opinion that he ought to reserve all his strength for the invasion of Italy and not fritter any of it away beforehand. The bulk of his army had not forgotten the previous war and looked forward with dismay to meeting their old enemy, but what appalled them much more was the prospect of an endless journey over the Alps, which rumor said was, to those at all events who had never tried it, a thing to be dreaded.

30. When Hannibal had made up his mind to go forward and lose no time in reaching Italy, his goal, he ordered a muster of his troops and addressed them in tones of mingled rebuke and encouragement. "I am astonished," he said, "to see how hearts that have been always dauntless have now suddenly become a prey to fear. Think of the many victorious campaigns you have gone through, and remember that you did not leave Spain before you had added to the Carthaginian empire all the tribes in the country washed by two widely remote seas. The Roman people made a demand for all who had taken part in the siege of Saguntum to be given up to them, and you, to avenge the insult, have crossed the Ebro to wipe out the name of Rome and bring freedom to the world. When you commenced your march, from the setting to the rising sun, none of you thought it too much for you, but now when you see that by far the greater part of the way has been accomplished; the passes of the Pyrenees, which were held by most warlike tribes, surmounted; the Rhone, that mighty stream, crossed in the face of so many thousand Gauls, and the rush of its waters checked—now that you are within sight of the Alps, on the other side of which lies Italy, you have become weary and are arresting your march in the very gates of the enemy. What do you imagine the Alps to be other than lofty mountains? Suppose them to be higher than the peaks of the Pyrenees, surely no region in the world can touch the sky or be impassable to man. Even the Alps are inhabited and cultivated, animals are bred and reared there, their gorges and ravines can be traversed by armies. Why, even the envoys whom you see here did not cross the Alps by flying through the air, nor were their ancestors native to the soil. They came into Italy as emigrants looking for a land to settle in, and they crossed the Alps often in immense bodies with their wives and children and all their belongings. What can be inaccessible or insuperable to the soldier who carries nothing with him but his weapons of war? What toils and perils you went through for eight months to effect the capture of Saguntum! And now that Rome, the capital of the world, is your goal, can you deem anything so difficult or so arduous that it should prevent you from reaching it? Many years ago the Gauls captured the place which Carthaginians despair of approaching; either you must confess yourselves inferior in courage and enterprise to a people whom you have conquered again and again, or else you must look forward to finishing your march on the ground between the Tiber and the walls of Rome."

31. After this rousing appeal he dismissed them with orders to prepare themselves by food and rest for the march. The next day they advanced up the left bank of the Rhone towards the central districts of Gaul, not because

this was the most direct route to the Alps, but because he thought that there would be less likelihood of the Romans meeting him, for he had no desire to engage them before he arrived in Italy. Four days' marching brought him to the "Island." Here the Isère and the Rhone, flowing down from different points in the Alps, enclose a considerable extent of land and then unite their channels; the district thus enclosed is called the "Island." The adjacent country was inhabited by the Allobroges, a tribe who even in those days were second to none in Gaul in power and reputation. At the time of Hannibal's visit a quarrel had broken out between two brothers who were each aspiring to the sovereignty. The elder brother, whose name was Brancus, had hitherto been the chief, but was now expelled by a party of the younger men, headed by his brother, who found an appeal to violence more successful than an appeal to right. Hannibal's timely appearance on the scene led to the question being referred to him; he was to decide who was the legitimate claimant to the kingship. He pronounced in favor of the elder brother, who had the support of the senate and the leading men. In return for this service he received assistance in provisions and supplies of all kinds, especially of clothing, a pressing necessity in view of the notorious cold of the Alps. After settling the feud amongst the Allobroges, Hannibal resumed his march. He did not take the direct course to the Alps, but turned to the left towards the Tricastini; then, skirting the territory of the Vocontii, he marched in the direction of the Tricorii. Nowhere did he meet with any difficulty until he arrived at the Durance. This river, which also takes its rise in the Alps, is of all the rivers of Gaul the most difficult to cross. Though carrying down a great volume of water, it does not lend itself to navigation, for it is not kept in by banks, but flows in many separate channels. As it is constantly shifting its bottom and the direction of its currents, the task of fording it is a most hazardous one, whilst the shingle and boulders carried down make the foothold insecure and treacherous. It happened to be swollen by rain at the time, and the men were thrown into much disorder whilst crossing it, whilst their fears and confused shouting added considerably to their difficulties.

32. Three days after Hannibal had left the banks of the Rhone, P. Cornelius Scipio arrived at the deserted camp with his army in battle order, ready to engage at once. When, however, he saw the abandoned lines and realized that it would be no easy matter to overtake his opponent after he had got such a long start, he returned to his ships. He considered that the easier and safer course would be to meet Hannibal as he came down from the Alps. Spain was the province allotted to him, and to prevent its being entirely denuded of Roman troops he sent his brother Cn. Scipio with the greater part of his army to act against Hasdrubal, not only to keep the old allies and win new ones, but to drive Hasdrubal out of Spain. He himself sailed for Genoa with a very small force, intending to defend Italy with the army lying in the valley of the Po. From the Durance Hannibal's route lay mostly through open level country, and he reached the Alps without meeting with any opposition from the Gauls who inhabited the district. But the sight of the Alps revived the terrors in the minds of his men. Although rumor, which generally magnifies untried dangers, had filled them with gloomy forebodings, the nearer view proved much more fearful. The height of the mountains now so close, the snow which was almost lost in the sky, the wretched huts perched on the rocks, the flocks and herds shriveled and stunted with the cold, the men wild and unkempt, everything animate and inanimate stiff with frost, together with other sights dreadful beyond description—all helped to increase their alarm.

As the head of the column began to climb the nearest slopes, the natives appeared on the heights above; had they concealed themselves in the ravines and then rushed down they would have caused frightful panic and bloodshed. Hannibal called a halt and sent on some Gauls to examine the ground, and when he learnt that advance was impossible in that direction he formed his camp in the widest part of the valley that he could find; everywhere around the ground was broken and precipitous. The Gauls who had been sent to reconnoiter got into conversation with the natives, as there was little difference between their speech or their manners, and they brought back word to Hannibal that the pass was only occupied in the daytime, at nightfall the natives all dispersed to their homes. Accordingly, at early dawn he began the ascent as though determined to force the pass in broad daylight, and spent the day in movements designed to conceal his real intentions and in fortifying the camp on the spot where they had halted. As soon as he observed that the natives had left the heights and were no longer watching his movements, he gave orders, with the view of deceiving the enemy, for a large number of fires to be lighted, larger in fact than would be required by those remaining in camp. Then, leaving the baggage with the cavalry and the greater part of the infantry in camp, he himself with a specially selected body of troops in light marching order rapidly moved out of the defile and occupied the heights which the enemy had held.

33. The following day the rest of the army broke camp in the gray dawn and commenced its march. The natives were beginning to assemble at their customary post of observation when they suddenly became aware that some of the enemy were in possession of their stronghold right over their heads, whilst others were advancing on the path beneath. The double impression made on their eyes and imagination kept them for a few moments motionless, but when they saw the column falling into disorder mainly through the horses becoming frightened, they thought that if they increased the confusion and panic it would be sufficient to destroy it. So they charged down from rock to rock, careless as to whether there were paths or not, for they were

familiar with the ground. The Carthaginians had to meet this attack at the same time that they were struggling with the difficulties of the way, and as each man was doing his best for himself to get out of the reach of danger, they were fighting more amongst themselves than against the natives. The horses did the most mischief; they were terrified at the wild shouts, which the echoing woods and valleys made all the louder, and when they happened to be struck or wounded they created terrible havoc amongst the men and the different baggage animals. The road was flanked by sheer precipices on each side, and in the crowding together many were pushed over the edge and fell an immense depth. Amongst these were some of the soldiers; the heavily-laden baggage animals rolled over like falling houses. Horrible as the sight was, Hannibal remained quiet and kept his men back for some time, for fear of increasing the alarm and confusion, but when he saw that the column was broken and that the army was in danger of losing all its baggage, in which case he would have brought them safely through to no purpose, he ran down from his higher ground and at once scattered the enemy. At the same time, however, he threw his own men into still greater disorder for the moment, but it was very quickly allayed now that the passage was cleared by the flight of the natives. In a short time the whole army had traversed the pass, not only without any further disturbance, but almost in silence. He then seized a fortified village, the head place of the district, together with some adjacent hamlets, and from the food and cattle thus secured he provided his army with rations for three days. As the natives, after their first defeat, no longer impeded their march, whilst the road presented little difficulty, they made considerable progress during those three days.

34. They now came to another canton which, considering that it was a mountain district, had a considerable population. Here he narrowly escaped destruction, not in fair and open fighting, but by the practices which he himself employed—falsehood and treachery. The head men from the fortified villages, men of advanced age, came as a deputation to the Carthaginian and told him that they had been taught by the salutary example of other people's misfortunes to seek the friendship of the Carthaginians rather than to feel their strength. They were accordingly prepared to carry out his orders; he would receive provisions and guides, and hostages as a guarantee of good faith. Hannibal felt that he ought not to trust them blindly nor to meet their offer with a flat refusal, in case they should become hostile. So he replied in friendly terms, accepted the hostages whom they placed in his hands, made use of the provisions with which they supplied him on the march, but followed their guides with his army prepared for action, not at all as though he were going through a peaceable or friendly country. The elephants and cavalry were in front, he himself followed with the main body of the infantry, keeping a sharp and anxious look-out in all directions. Just as they reached a

part of the pass where it narrowed and was overhung on one side by a wall of rock, the barbarians sprang up from ambush on all sides and assailed the column in front and rear, at close quarters, and at a distance by rolling huge stones down on it. The heaviest attack was made in the rear, and as the infantry faced round to meet it, it became quite obvious that if the rear of the column had not been made exceptionally strong, a terrible disaster must have occurred in that pass. As it was, they were in the greatest danger, and within an ace of total destruction. For whilst Hannibal was hesitating whether to send his infantry on into the narrow part of the pass—for whilst protecting the rear of the cavalry they had no reserves to protect their own rear—the mountaineers, making a flank charge, burst through the middle of the column and held the pass so that Hannibal had to spend that one night without his cavalry or his baggage.

35. The next day, as the savages attacked with less vigor, the column closed up, and the pass was surmounted, not without loss, more, however, of baggage animals than of men. From that time the natives made their appearance in smaller numbers and behaved more like banditti than regular soldiers; they attacked either front or rear just as the ground gave them opportunity, or as the advance or halt of the column presented a chance of surprise. The elephants caused considerable delay, owing to the difficulty of getting them through narrow or precipitous places; on the other hand, they rendered that part of the column safe from attack where they were, for the natives were unaccustomed to the sight of them and had a great dread of going too near them. Nine days from their commencing the ascent they arrived at the highest point of the Alps, after traversing a region mostly without roads and frequently losing their way either through the treachery of their guides or through their own mistakes in trying to find the way for themselves. For two days they remained in camp on the summit, whilst the troops enjoyed a respite from fatigue and fighting. Some of the baggage animals which had fallen amongst the rocks and had afterwards followed the track of the column came into camp. To add to the misfortunes of the worn-out troops, there was a heavy fall of snow—the Pleiads were near their setting—and this new experience created considerable alarm. In the early morning of the third day the army recommenced its heavy march over ground everywhere deep in snow. Hannibal saw in all faces an expression of listlessness and despondency. He rode on in front to a height from which there was a wide and extensive view, and halting his men, he pointed out to them the land of Italy and the rich valley of the Po lying at the foot of the Alps. "You are now," he said, "crossing the barriers not only of Italy, but of Rome itself. Henceforth all will be smooth and easy for you; in one or, at the most, two battles, you will be masters of the capital and stronghold of Italy." Then the army resumed its advance with no annoyance from the enemy beyond occasional attempts at plunder. The remainder of the march, however, was attended with much greater difficulty than they had experienced in the ascent, for the distance to the plains on the Italian side is shorter, and therefore the descent is necessarily steeper. Almost the whole of the way was precipitous, narrow, and slippery, so that they were unable to keep their footing, and if they slipped they could not recover themselves; they kept falling over each other, and the baggage animals rolled over on their drivers.

36. At length they came to a much narrower pass which descended over such sheer cliffs that a light-armed soldier could hardly get down it even by hanging on to projecting roots and branches. The place had always been precipitous, and a landslide had recently carried away the road for 1,000 feet. The cavalry came to a halt here as though they had arrived at their journey's end, and whilst Hannibal was wondering what could be causing the delay he was informed that there was no passage. Then he went forward to examine the place and saw that there was nothing for it but to lead the army by a long circuitous route over pathless and untrodden snow. But this, too, soon proved to be impracticable. The old snow had been covered to a moderate depth by a fresh fall, and the first comers planted their feet firmly on the new snow, but when it had become melted under the tread of so many men and beasts there was nothing to walk on but ice covered with slush. Their progress now became one incessant and miserable struggle. The smooth ice allowed no foothold, and as they were going down a steep incline they were still less able to keep on their legs, whilst, once down, they tried in vain to rise, as their hands and knees were continually slipping. There were no stumps or roots about for them to get hold of and support themselves by, so they rolled about helplessly on the glassy ice and slushy snow. The baggage animals as they toiled along cut through occasionally into the lowest layer of snow, and when they stumbled they struck out their hoofs in their struggles to recover themselves and broke through into the hard and congealed ice below, where most of them stuck as though caught in a gin.

37. At last, when men and beasts alike were worn out by their fruitless exertions, a camp was formed on the summit, after the place had been cleared with immense difficulty owing to the quantity of snow that had to be removed. The next thing was to level the rock through which alone a road was practicable. The soldiers were told off to cut through it. They built up against it an enormous pile of tall trees which they had felled and lopped, and when the wind was strong enough to blow up the fire they set light to the pile. When the rock was red hot they poured vinegar upon it to disintegrate it. After thus treating it by fire they opened a way through it with their tools, and eased the steep slope by winding tracks of moderate gradient, so that not only the baggage animals but even the elephants could be led down. Four days were spent over the rock, and the animals were almost starved to death,

for the heights are mostly bare of vegetation and what herbage there is buried beneath the snow. In the lower levels there were sunny valleys and streams flowing through woods, and spots more deserving of human inhabitants. Here the beasts were turned loose to graze, and the troops, worn out with their engineering, were allowed to rest. In three days more they reached the open plains and found a pleasanter country and pleasanter people living in it

38. Such, in the main, was the way in which they reached Italy, five months, according to some authorities, after leaving New Carthage, fifteen days of which were spent in overcoming the difficulties of the Alps. The authorities are hopelessly at variance as to the number of the troops with which Hannibal entered Italy. The highest estimate assigns him 100,000 infantry and 20,000 cavalry; the lowest puts his strength at 20,000 infantry and 6000 cavalry. L. Cincius Alimentus tells us that he was taken prisoner by Hannibal, and I should be most inclined to accept his authority if he had not confused the numbers by adding in the Gauls and Ligurians; if these are included there were 80,000 infantry and 10,000 cavalry. It is, however, more probable that these joined Hannibal in Italy, and some authorities actually assert this. Cincius also states that he had heard Hannibal say that subsequently to his passage of the Rhone he lost 36,000 men, besides an immense number of horses and other animals. The first people he came to were the Taurini, a semi-Gallic tribe. As tradition is unanimous on this point I am the more surprised that a question should be raised as to what route Hannibal took over the Alps, and that it should be generally supposed that he crossed over the Poenine range, which is said to have derived its name from that circumstance. Coelius asserts that he crossed by the Cremonian range. These two passes, however, would not have brought him to the Taurini but through the Salassi, a mountain tribe, to the Libuan Gauls. It is highly improbable that those routes to Gaul were available at that time, and in any case the Poenine route would have been closed by the semi-German tribes who inhabited the district. And it is perfectly certain, if we accept their authority, that the Seduni and Veragri, who inhabit that range, say that the name of Poenine was not given to it from any passage of the Carthaginians over it but from the deity Poeninus, whose shrine stands on the highest point of the range.

39. It was a very fortunate circumstance for Hannibal at the outset of his campaign that the Taurini, the first people he came to, were at war with the Insubres. But he was unable to bring his army into the field to assist either side, for it was whilst they were recovering from the ills and misfortunes which had gathered upon them that they felt them most. Rest and idleness instead of toil, plenty following upon starvation, cleanliness and comfort after squalor and emaciation, affected their filthy and well-nigh bestialised bodies in various ways. It was this state of things which induced P. Cornelius

Scipio, the consul, after he had arrived with his ships at Pisa and taken over from Manlius and Atilius an army of raw levies disheartened by their recent humiliating defeats, to push on with all speed to the Po that he might engage the enemy before he had recovered his strength. But when he reached Placentia Hannibal had already left his encampment and taken by storm one of the cities of the Taurini, their capital, in fact, because they would not voluntarily maintain friendly relations with him. He would have secured the adhesion of the Gauls in the valley of the Po, not by fear but by their own choice, if the sudden arrival of the consul had not taken them by surprise whilst they were waiting for a favorable moment to revolt. Just at the time of Scipio's arrival, Hannibal moved out of the country of the Taurini, for, seeing how undecided the Gauls were as to whose side they should take, he thought that if he were on the spot they would follow him. The two armies were now almost within sight of one another, and the commanders who were confronting each other, though not sufficiently acquainted with each other's military skill, were even then imbued with mutual respect and admiration. Even before the fall of Saguntum the name of Hannibal was on all men's lips in Rome, and in Scipio Hannibal recognized a great leader, seeing that he had been chosen beyond all others to oppose him. This mutual esteem was enhanced by their recent achievements; Scipio, after Hannibal had left him in Gaul, was in time to meet him on his descent from the Alps; Hannibal had not only dared to attempt but had actually accomplished the passage of the Alps. Scipio, however, made the first move by crossing the Po and shifting his camp to the Ticinus. Before leading his men into battle he addressed them in a speech full of encouragement, in the following terms:

40. "If, soldiers, I were leading into battle the army which I had with me in Gaul, there would have been no need for me to address you. For what encouragement would those cavalry need who had won such a brilliant victory over the enemy's cavalry at the Rhone or those legions of infantry with whom I pursued this same enemy, who by his running away and shirking an engagement acknowledged that I was his conqueror? That army, raised for service in Spain, is campaigning under my brother, Cn. Scipio, who is acting as my deputy in the country which the senate and people of Rome have assigned to it. In order, therefore, that you might have a consul to lead you against Hannibal and the Carthaginians, I have volunteered to command in this battle, and as I am new to you and you to me I must say a few words to you.

"Now as to the character of the enemy and the kind of warfare which awaits you. You have to fight, soldiers, with the men whom you defeated in the former war by land and sea, from whom you have exacted a war indemnity for the last twenty years, and from whom you wrested Sicily and Sardinia as the prizes of war. You, therefore, will go into this battle with the exultation of victors, they with the despondency of the vanquished. They are not going to fight now because they are impelled by courage but through sheer necessity; unless indeed you suppose that, after shirking a contest when their army was at its full strength, they have gained more confidence now that they have lost two-thirds of their infantry and cavalry in their passage over the Alps, now that those who survive are fewer than those who have perished.

"'Yes,' it may be said, 'they are few in number, but they are strong in courage and physique, and possess a power of endurance and vigor in attack which very few can withstand.' No, they are only semblances or rather ghosts of men, worn out with starvation, cold, filth, and squalor, bruised and enfeebled amongst the rocks and precipices, and, what is more, their limbs are frostbitten, their thews and sinews cramped with cold, their frames shrunk and shriveled with frost, their weapons battered and shivered, their horses lame and out of condition. This is the cavalry, this the infantry with whom you are going to fight; you will not have an enemy but only the last vestiges of an enemy to meet. My only fear is that when you have fought it will appear to be the Alps that have conquered Hannibal. But perhaps it was right that it should be so, and that the gods, without any human aid, should begin and all but finish this war with a people and their general who have broken treaties, and that to us, who next to the gods have been sinned against, it should be left to complete what they began.

41. "I am not afraid of any one thinking that I am saying this in a spirit of bravado for the sake of putting you in good heart, whilst my real feelings and convictions are far otherwise. I was at perfect liberty to go with my army to Spain, for which country I had actually started, and which was my assigned province. There I should have had my brother to share my plans and dangers; I should have had Hasdrubal rather than Hannibal as my foe, and undoubtedly a less serious war on my hands. But as I was sailing along the coast of Gaul I heard tidings of this enemy, and at once landed, and after sending on cavalry in advance moved up to the Rhone. A cavalry action was fought—that was the only arm I had the opportunity of employing—and I defeated the enemy. His infantry were hurrying away like an army in flight, and as I could not come up with them overland, I returned to my ships with all possible speed, and after making a wide circuit by sea and land have met this dreaded foe almost at the foot of the Alps. Does it seem to you that I have unexpectedly fallen in with him whilst I was anxious to decline a contest and not rather that I am meeting him actually on his track and challenging and dragging him into action? I shall be glad to learn whether the earth has suddenly within the last twenty years produced a different breed of Carthaginians, or whether they are the same as those who fought at the Aegates, and whom you allowed to depart from Eryx on payment of eighteen denarii a head, and whether this Hannibal is, as he gives out, the rival of Hercules in his journeys, or whether he has been left by his father to pay tax and tribute and to be the slave of the Roman people. If his crime at Saguntum were not driving him on, he would surely have some regard, if not for his conquered country, at all events for his house and his father, and the treaties signed by that Hamilcar who at the order of our consul withdrew his garrison from Eryx, who with sighs and groans accepted the hard conditions imposed on the conquered Carthaginians, and who agreed to evacuate Sicily and pay a war indemnity to Rome. And so I would have you, soldiers, fight not merely in the spirit which you are wont to show against other foes, but with feelings of indignant anger as though you saw your own slaves bearing arms against you. When they were shut up in Eryx we might have inflicted the most terrible of human punishments and starved them to death; we might have taken our victorious fleet across to Africa, and in a few days destroyed Carthage without a battle. We granted pardon to their prayers, we allowed them to escape from the blockade, we agreed to terms of peace with those whom we had conquered, and afterwards when they were in dire straits through the African war we took them under our protection. To requite us for these acts of kindness they are following the lead of a young madman and coming to attack our fatherland. I only wish this struggle were for honor alone and not for safety. It is not about the possession of Sicily and Sardinia, the old subjects of dispute, but for Italy that you have to fight. There is no second army at our back to oppose the enemy if we fail to win, there are no more Alps to delay his advance while a fresh army can be raised for defense. Here it is, soldiers, that we have to resist, just as though we were fighting before the walls of Rome. Every one of you must remember that he is using his arms to protect not himself only but also his wife and little children; nor must his anxiety be confined to his home, he must realize, too, that the senate and people of Rome are watching our exploits today. What our strength and courage are now here, such will be the fortune of our City yonder and of the empire of Rome."

42. Such was the language which the consul used towards the Romans. Hannibal thought that the courage of his men ought to be roused by deeds first rather than by words. After forming his army into a circle to view the spectacle, he placed in the center some Alpine prisoners in chains, and when some Gaulish arms had been thrown down at their feet he ordered an interpreter to ask if any one of them was willing to fight if he were freed from his chains and received arms and a horse as the reward of victory. All to a man demanded arms and battle, and when the lot was cast to decide who should fight, each wished that he might be the one whom Fortune should select for the combat. As each man's lot fell, he hastily seized his arms full of eagerness and exultant delight, amidst the congratulations of his comrades and danced after the custom of his country. But when they began to fight, such was the state of feeling not only amongst the men who had accepted this condition, but amongst the spectators generally that the good fortune of those who died bravely was lauded quite as much as that of those who were victorious.

43. After his men had been impressed by watching several pairs of combatants Hannibal dismissed them, and afterwards summoned them round him, when he is reported to have made the following speech: "Soldiers, you have seen in the fate of others an example how to conquer or to die. If the feelings with which you watched them lead you to form a similar estimate of your own fortunes we are victors. That was no idle spectacle but a picture, as it were, of your own condition. Fortune, I am inclined to think has bound you in heavier chains and imposed upon you a sterner necessity than on your captives. You are shut in on the right hand and on the left by two seas, and you have not a single ship in which to make your escape; around you flows the Po, a greater river than the Rhone and a more rapid one; the barrier of the Alps frowns upon you behind, those Alps which you could hardly cross when your strength and vigor were unimpaired. Here, soldiers, on this spot where you have for the first time encountered the enemy you must either conquer or die. The same Fortune which has imposed upon you the necessity of fighting also holds out rewards of victory, rewards as great as any which men are wont to solicit from the immortal gods. Even if we were only going to recover Sicily and Sardinia, possessions which were wrested from our fathers, they would be prizes ample enough to satisfy us. Everything that the Romans now possess, which they have won through so many triumphs, all that they have amassed, will become yours, together with those who own it. Come then, seize your arms and with the help of heaven win this splendid reward. You have spent time enough in hunting cattle on the barren mountains of Lusitania and Celtiberia, and finding no recompense for all your toils and dangers; now the hour has come for you to enter upon rich and lucrative campaigns and to earn rewards which are worth the earning, after your long march over all those mountains and rivers, and through all those nations in arms. Here Fortune has vouchsafed an end to your toils, here she will vouchsafe a reward worthy of all your past services.

"Do not think because the war, being against Rome, bears a great name, that therefore victory will be correspondingly difficult. Many a despised enemy has fought a long and costly fight; nations and kings of high renown have been beaten with a very slight effort. For, setting aside the glory which surrounds the name of Rome, what point is there in which they can be compared to you? To say nothing of your twenty years' campaigning earned on with all your courage, all your good fortune, from the pillars of Hercules, from the shores of the ocean, from the furthest corners of the earth, through the midst of all the most warlike peoples of Spain and Gaul, you have arrived here as victors. The army with which you will fight is made up of raw levies

who were beaten, conquered, and hemmed in by the Gauls this very summer, who are strangers to their general, and he a stranger to them. I, reared
as I was, almost born, in the headquarters tent of my father, a most distinguished general, I, who have subjugated Spain and Gaul, who have conquered not only the Alpine tribes, but, what is a much greater task, the Alps
themselves—am I to compare myself with this six months' general who has
deserted his own army, who, if any one were to point out to him the Romans
and the Carthaginians after their standards were removed, would, I am quite
certain, not know which army he was in command of as consul? I do not
count it a small matter, soldiers, that there is not a man amongst you before
whose eyes I have not done many a soldierly deed, or to whom I, who have
witnessed and attested his courage, could not recount his own gallant
exploits and the time and place where they were performed. I was your pupil
before I was your commander, and I shall go into battle surrounded by men
whom I have commended and rewarded thousands of times against those
who know nothing of each other, who are mutual strangers.

44. "Wherever I turn my eyes I see nothing but courage and strength, a
veteran infantry, a cavalry, regular and irregular alike, drawn from the noblest
tribes, you, our most faithful and brave allies, you, Carthaginians, who are
going to fight for your country, inspired by a most righteous indignation. We
are taking the aggressive, we are descending in hostile array into Italy, prepared to fight more bravely and more fearlessly than our foe because he who
attacks is animated by stronger hopes and greater courage than he who
meets the attack. Besides, we are smarting from a sense of injustice and
humiliation. First they demanded me, your general, as their victim, then they
insisted that all of you who had taken part in the siege of Saguntum should
be surrendered; had you been given up they would have inflicted upon you
the most exquisite tortures. That outrageously cruel and tyrannical nation
claims everything for itself, makes everything dependent on its will and pleasure; they think it right to dictate with whom we are to make war or peace.
They confine and enclose us within mountains and rivers as boundaries, but
they do not observe the limits which they themselves have fixed. 'Do not
cross the Ebro, see that you have nothing to do with the Saguntines.' 'But
Saguntum is not on the Ebro.' 'You must not move a step anywhere.' 'Is it a
small matter, your taking from me my oldest provinces, Sicily and Sardinia?
Will you cross over into Spain as well, and if I withdraw from there, will you
cross over into Africa? Do I say, will cross over? You have crossed over.' They
have sent the two consuls for this year, one to Africa, the other to Spain.
There is nothing left to us anywhere except what we claim by force of arms.
Those may be allowed to be cowards and dastards who have something to fall
back upon, whom their own land, their own territory will receive as they flee
through its safe and peaceful roads; you must of necessity be brave men,

every alternative between victory and death has been broken off by the resolve of despair, and you are compelled either to conquer, or if Fortune wavers, to meet death in battle rather than in flight. If you have all made up your minds to this, I say again you are victors, no keener weapon has been put into men's hands by the immortal gods than a contempt for death."

45. After the fighting spirit of both armies had been roused by these harangues, the Romans threw a bridge over the Ticinus and constructed a blockhouse for its defense. Whilst they were thus occupied, the Carthaginian sent Maharbal with a troop of 500 Numidian horse to ravage the lands of the allies of Rome, but with orders to spare those of the Gauls as far as possible, and to win over their chiefs to his side. When the bridge was completed the Roman army crossed over in the territory of the Insubres and took up a position five miles from Ictumuli, where Hannibal had his camp. As soon as he saw that a battle was imminent, he hastily recalled Maharbal and his troopers. Feeling that he could never say enough by way of admonition and encouragement to his soldiers, he ordered an assembly, and before the whole army offered definite rewards in the hope of which they were to fight. He said that he would give them land wherever they wished, in Italy, Africa, or Spain, which would be free from all taxation for the recipient and for his children; if any preferred money to land, he would satisfy his desires; if any of the allies wished to become Carthaginian citizens he would give them the opportunity; if any preferred to return to their homes he would take care that their circumstances should be such that they would never wish to exchange them with any of their countrymen. He even promised freedom to the slaves who followed their masters, and to the masters, for every slave freed, two more as compensation. To convince them of his determination to carry out these promises, he held a lamb with his left hand and a flint knife in his right and prayed to Jupiter and the other gods, that, if he broke his word and forswore himself they would slay him as he had slain the lamb. He then crushed the animal's head with the flint. They all felt then that the gods themselves would guarantee the fulfillment of their hopes, and looked upon the delay in bringing on an action as delay in gaining their desires; with one mind and one voice they clamored to be led into battle.

46. The Romans were far from showing this alacrity. Amongst other causes of alarm they had been unnerved by some portents which had happened lately. A wolf had entered the camp and after worrying all it met had got away unhurt. A swarm of bees, too, had settled on a tree which overhung the headquarters tent. After the necessary propitiation had been made Scipio moved out with a force of cavalry and light-armed javelin men towards the enemy's camp to get a nearer view and to ascertain the number and nature of his force. He fell in with Hannibal who was also advancing with his cavalry to explore the neighborhood. Neither body at first saw the other; the first indication of a hostile approach was given by the unusually dense cloud of dust which was raised by the tramp of so many men and horses. Each party halted and made ready for battle. Scipio placed the javelin men and the Gaulish cavalry in the front, the Roman horse and the heavy cavalry of the allies as reserves. Hannibal formed his center with his regular cavalry, and posted the Numidians on the flanks. Scarcely had the battle shout been raised before the javelin men retired to the second line amongst the reserves. For some time the cavalry kept up an equal fight, but as the foot-soldiers became mixed up with the mounted men they made their horses unmanageable, many were thrown or else dismounted where they saw their comrades in difficulty, until the battle was mainly fought on foot. Then the Numidians on the flanks wheeled round and appeared on the rear of the Romans, creating dismay and panic amongst them. To make matters worse the consul was wounded and in danger; he was rescued by the intervention of his son who was just approaching manhood. This was the youth who afterwards won the glory of bringing this war to a close, and gained the sobriquet of Africanus for his splendid victory over Hannibal and the Carthaginians. The javelin men were the first to be attacked by the Numidians and they fled in disorder, the rest of the force, the cavalry, closed round the consul, shielding him as much by their persons as by their arms, and returned to camp in orderly retirement. Caelius assigns the honor of saving the consul to a Ligurian slave, but I would rather believe that it was his son; the majority of authors assert this and the tradition is generally accepted.

47. This was the first battle with Hannibal, and the result made it quite clear that the Carthaginian was superior in his cavalry, and consequently that the open plains which stretch from the Po to the Alps were not a suitable battlefield for the Romans. The next night accordingly, the soldiers were ordered to collect their baggage in silence, the army moved away from the Ticinus and marched rapidly to the Po, which they crossed by the pontoon bridge which was still intact, in perfect order and without any molestation by the enemy. They reached Placentia before Hannibal knew for certain that they had left the Ticinus; however, he succeeded in capturing some 600, who were loitering on his side of the Po, and were slowly unfastening the end of the bridge. He was unable to use the bridge for crossing, as the ends had been unfastened and the whole was floating down-stream. According to Caelius, Mago with the cavalry and Spanish infantry at once swam across, whilst Hannibal himself took his army across higher up the river where it was fordable, the elephants being stationed in a row from bank to bank to break the force of the current. Those who know the river will hardly believe this for it is highly improbable that the cavalry could have stood against so violent a river without damage to their horses and arms, even supposing that the Spaniards had been carried across by their inflated skins, and it would have required a

march of many days to find a ford in the Po where an army loaded with baggage could be taken across. I attach greater weight to those authorities who state that it took them at least two days to find a spot where they could throw a bridge over the river, and that it was there that Mago's cavalry and the Spanish light infantry crossed. Whilst Hannibal was waiting near the river to give audience to deputations from the Gauls, he sent his heavy infantry across, and during this interval Mago and his cavalry advanced a day's march from the river in the direction of the enemy at Placentia. A few days later Hannibal entrenched himself in a position six miles from Placentia, and the next day he drew out his army in battle order in full view of the enemy and gave him the opportunity of fighting.

48. The following night a murderous outbreak took place amongst the Gaulish auxiliaries in the Roman camp; there was, however, more excitement and confusion than actual loss of life. About 2,000 infantry and 200 horsemen massacred the sentinels and deserted to Hannibal. The Carthaginian gave them a kind reception and sent them to their homes with the promise of great rewards if they would enlist the sympathies of their countrymen on his behalf. Scipio saw in this outrage a signal of revolt for all the Gauls, who, infected by the madness of this crime, would at once fly to arms, and though still suffering severely from his wound, he left his position in the fourth watch of the following night, his army marching in perfect silence, and shifted his camp close to the Trebia on to higher ground where the hills were impracticable for cavalry. He was less successful in escaping the notice of the enemy than he had been at the Ticinus, Hannibal sent first the Numidians, then afterwards the whole of his cavalry in pursuit and would have inflicted disaster upon the rear of the column at all events, had not the Numidians been tempted by their desire for plunder to turn aside to the deserted Roman camp. Whilst they were wasting their time in prying into every corner of the camp, without finding anything worth waiting for, the enemy slipped out of their hands, and when they caught sight of the Romans they had already crossed the Trebia and were measuring out the site for their camp. A few stragglers whom they caught on their side the river were killed. Unable any longer to endure the irritation of his wound, which had been aggravated during the march, and also thinking that he ought to wait for his colleague—he had already heard that he had been recalled from Sicily—Scipio selected what seemed the safest position near the river, and formed a standing camp which was strongly entrenched. Hannibal had encamped not far from there, and in spite of his elation at his successful cavalry action he felt considerable anxiety at the shortness of supplies which, owing to his marching through hostile territory where no stores were provided, became more serious day by day. He sent a detachment to the town of Clastidium where the Romans had accumulated large quantities of corn. Whilst they were preparing to attack the place they were led to hope that it would be betrayed to them. Dasius, a Brundisian, was commandant of the garrison, and he was induced by a moderate bribe of 400 gold pieces to betray Clastidium to Hannibal. The place was the granary of the Carthaginians while they were at the Trebia. No cruelty was practiced on the garrison, as Hannibal was anxious to win a reputation for clemency at the outset.

§

52. The fact that both consuls and all the available strength that Rome possessed were now brought up to oppose Hannibal, was a pretty clear proof that either that force was adequate for the defense of Rome or that all hope of its defense must be abandoned. Nevertheless, one consul, depressed after his cavalry defeat, and also by his wound, would rather that battle should be deferred. The other, whose courage had suffered no check and was therefore all the more eager to fight, was impatient of any delay. The country between the Trebia and the Po was inhabited by Gauls who in this struggle between two mighty peoples showed impartial goodwill to either side, with the view, undoubtedly, of winning the victor's gratitude. The Romans were quite satisfied with this neutrality if only it was maintained and the Gauls kept quiet, but Hannibal was extremely indignant, as he was constantly giving out that he had been invited by the Gauls to win their freedom. Feelings of resentment and, at the same time, a desire to enrich his soldiers with plunder prompted him to send 2,000 infantry and 1,000 cavalry, made up of Gauls and Numidians, mostly the latter, with orders to ravage the whole country, district after district, right up to the banks of the Po. Though the Gauls had hitherto maintained an impartial attitude, they were compelled in their need of help to turn from those who had inflicted these outrages to those who they hoped would avenge them. They sent envoys to the consuls to beg the Romans to come to the rescue of a land which was suffering because its people had been too loyal to Rome. Cornelius Scipio did not consider that either the grounds alleged or the circumstances justified his taking action. He regarded that nation with suspicion on account of their many acts of treachery, and even if their past faithlessness could have been forgotten through lapse of time, he could not forget the recent treachery of the Boii. Sempronius, on the other hand, was of opinion that the most effective means of preserving the fidelity of their allies was to defend those who first asked for their help. As his colleague still hesitated, he sent his own cavalry supported by about a thousand javelin men to protect the territory of the Gauls on the other side of the Trebia. They attacked the enemy suddenly whilst they were scattered and in disorder, most of them loaded with plunder, and after creating a great panic amongst them, and inflicting severe losses upon them, they drove them in flight to their camp. The fugitives were driven back by their comrades who poured in great numbers out of the camp, and thus reinforced they renewed the fighting. The battle wavered as each side retired or pursued, and up to the last the action was undecided. The enemy lost more men; the Romans claimed the victory.

53. To no one in the whole army did the victory appear more important or more decisive than to the consul himself. What gave him especial pleasure was that he had proved superior in that arm in which his colleague had been worsted. He saw that the spirits of his men were restored, and that there was no one but his colleague who wished to delay battle; he believed that Scipio was more sick in mind than in body, and that the thought of his wound made him shrink from the dangers of the battlefield. "But we must not be infected by a sick man's lethargy. What will be gained by further delay, or rather, by wasting time? Whom are we expecting as our third consul; what fresh army are we looking for? The camp of the Carthaginians is in Italy, almost in sight of the City. They are not aiming at Sicily and Sardinia, which they lost after their defeats, nor the Spain which lies on this side the Ebro; their sole object is to drive the Romans away from their ancestral soil, from the land on which they were born. What groans our fathers would utter, accustomed as they were to warring round the walls of Carthage, if they could see us, their descendants, with two consuls and two consular armies, cowering in our camp in the very heart of Italy, whilst the Carthaginian is annexing to his empire all between the Alps and the Apennines." This was the way he spoke when sitting by his incapacitated colleague, this the language he used before his soldiers as though he were haranguing the Assembly. He was urged on, too, by the near approach of the time for the elections, and the fear that the war, if delayed, might pass into the hands of the new consuls, as well as by the chance he had of monopolizing all the glory of it while his colleague was on the sick list. In spite, therefore, of the opposition of Cornelius he ordered the soldiers to get ready for the coming battle.

Hannibal saw clearly what was the best course for the enemy to adopt, and had very little hope that the consuls would do anything rash or ill-advised. When, however, he found that what he had previously learnt by hearsay was actually the case, namely, that one of the consuls was a man of impetuous and headstrong character, and that he had become still more so since the recent cavalry action, he had very little doubt in his own mind that he would have a favorable opportunity of giving battle. He was anxious not to lose a moment, in order that he might fight whilst the hostile army was still raw and the better of the two generals was incapacitated by his wound, and also whilst the Gauls were still in a warlike mood, for he knew that most of them would follow him with less alacrity the further they were dragged from their homes. These and similar considerations led him to hope that a battle was imminent, and made him desirous of forcing an engagement if there was any holding back on the other side. He sent out some Gauls to reconnoiter—as Gauls were serving in both armies they could be most safely trusted to find out what he wanted—and when they reported that the Romans had prepared for battle, the Carthaginian began to look out for ground which would admit of an ambuscade.

54. Between the two armies there was a stream with very high banks which were overgrown with marshy grass and the brambles and brushwood which are generally found on waste ground. After riding round the place and satisfying himself from personal observation that it was capable of concealing even cavalry, Hannibal, turning to his brother Mago, said, "This will be the place for you to occupy. Pick out of our whole force of cavalry and infantry a hundred men from each arm, and bring them to me at the first watch, now it is time for food and rest." He then dismissed his staff. Presently Mago appeared with his 200 picked men. "I see here," said Hannibal, "the very flower of my army, but you must be strong in numbers as well as in courage. Each of you therefore go and choose nine others like himself, from the squadrons and the maniples. Mago will show you the place where you are to lie in ambuscade, you have an enemy who are blindly ignorant of these practices in war." After sending Mago with his 1,000 infantry and 1,000 cavalry to take up his position, Hannibal gave orders for the Numidian cavalry to cross the Trebia in the early dawn and ride up to the gates of the Roman camp; then they were to discharge their missiles on the outposts and so goad the enemy on to battle. When the fighting had once started they were gradually to give ground and draw their pursuers to their own side of the river. These were the instructions to the Numidians; the other commanders, both infantry and cavalry, were ordered to see that all their men had breakfast, after which they were to wait for the signal, the men fully armed, the horses saddled and ready. Eager for battle, and having already made up his mind to fight, Sempronius led out the whole of his cavalry to meet the Numidian attack, for it was in his cavalry that he placed most confidence; these were followed by 6,000 infantry and at last the whole of his force marched on to the field. It happened to be the season of winter, a snowstorm was raging, and the district, situated between the Alps and the Apennines, was rendered especially cold by the vicinity of rivers and marshes. To make matters worse, men and horses alike had been hurriedly sent forward, without any food, without any protection against the cold, so they had no heat in them and the chilling blasts from the river made the cold still more severe as they approached it in their pursuit of the Numidians. But when they entered the water which had been swollen by the night's rain and was then breast high, their limbs became stiff with cold, and when they emerged on the other side they had hardly strength to hold their weapons; they began to grow faint from fatigue and as the day wore on, from hunger.

55. Hannibal's men, meanwhile, had made fires in front of their tents, oil had been distributed amongst the maniples for them to make their joints and limbs supple and they had time for an ample repast. When it was announced that the enemy had crossed the river they took their arms, feeling alert and active in mind and body, and marched to battle. The Balearic and light-armed infantry were posted in front of the standards; they numbered about 8,000; behind them the heavy-armed infantry, the mainstay and backbone of the army; on the flanks Hannibal distributed the cavalry, and outside them, again, the elephants. When the consul saw his cavalry, who had lost their order in the pursuit, suddenly meeting with an unsuspected resistance from the Numidians, he recalled them by signal and received them within his infantry. There were 18,000 Romans, 20,000 Latin allies, and an auxiliary force of Cenomani, the only Gallic tribe which had remained faithful. These were the forces engaged. The Balearics and light infantry opened the battle, but on being met by the heavier legions they were rapidly withdrawn to the wings, an evolution which at once threw the Roman horse into difficulties, for the 4,000 wearied troopers had been unable to offer an effective resistance to 10,000 who were fresh and vigorous, and now in addition they were over-whelmed by what seemed a cloud of missiles from the light infantry. More-over, the elephants, towering aloft at the ends of the line, terrified the horses not only by their appearance but by their unaccustomed smell, and created widespread panic. The infantry battle, as far as the Romans were concerned, was maintained more by courage than by physical strength, for the Carthaginians, who had shortly before been getting themselves into trim, brought their powers fresh and unimpaired into action, whilst the Romans were fatigued and hungry and stiff with cold. Still, their courage would have kept them up had it been only infantry that they were fighting against. But the light infantry, after repulsing the cavalry, were hurling their missiles on the flanks of the legions; the elephants had now come up against the center of the Roman line, and Mago and his Numidians, as soon as it had passed their ambuscade, rose up in the rear and created a terrible disorder and panic. Yet in spite of all the dangers which surrounded them, the ranks stood firm and immovable for some time, even, contrary to all expectation, against the elephants. Some skirmishers who had been placed where they could attack these animals flung darts at them and drove them off, and rushed after them, stabbing them under their tails, where the skin is soft and easily penetrated.

56. Maddened with pain and terror, they were beginning to rush wildly on their own men, when Hannibal ordered them to be driven away to the left wing against the auxiliary Gauls on the Roman right. There they instantly produced unmistakable panic and flight, and the Romans had fresh cause for alarm when they saw their auxiliaries routed. They now stood fighting in a square, and about 10,000 of them, unable to escape in any other direction, forced their way through the center of the African troops and the auxiliary Gauls who supported them and inflicted an immense loss on the enemy. They were prevented by the river from returning to their camp, and the rain made it impossible for them to judge where they could best go to the assistance of their comrades, so they marched away straight to Placentia. Then desperate attempts to escape were made on all sides; some who made for the river were swept away by the current or caught by the enemy while hesitating to cross; others, scattered over the fields in flight, followed the track of the main retreat and sought Placentia; others, fearing the enemy more than the river, crossed it and reached their camp. The driving sleet and the intolerable cold caused the death of many men and baggage animals, and nearly all the elephants perished. The Carthaginians stopped their pursuit at the banks of the Trebia and returned to their camp so benumbed with cold that they hardly felt any joy in their victory. In the night the men who had guarded the camp, and the rest of the soldiers, mostly wounded, crossed the Trebia on rafts without any interference from the Carthaginians, either because the roaring of the storm prevented them from hearing or because they were unable to move through weariness and wounds and pretended that they heard nothing. Whilst the Carthaginians were keeping quiet, Scipio led his army to Placentia and thence across the Po to Cremona, in order that one colony might not be burdened with providing winter quarters for the two armies.

57. This defeat so unnerved people in Rome that they believed the enemy was already advancing to attack the City, and that there was no help to be looked for, no hope of repelling him from their walls and gates. After one consul had been beaten at the Ticinus the other was recalled from Sicily, and now both consuls and both consular armies had been worsted. What fresh generals, men asked, what fresh legions could be brought to the rescue? Amidst this universal panic Sempronius arrived. He had slipped through the enemy's cavalry at immense risk while they were dispersed in quest of plunder, and owed his escape rather to sheer audacity than to cleverness, for he had little hope of eluding them or of successful resistance if he failed to do so. After conducting the elections, which was the pressing need for the moment, he returned to winter quarters. The consuls elected were Cneius Servilius and C. Flaminius. Even in their winter quarters the Romans were not allowed much quiet; the Numidian horse were roaming in all directions, or where the ground was too rough for them, the Celtiberians and Lusitanians. They were, therefore, cut off from supplies on every side, except what were brought in ships on the Po. Near Placentia there was a place called Emporium, which had been carefully fortified and occupied by a strong garrison. In the hope of capturing the place, Hannibal approached with cavalry and light-armed troops, and as he trusted mainly to secrecy for success, he marched thither by night. But he did not escape the observation of the sentinels, and such a shouting suddenly arose that it was actually heard at Placentia. By daybreak the consul was on the spot with his cavalry, having given orders for the legions of infantry to follow in battle formation. A cavalry action followed in which Hannibal was wounded, and his retirement from the field discomfited the enemy; the position was admirably defended.

After taking only a few days' rest, before his wound was thoroughly healed Hannibal proceeded to attack Victumviae. During the Gaulish war this place had served as an emporium for the Romans; subsequently, as it was a fortified place, a mixed population from the surrounding country had settled there in considerable numbers, and now the terror created by the constant depredations had driven most of the people from the fields into the town. This motley population, excited by the news of the energetic defense of Placentia, flew to arms and went out to meet Hannibal. More like a crowd than an army they met him on his march, and as on the one side there was nothing but an undisciplined mob, and on the other a general and soldiers who had perfect confidence in each other, a small body routed as many as 35,000 men. The next day they surrendered and admitted a Carthaginian garrison within their walls. They had just completed the surrender of their arms in obedience to orders, when instructions were suddenly given to the victors to treat the city as though it had been carried by storm, and no deed of blood, which on such occasions historians are wont to mention, was left undone, so awful was the example set of every form of licentiousness and cruelty and brutal tyranny towards the wretched inhabitants. Such were the winter operations of Hannibal.

58. The soldiers rested whilst the intolerable cold lasted; it did not, however, last long, and at the first doubtful indications of spring Hannibal left his winter quarters for Etruria with the intention of inducing that nation to join forces with him, either voluntarily or under compulsion. During his passage of the Apennines he was overtaken by a storm of such severity as almost to surpass the horrors of the Alps. The rain was driven by the wind straight into the men's faces, and either they had to drop their weapons or if they tried to struggle against the hurricane it caught them and dashed them to the ground, so they came to a halt. Then they found that it was stopping their respiration so that they could not breathe, and they sat down for a short time with their backs to the wind. The heavens began to reverberate with terrific roar, and amidst the awful din lightning flashed and quivered. Sight and sound alike paralyzed them with terror. At last, as the force of the gale increased owing to the rain having ceased, they saw that there was nothing for it but to pitch their camp on the ground where they had been caught by the storm. Now all their labor had to begin over again, for they could neither unroll anything nor fix anything, whatever was fixed did not stand, the wind tore everything into shreds and carried it off. Soon the moisture in the upper air above the cold mountain peaks froze and discharged such a shower of snow and hail that the men, giving up all further attempts, lay down as best they could, buried beneath their coverings rather than protected by them. This was followed by such intense cold that when any one attempted to rise out of that pitiable crowd of prostrate men and beasts it was a long time before he could get up, for his muscles being cramped and stiff with cold, he could hardly bend his limbs. At length, by exercising their arms and legs, they were able to move about, and began to recover their spirits; here and there fires were lighted, and those who were most helpless turned to their colleagues for help. They remained on that spot for two days like a force blockaded; many men and animals perished; of the elephants which survived the battle of the Trebia they lost seven.

59. After descending from the Apennines Hannibal advanced towards Placentia, and after a ten miles' march formed camp. The following day he marched against the enemy with 12,000 infantry and 5,000 cavalry. Sempronius had by this time returned from Rome, and he did not decline battle. That day the two camps were three miles distant from each other; the following day they fought, and both sides exhibited the most determined courage, but the action was indecisive. At the first encounter the Romans were so far superior that they not only conquered in the field, but followed the routed enemy to his camp and soon made an attack upon it. Hannibal stationed a few men to defend the rampart and the gates, the rest he massed in the middle of the camp, and ordered them to be on the alert and wait for the signal to make a sortie. It was now about three o'clock; the Romans were worn out with their fruitless efforts as there was no hope of carrying the camp, and the consul gave the signal to retire. As soon as Hannibal heard it and saw that the fighting had slackened and that the enemy were retiring from the camp, he immediately launched his cavalry against them right and left, and sallied in person with the main strength of his infantry from the middle of the camp. Seldom has there been a more equal fight, and few would have been rendered more memorable by the mutual destruction of both armies had the daylight allowed it to be sufficiently prolonged; as it was, night put an end to a conflict which had been maintained with such determined courage. There was greater fury than bloodshed, and as the fighting had been almost equal on both sides, they separated with equal loss. Not more than 600 infantry and half that number of cavalry fell on either side, but the Roman loss was out of proportion to their numbers; several members of the equestrian order and five military tribunes as well as three prefects of the allies were killed. Immediately after the battle Hannibal withdrew into Liguria, and Sempronius to Luca. Whilst Hannibal was entering Liguria, two Roman quaestors who had been ambushed and captured, C. Fulvius and L. Lucretius, together with three military tribunes and five members of the equestrian order, most of them sons of senators, were given up to him by the Gauls in order that he might feel more confidence in their maintenance of peaceful relations, and their determination to give him active support.

60. While these events were in progress in Italy, Cn. Cornelius Scipio, who had been sent with a fleet and an army to Spain, commenced operations in that country. Starting from the mouth of the Rhone, he sailed round the eastward end of the Pyrenees and brought up at Emporiae. Here he disembarked his army, and beginning with the Laeetani, he brought the whole of the maritime populations as far as the Ebro within the sphere of Roman influence by renewing old alliances and forming new ones. He gained in this way a reputation for clemency which extended not only to the maritime populations but to the more warlike tribes in the interior and the mountain districts. He established peaceable relations with these, and more than that, he secured their support in arms and several strong cohorts were enrolled from amongst them. The country on this side of the Ebro was Hanno's province, Hannibal had left him to hold it for Carthage. Considering that he ought to oppose Scipio's further progress before the whole province was under Roman sway, he fixed his camp in full view of the enemy and offered battle. The Roman general, too, thought that battle ought not to be delayed; he knew he would have to fight both Hanno and Hasdrubal, and preferred dealing with each singly rather than meeting them both at once. The battle was not a hard-fought one. The enemy lost 6,000; 2,000, including those who were guarding the camp, were made prisoners; the camp itself was carried and the general with some of his chiefs was taken; Cissis, a town near the camp, was successfully attacked. The plunder, however, as it was a small place, was of little value, consisting mainly of the barbarians' household goods and some worthless slaves. The camp, however, enriched the soldiers with the property belonging not only to the army they had defeated but also to the one serving with Hannibal in Italy. They had left almost all their valuable possessions on the other side of the Pyrenees, that they might not have heavy loads to carry.

61. Before he had received definite tidings of this defeat, Hasdrubal had crossed the Ebro with 8,000 infantry and 1,000 cavalry, hoping to encounter the Romans as soon as they landed, but after hearing of the disaster at Cissis and the capture of the camp, he turned his route to the sea. Not far from Tarracona he found our marines and seamen wandering at will through the fields, success as usual producing carelessness. Sending his cavalry in all directions amongst them, he made a great slaughter and drove them pell-mell to their ships. Afraid to remain any longer in the neighborhood lest he should be surprised by Scipio, he retreated across the Ebro. On hearing of this fresh enemy Scipio came down by forced marches, and after dealing summary punishment to some of the naval captains, returned by sea to Emporiae, leav-

ing a small garrison in Tarracona. He had scarcely left when Hasdrubal appeared on the scene, and instigated the Ilergetes, who had given hostages to Scipio, to revolt, and in conjunction with the warriors of that tribe ravaged the territories of those tribes who remained loyal to Rome. This roused Scipio from his winter quarters, on which Hasdrubal again disappeared beyond the Ebro, and Scipio invaded in force the territory of the Ilergetes, after the author of the revolt had left them to their fate. He drove them all into Antanagrum, their capital, which he proceeded to invest, and a few days later he received them into the protection and jurisdiction of Rome, after demanding an increase in the number of hostages and inflicting a heavy fine upon them. From there he advanced against the Ausetani, who lived near the Ebro and were also in alliance with the Carthaginians, and invested their city. The Laeetani whilst bringing assistance to their neighbors by night were ambushed not far from the city which they intended to enter. As many as 12,000 were killed, almost all the survivors threw away their arms and fled to their homes in scattered groups all over the country. The only thing which saved the invested city from assault and storm was the severity of the weather. For the thirty days during which the siege lasted the snow was seldom less than four feet deep, and it covered up the mantlets and vineae so completely that it even served as a sufficient protection against the firebrands which the enemy discharged from time to time. At last, after their chief, Amusicus, had escaped to Hasdrubal's quarters, they surrendered and agreed to pay an indemnity of twenty talents. The army returned to its winter quarters at Tarracona.

62. During this winter many portents occurred in Rome and the neighborhood, or at all events, many were reported and easily gained credence, for when once men's minds have been excited by superstitious fears they easily believe these things. A six-months-old child, of freeborn parents, is said to have shouted "Io Triumphe" in the vegetable market, whilst in the Forum Boarium an ox is reported to have climbed up of its own accord to the third story of a house, and then, frightened by the noisy crowd which gathered, it threw itself down. A phantom navy was seen shining in the sky; the temple of Hope in the vegetable market was struck by lightning; at Lanuvium Juno's spear had moved of itself, and a crow had flown down to her temple and settled upon her couch; in the territory of Amiternum beings in human shape and clothed in white were seen at a distance, but no one came close to them; in the neighborhood of Picenum there was a shower of stones; at Caere the oracular tablets had shrunk in size; in Gaul a wolf had snatched a sentinel's sword from its scabbard and run off with it. With regard to the other portents, the decemvirs were ordered to consult the Sacred Books, but in the case of the shower of stones at Picenum a nine days' sacred feast was proclaimed, at the close of which almost the whole community busied itself with the expiation of the others. First of all the City was purified, and full-grown victims were sacrificed to the deities named in the Sacred Books; an offering of forty pounds' weight of gold was conveyed to Juno at Lanuvium, and the matrons dedicated a bronze statue of that goddess on the Aventine. At Caere, where the tablets had shrunk, a lectisternium was enjoined, and a service of intercession was to be rendered to Fortuna on Algidus. In Rome also a lectisternium was ordered for Juventas and a special service of intercession at the temple of Hercules, and afterwards one in which the whole population were to take part at all the shrines. Five full-grown victims were sacrificed to the Genius of Rome, and C. Atilius Serranus, the praetor, received instructions to undertake certain vows which were to be discharged should the commonwealth remain in the same condition for ten years. These ceremonial observances and vows, ordered in obedience to the Sacred Books, did much to allay the religious fears of the people.

63. One of the consuls elect was C. Flaminius, and to him was assigned by lot the command of the legions at Placentia. He wrote to the consul giving orders for the army to be in camp at Ariminum by the 15th of March. The reason was that he might enter upon his office there, for he had not forgotten his old quarrels with the senate, first as tribune of the people, then afterwards about his consulship, the election to which had been declared illegal, and finally about his triumph. He further embittered the senate against him by his support of C. Claudius; he alone of all the members was in favor of the measure which that tribune introduced. Under its provisions no senator, no one whose father had been a senator, was allowed to possess a vessel of more than 300 amphorae burden. This was considered quite large enough for the conveyance of produce from their estates, all profit made by trading was regarded as dishonorable for the patricians. The question excited the keenest opposition and brought Flaminius into the worst possible odium with the nobility through his support of it, but on the other hand made him a popular favorite and procured for him his second consulship. Suspecting, therefore, that they would endeavor to detain him in the City by various devices, such as falsifying the auspices or the delay necessitated by the Latin Festival, or other hindrances to which as consul he was liable, he gave out that he had to take a journey, and then left the City secretly as a private individual and so reached his province. When this got abroad there was a fresh outburst of indignation on the part of the incensed senate; they declared that he was carrying on war not only with the senate but even with the immortal gods. "On the former occasion," they said, "when he was elected consul against the auspices and we recalled him from the very field of battle, he was disobedient to gods and men. Now he is conscious that he has despised them and has fled from the Capitol and the customary recital of solemn vows. He refuses to approach the temple of Jupiter Optimus Maximus on the day of his entrance upon office, to see and consult the senate, to whom he is so odious and whom he alone of all men detests, to proclaim the Latin Festival and offer sacrifice to Jupiter Latiaris on the Alban Mount, to proceed to the Capitol and after duly taking the auspices recite the prescribed vows, and from thence, vested in the paludamentum and escorted by lictors, go in state to his province. He has stolen away furtively without his insignia of office, without his lictors, just as though he were some menial employed in the camp and had quitted his native soil to go into exile. He thinks it, forsooth, more consonant with the greatness of his office to enter upon it at Ariminum rather than in Rome, and to put on his official dress in some wayside inn rather than at his own hearth and in the presence of his own household gods." It was unanimously decided that he should be recalled, brought back if need be by force, and compelled to discharge, on the spot, all the duties he owed to God and man before he went to the army and to his province. Q. Terentius and M. Antistius were delegated for this task, but they had no more influence with him than the dispatch of the senate in his former consulship. A few days afterwards he entered upon office, and whilst offering his sacrifice, the calf, after it was struck, bounded away out of the hands of the sacrificing priests and bespattered many of the bystanders with its blood. Amongst those at a distance from the altar who did not know what the commotion was about there was great excitement; most people regarded it as a most alarming omen. Flaminius took over the two legions from Sempronius, the late consul, and the two from C. Atilius, the praetor, and commenced his march to Etruria through the passes of the Apennines.

BOOK XXII 3–7; 44–51

Hannibal inflicted defeats on the Roman army at Lake Trasimene (217 B.C.E.) north of Rome, and at Cannae in the south. (216 B.C.E.)

3. After losing many men and beasts under these frightful circumstances, he at last got clear of the marshes, and as soon as he could find some dry ground he pitched his camp. The scouting parties he had sent out reported that the Roman army was lying in the neighborhood of Arretium. His next step was to investigate as carefully as he possibly could all that it was material for him to know—what mood the consul was in, what designs he was forming, what the character of the country and the kind of roads it possessed, and what resources it offered for the obtaining of supplies. The district was amongst the most fertile in Italy; the plains of Etruria, which extend from Faesulae to Arretium, are rich in corn and live stock and every kind of produce. The consul's overbearing temper, which had grown steadily worse since his last consulship, made him lose all proper respect and reverence even for the gods, to say nothing of the majesty of the senate and the laws, and this self-willed and obstinate side of his character had been aggravated by the successes he had achieved both at home and in the field. It was perfectly obvious that he would not seek counsel from either God or man, and whatever he did would be done in an impetuous and headstrong manner. By way of making him show these faults of character still more flagrantly, the Carthaginian prepared to irritate and annoy him. He left the Roman camp on his left, and marched in the direction of Faesulae to plunder the central districts of Etruria. Within actual view of the consul he created as widespread a devastation as he possibly could, and from the Roman camp they saw in the distance an extensive scene of fire and massacre.

Flaminius had no intention of keeping quiet even if the enemy had done so, but now that he saw the possessions of the allies of Rome plundered and pillaged almost before his very eyes, he felt it to be a personal disgrace that an enemy should be roaming at will through Italy and advancing to attack Rome with none to hinder him. All the other members of the council of war were in favor of a policy of safety rather than of display; they urged him to wait for his colleague, that they might unite their forces and act with one mind on a common plan, and pending his arrival they should check the wild excesses of the plundering enemy with cavalry and the light-armed auxiliaries. Enraged at these suggestions he dashed out of the council and ordered the trumpets to give the signal for march and battle; exclaiming at the same time: "We are to sit, I suppose, before the walls of Arretium, because our country and our household gods are here. Now that Hannibal has slipped through our hands, he is to ravage Italy, destroy and burn everything in his way till he reaches Rome, while we are not to stir from here until the senate summons C. Flaminius from Arretium as they once summoned Camillus from Veii." During this outburst, he ordered the standards to be pulled up with all speed and at the same time mounted his horse. No sooner had he done so than the animal stumbled and fell and threw him over its head. All those who were standing round were appalled by what they took to be an evil omen at the beginning of a campaign, and their alarm was considerably increased by a message brought to the consul that the standard could not be moved though the standard-bearer had exerted his utmost strength. He turned to the messenger and asked him: "Are you bringing a dispatch from the senate, also, forbidding me to go on with the campaign? Go, let them dig out the standard if their hands are too benumbed with fear for them to pull it up." Then the column began its march. The superior officers, besides being absolutely opposed to his plans, were thoroughly alarmed by the double portent, but the great body of the soldiers were delighted at the spirit their general had shown; they shared his confidence without knowing on what slender grounds it rested.

4. In order still further to exasperate his enemy and make him eager to avenge the injuries inflicted on the allies of Rome, Hannibal laid waste with all the horrors of war the land between Cortona and Lake Trasimene. He had now reached a position eminently adapted for surprise tactics, where the lake comes up close under the hills of Cortona. There is only a very narrow road here between the hills and the lake, as though a space had been purposely left for it. Further on there is a small expanse of level ground flanked by hills, and it was here that Hannibal pitched camp, which was only occupied by his Africans and Spaniards, he himself being in command. The Balearics and the rest of the light infantry he sent behind the hills; the cavalry, conveniently screened by some low hills, he stationed at the mouth of the defile, so that when the Romans had entered it they would be completely shut in by the cavalry, the lake, and the hills. Flaminius had reached the lake at sunset. The next morning, in a still uncertain light, he passed through the defile, without sending any scouts on to feel the way, and when the column began to deploy in the wider extent of level ground the only enemy they saw was the one in front, the rest were concealed in their rear and above their heads. When the Carthaginian saw his object achieved and had his enemy shut in between the lake and the hills with his forces surrounding them, he gave the signal for all to make a simultaneous attack, and they charged straight down upon the point nearest to them. The affair was all the more sudden and unexpected to the Romans because a fog which had risen from the lake was denser on the plain than on the heights; the bodies of the enemy on the various hills could see each other well enough, and it was all the easier for them to charge all at the same time. The shout of battle rose round the Romans before they could see clearly from whence it came, or became aware that they were surrounded. Fighting began in front and flank before they could form line or get their weapons ready or draw their swords.

5. In the universal panic, the consul displayed all the coolness that could be expected under the circumstances. The ranks were broken by each man turning towards the discordant shouts; he re-formed them as well as time and place allowed, and wherever he could be seen or heard, he encouraged his men and bade them stand and fight. "It is not by prayers or entreaties to the gods that you must make your way out," he said, "but by your strength and your courage. It is the sword that cuts a path through the middle of the enemy, and where there is less fear there is generally less danger." But such was the uproar and confusion that neither counsel nor command could be heard, and so far was the soldier from recognizing his standard or his company or his place in the rank, that he had hardly sufficient presence of mind

to get hold of his weapons and make them available for use, and some who found them a burden rather than a protection were overtaken by the enemy. In such a thick fog ears were of more use than eyes; the men turned their gaze in every direction as they heard the groans of the wounded and the blows on shield or breastplate, and the mingled shouts of triumph and cries of panic. Some who tried to fly ran into a dense body of combatants and could get no further; others who were returning to the fray were swept away by a rush of fugitives. At last, when ineffective charges had been made in every direction and they found themselves completely hemmed in, by the lake and the hills on either side, and by the enemy in front and rear, it became clear to every man that his only hope of safety lay in his own right hand and his sword. Then each began to depend upon himself for guidance and encouragement, and the fighting began afresh, not the orderly battle with its three divisions of principes, hastati, and triarii, where the fighting line is in front of the standards and the rest of the army behind, and where each soldier is in his own legion and cohort and maniple. Chance massed them together, each man took his place in front or rear as his courage prompted him, and such was the ardor of the combatants, so intent were they on the battle, that not a single man on the field was aware of the earthquake which leveled large portions of many towns in Italy, altered the course of swift streams, brought the sea up into the rivers, and occasioned enormous landslides amongst the mountains.

6. For almost three hours the fighting went on; everywhere a desperate struggle was kept up, but it raged with greater fierceness round the consul. He was followed by the pick of his army, and wherever he saw his men hard pressed and in difficulties he at once went to their help. Distinguished by his armor he was the object of the enemy's fiercest attacks, which his comrades did their utmost to repel, until an Insubrian horseman who knew the consul by sight—his name was Ducarius—cried out to his countrymen, "Here is the man who slew our legions and laid waste our city and our lands! I will offer him in sacrifice to the shades of my foully murdered countrymen." Digging spurs into his horse he charged into the dense masses of the enemy, and slew an armor-bearer who threw himself in the way as he galloped up lance in rest, and then plunged his lance into the consul; but the triarii protected the body with their shields and prevented him from despoiling it. Then began a general flight, neither lake nor mountain stopped the panic-stricken fugitives, they rushed like blind men over cliff and defile, men and arms tumbled pell-mell on one another. A large number, finding no avenue of escape, went into the water up to their shoulders; some in their wild terror even attempted to escape by swimming, an endless and hopeless task in that lake. Either their spirits gave way and they were drowned, or else finding their efforts fruitless, they regained with great difficulty the shallow water at the edge of the lake and were butchered in all directions by the enemy's cavalry who had ridden into the water. About 6,000 men who had formed the head of the line of march cut their way through the enemy and cleared the defile, quite unconscious of all that had been going on behind them. They halted on some rising ground, and listened to the shouting below and the clash of arms, but were unable, owing to the fog, to see or find out what the fortunes of the fight were. At last, when the battle was over and the sun's heat had dispelled the fog, mountain and plain revealed in the clear light the disastrous overthrow of the Roman army and showed only too plainly that all was lost. Fearing lest they should be seen in the distance and cavalry be sent against them, they hurriedly took up their standards and disappeared with all possible speed. Maharbal pursued them through the night with the whole of his mounted force, and on the morrow, as starvation, in addition to all their other miseries, was threatening them, they surrendered to Maharbal, on condition of being allowed to depart with one garment apiece. This promise was kept with Punic faith by Hannibal, and he threw them all into chains.

7. This was the famous battle at Trasimene, and a disaster for Rome memorable as few others have been. Fifteen thousand Romans were killed in action; 1,000 fugitives were scattered all over Etruria and reached the City by divers routes; 2,500 of the enemy perished on the field, many in both armies afterwards of their wounds. Other authors give the loss on each side as many times greater, but I refuse to indulge in the idle exaggerations to which writers are far too much given, and what is more, I am supported by the authority of Fabius, who was living during the war. Hannibal dismissed without ransom those prisoners who belonged to the allies and threw the Romans into chains. He then gave orders for the bodies of his own men to be picked out from the heaps of slain and buried; careful search was also made for the body of Flaminius that it might receive honorable interment but it was not found. As soon as the news of this disaster reached Rome the people flocked into the Forum in a great state of panic and confusion. Matrons were wandering about the streets and asking those they met what recent disaster had been reported or what news was there of the army. The throng in the Forum, as numerous as a crowded Assembly, flocked towards the Comitium and the Senate-house and called for the magistrates. At last, shortly before sunset, M. Pomponius, the praetor, announced, "We have been defeated in a great battle." Though nothing more definite was heard from him, the people, full of the reports which they had heard from one another, carried back to their homes the information that the consul had been killed with the greater part of his army; only a few survived, and these were either dispersed in flight throughout Etruria or had been made prisoners by the enemy.

The misfortunes which had befallen the defeated army were not more numerous than the anxieties of those whose relatives had served under C.

Flaminius, ignorant as they were of the fate of each of their friends, and not in the least knowing what to hope for or what to fear. The next day and several days afterwards, a large crowd, containing more women than men, stood at the gates waiting for some one of their friends or for news about them, and they crowded round those they met with eager and anxious inquiries, nor was it possible to get them away, especially from those they knew, until they had got all the details from first to last. Then as they came away from their informants you might see the different expressions on their faces, according as each had received good or bad news, and friends congratulating or consoling them as they wended their way homewards. The women were especially demonstrative in their joy and in their grief. They say that one who suddenly met her son at the gate safe and sound expired in his arms, whilst another who had received false tidings of her son's death and was sitting as a sorrowful mourner in her house, no sooner saw him returning than she died from too great happiness. For several days the praetors kept the senate in session from sunrise to sunset, deliberating under what general or with what forces they could offer effective resistance to the victorious Carthaginian.

§

44. The consuls followed the Carthaginians, carefully examining the roads as they marched, and when they reached Cannae and had the enemy in view they formed two entrenched camps separated by the same interval as at Gereonium, and with the same distribution of troops in each camp. The river Aufidus, flowing past the two camps, furnished a supply of water which the soldiers got as they best could, and they generally had to fight for it. The men in the smaller camp, which was on the other side of the river, had less difficulty in obtaining it, as that bank was not held by the enemy. Hannibal now saw his hopes fulfilled, that the consuls would give him an opportunity of fighting on ground naturally adapted for the movements of cavalry, the arm in which he had so far been invincible, and accordingly he placed his army in order of battle, and tried to provoke his foe to action by repeated charges of his Numidians. The Roman camp was again disturbed by a mutinous soldiery and consuls at variance, Paulus bringing up against Varro the fatal rashness of Sempronius and Flaminius, Varro retorting by pointing to Fabius as the favorite model of cowardly and inert commanders, and calling gods and men to witness that it was through no fault of his that Hannibal had acquired, so to speak, a prescriptive right to Italy; he had had his hands tied by his colleague; his soldiers, furious and eager for fight, had had their swords and arms taken away from them. Paulus, on the other hand, declared that if anything happened to the legions flung recklessly and betrayed into an ill-considered and imprudent action, he was free from all responsibility for it, though he would have to share in all the consequences. "See to it," he said to Varro, "that those who are so free and ready with their tongues are equally so with their hands in the day of battle."

45. Whilst time was thus being wasted in disputes instead of deliberation, Hannibal withdrew the bulk of his army, who had been standing most of the day in order of battle, into camp. He sent his Numidians, however, across the river to attack the parties who were getting water for the smaller camp. They had hardly gained the opposite bank when with their shouting and uproar they sent the crowd flying in wild disorder, and galloping on as far as the outpost in front of the rampart, they nearly reached the gates of the camp. It was looked upon as such an insult for a Roman camp to be actually terrorized by irregular auxiliaries that one thing, and one thing alone, held back the Romans from instantly crossing the river and forming their battle line—the supreme command that day rested with Paulus. The following day Varro, whose turn it now was, without any consultation with his colleague, exhibited the signal for battle and led his forces drawn up for action across the river. Paulus followed, for though he disapproved of the measure, he was bound to support it. After crossing, they strengthened their line with the force in the smaller camp and completed their formation. On the right, which was nearest to the river, the Roman cavalry were posted, then came the infantry; on the extreme left were the cavalry of the allies, their infantry were between them and the Roman legions. The javelin men with the rest of the light-armed auxiliaries formed the front line. The consuls took their stations on the wings, Terentius Varro on the left, Aemilius Paulus on the right.

46. As soon as it grew light Hannibal sent forward the Balearics and the other light infantry. He then crossed the river in person and as each division was brought across he assigned it its place in the line. The Gaulish and Spanish horse he posted near the bank on the left wing in front of the Roman cavalry; the right wing was assigned to the Numidian troopers. The center consisted of a strong force of infantry, the Gauls and Spaniards in the middle, the Africans at either end of them. You might fancy that the Africans were for the most part a body of Romans from the way they were armed, they were so completely equipped with the arms, some of which they had taken at the Trebia, but the most part at Trasimene. The Gauls and Spaniards had shields almost of the same shape; but their swords were totally different, those of the Gauls being very long and without a point, the Spaniard, accustomed to thrust more than to cut, had a short handy sword, pointed like a dagger. These nations, more than any other, inspired terror by the vastness of their stature and their frightful appearance: the Gauls were naked above the waist, the Spaniards had taken up their position wearing white tunics embroidered with purple, of dazzling brilliancy. The total number of infantry in the field was 40,000, and there were 10,000 cavalry. Hasdrubal was in command of the left wing, Maharbal of the right; Hannibal himself with his brother Mago commanded the center. It was a great convenience to both armies that the sun shone obliquely on them, whether it was that they had purposely so placed themselves, or whether it happened by accident, since the Romans faced the north, the Carthaginans the South. The wind, called by the inhabitants the Vulturnus, was against the Romans, and blew great clouds of dust into their faces, making it impossible for them to see in front of them.

47. When the battle shout was raised the auxiliaries ran forward, and the battle began with the light infantry. Then the Gauls and Spaniards on the left engaged the Roman cavalry on the right; the battle was not at all like a cavalry fight, for there was no room for maneuvering, the river on the one side and the infantry on the other hemming them in, compelled them to fight face to face. Each side tried to force their way straight forward, till at last the horses were standing in a closely pressed mass, and the riders seized their opponents and tried to drag them from their horses. It had become mainly a struggle of infantry, fierce but short, and the Roman cavalry was repulsed and fled. Just as this battle of the cavalry was finished, the infantry became engaged, and as long as the Gauls and Spaniards kept their ranks unbroken, both sides were equally matched in strength and courage. At length after long and repeated efforts the Romans closed up their ranks, echeloned their front, and by the sheer weight of their deep column bore down the division of the enemy which was stationed in front of Hannibal's line, and was too thin and weak to resist the pressure. Without a moment's pause they followed up their broken and hastily retreating foe till they took to headlong flight. Cutting their way through the mass of fugitives, who offered no resistance, they penetrated as far as the Africans who were stationed on both wings, somewhat further back than the Gauls and Spaniards who had formed the advanced center. As the latter fell back the whole front became level, and as they continued to give ground it became concave and crescent-shaped, the Africans at either end forming the horns. As the Romans rushed on incautiously between them, they were enfiladed by the two wings, which extended and closed round them in the rear. On this, the Romans, who had fought one battle to no purpose, left the Gauls and Spaniards, whose rear they had been slaughtering, and commenced a fresh struggle with the Africans. The contest was a very one-sided one, for not only were they hemmed in on all sides, but wearied with the previous fighting they were meeting fresh and vigorous opponents.

48. By this time the Roman left wing, where the allied cavalry were fronting the Numidians, had become engaged, but the fighting was slack at first owing to a Carthaginian stratagem. About 500 Numidians, carrying, besides their usual arms and missiles, swords concealed under their coats of mail, rode out from their own line with their shields slung behind their backs as though they were deserters, and suddenly leaped from their horses and flung their shields and javelins at the feet of their enemy. They were received into their ranks, conducted to the rear, and ordered to remain quiet. While the battle was spreading to the various parts of the field they remained quiet, but when the eyes and minds of all were wholly taken up with the fighting they seized the large Roman shields which were lying everywhere amongst the heaps of slain and commenced a furious attack upon the rear of the Roman line. Slashing away at backs and hips, they made a great slaughter and a still greater panic and confusion. Amidst the rout and panic in one part of the field and the obstinate but hopeless struggle in the other, Hasdrubal, who was in command of that arm, withdrew some Numidians from the center of the right wing, where the fighting was feebly kept up, and sent them in pursuit of the fugitives, and at the same time sent the Spanish and Gaulish horse to the aid of the Africans, who were by this time more wearied by slaughter than by fighting.

49. Paulus was on the other side of the field. In spite of his having been seriously wounded at the commencement of the action by a bullet from a sling, he frequently encountered Hannibal with a compact body of troops, and in several places restored the battle. The Roman cavalry formed a bodyguard round him, but at last, as he became too weak to manage his horse, they all dismounted. It is stated that when some one reported to Hannibal that the consul had ordered his men to fight on foot, he remarked, "I would rather he handed them over to me bound hand and foot." Now that the victory of the enemy was no longer doubtful this struggle of the dismounted cavalry was such as might be expected when men preferred to die where they stood rather than flee, and the victors, furious at them for delaying the victory, butchered without mercy those whom they could not dislodge. They did, however, repulse a few survivors exhausted with their exertions and their wounds. All were at last scattered, and those who could regained their horses for flight. Cn. Lentulus, a military tribune, saw, as he rode by, the consul covered with blood sitting on a boulder. "Lucius Aemilius," he said, "the one man whom the gods must hold guiltless of this day's disaster, take this horse while you have still some strength left, and I can lift you into the saddle and keep by your side to protect you. Do not make this day of battle still more fatal by a consul's death, there are enough tears and mourning without that." The consul replied: "Long may you live to do brave deeds, Cornelius, but do not waste in useless pity the few moments left in which to escape from the hands of the enemy. Go, announce publicly to the senate that they must fortify Rome and make its defense strong before the victorious enemy approaches, and tell Q. Fabius privately that I have ever remembered his precepts in life and in death. Suffer me to breathe my last among my slaughtered soldiers, let me not have to defend myself again when I am no longer consul, or appear as the accuser of my colleague and protect my own innocence by throwing the guilt on another." During this conversation a crowd of fugitives came suddenly upon them, followed by the enemy, who, not knowing who the consul was, overwhelmed him with a shower of missiles. Lentulus escaped on horseback in the rush. Then there was flight in all directions; 7,000 men escaped to the smaller camp, 10,000 to the larger, and about 2,000 to the village of Cannae. These latter were at once surrounded by Carthalo and his cavalry, as the village was quite unfortified. The other consul, who either by accident or design had not joined any of these bodies of fugitives, escaped with about fifty cavalry to Venusia; 45,500 infantry, 2,700 cavalry—almost an equal proportion of Romans and allies—are said to have been killed. Amongst the number were both the quaestors attached to the consuls, L. Atilius and L. Furius Bibaculus, twenty-nine military tribunes, several ex-consuls, ex-praetors, and ex-aediles (amongst them are included Cn. Servilius Geminus and M. Minucius, who was Master of the Horse the previous year and, some years before that, consul), and in addition to these, eighty men who had either been senators or filled offices qualifying them for election to the senate and who had volunteered for service with the legions. The prisoners taken in the battle are stated to have amounted to 3,000 infantry and 1,500 cavalry.

50. Such was the battle of Cannae, a battle as famous as the disastrous one at the Allia; not so serious in its results, owing to the inaction of the enemy, but more serious and more horrible in view of the slaughter of the army. For the flight at the Allia saved the army though it lost the City, whereas at Cannae hardly fifty men shared the consul's flight, nearly the whole army met their death in company with the other consul. As those who had taken refuge in the two camps were only a defenseless crowd without any leaders, the men in the larger camp sent a message to the others asking them to cross over to them at night when the enemy, tired after the battle and the feasting in honor of their victory, would be buried in sleep. Then they would go in one body to Canusium. Some rejected the proposal with scorn. "Why," they asked, "cannot those who sent the message come themselves, since they are quite as able to join us as we to join them? Because, of course, all the country between us is scoured by the enemy and they prefer to expose other people to that deadly peril rather than themselves." Others did not disapprove of the proposal, but they lacked courage to carry it out. P. Sempronius Tuditanus protested against this cowardice. "Would you," he asked, "rather be taken prisoners by a most avaricious and ruthless foe and a price put upon your heads and your value assessed after you have been asked whether you are a Roman citizen or a Latin ally, in order that another may win honor from your misery and disgrace? Certainly not, if you are really the fellow-countrymen of L. Aemilius, who chose a noble death rather than a life of degradation, and of all the brave men who are lying in heaps around him. But, before daylight overtakes us and the enemy gathers in larger force to bar our path, let us cut our way through the men who in disorder and confusion are clamoring at our gates. Good swords and brave hearts make a way through enemies, however densely they are massed. If you march shoulder to shoulder you will scatter this loose and disorganized force as easily as if nothing opposed you. Come then with me, all you who want to preserve yourselves and the State." With these words he drew his sword, and with his men in close formation marched through the very midst of the enemy. When the Numidians hurled their javelins on the right, the unprotected side, they transferred their shields to their right arms, and so got clear away to the larger camp. As many as 600 escaped on this occasion, and after another large body had joined them they at once left the camp and came through safely to Canusium. This action on the part of defeated men was due to the impulse of natural courage or of accident rather than to any concerted plan of their own or any one's generalship.

51. Hannibal's officers all surrounded him and congratulated him on his victory, and urged that after such a magnificent success he should allow himself and his exhausted men to rest for the remainder of the day and the following night. Maharbal, however, the commandant of the cavalry, thought that they ought not to lose a moment. "That you may know," he said to Hannibal, "what has been gained by this battle I prophesy that in five days you will be feasting as victor in the Capitol. Follow me; I will go in advance with the cavalry; they will know that you are come before they know that you are coming." To Hannibal the victory seemed too great and too joyous for him to realize all at once. He told Maharbal that he commended his zeal, but he needed time to think out his plans. Maharbal replied: "The gods have not given all their gifts to one man. You know how to win victory, Hannibal, you do not how to use it." That day's delay is believed to have saved the City and the empire. The next day, as soon as it grew light, they set about gathering the spoils on the field and viewing the carnage, which was a ghastly sight even for an enemy. There all those thousands of Romans were lying, infantry and cavalry indiscriminately as chance had brought them together in the battle or the flight. Some covered with blood raised themselves from amongst the dead around them, tortured by their wounds which were nipped by the cold of the morning, and were promptly put an end to by the enemy. Some they found lying with their thighs and knees gashed but still alive; these bared their throats and necks and bade them drain what blood they still had left. Some were discovered with their heads buried in the earth, they had evidently suffocated themselves by making holes in the ground and heaping the soil over their faces. What attracted the attention of all was a Numidian who was dragged alive from under a dead Roman lying across him; his ears and

nose were torn, for the Roman with hands too powerless to grasp his weapon had, in his mad rage, torn his enemy with his teeth, and while doing so expired.

BOOK XXX   28–37

After Hannibal has withdrawn his army from Italy and retreated to Africa, the Roman commander Scipio (later called "Africanus" in honor of his victory) invaded Africa and defeated the Carthaginian forces at Zama (202 B.C.E.).

28. All through this time there was a growing tension of feeling, hopes and fears alike were becoming stronger. Men could not make up their minds whether they had more to rejoice over in the fact that at the end of sixteen years Hannibal had finally evacuated Italy and left the unchallenged possession of it to Rome, or more to fear from his having landed in Africa with his military strength unimpaired. "The seat of danger," they said, "is changed, but not the danger itself. Quintus Fabius, who has just died, foretold how great the struggle would be when he declared in oracular tones that Hannibal would be a more formidable foe in his own country than he had been on alien soil. Scipio has not to do with Syphax, whose subjects are undisciplined barbarians and whose army was generally led by Statorius, who was little more than a camp menial, nor with Syphax's elusive father-in-law, Hasdrubal, nor with a half-armed mob of peasants hastily collected from the fields. It is Hannibal whom he has to meet, who was all but born in the headquarters of his father, that bravest of generals; reared and brought up in the midst of arms, a soldier whilst still a boy, and when hardly out of his teens in high command. He has passed the prime of his manhood in victory after victory and has filled Spain and Gaul and Italy from the Alps to the southern sea with memorials of mighty deeds. The men he is leading are his contemporaries in arms, steeled by innumerable hardships such as it is hardly credible that men can have gone through, bespattered, times without number, with Roman blood, laden with spoils stripped from the bodies, not of common soldiers only, but even of commanders-in-chief. Scipio will meet many on the field of battle who with their own hands have slain the praetors, the commanders, the consuls of Rome, and who are now decorated with mural and vallarian wreaths after roaming at will through the camps and cities of Rome which they captured. All the fasces borne before Roman magistrates today are not so many in number as those which Hannibal might have had borne before him, taken on the field of battle when the commander-in-chief was slain." By dwelling on such gloomy prognostications they increased their fears and anxieties. And there was another ground for apprehension. They had been accustomed to seeing war going on first in one part of Italy and then in another without much hope of its being soon brought to a close. Now, however, all thoughts were turned on Scipio and Hannibal, they seemed as though purposely pitted against each other for a final and decisive struggle. Even those who felt the greatest confidence in Scipio and entertained the strongest hopes that he would be victorious became more nervous and anxious as they realized that the fateful hour was approaching. The Carthaginians were in a very similar mood. When they thought of Hannibal and the greatness of the deeds he had done they regretted that they had sued for peace, but when they reflected that they had been twice worsted in the open field, that Syphax was a prisoner, that they had been driven out of Spain and then out of Italy, and that all this was the result of one man's resolute courage, and that man Scipio, they dreaded him as though he had been destined from his birth to be their ruin.

29. Hannibal had reached Hadrumetum where he remained a few days for his men to recover from the effects of the voyage, when breathless couriers announced that all the country round Carthage was occupied by Roman arms. He at once hurried by forced marches to Zama. Zama is a five days' march from Carthage. The scouts whom he had sent forward to reconnoiter were captured by the Roman outposts and conducted to Scipio. Scipio placed them in charge of the military tribunes and gave orders for them to be taken round the camp where they were to look at everything they wished to see without fear. After asking them whether they had examined all to their satisfaction, he sent them back with an escort to Hannibal. The report they gave was anything but pleasant hearing for him, for as it happened Masinissa had on that very day come in with a force of 6,000 infantry and 4,000 cavalry. What gave him most uneasiness was the confidence of the enemy which he saw too clearly was not without good grounds. So, although he had been the cause of the war, though his arrival had upset the truce and diminished the hope of any peace being arranged, he still thought that he would be in a better position to obtain terms if he were to ask for peace while his strength was still unbroken than after a defeat. Accordingly he sent a request to Scipio to grant him an interview. Whether he did this on his own initiative or in obedience to the orders of his government I am unable to say definitely. Valerius Antias says that he was defeated by Scipio in the first battle with a loss of 12,000 killed and 1,700 taken prisoners, and that after this he went in company with ten delegates to Scipio's camp. However this may be, Scipio did not refuse the proposed interview, and by common agreement the two commanders advanced their camps towards each other that they might meet more easily. Scipio took up his position not far from the city of Naragarra on ground which, in addition to other advantages, afforded a supply of water within range of missiles from the Roman lines. Hannibal selected some ris-

ing ground about four miles away, a safe and advantageous position, except
that water had to be obtained from a distance. A spot was selected midway
between the camps, which, to prevent any possibility of treachery, afforded a
view on all sides.

30. When their respective escorts had withdrawn to an equal distance,
the two leaders advanced to meet each other, each accompanied by an interpreter—the greatest commanders not only of their own age but of all who
are recorded in history before their day, the peers of the most famous kings
and commanders that the world had seen. For a few moments they gazed
upon one another in silent admiration. Hannibal was the first to speak. "If,"
he said, "Destiny has so willed it that I, who was the first to make war on
Rome and who have so often had the final victory almost within my grasp,
should now be the first to come to ask for peace, I congratulate myself that
Fate has appointed you, above all others, as the one from whom I am to ask
it. Amongst your many brilliant distinctions this will not be your smallest
title to fame, that Hannibal, to whom the gods have given the victory over so
many Roman generals, has yielded to you, that it has fallen to your lot to put
an end to a war which has been more memorable for your defeats than for
ours. This is indeed the irony of fortune, that after taking up arms when your
father was consul, and having him for my opponent in my first battle, it
should be his son to whom I come unarmed to ask for peace. It would have
been far better had the gods endowed our fathers with such a disposition that
you would have been contented with the sovereignty of Italy, whilst we were
contented with Africa. As it is, even for you, Sicily and Sardinia are no adequate compensation for the loss of so many fleets, so many armies, and so
many splendid generals. But it is easier to regret the past than to repair it. We
coveted what belonged to others, consequently we had to fight for our own
possessions; not only has war assailed you in Italy and us in Africa, but you
have seen the arms and standards of an enemy almost within your gates and
on your walls while we hear in Carthage the murmur of the Roman camp. So
the thing which we detest most of all, which you would have wished for
before everything, has actually come about, the question of peace is raised
when your fortunes are in the ascendant. We who are most concerned in
securing peace are the ones to propose it, and we have full powers to treat,
whatever we do here our governments will ratify. All we need is a temper to
discuss things calmly. As far as I am concerned, coming back to a country
which I left as a boy, years and a chequered experience of good and evil fortune have so disillusioned me that I prefer to take reason rather than Fortune
as my guide. As for you, your youth and unbroken success will make you, I
fear, impatient of peaceful counsels. It is not easy for the man whom Fortune
never deceives to reflect on the uncertainties and accidents of life. What I
was at Thrasymenus and at Cannae, that you are today. You were hardly old

enough to bear arms when you were placed in high command, and in all your enterprises, even the most daring, Fortune has never played you false. You avenged the deaths of your father and your uncle, and that disaster to your house became the occasion of your winning a glorious reputation for courage and filial piety. You recovered the lost provinces of Spain after driving four Carthaginian armies out of the country. Then you were elected consul, and whilst your predecessors had hardly spirit enough to protect Italy, you crossed over to Africa, and after destroying two armies and capturing and burning two camps within an hour, taking the powerful monarch Syphax prisoner, and robbing his dominions and ours of numerous cities you have at last dragged me away from Italy after I had kept my hold upon it for sixteen years. It is quite possible that in your present mood you should prefer victory to an equitable peace; I, too, know the ambition which aims at what is great rather than at what is expedient; on me, too, a fortune such as yours once shone. But if in the midst of success the gods should also give us wisdom, we ought to reflect not only on what has happened in the past but also upon what may happen in the future. To take only one instance, I myself am a sufficient example of the fickleness of fortune. Only the other day I had placed my camp between your city and the Anio and was advancing my standards against the walls of Rome—here you see me, bereaved of my two brothers, brave soldiers and brilliant generals as they were, in front of the walls of my native place which is all but invested, and begging on behalf of my city that it may be spared the fate with which I have threatened yours. The greater a man's good fortune the less ought he to count upon it. Success attends you and has deserted us, and this will make peace all the more splendid to you who grant it; to us who ask for it is a stern necessity rather than an honorable surrender. Peace once established is a better and safer thing than hoping for victory; that is in your hands, this in the hands of the gods. Do not expose so many years' good fortune to the hazard of a single hour. You think of your own strength, but think too of the part which fortune plays and the even chances of battle. On both sides there will be swords and men to use them, nowhere does the event less answer expectation than in war. Victory will not add so much to the glory which you can now win by granting peace, as defeat will take away from it. The chances of a single hour can annihilate all the honors you have gained and all you can hope for. If you cement a peace, P. Cornelius, you are master of all, otherwise you will have to accept whatever fortune the gods send you. M. Atilius Regulus on this very soil would have afforded an almost unique instance of the success which waits on merit, had he in the hour of victory granted peace to our fathers when they asked for it. But as he would set no bounds to his prosperity, nor curb his elation at his good fortune, the height to which he aspired only made his fall the more terrible.

"It is for him who grants peace, not for him who seeks it, to name the terms, but perhaps it may not be presumptuous in us to assess our own penalty. We consent to everything remaining yours for which we went to war —Sicily, Sardinia, Spain and all the islands that lie between Africa and Italy. We Carthaginians, confined within the shores of Africa, are content, since such is the will of the gods, to see you ruling all outside our frontiers by sea and land as your dominions. I am bound to admit that the lack of sincerity lately shown in the request for peace and in the non-observance of the truce justified your suspicions as to the good faith of Carthage. But, Scipio, the loyal observance of peace depends largely upon the character of those through whom it is sought. I hear that your senate have sometimes even refused to grant it because the ambassadors were not of sufficient rank. Now it is Hannibal who seeks it, and I should not ask for it if I did not believe it to be advantageous to us, and because I believe it to be so I shall keep it inviolate. As I was responsible for beginning the war and as I conducted it in a way which no one found fault with until the gods were jealous of my success, so I shall do my utmost to prevent any one from being discontented with the peace which I shall have been the means of procuring."

31. To these arguments the Roman commander made the following reply: "I was quite aware, Hannibal, that it was the hope of your arrival that led the Carthaginians to break the truce and cloud all prospect of peace. In fact, you yourself admit as much, since you are eliminating from the terms formerly proposed all that has not already been long in our power. However, as you are anxious that your countrymen should realize what a great relief you are bringing them, I must make it my care that they shall not have the conditions they formerly agreed to struck out today as a reward for their perfidy. You do not deserve to have the old proposals still open and yet you are seeking to profit by dishonesty! Our fathers were not the aggressors in the war for Sicily, nor were we the aggressors in Spain, but the dangers which threatened our Mamertine allies in the one case and the destruction of Saguntum in the other made our case a righteous one and justified our arms. That you provoked the war in each case you yourself admit, and the gods bear witness to the fact; they guided the former war to a just and righteous issue, and they are doing and will do the same with this one. As for myself, I do not forget what weak creatures we men are; I do not ignore the influence which Fortune exercises and the countless accidents to which all our doings are liable. Had you of your own free will evacuated Italy and embarked your army before I sailed for Africa and then come with proposals for peace, I admit that I should have acted in a high-handed and arbitrary spirit if I had rejected them. But now that I have dragged you to Africa like a reluctant and tricky defendant I am not bound to show you the slightest consideration. So then, if in addition to the terms on which peace might have been concluded previously, there is the further condition of an indemnity for the attack on our transports and the ill-treatment of our envoys during the armistice, I shall have something to lay before the councils. If you consider this unacceptable, then prepare for war as you have been unable to endure peace." Thus, no understanding was arrived at and the commanders rejoined their armies. They reported that the discussion had been fruitless, that the matter must be decided by arms, and the result left to the gods.

32. On their return to their camps, the commanders-in-chief each issued an order of the day to their troops. "They were to get their arms ready and brace up their courage for a final and decisive struggle; if success attended them they would be victors not for a day only but for all time; they would know before the next day closed whether Rome or Carthage was to give laws to the nations. For not Africa and Italy only—the whole world will be the prize of victory. Great as is the prize, the peril in case of defeat will be as great." For no escape lay open to the Romans in a strange and unknown land; and Carthage was making her last effort, if that failed, her destruction was imminent. On the morrow they went out to battle—the two most brilliant generals and the two strongest armies that the two most powerful nations possessed—to crown on that day the many honors they had won, or for ever lose them. The soldiers were filled with alternate hopes and fears as they gazed at their own and then at the opposing lines and measured their comparative strength with the eye rather than the mind, cheerful and despondent in turn. The encouragement which they could not give to themselves their generals gave them in their exhortations. The Carthaginian reminded his men of their sixteen years' successes on Italian soil, of all the Roman generals who had fallen and all the armies that had been destroyed, and as he came to each soldier who had distinguished himself in any battle, he recounted his gallant deeds. Scipio recalled the conquest of Spain and the recent battles in Africa and showed up the enemies' confession of weakness, since their fears compelled them to sue for peace and their innate faithlessness prevented them from abiding by it. He turned to his own purpose the conference with Hannibal, which being private allowed free scope for invention. He drew an omen and declared that the gods had vouchsafed the same auspices to them as those under which their fathers fought at the Aegates. The end of the war and of their labors, he assured them, had come; the spoils of Carthage were in their hands, and the return home to their wives and children and household gods. He spoke with uplifted head and a face so radiant that you might suppose he had already won the victory.

33. Then he drew up his men, the hastati in front, behind them the principes, the triarii closing the rear. He did not form the cohorts in line before their respective standards, but placed a considerable interval between the maniples in order that there might be space for the enemy elephants to be driven through without breaking the ranks. Laelius, who had been one of his staff-officers and was now by special appointment of the senate acting as quaestor, was in command of the Italian cavalry on the left wing, Masinissa and his Numidians being posted on the right. The velites, the light infantry of those days, were stationed at the head of the lanes between the columns of maniples with instructions to retire when the elephants charged and shelter themselves behind the lines of maniples, or else run to the right and left behind the standards and so allow the monsters to rush on to meet the darts from both sides. To make his line look more menacing Hannibal posted his elephants in front. He had eighty altogether, a larger number than he had ever brought into action before. Behind them were the auxiliaries, Ligurians and Gauls, with an admixture of Balearics and Moors. The second line was made up of Carthaginians and Africans together with a legion of Macedonians. A short distance behind these were posted his Italian troops in reserve. These were mainly Bruttians who had followed him from Italy more from the compulsion of necessity than of their own free will. Like Scipio, Hannibal covered his flanks with his cavalry, the Carthaginians on the right, the Numidians on the left.

Different words of encouragement were required in an army composed of such diverse elements, where the soldiers had nothing in common, neither language nor custom nor laws nor arms nor dress, nor even the motive which brought them into the ranks. To the auxiliaries he held out the attraction of the pay which they would receive, and the far greater inducement of the booty they would secure. In the case of the Gauls he appealed to their instinctive and peculiar hatred of the Romans. The Ligurians, drawn from wild mountain fastnesses, were told to look upon the fruitful plains of Italy as the rewards of victory. The Moors and Numidians were threatened by the prospect of being under the unbridled tyranny of Masinissa. Each nationality was swayed by its hopes or fears. The Carthaginians had placed before their eyes, their city walls, their homes, their fathers' sepulchers, their wives and children, the alternative of either slavery and destruction or the empire of the world. There was no middle course, they had either everything to hope for or everything to fear. Whilst the commander-in-chief was thus addressing the Carthaginians, and the officers of the various nationalities were conveying his words to their own people and to the aliens mingled with them mostly through interpreters, the trumpets and horns of the Romans were sounded and such a clangor arose that the elephants, mostly those in front of the left wing, turned upon the Moors and Numidians behind them. Masinissa had no difficulty in turning this disorder into flight and so clearing the Carthaginian left of its cavalry. A few of the animals, however, showed no fear and were urged forward upon the ranks of velites, amongst whom, in spite of the many wounds they received, they did considerable execution.

The velites, to avoid being trampled to death, sprang back to the maniples and thus allowed a path for the elephants, from both sides of which they rained their darts on the beasts. The leading maniples also kept up a fusillade of missiles until these animals too were driven out of the Roman lines on to their own side and put the Carthaginian cavalry, who were covering the right flank, to flight. When Laelius saw the enemy's horse in confusion he at once took advantage of it.

34. When the infantry lines closed, the Carthaginians were exposed on both flanks, owing to the flight of the cavalry, and were losing both confidence and strength. Other circumstances, too, seemingly trivial in themselves but of considerable importance in battle, gave the Romans an advantage. Their cheers formed one united shout and were therefore fuller and more intimidating; those of the enemy, uttered in many languages, were only dissonant cries. The Romans kept their foothold as they fought and pressed the enemy by the sheer weight of their arms and bodies; on the other side there was much more agility and nimbleness of foot than actual fighting strength. As a consequence, the Romans made the enemy give ground in their very first charge, then pushing them back with their shields and elbows and moving forward on to the ground from which they had dislodged them, they made a considerable advance as though meeting with no resistance. When those in the rear became aware of the forward movement they too pressed on those in front thereby considerably increasing the weight of the thrust. This retirement on the part of the enemy's auxiliaries was not checked by the Africans and Carthaginians who formed the second line. In fact, so far were they from supporting them that they too fell back, fearing lest the enemy, after overcoming the obstinate resistance of the first line, should reach them. On this the auxiliaries suddenly broke and turned tail; some took refuge within the second line, others, not allowed to do so, began to cut down those who refused to admit them after refusing to support them. There were now two battles going on, the Carthaginians had to fight with the enemy, and at the same time with their own troops. Still, they would not admit these maddened fugitives within their ranks, they closed up and drove them to the wings and out beyond the fighting ground, fearing lest their fresh and unweakened lines should be demoralized by the intrusion of panic-stricken and wounded men. The ground where the auxiliaries had been stationed had become blocked with such heaps of bodies and arms that it was almost more difficult to cross it than it had been to make way through the masses of the enemy. The hastati who formed the first line followed up the enemy, each man advancing as best he could over the heaps of bodies and arms and the slippery bloodstained ground until the standards and maniples were all in confusion. Even the standards of the principes began to sway to and fro when they saw how irregular the line in front had become. As soon as

Scipio observed this he ordered the call to be sounded for the hastati to retire, and after withdrawing the wounded to the rear he brought up the principes and triarii to the wings, in order that the hastati in the center might be supported and protected on both flanks. Thus the battle began entirely afresh, as the Romans had at last got to their real enemies, who were a match for them in their arms, their experience and their military reputation, and who had as much to hope for and to fear as themselves. The Romans, however, had the superiority in numbers and in confidence, since their cavalry had already routed the elephants and they were fighting with the enemy's second line after defeating his first.

35. Laelius and Masinissa, who had followed up the defeated cavalry a considerable distance, now returned from the pursuit at the right moment and attacked the enemy in the rear. This at last decided the action. The enemy were routed, many were surrounded and killed in action, those who dispersed in flight over the open country were killed by the cavalry who were in possession of every part. Above 20,000 of the Carthaginians and their allies perished on that day and almost as many were made prisoners. 132 standards were secured and 11 elephants. The victors lost 1,500 men. Hannibal escaped in the melee with a few horsemen and fled to Hadrumetum. Before quitting the field he had done everything possible in the battle itself and in the preparation for it. Scipio himself acknowledged and all experienced soldiers agreed that Hannibal had shown singular skill in the disposition of his troops. He placed his elephants in front so that their irregular charge and irresistible force might make it impossible for the Romans to keep their ranks and maintain the order of their formation, in which their strength and confidence mainly lay. Then he posted the mercenaries in front of his Carthaginians, in order that this motley force drawn from all nations, held together not by a spirit of loyalty but by their pay, might not find it easy to run away. Having to sustain the first onset they might wear down the impetuosity of the enemy, and if they did nothing else they might blunt his sword by their wounds. Then came the Carthaginian and African troops, the mainstay of his hopes. They were equal in all respects to their adversaries and even had the advantage inasmuch as they would come fresh into action against a foe weakened by wounds and fatigue. As to the Italian troops, he had his doubts as to whether they would turn out friends or foes and withdrew them consequently into the rearmost line. After giving this final proof of his great abilities, Hannibal fled, as has been stated, to Hadrumetum. From here he was summoned to Carthage, to which city he returned thirty-six years after he had left it as a boy. He told the senate frankly that he had lost not a battle merely but the whole war, and that their only chance of safety lay in obtaining peace.

36. From the battlefield Scipio proceeded at once to storm the enemies'

camp, where an immense quantity of plunder was secured. He then returned to his ships, having received intelligence that P. Lentulus had arrived off Utica with 50 warships and 100 transports loaded with supplies of every kind. Laelius was sent to carry the news of the victory to Scipio, who, thinking that the panic in Carthage ought to be increased by threatening the city on all sides, ordered Octavius to march the legions thither overland while he himself sailed from Utica with his old fleet strengthened by the division which Lentulus had brought, and steered for the harbor of Carthage. As he was approaching it he was met by a vessel hung with bands of white wool and branches of olive. In it there were the ten foremost men of the State, who, on Hannibal's advice, had been sent as an embassy to sue for peace. As soon as they were near the stern of the general's vessel they held up the suppliant emblems, and made imploring appeals to Scipio for his pity and protection. The only answer vouchsafed them was that they were to go to Tunis, as Scipio was about to move his army to that place. Keeping on his course he entered the harbor of Carthage in order to survey the situation of the city, not so much for the purpose of acquiring information as of discouraging the enemy. He then sailed back to Utica and recalled Octavius thither also. As the latter was on his way to Tunis he was informed that Vermina, the son of Syphax, was coming to the aid of the Carthaginians with a force consisting mainly of cavalry. Octavius attacked the Numidians whilst on the march with a portion of his infantry and the whole of his cavalry. The action took place on December 17, and soon ended in the utter rout of the Numidians. As they were completely surrounded by the Roman cavalry all avenues of escape were closed; 15,000 were killed and 1,200 taken prisoners, 1,500 horses were also secured and 72 standards. The prince himself escaped with a few horsemen. The Romans then reoccupied their old position at Tunis, and here an embassy consisting of thirty delegates had an interview with Scipio. Though they adopted a much humbler tone than on the previous occasion, as indeed their desperate condition demanded, they were listened to with much less sympathy on account of their recent breach of faith. At first the council of war, moved by a righteous indignation, were in favor of the complete destruction of Carthage. When, however, they reflected on the greatness of the task and the length of time which the investment of so strong and well-fortified a city would occupy, they felt considerable hesitation. Scipio himself too was afraid that his successor might come and claim the glory of terminating the war, after the way had been prepared for it by another man's toils and dangers. So there was a unanimous verdict in favor of peace being made.

37. The next day the envoys were again summoned before the council and severely taken to task for their want of truth and honesty, and they were admonished to lay to heart the lesson taught by their numerous defeats and

to believe in the power of the gods and the sanctity of oaths. The conditions of peace were then stated to them. They were to be a free State, living under their own laws; all the cities, all the territory and all the frontiers that they had held before the war they were to continue to hold, and the Romans would on that day cease from all further depredations. They were to restore to the Romans all the deserters, refugees and prisoners, to deliver up their warships, retaining only ten triremes and all their trained elephants, at the same time undertaking not to train any more. They were not to make war either within or beyond the frontiers of Africa without the permission of Rome. They were to restore all his possessions to Masinissa and make a treaty with him. Pending the return of the envoys from Rome they were to supply corn and pay to the auxiliaries in the Roman army. They were also to pay a war indemnity of 10,000 talents of silver, the payment to be in equal annual installments, extending over fifty years. One hundred hostages were to be handed over, to be selected by Scipio between the ages of fourteen and thirty years. Finally, he undertook to grant them an armistice if the transports which had been seized during the previous truce were restored with all that they contained. Otherwise there would be no armistice, nor any hopes of peace.

When the envoys brought these terms back and laid them before the Assembly, Gisgo came forward and protested against any proposals for peace. The populace, alike opposed to peace and incapable of war, were giving him a favorable hearing when Hannibal, indignant at such arguments being urged at such a crisis, seized him and dragged him by main force off the platform. This was an unusual sight in a free community, and the people were loud in their disapproval. The soldier, taken aback by the free expression of opinion on the part of his fellow-citizens, said, "I left you when I was nine years old, and now after thirty-six years' absence I have returned. The art of war which I have been taught from my boyhood, first as a private soldier and then in high command, I think I am fairly well acquainted with. The rules and laws and customs of civic life and of the forum I must learn from you." After this apology for his inexperience, he discussed the terms of peace and showed that they were not unreasonable and that their acceptance was a necessity. The greatest difficulty of all concerned the transports seized during the armistice, for nothing was to be found but the ships themselves, and any investigation would be difficult, as those who would be charged were the opponents of peace. It was decided that the ships should be restored and that in any case search should be made for the crews. It was left to Scipio to put a value on whatever else was missing and the Carthaginians were to pay the amount in cash. According to some writers, Hannibal went down to the coast straight from the battlefield, and going on board a ship which was in readiness, set sail immediately for the court of King Antiochus, and when Scipio insisted before all else upon his surrender, he was told that Hannibal was not in Africa.

BOOK XXXI 1–9

Soon after peace was concluded with Carthage in 202 B.C.E., the Romans embarked on the Second Macedonian War (200–197 B.C.E.) against King Philip V.

1. I, too, feel as much relief in having reached the end of the Punic War as if I had taken a personal part in its toils and dangers. It ill befits one who has had the courage to promise a complete history of Rome to find the separate sections of such an extensive work fatiguing. But when I consider that the sixty-three years from the beginning of the First Punic War to the end of the Second take up as many books as the four hundred and eighty-seven years from the foundation of the City to the consulship of Appius Claudius (266 B.C.E.) under whom the First Punic War commenced, I see that I am like people who are tempted by the shallow water along the beach to wade out to sea; the further I progress, the greater the depth, as though it were a bottomless sea, into which I am carried. I imagined that as I completed one part after another the task before me would diminish; as it is, it almost becomes greater. The peace with Carthage was very soon followed by war with Macedonia. There is no comparison between them as regards the critical nature of the contest, or the personality of the commander or the fighting quality of the troops. But the Macedonian war was, if anything, more noteworthy owing to the brilliant reputation of the former kings, the ancient fame of the nation and the vast extent of its dominion when it held sway over a large part of Europe and a still larger part of Asia. The war with Philip which had commenced some ten years previously had been suspended for the last three years, and both the war and its cessation were due to the action of the Aetolians. The peace with Carthage now left the Romans free. They were angry with Philip for his attacking the Aetolians and the other friendly States in Greece while he was nominally at peace with Rome, and also for his having given assistance in both men and money to Hannibal and Carthage. He had ravaged the Athenian territory and driven the inhabitants into the city, and it was their request for help which decided the Romans to recommence the war.

2. Just about the same time envoys arrived from King Attalus and also from Rhodes with the information that Philip was trying to gain the States of Asia Minor. The reply made to both deputations was that the situation in

Asia was engaging the attention of the senate. The question of war with Macedonia was referred to the consuls, who were at the time in their respective provinces. In the meanwhile, C. Claudius Nero, M. Aemilius Lepidus and P. Sempronius Tuditanus were sent on a mission to Ptolemy, king of Egypt, to announce the final defeat of Hannibal and the Carthaginians and to thank the king for having remained a staunch friend to Rome at a critical time, when even her nearest allies deserted her. They were further to request him, in case Philip's aggressions compelled them to declare war against him, that he would maintain his old friendly attitude towards the Romans. During this period P. Aelius, the consul who was commanding in Gaul, learnt that the Boii, prior to his arrival, had been raiding the territories of friendly tribes. He hastily raised a force of two legions in view of this disturbance and strengthened it with four cohorts from his own army. This force, thus hurriedly collected, he entrusted to C. Ampius, a prefect of allies, and ordered him to march through the canton of Umbria called Sapinia and invade the country of the Boii. He himself marched over the mountains by an open road. Ampius crossed the enemy's frontier, and after devastating his country without meeting any resistance, he selected a position at the fortified post of Mutilum as a suitable place for cutting the corn which was now ripe. He commenced the task without previously examining the neighborhood or posting armed parties in sufficient strength to protect the foragers, who had laid aside their weapons and were intent on their work. Suddenly he and his foragers were surprised by the Gauls who appeared on all sides. The panic and disorder extended to the men on guard; 7,000 men who were dispersed through the cornfields were killed, amongst them C. Ampius himself, the rest fled to the camp. The following night the soldiers, as they had no regular commander, decided to act for themselves, and leaving most of their possessions behind made their way through almost impassable forests to the consul. Beyond ravaging the Boian country and making a league with the Ligurian Ingauni the consul did nothing worth mentioning in his province before his return to Rome.

3. At the first meeting of the senate after his return there was a general demand that the action of Philip and the grievances of the friendly States should take precedence of all other business. The question was at once put in a crowded House and a decree was made that the consul P. Aelius should send the man whom he thought best, with full command to take over the fleet which Cn. Octavius was bringing back from Africa and proceed to Macedonia. He selected M. Valerius Laevinus, who was sent with the rank of propraetor. Laevinus took thirty-eight of Octavius' ships which were lying at anchor off Vibo and with these he sailed for Macedonia. He was met by M. Aurelius, who gave him details about the strength of the land and sea forces which the king had got together and the extent to which he was securing armed assistance not only from the cities on the mainland, but also from the islands in the Aegean, partly by his own personal influence, partly through his agents. Aurelius pointed out that the Romans would have to display far greater energy in the prosecution of this war, or else Philip, encouraged by their slackness, would venture on the same enterprise which Pyrrhus, whose kingdom was considerably smaller, had ventured on before. It was decided that Aurelius should send this information in a dispatch to the consuls and the senate.

4. Towards the close of the year the question was brought up as to the holdings which were to be assigned to the veteran soldiers who had served with Scipio in Africa. The senator decreed that M. Junius, the City praetor, should at his discretion appoint ten commissioners for the purpose of measuring and allotting that portion of the Samnite and Apulian territory which had become State domain. The commissioners were P. Servilius, Q. Caecilius Marcellus, the two Servilii, Caius and Marcus—who were known as "The Twins"—the two Hostilii Catones, Lucius and Aulus, P. Villius Tappulus, M. Fulvius Flaccus, P. Aelius Paetus and T. Quinctius Flamininus. The elections were conducted by the consul P. Aelius. The consuls-elect were P. Sulpicius Galba and C. Aurelius Cotta. The new praetors were Q. Minucius Rufus, L. Furius Purpureo, Q. Fulvius Gillo and C. Sergius Plancus. The Roman Scenic Games were celebrated this year with unusual splendor by the curule aediles, L. Valerius Flaccus and T. Quinctius Flamininus, and were repeated for a second day. They also distributed to the people with strict impartiality and to the general satisfaction a vast quantity of corn which Scipio had sent from Africa. It was sold at four asses the modius. The Plebeian Games were also exhibited on three separate occasions by the aediles L. Apustius Fullo and Q. Minucius Rufus; the latter after serving his aedileship was one of the newly-elected praetors. The Festival of Jupiter was also celebrated.

5. In the 551st year from the foundation of the City, during the consulship of P. Sulpicius Galba and C. Aurelius (202 B.C.E.) and within a few months of the conclusion of peace with Carthage, the war with King Philip began. On March 15, the day on which the consuls entered office, P. Sulpicius made this the first business before the senate. A decree was made that the consuls should sacrifice full-grown victims to those deities whom they might decide upon, and should offer up the following prayer: "May the will and purpose of the senate and people of Rome as regards the commonwealth and the entrance upon a new war have a prosperous and happy issue both for the Roman people and for the Latin allies!" After the sacrifice and prayer the consuls were to consult the senate as to the policy to be pursued and the allocation of provinces. Just at this time the war-spirit was stimulated by the receipt of the dispatches from M. Aurelius and M. Valerius Laevinus as well as by a fresh embassy from Athens which announced that the king was nearing their frontiers and would soon be master of their territory and of their city as well if Rome did not come to the rescue. The consuls reported the due performance of the sacrifices and the declaration of the augurs that the gods had listened to their prayer, for the victims had given favorable omens and portended victory, triumph, and an enlargement of the dominion of Rome. Then the dispatches from Valerius and Aurelius were read and an audience given to the Athenian envoys. A resolution was passed by the senate that thanks be given to their allies for remaining loyal in spite of continual attempts to seduce them and even when threatened with a siege. With regard to giving active assistance the senate deferred a definite answer until the consuls had balloted for their provinces, and the one to whom the Macedonian province fell had submitted to the people the question of declaring war against Philip of Macedon.

6. This province fell to P. Sulpicius, and he gave notice that he should propose to the Assembly that "owing to the lawless actions and armed attacks committed against the allies of Rome, it is the will and order of the Roman people that war be proclaimed against Philip, King of Macedonia, and against his people, the Macedonians." The other consul, Aurelius, received Italy for his province. Then the praetors balloted for their respective commands. C. Sergius Plancus drew the City; Q. Fulvius Gillo, Sicily; Q. Minucius Rufus, Bruttium, and L. Furius, Gaul. The proposed declaration of war against Macedonia was almost unanimously rejected at the first meeting of the Assembly. The length and exhausting demands of the late war had made men weary of fighting and they shrank from incurring further toils and dangers. One of the tribunes of the plebs, Q. Baebius, too, had adopted the old plan of abusing the patricians for perpetually sowing the seeds of fresh wars to prevent the plebeians from ever enjoying any rest. The patricians were extremely angry and the tribune was bitterly attacked in the senate, each of the senators in turn urging the consul to call another meeting of the Assembly to consider the proposal afresh and at the same time to rebuke the people for their want of spirit and show them what loss and disgrace would be entailed by the postponement of that war.

7. The Assembly was duly convened in the Campus Martius, and before the question was put to the vote, the consul addressed the centuries in the following terms: "You seem to be unaware, Quirites, that what you have to decide is not whether you will have peace or war; Philip will not leave you any option as to that, he is preparing war on an enormous scale both by land and sea. The only question is whether you will transport the legions into Macedonia or wait for the enemy in Italy. You have learnt by experience, if not before, at all events in the late Punic War, what a difference it makes which you decide upon. When Saguntum was besieged and our allies were imploring us for help, who doubts that if we had sent prompt assistance, as our fathers did to the Mamertines, we should have confined within the borders of Spain that war which, most disastrously for ourselves, we allowed through procrastination to enter Italy. Why, this very Philip had entered into an agreement with Hannibal through his agents and in his dispatches that he would invade Italy, and there is not the smallest doubt that we kept him in Macedonia by sending Laevinus with a fleet to take the offensive against him. Are we hesitating to do now what we did then, when we had Hannibal for our enemy in Italy—now that Hannibal has been driven out of Italy and out of Carthage, and Carthage itself is completely vanquished? If we allow the king to make proof of our slackness by storming Athens as we allowed Hannibal to do by storming Saguntum, it will not be in five months—the time Hannibal took from Saguntum—but in five days after he sails from Corinth that he will set foot in Italy.

"Perhaps you do not put Philip on a par with Hannibal or consider the Macedonians equal to the Carthaginians. At all events you will consider him the equal of Pyrrhus. Equal, do I say? How greatly the one man surpasses the other, how superior is the one nation to the other! Epirus always has been and is today a very small accession to the kingdom of Macedonia. The whole of the Peloponnese is under the sway of Philip, not excepting even Argos, famous for the death of Pyrrhus, quite as much as for its ancient glory. Now compare our position. Consider the flourishing state of Italy when all those generals and armies were safe and sound which have been since swept away by the Punic War. And yet when Pyrrhus attacked it, he shook it to its foundations and all but reached Rome itself in his victorious career! Not only did the Tarentines revolt from us and the whole of that coastal district of Italy called Magna Graecia, which you would naturally suppose would follow a leader of the same language and nationality as themselves, but the Lucanians, the Bruttians and the Samnites did the same. Do you suppose that if Philip landed in Italy, these nations would remain quiet and true to us? They showed their loyalty, I suppose, in the Punic War. No, those nations will never fail to revolt from us, unless there is no longer any one to whom they can revolt. If you had thought it too much to go to Africa you would have had Hannibal and his Carthaginians in Italy today. Let Macedonia rather than Italy be the seat of war, let it be the enemy's cities and fields that are devastated with fire and sword. We have learnt by this time that our arms are more potent and more successful abroad than they are at home. Go to the poll with the help of the gods, and confirm the decision of the senate. It is not your consul only who urges you to take this course, the immortal gods also bid you do it, for when I was offering up the sacrifices and praying that this war might end happily for the senate, for myself, for you, for our allies and Latin confederates, for our fleets and armies, the gods vouchsafed every cheering and happy omen."

8. After this speech they separated for the voting. The result was in favor of the consul's proposal, they resolved on war. Thereupon, the consuls, acting on a resolution of the senate, ordered special prayers and supplications for three days, and at all the shrines intercessions were offered up that the war which the Roman people had ordered against Philip might have a happy and prosperous issue. The fetials were consulted by the consul as to whether it was necessary for the declaration of war to be conveyed personally to King Philip, or whether it would be sufficient if it were published in one of his frontier garrison towns. They declared that either mode of procedure would be correct. The senate left it to the consul to select at his discretion one of them, not being a member of the senate, to make the declaration of war. The next business was the formation of the armies for the consuls and praetors. The consuls were ordered to disband the old armies and, each of them, to raise two fresh legions. As the conduct of the new war, which was felt to be a very serious one, was entrusted to Sulpicius, he was allowed to reenlist as volunteers as many as he could out of the army which P. Scipio had brought back from Africa, but on no account to compel any of the veterans to join against his will. The consuls were to give to each of the praetors, L. Furius Purpurio and Q. Minucius Rufus, 5,000 men from the Latin contingents as an army of occupation for their provinces, the one in Gaul, the other in Bruttium. Q. Fulvius Gillo also was ordered to select men belonging to the Latin and allied contingents from the army which the consul P. Aelius had commanded, beginning with those who had seen the shortest service until he had made up a force of 5,000 men. This army was for the defense of Sicily. M. Valerius Falto, who had had Campania for his province during the previous year, was to make a similar selection from the army in Sardinia, which province he was to take charge of as propraetor. The consuls received instructions to raise two legions in the City as a reserve to be sent wherever there was need for their services, as many of the Italian nationalities had taken the side of Carthage in the late war, and were seething with anger.

9. In the midst of these preparations for war a deputation came from King Ptolemy to bring information that the Athenians had sought his aid against Philip. Although both States were allies of Rome, the king would not —so the deputies stated—send either fleet or army to Greece to protect or attack any one without the consent of Rome. If the Romans were at liberty to defend their allies he should remain quietly in his kingdom; if on the other hand the Romans preferred to remain inactive he would himself send such assistance as would easily protect the Athenians against Philip. The senate passed a vote of thanks to the king and assured the deputation that it was the intention of the Roman people to protect their allies; if the need arose they would point it out to the king, and they were fully aware that the resources of his kingdom would prove a steady and loyal support for their commonwealth. To each of the deputies the senate presented 5000 asses. While the consuls were raising troops and preparing for war, the citizens were occupied with religious observances, especially those which were usual when a fresh war began. The special intercessions and prayers at all the shrines had been duly offered, but that nothing might be omitted the consul to whom Macedonia was allotted was authorized to vow Games in honor of Jupiter and an offering to his temple. This matter was delayed through the action of the Pontifex Maximus, Licinius, who laid it down that no vow ought to be made unless the sum required to discharge it was paid, because the money so appropriated could not be used in connection with the war, and ought to be at once set apart and not mixed up with other money. Unless this were done, the vow could not be duly discharged. Although the pontiff's authority and the reasons he gave had great weight, the consul was instructed to refer the question to the whole pontifical college as to whether a vow could be properly undertaken when the expense incurred was left uncertain. The pontiffs declared that it could, and would be made with even greater propriety under these conditions. The consul recited the words of the vow after the Pontifex Maximus in the same form in which vows to be discharged after an interval of five years were usually recited, the exception being that the senate was to determine the cost of its fulfillment at the time when it was discharged. Up to this time when the Games and offerings were vowed a definite sum had always been named; this was the first instance where the cost was not fixed at the time.

BOOK XXXIII   6–10; 30–33; 38–40

The Roman general Titus Quinctius Flamininus defeated King Philip at Cynoscephelae (197 B.C.E.) and, after the conclusion of the peace treaty, he proclaimed the freedom of all the cities of Greece. Roman negotiations with King Antiochus of Asia.

6. Quinctius resumed his march on the following day, but as the soldiers were carrying the timber for a stockade, so that they might be ready to form an entrenched camp anywhere, the day's march was not a long one. The position he selected was about six miles from Pherae, and after fixing his camp he sent out reconnoitering parties to find out in what part of Thessaly the enemy was, and what were his intentions. Philip was in the neighborhood of Larisa and had already received information that the Romans had left Thebes for Pherae. He, too, was anxious to bring matters to a decision and determined to make straight for the enemy, and finally fixed his camp some four miles from Pherae. The next day light infantry from both sides moved out to seize some hills which commanded the city, but when they caught sight of one another they halted and sent to their respective camps for instructions as to what they were to do now that they had come unexpectedly upon the enemy. As they awaited their return without moving the day passed without any fighting and these detachments were recalled to camp. The next day there was a cavalry action near those hills, in which Philip's troops were routed and driven back to their camp; a success in which the Aetolians had the greatest share. Both sides were greatly hampered in their movements by the nature of the ground, which was thickly planted with trees, and by the gardens which are usually found in suburban districts, the roads being enclosed between walls and in some cases blocked. Both commanders alike determined to get out of the neighborhood, and as though by mutual agreement they both made for Scotusa: Philip, in the hope of obtaining a supply of corn there; Quinctius, with the intention of forestalling his adversary and destroying his corn. The armies marched the whole day without once getting sight of each other owing to a continuous range of hills which lay between them. The Romans encamped at Eretria in Phthiotis, Philip fixed his camp by the river Onchestus. The next day Philip encamped at Melambium in the territory of Scotusa and Quinctius at Thetideum in the neighborhood of Pharsalia, but not even then did either side know for certain where their enemy was. The third day heavy clouds came up, followed by a darkness as black as night which kept the Romans in their camp for fear of a surprise attack.

7. Eager to press on, Philip was not in the least deterred by the clouds which had descended to the earth after the rain, and he ordered the standard-bearers to march out. But so thick a fog had blotted out the daylight that the standard-bearers could not see their way, nor could the men see their standards. Misled by the confused shouts, the column was thrown into as great disorder as if it had lost its way in a night march. When they had surmounted the range of hills called Cynoscephalae, where they left a strong force of infantry and cavalry in occupation, they formed their camp. The Roman general was still in camp at Thetideum; he sent out, however, ten squadrons of cavalry and a thousand velites to reconnoiter and warned them to be on their guard against an ambuscade, which owing to the darkened daylight might not be detected even in open country. When they reached the heights where the enemy were posted both sides stood stock-still as though paralyzed by mutual fear. As soon as their alarm at the unexpected sight subsided they sent messages to their generals in camp and did not hesitate any longer to engage. The action was begun by the advanced patrols, and then as the supports came up the fighting became general. The Romans were by no means a match for their opponents, and they sent message after message to their general to inform him that they were being overpowered. A reinforcement of

500 cavalry and 2,000 infantry, mostly Aetolians, under two military tribunes, was hastily dispatched and restored the battle, which was going against the Romans. This turn of fortune threw the Macedonians into difficulties and they sent to their king for help. But as owing to the darkness a battle was the last thing he had looked for on that day, and as a large number of men of all ranks had been sent out to forage, he was for a considerable time at a loss what to do. The messages became more and more importunate, and as the fog had now cleared away and revealed the situation of the Macedonians who had been driven to the topmost height and were finding more safety in their position than in their arms, Philip felt that he ought to risk a general and decisive engagement rather than let a part of his force be lost through want of support. Accordingly he sent Athenagoras, the commander of the mercenaries, with the whole of the foreign contingent, except the Thracians, and also the Macedonian and Thessalian cavalry. Their appearance resulted in the Romans being dislodged from the hill and compelled to retreat to lower ground. That they were not driven in disorderly flight was mainly owing to the Aetolian cavalry, which at that time was the best in Greece, though in infantry they were inferior to their neighbors.

8. This affair was reported to the king as a more important success than the facts warranted. Messenger after messenger ran back from the field shouting that the Romans were in flight, and though the king, reluctant and hesitating, declared that the action had been begun rashly and that neither the time nor the place suited him, he was at last driven into bringing the whole of his forces into the field. The Roman commander did the same, more because no other course was open to him than because he wished to seize the opportunity of a battle. He posted the elephants in front of his right wing, which he kept in reserve; the left, with the whole of the light infantry, he led in person against the enemy. As they advanced he reminded them that they were going to fight with the same Macedonians as those whom in spite of the difficult ground they had driven out of the pass leading into Epirus, protected though they were by the mountains and the river, and had thoroughly defeated; the same as those whom they had vanquished under P. Sulpicius when they tried to stop their march on Eordaea. The kingdom of Macedonia, he declared, stood by its prestige, not by its strength, and even its prestige had at last disappeared. By this time he had come up to his detachments who were standing at the bottom of the valley. They at once renewed the fight and by a fierce attack compelled the enemy to give ground. Philip with his caetrati and the infantry of his right wing, the finest body in his army, which they call "the phalanx," went at the enemy almost at a run; Nicanor, one of his courtiers, was ordered to follow at once with the rest of his force. As soon as he reached the top of the hill and saw a few of the enemy's bodies and weapons lying about, he concluded that there had been a battle there and that the Romans had been repulsed, and when he further saw that fighting was going on near the enemy's camp he was in a state of great exultation. Soon, however, when his men came back in flight and it was his turn to be alarmed, he was for a few moments anxiously debating whether he ought not to recall his troops to camp. Then, as the enemy were approaching, and especially as his own men were being cut down as they fled and could not be saved unless they were defended by fresh troops, and also as retreat was no longer safe, he found himself compelled to take the supreme risk, though half his force had not yet come up. The cavalry and light infantry who had been in action he stationed on his right; the caetrati and the men of the phalanx were ordered to lay aside their spears, the length of which only embarrassed them, and make use of their swords. To prevent his line from being quickly broken he halved the front and gave twice the depth to the files, so that the depth might be greater than the width. He also ordered the ranks to close up so that man might be in touch with man and arms with arms.

9. After the Roman troops who had been engaged had retired through the intervals between the leading maniples, Quinctius ordered the trumpets to sound the advance. Seldom, it is said, has such a battle-shout been raised at the beginning of an action, for both armies happened to shout at the same moment, not only those actually engaged, but even the Roman reserves and the Macedonians who were just then appearing on the field. On the right the king, aided mainly by the higher ground on which he was fighting, had the advantage. On the left, where that part of the phalanx which formed the rear was only just coming up, all was confusion and disorder. The center stood and looked on as though it were watching a fight in which it had no concern. The newly-arrived part of the phalanx, in column instead of in line of battle, in marching rather than in fighting formation, had hardly reached the crest of the hill. Though Quinctius saw that his men were giving ground on the left he sent the elephants against these unformed troops and followed up with a charge, rightly judging that the rout of a part would involve the rest. The result was not long in doubt; the Macedonians in front, terrified by the animals, instantly turned tail, and when these were repulsed the rest followed them. One of the military tribunes, seeing the position, suddenly made up his mind what to do, and leaving that part of his line which was undoubtedly winning, wheeled round with twenty maniples and attacked the enemy's right from behind. No army when attacked in the rear can fail to be shaken, but the inevitable confusion was increased by the inability of the Macedonian phalanx, a heavy and immobile formation, to face round on a new front. To make matters worse, they were at a serious disadvantage from the ground, for in following their repulsed enemy down the hill they had left the height for the enemy to make use of in his enveloping movement. Assailed on both sides they lost heavily, and in a short time they flung away their arms and took to flight.

10. With a small body of horse and foot Philip occupied the highest point on the hills in order to see what fortune his left wing had met with. When he became aware of their disorderly flight and saw the Roman standards and arms flashing on all the hills he too left the field. Quinctius, who was pressing on the retiring foe, saw the Macedonians suddenly holding their spears upright, and as he was doubtful as to what they intended by this unfamiliar maneuver he held up the pursuit for a few minutes. On learning that it was the Macedonian signal of surrender, he made up his mind to spare them. The soldiers, however, unaware that the enemy were no longer resisting and ignorant of their general's intention, commenced an attack upon them, and when those in front had been cut down the rest scattered in flight. Philip himself rode off at a hard gallop in the direction of Tempe and drew rein at Gomphi, where he remained for a day to pick up any survivors from the battle. The Romans broke into the hostile camp in hopes of plunder, but they found that it had to a large extent been cleared out by the Aetolians. 8,000 of the enemy perished that day; 5,000 were made prisoners. Of the victors about 700 fell. If we are to believe Valerius, who is given to boundless exaggeration, 40,000 of the enemy were killed and—here his invention is not so wild— 5,700 made prisoners and 249 standards captured. Claudius too writes that 32,000 of the enemy were killed and 4,300 made prisoners. We have taken the smaller number, not because it is the smaller, but because we have followed Polybius, who is no untrustworthy authority on Roman history especially when the scene of it is in Greece.

§

30. A few days later the ten commissioners arrived from Rome. On their advice peace was granted to Philip on the following terms: All the Greek communities in Europe and Asia were to be free and independent; Philip was to withdraw his garrisons from those which had been under his rule and after their evacuation hand them over to the Romans before the date fixed for the Isthmian Games. He was also to withdraw his garrisons from the following cities in Asia: Euromus, Pedasae, Bargyliae, Iasos, Myrina, Abydos, Thasos and Perinthus, for it was decided that these too should be free. With regard to the freedom of Cios, Quinctius undertook to communicate the decision of the senate and the commissioners to Prusias, King of Bithynia. The king was also to restore all prisoners and deserters to the Romans, and all his decked ships, save five, were to be surrendered, but he could retain his royal galley, which was all but unmanageable owing to its size and was propelled by sixteen banks of oars. His army was never to exceed 5000 men and he was not allowed to have a single elephant, nor was he permitted to make war beyond

his frontiers without the express sanction of the senate. The indemnity which he was required to pay amounted to 1,000 talents, half of it to be paid at once and the remainder in ten annual installments. Valerius Antias asserts that an annual tribute of 4,000 lbs. of silver was imposed on the king for ten years. Claudius says that the annual tribute amounted to 4,200 lbs. of silver and extended over thirty years, with an immediate payment of 2,000 lbs. He also says that an additional clause in the treaty expressly provided that Philip should not make war upon Eumenes, who had succeeded his father Attalus upon the throne. As a guarantee of the observance of these conditions hostages were taken by the Romans, amongst whom was Philip's son, Demetrius. Valerius Antias further states that the island of Aegina and the elephants were given to Attalus, and that Stratonice and the other cities in Caria which Philip had held were given to the Rhodians, and the islands of Lemnos, Imbros, Delos and Scyros to the Athenians.

31. Almost all the States of Greece welcomed peace on these terms. The Aetolians formed a solitary exception. They did not venture upon open opposition, but they criticized the commissioners' decision bitterly in private. It was, they said, a mere form of words vaguely suggesting the delusive image of pretended liberty. Why, they asked, were some cities to be given to the Romans without being named, and others which were named to retain their freedom, unless it was thought that the cities in Asia might be safely left free because of their remoteness, whilst those in Greece which are not even named might be appropriated, viz. Corinth, Chalcis, Oreus, together with Eretria and Demetrias? Nor was this charge altogether groundless, for there was much hesitation as to three of those cities. In the decree of the senate which the commissioners had brought with them the rest of the cities in Greece and Asia were unequivocally declared free, but in the case of Corinth, Chalcis and Demetrias the commissioners were instructed to do and determine as the interests of the commonwealth and the circumstances of the time and their own sense of duty required. It was Antiochus they had in their minds; they were convinced that as soon as he deemed his strength adequate he would invade Europe, and they did not intend to leave it open to him to occupy cities which would form such favorable bases of operations. Quinctius proceeded with the ten commissioners to Anticyra, and from there sailed across to Corinth. Here the commissioners discussed for days the measures for securing the freedom of Greece. Again and again Quinctius urged that the whole of Greece must be declared free if they wanted to stop the tongues of the Achaeans and inspire all with a true affection for Rome and an appreciation of her greatness—if, in fact, they desired to convince the Greeks that they had crossed the seas with the sole purpose of winning their freedom and not of transferring Philip's dominion over them to themselves. The commissioners took no exception to his insistence on making the cities free, but they

argued that it would be safer for the cities themselves to remain for a time under the protection of Roman garrisons rather than have to accept Antiochus as their master in the place of Philip. At last they came to a decision; the city of Corinth was to be restored to the Achaeans, but a garrison was to be placed in Acrocorinthus, and Chalcis and Demetrias were to be retained until the menace of Antiochus was removed.

32. The date fixed for the Isthmian Games was now close at hand. These Games always drew vast crowds, owing partly to the innate love of the nation for a spectacle in which they watched contests of every kind, competitions of artistic skill, and trials of strength and speed, and partly owing to the fact that its situation between two seas made it the common emporium of Greece and Asia, where supplies were to be obtained of everything necessary or useful to man. But on this occasion it was not the usual attractions alone that drew the people from every part of Greece; they were in a state of keen expectancy, wondering what would be the future position of the country, and what fortune awaited themselves. All sorts of conjectures were formed and openly expressed as to what the Romans would do, but hardly anybody persuaded himself that they would withdraw from Greece altogether.

When the spectators had taken their seats, a herald, accompanied by a trumpeter, stepped forward into the middle of the arena, where the Games are usually opened by the customary formalities, and after a blast from the trumpet had produced silence, made the following announcement: "THE SENATE OF ROME AND T. QUINCTIUS THEIR GENERAL, HAVING CONQUERED KING PHILIP AND THE MACEDONIANS DO NOW DECREE AND ORDAIN THAT THESE STATES SHALL BE FREE, SHALL BE RELEASED FROM THE PAYMENT OF TRIBUTE, AND SHALL LIVE UNDER THEIR OWN LAWS, NAMELY THE CORINTHIANS; THE PHOCIANS; ALL THE LOCRIANS TOGETHER WITH THE ISLAND OF EUBOEA; THE MAGNESIANS; THE THESSALIANS; THE PERRHAEBIANS, AND THE ACHAEANS OF PHTHIOTIS." This list comprised all those States which had been under the sway of Philip. When the herald had finished his proclamation the feeling of joy was too great for men to take it all in. They hardly ventured to trust their ears, and gazed wonderingly on one another, as though it were an empty dream. Not trusting their ears, they asked those nearest how their own interests were affected, and as everyone was eager not only to hear but also to see the man who had proclaimed their freedom, the herald was recalled and repeated his message. Then they realized that the joyful news was true, and from the applause and cheers which arose it was perfectly evident that none of life's blessings was dearer to the multitude than liberty. The Games were then hurried through; no man's eyes or ears were any longer fixed on them, so completely had the one master joy supplanted all other pleasurable sensations.

33. At the close of the Games, almost the entire assemblage ran to the spot where the Roman general was seated, and the rush of the crowd who

were trying to touch his hand and throw garlands and ribbons became almost dangerous. He was about thirty-three years old at the time, and not only the robustness of his manhood but the delight of reaping such a harvest of glory gave him strength. The universal rejoicing was not simply a temporary excitement; for many days it found expression in thoughts and words of gratitude. "There is," people said, "one nation which at its own cost, through its own exertions, at its own risk has gone to war on behalf of the liberty of others. It renders this service not to those across its frontiers, or to the peoples of neighboring States or to those who dwell on the same mainland, but it crosses the seas in order that nowhere in the wide world may injustice and tyranny exist, but that right and equity and law may be everywhere supreme. By this single proclamation of the herald all the cities in Greece and Asia recover their liberty. To have formed this design shows a daring spirit; to have brought it to fulfillment is a proof of exceptional courage and extraordinary good fortune."

§

38. During this year Antiochus, who had spent the winter in Ephesus, endeavored to reduce all the cities in Asia to their old condition of dependence. With the exception of Smyrna and Lampsacus, he thought that they would all accept the yoke without difficulty, since they either lay in open level country or were weakly defended by their walls and their soldiery. Smyrna and Lampsacus asserted their right to be free and there was danger, should their claim be allowed, of other cities in Aeolis and Ionia following the example of Smyrna, and those on the Hellespont the example of Lampsacus. Accordingly he dispatched a force from Ephesus to invest Smyrna and ordered the troops in Abydos to march to Lampsacus, only a small detachment being left to hold the place. But it was not only the threat of arms that he made use of, he sent envoys to make friendly overtures to the citizens, and whilst gently rebuking their rashness and obstinacy led them to hope that in a short time they would have what they wanted. It was, however, perfectly clear to them and to all the world that they would enjoy their liberty as the free gift of the king and not because they had seized a favorable opportunity of winning it. They told the envoys in reply that Antiochus must be neither surprised nor angry if they did not patiently resign themselves to the indefinite postponement of their hopes of liberty.

At the beginning of spring he set sail from Ephesus for the Hellespont and ordered his land army to proceed from Abydos to the Chersonese. He united his naval and military powers at Madytos, a city in the Chersonese, and as they had shut their gates against him he completely invested the place, and was on the point of bringing up his siege engines when the city surrendered. The fear which Antiochus thus inspired led the inhabitants of Sestos and the other cities in the Chersonese to make a voluntary surrender. His next objective was Lysimachia. When he arrived here with the whole of his land and sea forces he found the place deserted and little more than a heap of ruins, for some years previously the Thracians had captured and plundered the city and then burnt it. Finding it in this condition, Antiochus was seized by a desire to restore a city of such celebrity and so favorably situated, and he at once set about the various tasks which this involved. The houses and walls were rebuilt, some of the former inhabitants who had been made slaves were ransomed, others who were scattered as refugees throughout the Chersonese and the shores of the Hellespont were discovered and brought together, and new colonists were attracted by the prospect of the advantages they would receive. In fact every method was adopted of repopulating the city. To remove at the same time all apprehensions of trouble from the Thracians he proceeded with one half of his army to devastate the neighboring districts of Thrace, the other half and all the ships' crews he left to go on with the work of restoration.

39. Very shortly after this L. Cornelius, who had been sent by the senate to settle the differences between Antiochus and Ptolemy, made a halt at Selymbria, and three of the ten commissioners went to Lysimachia: P. Lentulus from Bargyliae, P. Villius and L. Terentius from Thasos. They were joined there by L. Cornelius from Selymbria, and a few days later by Antiochus, who returned from Thrace. The first meeting with the commissioners and the invitation which Antiochus gave them were kindly and hospitable, but when it came to discussing their instructions and the position of affairs in Asia a good deal of temper was shown on both sides. The Romans told Antiochus plainly that everything he had done since his fleet set sail from Syria met with the disapproval of the senate and they considered it right that all the cities which had been subject to Ptolemy should be restored to him. With regard to those cities which had formed part of Philip's possessions and which while he was preoccupied with the war against Rome Antiochus had seized the opportunity of appropriating himself, it was simply intolerable that after the Romans had sustained such risks and hardships by sea and land for all those years Antiochus should carry off the prizes of war. Granting that it was possible for the Romans to take no notice of his appearance in Asia as being no concern of theirs, what about his entrance into Europe with the whole of his army and navy? What difference was there between that and an open declaration of war against Rome? Even if he had landed in Italy he would say that he did not mean war, but the Romans were not going to wait until he was in a position to do that.

40. In his reply Antiochus expressed his surprise that the Romans should go so carefully into the question as to what Antiochus ought to do, whilst they never stopped to consider what limits were to be set to their own advance by land and sea. Asia was no concern of the senate, and they had no more right to ask what Antiochus was doing in Asia than he had to ask what the Roman people were doing in Italy. As for Ptolemy and their complaint that he had appropriated his cities, he and Ptolemy were on perfectly friendly terms and arrangements were being made for them to be connected by marriage shortly. He had not sought to take advantage of Philip's misfortunes nor had he come into Europe with any hostile intent against the Romans. After the defeat of Lysimachus all that belonged to him passed by the right of war to Seleucus, and therefore he counted it part of his dominion. Ptolemy, and after him Philip, alienated some of these places at a time when his (Antiochus') ancestors were devoting their care and attention to other matters. Could there be a shadow of doubt that the Chersonese and that part of Thrace which lies round Lysimachia once belonged to Lysimachus? To recover the ancient right over these was the object of his coming and also to rebuild from its foundations the city of Lysimachia, which had been destroyed by the Thracians, in order that his son Seleucus might have it as the seat of empire.

BOOK XXXIV 1–8

During the Punic War the Romans has passed the Oppian Law to restrict extravagant behavior among women. When its repeal was proposed in 195 B.C.E., the conservative consul Cato opposed repeal.

1. While the State was preoccupied by serious wars, some hardly yet over and others threatening, an incident occurred which though unimportant in itself resulted in a violent party conflict. Two of the tribunes of the plebs, M. Fundanius and L. Valerius, had brought in a proposal to repeal the Oppian Law. This law had been made on the motion of M. Oppius, a tribune of the plebs, during the consulship of Q. Fabius and Tiberius Sempronius, when the strain of the Punic War was most severely felt. It forbade any woman to have in her possession more than half an ounce of gold, to wear a dress of various colors or to ride in a two-horsed vehicle within a mile of the City or of any Roman town unless she was going to take part in some religious function. The two Brutuses—M. Junius and T. Junius—both tribunes of the plebs, defended the law and declared that they would not allow it to be repealed; many of the nobility came forward to speak in favor of the repeal or against it; the Capitol was crowded with supporters and opponents of the proposal; the matrons could not be kept indoors either by the authority of the magistrates or the orders of their husbands or their own sense of propriety. They filled all the streets and blocked the approaches to the Forum; they implored

the men who were on their way thither to allow the women to resume their former adornments now that the commonwealth was flourishing and private fortunes increasing every day. Their numbers were daily augmented by those who came up from the country towns. At last they ventured to approach the consuls and praetors and other magistrates with their demands. One of the consuls at all events was inexorably opposed to their request—M. Porcius Cato. He spoke as follows in defense of the law:

2. "If we had, each one of us, made it a rule to uphold the rights and authority of the husband in our own households we should not now have this trouble with the whole body of our women. As things are now our liberty of action, which has been checked and rendered powerless by female despotism at home, is actually crushed and trampled on here in the Forum, and because we were unable to withstand them individually we have now to dread their united strength. I used to think that it was a fabulous story which tells us that in a certain island the whole of the male sex was extirpated by a conspiracy amongst the women; there is no class of women from whom the gravest dangers may not arise, if once you allow intrigues, plots, secret cabals to go on. I can hardly make up my mind which is worse, the affair itself or the disastrous precedent set up. The latter concerns us as consuls and magistrates; the former has to do more with you, Quirites. Whether the measure before you is for the good of the commonwealth or not is for you to determine by your votes; this tumult amongst the women, whether a spontaneous movement or due to your instigation, M. Fundanius and L. Valerius, certainly points to failure on the part of the magistrates, but whether it reflects more on you tribunes or on the consuls I do not know. It brings the greater discredit on you if you have carried your tribunitian agitation so far as to create unrest among the women, but more disgrace upon us if we have to submit to laws being imposed upon us through fear of a secession on their part, as we had to do formerly on occasions of the secession of the plebs. It was not without a feeling of shame that I made my way into the Forum through a regular army of women. Had not my respect for the dignity and modesty of some amongst them, more than any consideration for them as a whole, restrained me from letting them be publicly rebuked by a consul, I should have said, 'What is this habit you have formed of running abroad and blocking the streets and accosting men who are strangers to you? Could you not each of you put the very same question to your husbands at home? Surely you do not make yourselves more attractive in public than in private, to other women's husbands more than to your own? If matrons were kept by their natural modesty within the limits of their rights, it would be most unbecoming for you to trouble yourselves even at home about the laws which may be passed or repealed here.' Our ancestors would have no woman transact even private business except through her guardian, they placed them under the tutelage of parents or brothers or husbands. We suffer them now to dabble in politics and mix themselves up with the business of the Forum and public debates and election contests. What are they doing now in the public roads and at the street corners but recommending to the plebs the proposal of their tribunes and voting for the repeal of the law? Give the reins to a headstrong nature, to a creature that has not been tamed, and then hope that they will themselves set bounds to their license if you do not do it yourselves. This is the smallest of those restrictions which have been imposed upon women by ancestral custom or by laws, and which they submit to with such impatience. What they really want is unrestricted freedom, or to speak the truth, license, and if they win on this occasion what is there that they will not attempt?

3. "Call to mind all the regulations respecting women by which our ancestors curbed their license and made them obedient to their husbands, and yet in spite of all those restrictions you can scarcely hold them in. If you allow them to pull away these restraints and wrench them out one after another, and finally put themselves on an equality with their husbands, do you imagine that you will be able to tolerate them? From the moment that they become your fellows they will become your masters. But surely, you say, what they object to is having a new restriction imposed upon them, they are not deprecating the assertion of a right but the infliction of a wrong. No, they are demanding the abrogation of a law which you enacted by your suffrages and which the practical experience of all these years has approved and justified. This they would have you repeal; that means that by rescinding this they would have you weaken all. No law is equally agreeable to everybody, the only question is whether it is beneficial on the whole and good for the majority. If everyone who feels himself personally aggrieved by a law is to destroy it and get rid of it, what is gained by the whole body of citizens making laws which those against whom they are enacted can in a short time repeal? I want, however, to learn the reason why these excited matrons have run out into the streets and scarcely keep away from the Forum and the Assembly. Is it that those taken prisoners by Hannibal—their fathers and husbands and children and brothers—may be ransomed? The republic is a long way from this misfortune, and may it ever remain so! Still, when this did happen, you refused to do so in spite of their dutiful entreaties. But, you may say, it is not dutiful affection and solicitude for those they love that has brought them together; they are going to welcome Mater Idaea on her way from Phrygian Pessinus. What pretext in the least degree respectable is put forward for this female insurrection? 'That we may shine,' they say, 'in gold and purple, that we may ride in carriages on festal and ordinary days alike, as though in triumph for having defeated and repealed a law after capturing and forcing from you your votes.'

4. "You have often heard me complain of the expensive habits of women and often, too, of those of men, not only private citizens but even magistrates, and I have often said that the community suffers from two opposite vices—avarice and luxury—pestilential diseases which have proved the ruin of all great empires. The brighter and better the fortunes of the republic become day by day, and the greater the growth of its dominion—and now we are penetrating into Greece and Asia, regions filled with everything that can tempt appetite or excite desire, and are even laying hands on the treasures of kings—so much the more do I dread the prospect of these things taking us captive rather than we them. It was a bad day for this City, believe me, when the statues were brought from Syracuse. I hear far too many people praising and admiring those which adorn Athens and Corinth and laughing at the clay images of our gods standing in front of their temples. I for my part prefer these gods who are propitious to us, and I trust that they will continue to be so as long as we allow them to remain in their present abodes.

In the days of our forefathers Pyrrhus attempted, through his ambassador Cineas, to tamper with the loyalty of women as well as men by means of bribes. The Law of Oppius in restraint of female extravagance had not then been passed, still not a single woman accepted a bribe. What do you think was the reason? The same reason which our forefathers had for not making any law on the subject; there was no extravagance to be restrained. Diseases must be recognized before remedies are applied, and so the passion for self-indulgence must be in existence before the laws which are to curb it. What called out the Licinian Law which restricted estates to 500 jugera except the keen desire of adding field to field? What led to the passing of the Cincian Law concerning presents and fees except the condition of the plebeians who had become tributaries and taxpayers to the senate? It is not therefore in the least surprising that neither the Oppian nor any other law was in those days required to set limits to the expensive habits of women when they refused to accept the gold and purple that was freely offered to them. If Cineas were to go in these days about the City with his gifts, he would find women standing in the streets quite ready to accept them.

There are some desires of which I cannot penetrate either the motive or the reason. That what is permitted to another should be forbidden to you may naturally create a feeling of shame or indignation, but when all are upon the same level as far as dress is concerned why should any one of you fear that you will not attract notice? The very last things to be ashamed of are thriftiness and poverty, but this law relieves you of both since you do not possess what it forbids you to possess. The wealthy woman says, 'This leveling down is just what I do not tolerate. Why am I not to be admired and looked at for my gold and purple? Why is the poverty of others disguised under this appearance of law so that they may be thought to have possessed, had the law allowed it, what it was quite out of their power to possess?'

Do you want, Quirites, to plunge your wives into a rivalry of this nature, where the rich desire to have what no one else can afford, and the poor, that they may not be despised for their poverty, stretch their expenses beyond their means? Depend upon it, as soon as a woman begins to be ashamed of what she ought not to be ashamed of she will cease to feel shame at what she ought to be ashamed of. She who is in a position to do so will get what she wants with her own money, she who cannot do this will ask her husband. The husband is in a pitiable plight whether he yields or refuses; in the latter case he will see another giving what he refused to give. Now they are soliciting other women's husbands, and what is worse they are soliciting votes for the repeal of a law, and are getting them from some, against the interest of you and your property and your children. When once the law has ceased to fix a limit to your wife's expenses, you will never fix one. Do not imagine that things will be the same as they were before the law was made. It is safer for an evil-doer not to be prosecuted than for him to be tried and then acquitted, and luxury and extravagance would have been more tolerable had they never been interfered with than they will be now, just like wild beasts which have been irritated by their chains and then released. I give my vote against every attempt to repeal the law, and pray that all the gods may give your action a fortunate result."

5. After this the tribunes of the plebs who had announced their intention of vetoing the repeal spoke briefly to the same effect. Then L. Valerius made the following speech in defense of his proposal: "If it had been only private citizens who came forward to argue in favor of, or against, the measure we have brought in, I should have awaited your votes in silence as I should have considered that enough had been said on either side. But now, when a man of such weight of character as M. Porcius, our consul, is opposing our bill, not simply by exerting his personal authority which, even had he remained silent, would have had very great influence, but also in a long and carefully thought out speech, it is necessary to make a brief reply. He spent, it is true, more time in castigating the matrons than in arguing against the bill, and he even left it doubtful whether the action of the matrons which he censured was due to their own initiative or to our instigation. I shall defend the measure and not ourselves, for that was thrown out as a suggestion rather than as an actual charge. Because we are now enjoying the blessings of peace and the commonwealth is flourishing and happy, the matrons are making a public request to you that you will repeal a law which was passed against them under the pressure of a time of war. He denounces this action of theirs as a plot, a seditious movement, and he sometimes calls it a female secession. I know how these and other strong expressions are selected to bolster up a case, and we all know that, though naturally of a gentle disposition, Cato is a powerful speaker and sometimes almost menacing. What innovation have the matrons been guilty of by publicly assembling in such numbers for a cause which touches them so closely? Have they never appeared in public before? I will quote your own *Origines* against you. Hear how often they have done this and always to the benefit of the State.

"At the very beginning, during the reign of Romulus, after the capture of the Capitol by the Sabines, when a pitched battle had begun in the Forum, was not the conflict stopped by the matrons rushing between the lines? And when after the expulsion of the kings the Volscian legions under their leader Caius Marcius had fixed their camp at the fifth milestone from the City, was it not the matrons who warded off that enemy by whom otherwise this City would have been laid in ruins? When it had been captured by the Gauls, how was it ransomed? By the matrons, of course, who by general agreement brought their contributions to the treasury. And without searching for ancient precedents, was it not the case that in the late war when money was needed the treasury was assisted by the money of the widows? Even when new deities were invited to help us in the hour of our distress did not the matrons go in a body down to the shore to receive Mater Idaea? You say that they were actuated by different motives then. It is not my purpose to establish the identity of motives, it is sufficient to clear them from the charge of strange unheard-of conduct. And yet, in matters which concern men and women alike, their action occasioned surprise to no one; why then should we be surprised at their taking the same action in a cause which especially interests them? But what have they done? We must, believe me, have the ears of tyrants if, whilst masters condescend to listen to the prayers of their slaves we deem it an indignity to be asked a favor by honorable women.

6. "I come now to the matter of debate. Here the consul adopted a twofold line of argument, for he protested against any law being repealed and in particular against the repeal of this law which had been passed to restrain female extravagance. His defense of the laws as a whole seemed to me such as a consul ought to make and his strictures on luxury were quite in keeping with his strict and severe moral code. Unless, therefore, we show the weakness of both lines of argument there is some risk of your being led into error. As to laws which have been made not for a temporary emergency, but for all time as being of permanent utility, I admit that none of them ought to be repealed except where experience has shown it to be hurtful or political changes have rendered it useless. But I see that the laws which have been necessitated by particular crises are, if I may say so, mortal and subject to change with the changing times. Laws made in times of peace war generally repeals, those made during war peace rescinds, just as in the management of a ship some things are useful in fair weather and others in foul. As these two classes of laws are distinct in their nature, to which class would the law which we are repealing appear to belong? Is it an ancient law of the kings, coeval with the City, or, which is the next thing to it, did the decemviri who were appointed to codify the laws inscribe it on the Twelve Tables as an enactment without which our forefathers thought that the honor and dignity of our matrons could not be preserved, and if we repeal it shall we have reason to fear that we shall destroy with it the self-respect and purity of our women? Who does not know that this is quite a recent law passed twenty years ago in the consulship of Q. Fabius and Tiberius Sempronius? If the matrons led exemplary lives without it, what danger can there possibly be of their plunging into luxury if it is repealed? If that law had been passed with the sole motive of limiting female excesses there might be some ground for apprehension that the repeal might encourage them, but the circumstances under which it was passed will reveal its object.

"Hannibal was in Italy; he had won the victory of Cannae; he was now master of Tarentum, Arpi and Capua; there was every likelihood that he would bring his army up to Rome. Our allies had fallen away from us, we had no reserves from which to make good our losses, no seamen to render our navy effective, and no money in the treasury. We had to arm the slaves and they were bought from their owners on condition that the purchase money should be paid at the end of the war; the contractors undertook to supply corn and everything else required for the war, to be paid for at the same date. We gave up our slaves to act as rowers in numbers proportionate to our assessment and placed all our gold and silver at the service of the State, the senators setting the example. Widows and minors invested their money in the public funds and a law was passed fixing the maximum of gold and silver coinage which we were to keep in our houses. Was it at such a crisis as this that the matrons were so given to luxury that the Oppian Law was needed to restrain them, when, owing to their being in mourning, the sacrificial rites of Ceres had been intermitted and the senate in consequence ordered the mourning to be terminated in thirty days? Who does not see that the poverty and wretched condition of the citizens, every one of whom had to devote his money to the needs of the commonwealth, were the real enactors of that law which was to remain in force as long as the reason for its enactment remained in force? If every decree made by the senate and every order made by the people to meet the emergency is to remain in force for all time, why are we repaying to private citizens the sums they advanced? Why are we making public contracts on the basis of immediate payment? Why are slaves not being purchased to serve as soldiers, and each of us giving up our slaves to serve as rowers as we did then?

7. "All orders of society, all men will feel the change for the better in the condition of the republic; are our wives alone to be debarred from the enjoyment of peace and prosperity? We, their husbands, shall wear purple, the toga praetexta will mark those holding magisterial and priestly offices, our

children will wear it, with its purple border; the right to wear it belongs to the magistrates in the military colonies and the municipal towns. Nor is it only in their lifetime that they enjoy this distinction; when they die they are cremated in it. You husbands are at liberty to wear a purple wrap over your dress, will you refuse to allow your wives to wear a purple mantle? Are the trappings of your horses to be more gorgeous than the dress of your wives? Purple fabrics, however, become frayed and worn out, and in their case I recognize some reason, though a very unfair one, for his opposition; but what is there to offend with regard to gold, which suffers no waste except on the cost of working it? On the contrary, it rather protects us in the time of need and forms a resource available for either public or private requirements, as you have learnt by experience. Cato said that there was no individual rivalry amongst them since none possessed what might make others jealous. No, but most certainly there is general grief and indignation felt among them when they see the wives of our Latin allies permitted to wear ornaments which they have been deprived of, when they see them resplendent in gold and purple and driving through the City while they have to follow on foot, just as though the seat of empire was in the Latin cities and not in their own. This would be enough to hurt the feelings of men, what then think you must be the feelings of poor little women who are affected by small things? Magistracies, priestly functions, triumphs, military decorations and rewards, spoils of war—none of these fall to their lot. Neatness, elegance, personal adornment, attractive appearance and looks—these are the distinctions they covet, in these they delight and pride themselves; these things our ancestors called the ornament of women. What do they lay aside when they are in mourning except their gold and purple, to resume them when they go out of mourning? How do they prepare themselves for days of public rejoicing and thanksgiving beyond assuming richer personal adornment? I suppose you think that if you repeal the Oppian Law, and should wish to forbid anything which the law forbids now, it will not be in your power to do so, and that some will lose all legal rights over their daughters and wives and sisters. No; women are never freed from subjection as long as their husbands and fathers are alive; they deprecate the freedom which orphanhood and widowhood bring. They would rather leave their personal adornment to your decision than to that of the law. It is your duty to act as their guardians and protectors and not treat them as slaves; you ought to wish to be called fathers and husbands, instead of lords and masters. The consul made use of invidious language when he spoke of female sedition and secession. Do you really think there is any danger of their seizing the Sacred Mount as the exasperated plebs once did, or of their taking possession of the Aventine? Whatever decision you come to, they in their weakness will have to submit to it. The greater your power, so much the more moderate ought you to be in exercising it."

8. After these speeches in support of and against the law the women poured out into the streets the next day in much greater force and went in a body to the house of the two Brutuses, who were vetoing their colleagues' proposal, and beset all the doors, nor would they desist till the tribunes had abandoned their opposition. There was no doubt now that the tribes would be unanimous in rescinding the law. It was abrogated twenty years after it had been made. After this matter was settled Cato at once left the City and with twenty-five ships of war, five of which belonged to the allies, sailed to the port of Luna, where the army had also received orders to muster. He had published an edict through the whole length of the coast requiring ships of every description to be assembled at Luna, and there he left orders that they should follow him to the Port of the Pyrenees, it being his intention to advance against the enemy with his full naval strength. Sailing past the Ligurian coast and the Gulf of Gaul, they assembled there by the appointed day. Cato sailed on to Rhoda and expelled the Spanish garrison who were holding the fort. From Rhoda a favorable wind brought him to Emporiae. Here he disembarked the whole of his force with the exception of the crews of the vessels.

BOOK XXXVI **15–19**

King Antiochus confronted the Romans at the pass of Thermopylae, where he was defeated and driven from Greece.

15. Antiochus was all this time at Chalcis (191 B.C.E.), having at last discovered that he had gained nothing from Greece beyond a pleasant winter at Chalcis and a disreputable marriage. He now accused the Aetolians of having made empty promises and admired Hannibal, not only as a man of prudence and foresight, but also as little short of a prophet, seeing how he had foretold everything which was happening. In order that his reckless adventure might not be ruined through his own inactivity, he sent a message to the Aetolians requesting them to concentrate all their fighting strength at Lamia, where he himself joined them with about 10,000 infantry, made up largely of troops which had come from Asia, and 500 cavalry. The Aetolians mustered in considerably smaller numbers than on any previous occasion, only the leading men with a few of their dependents were present. They said that they had done their utmost to call up as many as possible from their respective cities, but their personal influence, their appeals, their official authority, were alike powerless against those who declined to serve. Finding himself deserted on all sides by his own troops, who were hanging back in Asia, and by his allies, who were not doing what they undertook to do when they invited him, he withdrew into the pass of Thermopylae. This mountain range cuts Greece in two, just as Italy is intersected by the Apennines. To the north of the pass are situated Epirus, Perrhaebia, Magnesia, Thessaly, the Achaeans of Phthiotis, and the Malian Gulf. South of it lie the greater part of Aetolia, Acarnania, Locris, Phocis, Boeotia, the adjoining island of Euboea, and Attica, which projects into the sea like a promontory; beyond these is the Peloponnese. This range extends from Leucas on the western sea through Aetolia to the eastern sea, and is so rugged and precipitous that even light infantry—let alone an army—would have great difficulty in finding any paths by which to cross it. The eastern end of the range is called Oeta, and its highest peak bears the name of Callidromus. The road running through the lower ground between its base and the Maliac Gulf is not more than sixty paces broad and is the only military road which can be traversed by an army, and then only if it meets with no opposition. For this reason the place is called Pylae, and also Thermopylae, from the hot springs there, and is famous for the battle against the Persians, but still more so for the glorious death of the Lacedaemonians who fought there.

16. In a state of mind very unlike theirs Antiochus pitched his camp inside the narrowest part of the pass and barricaded it with defensive works, protecting every part of it with a double line of fosse and rampart and where it seemed necessary with a wall built up from the stones which were lying about everywhere. He felt pretty confident that the Roman army would never force a passage there, and so he sent two detachments out of the 4,000 Aetolians who had joined him, one to hold Heraclea, a place just in front of the pass, the other to Hypata. He quite expected that the consul would attack Heraclea; and from Hypata numerous messages had come stating that the whole of the surrounding country was being laid waste. The consul ravaged the territory of Hypata first and then that of Heraclea; in neither place did the Aetolians prove of the slightest use, and finally encamped opposite the king in the mouth of the pass at the hot springs. Both the Aetolian detachments shut themselves up in Heraclea. Before the actual appearance of his enemy Antiochus thought that the whole of the pass was fortified and blocked by his troops, but now he felt anxious lest the Romans might find some paths on the surrounding heights by which they could turn his defenses, for the Lacedaemonians were stated to have been similarly taken in the rear by the Persians, and Philip quite recently by the Romans. Accordingly he sent a message to the Aetolians at Heraclea asking them to do him this service at least in the war, namely, to seize and hold the crests of the surrounding mountains and prevent the Romans from crossing them anywhere. On the receipt of this message there was a sharp difference of opinion among the Aetolians. Some thought that they ought to comply with the king's request and go; others were in favor of remaining in their quarters at

Heraclea, prepared for either eventuality. If the king were defeated they would then have their forces intact and be able to assist in the defense of the cities round them, if on the other hand he were victorious they would then be in a position to take up the pursuit of the fugitive Romans. Each party held to its opinion, and not only held to it but acted upon it; 2,000 remained in Heraclea, and the others, formed into three divisions, occupied the three heights of Callidromus, Rhoduntia, and Tichius.

17. When the consul saw that the heights were occupied by the Aetolians he sent M. Porcius Cato and L. Valerius Flaccus, men of consular rank commanding under him, to attack their fortified positions, Flaccus against Rhoduntia and Tichius, and Cato against Callidromus. They each took a picked force of 2,000 infantry. Before making his general advance against the enemy, the consul called his men on parade and addressed a few words to them. "Soldiers," he said, "I see that there are very many amongst you, men of all ranks, who have campaigned in this very province under the leadership and auspices of T. Quinctius. In the Macedonian war the pass at the Aous was more difficult to force than this one, for here we have gates and this passage as though provided by nature is the only one available, every other route between the two seas being closed to us. On that occasion, too, the enemy defenses were stronger and constructed on more advantageous ground; the hostile army was more numerous and made up of far better soldiery; there were in that army Macedonians, Thracians and Illyrians, all very warlike tribes; here there are Syrians and Asiatic Greeks, the meanest of mankind, and born only for slavery. The monarch who was opposed to us then was a true soldier, trained from his youth in wars with the Thracians and the Illyrians and all the nations round him; this man—to say nothing of his previous life—has done nothing during the whole of the winter months more memorable than marrying a girl for love out of a private family and, even when compared with their fellow-townsmen, of obscure origin, and now the newly-wedded bridegroom, fattened up as it were with marriage feasts, has come out to fight. His main hope was in the Aetolians, they were his chief strength, and you have already learnt by experience as Antiochus is learning now what an untrustworthy and ungrateful race they are. They have not come in any considerable number, it was impossible to keep them in camp, they are at loggerheads among themselves, and after insisting that Hypata and Heraclea must be defended they refused to defend either place and took refuge on the mountain heights, some shutting themselves up in Heraclea. The king himself has shown clearly that he durst not venture to meet us on fair ground, he is not even fixing his camp in open country; he has abandoned the whole of the district in front of him which he boasts of having taken from us and from Philip, and has hidden himself amongst the rocks. His camp is not even placed at the entrance to the path, as we are told the

Lacedaemonians placed theirs, but is withdrawn far within it. What difference is there, as a visible proof of fear, between his shutting himself up here
or behind the walls of a besieged city? The pass, however, will not protect
Antiochus, nor will the heights which the Aetolians have seized protect
them. Sufficient caution and foresight have been exercised to prevent your
having anything to fight against but the actual enemy. You must bear in mind
that you are not fighting only for the freedom of Greece, though it will be a
splendid record to deliver out of the hands of the Aetolians and Antiochus
the country which you formerly rescued from Philip. Nor will it be only the
spoil in the enemy's camp that will fall to you as a prize; all the stores and
material which he is daily looking for from Ephesus will be your booty; you
will open up Asia and Syria and all the wealthiest realms to the furthest East
to the supremacy of Rome. What will then prevent us from extending our
dominion from Gades to the Red Sea with no limit but the Ocean which
enfolds the world, and making the whole human race look up to Rome with
a reverence only second to that which they pay to the gods? Show yourselves
worthy in heart and mind of such vast rewards so that we may take the field
tomorrow assured that the gods will help us."

18. After this address the soldiers were dismissed and got their armor and
weapons ready before they took food and rest. As soon as it began to grow
light the consul hung out the signal for battle and formed his line on a narrow
front to suit the confined limits of the ground. When the king saw the standards of the enemy he also led out his men. Part of his light infantry he stationed in front of their rampart to form the first line. Behind them in support
he posted the Macedonians with long spears, the main strength of his army;
they extended across the whole length of the rampart. To the left of them
were posted a body of javelin men, bowmen and slingers immediately under
the foot of the mountains, so that they might from their higher ground
harass the unprotected flank of the enemy. On the right of the Macedonians,
towards the end of his lines, where the ground beyond down to the sea is
impassable owing to bogs and quicksands, he posted the elephants with their
usual guard, and behind them the cavalry, and a short distance behind them
again the rest of his troops. The Macedonians in front of the rampart had no
difficulty at first in resisting the Romans, who were trying at all points to
break through, and they received considerable assistance from those on the
higher ground, who discharged bullets from their slings, arrows and javelins
all at once, a perfect cloud of missiles. But as the enemy's pressure increased
and the attack was made in greater force they gradually fell back to their rampart, and standing upon it made practically a second rampart with their leveled spears. The rampart, owing to its moderate height, not only offered a
higher position from which to fight, but also enabled them to reach the
enemy below with their long spears. Many in their reckless attempts to

mount the rampart were run through, and they would have had either to retire baffled or sustain serious losses had not M. Porcius appeared on a hill which commanded the camp. He had dislodged the Aetolians from the crest of Callidromus and killed the greater part of them, attacking them when they were off their guard and most of them asleep.

19. Flaccus was not so fortunate, his attempt to reach the fortified posts on Tichius and Rhoduntia was a failure. The Macedonians and the other troops in the king's camp could at first only make out a moving mass of men in the distance, and were under the impression that the Aetolians had seen the fighting from afar and were coming to their assistance. When, however, they recognized the approaching standards and arms and discovered their mistake, they were so panic-stricken that they flung away their weapons and fled. The pursuit was impeded by the entrenchments of the camp and the confined space through which the pursuers had to pass, but the elephants were the greatest hindrance, for it was difficult for the infantry to get past them, and impossible for the cavalry; the frightened horses created more confusion than in the actual battle. The plunder of the camp still further delayed the pursuit. However, they followed up the enemy as far as Scarphea, after which they returned to camp. Large numbers of men and horses had been either killed or captured on the way, and even the elephants, which they were unable to secure, had been killed. While the battle was going on the Aetolians who had been holding Heraclea made an attempt on the Roman camp, but they gained nothing from their enterprise, which was certainly not lacking in audacity. At the third watch of the following night the consul sent the cavalry to continue the pursuit, and at daybreak he put the legions in motion. The king had gained a considerable start, as he did not stop in his headlong ride till he reached Elatia. Here he collected what was left of his army out of the battle and the flight and retreated with a very small body of half-armed soldiers to Chalcis. The Roman cavalry did not succeed in overtaking the king himself at Elatia, but they cut off a large part of his army, who were unable to go any further through sheer fatigue, or else had lost their way in an unknown country, with none to guide them. Out of the whole army not a single man escaped beyond the 500 who formed the king's bodyguard, an insignificant number even if we accept Polybius' statement which I have mentioned above that the force the king brought with him out of Asia did not exceed 10,000 men. What proportion would it be if we are to believe Valerius Antias, that there were 60,000 men in the king's army, of whom 40,000 fell and over 5,000 made prisoners, and 230 standards captured? In the battle itself the Roman losses amounted to 150, and in the defense of the camp against the Aetolians not more than 50 were killed.

BOOK XXXVIII 37–38

The terms of the Peace of Apamea (188 B.C.E.) between Rome and King Antiochus.

37. During this winter Cn. Manlius, who was passing the season in Asia first as consul and then as proconsul, was visited by deputations from all the cities and nationalities west of the Taurus. Whilst the Romans regarded their victory over Antiochus as a more notable one than their subsequent victory over the Gauls, their Asiatic allies rejoiced more over the latter than the former. Subjection to the king was a much easier thing to bear than the ferocity of the ruthless barbarians and the terror which haunted them from one day to another, for they never knew in what direction that ferocity might sweep them like a storm upon plundering and devastating raids. They had regained their liberty through the repulse of Antiochus and their peace through the subjugation of the Gauls, and now they brought to the consul not only their congratulations and thanks but also golden crowns, each according to their ability. Delegates came, too, from Antiochus and even from the Gauls themselves to learn the conditions of peace. Ariarathes also sent envoys from Cappadocia to sue for forgiveness and offer a pecuniary atonement for his offense in assisting Antiochus. He was ordered to pay 600 talents of silver and the Gauls were told that when Eumenes arrived they would have the conditions of peace given to them. The delegations from the various cities were dismissed with gracious replies and went away even happier than they had come. Those from Antiochus received instructions to convey money and corn into Pamphylia, as agreed with L. Scipio, as the consul was going there with his army.

At the beginning of spring, therefore, after performing the purification rites on behalf of his army, he commenced his march, and after eight days reached Apamea. Here he remained encamped for three days, and then advanced into Pamphylia where he had ordered the king's envoys to deposit the money and the corn. He received 1,500 talents of silver which were taken to Apamea; the corn was distributed amongst the soldiers. From there he advanced to Perga, the only city in that country which was held by a garrison of the king's troops. On his approach he was met by the commandant who asked for a respite of thirty days that he might consult Antiochus about surrendering the city. He was allowed the interval and on the thirtieth day the garrison evacuated the place. Whilst the consul was at Perga he sent his brother L. Manlius with a force of 4,000 men to Oroanda to exact the rest of the money which, according to the stipulation, was to be paid. On learning that Eumenes and the ten commissioners from Rome had arrived at Ephesus, he led his army back to Apamea and ordered the envoys from Antiochus to follow him.

38. Here the treaty as settled by the ten commissioners was drawn up. The substance of it was as follows: "There shall be peace and amity between King Antiochus and the Roman people on these terms and conditions: The king shall not suffer any army purposing to levy war on the Roman people or their allies to pass through the borders of his kingdom or of any subject to him, nor shall he assist it with provisions or in any other way whatever. The Romans and their allies shall act in like manner towards Antiochus and those under his sway. Antiochus shall have no right to levy war upon those who dwell in the islands, or to sail across to Europe. He shall withdraw from all the cities, lands, villages and forts west of the Taurus as far as the Halys and extending from the lowlands of the Taurus up to the range which stretches towards Lycaonia. He shall not carry any arms from the aforesaid towns and lands and forts from which he withdraws; if he has carried any away he shall duly restore them to whatever place they belong. He shall not reclaim any soldier or any other person whatever from the kingdom of Eumenes. If any citizens belonging to the cities which are passing from under his rule are with Antiochus or within the boundaries of his realm, they shall all return to Apamea by a certain day; if any of Antiochus' subjects are with the Romans and their allies they shall be at liberty to depart or to remain. He shall restore to the Romans and their allies the slaves, whether fugitives or prisoners of war, or any free man who has been taken captive or is a deserter. He shall give up his elephants and not procure any more. He shall likewise make over his ships of war and all their tackle, nor shall he possess more than ten light decked ships, none of which may be propelled by more than thirty oars, and no smaller ones for use in any war which he may undertake. He shall not take his ships west of the headlands of the Calycadnus or the Sorpedon, save only such ships as shall carry money or tribute or envoys or hostages. Antiochus shall not have the right to hire mercenary troops from those nations which shall be under the suzerainty of Rome nor to accept them even as volunteers. Such houses and buildings as belonged to the Rhodians and their allies within the dominions of Antiochus shall be held by them on the same right as before the war. If any moneys are due to them they shall have the same right to exact them, if aught has been taken from them, they shall have the right of search and recovery. Whatever cities amongst those that are to be surrendered they hold as a gift from Antiochus; he shall withdraw the garrisons from them and provide for their due surrender. He shall pay 12,000 Attic talents of sterling silver in equal installments over twelve years—the talent shall weigh not less than 80 Roman pounds—and 540,000 modii of wheat. To King Eumenes he shall pay 350 talents within five years, and in place of corn its value in money, 127 talents. He shall give twenty hostages to the Romans and exchange them for others in three years, that none may be less than eighteen or more than forty-five years of age. If any of the allies of Rome shall wantonly and without provocation make war on Antiochus, he shall have the right to repel them by force of arms, always providing that he shall not hold any city by right of war or receive it into friendship and amity. Disputes shall be determined before a judicial tribunal, or if both parties shall so will it, by war." There was an additional clause dealing with the surrender of Hannibal, Thoas and Mnasilochus, as well as Eubulidas and Philo of Chalcidaea, and also a proviso that if it should afterwards be decided to add to, or repeal, or alter any of the articles, that should be done without impairing the validity of the treaty.

BOOK XXXIX 51

The death of Hannibal in 183 B.C.E.

51. King Prusias of Bithynia had for some time fallen under suspicion in Rome, partly owing to his having sheltered Hannibal after the flight of Antiochus and partly because he had started a war with Eumenes. T. Quinctius Flamininus was accordingly sent on a special mission to him. He charged Prusias, amongst other things, with admitting to his court the man who of all men living was the most deadly foe to the People of Rome, who had instigated first his own countrymen and then, when their power was broken, King Antiochus to levy war on Rome. Either owing to the menacing language of Flamininus or because he wished to ingratiate himself with Flamininus and the Romans, he formed the design of either putting Hannibal to death or delivering him up to them. In any case, immediately after his first interview with Flamininus he sent soldiers to guard the house in which Hannibal was living. Hannibal had always looked forward to such a fate as this; he fully realized the implacable hatred which the Romans felt towards him, and he put no trust whatever in the good faith of monarchs. He had already had experience of Prusias' fickleness of temper and he had dreaded the arrival of Flamininus as certain to prove fatal to himself. In face of the dangers confronting him on all sides he tried to keep open some one avenue of escape. With this view he had constructed seven exits from his house, some of them concealed, so that they might not be blocked by the guard. But the tyranny of kings leaves nothing hidden which they want to explore. The guards surrounded the house so closely that no one could slip out of it. When Hannibal was informed that the king's soldiers were in the vestibule, he tried to escape through a postern gate which afforded the most secret means of exit. He found that this too was closely watched and that guards were posted all round the place. Finally he called for the poison which he had long kept in readiness for such an emergency. "Let us," he said, "relieve the Romans from the anxiety they have so long experienced, since they think it tries their patience too much to wait for an old man's death. The victory which Flamininus will win over a defenseless fugitive will be neither great nor memorable; this day will show how vastly the moral of the Roman People has changed. Their fathers warned Pyrrhus, when he had an army in Italy, to beware of poison, and now they have sent a man of consular rank to persuade Prusias to murder his guest." Then, invoking curses on Prusias and his realm and appealing to the gods who guard the rights of hospitality to punish his broken faith, he drained the cup. Such was the close of Hannibal's life.

BOOK XLV 12; 20–25

The arrogant behavior of Roman ambassadors in Egypt, and towards the island city of Rhodes, Rome's long-time ally.

12. When the time for the suspension of hostilities had elapsed he marched through the desert of Arabia, while his fleet was sailing up the mouth of the Nile to Pelusium. After receiving the submission of the inhabitants of Memphis and of the rest of the Egyptian people, some submitting voluntarily, others under threats, he marched by easy stages towards Alexandria. After crossing the river at Eleusis, about four miles from Alexandria, he was met by the Roman commissioners, to whom he gave a friendly greeting and held out his hand to Popilius. Popilius, however, placed in his hand the tablets on which was written the decree of the senate and told him first of all to read that. After reading it through he said he would call his friends into council and consider what he ought to do. Popilius, stern and imperious as ever, drew a circle round the king with the stick he was carrying and said, "Before you step out of that circle give me a reply to lay before the senate." For a few moments he hesitated, astounded at such a peremptory order, and at last replied, "I will do what the senate thinks right." Not till then did Popilius extend his hand to the king as to a friend and ally. Antiochus evacuated Egypt at the appointed date, and the commissioners exerted their authority to establish a lasting concord between the brothers, as they had as yet hardly made peace with each other. They then sailed to Cyprus and sent home the fleet of Antiochus which had defeated the Egyptian ships in a naval engagement. The work of the commissioners won great renown amongst the nations, for it was undoubtedly owing to this that Egypt had been rescued out of the hands of Antiochus and the crown restored to the Ptolemaic dynasty. Whilst one of the consuls for the year had signalized his consulship by a famous victory, the other remained in comparative obscurity because he had no opportunity of distinguishing himself. At the outset, in fixing the day for the muster of his legions, he did so in a place where the auspices had not been taken. The matter was referred to the augurs, who announced that the proceeding was invalid. After his departure into Gaul he selected a spot near the Macrian Plain at the foot of Mount Sicimina and Papinus for his standing camp and then went into winter quarters in the same neighborhood with the troops of the Latin allies; the Roman legions owing to the informality in appointing the day for their assembling, remained in Rome. The praetors, with the exception of C. Papirius Carbo, went to their respective provinces. Sardinia had been allotted to him, but the senate decided that he should exercise the alien jurisdiction in Rome, for this, too, the ballot had assigned to him.

§

20. These arguments prevailed with Attalus. Accordingly, when introduced to the senate he offered his congratulations on the victory, and alluded to the services, such as they were, which he and his brothers had rendered. He then described the serious unrest among the Gauls which had brought about a revolt and begged the senate to send envoys to them with sufficient influence and authority to induce them to lay down their arms. Having carried out his instructions so far as they affected the welfare of the kingdom, he asked that Aenus and Maronea might be assigned to him. So, to the disappointment of those who supposed that after bringing charges against his brother he would ask for the kingdom to be divided between them, he left the senate-house. Seldom at any time has either king or private citizen been listened to with such universal pleasure and approval; all honors and gifts were showered upon him during his stay, and his departure was witnessed by large crowds. Amongst the numerous delegations from Greece the one from Rhodes excited the greatest interest. They appeared in white garments as befitted their mission of congratulation, and indeed if they had shown themselves in mourning it might have looked as though they were lamenting the fall of Perseus. When the consul, M. Junius, consulted the senate as to whether they would grant them free quarters and hospitality and an audience, the House decided that the obligations of hospitality should not be discharged in their case. The envoys meanwhile were standing in the Comitium, and when the consul came out of the senate-house they told him that they had come to offer their congratulations on the victory and to rebut the accusations of treason, and they begged that the senate would grant them an audience. The consul told them plainly that it was to friends and allies that the Romans were wont to give a hospitable welcome and grant an audience of the senate. The conduct of the Rhodians during the war had not been such that they deserved to be counted amongst the friends and allies of Rome. On hearing this, they all prostrated themselves to the ground and implored the consul and all who were present not to think it just and right that the new charges which were falsely made against them should outweigh their services in the past, services to which the Romans themselves could testify. They lost no time in putting on mourning garments and visiting the residences of the principal men, whom they implored not to condemn them without a hearing.

21. M. Juventius Thalna, who was the praetor in charge of the alien jurisdiction, was inciting the populace against the Rhodians and had proposed a resolution that war should be declared against Rhodes, and that one of the magistrates for the year should be chosen to command the fleet, hoping that he himself would be appointed. Two of the tribunes of the plebs, M. Antonius and M. Pomponius, opposed this proceeding. The praetor himself had acted in defiance of precedent, for he was making the proposal on his own initiative without consulting the senate or informing the consuls of the question he was going to put, viz. whether it was the will and order of the people of Rome that war should be declared against Rhodes. Hitherto the senate had always been consulted on the question of war, and then, if the senate gave their sanction, the question was submitted to the popular Assembly. The tribunes of the plebs, too, were in the wrong, because the traditional usage was that no one should veto a measure until the citizens had had the opportunity of speaking for or against it. Hence it had very frequently happened that those who had asserted that they would not interpose their veto did interpose after the opponents of the measure had made them aware of its defects, whilst on the other hand those who had come prepared to veto a measure were convinced by the arguments of its supporters and withdrew their veto. On this occasion the praetors and the tribunes vied with each other as to who could act most precipitately; the tribunes forestalled the praetor by interposing their veto before the right time . . .

22. "So far it is a question whether we have or have not been guilty of any offense; all the penalty, the humiliation we are suffering from already. In the past, when we visited Rome after the Carthaginians were defeated, after Philip and Antiochus had been overcome, we went from our quarters where we were the guests of the State to offer our congratulations in the senate house, and from there we went up to the Capitol with gifts for your gods. Now we have come away from a miserable inn where we could hardly get admittance, ordered as we are to remain outside the City almost as though we were enemies. In this squalid plight we have come into the Roman senate-house—we Rhodians to whom not long ago you granted the provinces of Lycia and Caria, and upon whom you have bestowed the greatest distinctions and rewards. According to what we hear, you are ordaining that the Macedonians and Illyrians shall be free peoples, though before they went to war with you they were in servitude—not that we envy any one's good fortunes, on the contrary we recognize the clemency of Rome—but the Rhodians simply remained quiet, and are you going to convert friends into enemies by this proposed war? Surely you are the same Romans who make it your boast that your wars are successful because they are just, and pride yourselves not so much upon bringing them to a close as victors as upon never beginning them without just cause. The attack on Messana in Sicily made the Carthaginians your enemy; his attack on Athens, his attempt to enslave Greece, the assistance rendered to Hannibal in money and troops made Philip your enemy. Antiochus, on the invitation of the Aetolians, who were your enemies, sailed in person with his fleet from Asia to Greece, seized Demetrias, Chalcis and the Pass of Thermopylae and tried to dispossess you of your empire. Your grounds for the war with Perseus were the attacks on your allies, or the murder of the princes and leading men in different communities and nationalities. What pretext or justification will there be for our ruin, if we are to perish? So far I do not make any difference between the case of our city as a whole and that of our fellow-citizens Polyaratus and Dino and the others whom we have brought with us to deliver up to you. Suppose all we Rhodians were equally guilty, what charge would be brought against us with regard to this war? You say we took the side of Perseus, and just as in the wars against Philip and Antiochus we stood by you against those monarchs, so now we stood by the king against you. Ask the commanders of your fleets in Asia, C. Livius, L. Aemilius Regillus, how we were wont to help our allies and with what energy we prosecuted the war. Your ships never fought without us to help you; we fought single-handed at Samos and a second time off Pamphylia against Hannibal, who was in command. And this victory was all the more glorious for us because after losing a large proportion of our ships and the flower of our youth in the defeat at Samos, we were not daunted even by that disaster, and we met the king's fleet on its way from Syria. I am not recounting these incidents in a spirit of boasting—our present circumstances forbid that—but to remind you how the Rhodians have been accustomed to help their allies.

23. "After the final defeat of Philip and of Antiochus we received the most splendid rewards from you. If the good fortune which, through the kindness of heaven and your own courage, is now yours had fallen to the lot of Perseus and we had gone to Macedonia to meet the victorious king and ask him for rewards, what could we possibly say for ourselves? That he had received assistance from us in money or corn? Or in naval and military contingents? Or that we had held any fortified position for him? Or that we had fought any battles for him either under his generals or on our own account? If

he were to ask where our soldiers were supplying his garrison or our ships joining his fleet, we should, perhaps, make the same defense before the victor that we are now making before you. This is what we have gained by sending envoys to both parties to urge peace—we have won the gratitude of neither, and from one side we have incurred suspicion and danger. And yet Perseus truly might bring a charge against us which you, senators, cannot bring. At the outset of the war we sent a deputation to promise assistance with whatever was needful for the war, and to assure you that everything was in readiness, our naval forces, our munitions of war, our fighting men, just as in the former wars. It was owing to you that we did not supply them; whatever the reason was, you refused our assistance. So then not only did we show no hostility to you, but we were not lacking in our duty as faithful allies, though you prohibited us from discharging it.

"Some one may say, 'What then? Has nothing been done or said in your City which you disapproved of and which was such as to give just offense to the people of Rome?' I am not here now to defend what has been done—I am not so mad—but I shall draw a distinction between the cause of the State as a whole and the guilty conduct of individual citizens. There is no State which does not at some time possess bad citizens and at all times an ignorant populace. I have heard that even amongst you there have been men who made their way by flattering the mob, and that there have occasionally been secessions of the plebs when the government was no longer in your hands. If these things could happen in so well-ordered a State as this, can any one feel surprised that there have been amongst us a few men who in their desire to win the friendship of the king have led our plebs astray by their evil counsels? All the same, they did not effect anything more than make us slacken in our duty. I will not pass over what is the most serious charge brought against us with regard to this war. We sent embassies to you and to Perseus simultaneously to urge peace. This unfortunate policy has been, as we have heard, held up as abject folly by a furious orator, who it is admitted spoke in such a tone that he might have been C. Popilius, your envoy, whom you commissioned to dissuade Antiochus and Ptolemy from war. Still, whether we are to call it arrogance or folly, our policy towards you was the same as towards Perseus.

"States, like individuals, have their distinctive characters, some are hottempered, others bold and enterprising; some are of a timid disposition, others more prone to sensual indulgence. The people of Athens are generally reported to be quick and impulsive and venture upon enterprises beyond their strength: the Lacedaemonians are said to be slow in action and only with difficulty are they brought to engage in undertakings in which they feel perfectly safe. I quite admit that Asia as a whole produces somewhat empty heads and that the language of my countrymen is somewhat inflated because we fancy ourselves superior to our neighbors. This in itself is due more to the honors which you have judged us worthy to receive than to any strength which we ourselves possessed. Surely that embassy was sufficiently chastised when it was dismissed without any reply. If the humiliation then inflicted was not enough, this embassy, at all events, with its piteous and suppliant appeal will be an adequate atonement for an even more peremptory set of negotiators than that one was. Arrogance, especially in language, is bitterly resented by hot-tempered people and laughed at by sensible people, particularly when shown by inferiors towards a superior, but no one has ever regarded it as a capital offense. Possibly some one imagined that the Rhodians felt a contempt for the Romans. Some men even abuse the gods in presumptuous language, but we do not hear of any one being struck by lightning for it.

24. "If no hostile act can be imputed to us, if the pompous language of our envoy, offensive as it was to listen to, did not merit the destruction of our city, what is there left from which we have to clear ourselves? I hear, senators, that you are discussing the amount of the fine which is to be imposed upon us for our unspoken wishes. It is alleged that our sympathies were with the king and that we should have preferred to see him victorious, so, some of you think we ought to be punished by war, others hold that while that was our wish we ought not on that account to be punished. In no State has it been laid down either by traditional usage or by positive enactment that whoever wishes the destruction of an enemy, but does nothing to bring it about, shall still suffer capital punishment. To those of you who are for freeing us from the penalty though not from the charge we are grateful; we assert this principle for ourselves—if, as is alleged, this was the universal wish, we do not distinguish between will and deed, we are all involved. If some of our leaders were on your side and others on the side of the king, I do not ask that the supporters of the king should enjoy immunity on account of us who were on your side; what I do ask is that we should not perish on account of them. You are not more angry with them than our State itself is, and, knowing this, most of them have either fled or taken their own lives; others whom we have found guilty will be in your hands, senators. Though the conduct of the rest of us during the war has merited no gratitude, it certainly has not merited punishment. Let the accumulation of our former services outweigh this failure in our duty. During these late years you have been engaged in war with three kings; let not the fact that we gave no assistance in one war count more against us than the fact that we fought for you in two wars counts for us. Let Philip, Antiochus and Perseus stand for three separate verdicts; two acquit us, one is so doubtful as to be adverse. If they were our judges we should be pronounced guilty; you, senators, are now acting as judges as to whether Rhodes is to remain in the world or be utterly blotted out. The question before you is not one of war; you can commence one, but you cannot continue it, since not a single Rhodian is going to bear arms against you. If you persist in nurs-

ing your wrath against us we shall ask for time to carry the tidings of this fatal embassy home. All of us every free person, every man and woman in Rhodes, will go on board our ships with all the money we possess, and bidding farewell to our national and our household gods, we shall come to Rome. All the gold and silver belonging to the State, all that individual citizens possess, will be placed in a heap on the Comitium, on the threshold of your senate-house, and we shall deliver up ourselves, our wives and children to you, prepared to suffer whatever may be in store for us. Far removed from our eyes, let our city be plundered and burnt. The Romans have it in their power to judge the Rhodians to be public enemies, we too can pass some judgment on ourselves; we shall never judge ourselves to be your enemies, nor will we commit a single hostile act, even if we have to suffer everything that you can inflict upon us."

25. Such was the speech. At its close they all again prostrated themselves, waving their suppliant olive branches to and fro. At last they rose and left the senate-house. Then the senators were asked to state their view. The bitterest opponents of the Rhodians were those who as consuls or praetors or staff officers had taken part in the war. The one who did most to help them was M. Porcius Cato, who though naturally stern and inflexible acted on this occasion the part of a lenient and conciliatory senator. I will not insert a specimen of his fluency and eloquence by transcribing his speech, it is extant in the Fifth Book of his *Origines*. The reply made to the Rhodians was to the effect that they would neither be declared enemies nor allowed to remain as allies. The leaders of the deputation were Philocrates and Astymedes. Some of the delegates decided to accompany Philocrates back to Rhodes with the report of the proceedings, others elected to remain in Rome with Astymedes so that they could find out what was going on and inform their countrymen. For the time being they were only required to withdraw their governors from Lycia and Caria. This would in itself have created a painful impression, but as they were relieved from the apprehension of a worse evil, that of war, the announcement was received with joy. They at once decreed a crown of 20,000 gold pieces in value and sent it to Theaetetus, the commandant of the fleet, for him to carry it to Rome. They wished him to press for an alliance with Rome, but in such a way that the terms would not be submitted to the people, nor reduced to writing, because in case he was unsuccessful the failure would be all the more humiliating. It was the sole prerogative of the commandant of the fleet to act in these matters without any formal decree being made. For all those years they had maintained friendly relations with Rome without binding themselves by an express treaty of alliance, their only reason being that they did not wish to preclude the kings from all hopes of their assistance should it ever be needed, nor themselves from the advantage to be derived from the bounty and good fortune of those monarchs. Under present circumstances it seemed especially desirable that an alliance should be formed, not to give them additional security against other nations—for they feared none but the Romans—but to make them less suspected by the Romans themselves. Just at this time the Caunians revolted from them and the Mylasensians seized the towns of the Euromensians. The Rhodian government was not so broken in spirit as not to become aware that if Lycia and Caria had been taken from them by Rome the other subject countries would either win their freedom by revolt or be seized by their neighbors, and they themselves would be shut up in a small and unfertile island which was quite incapable of supporting the population of so large a city. A body of troops was accordingly dispatched to the disaffected districts and reduced the Caunians to submission, though they had summoned help from the Cibyratae. They also defeated in an action near Orthosia the Mylasensians and Alabandians who had joined forces to wrest from them the province of Euromos.

AUGUSTUS

Life

C. Octavius (63 B.C.E.–14 C.E.) was raised by his mother Atia, since his father died a few years after his birth. Atia's uncle, Julius Caesar, became fond of the boy and introduced him to public life. At the age of 12 he pronounced the funeral address for his grandmother Julia, Caesar's sister, and he accompanied his great-uncle in his triumph of 46. When he learned of Caesar's assassination in 44 and his own designation in Caesar's will as his adopted son and heir, the 18-year-old youth called himself C. Julius Caesar Octavianus (thus called "Octavian") and recruited Caesar's veterans to fight for vengeance. First he sought the support of the senatorial forces, but he finally allied with Caesar's deputy Marc Antony to crush the forces of the Caesar's murderers at Philippi. Octavian allowed Antony free reign to murder his enemies, including the distinguished senator Cicero. After a decade of uneasy alliance, Octavian defeated Antony and his ally the Egyptian queen Cleopatra in 30.

In 27 Octavian took the name of "Augustus" and such a collection of powers that the Roman Empire might be said to have begun. Augustus brought Egypt into the Roman Empire and ruled over the entire Mediterranean for two generations. His principal concerns were to settle the vast armies after the civil war, create a new administrative and financial structure, and secure the succession within the Julian family. This ruthless young man later was represented as patron of the arts, upholder of morality, and the benevolent father of his country. Though he had always been sickly and often was desperately ill, Augustus outlived at least four designated successors until his death in 14 C.E. brought to power his stepson Tiberius.

Work

Augustus wrote an autobiography that has not survived, but we do have his Res Gestae—*a reckoning of his stewardship placed on bronze tablets in front of Augustus' mausoleum. It survives only in inscriptions carved on the side of temples. This document has a magisterial disregard for the embarrassing factual details of the civil wars, where the republican leader Sextus Pompey is referred to simply as a pirate. Nor is Antony's name even mentioned. Constitutional issues are also blurred; the document is a rose-colored glorification of the reign from the perspective of his 77th (and final) year.*

THE ACHIEVEMENTS OF THE DEIFIED AUGUSTUS*

(RES GESTAE DIVI AUGUSTI)

Below is a copy of *The Achievements of the Divine Augustus*, by which he subjected the entire world to imperial power of the Roman people, and of the expenses which he incurred for the state and people of Rome; the original text has been inscribed on two bronze pillars set up at Rome.

1. When I was nineteen year old, on my own initiative and at my own expense I raised an army, with which I restored freedom to the state which was oppressed by the power of a clique. For that reason the senate passed honorary decrees enrolling me in its order in the consulship of Gaius Pansa and Aulus Hirtius (43 B.C.E.), granting me the privilege of speaking among the ex-consuls and giving me *imperium*—the right of military command. It ordered me as a propraetor together with the consuls to ensure that the state should suffer no harm. In the same year, when both consuls had fallen in battle, the people named me consul and appointed me one of a commission of three(*triumvir*) for the re-establishment of the Republic.

2. I drove the murderers of my father into exile, and avenged their crime through legal tribunals; and afterwards, when they made war on the republic, I twice defeated them in battle.[1]

---

*Translated by Ronald Mellor (1997).

[1]Brutus, Cassius, and other senators assassinated Julius Caesar. Two years later the triumvirs (Octavian, Marc Antony, and Lepidus) defeated them in the two battles at Philippi.

3. I undertook civil and foreign wars by land and sea throughout the whole world, and as victor I spared the lives of all citizens who sought pardon. When foreign nations could safely be pardoned I preferred to preserve rather than to destroy them. 500,000 Roman citizens took a military oath of obedience to me. Of this number, I settled more than 300,000 in colonies or sent them back to their home towns after their service was completed; to all I gave lands or money as a reward for their military service. I captured six hundred ships, not counting those smaller than triremes.

4. Twice I was honored with ovations and I celebrated three curule triumphs and I was twenty-one times saluted as *imperator*. When the senate decreed still more triumphs in my honor, I declined them all. After I had fulfilled the vows I made in each war, I laid the bay leaves from my *fasces* in the Capitol. Fifty-five times the senate decreed that thanks be offered to the immortal gods on account of successes on land and sea gained by me or by lieutenants acting under my command. The thanksgivings decreed by the senate occupied 890 days. In my triumphs nine kings or children of kings paraded before my chariot. When I was writing these words, I had been consul thirteen times and was in the thirty-seventh year of tribunician power (14 B.C.E.).

5. In the consulship of Marcus Marcellus and Lucius Arruntius (22 B.C.E.), the people and the senate both offered me the dictatorship, both in my absence and when I was at Rome, but I refused it. During the great famine I did take charge of the grain-supply, which I so administered that, in a few days and at my own expense, I freed the whole city from the fear and present danger of starvation. At that time the consulship was offered to me, to be held each year for life, but I refused it.

6. In the consulship of Marcus Vinicius and Quintus Lucretius (19 B.C.E.), and afterwards in that of Publius and Gnaeus Lentulus (18 B.C.E.), and thirdly in that of Paullus Fabius Maximus and Quintus Tubero (11 B.C.E.), the senate and the Roman people agreed that I should be appointed sole guardian of laws and morals with supreme power, but I refused any office offered to me that was contrary to the custom of our ancestors. The actions that the senate which me to take I carried out in virtue of my tribunician power. On five occasions, at my own request, I received from the senate a colleague in that office.

7. I was triumvir for the re-establishment of the Republic for ten consecutive years. Up to the day of writing I have been *princeps senatus* for forty years. I am High Priest, *augur*, member of the religious board of fifteen, board of seven for religious feasts, Arval brother, *sodalis Titius*, Fetial priest.

8. In my fifth consulship (29 B.C.E.) I increased the number of patricians at the command of the people and the senate. I revised the roll of the senate three times. In my sixth consulship (28 B.C.E.) with Marcus Agrippa as colleague, I held a census of the people, and I performed a *lustrum* after a lapse of forty-one years; at that *lustrum* 4,063,000 Roman citizens were enrolled. Then I performed a second *lustrum* with consular *imperium* and without a colleague, in the consulship of Gaius Censorinus and Gaius Asinius (8 B.C.E.); at that *lustrum* 4,233,000 citizens were registered. Thirdly I performed a *lustrum* with consular *imperium*, with my son Tiberius Caesar as colleague, in the consulship of Sextus Pompeius and Sextus Appuleius (14 C.E.); at that *lustrum* 4,937,000 citizens were registered. By new laws which I proposed, I restored many exemplary practices of our ancestors which were falling out of use in our own time, and I myself transmitted many exemplars to be imitated by posterity.

9. The senate decreed that every fifth year the consuls and priests should undertake vows for my health. In fulfillment of these vows games were often celebrated in my lifetime, sometimes by the four most distinguished colleges of priests, sometimes by the consuls. Moreover, all the citizens, individually and on behalf of their towns, have unanimously and continuously offered sacrifices for my health at all the seats of the gods.

10. By decree of the senate my name was inserted in the Salian hymn, and it was enacted by law that my person should be forever inviolable and that I should hold the tribunician power as long as I live. When the people offered me the High Priesthood which my father had held, I refused to replace in that office my colleague who was still alive. Several years later, after the death of the man[2] who had seized it during civil disturbance, I accepted this priesthood, in the consulship of Publius Sulpicius and Gaius Valgius (12 B.C.E.), and such a crowd from all of Italy assembled for to my election as was never before recorded at Rome.

11. In honor of my return the senate consecrated the altar of *Fortuna Redux* (Fortune Who Brings Back) before the temples of Honor and Virtue at the Porta Capena, and it ordered that the priests and Vestal virgins should make a sacrifice there each year on the anniversary of my return to the city from Syria in the consulship of Quintus Lucretius and Marcus Vinicius (19 B.C.E.), and it named the day the Augustalia from my name.

12. At the same time, by decree of the senate, some of the praetors and tribunes of the plebs, with the consul Quintus Lucretius and the leading men, were sent to Campania to meet me, an honor that has been decreed to no one else up to the present day. After I successfully handled affairs in Spain and Gaul and returned to Rome in the consulship of Tiberius Nero and Publius Quintilius (13 B.C.E.), the senate decreed that an altar of the Augustan Peace (*Ara Pacis Augustae*) should be consecrated in the Campus Martius in

---

[1] Marcus Lepidus.

honor of my return, at which the magistrates, priests, and Vestal virgins were ordered to make an annual sacrifice.

13. Our ancestors wished that the gateway of Janus Quirinus should be shut whenever victory had secured peace on land and sea throughout the whole empire of the Roman people. From the foundation of the city down to my birth, the tradition is that it was shut only twice, but while I was *princeps* the senate voted to shut it on three occasions.[1]

14. To honor me, the senate and Roman people designated my sons Gaius and Lucius Caesar, whom Fortune took from me as young men, as consuls when they were fourteen, providing that they should only enter that magistracy after five years. And the senate decreed that from the day when they entered into public life they should take part in the councils of state. Furthermore the whole body of Roman knights hailed each one as Leader of the Youth and presented them with silver shields and spears.

15. To the Roman plebs I paid each man 300 sesterces under my father's will, and in my own name I gave them 400 each from the booty of war in my fifth consulship (29 B.C.E.). In my tenth consulship (24 B.C.E.) I again paid out of my own inheritance a bonus of 400 sesterces to each man, and in my eleventh consulship (23 B.C.E.) I bought grain with my own money and made twelve food distributions. In the twelfth year of my tribunician power (12 B.C.E.) I gave every man 400 sesterces for the third time. These grants of mine never reached fewer than 250,000 persons. In the eighteenth year of my tribunician power and my twelfth consulship (5 B.C.E.), I gave 240 sesterces apiece to 320,000 members of the urban plebs. In my fifth consulship I gave 1,000 sesterces out of booty to every one of the colonists drawn from my soldiers; about 120,000 men in colonies received this bonus at the time of my triumph. In my thirteenth consulship (2 B.C.E.) I gave 240 sesterces apiece to the plebs who then received public grain; there were a bit more than 200,000 persons.

16. I paid cash to the towns for the lands that I granted to soldiers in my fourth consulship (30 B.C.E.), and later in the consulship of Marcus Crassus and Gnaeus Lentulus (14 B.C.E.). I paid a total of about 600,000,000 sesterces for Italian land, and about 260,000,000 sesterces for provincial lands. In the recollection of my contemporaries, I was the first and only one to have done this of all who founded military colonies in Italy or the provinces.[2] Later, in

---

[1] It had been closed under King Numa and after the First Punic War in 235 B.C.E. Under Augustus it was closed after the battle of Actium, in 25 B.C.E. after his war in Spain. The third time is uncertain.

[2] Previously generals, including Octavian/Augustus himself in 41 B.C.E., had confiscated land for their soldiers without compensation.

the consulships of Tiberius Nero and Gnaeus Piso, of Gaius Antistius and Decimus Laelius, of Gaius Calvisius and Lucius Pasienus, of Lucius Lentulus and Marcus Messalla and of Lucius Caninius and Quintus Fabricius I paid cash bonuses to soldiers whom I settled in their home towns after discharge, and for this I spent about 400,000,000 sesterces.

17. Four times I helped the treasury with my own money, so that I transferred to the administrators of the treasury 150,000,000 sesterces. In the consulship of Marcus Lepidus and Lucius Arruntius, I paid 170,000,000 sesterces from my inheritance to the military treasury which was founded by my advice so that cash bonuses could be paid to soldiers who had served for twenty years or more.

18. Beginning in the consulship of Gnaeus and Publius Lentulus (18 B.C.E.), whenever the taxes were inadequate, I distributed from my own funds and my inheritance both grain and money, sometimes to 100,000 persons, sometimes to many more.

19. I built the Senate House, and the Chalcidicum next to it, the temple of Apollo on the Palatine with its porticoes, the temple of the deified Julius, the Lupercal, the portico at the Flaminian circus, which I permitted to bear the name of the portico of Octavius after the man who erected an earlier portico on the same site, the imperial box at the Circus Maximus, the temples of Jupiter the Subduer and Jupiter the Thunderer on the Capitol, the temple of Quirinus, the temples of Minerva, of Queen Juno and of Jupiter Libertas on the Aventine, the temple of the Lares at the head of the Sacred Way, the temple of the Di Penates on the Velia, the temple of Youth, and the temple of the Great Mother on the Palatine.

20. I rebuilt the Capitol and the theater of Pompey—both at great expense—without inscribing my own name. I repaired the channels of the aqueducts, which in several places were collapsing through age, and I doubled the supply of the Marcian aqueduct, by bringing in a new spring. I completed the Forum Julium and the basilica between the temples of Castor and Saturn, works begun and almost finished by my father, and when that same basilica was destroyed by fire, I began to rebuild it on an enlarged site, in the name of my sons, and in case I do not finish it in my life-time, I have ordered my heirs to complete it. In my sixth consulship (28 B.C.E.) I restored eighty-two temples of the gods in the city on the authority of the senate, neglecting none that needed repair at that time. In my seventh consulship (27 B.C.E.) I rebuilt the Via Flaminia from the city to Rimini, and all the bridges except the Mulvian and the Minucian.

21. I built the temple of Mars the Avenger and the Forum Augustum on my own land from the proceeds of booty. On ground largely bought from private owners, I built a theater next to the temple of Apollo, and called it after my son-in-law Marcus Marcellus. From the booty of war I consecrated

dedications on the Capitol and in the temples of the deified Julius, of Apollo, of Vesta and of Mars the Avenger, which cost me about 100,000,000 sesterces. In my fifth consulship I gave back 35,000 pounds of gold crowns contributed by the cities and colonies of Italy to my triumphal celebrations, and thereafter, whenever I was saluted as *imperator*, I refused the gold crowns which the cities and colonies continued to vote with the same kindness as before.

22. I presented three gladiatorial games in my own name and five in the name of my sons or grandsons; at these games about 10,000 men fought. Twice in my own name and a third time in that of my grandson I presented to the people spectacles of athletes summoned from all parts. I gave games in my own name four times and, in place of other magistrates, twenty-three times. For the board of fifteen, as its president with Marcus Agrippa as my colleague, I presented the Secular Games in the consulship of Gaius Furnius and Gaius Silanus (17 B.C.E.). In my thirteenth consulship (2 B.C.E.) I was the first to present the games of Mars, which since that time have been given annually by the consuls by a decree of the senate. Twenty-six times I presented in my own name or in that of my sons and grandsons beast-hunts with African animals in the circus, forum or amphitheater, during which about 3,500 beasts were killed.

23. I presented a display of a naval battle as a show for the people across the Tiber in a place now occupied by the grove of the Caesars, where a site 1,800 feet long and 1,200 broad was excavated. In that spot thirty beaked triremes or biremes and more smaller vessels engaged in battle. In these fleets about 3,000 men fought in addition to the rowers.

24. After my victory, I replaced in the temples of all the cities of the province of Asia the ornaments which my former enemy, after looting those temples, had taken for his private use.[1] Some eighty silver statues of me, standing, mounted, and in four-horse chariots, were set up in Rome; I myself removed them, and with the money from them I placed golden offerings in the temple of Apollo, in my name and in the name of those who had honored me with the statues.

25. I freed the sea of pirates.[2] In that war I captured about 30,000 slaves who had fled from their masters and taken up arms against the state, and I returned them to their masters for punishment. The whole of Italy voluntarily swore an oath of allegiance to me and demanded me to be Leader in the war which I won at Actium. The Gallic and Spanish provinces, Africa, Sicily and Sardinia swore the same oath. More than 700 senators fought under my standards at that time, including eighty-three who previously or subse-

---

[1] Even forty-five years after the battle of Actium in 31 B.C.E., Augustus refuses to refer to Marc Antony by name.

[2] Augustus refers to his war against Sextus Pompey in 36 B.C.E.

quently (down to the day this was written) were made consuls, and about one hundred and seventy who were appointed priests.

26. I expanded the frontiers of all those provinces of the Roman people bordered by peoples not subject to our government. I brought peace to the Gallic and Spanish provinces as well as to Germany, an area bounded by the Ocean from Cadiz to the mouth of the Elbe. I brought peace to the Alps, from the region near the Adriatic all the way to the Tuscan sea, yet without waging an unjust war on any people. My fleet sailed through the Ocean from the mouth of the Rhine eastwards to the territory of the Cimbri, a region which no Roman had visited before either by land or sea, and the Cimbri, Charydes, Semnones and other German peoples of that region sent envoys to seek my friendship and that of the Roman people. At my command and under my auspices two armies were led about the same time into Ethiopia and Arabia Felix; vast enemy forces of both peoples were cut down in battle and many towns were captured. Ethiopia was invaded as far as the town of Nabata, which is next to Meroë; in Arabia the army advanced into the territory of the Sabaeans to the town of Mariba.

27. I added Egypt to the empire of the Roman people. I might have made Greater Armenia a province after its king, Artaxes, was killed, but I preferred, following the precedent of our ancestors, to give that kingdom to Tigranes, son of King Artavasdes and grandson of King Tigranes, acting through Tiberius Nero, who was then my stepson. When the same people later rebelled and were subdued by my son Gaius, I handed them over to be ruled by King Ariobarzanes, son of Artabazus, King of the Medes, and after his death by his son Artavasdes. When he was murdered, I sent Tigranes, a heir of the royal Armenian house, into that kingdom. I recovered all the provinces east of the Adriatic sea, together with Cyrene, the greater part of them being then occupied by kings.[1] I had earlier recovered Sicily and Sardinia which had been seized in the slave war.[2]

28. I established colonies of soldiers in Africa, Sicily, Macedonia, both Spanish provinces, Achaea, Asia, Syria, Gallia Narbonensis and Pisidia. Italy also has twenty-eight colonies founded under my authority, which have become densely populated in my lifetime.

29. By defeating my enemies I recovered in Spain, in Gaul, and from the Dalmatians military standards lost by other commanders. I forced the Parthians to restore to me the spoils and standards of three Roman armies and to beg as suppliants for the friendship of the Roman people.[3] Those standards I

---

[1] Antony had allowed kings (like Herod of Judaea) to administer Roman provinces.

[2] Another derogatory reference to the war with Sextus Pompey.

[3] Standards lost by Crassus at Carrhae (53 B.C.E.) and Marc Antony in 40 and 36 B.C.E. They were returned in 20 B.C.E.

placed in the inner shrine of the temple of Mars the Avenger.

30. The Pannonian tribes, which a Roman army had never approached before I was *princeps*, were conquered by Tiberius Nero, who was then my stepson and legate. I added them to the empire of the Roman people, and extended the frontier of Illyricum to the bank of the Danube river. When an army of Dacians crossed to this side of the Danube, it was defeated and routed under my auspices, and later my army crossed the Danube and forced the Dacian peoples to submit to the orders of the Roman people.

31. Embassies were often sent to me from kings in India, which had never been seen by any Roman leader. The Bastarnae, Scythians and the kings of the Sarmatians who live on both sides of the river Don, and the kings of the Albanians and the Iberians and the Medes sent embassies to seek our friendship.

32. The following kings fled to me as suppliants: Tiridates, King of Parthia, and later Phraates son of King Phraates; Artavasdes, King of the Medes; Artaxares, King of the Adiabeni; Dumnobellaunus and Tincommius, Kings of the Britons; Maelo, King of the Sugambri; and the King of the Marcomanni and Suebi. The king of Parthia, Phraates, son of Orodes, sent all his sons and grandsons to me in Italy, not because he had been overcome in war, but because he sought our friendship by pledging his children. While I was the *princeps* very many other peoples, who had never previously exchanged embassies or had friendly relations with us, have experienced the good faith of the Roman people.

33. The Parthians and Medians sent to me noble ambassadors who sought and received kings from me, for the Parthians Vonones, son of King Phraates, grandson of King Orodes, and for the Medes, Ariobarzanes, son of King Artavasdes, grandson of King Ariobarzanes.

34. In my sixth and seventh consulships (28–27 B.C.E.), after I had extinguished civil war, and with the consent of all I was in complete control of affairs, I transferred the republic from my power to the authority of the senate and Roman people.[1] For this service of mine I was called Augustus by decree of the senate, and the door-posts of my house were publicly decorated with bay leaves, a civic crown was fixed over my door, and a golden shield was placed in the Curia Julia, whose inscription attests that it was given me by the senate and Roman people because of my courage, clemency, justice and piety. Thereafter I excelled all in authority, although I possessed no more official power than others who were my colleagues in each office.

35. In my thirteenth consulship (2 B.C.E.), the senate, the equestrian order and the entire Roman people called me "Father of the Country," and decreed

---

[1] Though Augustus referred to the events of 27 B.C.E. as the restoration of the Republic, he in fact retained all effective power.

that this title should be inscribed on the porch of my house, in the Senate House, and in the Forum Augustum below the four-horse chariot which was placed there in my honor by decree of the senate. At the time of writing I was in my seventy-sixth year.

APPENDIX

1 The sum of money that he gave to the treasury or to the Roman *plebs* or to discharged soldiers was 2,400,000,000 sesterces. **2** He built these new structures: the temples of Mars, of Jupiter the Thunderer and the Subduer, of Apollo, of the deified Julius, of Quirinus, of Minerva, of Queen Juno, of Jupiter Libertas, of the Lares, of the Di Penates, of the Youth, of the Great Mother, the Lupercal, the imperial box at the Circus, the Senate House with the Chalcidicum, the Forum Augustum, the Basilica Julia, the theater of Marcellus, the Octavian portico, the grove of the Caesars beyond the Tiber. **3** He restored the Capitol and sacred buildings to the number of eighty-two, the theater of Pompey, the aqueducts and the Via Flaminia. **4** The expenditure that he devoted to dramatic shows, to gladiatorial contests, to athletic games and hunts and the sea battle, and the money granted to colonies, cities, towns destroyed by earthquake and fire, or to individual friends and senators to whose property requirement he contributed, are incalculable.

SUETONIUS

Life and Work

Gaius Suetonius Tranquillus (c. 70–140 C.E.) was born to a distinguished family in north Africa; his uncle had served as governor of Britain. Suetonius pursued a civil service career in the imperial archives. As chief librarian, he moved among the intellectuals of Trajan's court and was admired by the writer, Pliny, who called him "most learned." Suetonius wrote biographies of many illustrious men grouped by profession; some lives of poets and grammarians survive. His most important book was Lives of the Twelve Caesars, *which began with Julius Caesar (died 44 B.C.E.) and stretched to the reign of Domitian (81–96 C.E.). He made much use of official archives in his biographies, until he was dismissed from his position in 122 by the emperor Hadrian for disrespect to the empress Sabina. Perhaps it was the unavailability of the archives that makes the later lives much less detailed.*

Roman historians saw themselves as literary artists who promoted moral standards and a political perspective in their work. Suetonius stands outside that tradition and includes vulgar stories that would not be suitable for literary history.

After a brief chronological narrative, he organized the material in his biographies by topic: achievements; awful acts; personal characteristics; games; wars; etc. As he presents anecdotes to illustrate each point, he almost seems to be a modern researcher with a card index. Though he does aspire to the narrative skill of an history, he can at times be a fine story-teller. Though sometimes regarded as little more than a gossip-monger, Suetonius is especially valuable for his many references to cultural, literary, and even scientific developments which cannot be found elsewhere.

LIFE OF GAIUS CALIGULA*

Suetonius' Life of Caligula is particularly valuable since the section of Tacitus which treated Caligula's reign is lost. Gaius Caligula (37–41 C.E.) was the great-grandson of both Augustus and Marc Antony.

1. Germanicus, father of Gaius Caesar, son of Drusus and the younger Antonia, after being adopted by his paternal uncle Tiberius, held the quaestorship five years before the legal age and passed directly to the consulship. When the death of Augustus was announced, he was sent to the army in Germany, where it is hard to say whether his filial piety or his courage was more conspicuous; for although all the legions obstinately refused to accept Tiberius as emperor, and offered him the rule of the state, he held them to their allegiance. And later he won a victory over the enemy and celebrated a triumph. Then chosen consul for a second time, before he entered on his term he was hurried off to restore order in the Orient, and after vanquishing the king of Armenia and reducing Cappadocia to the form of a province, died of a lingering illness at Antioch, in the thirty-fourth year of his age. There was some suspicion that he was poisoned; for besides the dark spots which appeared all over his body and the froth which flowed from his mouth, after he had been reduced to ashes his heart was found entire among his bones; and it is supposed to be a characteristic of that organ that when steeped in poison it cannot be destroyed by fire.

2. Now the belief was that he met his death through the wiles of Tiberius, aided and abetted by Gn. Piso. This man had been made governor of Syria at about that time, and realizing that he must give offense either to the father or the son, as if there were no alternative, he never ceased to show the bitterest enmity towards Germanicus in word and deed, even after the latter fell ill. In consequence Piso narrowly escaped being torn to pieces by the people on his return to Rome, and was condemned to death by the senate.

3. It is the general opinion that Germanicus possessed all the highest qualities of body and mind, to a degree never equaled by anyone; a handsome person, unequaled valor, surpassing ability in the oratory and learning of Greece and Rome, unexampled kindliness, and a remarkable desire and capacity for winning men's regard and inspiring their affection. His legs were too slender for the rest of his figure, but he gradually brought them to proper proportions by constant horseback riding after meals. He often slew a foe in

*Suetonius. 1913. *Suetonius*. Vol. 1. Translated by J.C. Rolfe. Loeb Classical Library.

hand-to-hand combat. He pleaded causes even after receiving the triumphal regalia; and among other fruits of his studies he left some Greek comedies. Unassuming at home and abroad, he always entered the free and federate towns without lictors. Wherever he came upon the tombs of distinguished men, he always offered sacrifice to their shades. Planning to bury in one mound the old and scattered relics of those who fell in the overthrow of Varus, he was the first to attempt to collect and assemble them with his own hand. Even towards his detractors, whosoever they were and whatever their motives, he was so mild and lenient, that when Piso was annulling his decrees and maltreating his dependents, he could not make up his mind to break with him, until he found himself assailed also by potions and spells. Even then he went no farther than formally to renounce Piso's friendship in the old-time fashion, and to bid his household avenge him, in case anything should befall him.

4. He reaped plentiful fruit from these virtues, for he was so respected and beloved by his kindred that Augustus (to say nothing of the rest of his relatives) after hesitating for a long time whether to appoint him his successor, had him adopted by Tiberius. He was so popular with the masses, that, according to many writers, whenever he came to any place or left one, he was sometimes in danger of his life from the crowds that met him or saw him off; in fact, when he returned from Germany after quelling the outbreak, all the cohorts of the praetorian guard went forth to meet him, although orders had been given that only two should go, and the whole populace, regardless of age, sex, or rank, poured out of Rome as far as the twentieth milestone.

5. Yet far greater and stronger tokens of regard were shown at the time of his death and immediately afterwards. On the day when he passed away the temples were stoned and the altars of the gods thrown down, while some flung their household gods into the street and cast out their newly born children. Even barbarian peoples, so they say, who were engaged in war with us or with one another, unanimously consented to a truce, as if all in common had suffered a domestic tragedy. It is said that some princes cut off their beards and had their wives' heads shaved, as a token of the deepest mourning; that even the king of kings suspended his exercise at hunting and the banquets with his grandees, which among the Parthians is a sign of public mourning.

6. At Rome when the community, in grief and consternation at the first report of his illness, was awaiting further news, and suddenly after nightfall a report at last spread abroad, on doubtful authority, that he had recovered, a general rush was made from every side to the Capitol with torches and victims, and the temple gates were all but torn off, that nothing might hinder them in their eagerness to pay their vows. Tiberius was roused from sleep by the cries of the rejoicing throng, who all united in singing:

"Safe is Rome, safe too our country, for Germanicus is safe."

But when it was at last made known that he was no more, the public grief could be checked neither by any consolation nor edict, and it continued even during the festal days of the month of December.

The fame of the deceased and regret for his loss were increased by the horror of the times which followed, since all believed, and with good reason, that the cruelty of Tiberius, which soon burst forth, bad been held in check through his respect and awe for Germanicus.

7. He had to wife Agrippina, daughter of Marcus Agrippa and Julia, who bore him nine children. Two of these were taken off when they were still in infancy, and one just as he was reaching the age of boyhood, a charming chill, whose statue, in the guise of Cupid, Livia dedicated in the temple of the Capitoline Venus, while Augustus had another placed in his bed chamber and used to kiss it fondly whenever he entered the room. The other children survived their father, three girls, Agrippina, Drusilla, and Livilla, born in successive years, and three boys, Nero, Drusus, and Gaius Caesar. Nero and Drusus were adjudged public enemies by the senate on the accusation of Tiberius.

8. Gaius Caesar was born the day before the Kalends of September in the consulship of his father and Gaius Fonteius Capito. Conflicting testimony makes his birthplace uncertain. Gn. Lentulus Gaetulicus writes that he was born at Tibur, Pliny among the Treveri, in a village called Ambitarvium north in Gaul. Pliny adds as proof that altars are shown there, inscribed "For the Delivery of Agrippina." Verses which were in circulation soon after he became emperor indicate that he was begotten in the winter-quarters of the legions:

"He who was born in the camp and reared 'mid his country's arms,
Gave at the outset a sign that he was fated to rule."

I myself find in the gazette that he first saw the light at Antium south of Rome. Gaetulicus is shown to be wrong by Pliny, who says that he told a flattering lie, to add some luster to the fame of a young and vainglorious prince from the city sacred to Hercules; and that he lied with the more assurance because Germanicus really did have a son born to him at Tibur, also called Gaius Caesar, of whose lovable disposition and untimely death I have already spoken. Pliny has erred in his chronology; for the historians of Augustus agree that Germanicus was not sent to Germany until the close of his consulship, when Gaius was already born. Moreover, the inscription on the altar adds no strength to Pliny's view, for Agrippina twice gave birth to daughters in that region, and any childbirth, regardless of sex, is called *puerperium*, since the men of old called girls *puerae*, just as called boys *puelli*. Furthermore, we have a letter written by Augustus to his granddaughter Agrippina, a few months before he died, about the Gaius in question (for no other child of the name was still alive at that time), reading as follows: "Yesterday I arranged with Talarius and Asillius to bring your boy Gaius on the fifteenth day before the Kalends of June, if it be the will of the gods. I send with him besides one of my slaves who is a physician, and I have written Germanicus to keep him if he wishes. Farewell, my Agrippina, and take care to come in good health to your Germanicus."

I think it is clear enough that Gaius could not have been born in a place to which he was first taken from Rome when he was nearly two years old. This letter also weakens our confidence in the verses, the more so because they are anonymous. We must then accept the only remaining testimony, that of the public record, particularly since Gaius loved Antium as if it were his native soil, always preferring it to all other places of retreat, and even thinking, it is said, of transferring thither the seat and abode of the empire through weariness of Rome.

9. His surname Caligula he derived from a joke of the troops, because he was brought up in their midst in the dress of a common soldier. To what extent besides he won their love and devotion by being reared in fellowship with them is especially evident from the fact that when they threatened mutiny after the death of Augustus they were ready for any act of madness, the mere sight of Gaius unquestionably calmed them. For they did not become quiet until they saw that he was being spirited away because of the danger from their outbreak and taken for protection to the nearest town. Then at last they became contrite, and laying hold of the carriage and stopping it, begged to be spared the disgrace which was being put upon them.

10. He attended his father also on his expedition to Syria. On his return from there he first lived with his mother and after her banishment, with his great-grandmother Livia; and when Livia died, though he was not yet of age, he spoke her eulogy from the rostra. Then he fell to the care of his grandmother Antonia and in the nineteenth year of his age he was called to Capri by Tiberius, on the same day assuming the gown of manhood and shaving his first beard, but without any such ceremony as had attended the coming of age of his brothers. Although at Capri every kind of wile was resorted to by those who tried to lure him or force him to utter complaints, he never gave them any satisfaction, ignoring the ruin of his kindred as if nothing at all had happened, passing over his own ill-treatment with an incredible presence of indifference, and so obsequious towards his grandfather and his household, that it was well said of him that no one had ever been a better slave or a worse master.

11. Yet even at that time he could not control his natural cruelty and viciousness, but he was a most eager witness of the tortures and executions of those who suffered punishment, reveling at night in gluttony and adultery, disguised in a wig and a long robe, passionately devoted besides to the theatrical arts of dancing and singing, in which Tiberius very willingly indulged him, in the hope that through these his savage nature might be softened. This last was so clearly evident to the shrewd old man, that he used to say now and then that to allow Gaius to live would prove the ruin of himself and of all men, and that he was rearing a viper for the Roman people and a Phaethon for the world.

12. Not so very long afterward Gaius took to wife Junia Claudilla, daughter of Marcus Silanus, a man of noble rank. Then appointed augur in place of his brother Drusus, before he was invested with the office he was advanced to that of pontiff, with strong commendation of his dutiful conduct and general character; for since the court was deserted and deprived of its other supports, after Sejanus had been suspected of hostile designs and presently put out of the way he was little by little encouraged to look forward to succession. To have a better chance of realizing this, after losing Junia in childbirth, he seduced Ennia Naevia, wife of Macro, who at that time commanded the praetorian guard, even promising to marry her if he became emperor, and guaranteeing this promise by an oath and a written contract. Having through her wormed himself into Macro's favor, he poisoned Tiberius, as some think, and ordered that his ring be taken from him while he still breathed, and then suspecting that he was trying to hold fast to it, that a pillow be put over his face; or even strangled the old man with his own hand, immediately ordering the crucifixion of a freedman who cried out at the awful deed. And this is likely enough; for some writers say that Caligula himself later admitted, not, it is true, that he had committed parricide, but that he had at least meditated it at one time; for they say that he constantly boasted, in speaking of his filial piety, that he had entered the bedchamber of the sleeping Tiberius dagger in hand, to avenge the death of his mother and brothers; but that, seized with pity, he threw down the dagger and went out again; and that through Tiberius knew of this, he had never dared to make any inquiry or take any action.

13. By thus gaining the throne he fulfilled the highest hopes of the Roman people, or I may say of all mankind, since he was the prince most earnestly desired by the great part of the provincials and soldiers, many of whom had known him in his infancy, as well as by the whole body of the city populace, because of the memory of his father Germanicus and pity for a family that was all but extinct. Accordingly, when he set out from Misenum, though he was in mourning garb and escorting the body of Tiberius, yet his progress was marked by altars, victims, and blazing torches, and he was met by a dense and joyful throng, who called him besides other propitious names their "star," their "chick," their "babe," and their "nursling."

14. When he entered the city, full and absolute power was at once put into his hands by the unanimous consent of the senate and of the mob, which forced its way into the House, and no attention was paid to the wish of Tiberius, who in his will had named his other grandson, still a boy, joint heir with Caligula. So great was the public rejoicing, that within the next three months, or less than that, more than a hundred and sixty thousand victims are said to have been slain in sacrifice. A few days after this, when he crossed to the islands near Campania, vows were put up for his safe return, while no one let slip even the slightest chance of giving testimony to his anxiety and regard for his safety. But when he fell ill, they all spent the whole night about the Palace; some even vowed to fight as gladiators, and others posted placards offering their lives, if the ailing prince were spared. To this unbounded love of his citizens was added marked devotion from foreigners. Artabanus, for example, king of the Parthians, who was always outspoken in his hatred and contempt for Tiberius, voluntarily sought Caligula's friendship and came to a conference with the consular governor; then crossing the Euphrates, he paid homage to the Roman eagles and to the statues of the Caesars.

15. Gaius himself tried to rouse men's devotion by courting popularity in every way. After eulogizing Tiberius with many tears before the assembled people and giving him a magnificent funeral, he at once posted off to Pandateria and the Pontian islands, to remove the ashes of his mother and brother to Rome; and in stormy weather, too, to make his filial piety the more conspicuous. He approached them with reverence and placed them in the urns with his own hands. With no less theatrical effect he brought them to Ostia in a bireme with a banner set in the stern, and from there up the Tiber to Rome, where he had them carried to the Mausoleum on two biers by the most distinguished men of the order of knights, in the middle of the day, when the streets were crowded. He appointed funeral sacrifices, too, to be offered each year with due ceremony, as well as games in the Circus in honor of his mother, providing a carriage to carry her image in the procession. But in memory of his father he gave to the month of September the name of Germanicus. After this, by a single decree of the senate, he heaped upon his grandmother Antonia whatever honors Livia Augusta had ever enjoyed; took his uncle Claudius, who up to that time had been a Roman knight, as his colleague in the consulship; adopted his brother Tiberius on the day that he assumed the gown of manhood, and gave him the title of Chief of the Youth. He caused the names of his sisters to be included in all oaths: "And I will not hold myself and my children dearer shall I do Gaius and his sisters;" as well as in the propositions of the consuls: "Favor and good fortune attend Gaius Caesar and his sisters."

With the same degree of popularity he recalled those who had been condemned to banishment; took no cognizance of any charges that remained untried from an earlier time; had all documents relating to the cases of his mother and brothers carried to the Forum and burned, to give no informer or witness occasion for further fear, having first loudly called the gods to witness that he had neither read nor touched any of them. He refused a note which was offered him regarding his own safety, maintaining that he had done nothing to make anyone hate him, and that he had no ears for informers.

16. He banished from the city the sexual perverts called, *spintriae*, barely persuaded not to sink them in the sea. The writings of Titus Labienus, Cremutius Cordus, and Cassius Severus, which had been suppressed by decrees of the senate, he allowed to be hunted up, circulated, and read, saying that it was wholly to his interest that everything which happened be handed down to posterity. He published the accounts of the empire, which had regularly been made public by Augustus, a practice discontinued by Tiberius. He allowed the magistrates unrestricted jurisdiction, without appeal to himself. He revised the lists of the Roman knights strictly and scrupulously, yet with due moderation, publicly taking their horses from those guilty of any wicked or scandalous act, but merely omitting to read the names of men convicted of lesser offenses. To lighten the labor of the jurors, he added a fifth division to the previous four. He tried also to restore the suffrage to the people by reviving the custom of elections. He at once paid faithfully and without dispute the legacies named in the will of Tiberius, though this had been set aside, as well as in that of Julia Augusta, which Tiberius had suppressed. He remitted the tax of a two-hundredth on auction sales in Italy; made good to many their losses from fires; and whenever he restored kings to their thrones, he allowed them all the arrears of their taxes and their revenue for the meantime; for example, to Antiochus of Commagene, a hundred million sesterces that had accrued to the Treasury. To make it known that he encouraged every kind of noble action, he gave 800,000 sesterces to a freedwoman, because she had kept silence about the guilt of her patron, though subjected to the utmost torture. Because of these acts, besides other honors, a golden shield was voted him, which was to be borne every year to the Capitol on an appointed day by the colleges of priests, escorted by the senate, while boys and girls of noble birth sang the praises of his virtues in a choral ode. It was also decreed that the day on which he began to reign should be called Parilia, as a sign that the city had been founded a second time.

17. He held four consulships, one from the Kalends of July for two months, a second from the Kalends of January for thirty days, a third up to the Ides of January, and the fourth until the seventh day before the Ides of the same month. Of all these only the last two were continuous. The third he assumed at Lugdunum without a colleague, not, as some think, through arrogance or disregard of precedent, but because at that distance from Rome he had been unable to get news of the death of the other consul just before the day of the Kalends. He twice gave the people a bonus of three hundred sesterces each, and twice a lavish banquet to the senate and the equestrian order, together with their wives and children. At the former of these he also distributed togas to the men, and to the women and children scarves of red and scarlet. Furthermore, to make a permanent addition to the public gaiety, he added a day to the Saturnalia, and called it *Juvenalis.*

18. He gave several gladiatorial shows, some in the amphitheater of Taurus and some in the Saepta, in which he introduced pairs of African and Campanian boxers, the pick of both regions. He did not always preside at the games in person, but sometimes assigned the honor to the magistrates or to friends. He exhibited stage-plays continually, of various kinds and in many different places, some times even by night, lighting up the whole city. He also threw about gifts of various kinds, and gave each man a basket of victuals. During the feasting he sent his share to a Roman knight opposite him, who was eating with evident relish and appetite, while to a senator for the same reason he gave a commission naming him praetor out of the regular order. He also gave many games in the Circus, lasting from early morning until evening, introducing between the races now a baiting of panthers and now the "Trojan game;" some, too, of special splendor, in which the Circus was strewn with red and green, while the charioteers were all men of senatorial rank. He also started some games off-hand, when a few people called for them from the neighboring balconies, as he was inspecting the outfit of the Circus from the Gelotian house.

19. Besides this, he devised a novel and unheard of kind of pageant; for he bridged the gap between Baiae and the mole at Puteoli, a distance of about thirty-six hundred paces, by bringing together merchant ships from all sides and anchoring them in a double line, after which a mound of earth was heaped upon them and fashioned in the manner of the Appian Way. Over this bridge he rode back and forth for two successive days, the first day on a caparisoned horse, himself resplendent in a crown of oak leaves, a buckler, a sword, and a cloak of cloth of gold; on the second, dressed as a charioteer in a car drawn by a pair of famous horses, carrying before him a boy named Dareus, a hostage from Parthia, and attended by the entire praetorian guard and a company of his friends in Gallic chariots. I know that many have supposed that Gaius devised this kind of bridge in rivalry of Xerxes, who excited no little admiration by bridging the much narrower Hellespont; others, that it was to inspire fear in Germany and Britain, on which he had designs, by the fame of some stupendous work. But when I was a boy, I used to hear my grandfather say that the reason for the work, as revealed by the emperor's confidential courtiers, was that Thrasyllus the astrologer had declared to Tiberius, when he was worried about his successor and inclined towards his natural grandson, that Gaius had no more chance of becoming emperor than of riding about over the gulf of Baiae with horses.

20. He also gave shows in foreign lands, Athenian games at Syracuse in Sicily, and miscellaneous games at Lugdunum in Gaul; at the latter place also a contest in Greek and Latin oratory, in which, they say, the losers gave prizes to the victors and were forced to compose eulogies upon them, while those who were least successful were ordered to erase their writings with a sponge or with their tongue, unless they elected rather to be beaten with rods or thrown into the neighboring river.

21. He completed the public works which had been half finished under Tiberius: the temple of Augustus and the theater of Pompey. He likewise began an aqueduct in the region near Tibur and an amphitheater beside the Saepta, the former finished by his successor Claudius, while the latter was abandoned. At Syracuse he repaired the city walls, which had fallen into ruin through lapse of time, and the temples of the gods. He had planned, besides, to rebuild the palace of Polycrates at Samos, to finish the temple of Didymaean Apollo at Ephesus, to found a city high up in the Alps, but, above all, to dig a canal through the Isthmus in Greece, and he had already sent a chief centurion to survey the work.

22. So much for Caligula as emperor; we must now tell of his career as a monster. After he had assumed various surnames (for he was called "Pious," "Child of the Camp," "Father of the Armies," and "Greatest and Best of Caesars"), chancing to overhear some kings, who had come to Rome to pay their respects to him, disputing at dinner about the nobility of their descent, he cried: "Let there be one Lord, one King!" And he came near assuming a crown at once and changing the semblance of a principate into the form of a monarchy. But on being reminded that he had risen above the elevation both of princes and kings, he began from that time on to lay claim to divine majesty; for after giving orders that such statues of the gods as were especially famous for their sanctity or their artistic merit, including that of Jupiter of Olympia, should be brought from Greece, in order to remove their beads and put his own in their place, he built out a part of the Palace as far as the Forum, and making the temple of Castor and Pollux its vestibule, he often took his place between the divine brethren, and exhibited himself there to be worshipped by those who presented themselves; and some hailed him as Jupiter Latiaris. He also set up a special temple to his own godhead, with priests and with victims of the choicest kind. In this temple was a life-sized statue of the emperor in gold, which was dressed each day in clothing such as he wore himself. The richest citizens used all their influence to secure the priesthoods of his cult and bid high for the honor. The victims were flamingoes, peacocks, black grouse, guinea-hens and pheasants, offered daily each after its own kind. At night he used constantly to invite the full and radiant

moon to his embraces and his bed, while in the daytime he would talk confidentially with Jupiter Capitolinus, now whispering and then in turn putting
his ear to the mouth of the god, now in louder and even angry language; for
he was heard to make the threat: "Lift me up, or I'll lift thee." But finally won
by entreaties, as he reported, and even invited to live with the god, he built a
bridge over the temple of the Deified Augustus, and thus joined his Palace to
the Capitol. Presently, to be nearer yet, he laid the foundations of a new
house in the court of the Capitol.

23. He did not wish to be thought the grandson of Agrippa, or called so,
because of the latter's humble origin; and he grew very angry if anyone in a
speech or a song included Agrippa among the ancestors of the Caesars. He
even boasted that his own mother was born in incest, which Augustus had
committed with his daughter Julia; and not content with this slur on the
memory of Augustus, he forbade the celebration of his victories at Actium
and off Sicily by annual festivals, on the ground that they were disastrous and
ruinous to the Roman people. He often called his great-grandmother Livia
Augusta "a Ulysses in petticoats," and he had the audacity to accuse her of
low birth in a letter to the senate, alleging that her maternal grandfather had
been nothing but a decurion of Fundi; whereas it is proved by public records
that Aufidius Lurco held high offices at Rome. When his grandmother Antonia asked for a private interview, he refused it except in the presence of the
prefect Macro, and by such indignities and annoyances he caused her death;
although some think that he also gave her poison. After she was dead, he paid
her no honor, but viewed her burning pyre from his dining-room. He had his
brother Tiberius put to death without warning, suddenly sending a tribune
of the soldiers to do the deed; besides driving his father-in-law Silanus to end
his life by cutting his throat with a razor. His charge against the latter was
that Silanus had not followed him when he put to sea in stormy weather, but
had remained behind in the hope of taking possession of the city in case he
should be lost in the storm; against Tiberius, that his breath smelled of an
antidote, which he had taken to guard against being poisoned at his hand.
Now as a matter of fact, Silanus was subject to sea-sickness and wished to
avoid the discomforts of the voyage, while Tiberius had taken medicine for a
chronic cough, which was growing worse. As for his uncle Claudius, he
spared him merely as a laughing-stock.

24. He lived in habitual incest with all his sisters, and at a large banquet
he placed each of them in turn below him, while his wife reclined above. Of
these he is believed to have violated Drusilla when he was still a minor, and
even to have been caught lying with her by his grandmother Antonia, at
whose house they were brought up in company. Afterwards, when she was
the wife of Lucius Cassius Longinus, an ex-consul, he took her from him and
openly treated her as his lawful wife; and when ill, he made her heir to his

property and the throne. When she died, he appointed a season of public mourning, during which it was a capital offense to laugh, bathe, or dine in company with one's parents, wife, or children. He was so beside himself with grief that suddenly fleeing the city by night and traversing Campania, he went to Syracuse and hurriedly returned from there without cutting his hair or shaving his beard. And he never afterwards took oath about matters of the highest moment, even before the assembly of the people or in the presence of the soldiers, except by the godhead of Drusilla. The rest of his sisters he did not love with so great affection, nor honor so highly, but often prostituted them to his favorites: so that he was the readier at the trial of Aemilius Lepidus to condemn them, as adulteresses and privy to the conspiracies against him; and he not only made public letters in the handwriting of all of them, procured by fraud and seduction, but also dedicated to Mars the Avenger, with an explanatory inscription, three swords designed to take his life.

25. It is not easy to decide whether he acted more basely in contracting his marriages, in annulling them, or as a husband. At the marriage of Livia Orestilla to Gaius Piso, he attended the ceremony himself, gave orders that the bride be taken to his own house, and within a few days divorced her; two years later he banished her, because of a suspicion that in the meantime she had gone back to her former husband. Others write that being invited to the wedding banquet, he sent word to Piso, who reclined opposite to him: "Don't take liberties with my wife," and at once carried her off with him from the table, the next day issuing a proclamation that he had got himself a wife in the manner of Romulus and Augustus. When the statement was made that the grandmother of Lollia Paulina, who was married to Gaius Memmius, an ex-consul commanding armies, had once been a remarkably beautiful woman, he suddenly called Lollia from the province, separated her from her husband, and married her; then in a short time he put her away, with the command never to have intercourse with anyone. Though Caesonia was neither beautiful nor young, and was already mother of three daughters by another, besides being a woman of reckless extravagance and wantonness, he loved her not only more passionately but more faithfully, often exhibiting her to the soldiers riding by his side, decked with cloak, helmet and shield, and to his friends even in a state of nudity. He did not honor her with the title of wife until she had borne him a child, announcing on the selfsame day that he had married her and that he was the father of her babe. This babe, whom he named Julia Drusilla, he carried to the temples of all the goddesses, finally placing her in the lap of Minerva and commending to her the child's nurture and training. And no evidence convinced him so positively that she was sprung from his own loins as her savage temper, which was even then so violent that she would try to scratch the faces and eyes of the little children who played with her.

26. It would be trivial and pointless to add to this an account of his treatment of his relatives and friends, Ptolemy, son of king Juba, his cousin (for he was the grandson of Mark Antony by Antony's daughter Selene), and in particular Macro himself and even Ennia, who helped him to the throne; all these were rewarded for their kinship and their faithful services by a bloody death. He was no whit more respectful or mild towards the senate, allowing some who had held the highest offices to run in their togas for several miles beside his chariot and to wait on him at table, standing napkin in hand either at the head of his couch, or at his feet. Others he secretly put to death, yet continued to send for them as if they were alive, after a few days falsely asserting that they had committed suicide. When the consuls forgot to make proclamation of his birthday, he deposed them, and left the state for three days without its highest magistrates. He flogged his quaestor, who was charged with conspiracy, stripping off the man's clothes and spreading them under the soldiers' feet, to give them a firm footing as they beat him.

He treated the other orders with like insolence and cruelty. Being disturbed by the noise made by those who came in the middle of the night to secure the free seats in the Circus, he drove them all out with cudgels; in the confusion more than twenty Roman knights were crushed to death, with as many matrons and a countless number of others. At the plays in the theater, sowing discord between the commons and the knights, he scattered the gift tickets ahead of time, to induce the rabble to take the seats reserved for the equestrian order. At a gladiatorial show he would sometimes draw back the awnings when the sun was hottest and give orders that no one be allowed to leave; then removing the usual equipment, he would match worthless and decrepit gladiators against mangy wild beasts, and have sham fights between householders who were of good repute, but conspicuous for some bodily infirmity. Sometimes too he would shut up the granaries and condemn the people to hunger.

27. The following are special instances of his innate brutality. When cattle to feed the wild beasts which he had provided for a gladiatorial show were rather costly, he selected criminals to be devoured, and reviewing the line of prisoners without examining the charges, but merely taking his place in the middle of a colonnade, he bade them be led away "from baldhead to baldhead." A man who had made a vow to fight in the arena, if the emperor recovered, he compelled to keep his word, watched him as he fought sword in hand, and would not let him go until he was victorious, and then only after many entreaties. Another who had offered his life for the same reason, but delayed to kill himself, he turned over to his slaves, with orders to drive him through the streets decked with sacred boughs and fillets, calling for the fulfillment of his vow, and finally hurl him from the embankment. Many men of honorable rank were first disfigured with the marks of branding-irons and then condemned to the mines, to work at building roads, or to be thrown to the wild beasts; or else he shut them up in cages on all fours, like animals, or had them sawed asunder. Not all these punishments were for serious offenses, but merely for criticizing one of his shows, or for never having sworn by his Genius. He forced parents to attend the executions of their sons, sending a litter for one man who pleaded ill health, and inviting another to dinner immediately after witnessing the death, and trying to rouse him to gaiety and jesting by a great show of affability. He had the manager of his gladiatorial shows and beast-battings beaten with chains in his presence for several successive days, and would not kill him until he was disgusted at the stench of his putrefied brain. He burned a writer of Atellan farces alive in the middle of the arena of the amphitheater, because of a humorous line of double meaning. When a Roman knight on being thrown to the wild beasts loudly protested his innocence, he took him out, cut off his tongue, and put him back again.

28. Having asked a man who had been recalled from an exile of long standing, how in the world he spent his time there, the man replied by way of flattery: "I constantly prayed the gods for what has come to pass, that Tiberius might die and you become emperor." Thereupon Caligula, thinking that his exiles were likewise praying for his death, sent emissaries from island to island to butcher them all. Wishing to have one of the senators torn to pieces, he induced some of the members to assail him suddenly, on his entrance into the House, with the charge of being a public enemy, to stab him with their styles, and turn him over to the rest to be mangled; and his cruelty was not sated until he saw the man's limbs, members, and bowels dragged through the streets and heaped up before him.

29. He added to the enormity of his crimes by the brutality of his language. He used to say that there was nothing in his own character which he admired and approved more highly than what he called, in Greek, his "shameless impudence." When his grandmother Antonia gave him some advice, he was not satisfied merely not to listen but replied: "Remember that I have the right to do anything to anybody." When he was on the point of killing his brother, and suspected that he had taken drugs as a precaution against poison, he cried: "What! an antidote against Caesar?" After banishing his sisters, he made the threat that he not only had islands, but swords as well. An ex-praetor who had retired to Anticyra for his health, sent frequent requests for an extension of his leave, but Caligula had him put to death, adding that a man who had not been helped by so long a course of hellebore needed to be bled. On signing the list of prisoners who were to be put to death later, he said that he was clearing his accounts. Having condemned several Gauls and Greeks to death in a body, he boasted that he had subdued Gallograecia.

30. He seldom had anyone put to death except by numerous slight wounds, his constant order, which soon became well-known, being: "Strike so that he may feel that he is dying." When a different man than he had intended had been killed, through a mistake in the names, he said that the victim too had deserved the same fate. He often uttered the familiar line of the tragic poet: "Let them hate me, as long as they fear me." He often inveighed against all the senators alike, as adherents of Sejanus and informers against his mother and brothers, producing the documents which he pretended to have burned, and upholding the cruelty of Tiberius as forced upon him, since he could not but believe so many accusers. He constantly tongue-lashed the equestrian order as devotees of the stage and the arena. Angered at the rabble for applauding a faction which he opposed, he cried: "I wish the Roman people had but a single neck," and when the brigand Tetrinius was demanded, he said that those who asked for him were Tetriniuses also. Once a band of five net-fighters[1] in tunics, matched against the same number of swordsmen, yielded without a struggle; but when their death was ordered, one of them caught up his trident and slew all the victors. Caligula bewailed this in a public proclamation as a most cruel murder, and expressed his horror of those who had had the heart to witness it.

31. He even used openly to deplore the state of his times, because they had been marked by no public disasters, saying that the rule of Augustus had been made famous by the Varus massacre, and that of Tiberius by the collapse of the amphitheater at Fidenae, while his own was threatened with oblivion because of its prosperity; and every now and then he wished for the destruction of his armies, for famine, pestilence, fires, or a great earthquake.

32. His acts and words were equally cruel, even when he was indulging in relaxation and given up to amusement and feasting. While he was lunching or reveling capital examinations by torture were often made in his presence, and a soldier who was an adept at decapitation cut off the heads of those who were brought from prison. At Puteoli, at the dedication of the bridge that he contrived, as has been said, after inviting a number to come to him from the shore, on a sudden he had them all thrown overboard; and when some caught hold of the rudders of the ships, he pushed them off into the sea with boathooks and oars. At a public banquet in Rome he immediately handed a slave over to the executioners for stealing a strip of silver from the couches, with orders that his hands be cut off and hung from his neck upon his breast, and that he then be led about among the guests, preceded by a placard giving the reason for his punishment. When a gladiator fought with him with wooden swords and fell on purpose, he stabbed him with a real

---

[1] Gladiators, armed with nets for trapping and trident-spears, were often matched against other gladiators with swords.

dagger and then ran about with a palm-branch, as victors do. Once when he stood by the altar dressed as a priest, and a victim was brought up, he raised his mallet on high and slew the knife-bearer instead. At one of his more sumptuous banquets he suddenly burst into a fit of laughter, and when the consuls, who were reclining next him, politely inquired at what he was laughing, he replied: "What do you suppose, except that at a single nod of mine both of you could have your throats cut on the spot."

33. As a sample of his humor, he took his place beside a statue of Jupiter, and asked the tragic actor which of the two seemed to him the greater, and when he hesitated, Caligula had him flayed with whips, extolling his voice from time to time, when the wretch begged for mercy, as passing sweet even in his groans. Whenever he kissed the neck of his wife or sweetheart, he would say: "Off comes this beautiful head whenever I give the word." He even used to threaten now and then that he would resort to torture if necessary, to find out from his dear Caesonia why he loved her so passionately.

34. He assailed mankind of almost every epoch with no less envy and malice than insolence and cruelty. He threw down the statues of famous men, which for lack of room Augustus had moved from the court of the Capitol to the Campus Martius, and so utterly demolished them that they could not be set up again with their inscriptions entire; and thereafter he forbade the erection of the statue of any living man anywhere, without his knowledge and consent. He even thought of destroying the poems of Homer, asking why he should not have the same privilege as Plato, who excluded Homer from his ideal commonwealth. More than that, he all but removed the writings and the busts of Vergil and of Livy from all the libraries, railing at the former as a man of no talent and very little learning, and the latter as a verbose and careless historian. With regard to lawyers too, as if intending to do away with any practice of their profession, he often threatened that he would see to it, by Heaven, that they could give no advice contrary to his wish.

35. He took from all the noblest of the city, the ancient devices of their families, from Torquatus his collar, from Cincinnatus his lock of hair, from Gn. Pompeius the surname Great belonging to his ancient race. After inviting Ptolemy, whom I have mentioned before, to come from his kingdom and receiving him with honor, he suddenly had him executed for no other reason than that when giving a gladiatorial show, he noticed that Ptolemy on entering the theater attracted general attention by the splendor of his purple cloak. Whenever he ran across handsome men with fine heads of hair, he disfigured them by having the backs of their heads shaved. There was a certain Aesius Proculus, son of a chief centurion, called Colosseros because of his remarkable size and handsome appearance; this man Caligula ordered to be suddenly dragged from his seat in the amphitheater and led into the arena, where he matched him first against a Thracian and then against a heavy-armed gladiator; when Proculus was victor in both contests, Caligula gave orders that he be bound at once, clad in rags, and then put to death, after first being led about the streets and exhibited to the women. In short, there was no one of such low condition or such abject fortune that he did not envy him such advantages as he possessed. Since the king of Nemi had not held his priesthood for many years, he hired a stronger adversary to attack him. When an charioteer-gladiator called Porius was vigorously applauded on the day of one of the games for setting his slave free after a victory, Caligula rushed from the amphitheater in such haste that he trod on the fringe of his toga and went headlong down the steps, fuming and shouting: "The people that rule the world give more honor to a gladiator for a trifling act than to their deified emperors or to the one still present with them."

36. He respected neither his own chastity nor that of anyone else. He is said to have had unnatural relations with Marcus Lepidus, the pantomimic actor Mnester, and certain hostages. Valerius Catullus, a young man of a consular family, publicly proclaimed that he had violated the emperor and worn himself out in commerce with him. To say nothing of his incest with his sisters and his notorious passion for the concubine Pyrallis, there was scarcely any woman of rank whom he did not approach. These as a rule he invited to dinner with their husbands, and as they passed by the foot of his couch, he would inspect them critically and deliberately, as if buying slaves, even putting out his hand and lifting up the face of anyone who looked down in modesty; then as often as the fancy took him he would leave the room, sending for the one who pleased him best, and returning soon afterward with evident signs of what had occurred, he would openly commend or criticize his partner, recounting her charms or defects and commenting on her conduct. To some he personally sent a bill of divorce in the name of their absent husbands, and had it entered in the public records.

37. In reckless extravagance he outdid the prodigals of all times in ingenuity, inventing a new sort of baths and unnatural varieties of food and feasts; for he would bathe in hot or cold perfumed oils, drink pearls of great price dissolved in vinegar, and set before his guests loaves and meats of gold, declaring that a man ought either to be frugal or Caesar. He even scattered large sums of money among the commons from the roof of the basilica Julia for several days in succession. He also built Liburnian galleys with ten banks of oars, until sterns set with gems, parti-colored sails, huge spacious baths, colonnades, and banquet-halls, and even a great variety of vines and fruit trees; that on board of them he might recline at table from an early hour, and coast along the shores of Campania amid songs and choruses. He built villas and country houses with utter disregard of expense, caring for nothing so much as to do what men said was impossible. So he built moles out into the deep and stormy sea, tunneled rocks of hardest flint, built up plains to the height of mountains and razed mountains to the level of the plain; all with incredible dispatch, since the penalty for delay was death. To make a long story short, vast sums of money, including the 2,700,000,000 sesterces which Tiberius Caesar had amassed, were squandered by him in less than the revolution of a year.

38. Having thus impoverished himself, from very need he turned his attention to pillage through a complicated and cunningly devised system of false accusations, auction sales, and imposts. He ruled that Roman citizenship could not lawfully be enjoyed by those whose forefathers had obtained it for themselves and their descendants, except in the case of sons, since "descendants" ought not to be understood as going beyond that degree; and when certificates of the deified Julius and Augustus were presented to him, he waved them aside as old and out of date. He also charged that those estates had been falsely returned, to which any addition had later been made from any cause whatever. If any chief centurions since the beginning of Tiberius' reign had not named that emperor or himself among their heirs, he set aside their wills on the ground of ingratitude; also the testaments of all others, as null and void, if anyone said that they had intended to make Caesar their heir when they died. When he had roused such fear in this way that he came to be named openly as heir by strangers among their intimates and by parents among their children, he accused them of making game of him by continuing to live after such a declaration, and to many of them he sent poisoned dainties. He used further to conduct the trial of such cases in person, naming in advance the sum which he proposed to raise at each sitting, and not rising until it was made up. Impatient of the slightest delay, he once condemned in a single sentence more than forty who were accused on different counts, boasting to Caesonia, when she woke after a nap, of the great amount of business he had done while she was taking her siesta.

Appointing an auction, he put up and sold what was left from all the shows, personally soliciting bids and running them up so high, that some who were forced to buy articles at an enormous price and were thus stripped of their possessions, opened their veins. A well-known incident is that of Aponius Saturninus; he fell asleep on one of the benches, and as the auctioneer was warned by Gaius not to overlook the praetorian gentlemen who kept nodding to him, the bidding was not stopped until thirteen gladiators were knocked down to the unconscious sleeper at nine million sesterces.

39. When he was in Gaul and had sold at immense figures the jewels, furniture, slaves and even the freedmen of his sisters who had been condemned to death, finding the business so profitable, he sent to the city for all the paraphernalia of the old palace, seizing for its transportation even public carriages and animals from the bakeries; with the result that bread was often scarce at Rome and many who had cases in court lost them from inability to appear and meet their bail. To get rid of this furniture, he resorted to every kind of trickery and wheedling, now railing at the bidders for avarice and because they were not ashamed to be richer than he, and now feigning regret for allowing common men to acquire the property of princes. Having learned that a rich provincial had paid those who issued the emperor's invitations two hundred thousand sesterces, to be smuggled in among the guests at one of his dinner-parties, he was not in the least displeased that the honor of dining with him was rated so high; but when next day the man appeared at his auction, he sent a messenger to hand him some trifle or other at the price of two hundred thousand sesterces and say that he should dine with Caesar on his personal invitation.

40. He levied new and unheard of taxes, at first through the publicans and then, because their profit was so great, through the centurions and tribunes of the praetorian guard; and there was no class of commodities or men on which he did not impose some form of tariff: on all eatables sold in any of the city he levied a fixed and definite charge, on lawsuits and legal processes begun anywhere, a fortieth part of the sum involved, providing a penalty in case anyone was found guilty of compromising or abandoning a suit; on the daily wages of porters, an eighth; on the earnings of prostitutes, as much as each received for one embrace; and a clause was added to this chapter of the law, providing that those who had ever been prostitutes or acted as panders should be liable to this public tax, and that even matrimony should not be exempt.

41. When taxes of this kind had been proclaimed, but not published in writing, inasmuch as many offenses were committed through ignorance of the letter of the law, he at last, on the urgent demand of the people, had the law posted up, but in a very narrow place and in excessively small letters, to prevent the making of a copy. To leave no kind of plunder untried, he opened a brothel in his palace, setting apart a number of rooms and furnishing them to suit the grandeur of the place, where matrons and freeborn youths should stand exposed. Then he sent his pages all about the fora and basilicas, to invite young men and old to enjoy themselves, lending money on interest to those who came and having clerks openly take down their names, as contributors to Caesar's revenues. He did not even disdain to make money from play, and to increase his gains by falsehood and even by perjury. Having on one occasion given up his place to the player next him and gone into the courtyard, he spied two wealthy Roman knights passing by; he ordered them to be seized at once and their property confiscated and came back exultant, boasting that he had never played in better luck.

42. But when his daughter was born, complaining of his narrow means, and no longer merely of the burdens of a ruler but of those of a father as

well, he took up contributions for the girl's maintenance and dowry. He also made proclamation that he would receive New Year's gifts and on the Kalends of January took his place in the entrance to the Palace, to clutch the coins which a throng of people of all classes showered on him by handfuls and lapfuls. Finally, seized with a mania for feeling the touch of money, he would often pour out huge piles of goldpieces in some open place, walk over them barefooted, and wallow in them for a long time with his whole body.

43. He had but one experience with military affairs or war, and then on a sudden impulse; for having gone to Mevania to visit the river Clitumnus and its grove, he was reminded of the necessity of recruiting his body-guard of Batavians and was seized with the idea of an expedition to Germany. So without delay he assembled legions and auxiliaries from all quarters, holding levies everywhere with the utmost strictness, and collecting provisions of every kind on an unheard of scale. Then he began his march and made it now so hurriedly and rapidly, that the praetorian cohorts were forced, contrary to all precedent, to lay their standards on the pack-animals and thus to follow him; again he was so lazy and luxurious that he was carried in a litter by eight bearers, requiring the inhabitants of the towns through which he passed to sweep the roads for him and sprinkle them to lay the dust.

44. On reaching his camp, to show his vigilance and strictness as a commander, he dismissed in disgrace the generals who were late in bringing in the auxiliaries from various places, and in reviewing his troops he deprived many of the chief centurions who were well on in years of their rank, in some cases only a few days before they would have served their time, giving as a reason their age and infirmity; then railing at the rest for their avarice, he reduced the rewards given on completion of full military service to six thousand sesterces.

All that he accomplished was to receive the surrender of Adminius, son of Cynobellinus king of the Britons, who had been banished by his father and had deserted to the Romans with a small force; yet as if the entire island had submitted to him, he sent a grandiloquent letter to Rome, commanding the couriers who carried it to ride in their post-chaise all the way to the Forum and the House, and not to deliver it to anyone except the consuls, in the temple of Mars the Avenger, before a full meeting of the senate.

45. Presently, finding no one to fight with, he had a few Germans of his body-guard taken across the river and concealed there, and word brought him after luncheon with great bustle and confusion that the enemy were close at hand. Upon this he rushed out with his friends and a part of the praetorian cavalry to the woods close by, and after cutting the branches from some trees and adorning them like trophies, he returned by torchlight, taunting those who had not followed him as timorous and cowardly, and presenting his companions and the partners in his victory with crowns of a new kind

and of a new name, ornamented with figures of the sun, moon and stars, and called *exploratoriae*. Another time some hostages were taken from a common school and secretly sent on ahead of him, when he suddenly left a banquet and pursued them with the cavalry as if they were runaways, caught them, and brought them back in fetters, in this farce too showing immoderate extravagance. On coming back to the table, when some announced that the army was assembled, he urged them to take their places just as they were, in their coats of mail. He also admonished them in the familiar line of Vergil to "bear up and save themselves for better days."

Meanwhile he rebuked the absent senate and people in a stern edict because "while Caesar was fighting and exposed to such dangers they were indulging in revels and frequenting the theaters and their pleasant villas."

46. Finally, as if he intended to bring the war to an end, he drew up a line of battle on the shore of the Ocean, arranging his ballistas and other artillery; and when no one knew or could imagine what he was going to do, he suddenly bade them gather shells and fill their helmets and the folds of their gowns, calling them "spoils from the Ocean, due to the Capitol and Palatine." As a monument of his Victory he erected a lofty tower, from which lights were to shine at night to guide the course of ships, as from the Pharos. Then promising the soldiers a gratuity of a hundred denarii each, as if he had shown unprecedented liberality, he said, "Go your way happy; go your way rich."

47. Then turning his attention to his triumph, in addition to a few captives and deserters from the barbarians he chose all the tallest of the Gauls, and as he expressed it, those who were "worthy of a triumph," as well as some of the chiefs. These he reserved for his parade, compelling them not only to dye their hair red and to let it grow long, but also to learn the language of the Germans and assume barbarian names. He also had the triremes in which he had entered the Ocean carried overland to Rome for the greater part of the way. He wrote besides to his financial agents to prepare for a triumph at the smallest possible cost, but on a grander scale than had ever before been known, since the goods of all were at their disposal.

48. Before leaving the province he formed a design of unspeakable cruelty, that of butchering the legions that had begun the mutiny years before just after the death of Augustus, because they had beleaguered his father Germanicus, their leader, and himself, at the time an infant; and though he was with difficulty turned from this mad purpose, he could by no means be prevented from persisting in his desire to decimate them. Accordingly he summoned them to an assembly without their arms, not even wearing their swords, and surrounded them with armed horsemen. But seeing that some of the legionaries, suspecting his purpose, were stealing off to resume their arms, in case any violence should be offered them, he fled from the assembly and set out for the city in a hurry, turning all his ferocity upon the senate, against which he uttered open threats, in order to divert the gossip about his own dishonor. He complained among other things that he had been cheated of his fairly earned triumph; whereas a short time before he had himself given orders that on pain of death no action should be taken about his honors.

49. Therefore when he was met on the road by envoys from that distinguished body, begging him to hasten his return, he roared, "I will come, and this will be with me," frequently smiting the hilt of the sword which he wore at his side. He also made proclamation that he was returning, but only to those who desired his presence, the equestrian order and the people, for to the senate he would never more be fellow-citizen nor prince. He even forbade anyone of the senators to meet him. Then giving up or postponing his triumph, he entered the city on his birthday in an ovation; and within four months he perished, having dared great crimes and meditating still greater ones. For he had made up his mind to move to Antium, and later to Alexandria, after first slaying the noblest members of the two orders. That no one may doubt this, let me say that among his private papers two notebooks were found with different titles, one called "The Sword" and the other "The Dagger," and both containing the names and marks of identification of those whom he had doomed to death. There was found besides a great chest full of divers kinds of poisons, which they say were later thrown into the sea by Claudius and so infected it as to kill the fish, which were thrown up by the tide upon the neighboring shores.

50. He was very tall and extremely pale, with an unshapely body, but very thin neck and legs. His eyes and temples were hollow, his forehead broad and grim, his hair thin and entirely gone on the top of his head, though his body was hairy. Because of this to look upon him from a higher place as he passed by, or for any reason whatever to mention a goat, was treated as a capital offense. While his face was naturally forbidding and ugly, he purposely made it even more savage, practicing all kinds of terrible and fearsome expressions before a mirror.

He was sound neither of body nor mind. As a boy he was troubled with the falling sickness, and while in his youth he had some endurance, yet at times because of sudden faintness he was hardly able to walk, to stand up, to collect his thoughts, or to hold up his head. He himself realized his mental infirmity, and thought at times of going into retirement and clearing his brain. It is thought that his wife Caesonia gave him a drug intended for a love potion, which however had the effect of driving him mad. He was especially tormented with sleeplessness; for he never rested more than three hours at night, and even for that length of time he did not sleep quietly, but was terrified by strange apparitions, once for example dreaming that the spirit of the

Ocean talked with him. Therefore weary of lying in bed wide awake during the greater part of the night, he would now sit upon his couch, and now wander through the long colonnades, crying out from time to time for daylight and longing for its coming.

51. I think I may fairly attribute to mental weakness the existence of two exactly opposite faults in the same person, extreme assurance and, on the other hand, excessive timorousness. For this man, who so utterly despised the gods, was wont at the slightest thunder and lightning to shut his eyes, to muffle up his head, and if they increased, to leap from his bed and hide under it. In his journey through Sicily, though he made all manner of full of the miracles in various places, he suddenly fled from Messana by night, panic-stricken by the smoke and roaring from Etna's crater. Full of threats as he was also against the barbarians, when he was riding in a chariot through a narrow defile on the far side of the Rhine, and someone said that there would be no slight panic if the enemy should appear anywhere, he immediately mounted a horse and hastily returned to the bridges. Finding them crowded with camp servants and baggage, in his impatience of any delay he was passed along from hand to hand over the men's heads. Soon after, hearing of an uprising in Germany, he made preparations to flee from the city and equipped fleets for the purpose, finding comfort only in the thought that the provinces across the sea would at any rate be left him, in case the enemy should be victorious and take possession of the summits of the Alps, as the Cimbri, or even of the city, as the Senones had once done. And it was this, I think, that later inspired his assassins with the idea of pretending to the riotous soldiers that he had laid hands on himself in terror at the report of a defeat.

52. In his clothing, his shoes, and the rest of his attire he did not follow the usage of his country and his fellow-citizens; not always even that of his sex; or in fact, that of an ordinary mortal. He often appeared in public in embroidered cloaks covered with precious stones, with a long-sleeved tunic and bracelets; sometimes in silk and in a woman's robe; now in slippers or buskins, again in boots, such as the emperor's body-guard wear, and at times in the low shoes which are used by females. But oftentimes he exhibited himself with a golden beard, holding in his hand a thunderbolt, a trident, or a caduceus, emblems of the gods, and even in the garb of Venus. He frequently wore the dress of a triumphing general, even before his campaign, and sometimes the breastplate of Alexander the Great, which he had taken from his sarcophagus.

53. As regards liberal studies, he gave little attention to literature but a great deal to oratory, and he was as ready of speech and eloquent as you please, especially if he had occasion to make a charge against anyone. For when he was angry, he had an abundant flow of words and thoughts, and his voice and delivery were such that for very excitement he could not stand still and he was clearly heard by those at a distance. When about to begin an harangue, he threatened to draw the sword of his nightly labors, and he had such scorn of a polished and elegant style that he used to say that Seneca, who was very popular just then, composed "mere school exercises," and that he was "sand without lime." He had the habit too of writing replies to the successful pleas of orators and composing accusations and defenses of important personages who were brought to trial before the senate; and according as his pen had run most easily, he brought ruin or relief to each of them by his speech, while he would also invite the equestrian order by proclamation to come in and hear him.

54. Moreover he devoted himself with much enthusiasm to arts of other kinds and of great variety, appearing as a Thracian gladiator, as a charioteer, and even as a singer and dancer, fighting with the weapons of actual warfare, and driving in circuses built in various places; so carried away by his interest in singing and dancing that even at the public performances he could not refrain from singing with the tragic actor as he delivered his lines, or from openly imitating his gestures by way of praise or correction. Indeed, on the day when he was slain he seems to have ordered an all-night vigil for the sole purpose of taking advantage of the license of the occasion to make his first appearance on the stage. Sometimes he danced even at night, and once he summoned three consulars to the Palace at the close of the second watch, and when they arrived in great and deathly fear, he seated them on a stage and then of a sudden burst out with a great din of flutes and clogs, dressed in a cloak and a tunic reaching to his heels, and after dancing a number went off again. And yet varied as were his accomplishments, the man could not swim.

55. Toward those to whom he was devoted his partiality became madness. He used to kiss Mnester, an actor of pantomimes, even in the theater, and if anyone made even the slightest sound while his favorite was dancing, he had him dragged from is seat and scourged him with his own hand. When a Roman knight created a disturbance, he sent a centurion to bid him go without delay to Ostia and carry a message for him to King Ptolemy in Mauretania; and its purport was this: "Do neither good nor ill to the man whom I have sent you." He gave some Thracian gladiators command of his German body-guard. He reduced the amount of armor of other gladiators. When a certain Columbus had won a victory, but had suffered a slight wound, he had the place rubbed with a poison which he henceforth called "Columbinum"; at least that name was found included in his list of poisons. He was so passionately devoted to the green faction that he constantly dined and spent the night in their stable, and in one of his revels with them he gave the driver Eutychus two million sesterces in gifts. He used to send his soldiers on the day before the games and order silence in the neighborhood, to prevent the

horse Incitatus from being disturbed. Besides a stall of marble, a manger of ivory, purple blankets and a collar of precious stones, he even gave this horse a house, a troop of slaves and furniture, for the more elegant entertainment of the guests invited in his name; and it is also said that he planned to make him consul.

56. During this frantic and riotous career several thought of attempting his life. But when one or two conspiracies had been detected and the rest were waiting for a favorable opportunity, two men made common cause and succeeded, with the connivance of his most influential freedmen and the officers of the praetorian guard; for although the charge that these last were privy to one of the former conspiracies was false, they realized that Caligula hated and feared them. In fact, he exposed them to great odium by at once taking them aside and declaring, drawn sword in hand, that he would kill himself, if they too thought he deserved death; and from that time on he never ceased accusing them one to the other and setting them all at odds.

When they had decided to attempt his life at the exhibition of the Palatine games, as he went out at noon, Cassius Chaerea, tribune of a cohort of the praetorian guard, claimed for himself the principal part; for Gaius used to taunt him, a man already well on in years, with voluptuousness and effeminacy by every form of insult. When he asked for the watchword Gaius would give him "Priapus" or "Venus," and when Chaerea had occasion to thank him for anything, he would hold out his hand to kiss, forming and moving it in an obscene fashion.

57. His approaching murder was foretold by many prodigies. The statue of Jupiter at Olympia, which he had ordered to be taken to pieces and moved to Rome, suddenly uttered such a peal of laughter that the scaffoldings collapsed and the workmen took to their heels; and at once a man called Cassius turned up, who declared that he had been bidden in a dream to sacrifice a bull to Jupiter. The Capitol at Capua was struck by lightning on the Ides of March, and also the room of the doorkeeper of the Palace at Rome. Some inferred from the latter omen that danger was threatened to the owner at the hands of his guards; and from the former, the murder of a second distinguished personage, such as had taken place long before on that same day. The soothsayer Sulla too, when Gaius consulted him about his horoscope, declared that inevitable death was close at hand. The lots of Fortune at Antium warned him to beware of Cassius, and he accordingly ordered the death of Cassius Longinus, who was at the time proconsul of Asia, forgetting that the family name of Chaerea was Cassius. The day before he was killed he dreamt that he stood in heaven beside the throne of Jupiter and that the god struck him with the toe of his right foot and hurled him to earth. Some things which had happened on that very day shortly before he was killed were also regarded as portents. As he was sacrificing, he was sprinkled with the blood of a flamingo, and the pantomimic actor Mnester danced a tragedy which the tragedian Neoptolemus had acted years before during the games at which Philip king of the Macedonians was assassinated. In a farce called "Laureolus," in which the chief actor falls as he is making his escape and vomits blood, several understudies so vied with one another in giving evidence of their proficiency that the stage swam in blood. A nocturnal performance besides was rehearsing, in which scenes from the lower world were represented by Egyptians and Aethiopians.

58. On the ninth day before the Kalends of February at about the seventh hour he hesitated whether or not to get up for luncheon, since his stomach was still disordered from excess of food on the day before, but at length he came out at the persuasion of his friends. In the covered passage through which he had to pass, some boys of good birth, who had been summoned from Asia to appear on the stage, were rehearsing their parts, and he stopped to watch and encourage them; and had not the leader of the troop complained that he had a chill he would have returned and had the performance given at once. From this point there are two versions of the story: some say that as he was talking with the boys, Chaerea came up behind, and gave him a deep cut in the neck, having first cried, "Take that," and that then the tribune Cornelius Sabinus, who was the other conspirator and faced Gaius, stabbed him in the breast. Others say that Sabinus, after getting rid of the crowd through centurions who were in the plot, asked for the watchword, as soldiers do; and that when Gaius gave him "Jupiter," he cried "So be it," and as Gaius looked around, he split his jawbone with a blow of his sword. As he lay upon the ground and with writhing limbs called out that he still lived, the others dispatched him with thirty wounds; for the general signal was "Strike again." Some even thrust their swords through his privates. At the beginning of the disturbance his bearers ran to his aid with their poles, and presently the Germans of his body-guard, and they slew several of his assassins, as well as some inoffensive senators.

59. He lived twenty-nine years and ruled three years, ten months and eight days. His body was conveyed secretly to the gardens of the Lamian family, where it was partly consumed on a hastily erected pyre and buried beneath a light covering of turf; later his sisters on their return from exile dug it up, cremated it, and consigned it to the tomb. Before this was done, it is well known that the caretakers of the gardens were disturbed by ghosts, and that in the house where he was slain not a night passed without some fearsome apparition, until at last the house itself was destroyed by fire. With him died his wife Caesonia, stabbed with a sword by a centurion, while his daughter's brains were dashed out against a wall.

60. One may form an idea of the state of those times by what followed. Not even after the murder was made known was it at once believed that he

was dead, but it was suspected that Gaius himself had made up and circulated the report, to find out by that means how men felt towards him. The conspirators too had not agreed on a successor, and the senate was so unanimously in favor of re-establishing the republic that the consuls called the first meeting, not in the senate house, because it had the name Julia, but in the Capitol; while some in expressing their views proposed that the memory of the Caesars be done away with and their temples destroyed. Men further observed and commented on the fact that all the Caesars whose forename was Gaius perished by the sword, beginning with the one who was slain in the times of Cinna.

TACITUS*

Life and Works

Cornelius Tacitus was born about 55 C.E. in southern Gaul to a highly romanized family; his father was an imperial tax official. His outstanding oratorical ability, and his favorable marriage to the daughter of the Gallic senator Julius Agricola, allowed Tacitus to advance rapidly to high office under the Flavian emperors. He was praetor under Domitian, but withdrew from Rome during the worst period of the emperor's terror. After the assassination of Domitian in 96, Tacitus served as consul for 97 and was on friendly terms with the emperors Nerva (96–98) and Trajan (98–117). He probably died in 117.

Tacitus' strong political views were formed under Domitian, and it is the tyrant Domitian that we find projected back into the portrait of Tiberius. Though the historian bemoans the loss of liberty and free speech under the emperors, he cannot be called a "republican" since he well understood the dangers of civil war and would detest "mob rule."

His first books, the Agricola and the Germania, were published in 98 and were trial runs for his great narrative histories. The Germania is an ethnographic and geographic monograph which shows a certain admiration for Rome's German enemies. The book allows Tacitus to criticize the social and moral decline in Rome of his own day.

With his Histories and Annals Tacitus became the greatest historian that Rome ever produced. He wrote history to pass moral and political judgments on the past and thereby affect the future. In these books Tacitus creates a psychological portrait of the tyrant and his flatterers. The historian has no interest in

*Tacitus. 1886. *The Works of Tacitus.* Translated by A.J. Church and W.J. Brodribb. London: MacMillan.

sociological or economic explanations; he is concerned with political life, the loss of liberty, and the pathology of power.

Tacitus took the intense, asymmetrical style of Sallust and honed it to a knife-edge. His words analyze and reveal, they do not conceal. Though he draws on such poets as Vergil and Lucan, the biting wit and devastating epigrams are uniquely Tacitean. His rhetorical training is obvious throughout. Characterizations of tyrants, victims, and martyrs often rely on descriptions of type-characters known from school exercises. But Tacitus goes far beyond this in his great, subtle portraits of Nero and Tiberius as well as the wonderful vignettes scattered through the books: Petronius, Galba, Messalina, and Agrippina.

THE LIFE OF AGRICOLA

The biography of Tacitus' father-in-law Agricola is a highly personal work. In addition to family eulogy, the apprentice historian includes material on the wars in Britain and an ethnography of that island. It also contains Tacitus' vivid recollections of the years of Domitian's tyranny between 81 and 96 C.E.

1. To bequeath to posterity a record of the deeds and characters of distinguished men is an ancient practice which even the present age, careless as it is of its own sons, has not abandoned whenever some great and conspicuous excellence has conquered and risen superior to that failing, common to petty and to great states, blindness and hostility to goodness. But in days gone by, as there was a greater inclination and a more open path to the achievement of memorable actions, so the man of highest genius was led by the simple reward of a good conscience to hand on without partiality or self-seeking the remembrance of greatness. Many too thought that to write their own lives showed the confidence of integrity rather than presumption. Of Rutilius and Scaurus no one doubted the honesty or questioned the motives. So true is it that merit is best appreciated by the age in which it thrives most easily. But in these days, I, who have to record the life of one who has passed away, must crave an indulgence, which I should not have had to ask had I only to inveigh against an age so cruel, so hostile to all virtue.

2. We have read that the panegyrics pronounced by Arulenus Rusticus on Paetus Thrasea, and by Herennius Senecio on Priscus Helvidius, were made capital crimes, that not only their persons but their very books were objects of rage, and that the triumvirs were commissioned to burn in the forum those works of splendid genius. They fancied, in fact, that in that fire

the voice of the Roman people, the freedom of the Senate, and the con-science of the human race were perishing, while at the same time they ban-ished the teachers of philosophy, and exiled every noble pursuit, that nothing good might anywhere confront them. Certainly we showed a magnificent example of patience; as a former age had witnessed the extreme of liberty, so we witnessed the extreme of servitude, when the informer robbed us of the interchange of speech and hearing. We should have lost memory as well as voice, had it been as easy to forget as to keep silence.

3. Now at last our spirit is returning. And yet, though at the dawn of a most happy age Nerva Caesar blended things once irreconcilable, sover-eignty and freedom, though Nerva Trajan is now daily augmenting the pros-perity of the time, and though the public safety has not only our hopes and good wishes, but has also the certain pledge of their fulfillment, still, from the necessary condition of human frailty, the remedy works less quickly than the disease. As our bodies grow but slowly, perish in a moment, so it is easier to crush than to revive genius and its pursuits. Besides, the charm of indo-lence steals over us, and the idleness which at first we loathed we afterwards love. What if during those fifteen years, a large portion of human life, many were cut off by ordinary casualties, and the ablest fell victims to the Emperor's rage, if a few of us survive, I may almost say, not only others but ourselves, survive, though there have been taken from the midst of life those many years which brought the young in dumb silence to old age, and the old almost to the very verge and end of existence! Yet we shall not regret that we have told, though in language unskillful and unadorned, the story of past servitude, and borne our testimony to present happiness. Meanwhile this book, intended to do honor to Agricola, my father-in-law, will, as an expres-sion of filial regard, be commended, or at least excused.

4. Cn. Julius Agricola was born at the ancient and famous colony of Forum Julii. Each of his grandfathers was an Imperial procurator, that is, of the highest equestrian rank. His father, Julius Graecinus, a member of the Senatorial order, and distinguished for his pursuit of eloquence and philoso-phy, earned for himself by these very merits the displeasure of C. Caesar. He was ordered to impeach Marcus Silanus, and because he refused was put to death. His mother was Julia Procilla, a lady of singular virtue. Brought up by her side with fond affection, he passed his boyhood and youth in the cultiva-tion of every worthy attainment. He was guarded from the enticements of the profligate not only by his own good and straightforward character, but also by having, when quite a child, for the scene and guide of his studies, Massilia, a place where refinement and provincial frugality were blended and happily combined. I remember that he used to tell us how in his early youth he would have imbibed a keener love of philosophy than became a Roman and a senator, had not his mother's good sense checked his excited and ardent

spirit. It was the case of a lofty and aspiring soul craving with more eagerness than caution the beauty and splendor of great and glorious renown. But it was soon mellowed by reason and experience, and he retained from his learning that most difficult of lessons—moderation.

5. He served his military apprenticeship in Britain to the satisfaction of Suetonius Paullinus, a painstaking and judicious officer, who, to test his merits, selected him to share his tent. Without the recklessness with which young men often make the profession of arms a mere pastime, and without indolence, he never availed himself of his tribune's rank or his inexperience to procure enjoyment or to escape from duty. He sought to make himself acquainted with the province and known to the army; he would learn from the skillful, and keep pace with the bravest, would attempt nothing for display, would avoid nothing from fear, and would be at once careful and vigilant.

Never indeed had Britain been more excited, or in a more critical condition. Veteran soldiers had been massacred, colonies burnt, armies cut off. The struggle was then for safety; it was soon to be for victory. And though all this was conducted under the leadership and direction of another, though the final issue and the glory of having won back the province belonged to the general, yet skill, experience, and ambition were acquired by the young officer. His soul too was penetrated with the desire of warlike renown, a sentiment unwelcome to an age which put a sinister construction on eminent merit, and made glory as perilous as infamy.

6. From Britain he went to Rome, to go through the regular course of office, and there allied himself with Domitia Decidiana, a lady of illustrious birth. The marriage was one which gave a man ambitious of advancement distinction and support. They lived in singular harmony, through their mutual affection and preference of each other to self. However the good wife deserves the greater praise, just as the bad incurs a heavier censure.

Appointed quaestor, the ballot gave him Asia for his province, Salvius Titianus for his proconsul. Neither the one nor the other corrupted him, though the province was rich and an easy prey to the wrongdoer, while the proconsul, a man inclined to every species of greed, was ready by all manner of indulgence to purchase a mutual concealment of guilt.

A daughter was there added to his family to be his stay and comfort, for shortly after he lost the son that had before been born to him. The year between his quaestorship and tribunate, as well as the year of the tribunate itself, he passed in retirement and inaction, for he knew those times of Nero when indolence stood for wisdom. His praetorship was passed in the same consistent quietude, for the usual judicial functions did not fall to his lot. The games and the pageantry of his office he ordered according to the mean between strictness and profusion, avoiding extravagance, but not missing distinction. He was afterwards appointed by Galba to draw up an account of the temple offerings, and his searching scrutiny relieved the conscience of the state from the burden of all sacrileges but those committed by Nero.

7. The following year inflicted a terrible blow on his affections and his fortunes. Otho's fleet, while cruising idly about, cruelly ravaged Intemelii, a district of Liguria; his mother, who was living here on her own estate, was murdered. The estate itself and a large part of her patrimony were plundered. This was indeed the occasion of the crime. Agricola, who instantly set out to discharge the duties of affection, was overtaken by the tidings that Vespasian was aiming at the throne. He at once joined his party. Vespasian's early policy, and the government of Rome were directed by Mucianus, for Domitian was a mere youth, and from his father's elevation sought only the opportunities of indulgence. Agricola, having been sent by Mucianus to conduct a levy of troops, and having done his work with integrity and energy, was appointed to command the 20th Legion, which had been slow to take the new oath of allegiance, and the retiring officer of which was reported to be acting disloyally. It was a trying and formidable charge for even officers of consular rank, and the late praetorian officer, perhaps from his own disposition, perhaps from that of the soldiers, was powerless to restrain them. Chosen thus at once to supersede and to punish, Agricola, with a singular moderation, wished it to be thought that he had found rather than made an obedient soldiery.

8. Britain was then under Vettius Bolanus, who governed more mildly than suited so turbulent a province. Agricola moderated his energy and restrained his ardor, that he might not grow too important, for he had learnt to obey, and understood well how to combine expediency with honor. Soon afterwards Britain received for its governor a man of consular rank, Petilius Cerialis. Agricola's merits had now room for display. Cerialis let him share at first indeed only the toils and dangers, but before long the glory of war, often by way of trial, putting him in command of part of the army and sometimes, on the strength of the result, of larger forces: Never to enhance his own renown did Agricola boast of his exploits; he always referred his success, as though he were but an instrument, to his general and director. Thus by his valor in obeying orders and by his modesty of speech he escaped jealousy without losing distinction.

9. As he was returning from the command of the legion, Vespasian admitted him into the patrician order, and then gave him the province of Aquitania, a preeminently splendid appointment both from the importance of its duties and the prospect of the consulate to which the Emperor destined him. Many think the genius of the soldier wants subtlety, because military

law, which is summary and blunt, and apt to appeal to the sword, finds no exercise for the refinements of the forum. Yet Agricola, from his natural good sense, though called to act among civilians, did his work with ease and correctness. And, besides, the times of business and relaxation were kept distinct. When his public and judicial duties required it, he was dignified, thoughtful, austere, and yet often merciful; when business was done with, he wore no longer the official character. He was altogether without harshness, pride, or the greed of gain. With a most rare felicity, his good nature did not weaken his authority, nor his strictness the attachment of his friends. To speak of uprightness and purity in such a man would be an insult to his virtues. Fame itself, of which even good men are often weakly fond, he did not seek by an ostentation of virtue or by artifice. He avoided rivalry with his colleagues, contention with his procurator, thinking such victories no honor and defeat disgrace. For somewhat less than three years he was kept in his governorship, and was then recalled with an immediate prospect of the consulate. A general belief went with him that the province of Britain was to be his, not because he had himself hinted it, but because he seemed worthy of it. Public opinion is not always mistaken; sometimes even it chooses the right man. He was consul, and I but a youth, when he betrothed to me his daughter, a maiden even then of noble promise. After his consulate he gave her to me in marriage, and was then at once appointed to the government of Britain, with the addition of the sacred office of the pontificate.

10. The geography and inhabitants of Britain, already described by many writers, I will speak of, not that my research and ability may be compared with theirs, but because the country was then for the first time thoroughly subdued. And so matters, which as being still not accurately known my predecessors embellished with their eloquence, shall now be related on the evidence of facts.

Britain, the largest of the islands which Roman geography includes, is so situated that it faces Germany on the east, Spain on the west; on the south it is even within sight of Gaul; its northern extremities, which have no shores opposite to them, are beaten by the waves of a vast open sea. The form of the entire country has been compared by Livy and Fabius Rusticus, the most graphic among ancient and modern historians, to an oblong shield or battle-axe. And this no doubt is its shape without Caledonia, so that it has become the popular description of the whole island. There is, however, a large and irregular tract of land which juts out from its furthest shores, tapering off in a wedge-like form. Round these coasts of remotest ocean the Roman fleet then for the first time sailed, ascertained that Britain is an island, and simultaneously discovered and conquered what are called the Orkneys, islands hitherto unknown. Thule too was descried in the distance, which as yet had been hidden by the snows of winter. Those waters, they say, are sluggish, and yield with difficulty to the oar, and are not even raised by the wind as other seas. The reason, I suppose, is that lands and mountains, which are the cause and origin of storms, are here comparatively rare, and also that the vast depths of that unbroken expanse are more slowly set in motion. But to investigate the nature of the ocean and the tides is no part of the present work, and many writers have discussed the subject. I would simply add, that nowhere has the sea a wider dominion, that it has many currents running in every direction, that it does not merely flow and ebb within the limits of the shore, but penetrates and winds far inland, and finds a home among hills and mountains as though in its own domain.

11. Who were the original inhabitants of Britain, whether they were indigenous or foreign, is, as usual among barbarians, little known. Their physical characteristics are various, and from these conclusions may be drawn. The red hair and large limbs of the inhabitants of Caledonia point clearly to a German origin. The dark complexion of the Silures, their usually curly hair, and the fact that Spain is the opposite shore to them, are an evidence that Iberians of a former date crossed over and occupied these parts. Those who are nearest to the Gauls are also like them, either from the permanent influence of original descent, or, because in countries which run out so far to meet each other, climate has produced similar physical qualities. But a general survey inclines me to believe that the Gauls established themselves in an island so near to them. Their religious belief may be traced in the strongly-marked British superstition. The language differs but little; there is the same boldness in challenging danger, and, when it is near, the same timidity in shrinking from it. The Britons, however, exhibit more spirit, as being a people whom a long peace has not yet enervated. Indeed we have understood that even the Gauls were once renowned in war; but, after a while, sloth following on ease crept over them, and they lost their courage along with their freedom. This too has happened to the long-conquered tribes of Britain; the rest are still what the Gauls once were.

12. Their strength is in infantry. Some tribes fight also with the chariot. The higher in rank is the charioteer; the dependents fight. They were once ruled by kings, but are now divided under chieftains into factions and parties. Our greatest advantage in coping with tribes so powerful is that they do not act in concert. Seldom is it that two or three states meet together to ward off a common danger. Thus while they fight singly, all are conquered.

Their sky is obscured by continual rain and cloud. Severity of cold is unknown. The days exceed in length those of our part of the world; the nights are bright, and in the extreme north so short that between sunlight and dawn you can perceive but a slight distinction. It is said that, if there are no clouds in the way, the splendor of the sun can be seen throughout the night, and that he does not rise and set, but only crosses the heavens. The truth is, that the low shadow thrown from the flat extremities of the earth's surface does not raise the darkness to any height, and the night thus fails to reach the sky and stars.

With the exception of the olive and vine, and plants which usually grow in warmer climates, the soil will yield, and even abundantly, all ordinary produce. It ripens indeed slowly, but is of rapid growth, the cause in each case being the same, namely, the excessive moisture of the soil and of the atmosphere. Britain contains gold and silver and other metals, as the prize of conquest. The ocean, too, produces pearls, but of a dusky and bluish hue. Some think that those who collect them have not the requisite skill, as in the Red Sea the living and breathing pearl is torn from the rocks, while in Britain they are gathered just as they are thrown up. I could myself more readily believe that the natural properties of the pearls are in fault than our keenness for gain.

13. The Britons themselves bear cheerfully the conscription, the taxes, and the other burdens imposed on them by the Empire, if there be no oppression. Of this they are impatient; they are reduced to subjection, not as yet to slavery. The deified Julius was the very first Roman who entered Britain with an army. By a successful engagement he struck terror into the inhabitants and gained possession of the coast, but he must be regarded as having discovered the island rather than conquered it for future generations. Then came the civil wars, and the arms of our leaders were turned against their country, and even when there was peace, there was a long neglect of Britain. This Augustus spoke of as policy, Tiberius as an inherited maxim. That C. Caesar meditated an invasion of Britain is perfectly clear, but his purposes, rapidly formed, were easily changed, and his vast attempts on Germany had failed. Claudius was the first to renew the attempt, and conveyed over into the island some legions and auxiliaries, choosing Vespasian to share with him the campaign, whose approaching elevation had this beginning. Several tribes were subdued and kings made prisoners, and destiny learnt to know its favorite.

14. Aulus Plautius was the first governor of consular rank, and Ostorius Scapula the next. Both were famous soldiers, and by degrees the nearest portions of Britain were brought into the condition of a province, and a colony of veterans was also introduced. Some of the states were given to King Cogidumnus, who lived down to our day a most faithful ally. So was maintained the ancient and long-recognized practice of the Roman people, which seeks to secure among the instruments of dominion even kings themselves. Soon after, Didius Gallus consolidated the conquests of his predecessors, and advanced a very few positions into parts more remote, to gain the credit of having enlarged the sphere of government. Didius was succeeded by Veranius, who died within the year. Then Suetonius Paullinus enjoyed success for

two years; he subdued several tribes and strengthened our military posts. Thus encouraged, he made an attempt on the island of Anglesey, as a place from which the rebels drew reinforcements; but in doing this he left his rear open to attack.

15. Relieved from apprehension by the legate's absence, the Britons dwelt much among themselves on the miseries of subjection, compared their wrongs, and exaggerated them in the discussion. "All we get by patience," they said, "is that heavier demands are exacted from us, as from men who will readily submit. A single king once ruled us; now two are set over us; a legate to tyrannize over our lives, a procurator to tyrannize over our property. Their quarrels and their harmony are alike ruinous to their subjects. The centurions of the one, the slaves of the other, combine violence with insult. Nothing is now safe from their avarice, nothing from their lust. In war it is the strong who plunders; now, it is for the most part by cowards and poltroons that our homes are rifled, our children torn from us, the conscription enforced, as though it were for our country alone that we could not die. For, after all, what a mere handful of soldiers has crossed over, if we Britons look at our own numbers. Germany did thus actually shake off the yoke, and yet its defense was a river, not the ocean. With us, fatherland, wives, parents, are the motives to war; with them, only greed and profligacy. They will surely fly, as did the now deified Julius, if once we emulate the valor of our sires. Let us not be panic-stricken at the result of one or two engagements. The miserable have more fury and greater resolution. Now even the gods are beginning to pity us, for they are keeping away the Roman general, and detaining his army far from us in another island. We have already taken the hardest step; we are deliberating. And indeed, in all such designs, to dare is less perilous than to be detected."

16. Rousing each other by this and like language, under the leadership of Boudicea, a woman of kingly descent (for they admit no distinction of sex in their royal successions), they all rose in arms. They fell upon our troops, which were scattered on garrison duty, stormed the forts, and burst into the colony itself, the head-quarters, as they thought, of tyranny. In their rage and their triumph, they spared no variety of a barbarian's cruelty. Had not Paullinus on hearing of the outbreak in the province rendered prompt succor, Britain would have been lost. By one successful engagement, he brought it back to its former obedience, though many, troubled by the conscious guilt of rebellion and by particular dread of the legate, still clung to their arms. Excellent as he was in other respects, his policy to the conquered was arrogant, and exhibited the cruelty of one who was avenging private wrongs. Accordingly Petronius Turpilianus was sent out to initiate a milder rule. A stranger to the enemy's misdeeds and so more accessible to their penitence, he put an end to old troubles, and, attempting nothing more, handed the

province over to Trebellius Maximus. Trebellius, who was somewhat indolent, and never ventured on a campaign, controlled the province by a certain
courtesy in his administration. Even the barbarians now learnt to excuse
many attractive vices, and the occurrence of the civil war gave a good pretext
for inaction. But we were sorely troubled with mutiny as troops habituated
to service grew demoralized by idleness. Trebellius, who had escaped the soldiers' fury by flying and hiding himself, governed henceforth on sufferance, a
disgraced and humbled man. It was a kind of bargain; the soldiers had their
license, the general had his life; and so the mutiny cost no bloodshed. Nor did
Vettius Bolanus, during the continuance of the civil wars, trouble Britain
with discipline. There was the same inaction with respect to the enemy, and
similar unruliness in the camp, only Bolanus, an upright man, whom no misdeeds made odious, had secured affection in default of the power of control.

17. When however Vespasian had restored to unity Britain as well as the
rest of the world, in the presence of great generals and renowned armies the
enemy's hopes were crushed. They were at once panic-stricken by the attack
of Petilius Cerialis on the state of the Brigantes, said to be the most prosperous in the entire province. There were many battles, some by no means
bloodless, and his conquests, or at least his wars, embraced a large part of the
territory of the Brigantes. Indeed he would have altogether thrown into the
shade the activity and renown of any other successor; but Julius Frontinus
was equal to the burden, a great man as far as greatness was then possible,
who subdued by his arms the powerful and warlike tribe of the Silures, sur-
mounting the difficulties of the country as well as the velour of the enemy.

18. Such was the state of Britain, and such were the vicissitudes of the
war, which Agricola found on his crossing over about midsummer. Our soldiers made it a pretext for carelessness, as if all fighting was over, and the
enemy were biding their time. The Ordovices, shortly before Agricola's
arrival, had destroyed nearly the whole of a squadron of allied cavalry quartered in their territory. Such a beginning raised the hopes of the country, and
all who wished for war approved the precedent, and anxiously watched the
temper of the new governor. Meanwhile Agricola, though summer was past
and the detachments were scattered throughout the province, though the
soldiers' confident anticipation of inaction for that year would be a source of
delay and difficulty in beginning a campaign, and most advisers thought it
best simply to watch all weak points, resolved to face the peril. He collected a
force of veterans and a small body of auxiliaries; then as the Ordovices would
not venture to descend into the plain, he put himself in front of the ranks to
inspire all with the same courage against a common danger, and led his
troops up a hill. The tribe was all but exterminated.

Well aware that he must follow up the prestige of his arms, and that in
proportion to his first success would be the terror of the other tribes, he

formed the design of subjugating the island of Anglesey, from the occupation of which Paullinus had been recalled, as I have already related, by the rebellion of the entire province. But, as his plans were not matured, he had no fleet. The skill and resolution of the general accomplished the passage. With some picked men of the auxiliaries, disencumbered of all baggage, who knew the shallows and had that national experience in swimming which enables the Britons to take care not only of themselves but of their arms and horses, he delivered so unexpected an attack that the astonished enemy who were looking for a fleet, a naval armament, and an assault by sea, thought that to such assailants nothing could be formidable or invincible. And so, peace having been sued for and the island given up, Agricola became great and famous as one who, when entering on his province, a time which others spend in vain display and a round of ceremonies, chose rather toil and danger. Nor did he use his success for self-glorification, or apply the name of campaigns and victories to the repression of a conquered people. He did not even describe his achievements in a laurelled letter. Yet by thus disguising his renown he really increased it, for men inferred the grandeur of his aspirations from his silence about services so great.

19. Next, with thorough insight into the feelings of his province, and taught also, by the experience of others, that little is gained by conquest if followed by oppression, he determined to root out the causes of war. Beginning first with himself and his dependents, he kept his household under restraint, a thing as hard to many as ruling a province. He transacted no public business through freedmen or slaves; no private leanings, no recommendations or entreaties of friends, moved him in the selection of centurions and soldiers, out it was ever the best man whom he thought most trustworthy. He knew everything, but did not always act on his knowledge. Trifling errors he treated with leniency, serious offenses with severity. Nor was it always punishment, but far oftener penitence, which satisfied him. He preferred to give office and power to men who would not transgress, rather than have to condemn a transgressor. He lightened the exaction of corn and tribute by an equal distribution of the burden, while he got rid of those contrivances for gain which were more intolerable than the tribute itself. Hitherto the people had been compelled to endure the farce of waiting by the closed granary and of purchasing corn unnecessarily and raising it to a fictitious price. Difficult byroads and distant places were fixed for them, so that states with a winter-camp close to them had to carry corn to remote and inaccessible parts of the country, until what was within the reach of all became a source of profit to the few.

20. Agricola, by the repression of these abuses in his very first year of office, restored to peace its good name, when, from either the indifference or the harshness of his predecessors, it had come to be as much dreaded as war.

When however, summer came, assembling his forces, he continually showed himself in the ranks, praised good discipline, and kept the stragglers in order. He would himself choose the position of the camp, himself explore the estuaries and forests. Meanwhile he would allow the enemy no rest, laying waste his territory with sudden incursions, and, having sufficiently alarmed him, would then by forbearance display the allurements of peace. In consequence, many states, which up to that time had been independent, gave hostages, and laid aside their animosities; garrisons and forts were established among them with a skill and diligence with which no newly-acquired part of Britain had before been treated.

21. The following winter passed without disturbance, and was employed in salutary measures. For, to accustom to rest and repose through the charms of luxury a population scattered and barbarous and therefore inclined to war, Agricola gave private encouragement and public aid to the building of temples, courts of justice and dwelling-houses, praising the energetic, and reproving the indolent. Thus an honorable rivalry took the place of compulsion. He likewise provided a liberal education for the sons of the chiefs, and showed such a preference for the natural powers of the Britons over the industry of the Gauls that they who lately disdained the tongue of Rome now coveted its eloquence. Hence, too, a liking sprang up for our style of dress, and the "toga" became fashionable. Step by step they were led to things which dispose to vice, the lounge, the bath, the elegant banquet. All this in their ignorance, they called civilization, when it was but a part of their servitude.

22. The third year of his campaigns opened up new tribes, our ravages on the native population being earned as far as the Taus, an estuary so called. This struck such terror into the enemy that he did not dare to attack our army, harassed though it was by violent storms; and there was even time for the erection of forts. It was noted by experienced officers that no general had ever shown more judgment in choosing suitable positions, and that not a single fort established by Agricola was either stormed by the enemy or abandoned by capitulation or flight. Sorties were continually made; for these positions were secured from protracted siege by a year's supply. So winter brought with it no alarms, and each garrison could hold its own, as the baffled and despairing enemy, who had been accustomed often to repair his summer losses by winter successes, found himself repelled alike both in summer and winter.

Never did Agricola in a greedy spirit appropriate the achievements of others; the centurion and the prefect both found in him an impartial witness of their every action. Some persons used to say that he was too harsh in his reproofs, and that he was as severe to the bad as he was gentle to the good. But his displeasure left nothing behind it; reserve and silence in him were not to be dreaded. He thought it better to show anger than to cherish hatred.

23. The fourth summer he employed in securing what he had overrun. Had the valor of our armies and the renown of the Roman name permitted it, a limit to our conquests might have been found in Britain itself. Clota and Bodotria, estuaries which the tides of two opposite seas carry far back into the country, are separated by but a narrow strip of land. This Agricola then began to defend with a line of forts, and, as all the country to the south was now occupied, the enemy were pushed into what might be called another island.

24. In the fifth year of the war Agricola, himself in the leading ship, crossed the Clota, and subdued in a series of victories tribes hitherto unknown. In that part of Britain which looks towards Ireland, he posted some troops, hoping for fresh conquests rather than fearing attack, inasmuch as Ireland, being between Britain and Spain and conveniently situated for the seas round Gaul, might have been the means of connecting with great mutual benefit the most powerful parts of the empire. Its extent is small when compared with Britain, but exceeds the islands of our seas. In soil and climate, in the disposition, temper, and habits of its population, it differs but little from Britain. We know most of its harbors and approaches, and that through the intercourse of commerce. One of the petty kings of the nation, driven out by internal faction, had been received by Agricola, who detained him under the semblance of friendship till he could make use of him. I have often heard him say that a single legion with a few auxiliaries could conquer and occupy Ireland, and that it would have a salutary effect on Britain for the Roman arms to be seen everywhere, and for freedom, so to speak, to be banished from its sight.

25. In the summer in which he entered on the sixth year of his office, his operations embraced the states beyond Bodotria, and, as he dreaded a general movement among the remoter tribes, as well as the perils which would beset an invading army, he explored the harbors with a fleet, which at first employed by him as an integral part of his force, continued to accompany him. The spectacle of war thus pushed on at once by sea and land was imposing; while often infantry, cavalry, and marines, mingled in the same encampment and joyously sharing the same meals, would dwell on their own achievements and adventures, comparing, with a soldier's boastfulness, at one time the deep recesses of the forest and the mountain with the dangers of waves and storms, or, at another, battles by land with victories over the ocean. The Britons too, as we learnt from the prisoners, were confounded by the sight of a fleet, as if, now that their inmost seas were penetrated, the conquered had their last refuge closed against them. The tribes inhabiting Caledonia flew to arms, and with great preparations, made greater by the rumors which always exaggerate the unknown, themselves advanced to attack our fortresses, and thus challenging a conflict, inspired us with alarm. To retreat south of the Bodotria, and to retire rather than to be driven out, was the advice of timid pretenders to prudence, when Agricola learnt that the enemy's attack would be made with more than one army. Fearing that their superior numbers and their knowledge of the country might enable them to hem him in, he too distributed his forces into three divisions, and so advanced.

26. This becoming known to the enemy, they suddenly changed their plan, and with their whole force attacked by night the ninth Legion, as being the weakest, and cutting down the sentries, who were asleep or panic-stricken, they broke into the camp. And now the battle was raging within the camp itself, when Agricola, who had learnt from his scouts the enemy's line of march and had kept close on his track, ordered the most active soldiers of his cavalry and infantry to attack the rear of the assailants, while the entire army were shortly to raise a shout. Soon his standards glittered in the light of daybreak. A double peril thus alarmed the Britons, while the courage of the Romans revived; and feeling sure of safety, they now fought for glory. In their turn they rushed to the attack, and there was a furious conflict within the narrow passages of the gates till the enemy were routed. Both armies did their utmost, the one for the honor of having given aid, the other for that of not having needed support. Had not the flying enemy been sheltered by morasses and forests, this victory would have ended the war.

27. Knowing this, and elated by their glory, our army exclaimed that nothing could resist their valor—that they must penetrate the recesses of Caledonia, and at length after an unbroken succession of battles, discover the furthest limits of Britain. Those who but now were cautious and prudent, became after the event eager and boastful. It is the singularly unfair peculiarity of war that the credit of success is claimed by all, while a disaster is attributed to one alone. But the Britons thinking themselves beaten, not so much by our valor as by our general's skillful use of an opportunity, abated nothing of their arrogant demeanor, arming their youth, removing their wives and children to a place of safety, and assembling together to ratify, with sacred rites a confederacy of all their states. Thus, with angry feelings on both sides, the combatants parted.

28. The same summer a Usipian cohort, which had been levied in Germany and transported into Britain, ventured on a great and memorable exploit. Having killed a centurion and some soldiers, who, to impart military discipline, had been incorporated with their ranks and were employed at once to instruct and command them, they embarked on board three swift galleys with pilots pressed into their service. Under the direction of one of them—for two of the three they suspected and consequently put to death—they sailed past the coast in the strangest way before any rumor about them

was in circulation. After a while, dispersing in search of water and provisions, they encountered many of the Britons, who sought to defend their property. Often victorious, though now and then beaten, they were at last reduced to such an extremity of want as to be compelled to eat, at first, the feeblest of their number, and then victims selected by lot. Having sailed round Britain and lost their vessels from not knowing how to manage them, they were looked upon as pirates and were intercepted, first by the Suevi and then by the Frisii. Some who were sold as slaves in the way of trade, and were brought through the process of barter as far as our side of the Rhine, gained notoriety by the disclosure of this extraordinary adventure.

29. Early in the summer Agricola sustained a domestic affliction in the loss of a son born a year before, a calamity which he endured, neither with the ostentatious fortitude displayed by many brave men, nor, on the other hand, with womanish tears and grief. In his sorrow he found one source of relief in war. Having sent on a fleet, which by its ravages at various points might cause a vague and wide-spread alarm, he advanced with a lightly equipped force, including in its ranks some Britons of remarkable bravery, whose fidelity had been tried through years of peace, as far as the Grampian mountains, which the enemy had already occupied. For the Britons, indeed, in no way cowed by the result of the late engagement, had made up their minds to be either avenged or enslaved, and convinced at length that a common danger must be averted by union, had, by embassies and treaties, summoned forth the whole strength of all their states. More than 30,000 armed men were now to be seen, and still there were pressing in all the youth of the country, with all whose old age was yet hale and vigorous, men renowned in war and bearing each decorations of his own. Meanwhile, among the many leaders, one superior to the rest in valor and in birth, Calgacus by name, is said to have thus harangued the multitude gathered around him and clamoring for battle:

30. "Whenever I consider the origin of this war and the necessities of our position, I have a sure confidence that this day, and this union of yours, will be the beginning of freedom to the whole of Britain. To all of us slavery is a thing unknown; there are no lands beyond us, and even the sea is not safe, menaced as we are by a Roman fleet. And thus in war and battle, in which the brave find glory, even the coward will find safety. Former contests, in which, with varying fortune, the Romans were resisted, still left in us a last hope of succor, inasmuch as being the most renowned nation of Britain, dwelling in the very heart of the country, and out of sight of the shores of the conquered, we could keep even our eyes unpolluted by the contagion of slavery. To us who dwell on the uttermost confines of the earth and of freedom, this remote sanctuary of Britain's glory has up to this time been a defense. Now, however, the furthest limits of Britain are thrown open, and the unknown always passes for the marvelous. But there are no tribes beyond us, nothing indeed but waves and rocks, and the yet more terrible Romans, from whose oppression escape is vainly sought by obedience and submission. Robbers of the world, having by their universal plunder exhausted the land, they rifle the deep. If the enemy be rich, they are rapacious; if he be poor, they lust for dominion; neither the east nor the west has been able to satisfy them. Alone among men they covet with equal eagerness poverty and riches. To robbery, slaughter, plunder, they give the lying name of empire; they make a solitude and call it peace.

31. "Nature has willed that every man's children and kindred should be his dearest objects. Yet these are torn from us by conscriptions to be slaves elsewhere. Our wives and our sisters, even though they may escape violation from the enemy, are dishonored under the names of friendship and hospitality. Our goods and fortunes they collect for their tribute, our harvests for their granaries. Our very hands and bodies, under the lash and in the midst of insult, are worn down by the toil of clearing forests and morasses. Creatures born to slavery are sold once for all, and are, moreover, fed by their masters; but Britain is daily purchasing, is daily feeding, her own enslaved people. And as in a household the last comer among the slaves is always the butt of his companions, so we in a world long used to slavery, as the newest and the most contemptible, are marked out for destruction. We have neither fruitful plains, nor mines, nor harbors, for the working of which we may be spared. Valor, too, and high spirit in subjects, are offensive to rulers; besides, remoteness and seclusion, while they give safety, provoke suspicion. Since then you cannot hope for quarter, take courage, I beseech you, whether it be safety or renown that you hold most precious. Under a woman's leadership the Brigantes were able to burn a colony, to storm a camp, and had not success ended in supineness, might have thrown off the yoke. Let us, then, a fresh and unconquered people, never likely to abuse our freedom, show forthwith at the very first onset what heroes Caledonia has in reserve.

32. "Do you suppose that the Romans will be as brave in war as they are licentious in peace? To our strifes and discords they owe their fame, and they turn the errors of an enemy to the renown of their own army, an army which, composed as it is of every variety of nations, is held together by success and will be broken up by disaster. These Gauls and Germans, and, I blush to say, these numerous Britons, who, though they lend their lives to support a stranger's rule, have been its enemies longer than its subjects, you cannot imagine to be bound by fidelity and affection. Fear and terror there certainly are, feeble bonds of attachment; remove them, and those who have ceased to fear will begin to hate. All the incentives to victory are on our side. The Romans have no wives to kindle their courage; no parents to taunt them with flight; many have either no country or one far away. Few in number, dismayed by their ignorance, looking around upon a sky, a sea, and forests which are all unfamiliar to them; hemmed in, as it were, and enmeshed, the Gods have delivered them into our hands. Be not frightened by idle display, by the glitter of gold and of silver, which can neither protect nor wound. In the very ranks of the enemy we shall find our own forces. Britons will acknowledge their own cause; Gauls will remember past freedom; the other Germans will abandon them, as but lately did the Usipii. Behind them there is nothing to dread. The forts are ungarrisoned; the colonies in the hands of aged men; what with disloyal subjects and oppressive rulers, the towns are ill-affected and rife with discord. On the one side you have a general and an army; on the other, tribute, the mines, and all the other penalties of an enslaved people. Whether you endure these forever, or instantly avenge them, this field is to decide. Think, therefore, as you advance to battle, at once of your ancestors and of your posterity."

33. They received his speech with enthusiasm, and as is usual among barbarians, with songs, shouts and discordant cries. And now was seen the assembling of troops and the gleam of arms, as the boldest warriors stepped to the front. As the line was forming, Agricola, who, though his troops were in high spirits and could scarcely be kept within the entrenchments, still thought it right to encourage them, spoke as follows:

"Comrades, this is the eighth year since, thanks to the greatness and good fortune of Rome and to your own loyalty and energy, you conquered Britain. In our many campaigns and battles, whether courage in meeting the foe, or toil and endurance in struggling, I may say, against nature herself, have been needed, I have ever been well satisfied with my soldiers, and you with your commander. And so you and I have passed beyond the limits reached by former armies or by former governors, and we now occupy the last confines of Britain, not merely in rumor and report, but with an actual encampment and armed force. Britain has been both discovered and subdued. Often on the march, when morasses, mountains, and rivers were wearing out your strength, did I hear our bravest men exclaim, 'When shall we have the enemy before us?—when shall we fight?' He is now here, driven from his lair, and your wishes and your valor have free scope, and everything favors the conqueror, everything is adverse to the vanquished. For as it is a great and glorious achievement, if we press on, to have accomplished so great a march, to have traversed forests and to have crossed estuaries, so, if we retire, our present most complete success will prove our greatest danger. We have not the same knowledge of the country or the same abundance of supplies, but we have arms in our hands, and in them we have everything. For myself I have long been convinced that neither for an army nor for a general is retreat safe. Better, too, is an honorable death than a life of shame, and safety and renown are for us to be found together. And it would be no inglorious end to perish on the extreme confines of earth and of nature.

34. "If unknown nations and an untried enemy confronted you, I should urge you on by the example of other armies. As it is, look back upon your former honors, question your own eyes. These are the men who last year under cover of darkness attacked a single legion, whom you routed by a shout. Of all the Britons these are the most confirmed runaways, and this is why they have survived so long. Just as when the huntsman penetrates the forest and the thicket, all the most courageous animals rush out upon him, while the timid and feeble are scared away by the very sound of his approach, so the bravest of the Britons have long since fallen; and the rest are a mere crowd of spiritless cowards. You have at last found them, not because they have stood their ground, but because they have been overtaken. Their desperate plight, and the extreme terror that paralyses them, have riveted their line to this spot, that you might achieve in it a splendid and memorable victory. Put an end to campaigns; crown your fifty years' service with a glorious day; prove to your country that her armies could never have been fairly charged with protracting a war or with causing a rebellion."

35. While Agricola was yet speaking, the ardor of the soldiers was rising to its height, and the close of his speech was followed by a great outburst of enthusiasm. In a moment they flew to arms. He arrayed his eager and impetuous troops in such a manner that the auxiliary infantry, 8,000 in number, strengthened his center, while 3,000 cavalry were posted on his wings. The legions were drawn up in front of the entrenched camp; his victory would be vastly more glorious if won without the loss of Roman blood, and he would have a reserve in case of repulse. The enemy, to make a formidable display, had posted himself on high ground; his van was on the plain, while the rest of his army rose in an arch-like form up the slope of a hill. The plain between resounded with the noise and with the rapid movements of chariots and cavalry. Agricola, fearing that from the enemy's superiority of force he would be simultaneously attacked in front and on the flanks, widened his ranks, and though his line was likely to be too extended, and several officers advised him to bring up the legions, yet, so sanguine was he, so resolute in meeting danger, he sent away his horse and took his stand on foot before the colors.

36. The action began with distant fighting. The Britons with equal steadiness and skill used their huge swords and small shields to avoid or to parry the missiles of our soldiers, while they themselves poured on us a dense shower of darts, till Agricola encouraged three Batavian and two Tungrian cohorts to bring matters to the decision of close fighting with swords. Such tactics were familiar to these veteran soldiers, but were embarrassing to an enemy armed with small bucklers and unwieldy weapons. The swords of the Britons are not pointed, and do not allow them to close with the foe, or to fight in the open field. No sooner did the Batavians begin to close with the enemy, to strike them with their shields, to disfigure their faces, and over-throwing the force on the plain to advance their line up the hill, than the other auxiliary cohorts joined with eager rivalry in cutting down all the near-est of the foe. Many were left behind half dead, some even unwounded, in the hurry of victory. Meantime the enemy's cavalry had fled, and the chario-teers had mingled in the engagement of the infantry. But although these at first spread panic, they were soon impeded by the close array of our ranks and by the inequalities of the ground. The battle had anything but the appearance of a cavalry action, for men and horses were carried along in con-fusion together, while chariots, destitute of guidance, and terrified horses without drivers, dashed as panic urged them, sideways, or in direct collision against the ranks.

37. Those of the Britons who, having as yet taken no part in the engage-ment, occupied the hill-tops, and who without fear for themselves sat idly disdaining the smallness of our numbers, had begun gradually to descend and to hem in the rear of the victorious army, when Agricola, who feared this very movement, opposed their advance with four squadrons of cavalry held in reserve by him for any sudden emergencies of battle. Their repulse and rout was as severe as their onset had been furious. Thus the enemy's design recoiled on himself, and the cavalry which by the general's order had wheeled round from the van of the contending armies, attacked his rear. Then, indeed, the open plain presented an awful and hideous spectacle. Our men pursued, wounded, made prisoners of the fugitives only to slaughter them when others fell in their way. And now the enemy, as prompted by their various dispositions, fled in whole battalions with arms in their hands before a few pursuers, while some, who were unarmed, actually rushed to the front and gave themselves up to death. Everywhere there lay scattered arms, corpses, and mangled limbs, and the earth reeked with blood. Even the con-quered now and then felt a touch of fury and of courage. On approaching the woods, they rallied, and as they knew the ground, they were able to pounce on the foremost and least cautious of the pursuers. Had not Agricola, who was present everywhere, ordered a force of strong and lightly-equipped cohorts, with some dismounted troopers for the denser parts of the forest, and a detachment of cavalry where it was not so thick, to scour the woods like a party of huntsmen, serious loss would have been sustained through the excessive confidence of our troops. When, however, the enemy saw that we again pursued them in firm and compact array, they fled no longer in masses as before, each looking for his comrade; but dispersing and avoiding one another, they sought the shelter of distant and pathless wilds. Night and weariness of bloodshed put an end to the pursuit. About 10,000 of the enemy were slain; on our side there fell 360 men, and among them Aulus Atticus, the

commander of the cohort, whose youthful impetuosity and mettlesome steed had borne him into the midst of the enemy.

38. Elated by their victory and their booty, the conquerors passed a night of merriment. Meanwhile the Britons, wandering amidst the mingled wailing of men and women, were dragging off their wounded, calling to the unhurt, deserting their homes, and in their rage actually firing them, choosing places of concealment only instantly to abandon them. One moment they would take counsel together, the next, part company, while the sight of those who were dearest to them sometimes melted their hearts, but oftener roused their fury. It was an undoubted fact that some of them vented their rage on their wives and children, as if in pity for their lot. The following day showed more fully the extent of the calamity, for the silence of desolation reigned everywhere: the hills were forsaken, houses were smoking in the distance, and no one was seen by the scouts. These were dispatched in all directions; and it having been ascertained that the track of the flying enemy was uncertain, and that there was no attempt at rallying, it being also impossible, summer was now over, to extend the war, Agricola led back his army into the territory of the Boresti. He received hostages from them, and then ordered the commander of the fleet to sail round Britain. A force for this purpose was given him, which great panic everywhere preceded. Agricola himself, leading his infantry and cavalry by slow marches, so as to overawe the newly-conquered tribes by the very tardiness of his progress, brought them into winter-quarters, while the fleet with propitious breezes and great renown entered the harbor of Trutulium, to which it had returned after having coasted along the entire southern shore of the island.

39. Of this series of events, though not exaggerated in the dispatches of Agricola by any boastfulness of language, Domitian heard, as was his wont, with joy in his face but anxiety in his heart. He felt conscious that all men laughed at his late mock triumph over Germany, for which there had been purchased from traders people whose dress and hair might be made to resemble those of captives, whereas now a real and splendid victory, with the destruction of thousands of the enemy, was being celebrated with just applause. It was, he thought, a very alarming thing for him that the name of a subject should be raised above that of the Emperor; it was to no purpose that he had driven into obscurity the pursuit of forensic eloquence and the graceful accomplishments of civil life, if another were to forestall the distinctions of war. To other glories he could more easily shut his eyes, but the greatness of a good general was a truly imperial quality. Harassed by these anxieties, and absorbed in an incommunicable trouble, a sure prognostic of some cruel purpose, he decided that it was best for the present to suspend his hatred until the freshness of Agricola's renown and his popularity with the army should begin to pass away.

40. For Agricola was still the governor of Britain. Accordingly the Emperor ordered that the usual triumphal decorations, the honor of a laurelled statue, and all that is commonly given in place of the triumphal procession, with the addition of many laudatory expressions, should be decreed in the senate, together with a hint to the effect that Agricola was to have the province of Syria, then vacant by the death of Atilius Rufus, a man of consular rank, and generally reserved for men of distinction. It was believed by many persons that one of the freedmen employed on confidential services was sent to Agricola, bearing a dispatch in which Syria was offered him, and with instructions to deliver it should he be in Britain; that this freedman in crossing the straits met Agricola, and without even saluting him made his way back to Domitian; though I cannot say whether the story is true, or is only a fiction invented to suit the Emperor's character.

Meanwhile Agricola had handed over his province in peace and safety to his successor. And not to make his entrance into Rome conspicuous by the concourse of welcoming throngs, he avoided the attentions of his friends by entering the city at night, and at night too, according to orders, proceeded to the palace, where, having been received with a hurried embrace and without a word being spoken, he mingled in the crowd of courtiers. Anxious henceforth to temper the military renown, which annoys men of peace, with other merits, he studiously cultivated retirement and leisure, simple in dress, courteous in conversation, and never accompanied but by one or two friends, so that the many who commonly judge of great men by their external grandeur, after having seen and attentively surveyed him, asked the secret of a greatness which but few could explain.

41. During this time he was frequently accused before Domitian in his absence, and in his absence acquitted. The cause of his danger lay not in any crime, nor in any complaint of injury, but in a ruler who was the foe of virtue, in his own renown, and in that worst class of enemies—the men who praise. And then followed such days for the commonwealth as would not suffer Agricola to be forgotten; days when so many of our armies were lost in Moesia, Dacia, Germany, and Pannonia, through the rashness or cowardice of our generals, when so many of our officers were besieged and captured with so many of our auxiliaries, when it was no longer the boundaries of empire and the banks of rivers which were imperiled, but the winter-quarters of our legions and the possession of our territories. And so when disaster followed upon disaster, and the entire year was marked by destruction and slaughter, the voice of the people called Agricola to the command; for they all contrasted his vigor, firmness, and experience in war, with the inertness and timidity of other generals. This talk, it is quite certain, assailed the ears of the Emperor himself, while affection and loyalty in the best of his freedmen, malice and envy in the worst, kindled the anger of a prince ever inclined to evil. And so at once, by his own excellence and by the faults of others, Agricola was hurried headlong to a perilous elevation.

42. The year had now arrived in which the pro-consulate of Asia or Africa was to fall to him by lot, and, as Civica had been lately murdered, Agricola did not want a warning, or Domitian a precedent. Persons well acquainted with the Emperor's feelings came to ask Agricola, as if on their own account, whether he would go. First they hinted their purpose by praises of tranquillity and leisure; then offered their services in procuring acceptance for his excuses; and at last, throwing off all disguise, brought him by entreaties and threats to Domitian. The Emperor, armed beforehand with hypocrisy, and assuming a haughty demeanor, listened to his prayer that he might be excused, and having granted his request allowed himself to be formally thanked, nor blushed to grant so sinister a favor. But the salary usually granted to a pro-consul, and which he had himself given to some governors, he did not bestow on Agricola, either because he was offended at its not having been asked, or was warned by his conscience that he might be thought to have purchased the refusal which he had commanded. It is, indeed, human nature to hate the man whom you have injured; yet the Emperor, notwithstanding his irascible temper and an implacability proportioned to his reserve, was softened by the moderation and prudence of Agricola, who neither by a perverse obstinacy nor an idle parade of freedom challenged fame or provoked his fate. Let it be known to those whose habit it is to admire the disregard of authority, that there may be great men even under bad emperors, and that obedience and submission, when joined to activity and vigor, may attain a glory which most men reach only by a perilous career, utterly useless to the state, and closed by an ostentatious death.

43. The end of his life, a deplorable calamity to us and a grief to his friends, was regarded with concern even by strangers and those who knew him not. The common people and this busy population continually inquired at his house, and talked of him in public places and in private gatherings. No man when he heard of Agricola's death could either be glad or at once forget it. Men's sympathy was increased by a prevalent rumor that he was destroyed by poison. For myself, I have nothing which I should venture to state for fact. Certainly during the whole of his illness the Emperor's chief freedmen and confidential physicians came more frequently than is usual with a court which pays its visits by means of messengers. This was, perhaps, solicitude, perhaps espionage. Certain it is, that on the last day the very agonies of his dying moments were reported by a succession of couriers, and no one believed that there would be such haste about tidings which would be heard with regret. Yet in his manner and countenance the Emperor displayed some signs of sorrow, for he could now forget his enmity, and it was easier to conceal his joy than his fear. It was well known that on reading the will, in which he was named co-heir with Agricola's excellent wife and most dutiful daughter, he expressed delight, as if it had been a complimentary choice. So blinded and perverted was his mind by incessant flattery, that he did not know that it was only a bad Emperor whom a good father would make his heir.

44. Agricola was born on the 13th of June, in the third consulate of C. Caesar; he died on the 23rd of August, during the consulate of Collega and Priscus, being in the fifty-sixth year of his age. Should posterity wish to know something of his appearance, it was graceful rather than commanding. There was nothing formidable in his appearance; a gracious look predominated. One would easily believe him a good man, and willingly believe him to be great. As for himself, though taken from us in the prime of a vigorous manhood, yet, as far as glory is concerned, his life was of the longest. Those true blessings, indeed, which consist in virtue, he had fully attained; and on one who had reached the honors of a consulate and a triumph, what more had fortune to bestow? Immense wealth had no attractions for him, and wealth he had, even to splendor. As his daughter and his wife survived him, it may be thought that he was even fortunate—fortunate, in that while his honors had suffered no eclipse, while his fame was at its height, while his kindred and his friends still prospered, he escaped from the evil to come. For, though to survive until the dawn of this most happy age and to see a Trajan on the throne was what he would speculate upon in previsions and wishes confided to my ears, yet he had this mighty compensation for his premature death, that he was spared those later years during which Domitian, leaving now no interval or breathing space of time, but, as it were, with one continuous blow, drained the life-blood of the Commonwealth.

45. Agricola did not see the senate-house besieged, or the senate hemmed in by armed men, or so many of our consulars falling at one single massacre, or so many of Rome's noblest ladies exiles and fugitives. Carus Metius had as yet the distinction of but one victory, and the noisy counsels of Messalinus were not heard beyond the walls of Alba and Massa Baebius was then answering for his life. It was not long before our hands dragged Helvidius to prison, before we gazed on the dying looks of Manricus and Rusticus, before we were steeped in Senecio's innocent blood. Even Nero turned his eyes away, and did not gaze upon the atrocities which he ordered; with Domitian it was the chief part of our miseries to see and to be seen, to know that our sighs were being recorded, to have, ever ready to note the pallid looks of so many faces, that savage countenance reddened with the hue with which he defied shame.

You were indeed fortunate, Agricola, not only in the splendor of your life, but in the opportune moment of your death. You submitted to your fate, so they tell us who were present to hear your last words, with courage and cheerfulness, seeming to be doing all you could to give thine Emperor full acquittal. As for me and your daughter, besides all the bitterness of a father's loss, it increases our sorrow that it was not permitted us to watch over your failing health, to comfort your weakness, to satisfy ourselves with those looks, those embraces. Assuredly we should have received some precepts, some utterances to fix in our inmost hearts. This is the bitterness of our sorrow, this the smart of our wound, that from the circumstance of so long an absence you were lost to us four years before. Doubtless, best of fathers, with that most loving wife at your side, all the dues of affection were abundantly paid you, yet with too few tears you were laid to your rest, and in the light of your last day there was something for which shine eyes longed in vain.

46. If there is any dwelling-place for the spirits of the just; if, as the wise believe, noble souls do not perish with the body, rest you in peace; and call us, your family, from weak regrets and womanish laments to the contemplation of your virtues, for which we must not weep nor beat the breast. Let us honor you not so much with transitory praises as with our reverence, and, if our powers permit us, with our emulation. That will be true respect, that the true affection of your nearest kin. This, too, is what I would enjoin on daughter and wife, to honor the memory of that father, that husband, by pondering in their hearts all his words and acts, by cherishing the features and lineaments of his character rather than those of his person. It is not that I would forbid the likenesses which are wrought in marble or in bronze; but as the faces of men, so all similitude of the face are weak and perishable things, while the fashion of the soul is everlasting, such as may be expressed not in some foreign substance, or by the help of art, but in our own lives. Whatever we loved, whatever we admired in Agricola, survives, and will survive in the hearts of men, in the succession of the ages, in the fame that waits on noble deeds. Over many indeed, of those who have gone before, as over the inglorious and ignoble, the waves of oblivion will roll; Agricola, made known to posterity by history and tradition, will live for ever.

ANNALS

Late in his life Tacitus began work on his masterpiece—a history of the Julio-Claudian emperors from the death of Augustus (14 C.E.) to the death of Nero (68 C.E.). The reigns of Tiberius, Caligula, Claudius, and Nero were contained in 18 books, but only 12 survive: Books 1-6 (with only a fragment of 5 surviving) treat the reign of Nero. Books 7-10 —the four-year reign of Caligula and the first years of Claudius— have been lost. The surviving books 11–16 cover the last years of Claudius and Nero to 66 C.E. The last two books, treating the army rebellions which brought down Nero, are also lost.

BOOK I 1–15

The Annals opens in 14 C.E. with the death of the Augustus. Tacitus briefly recalls the emperor's rise to power before giving an account of his funeral and the divergent judgments passed on him.

1. Rome at the beginning was ruled by kings. Freedom and the consulship were established by Lucius Brutus. Dictatorships were held for a temporary crisis. The power of the decemvirs did not last beyond two years, nor was the consular jurisdiction of the military tribunes of long duration. The despotisms of Cinna and Sulla were brief; the rule of Pompeius and of Crassus soon yielded before Caesar; the arms of Lepidus and Antonius before Augustus; who, when the world was wearied by civil strife, subjected it to empire under the title of "Prince." But the successes and reverses of the old Roman people have been recorded by famous historians; and fine intellects were not wanting to describe the times of Augustus, till growing sycophancy scared them away. The histories of Tiberius, Gaius Caligula, Claudius, and Nero, while they were in power, were falsified through terror, and after their death were written under the irritation of a recent hatred. Hence my purpose is to relate a few facts about Augustus—more particularly his last acts, then the reign of Tiberius, and all which follows, without either bitterness or partiality, from any motives to which I am far removed.

2. When after the destruction of Brutus and Cassius there was no longer any army of the Commonwealth, when Pompeius was crushed in Sicily, and when, with Lepidus pushed aside and Antonius slain, even the Julian faction had only Caesar left to lead it, then, dropping the title of triumvir, and giving out that he was a Consul, and was satisfied with a tribune's authority for the protection of the people, Augustus won over the soldiers with gifts, the populace with cheap corn, and all men with the sweets of repose, and so grew greater by degrees, while he concentrated in himself the functions of the Senate, the magistrates, and the laws. He was wholly unopposed, for the boldest spirits had fallen in battle, or in the proscription, while the remaining nobles, the readier they were to be slaves, were raised the higher by wealth and promotion, so that, aggrandized by revolution, they preferred the safety of the present to the dangerous past. Nor did the provinces dislike that condition of affairs, for they distrusted the government of the Senate and the people, because of the rivalries between the leading men and the rapacity of the officials, while the protection of the laws was unavailing, as they were continually deranged by violence, intrigue, and finally by corruption.

3. Augustus meanwhile, as supports to his despotism, raised to the pontificate and curule aedileship Claudius Marcellus, his sister's son, while a mere stripling, and Marcus Agrippa, of humble birth, a good soldier, and one who had shared his victory, to two consecutive consulships, and as Marcellus

soon afterwards died, he also accepted him as his son-in-law. Tiberius Nero and Claudius Drusus, his stepsons, he honored with imperial titles, although his own family was as yet undiminished. For he had admitted the children of Agrippa, Gaius and Lucius, into the house of the Caesars; and before they had yet laid aside the dress of boyhood he had most fervently desired, with an outward show of reluctance, that they should be entitled "princes of the youth," and be consuls-elect. When Agrippa died, and Lucius Caesar as he was on his way to our armies in Spain, and Gaius while returning from Armenia, still suffering from a wound, were prematurely cut off by destiny, or by their step-mother Livia's treachery, Drusus too having long been dead, Nero remained alone of the stepsons, and in him everything tended to center. He was adopted as a son, as a colleague in empire and a partner in the tribunitian power, and paraded through all the armies, no longer through his mother's secret intrigues, but at her open suggestion. For she had gained such a hold on the aged Augustus that he drove out as an exile into the island of Planasia, his only grandson, Agrippa Postumus, who, though devoid of worthy qualities, and having only the brute courage of physical strength, had not been convicted of any gross offense. And yet Augustus had appointed Germanicus, Drusus' offspring, to the command of eight legions on the Rhine, and required Tiberius to adopt him, although Tiberius had a son, now a young man, in his house; but he did it that he might have several safeguards to rest on. He had no war at the time on his hands except against the Germans, which was rather to wipe out the disgrace of the loss of Quintilius Varus[1] and his army than out of an ambition to extend the empire, or for any adequate recompense. At home all was tranquil, and there were magistrates with the same titles; there was a younger generation, sprung up since the victory of Actium, and even many of the older men had been born during the civil wars. How few were left who had seen the republic!

4. Thus the State had been revolutionized, and there was not a vestige left of the old sound morality. Stripped of equality, all looked up to the commands of a sovereign without the least apprehension for the present, while Augustus in the vigor of life, could maintain his own position, that of his house, and the general tranquillity. When in advanced old age, he was worn out by a sickly frame, and the end was near and new prospects opened, a few spoke in vain of the blessings of freedom, but most people dreaded and some longed for war. The popular gossip of the large majority fastened itself variously on their future masters. "Agrippa was savage, and had been exasperated by insult, and neither from age nor experience in affairs was equal to so great

---

[1] In 9 C.E. German insurgents ambushed Varus in the Teutoburg forest and destroyed three legions. It was the worst Roman defeat since Hannibal's triumph at Cannae in 216 B.C.E.

a burden. Tiberius Nero was of mature years, and had established his fame in war, but he had the old arrogance inbred in the Claudian family, and many symptoms of a cruel temper, though they were repressed, now and then broke out. He had also from earliest infancy been reared in an imperial house; consulships and triumphs had been heaped on him in his younger days; even in the years which, on the pretext of seclusion he spent in exile at Rhodes, he had had no thoughts but of wrath, hypocrisy, and secret sensuality. There was his mother too with a woman caprice. They must, it seemed, be subject to a female and to two striplings besides, who for a while would burden, and some day rend asunder the State."

5. While these and like topics were discussed, the infirmities of Augustus increased, and some suspected guilt on his wife's part. For a rumor had gone abroad that a few months before he had sailed to Planasia on a visit to Agrippa, with the knowledge of some chosen friends, and with one companion, Fabius Maximus; that many tears were shed on both sides, with expressions of affection, and that thus there was a hope of the young man being restored to the home of his grandfather. This, it was said, Maximus had divulged to his wife Marcia, she again to Livia. All was known to Caesar, and when Maximus soon afterwards died, by a death some thought to be self-inflicted, there were heard at his funeral wailings from Marcia, in which she reproached herself for having been the cause of her husband's destruction. Whatever the fact was, Tiberius as he was just entering Illyria was summoned home by an urgent letter from his mother, and it has not been thoroughly ascertained whether at the city of Nola he found Augustus still breathing or quite lifeless. For Livia had surrounded the house and its approaches with a strict watch, and favorable bulletins were published from time to time, till, provision having been made for the demands of the crisis, one and the same report told men that Augustus was dead and that Tiberius Nero was master of the State.

6. The first crime of the new reign was the murder of Postumus Agrippa. Though he was surprised and unarmed, a centurion of the firmest resolution dispatched him with difficulty. Tiberius gave no explanation of the matter to the Senate; he pretended that there were directions from his father ordering the tribune in charge of the prisoner not to delay the slaughter of Agrippa, whenever he should himself have breathed his last. Beyond a doubt, Augustus had often complained of the young man's character, and had thus succeeded in obtaining the sanction of a decree of the Senate for his banishment. But he never was hard-hearted enough to destroy any of his kinsfolk, nor was it credible that death was to be the sentence of the grandson in order that the stepson might feel secure. It was more probable that Tiberius and Livia, the one from fear, the other from a stepmother's enmity, hurried on the destruction of a youth whom they suspected and hated. When the centu-

rion reported, according to military custom, that he had executed the command, Tiberius replied that he had not given the command, and that the act must be justified to the Senate.

As soon as Sallustius Crispus who shared the secret (he had, in fact, sent the written order to the tribune) knew this, fearing that the charge would be shifted on himself, and that his peril would be the same whether he uttered fiction or truth, he advised Livia not to divulge the secrets of her house or the counsels of friends, or any services performed by the soldiers, nor to let Tiberius weaken the strength of imperial power by referring everything to the Senate, for "the condition," he said, "of holding empire is that an account cannot be balanced unless it be rendered to one person."

7. Meanwhile at Rome people plunged into slavery- consuls, senators, knights. The higher a man's rank, the more eager his hypocrisy, and his looks the more carefully studied, so as neither to betray joy at the decease of one emperor nor sorrow at the rise of another, while he mingled delight and lamentations with his flattery. Sextus Pompeius and Sextus Apuleius, the consuls, were the first to swear allegiance to Tiberius Caesar, and in their presence the oath was taken by Seius Strabo and Gaius Turranius, respectively the commander of the praetorian cohorts and the superintendent of the corn supplies. Then the Senate, the soldiers and the people did the same. For Tiberius would inaugurate everything with the consuls, as though the ancient constitution remained, and he hesitated about being emperor. Even the proclamation by which he summoned the senators to their chamber, he issued merely with the title of Tribune, which he had received under Augustus. The wording of the proclamation was brief, and in a very modest tone. "He would," it said, "provide for the honors due to his father, and not leave the lifeless body, and this was the only public duty he now claimed."

As soon, however, as Augustus was dead, he had given the watchword to the praetorian cohorts, as commander-in-chief. He had the guard under arms, with all the other adjuncts of a court; soldiers attended him to the forum; soldiers went with him to the senate-house. He sent letters to the different armies, as though supreme power was now his, and showed hesitation only when he spoke in the Senate. His chief motive was fear that Germanicus, who had at his disposal so many legions, such vast auxiliary forces of the allies, and such wonderful popularity, might prefer the possession to the expectation of empire. He looked also at public opinion, wishing to have the credit of having been called and elected by the State rather than of having crept into power through the intrigues of a wife and a dotard's adoption. It was subsequently understood that he assumed a wavering attitude, to test likewise the temper of the nobles. For he would twist a word or a look into a crime and treasure it up in his memory.

8. On the first day of the Senate he allowed nothing to be discussed but

the funeral of Augustus, whose will, which was brought in by the Vestal Virgins, named as his heirs Tiberius and Livia. The latter was to be admitted into the Julian family with the name of Augusta; next in expectation were the grand and great-grandchildren. In the third place, he had named the chief men of the State, most of whom he hated, simply out of ostentation and to win credit with posterity. His legacies were not beyond the scale of a private citizen, except a bequest of forty-three million five hundred thousand sesterces "to the people and populace of Rome," of one thousand to every praetorian soldier, and of three hundred to every man in the legionary cohorts composed of Roman citizens.

Next followed a deliberation about funeral honors. Of these the most imposing were thought fitting. The procession was to be conducted through "the gate of triumph," on the motion of Gallus Asinius; the titles of the laws passed, the names of the nations conquered by Augustus were to be borne in front, on that of Lucius Arruntius. Messala Valerius further proposed that the oath of allegiance to Tiberius should be yearly renewed, and when Tiberius asked him whether it was at his bidding that he had brought forward this motion, he replied that he had proposed it spontaneously, and that in whatever concerned the State he would use only his own discretion, even at the risk of offending. This was the only style of adulation which yet remained. The Senators unanimously exclaimed that the body ought to be borne on their shoulders to the funeral pile. The emperor left the point to them with disdainful moderation, he then admonished the people by a proclamation not to indulge in that tumultuous enthusiasm which had distracted the funeral of the Divine Julius, or express a wish that Augustus should be burnt in the Forum instead of in his appointed resting-place in the Campus Martius.

On the day of the funeral soldiers stood round as a guard, amid much ridicule from those who had either themselves witnessed or who had heard from their parents of the famous day when slavery was still something fresh, and freedom had been resought in vain, when the slaying of Caesar, the Dictator, seemed to some the vilest, to others, the most glorious of deeds. "Now," they said, "an aged sovereign, whose power had lasted long, who had provided his heirs with abundant means to coerce the State, requires the defense of soldiers that his burial may be undisturbed."

9. Then followed much talk about Augustus himself, and many expressed an idle wonder that the same day marked the beginning of his assumption of empire and the close of his life, and, again, that he had ended his days at Nola in the same house and room as his father Octavius. People extolled too the number of his consulships, in which he had equaled Valerius Corvus and Gaius Marius combined, the continuance for thirty-seven years of the tribunician power, the title of Imperator twenty-one times earned, and his other honors which had either frequently repeated or were wholly new. Sensible men, however, spoke variously of his life with praise and censure. Some said "that dutiful feeling towards a father, and the necessities of the State in which laws had then no place, drove him into civil war, which can neither be planned nor conducted on any right principles. He had often yielded to Antonius, while he was taking vengeance on his father's murderers, often also to Lepidus. When the latter sank into feeble dotage and the former had been ruined by his profligacy, the only remedy for his distracted country was the rule of a single man. Yet the State had been organized under the name neither of a kingdom nor a dictatorship, but under that of a prince. The ocean and remote rivers were the boundaries of the empire; the legions, provinces, fleets, all things were linked together; there was law for the citizens; there was respect shown to the allies. The capital had been embellished on a grand scale; only in a few instances had he resorted to force, simply to secure general tranquillity."

10. It was said, on the other hand, "that filial duty and State necessity were merely assumed as a mask. It was really from a lust of sovereignty that he had excited the veterans by bribery, had, when a young man and a subject, raised an army, tampered with the Consul's legions, and feigned an attachment to the faction of Pompeius. Then, when by a decree of the Senate he had usurped the high functions and authority of Praetor when Hirtius and Pansa were slain—whether they were destroyed by the enemy, or Pansa by poison infused into a wound, Hirtius by his own soldiers and Caesar's treacherous machinations—he at once possessed himself of both their armies, wrested the consulate from a reluctant Senate, and turned against the State the arms with which he had been entrusted against Antonius. Citizens were proscribed, lands divided, without so much as the approval of those who executed these deeds. Even granting that the deaths of Cassius and of the Bruti were sacrifices to a hereditary enmity (though duty requires us to waive private feuds for the sake of the public welfare), still Pompeius had been deluded by the phantom of peace, and Lepidus by the mask of friendship. Subsequently, Antonius had been lured on by the treaties of Tarentum and Brundisium, and by his marriage with the sister, and paid by his death the penalty of a treacherous alliance. No doubt, there was peace after all this, but it was a peace stained with blood; there were the disasters of Lollius and Varus, the murders at Rome of the Varros, Egnatii, and Juli."

The domestic life too of Augustus was not spared. "Nero's wife had been taken from him, and there had been the farce of consulting the pontiffs, whether, with a child conceived and not yet born, she could properly marry. There were the excesses of Quintus Tedius and Vedius Pollio; last of all, there was Livia, terrible to the State as a mother, terrible to the house of the Caesars as a stepmother. No honor was left for the gods, when Augustus chose to be himself worshipped with temples and statues, like those of the deities, and with flamens and priests. He had not even adopted Tiberius as his successor out of affection or any regard to the State, but, having thoroughly seen his arrogant and savage temper, he had sought glory for himself by a contrast of extreme wickedness." For, in fact, Augustus, a few years before, when he was a second time asking from the Senate the tribunician power for Tiberius, though his speech was complimentary, had thrown out certain hints as to his manners, style, and habits of life, which he meant as reproaches, while he seemed to excuse. However, when his obsequies had been duly performed, a temple with a religious ritual was decreed him.

11. After this all prayers were addressed to Tiberius. He, on his part, urged various considerations, the greatness of the empire, his distrust of himself. "Only," he said, "the intellect of the Divine Augustus was equal to such a burden. Called as he had been by him to share his anxieties, he had learnt by experience how exposed to fortune's caprices was the task of universal rule. Consequently, in a state which had the support of so many great men, they should not put everything on one man, as many, by uniting their efforts would more easily discharge public functions." There was more grand sentiment than good faith in such words. Tiberius' language even in matters which he did not care to conceal, either from nature or habit, was always hesitating and obscure, and now that he was struggling to hide his feelings completely, it was all the more involved in uncertainty and doubt. The Senators, however, whose only fear was lest they might seem to understand him, burst into complaints, tears, and prayers. They raised their hands to the gods, to the statue of Augustus, and to the knees of Tiberius, when he ordered a document to be produced and read. This contained a description of the resources of the State, of the number of citizens and allies under arms, of the fleets, subject kingdoms, provinces, taxes, direct and indirect, necessary expenses and customary bounties. All these details Augustus had written with his own hand, and had added a counsel, that the empire should be confined to its present limits, either from fear or out of jealousy.

12. Meantime, while the Senate stooped to the most abject supplication, Tiberius happened to say that although he was not equal to the whole burden of the State, yet he would undertake the charge of whatever part of it might be entrusted to him. Thereupon Asinius Gallus said, "I ask you, Caesar, what part of the State you wish to have entrusted to you?" Confounded by the sudden inquiry he was silent for a few moments; then, recovering his presence of mind, he replied that it would by no means become his modesty to choose or to avoid in a case where he would prefer to be wholly excused. Then Gallus again, who had inferred anger from his looks, said that the question had not been asked with the intention of dividing what could not be separated, but to convince him by his own admission that the body of the State

was one, and must be directed by a single mind. He further spoke in praise of Augustus, and reminded Tiberius himself of his victories, and of his admirable deeds for many years as a civilian. Still, he did not thereby soften the emperor's resentment, for he had long been detested from an impression that, as he had married Vipsania, daughter of Marcus Agrippa, who had once been the wife of Tiberius, he aspired to be more than a citizen, and kept up the arrogant tone of his father, Asinius Pollio.

13. Next, Lucius Arruntius, who differed but little from the speech of Gallus, gave like offense, though Tiberius had no old grudge against him, but simply mistrusted him, because he was rich and daring, had brilliant accomplishments, and corresponding popularity. For Augustus, when in his last conversations he was discussing who would refuse the highest place, though sufficiently capable, who would aspire to it without being equal to it, and who would unite both the ability and ambition, had described Marcus Lepidus as able but contemptuously indifferent, Gallus Asinius as ambitious and incapable, Lucius Arruntius as not unworthy of it, and, should the chance be given him, sure to make the venture. About the two first there is a general agreement, but instead of Arruntius some have mentioned Cn. Piso, and all these men, except Lepidus, were soon afterwards destroyed by various charges through the contrivance of Tiberius. Quintus Haterius too and Mamercus Scaurus ruffled his suspicious temper, Haterius by having said: "How long, Caesar, will you suffer the State to be without a head?" Scaurus by the remark that there was a hope that the Senate's prayers would not be fruitless, seeing that he had not used his right as Tribune to negative the motion of the Consuls. Tiberius instantly broke out into invective against Haterius; Scaurus, with whom he was far more deeply displeased, he passed over in silence. Wearied at last by the assembly's clamorous importunity and the urgent demands of individual Senators, he gave way by degrees, not admitting that he undertook empire, but yet ceasing to refuse it and to be entreated. It is known that Haterius having entered the palace to ask pardon, and thrown himself at the knees of Tiberius as he was walking, was almost killed by the soldiers, because Tiberius fell forward, accidentally or from being entangled by the suppliant's hands. Yet the peril of so great a man did not make him relent, till Haterius went with entreaties to Augusta, and was saved by her very earnest intercessions.

14. Great too was the Senate's sycophancy to Augusta. Some would have her styled "parent;" others "mother of the country," and a majority proposed that to the name of Caesar should be added "son of Julia." The emperor repeatedly asserted that there must be a limit to the honors paid to women, and that he would observe similar moderation in those bestowed on himself, but annoyed at the invidious proposal, and indeed regarding a woman's elevation as a slight to himself, he would not allow so much as a lictor to be

assigned her, and forbade the erection of an altar in memory of her adoption, and any like distinction. But for Germanicus Caesar he asked pro-consular powers, and envoys were dispatched to confer them on him, and also to express sympathy with his grief at the death of Augustus. The same request was not made for Drusus, because he was consul elect and present at Rome. Twelve candidates were named for the praetorship, the number which Augustus had handed down, and when the Senate urged Tiberius to increase it, he bound himself by an oath not to exceed it.

15. It was then for the first time that the elections were transferred from the Campus Martius to the Senate. For up to that day, though the most important rested with the emperor's choice, some were settled by the partialities of the tribes. Nor did the people complain of having the right taken from them, except in mere idle talk, and the Senate, being now released from the necessity of bribery and of degrading solicitations, gladly upheld the change, Tiberius confining himself to the recommendation of only four candidates who were to be nominated without rejection or canvass. Meanwhile the tribunes of the people asked leave to exhibit at their own expense games to be named after Augustus and added to the Calendar as the Augustales. Money was, however, voted from the exchequer, and though the use of the triumphal robe in the circus was prescribed, it was not allowed them to ride in a chariot. Soon the annual celebration was transferred to the praetor, to whose lot fell the administration of justice between citizens and foreigners.

BOOK I **33–53**

On the death of the emperor Augustus, his favorite (and grandson-in-law) Germanicus goes to suppress the mutiny of the German legions in the name of the new emperor Tiberius. Though Tacitus is sympathetic to Germanicus, the young prince's emotional behavior is quite different from earlier Roman heroes.

33. Meantime Germanicus, while, as I have related, he was collecting the taxes of Gaul, received news of the death of Augustus. He was married to the granddaughter of Augustus, Agrippina, by whom he had several children, and though he was himself the son of Drusus, brother of Tiberius, and grandson of Augusta, he was troubled by the secret hatred of his uncle and grandmother, the motives for which were the more venomous because unjust. For the memory of Drusus was held in honor by the Roman people, and they believed that had he obtained empire, he would have restored freedom. Hence they regarded Germanicus with favor and with the same hope. He was indeed a young man of unsparing temper, and of wonderful kindli-

ness, contrasting strongly with the proud and mysterious reserve that marked the conversation and the features of Tiberius. Then, there were feminine jealousies, Livia feeling a stepmother's bitterness towards Agrippina, and Agrippina herself too being rather excitable, only her purity and love of her husband gave a right direction to her otherwise imperious disposition.

34. But the nearer Germanicus was to the highest hope, the more laboriously did he exert himself for Tiberius, and he made the neighboring Sequani and all the Belgic states swear obedience to him. On hearing of the mutiny in the legions, he instantly went to the spot, and met them outside the camp, eyes fixed on the ground, and seemingly repentant. As soon as he entered the entrenchment, confused murmurs became audible. Some men, seizing his hand under pretense of kissing it, thrust his fingers into their mouths, that he might touch their toothless gums; others showed him their limbs bowed with age. He ordered the throng which stood near him, as it seemed a promiscuous gathering, to separate itself into its military companies. They replied that they would hear better as they were. The standards were then to be advanced, so that thus at least the cohorts might be distinguished. The soldiers obeyed reluctantly. Then beginning with a reverent mention of Augustus, he passed on to the victories and triumphs of Tiberius, dwelling with especial praise on his glorious achievements with those legions in Germany. Next, he extolled the unity of Italy, the loyalty of Gaul, the entire absence of turbulence or strife. He was heard in silence or with but a slight murmur.

35. As soon as he touched on the mutiny and asked what had become of soldierly obedience, of the glory of ancient discipline, whither they had driven their tribunes and centurions, they all bared their bodies and taunted him with the scars of their wounds and the marks of the lash. And then with confused exclamations they spoke bitterly of the prices of exemptions, of their scanty pay, of the severity of their tasks, with special mention of the entrenchment, the fosse, the conveyance of fodder, building-timber, firewood, and whatever else had to be procured from necessity, or as a check on idleness in the camp. The fiercest clamor arose from the veteran soldiers, who, as they counted their thirty campaigns or more, implored him to relieve worn-out men, and not let them die under the same hardships, but have an end of such harassing service, and repose without beggary. Some even claimed the legacy of the Divine Augustus, with words of good omen for Germanicus, and, should he wish for empire, they showed themselves abundantly willing. Thereupon, as though he were contracting the pollution of guilt, he leapt impetuously from the tribunal. The men opposed his departure with their weapons, threatening him repeatedly if he would not go back. But Germanicus protesting that he would die rather than cast off his loyalty, plucked his sword from his side, raised it aloft and was plunging it into his breast, when those nearest him seized his hand and held it by force. The remotest and most densely crowded part of the throng, and, what almost passes belief, some, who came close up to him, urged him to strike the blow, and a soldier, by name Calusidius, offered him a drawn sword, saying that it was sharper than his own. Even in their fury, this seemed to them a savage act and one of evil precedent, and there was a pause during which Caesar's friends hurried him into his tent.

36. There they took counsel how to heal matters. For news was also brought that the soldiers were preparing the dispatch of envoys who were to draw the upper army into their cause; that the capital of the Ubii was marked out for destruction, and that hands with the stain of plunder on them would soon be daring enough for the pillage of Gaul. The alarm was heightened by the knowledge that the enemy was aware of the Roman mutiny, and would certainly attack if the Rhine bank were undefended. Yet if the auxiliary troops and allies were to be armed against the retiring legions, civil war was in fact begun. Severity would be dangerous; profuse liberality would be scandalous. Whether all or nothing were conceded to the soldiery, the State was equally in jeopardy.

Accordingly, having weighed their plans one against each other, they decided that a letter should be written in the prince's name, to the effect that full discharge was granted to those who had served in twenty campaigns; that there was a conditional release for those who had served sixteen, and that they were to be retained under a standard with immunity from everything except actually keeping off the enemy; that the legacies which they had asked, were to be paid and doubled.

37. The soldiers perceived that all this was invented for the occasion, and instantly pressed their demands. The discharge from service was quickly arranged by the tribunes. Payment was put off till they reached their respective winter quarters. The men of the fifth and twenty-first legions refused to go till in the summer-camp where they stood the money was made up out of the purses of Germanicus himself and his friends, and paid in full. The first and twentieth legions were led back by their officer Caecina to the canton of the Ubii, marching in disgrace, since sums of money which had been extorted from the general were carried among the eagles and standards. Germanicus went to the Upper Army, and the second, thirteenth, and sixteenth legions, without any delay, accepted from him the oath of allegiance. The fourteenth hesitated a little, but their money and the discharge were offered even without their demanding it.

38. Meanwhile there was an outbreak among the Chauci, begun by some veterans of the mutinous legions on garrison duty. They were quelled for a time by the instant execution of two soldiers. Such was the order of Mennius, the camp-prefect, more as a salutary warning than as a legal act. Then, when the commotion increased, he fled and having been discovered, as his hiding place was now unsafe, he borrowed a resource from audacity. "It was not," he told them, "the camp-prefect, it was Germanicus, their general, it was Tiberius, their emperor, whom they were insulting." At the same moment, overawing all resistance, he seized the standard, faced round towards the river-bank, and exclaiming that whoever left the ranks, he would hold as a deserter, he led them back into their winter-quarters, disaffected indeed, but cowed.

39. Meanwhile envoys from the Senate had an interview with Germanicus, who had now returned, at the Altar of the Ubii. Two legions, the first and twentieth, with veterans discharged and serving under a standard, were there in winter-quarters. In the bewilderment of terror and conscious guilt they were penetrated by an apprehension that persons had come at the Senate's orders to cancel the concessions they had extorted by mutiny. And as it is the way with a mob to fix any charge, however groundless, on some particular person, they reproached Manatius Plancus, an ex-consul and the chief envoy, with being the author of the Senate's decree. At midnight they began to demand the imperial standard kept in Germanicus' quarters, and having rushed together to the entrance, burst the door, dragged Caesar from his bed, and forced him by menaces of death to give up the standard. Then roaming through the camp-streets, they met the envoys, who on hearing of the tumult were hastening to Germanicus. They loaded them with insults, and were on the point of murdering them, Plancus especially, whose high rank had deterred him from flight. In his peril he found safety only in the camp of the first legion. There clasping the standards and the eagle, he sought to protect himself under their sanctity. And had not the eagle-bearer, Calpurnius, saved him from the worst violence, the blood of an envoy of the Roman people, an occurrence rare even among our foes, would in a Roman camp have stained the altars of the gods.

At last, with the light of day, when the general and the soldiers and the whole affair were clearly recognized, Germanicus entered the camp, ordered Plancus to be conducted to him, and received him on the tribunal. He then upbraided them with their fatal infatuation, revived not so much by the anger of the soldiers as by that of heaven, and explained the reasons of the envoys' arrival. On the rights of ambassadors, on the dreadful and undeserved peril of Plancus, and also on the disgrace into which the legion had brought itself, he dwelt with the eloquence of pity, and while the throng was confounded rather than appeased, he dismissed the envoys with an escort of auxiliary cavalry.

40. Amid the alarm all condemned Germanicus for not going to the Upper Army, "Enough and more than enough blunders," they said, "had been made by granting discharges and money, indeed, by conciliatory measures. Even if Germanicus held his own life cheap, why should he keep a little son and a pregnant wife among madmen who outraged every human right? Let these, at least, be restored safely to their grandsire and to the State."

When his wife spurned the notion, protesting that she was a descendant of the Divine Augustus and could face peril with no degenerate spirit, he at last embraced her and the son of their love with many tears, and after long delay compelled her to depart. Slowly moved along a pitiable procession of women, a general's fugitive wife with a little son in her bosom, her friends' wives weeping round her, as with her they were dragging themselves from the camp. Not less sorrowful were those who remained.

41. There was no appearance of the triumphant general about Germanicus, and he seemed to be in a conquered city rather than in his own camp, while groans and wailings attracted the ears and looks even of the soldiers. They came out of their tents, asking "what was that mournful sound? What meant the sad sight? Here were ladies of rank, not a centurion to escort them, not a soldier, no sign of a prince's wife, none of the usual retinue. Could they be going to the Treveri, to be subjects of the foreigner?" Then they felt shame and pity, and remembered her father Agrippa, her grandfather Augustus, her father-in-law Drusus, her own glory as a mother of children, her noble purity.[1] And there was her little child too, born in the camp, brought up amid the tents of the legions, whom they used to call in soldiers' fashion, Caligula, because he often wore the shoe so called, to win the men's goodwill. But nothing moved them so much as jealousy towards the Treveri. They entreated, stopped the way, that Agrippina might return and remain, some running to meet her, while most of them went back to Germanicus. He, with a grief and anger that were yet fresh, thus began to address the throng around him:

42. "Neither wife nor son are dearer to me than my father and the State. But he will surely have the protection of his own majesty, the empire of Rome that of our other armies. My wife and children whom, were it a question of your glory, I would willingly expose to destruction, I now remove to a distance from your fury, so that whatever wickedness is thereby threatened, may be expiated by my blood only, and that you may not be made more guilty by the slaughter of a great-grandson of Augustus, and the murder of a daughter-in-law of Tiberius. For what have you not dared, what have you not profaned during these days? What name shall I give to this gathering? Am I to call you soldiers, you who have beset with entrenchment and arms your general's son, or citizens, when you have trampled under foot the authority of the Senate? Even the rights of public enemies, the sacred character of the

---

[1] Agrippina was the daughter of Agrippa and Augustus' only child, Julia. She and Germanicus had six children, including Gaius (called Caligula) and the younger Agrippina, who was later mother of Nero.

ambassador, and the law of nations have been violated by you. The Divine Julius once quelled an army's mutiny with a single word by calling those who were renouncing their military obedience 'citizens.' The Divine Augustus cowed the legions who had fought at Actium with one look of his face. Though I am not yet what they were, still, descended as I am from them, it would be a strange and unworthy thing should I be spurned by the soldiery of Spain or Syria. First and twentieth legions, you who received your standards from Tiberius, you, men of the twentieth who have shared with me so many battles and have been enriched with so many rewards, is not this a fine gratitude with which you are repaying your general? Are these the tidings which I shall have to carry to my father when he hears only joyful intelligence from our other provinces, that his own recruits, his own veterans are not satisfied with discharge or pay; that here only centurions are murdered, tribunes driven away, envoys imprisoned, camps and rivers stained with blood, while I am myself dragging on a precarious existence amid those who hate me?

43. "Why, on the first day of our meeting, why did you, my friends, wrest from me, in your blindness, the steel which I was preparing to plunge into my breast? Better and more loving was the act of the man who offered me the sword. At any rate I should have perished before I was as yet conscious of all the disgraces of my army, while you would have chosen a general who though he might allow my death to pass unpunished would avenge the death of Varus and his three legions. Never indeed may heaven suffer the Belgae, though they proffer their aid, to have the glory and honor of having rescued the name of Rome and quelled the tribes of Germany. It is your spirit, Divine Augustus, now received into heaven, your image, father Drusus, and the remembrance of you, which, with these same soldiers who are now stimulated by shame and ambition, should wipe out this blot and turn the wrath of civil strife to the destruction of the foe. You too, in whose faces and in whose hearts I perceive a change, if only you restore to the Senate their envoys, to the emperor his due allegiance, to myself my wife and son, do you stand aloof from pollution and separate the mutinous from among you. This will be a pledge of your repentance, a guarantee of your loyalty."

44. Thereupon, as suppliants confessing that his reproaches were true, they implored him to punish the guilty, pardon those who had erred, and lead them against the enemy. And he was to recall his wife, to let the nursling of the legions return and not be handed over as a hostage to the Gauls. As to Agrippina's return, he made the excuse of her approaching confinement and of winter. His son, he said, would come, and the rest they might settle themselves. Away they hurried hither and thither, altered men, and dragged the chief mutineers in chains to C. Caetronius commander of the first legion, who tried and punished them one by one in the following fashion. In front of the throng stood the legions with drawn swords. Each accused man was on a raised platform and was pointed out by a tribune. If they shouted out that he was guilty, he was thrown headlong and cut to pieces. The soldiers gloated over the bloodshed as though it gave them absolution. Nor did Caesar check them, seeing that without any order from himself the same men were responsible for all the cruelty and all the odium of the deed.

The example was followed by the veterans, who were soon afterwards sent into Raetia, nominally to defend the province against a threatened invasion of the Suevi but really that they might tear themselves from a camp stamped with the horror of a dreadful remedy no less than with the memory of guilt. Then the general revised the list of centurions. Each, at his summons, stated his name, his rank, his birthplace, the number of his campaigns, what brave deeds he had done in battle, his military rewards, if any. If the tribunes and the legion commended his energy and good behavior, he retained his rank; where they unanimously charged him with rapacity or cruelty, he was dismissed the service.

45. Quiet being thus restored for the present, a no less formidable difficulty remained through the turbulence of the fifth and twenty-first legions, who were in winter quarters sixty miles away at Old Camp, as the place was called. These, in fact, had been the first to begin the mutiny, and the most atrocious deeds had been committed by their hands. Unawed by the punishment of their comrades, and unmoved by their contrition, they still retained their resentment. Caesar accordingly proposed to send an armed fleet with some of our allies down the Rhine, resolved to make war on them should they reject his authority.

46. At Rome, meanwhile, when the result of affairs in Illyrium was not yet known, and men had heard of the commotion among the German legions, the citizens in alarm reproached Tiberius for the hypocritical irresolution with which he was fooling the senate and the people, feeble and disarmed as they were, while the soldiery were all the time in revolt, and could not be quelled by the yet imperfectly-matured authority of two striplings. "He ought to have gone himself and confronted with his imperial majesty those who would have soon yielded, when they once saw a sovereign of long experience, who was the supreme dispenser of rigor or of bounty. Could Augustus, with the feebleness of age on him, so often visit Germany, and is Tiberius, in the vigor of life, to sit in the Senate and criticize its members' words? He had taken good care that there should be slavery at Rome; he should now apply some soothing medicine to the spirit of soldiers, that they might be willing to endure peace."

47. Notwithstanding these remonstrances, it was the inflexible purpose of Tiberius not to quit the head-quarters of empire or to imperil himself and the State. Indeed, many conflicting thoughts troubled him. The army in Germany was the stronger; that in Pannonia the nearer; the first was supported by all the strength of Gaul; the latter menaced Italy. Which was he to prefer, without the fear that those whom he slighted would be infuriated by the affront? But his sons might alike visit both, and not compromise the imperial dignity, which inspired the greatest awe at a distance. There was also an excuse for mere youths referring some matters to their father, with the possibility that he could conciliate or crush those who resisted Germanicus or Drusus. What resource remained, if they despised the emperor? However, as if on the eve of departure, he selected his attendants, provided his camp-equipage, and prepared a fleet; then winter and matters of business were the various pretexts with which he amused, first, sensible men, then the populace, last, and longest of all, the provinces.

48. Germanicus meantime, though he had concentrated his army and prepared vengeance against the mutineers, thought that he ought still to allow them an interval, in case they might, with the late warning before them, regard their safety. He sent a dispatch to Caecina, which said that he was on the way with a strong force, and that, unless they forestalled his arrival by the execution of the guilty, he would resort to an indiscriminate massacre. Caecina read the letter confidentially to the eagle and standard-bearers, and to all in the camp who were least tainted by disloyalty, and urged them to save the whole army from disgrace, and themselves from destruction. "In peace," he said, "the merits of a man's case are carefully weighed; when war bursts on us, innocent and guilty alike perish."

Upon this, they sounded those whom they thought best for their purpose, and when they saw that a majority of their legions remained loyal, at the commander's suggestion they fixed a time for falling with the sword on all the vilest and foremost of the mutineers. Then, at a mutually given signal, they rushed into the tents, and butchered the unsuspecting men, none but those in the secret knowing what was the beginning or what was to be the end of the slaughter.

49. The scene was a contrast to all civil wars which have ever occurred. It was not in battle, it was not from opposing camps, it was from those same dwellings where day saw them at their common meals, night resting from labor, that they divided themselves into two factions, and showered on each other their missiles. Uproar, wounds, bloodshed, were everywhere visible; the cause was a mystery. All else was at the disposal of chance. Even some loyal men were slain, for, on its being once understood who were the objects of fury, some of the worst mutineers too had seized on weapons. Neither commander nor tribune was present to control them; the men were allowed license and vengeance to their heart's content. Soon afterwards Germanicus entered the camp, and exclaiming with a flood of tears, that this was destruction rather than remedy, ordered the bodies to be burnt.

Even then their savage spirit was seized with desire to march against the enemy, as an atonement for their frenzy, and it was felt that the shades of their fellow-soldiers could be appeased only by exposing such impious breasts to honorable scars. Caesar followed up the enthusiasm of the men, and having bridged over the Rhine, he sent across it 12,000 from the legions, with six-and-twenty allied cohorts, and eight squadrons of cavalry, whose discipline had been without a stain during the mutiny.

50. There was exultation among the Germans, not far off, as long as we were detained by the public mourning for the loss of Augustus, and then by our dissensions. But the Roman general in a forced march, cut through the Caesian forest and the barrier which had been begun by Tiberius, and pitched his camp on this barrier, his front and rear being defended by entrenchments, his flanks by timber barricades. He then penetrated some forest passes but little known, and, as there were two routes, he deliberated whether he should pursue the short and ordinary route, or that which was more difficult, unexplored, and consequently unguarded by the enemy. He chose the longer way, and hurried on every remaining preparation, for his scouts had brought word that among the Germans it was a night of festivity, with games, and one of their grand banquets. Caecina had orders to advance with some light cohorts, and to clear away any obstructions from the woods. The legions followed at a moderate interval. They were helped by a night of bright starlight, reached the villages of the Marsi, and threw their pickets round the enemy, who even then were stretched on beds or at their tables, without the least fear, or any sentries before their camp, so complete was their carelessness and disorder; and of war indeed there was no apprehension. Peace it certainly was not—merely the languid and heedless ease of half-intoxicated people.

51. Caesar, to spread devastation widely, divided his eager legions into four columns, and ravaged a space of fifty miles with fire and sword. Neither sex nor age moved his compassion. Everything, sacred or profane, the temple too of Tamfana, as they called it, the special resort of all those tribes, was leveled to the ground. There was not a wound among our soldiers, who cut down a half-asleep, an unarmed, or a straggling foe. The Bructeri, Tubantes, and Usipetes, were roused by this slaughter, and they beset the forest passes through which the army had to return. The general knew this, and he marched, prepared both to advance and to fight. Part of the cavalry, and some of the auxiliary cohorts led the van; then came the first legion, and, with the baggage in the center, the men of the twenty-first closed up the left, those of the fifth, the right flank. The twentieth legion secured the rear, and, next, were the rest of the allies.

Meanwhile the enemy moved not till the army began to defile in column through the woods, then made slight skirmishing attacks on its flanks and van, and with his whole force charged the rear. The light cohorts were thrown into confusion by the dense masses of the Germans, when Caesar rode up to the men of the twentieth legion, and in a loud voice exclaimed that this was the time for wiping out the mutiny. "Advance," he said, "and hasten to turn your guilt into glory." This fired their courage, and at a single dash they broke through the enemy, and drove him back with great slaughter into the open country. At the same moment the troops of the van emerged from the woods and entrenched a camp. After this their march was uninterrupted, and the soldiery, with the confidence of recent success, and forgetful of the past, were placed in winter-quarters.

52. The news was a source of joy and also of anxiety to Tiberius. He rejoiced that the mutiny was crushed, but the fact that Germanicus had won the soldiers' favor by lavishing money, and promptly granting the discharge, as well as his fame as a soldier, annoyed him. Still, he brought his achievements under the notice of the Senate, and spoke much of his greatness in language elaborated for effect, more so than could be believed to come from his inmost heart. He bestowed a briefer praise on Drusus, and on the termination of the disturbance in Illyricum, but he was more earnest, and his speech more hearty. And he confirmed, too, in the armies of Pannonia all the concessions of Germanicus.

53. That same year Julia ended her days. For her profligacy she had formerly been confined by her father Augustus in the island of Pandateria, and then in the town of the Regini on the shores of the straits of Sicily. She had been the wife of Tiberius while Caius and Lucius Caesar were in their glory, and had disdained him as an unequal match. This was Tiberius' special reason for retiring to Rhodes. When he obtained the empire, he left her in banishment and disgrace, deprived of all hope after the murder of Postumus Agrippa, and let her perish by a lingering death of destitution, with the idea that an obscurity would hang over her end from the length of her exile. He had a like motive for cruel vengeance on Sempronius Gracchus, a man of noble family, of shrewd understanding, and a perverse eloquence, who had seduced this same Julia when she was the wife of Marcus Agrippa. And this was not the end of the intrigue. When she had been handed over to Tiberius, her persistent paramour inflamed her with disobedience and hatred towards her husband; and a letter which Julia wrote to her father, Augustus, inveighing against Tiberius, was supposed to be the composition of Gracchus. He was accordingly banished to Cercina, where he endured an exile of fourteen years. Then the soldiers who were sent to slay him, found him on a promontory, expecting no good. On their arrival, he begged a brief interval in which to give by letter his last instructions to his wife Alliaria, and then offered his neck to the executioners, dying with a courage not unworthy of the Sempronian name, which his degenerate life had dishonored. Some have related that these soldiers were not sent from Rome, but by Lucius Asprenas, pro-

consul of Africa, on the authority of Tiberius, who had vainly hoped that the infamy of the murder might be shifted on Asprenas.

BOOK II **69–73**

Germanicus' travels in the eastern Mediterranean led to some conflict with Piso, the governor of Syria, which led to rumors when Germanicus died in Antioch.

69. Germanicus meanwhile, as he was returning from Egypt, found that all his directions to the legions and to the various cities had been repealed or reversed. This led to grievous insults on Piso, while he as savagely assailed the prince. Piso then resolved to quit Syria. Soon he was detained there by the failing health of Germanicus, but when he heard of his recovery, while people were paying the vows they had offered for his safety, he went attended by his lictors, drove away the victims placed by the altars with all the preparations for sacrifice, and the festal gathering of the populace of Antioch. Then he left for Seleucia and awaited the result of the illness which had again attacked Germanicus. The terrible intensity of the malady was increased by the belief that he had been poisoned by Piso. And certainly there were found hidden in the floor and in the walls disinterred remains of human bodies, incantations and spells, and the name of Germanicus inscribed on leaden tablets, half-burnt cinders smeared with blood, and other horrors by which in popular belief souls are devoted to the infernal deities. Piso too was accused of sending emissaries to note curiously every unfavorable symptom of the illness.

70. Germanicus heard of all this with anger, no less than with fear. "If my doors," he said, "are to be besieged, if I must gasp out my last breath under my enemies' eyes, what will then be the lot of my most unhappy wife, of my infant children? Poisoning seems tedious; he is in eager haste to have the sole control of the province and the legions. But Germanicus is not yet fallen so low, nor will the murderer long retain the reward of the fatal deed."

He then addressed a letter to Piso, renouncing his friendship, and, as many also state, ordered him to quit the province. Piso without further delay weighed anchor, slackening his course that he might not have a long way to return should Germanicus' death leave Syria open to him.

71. For a brief space the prince's hopes rose; then his frame became exhausted, and, as his end drew near, he spoke as follows to the friends by his side:

"Were I succumbing to nature, I should have just ground of complaint even against the gods for thus tearing me away in my youth by an untimely death from parents, children, country. Now, cut off by the wickedness of Piso and Plancina, I leave to your hearts my last entreaties. Describe to my father and brother, torn by what persecutions, entangled by what plots, I have ended by the worst of deaths the most miserable of lives. If any were touched by my bright prospects, by ties of blood, or even by envy towards me while I lived, they will weep that the once prosperous survivor of so many wars has perished by a woman's treachery. You will have the opportunity of complaint before the Senate, of an appeal to the laws. It is not the chief duty of friends to follow the dead with unprofitable laments, but to remember his wishes, to fulfill his commands. Tears for Germanicus even strangers will shed; vengeance must come from you, if you loved the man more than his fortune. Show the people of Rome her who is the granddaughter of the Divine Augustus, as well as my consort; set before them my six children. Sympathy will be on the side of the accusers, and to those who screen themselves under infamous orders belief or pardon will be refused."

His friends clasped the dying man's right hand, and swore that they would sooner lose life than revenge.

72. He then turned to his wife and implored her by the memory of her husband and by their common offspring to lay aside her high spirit, to submit herself to the cruel blows of fortune, and not, when she returned to Rome, to enrage by political rivalry those who were stronger than herself. This was said openly; other words were whispered, pointing, it was supposed, to his fears from Tiberius. Soon afterwards he expired, to the intense sorrow of the province and of the neighboring peoples. Foreign nations and kings grieved over him, so great was his courtesy to allies, his humanity to enemies. He inspired reverence alike by look and voice, and while he maintained the greatness and dignity of the highest rank, he had escaped the hatred that waits on arrogance.

73. His funeral, though it lacked the family statues and procession, was honored by panegyrics and a commemoration of his virtues. Some there were who, as they thought of his beauty, his age, and the manner of his death, the vicinity too of the country where he died, likened his end to that of Alexander the Great. Both had a graceful person and were of noble birth; neither had much exceeded thirty years of age, and both fell by the treachery of their own people in strange lands. But Germanicus was gracious to his friends, temperate in his pleasures, the husband of one wife, with only legitimate children. He was too no less a warrior, though rashness he had none, and, though after having cowed Germany by his many victories, he was hindered from crushing it into subjection. Had he had the sole control of affairs, had he possessed the power and title of a king, he would have attained military glory as much more easily as he had excelled Alexander in clemency, in self-restraint, and in all other virtues.

As to the body which, before it was burnt, lay bare in the forum at Antioch, its destined place of burial, it is doubtful whether it exhibited the marks of poisoning. For men according as they pitied Germanicus and were prepossessed with suspicion or were biased by partiality towards Piso, gave conflicting accounts.

BOOK III 1–18

Agrippina, the granddaughter of Augustus, returns to Rome with the ashes of her husband Germanicus. Piso is brought to trial and commits suicide.

1. Without pausing in her winter voyage Agrippina arrived at the island of Corcyra, facing the shores of Calabria. There she spent a few days to compose her mind, for she was wild with grief and knew not how to endure. Meanwhile on hearing of her arrival, all her intimate friends and several officers, everyone indeed who had served under Germanicus, many strangers too from the neighboring towns, some thinking it respectful to the emperor, and still more following their example, thronged eagerly to Brundisium, the nearest and safest landing place for a voyager.

As soon as the fleet was seen on the horizon, not only the harbor and the adjacent shores, but the city walls too and the roofs and every place which commanded the most distant prospect were filled with crowds of mourners, who incessantly asked one another, whether, when she landed, they were to receive her in silence or with some utterance of emotion. They were not agreed on what befitted the occasion when the fleet slowly approached, its crew, not joyous as is usual, but wearing all a studied expression of grief. When Agrippina descended from the vessel with her two children, clasping the funeral urn, with eyes riveted to the earth, there was one universal groan. You could not distinguish kinsfolk from strangers, or the laments of men from those of women; only the attendants of Agrippina, worn out as they were by long sorrow, were surpassed by the mourners who now met them, fresh in their grief.

2. The emperor had dispatched two praetorian cohorts with instructions that the magistrates of Calabria, Apulia, and Campania were to pay the last honors to his son's memory. Accordingly tribunes and centurions bore Germanicus' ashes on their shoulders. They were preceded by the standards unadorned and the faces reversed. As they passed colony after colony, the populace in black, the knights in their state robes, burnt vestments and perfumes with other usual funeral adjuncts, in proportion to the wealth of the place. Even those whose towns were out of the route, met the mourners,

offered victims and built altars to the dead, testifying their grief by tears and wailings. Drusus went as far as Tarracina with Claudius, brother of Germanicus, and had been at Rome. Marcus Valerius and Gaius Aurelius, the consuls, who had already entered on office, and a great number of the people thronged the road in scattered groups, everyone weeping as he felt inclined. Flattery there was none, for all knew that Tiberius could scarcely dissemble his joy at the death of Germanicus.

3. Tiberius and Augusta refrained from showing themselves, thinking it below their dignity to shed tears in public, or else fearing that, if all eyes scrutinized their faces, their hypocrisy would be revealed. I do not find in any historian or in the daily register that Antonia, Germanicus' mother, rendered any conspicuous honor to the deceased, though besides Agrippina, Drusus, and Claudius, all his other kinsfolk are mentioned by name. She may either have been hindered by illness, or with a spirit overpowered by grief she may not have had the heart to endure the sight of so great an affliction. But I can more easily believe that Tiberius and Augusta, who did not leave the palace, kept her within, that their sorrow might seem equal to hers, and that the grandmother and uncle might be thought to follow the mother's example in staying at home.

4. The day on which the remains were consigned to the tomb of Augustus, was now desolate in its silence, now distracted by lamentations. The streets of the city were crowded; torches were blazing throughout the Campus Martius. There the soldiers under arms, the magistrates without their symbols of office, the people in the tribes, were all incessantly exclaiming that the commonwealth was ruined, that not a hope remained, too boldly and openly to let one think that they remembered their rulers. But nothing impressed Tiberius more deeply than the enthusiasm kindled in favor of Agrippina, whom men spoke of as the glory of the country, the sole surviving offspring of Augustus, the solitary example of the old times, while looking up to heaven and the gods they prayed for the safety of her children and that they might outlive their oppressors.

5. Some there were who missed the grandeur of a state-funeral, and contrasted the splendid honors conferred by Augustus on Drusus, the father of Germanicus. "Then the emperor himself," they said, "went in the extreme rigor of winter as far as Ticinum, and never leaving the corpse entered Rome with it. Round the funeral bier were ranged the images of the Claudii and the Julii; there was weeping in the forum, and a panegyric before the rostra; every honor devised by our ancestors or invented by their descendants was heaped on him. But as for Germanicus, even the customary distinctions due to any noble had not fallen to his lot. Granting that his body, because of the distance of the journey, was burnt in any fashion in foreign lands, still all the more honors ought to have been afterwards paid him, because at first chance

had denied them. His brother had gone but one day's journey to meet him; his uncle, not even to the city gates. Where were all those usages of the past, the image at the head of the bier, the lays composed in commemoration of worth, the eulogies and laments, or at least the semblance of grief?"

6. All this was known to Tiberius, and, to silence popular talk, he reminded the people in a proclamation that many eminent Romans had died for their country and that none had been honored with such passionate regret. This regret was a glory both to himself and to all, provided only a due mean were observed; for what was becoming in humble homes and communities, did not befit princely personages and an imperial people. Tears and the solace found in mourning were suitable enough for the first burst of grief; but now they must brace their hearts to endurance, as in former days the Divine Julius after the loss of his only daughter, and the Divine Augustus when he was bereft of his grandchildren, had thrust away their sorrow. There was no need of examples from the past, showing how often the Roman people had patiently endured the defeats of armies, the destruction of generals, the total extinction of noble families. Princes were mortal; the State was everlasting. Let them then return to their usual pursuits, and, as the shows of the festival of the Great Goddess were at hand, even resume their amusements.

7. The suspension of business then ceased, and men went back to their occupations. Drusus was sent to the armies of Illyricum, amidst an universal eagerness to exact vengeance on Piso, and ceaseless complaints that he was meantime roaming through the delightful regions of Asia and Achaia, and was weakening the proofs of his guilt by an insolent and artful procrastination. It was indeed widely rumored that the notorious poisoner Martina, who, as I have related, had been dispatched to Rome by Cn. Sentius, had died suddenly at Brundisium; that poison was concealed in a knot of her hair, and that no symptoms of suicide were discovered on her person.

8. Piso meanwhile sent his son on to Rome with a message intended to pacify the emperor, and then made his way to Drusus, who would, he hoped, be not so much infuriated at his brother's death as kindly disposed towards himself in consequence of a rival's removal. Tiberius, to show his impartiality, received the youth courteously, and enriched him with the liberality he usually bestowed on the sons of noble families. Drusus replied to Piso that if certain insinuations were true, he must be foremost in his resentment, but he prefered to believe that they were false and groundless, and that Germanicus' death need be the ruin of no one. This he said openly, avoiding anything like secrecy. Men did not doubt that his answer was dictated to him by Tiberius, inasmuch as one who had generally all the simplicity and candor of youth, now had recourse to the artifices of old age.

9. Piso, after crossing the Dalmatian sea and leaving his ships at Ancona,

went through Picenum and along the Flaminian road, where he overtook a legion which was marching from Pannonia to Rome and was then to garrison Africa. It was a matter of common talk how he had repeatedly displayed himself to the soldiers on the road during the march. From Narnia, to avoid suspicion or because the plans of fear are uncertain, he sailed down the Nar, then down the Tiber, and increased the fury of the populace by bringing his vessel to shore at the tomb of the Caesars. In broad daylight, when the riverbank was thronged, he himself with a numerous following of dependents, and Plancina with a retinue of women, moved onward with joy in their countenances. Among other things which provoked men's anger was his house towering above the forum, gay with festal decorations, his banquets and his feasts, about which there was no secrecy, because the place was so public.

10. Next day, Fulcinius Trio asked the consul's leave to prosecute Piso. It was contended against him by Vitellius and Veranius and the others who had been the companions of Germanicus, that this was not Trio's proper part, and that they themselves meant to report their instructions from Germanicus, not as accusers, but as deponents and witnesses to facts. Trio, abandoning the prosecution on this count, obtained leave to accuse Piso's previous career, and the emperor was requested to undertake the inquiry. This even the accused did not refuse, fearing, as he did, the bias of the people and of the Senate; while Tiberius, he knew, was resolute enough to despise report, and was also entangled in his mother's complicity. Truth too would be more easily distinguished from perverse misrepresentation by a single judge, where a number would be swayed by hatred and ill-will.

Tiberius was not unaware of the formidable difficulty of the inquiry and of the rumors by which he was himself assailed. Having therefore summoned a few intimate friends, he listened to the threatening speeches of the prosecutors and to the pleadings of the accused, and finally referred the whole case to the Senate.

11. Drusus meanwhile, on his return from Illyricum, though the Senate had voted him an ovation for the submission of Maroboduus and the successes of the previous summer, postponed the honor and entered Rome. Then the defendant sought the advocacy of Lucius Arruntius, Marcus Vinicius, Asinius Gallus, Aeserninus Marcellus and Sextus Pompeius, and on their declining for different reasons, Marcus Lepidus, Lucius Piso, and Livineius Regulus became his counsel, amid the excitement of the whole country, which wondered how much fidelity would be shown by the friends of Germanicus, on what the accused rested his hopes, and how far Tiberius would repress and hide his feelings. Never were the people more keenly interested; never did they indulge themselves more freely in secret whispers against the emperor or in the silence of suspicion.

12. On the day the Senate met, Tiberius delivered a speech of studied

moderation. "Piso," he said, "was my father's representative and friend, and was appointed by myself, on the advice of the Senate, to assist Germanicus in the administration of the East. Whether he there had provoked the young prince by willful opposition and rivalry, and had rejoiced at his death or wickedly destroyed him, is for you to determine with minds unbiased. Certainly if a subordinate oversteps the bounds of duty and of obedience to his commander, and has exulted in his death and in my affliction, I shall hate him and exclude him from my house, and I shall avenge a personal quarrel without resorting to my power as emperor. If however a crime is discovered which ought to be punished, whoever the murdered man may be, it is for you to give just reparation both to the children of Germanicus and to us, his parents.

"Consider this too, whether Piso dealt with the armies in a revolutionary and seditious spirit; whether he sought by intrigue popularity with the soldiers; whether he attempted to repossess himself of the province by arms, or whether these are falsehoods which his accusers have published with exaggeration. As for them, I am justly angry with their intemperate zeal. For to what purpose did they strip the corpse and expose it to the pollution of the vulgar gaze, and circulate a story among foreigners that he was destroyed by poison, if all this is still doubtful and requires investigation? For my part, I sorrow for my son and shall always sorrow for him; still I would not hinder the accused from producing all the evidence which can relieve his innocence or convict Germanicus of any unfairness, if such there was. And I implore you not to take as proven charges alleged, merely because the case is intimately bound up with my affliction. Do you, whom ties of blood or your own true-heartedness have made his advocates, help him in his peril, everyone of you, as far as each man's eloquence and diligence can do so. To like exertions and like persistency I would urge the prosecutors. In this, and in this only, will we place Germanicus above the laws, by conducting the inquiry into his death in this house instead of in the forum, and before the Senate instead of before a bench of judges. In all else let the case be tried as simply as others. Let no one heed the tears of Drusus or my own sorrow, or any stories invented to our discredit."

13. Two days were then assigned for the bringing forward of the charges, and after six days' interval, the prisoner's defense was to occupy three days. Thereupon Fulcinius Trio began with some old and irrelevant accusations about intrigues and extortion during Piso's government of Spain. This, if proved, would not have been fatal to the defendant, if he cleared himself as to his late conduct, and, if refuted, would not have secured his acquittal, if he were convicted of the greater crimes. Next, Servaeus, Veranius, and Vitellius, all with equal earnestness, Vitellius with striking eloquence, alleged against Piso that out of hatred of Germanicus and a desire of revolution he had so

corrupted the common soldiers by license and oppression of the allies that he was called by the vilest of them "father of the legions" while on the other hand to all the best men, especially to the companions and friends of Germanicus, he had been savagely cruel. Lastly, he had, they said, destroyed Germanicus himself by sorcery and poison, and hence came those ceremonies and horrible sacrifices made by himself and Plancina; then he had threatened the State with war, and had been defeated in battle, before he could be tried as a prisoner.

14. On all points but one the defense broke down. That he had tampered with the soldiers, that his province had been at the mercy of the vilest of them, that he had even insulted his chief, he could not deny. It was only the charge of poisoning from which he seemed to have cleared himself. This indeed the prosecutors did not adequately sustain by merely alleging that at a banquet given by Germanicus, his food had been tainted with poison by the hands of Piso who sat next above him. It seemed absurd to suppose that he would have dared such an attempt among strange servants, in the sight of so many bystanders, and under Germanicus' own eyes. And, besides, the defendant offered his slaves to the torture, and insisted on its application to the attendants on that occasion. But the judges for different reasons were merciless, the emperor, because war had been made on a province, the Senate because they could not be sufficiently convinced that there had been no treachery about the death of Germanicus.

At the same time shouts were heard from the people in front of the Senate House, threatening violence if he escaped the verdict of the Senators. They had actually dragged Piso's statues to the Gemonian stairs, and were breaking them in pieces, when by the emperor's order they were rescued and replaced. Piso was then put in a litter and attended by a tribune of one of the Praetorian cohorts, who followed him, so it was variously rumored, to guard his person or to be his executioner.

15. Plancina was equally detested, but had stronger interest. Consequently it was considered a question how far the emperor would be allowed to go against her. While Piso's hopes were in suspense, she offered to share his lot, whatever it might be, and in the worst event, to be his companion in death. But as soon as she had secured her pardon through the secret intercessions of Augusta, she gradually withdrew from her husband and separated her defense from his. When the prisoner saw that this was fatal to him, he hesitated whether he should still persist, but at the urgent request of his sons braced his courage and once more entered the Senate. There he bore patiently the renewal of the accusation, the furious voices of the Senators, savage opposition indeed from every quarter, but nothing daunted him so much as to see Tiberius, without pity and without anger, resolutely closing

himself against any inroad of emotion. He was conveyed back to his house, where, seemingly by way of preparing his defense for the next day, he wrote a few words, sealed the paper and handed it to a freedman. Then he bestowed the usual attention on his person; after a while, late at night, his wife having left his chamber, he ordered the doors to be closed, and at daybreak was found with his throat cut and a sword lying on the ground.

16. I remember to have heard old men say that a document was often seen in Piso's hands, the substance of which he never himself divulged, but which his friends repeatedly declared contained a letter from Tiberius with instructions referring to Germanicus, and that it was his intention to produce it before the Senate and upbraid the emperor, had he not been deluded by vain promises from Sejanus. Nor did he perish, they said, by his own hand, but by that of one sent to be his executioner. Neither of these statements would I positively affirm; still it would not have been right for me to conceal what was related by those who lived up to the time of my youth.

The emperor, assuming an air of sadness, complained in the Senate that the purpose of such a death was to bring odium on himself, and he asked with repeated questionings how Piso had spent his last day and night. Receiving answers which were mostly judicious, though in part somewhat incautious, he read out a note written by Piso, nearly to the following effect:

"Crushed by a conspiracy of my foes and the odium excited by a lying charge, since my truth and innocence find no place here, I call the immortal gods to witness that towards you Caesar, I have lived loyally, and with like dutiful respect towards your mother. And I implore you to think of my children, one of whom, Gnaeus, is in no way implicated in my career, whatever it may have been, seeing that all this time he has been at Rome, while the other, Marcus Piso, dissuaded me from returning to Syria. Would that I had yielded to my young son rather than he to his aged father! And therefore I pray the more earnestly that the innocent may not pay the penalty of my wickedness. By forty-five years of obedience, by my association with you in the consulate, as one who formerly won the esteem of the Divine Augustus, your father, as one who is your friend and will never hereafter ask a favor, I implore you to save my unhappy son." About Plancina he added not a word.

17. Tiberius after this acquitted the young Piso of the charge of civil war on the ground that a son could not have refused a father's orders, showing compassion at the same time the high rank of the family and the terrible downfall even of Piso himself, however he might have deserved it. For Plancina he spoke with shame and conscious disgrace, alleging in excuse the intercession of his mother, secret complaints against whom from all good men were growing more and more vehement. "So it was the duty of a grandmother," people said, "to look a grandson's murderess in the face, to con-

verse with her and rescue her from the Senate. What the laws secure on behalf of every citizen, had to Germanicus alone been denied. The voices of a Vitellius and Veranius had bewailed a Caesar, while the emperor and Augusta had defended Plancina. She might as well now turn her poisonings, and her devices which had proved so successful, against Agrippina and her children, and thus sate this exemplary grandmother and uncle with the blood of a most unhappy house."

Two days were frittered away over this mockery of a trial, Tiberius urging Piso's children to defend their mother. While the accusers and their witnesses pressed the prosecution with rival zeal, and there was no reply, pity rather than anger was on the increase. Aurelius Cotta, the consul, who was first called on for his vote (for when the emperor put the question, even those in office went through the duty of voting), held that Piso's name ought to be erased from the public register, half of his property confiscated, half given up to his son, Cn. Piso, who was to change his first name; that Marcus Piso, stripped of his rank, with an allowance of five million sesterces, should be banished for ten years, Plancina's life being spared in consideration of Augusta's intercession.

18. Much of the sentence was mitigated by the emperor. The name of Piso was not to be struck out of the public register, since that of Marcus Antonius who had made war on his country, and that of Julius Antonius who had dishonored the house of Augustus, still remained. Marcus Piso too he saved from degradation, and gave him his father's property, for he was firm enough, as I have often related, against the temptation of money, and now for very shame at Plancina's acquittal, he was more than usually merciful. Again, when Valerius Messalinus and Caecina Severus proposed respectively the erection of a golden statue in the temple of Mars the Avenger and of an altar to Vengeance, he interposed, protesting that victories over the foreigner were commemorated with such monuments, but that domestic woes ought to be shrouded in silent grief.

There was a further proposal of Messalinus, that Tiberius, Augusta, Antonia, Agrippina and Drusus ought to be publicly thanked for having avenged Germanicus. He omitted all mention of Claudius. Thereupon he was pointedly asked by Lucius Asprenas before the Senate, whether the omission had been intentional, and it was only then that the name of Claudius was added. For my part, the wider the scope of my reflection on the present and the past, the more am I impressed by their mockery of human plans in every transaction. Clearly, the very last man marked out for empire by public opinion, expectation and general respect was he whom fortune was holding in reserve as the emperor of the future.

BOOK IV 1–12

Despite his distate for Tiberius, Tacitus here paints a picture of a well-administered empire until 21 c.e. In that year the praetorian prefect Aelius Sejanus became the most influential man at court.

1. The year when Gaius Asinius and Gaius Antistius were consuls was the ninth of Tiberius' reign, a period of tranquillity for the State and prosperity for his own house, for he counted Germanicus' death a happy incident. Suddenly fortune deranged everything; the emperor became a cruel tyrant, as well as an abettor of cruelty in others. Of this the cause and origin was Aelius Sejanus, commander of the praetorian cohorts, of whose influence I have already spoken. I will now fully describe his extraction, his character, and the daring wickedness by which he grasped at power.

Born at Vulsinii, the son of Seius Strabo, a Roman knight, he attached himself in his early youth to Gaius Caesar, grandson of the Divine Augustus, and the story went that he had sold his person to Apicius, a rich debauchee. Soon afterwards he won the heart of Tiberius so effectually by various artifices that the emperor, ever dark and mysterious towards others, was with Sejanus alone careless and freespoken. It was not through his craft, for it was by this very weapon that he was overthrown; it was rather from heaven's wrath against Rome, to whose welfare his elevation and his fall were alike disastrous. He had a body which could endure hardships, and a daring spirit. He was one who screened himself, while he was attacking others; he was as cringing as he was imperious; before the world he affected humility; in his heart he lusted after supremacy, for the sake of which he was sometimes lavish and luxurious, but oftener energetic and watchful, qualities quite as mischievous when hypocritically assumed for the attainment of sovereignty.

2. He strengthened the hitherto moderate powers of his office by concentrating the cohorts scattered throughout the capital into one camp, so that they might all receive orders at the same moment, and that the sight of their numbers and strength might give confidence to themselves, while it would strike terror into the citizens. His pretexts were the demoralization incident to a dispersed soldiery, the greater effectiveness of simultaneous action in the event of a sudden peril, and the stricter discipline which would be insured by the establishment of an encampment at a distance from the temptations of the city. As soon as the camp was completed, he crept gradually into the affections of the soldiers by mixing with them and addressing them by name, himself selecting the centurions and tribunes. With the Senate too he sought to ingratiate himself, distinguishing his partisans with offices and provinces, Tiberius readily yielding, and being so biased that not only in private conversation but before the senators and the people he spoke highly of him as the partner of his toils, and allowed his statues to be honored in theaters, in forums, and at the headquarters of our legions.

3. There were however obstacles to his ambition in the imperial house with its many princes, a son in youthful manhood and grown-up grandsons. As it would be unsafe to sweep off such a number at once by violence, while craft would necessitate successive intervals in crime, he chose, on the whole, the stealthier way and to begin with Drusus, against whom he had the stimulus of a recent resentment. Drusus, who could not brook a rival and was somewhat irascible, had, in a casual dispute, raised his fist at Sejanus, and, when he defended himself, had struck him in the face. On considering every plan Sejanus thought his easiest revenge was to turn his attention to Livia, Drusus' wife. She was a sister of Germanicus, and though she was not handsome as a girl, she became a woman of surpassing beauty. Pretending an ardent passion for her, he seduced her, and having won his first infamous triumph, and assured that a woman after having parted with her virtue will hesitate at nothing, he lured her on to thoughts of marriage, of a share in sovereignty, and of her husband's destruction. And she, the niece of Augustus, the daughter-in-law of Tiberius, the mother of children by Drusus, for a provincial paramour, foully disgraced herself, her ancestors, and her descendants, giving up honor and a sure position for prospects as base as they were uncertain. They took into their confidence Eudemus, Livia's friend and physician, whose profession was a pretext for frequent secret interviews. Sejanus, to avert his mistress' jealousy, divorced his wife Apicata, by whom he had had three children. Still the magnitude of the crime caused fear and delay, and sometimes a conflict of plans.

4. Meanwhile, at the beginning of this year, Drusus, one of the children of Germanicus, assumed the dress of manhood, with a repetition of the honors decreed by the Senate to his brother Nero. The emperor added a speech with warm praise of his son for sharing a father's affection to his brother's children. Drusus indeed, difficult as it is for power and mutual harmony to exist side by side, had the character of being kindly disposed or at least not unfriendly towards the lads. And now the old plan, so often insincerely broached, of a progress through the provinces, was again discussed. The emperor's pretext was the number of veterans on the eve of discharge and the necessity of fresh levies for the army. Volunteers were not forthcoming, and even if they were sufficiently numerous, they had not the same bravery and discipline, as it is chiefly the needy and the homeless who adopt by their own choice a soldier's life. Tiberius also rapidly enumerated the legions and the provinces which they had to garrison. I too ought, I think, to go through these details, and thus show what forces Rome then had under arms, what kings were our allies, and how much narrower then were the limits of our empire.

5. Italy on both seas was guarded by fleets, at Misenum and at Ravenna, and the contiguous coast of Gaul by ships of war captured in the victory of Actium, and sent by Augustus powerfully manned to the town of Forumjulium. But chief strength was on the Rhine, as a defense alike against Germans and Gauls, and numbered eight legions. Spain, lately subjugated, was held by three. Mauretania was King Juba's, who had received it as a gift from the Roman people. The rest of Africa was garrisoned by two legions, and Egypt by the same number. Next, beginning with Syria, all within the entire tract of country stretching as far as the Euphrates, was kept in restraint by four legions, and on this frontier were Iberian, Albanian, and other kings, to whom our greatness was a protection against any foreign power. Thrace was held by Rhoemetalces and the children of Cotys; the bank of the Danube by two legions in Pannonia, two in Moesia, and two also were stationed in Dalmatia, which, from the situation of the country, were in the rear of the other four, and, should Italy suddenly require aid, not too distant to be summoned. But the capital was garrisoned by its own special soldiery, three city, nine praetorian cohorts, levied for the most part in Etruria and Umbria, or ancient Latium and the old Roman colonies. There were besides, in commanding positions in the provinces, allied fleets, cavalry and light infantry, of but little inferior strength. But any detailed account of them would be misleading, since they moved from place to place as circumstances required, and had their numbers increased and sometimes diminished.

6. It is however, I think, a convenient opportunity for me to review the hitherto prevailing methods of administration in the other departments of the State, inasmuch as that year brought with it the beginning of a change for the worse in Tiberius' policy. In the first place, public business and the most important private matters were managed by the Senate: the leading men were allowed freedom of discussion, and when they stooped to flattery, the emperor himself checked them. He bestowed honors with regard to noble ancestry, military renown, or brilliant accomplishments as a civilian, letting it be clearly seen that there were no better men to choose. The consul and the praetor retained their prestige; inferior magistrates exercised their authority; the laws too, with the single exception of cases of treason, were properly enforced.

As to the duties on corn, the indirect taxes and other branches of the public revenue, they were in the hands of companies of Roman knights. The emperor entrusted his own property to men of the most tried integrity or to persons known only by their general reputation, and once appointed they were retained without any limitation, so that most of them grew old in the same employment. The city populace indeed suffered much from high prices, but this was no fault of the emperor, who actually endeavored to counteract barren soils and stormy seas with every resource of wealth and foresight. And he was also careful not to distress the provinces by new burdens, and to see that in bearing the old they were safe from any rapacity or oppression on the part of governors. Corporal punishments and confiscations of property were unknown.

7. The emperor had only a few estates in Italy, slaves on a moderate scale, and his household was confined to a few freedmen. If ever he had a dispute with a private person, it was decided in the law courts. All this, not indeed with any graciousness, but in a blunt fashion which often alarmed, he still kept up, until the death of Drusus changed everything. While he lived, the system continued, because Sejanus, as yet only in the beginning of his power, wished to be known as an upright counselor, and there was one whose vengeance he dreaded, who did not conceal his hatred and incessantly complained "that a stranger was invited to assist in the government while the emperor's son was alive. How near was the step of declaring the stranger a colleague! Ambition at first had a steep path before it; when once the way had been entered, zealous adherents were forthcoming. Already, at the pleasure of the commander of the guards, a camp had been established; the soldiers given into his hands; his statues were to be seen among the monuments of Cn. Pompeius; his grandsons would be of the same blood as the family of the Drusi. Henceforth they must pray that he might have self-control, and so be contented." So would Drusus talk, not infrequently, or only in the hearing of a few persons. Even his confidences, now that his wife had been corrupted, were betrayed.

8. Sejanus accordingly thought that he must be prompt, and chose a poison the gradual working of which might be mistaken for a natural disorder. It was given to Drusus by Lygdus, a eunuch, as was ascertained eight years later. As for Tiberius, he went to the senate-house during the whole time of the prince's illness, either because he was not afraid, or to show his strength of mind, and even in the interval between his death and funeral. Seeing the consuls, in token of their grief, sitting on the ordinary benches, he reminded them of their high office and of their proper place; and when the Senate burst into tears, suppressing a groan, he revived their spirits with a fluent speech. "He knew indeed that he might be reproached for thus encountering the gaze of the Senate after so recent an affliction. Most mourners could hardly bear even the soothing words of kinsfolk or to look on the light of day. And such were not to be condemned as weak. But he had sought a more manly consolation in the bosom of the commonwealth."

Then deploring the extreme age of Augusta, the childhood of his grandsons, and his own declining years, he begged the Senate to summon Germanicus' children, the only comfort under their present misery. The consuls went out, and having encouraged the young princes with kind words, brought them in and presented them to the emperor. Taking them by the hand he said: "Senators, when these boys lost their father, I committed them to their uncle, and begged him, though he had children of his own, to cherish and rear them as his own offspring, and train them for himself and for posterity. Drusus is now lost to us, and I turn my prayers to you, and before heaven and your country I adjure you to receive into your care and guidance the great-grandsons of Augustus, descendants of a most noble ancestry. So fulfill your duty and mine. To you, Nero and Drusus, these senators are as fathers. Such is your birth that your prosperity and adversity must alike affect the State."

9. There was great weeping at these words, and then many a benediction. Had the emperor set bounds to his speech, he must have filled the hearts of his hearers with sympathy and admiration. But he now fell back on those idle and often ridiculed professions about restoring the republic, and the wish that the consuls or some one else might undertake the government, and thus destroyed belief even in what was genuine and noble.

The same honors were decreed to the memory of Drusus as to that of Germanicus, and many more were added. Such is the way with flattery, when repeated. The funeral with its procession of statues was singularly grand. Aeneas, the father of the Julian house, all the Alban kings, Romulus, Rome's founder, then the Sabine nobility, Attus Clausus, and the busts of all the other Claudii were displayed in a long train.

10. In relating the death of Drusus I have followed the narrative of most of the best historians. But I would not pass over a rumor of the time, the strength of which is not even yet exhausted. Sejanus, it is said, having seduced Livia into crime, next secured, by the foulest means, the consent of Lygdus, the eunuch, as from his youth and beauty he was his master's favorite, and one of his principal attendants. When those who were in the secret had decided on the time and place of the poisoning, Sejanus, with the most consummate daring, reversed his plan, and, whispering an accusation against Drusus of intending to poison his father, warned Tiberius to avoid the first draught offered him as he was dining at his son's house. Thus deceived, the old emperor, on sitting down to the banquet, took the cup and handed it to Drusus. His suspicions were increased when Drusus, in perfect unconsciousness, drank it off with youthful eagerness, apparently, out of fear and shame, bringing on himself the death which he had plotted against his father.

11. These popular rumors, over and above the fact that they are not vouched for by any good writer, may be instantly refuted. For who, with moderate prudence, far less Tiberius with his great experience, would have thrust destruction on a son, without even hearing him, with his own hand too, and with an impossibility of returning to better thoughts. Surely he

would rather have had the slave who handed the poison, tortured, have sought to discover the traitor, in short, would have been as hesitating and tardy in the case of an only son hitherto unconvicted of any crime, as he was naturally even with strangers. But as Sejanus had the credit of contriving every sort of wickedness, the fact that he was the emperor's special favorite, and that both were hated by the rest of the world, procured belief for any monstrous fiction, and rumor too always has a dreadful side in regard to the deaths of men in power. Besides, the whole process of the crime was betrayed by Apicata, Sejanus' wife, and fully divulged, under torture, by Eudemus and Lygdus. No writer has been found sufficiently malignant to fix the guilt on Tiberius, though every circumstance was scrutinized and exaggerated. My object in mentioning and refuting this story is, by a conspicuous example, to put down hearsay, and to request all into whose hands my work shall come, not to catch eagerly at wild and improbable rumors in preference to genuine history which has not been perverted into romance.

12. Tiberius pronounced a panegyric on his son before the Rostra, during which the Senate and people, in appearance rather than in heart, put on the expression and accents of sorrow, while they inwardly rejoiced at the brightening future of the family of Germanicus. This beginning of popularity and the ill-concealed ambition of their mother Agrippina, hastened its downfall. Sejanus when he saw that the death of Drusus was not avenged on the murderers and was no grief to the people, grew bold in wickedness, and, now that his first attempt had succeeded, speculated on the possibility of destroying the children of Germanicus, whose succession to the throne was a certainty. There were three, and poison could not be distributed among them, because of the singular fidelity of their guardians and the unassailable virtue of Agrippina. So Sejanus inveighed against Agrippina's arrogance, and worked powerfully on Augusta's old hatred of her and on Livia's consciousness of recent guilt, and urged both these women to represent to the emperor that her pride as a mother and her reliance on popular enthusiasm were leading her to dream of empire. Livia availed herself of the cunning of accusers, among whom she had selected Julius Postumus, a man well suited to her purpose, as he had an intrigue with Mutilia Prisca, and was consequently in the confidence of Augusta, over whose mind Prisca had great influence. She thus made her aged grandmother, whose nature it was to tremble for her power, irreconcilably hostile to her grandson's widow. Agrippina's friends too were induced to be always inciting her proud spirit by mischievous talk.

BOOK IV **32–35**

Sejanus not only prosecutes political opponents but cannot tolerate the free speech of historians like Cremutius Cordus.

32. Much what I have related and shall have to relate, may perhaps, I am aware, seem petty trifles to record. But no one must compare my annals with the writings of those who have described Rome in old days. They told of great wars, of the storming of cities, of the defeat and capture of kings, or whenever they turned by preference to home affairs, they related, with a free scope for digression, the struggles of consuls with tribunes, land and corn-laws, and the struggles between the commons and the aristocracy. My labors are circumscribed and inglorious; peace wholly unbroken or but slightly disturbed, dismal misery in the capital, an emperor careless about the enlargement of the empire, such is my theme. Still it will not be useless to study those at first sight trifling events out of which the movements of vast changes often take their rise.

33. All nations and cities are ruled by the people, the nobility, or by one man. A constitution, formed by selection out of these elements, it is easy to commend but not to produce; or, if it is produced, it cannot be lasting. Formerly, when the people had power or when the patricians were in the ascendant, the popular temper and the methods of controlling it, had to be studied, and those who knew most accurately the spirit of the Senate and aristocracy, had the credit of understanding the age and of being wise men. So now, after a revolution, when Rome is nothing but the realm of a single despot, there must be good in carefully noting and recording this period, for it is but few who have the foresight to distinguish right from wrong or what is sound from what is hurtful, while most men learn wisdom from the fortunes of others. Still, though this is instructive, it gives very little pleasure. Descriptions of countries, the various incidents of battles, glorious deaths of great generals, enchain and refresh a reader's mind. I have to present in succession the merciless bidding of a tyrant, incessant prosecutions, faithless friendships, the ruin of innocence, the same causes issuing in the same results, and I am everywhere confronted by a wearisome monotony in my subject matter. Then, again, an ancient historian has but few disparagers, and no one cares whether you praise more heartily the armies of Carthage or Rome. But of many who endured punishment or disgrace under Tiberius, the descendants yet survive; or even though the families themselves may be now extinct, you will find those who, from a resemblance of character, imagine that the evil deeds of others are a reproach to themselves. Again, even honor and virtue make enemies, condemning, as they do, their opposites by too close a contrast. But I return to my work.

34. In the year of the consulship of Cornelius Cossus and Asinius Agrippa, Cremutius Cordus was arraigned on a new charge, now for the first time heard. He had published a history in which he had praised Marcus Brutus and called Gaius Cassius the last of the Romans. His accusers were Satrius Secundus and Pinarius Natta, creatures of Sejanus. This was enough to ruin the accused; and then too the emperor listened with an angry frown to his defense, which Cremutius, resolved to give up his life, began thus:

"It is my words, Senators, which are condemned, so innocent am I of any guilty act; yet these do not touch the emperor or the emperor's mother, who are alone comprehended under the law of treason. I am said to have praised Brutus and Cassius, whose careers many have described and no one mentioned without eulogy. Titus Livius, pre-eminently famous for eloquence and truthfulness, extolled Cn. Pompeius in such a panegyric that Augustus called him "Pompeian," and yet this was no obstacle to their friendship. Scipio, Afranius, this very Cassius, this same Brutus, he nowhere describes as brigands and traitors, terms now applied to them, but repeatedly as illustrious men. Asinius Pollio's writings too hand down a glorious memory of them, and Messala Corvinus used to speak with pride of Cassius as his general. Yet both these men prospered to the end with wealth and preferment. Again, that book of Marcus Cicero, in which he lauded Cato to the skies, how else was it answered by Caesar the dictator, than by a written oration in reply, as if he was pleading in court? The letters Antonius, the harangues of Brutus contain reproaches against Augustus, false indeed, but urged with powerful sarcasm; the poems which we read of Bibaculus and Catullus are crammed with invectives on the Caesars. Yet the Divine Julius, the Divine Augustus themselves bore all this and let it pass, whether in forbearance or in wisdom I cannot easily say. Assuredly what is despised is soon forgotten; when you resent a thing, you seem to recognize it."

35. "Of the Greeks I say nothing; with them not only liberty, but even license went unpunished, or if a person aimed at chastising, he retaliated on satire by satire. It has, however, always been perfectly open to us without any one to censure, to speak freely of those whom death has withdrawn alike from the partialities of hatred or esteem. Are Cassius and Brutus now in arms on the fields of Philippi, and am I with them rousing the people by harangues to stir up civil war? Did they not fall more than seventy years ago, and as they are known to us by statues which even the conqueror did not destroy, so too is not some portion of their memory preserved for us by historians? To every man posterity gives his due honor, and, if a fatal sentence hangs over me, there will be those who will remember me as well as Cassius and Brutus."

He then left the Senate and ended his life by starvation. His books, so the Senators decreed, were to be burnt by the aediles; but some copies were left which were concealed and afterwards published. And so one is all the more inclined to laugh at the stupidity of men who suppose that the despotism of the present can actually efface the remembrances of the next generation. On the contrary, the persecution of genius fosters its influence; foreign tyrants, and all who have imitated their oppression, have merely procured infamy for themselves and glory for their victims.

BOOK VI 50–51

The death of Tiberius in 14 C.E.

50. Tiberius' bodily powers were now leaving him, but not his skill in dissembling. There was the same stern spirit; he had his words and looks under strict control, and occasionally would try to hide his weakness, evident as it was, by a forced politeness. After frequent changes of place, he at last settled down on the promontory of Misenum in a country-house once owned by Lucius Lucullus. There it was noted, in this way, that he was drawing near his end. There was a physician, distinguished in his profession, of the name of Charicles, usually employed, not indeed to have the direction of the emperor's varying health, but to put his advice at immediate disposal. This man, as if he were leaving on business of his own, clasped his hand, with a show of homage, and touched his pulse. Tiberius noticed it. Whether he was displeased and strove the more to hide his anger, is a question; at any rate, he ordered the banquet to be renewed, and sat at the table longer than usual, by way, apparently, of showing honor to his departing friend. Charicles, however, assured Macro that his breath was failing and that he would not last more than two days. All was at once hurry; there were conferences among those on the spot and dispatches to the generals and armies. On the 15th of March, his breath failing, he was believed to have expired, and Caligula was going forth with a numerous throng of congratulating followers to take the first possession of the empire, when suddenly news came that Tiberius was recovering his voice and sight, and calling for persons to bring him food to revive him from his faintness. Then ensued a universal panic, and while the rest fled hither and thither, everyone feigning grief or ignorance, Caligula, in silent stupor, passed from the highest hopes to the extremity of apprehension. Macro, nothing daunted, ordered the old emperor to be smothered under a huge heap of clothes, and all to quit the entrance-hall.

51. And so died Tiberius, in the seventy-eighth year of his age. Nero was his father, and he was on both sides descended from the Claudian house, though his mother passed by adoption, first into the Livian, then into the Julian family. From earliest infancy, perilous vicissitudes were his lot. Himself

an exile, he was the companion of a proscribed father, and on being admitted as a stepson into the house of Augustus, he had to struggle with many rivals, so long as Marcellus and Agrippa and, subsequently, Gaius and Lucius Caesar were in their glory. Again his brother Drusus enjoyed in a greater degree the affection of the citizens. But he was more than ever on dangerous ground after his marriage with Julia, whether he tolerated or escaped from his wife's profligacy. On his return from Rhodes he ruled the emperor's now heirless house for twelve years, and the Roman world, with absolute sway, for about twenty-three. His character too had its distinct periods. It was a bright time in his life and reputation, while under Augustus he was a private citizen or held high offices; a time of reserve and crafty assumption of virtue, as long as Germanicus and Drusus were alive. Again, while his mother lived, he was a compound of good and evil; he was infamous for his cruelty, though he veiled his debaucheries, while he loved or feared Sejanus. Finally, he plunged into every wickedness and disgrace, when fear and shame being cast off, he simply indulged his own inclinations.

BOOK XI 23–38

The emperor Claudius delivers a speech in favor of the admission of romanized Gauls to the Senate. (The speech also survives on an inscription, which shows that Tacitus has remained true to the argument while polishing the style.) The emperor's adulterous wife, Messalina, embarks on such scandalous behavior that Claudius' advisors urge him to move against her.

23. In the consulship of Aulus Vitellius and Lucius Vipstanus the question of filling up the Senate was discussed, and the chief men of Gallia Comata, as it was called, who had long possessed the rights of allies and of Roman citizens, sought the privilege of obtaining public offices at Rome. There was much talk of every kind on the subject, and it was argued before the emperor with vehement opposition. "Italy," it was asserted, "is not so feeble as to be unable to furnish its own capital with a senate. Once our native-born citizens sufficed for peoples of our own kin, and we are by no means dissatisfied with the Rome of the past. To this day we cite examples, which under our old customs the Roman character exhibited as to valor and renown. Is it a small thing that Veneti and Insubres have already burst into the Senate-house, unless a mob of foreigners, a troop of captives, so to say, is now forced upon us? What distinctions will be left for the remnants of our noble houses, or for any impoverished senators from Latium? Every place will be crowded with these millionaires, whose ancestors of the second and third generations at the head of hostile tribes destroyed our armies with fire and sword, and actually besieged the divine Julius at Alesia. These are recent memories. What if there were to rise up the remembrance of those who fell in Rome's citadel and at her altar by the hands of these same barbarians! Let them enjoy indeed the title of citizens, but let them not vulgarize the distinctions of the Senate and the honors of office."

24. These and like arguments failed to impress the emperor. He at once addressed himself to answer them, and thus harangued the assembled Senate. "My ancestors, the most ancient of whom was made at once a citizen and a noble of Rome, encourage me to govern by the same policy of transferring to this city all conspicuous merit, wherever found. And indeed I know, as facts, that the Julii came from Alba, the Coruncanii from Camerium, the Porcii from Tusculum, and not to inquire too minutely into the past, that new members have been brought into the Senate from Etruria and Lucania and the whole of Italy, that Italy itself was at last extended to the Alps, to the end that not only single persons but entire countries and tribes might be united under our name. We had unshaken peace at home; we prospered in all our foreign relations, in the days when Italy beyond the Po was admitted to share our citizenship, and when, enrolling in our ranks the most vigorous of the provincials, under color of settling our legions throughout the world, we recruited our exhausted empire. Are we sorry that the Balbi came to us from Spain, and other men not less illustrious from southern Gaul? Their descendants are still among us, and do not yield to us in patriotism.

"What was the ruin of Sparta and Athens, but this, that mighty as they were in war, they spurned from them as aliens those whom they had conquered? Our founder Romulus, on the other hand, was so wise that he fought as enemies and then hailed as fellow-citizens several nations on the very same day. Strangers have reigned over us. That freedmen's sons should be entrusted with public offices is not, as many wrongly think, a sudden innovation, but was a common practice in the old commonwealth. But, it will be said, we have fought with the Senones. I suppose then that the Volsci and Aequi never stood in array against us. Our city was taken by the Gauls. Well, we also gave hostages to the Etruscans, and passed under the yoke of the Samnites. On the whole, if you review all our wars, never has one been finished in a shorter time than that with the Gauls. Thenceforth they have preserved an unbroken and loyal peace. United as they now are with us by manners, education, and intermarriage, let them bring us their gold and their wealth rather than enjoy it in isolation. Everything, Senators, which we now hold to be of the highest antiquity, was once new. Plebeian magistrates came after patrician; Latin magistrates after plebeian; magistrates of other Italian peoples after Latin. This practice too will establish itself, and what we are this day justifying by precedents, will be itself a precedent."

25. The emperor's speech was followed by a decree of the Senate, and the Aedui were the first to obtain the right of becoming senators at Rome. This compliment was paid to their ancient alliance, and to the fact that they alone of the Gauls cling to the name of brothers of the Roman people.

About the same time the emperor enrolled in the ranks of the patricians such senators as were of the oldest families, and such as had had distinguished ancestors. There were now but scanty relics of the Greater Houses of Romulus and of the Lesser Houses of Lucius Brutus, as they had been called, and those too were exhausted which the Dictator Caesar by the Cassian law, and the emperor Augustus by the Saenian law had chosen into their place. These acts, as being welcome to the State, were undertaken with hearty gladness by the imperial censor. Anxiously considering how he was to rid the Senate of men of notorious infamy, he preferred a gentle method, recently devised, to one which accorded with the sternness of antiquity, and advised each to examine his own case and seek the privilege of laying aside his rank. Permission, he said, would be readily obtained. He would publish in the same list those who had been expelled and those who had been allowed to retire, that by this confounding together of the decision of the censors and the modesty of voluntary resignation the disgrace might be softened.

For this, the consul Vipstanus moved that Claudius should be called "Father of the Senate." The title of "Father of the Country" had, he argued, been indiscriminately bestowed; new services ought to be recognized by unusual titles. The emperor, however, himself stopped the consul's flattery, as extravagant. He closed the lustrum, the census for which gave a total of 5,984,072 citizens. Then too ended his blindness as to his domestic affairs. He was soon compelled to notice and punish his wife's infamies, till he afterwards craved passionately for an unhallowed union.

26. Messalina, now grown weary of the very facility of her adulteries, was rushing into strange excesses, when even Silius, either through some fatal infatuation or because he imagined that, amid the dangers which hung over him, danger itself was the best safety, urged the breaking off of all concealment. "They were not," he said, "in such an extremity as to have to wait for the emperor's old age. Harmless measures were for the innocent. Crime once exposed had no refuge but in audacity. They had accomplices in all who feared the same fate. For himself, as he had neither wife nor child, he was ready to marry and to adopt Britannicus. Messalina would have the same power as before, with the additional advantage of a quiet mind, if only they took Claudius by surprise, who, though unsuspicious of treachery, was hasty in his wrath."

The suggestion was coldly received, not because the lady loved her husband, but from a fear that Silius, after attaining his highest hopes, would spurn an adulteress, and soon estimate at its true value the crime which in the midst of peril he had approved. But she craved the name of wife, for the sake of the monstrous infamy, that last source of delight to the reckless. She waited only till Claudius set out for Ostia to perform a sacrifice, and then celebrated all the solemnities of marriage.

27. I am well aware that it will seem a fable that any persons in the world could have been so obtuse in a city which knows everything and hides nothing, much more, that these persons should have been a consul-elect and the emperor's wife; that, on an appointed day, before witnesses duly summoned, they should have come together as if for the purpose of legitimate marriage; that she should have listened to the words of the bridegroom's friends, should have sacrificed to the gods, have taken her place among a company of guests, have lavished her kisses and caresses, and passed the night in the freedom which marriage permits. But this is no story to excite wonder; I do but relate what I have heard and what our fathers have recorded.

28. The emperor's court indeed shuddered, its powerful personages especially, the men who had much to fear from a revolution. From secret whisperings they passed to loud complaints. "When an actor," they said, "impudently thrust himself into the imperial chamber, it certainly brought scandal on the State, but we were a long way from ruin. Now, a young noble of stately beauty, of vigorous intellect, with the near prospect of the consulship, is preparing himself for a loftier ambition. There can be no secret about what is to follow such a marriage." Doubtless there was a thrill of alarm when they thought of the apathy of Claudius, of his devotion to his wife and of the many murders perpetrated at Messalina's bidding. On the other hand, the very good nature of the emperor inspired confident hope that if they could overpower him by the enormity of the charge, she might be condemned and crushed before she was accused. The critical point was this, that he should not hear her defense, and that his ears should be shut even against her confession.

29. At first Callistus, of whom I have already spoken in connection with the assassination of Gaius Caesar, Narcissus, who had contrived the death of Appius, and Pallas, who was then in the height of favor, debated whether they might not by secret threats turn Messalina from her passion for Silius, while they concealed all else. Then fearing that they would be themselves involved in ruin, they abandoned the idea, Pallas out of cowardice, and Callistus, from his experience of a former court, remembering that prudent rather than vigorous counsels insure the maintenance of power. Narcissus persevered, only so far changing his plan as not to make her aware beforehand by a single word what was the charge or who was the accuser. Then he eagerly watched his opportunity, and, as the emperor lingered long at Ostia, he sought two of the mistresses to whose society Claudius was especially partial, and, by gifts, by promises, by dwelling on power increased by the wife's fall, he induced them to undertake the work of the informer.

30. On this, Calpurnia (that was the woman's name), as soon as she was allowed a private interview, threw herself at the emperor's knees, crying out that Messalina was married to Silius. At the same time she asked Cleopatra, who was standing near and waiting for the question, whether she knew it. Cleopatra nodding assent, she begged that Narcissus might be summoned. Narcissus entreated pardon for the past, for having concealed the scandal while confined to a Vettius or a Plautius. Even now, he said, he would not make charges of adultery, and seem to be asking back the palace, the slaves, and the other belongings of imperial rank. These Silius might enjoy; only, he must give back the wife and annul the act of marriage. "Do you know," he said "of your divorce? The people, the army, the Senate saw the marriage of Silius. Act at once, or the new husband is master of Rome."

31. Claudius then summoned all his most powerful friends. First he questioned Turranius, superintendent of the corn market; next, Lusius Geta, who commanded the praetorians. When they confessed the truth, the whole company clamored in concert that he must go to the camp, must assure himself of the praetorian cohorts, must think of safety before he thought of vengeance. It is quite certain that Claudius was so overwhelmed by terror that he repeatedly asked whether he was indeed in possession of the empire, whether Silius was still a subject.

Messalina meanwhile, more wildly profligate than ever, was celebrating in mid-autumn a representation of the vintage in her new home. The presses were being trodden; the vats were overflowing; women girt with skins were dancing, as Bacchanals dance in their worship or their frenzy. Messalina with flowing hair shook the thyrsus, and Silius at her side, crowned with ivy and wearing the buskin, moved his head to some lascivious chorus. It is said that one Vettius Valens climbed a very lofty tree in sport, and when they asked him what he saw, replied, "A terrible storm from Ostia." Possibly such appearance had begun; perhaps, a word dropped by chance became a prophecy.

32. Meanwhile no mere rumor but messengers from all parts brought the news that everything was known to Claudius, and that he was coming, bent on vengeance. Messalina upon this went to the gardens of Lucullus; Silius, to conceal his fear, to his business in the forum. The other guests were flying in all directions when the centurions appeared and put everyone in irons where they found them, either in the public streets or in hiding. Messalina, though her peril took away all power of thought, promptly resolved to meet and face her husband, a course in which she had often found safety; while she bade Britannicus and Octavia hasten to embrace their father. She besought Vibidia, the eldest of the Vestal Virgins, to demand audience of the supreme pontiff and to beg for mercy. Meanwhile, with only three companions, so lonely did she find herself in a moment, she traversed the whole length of the city, and, mounting on a cart used to remove garden refuse, proceeded along the road to Ostia; not pitied, so overpoweringly hideous were her crimes, by a single person.

33. There was equal alarm on the emperor's side. They put but little trust in Geta, who commanded the praetorians, a man swayed with good case to good or evil. Narcissus in concert with others who dreaded the same fate, declared that the only hope of safety for the emperor lay in his transferring for that one day the command of the soldiers to one of the freedmen, and he offered to undertake it himself. And that Claudius might not be induced by Lucius Vitellius and Largus Caecina to repent, while he was riding into Rome, he asked and took a seat in the emperor's carriage.

34. It was currently reported in after times that while the emperor broke into contradictory exclamations, now inveighing against the infamies of his wife, and now, returning in thought to the remembrance of his love and of his infant children, Vitellius said nothing but, "What audacity! what wickedness!" Narcissus indeed kept pressing him to clear up his ambiguities and let the truth be known, but still he could not prevail upon him to utter anything that was not vague and susceptible of any meaning which might be put on it, or upon Largus Caecina, to do anything but follow his example. And now Messalina had presented herself, and was insisting that the emperor should listen to the mother of Octavia and Britannicus, when the accuser roared out at her the story of Silius and her marriage. At the same moment, to draw Caesar's eyes away from her, he handed him some papers which detailed her debaucheries. Soon afterwards, as he was entering Rome, his children by Messalina were to have shown themselves, had not Narcissus ordered their removal. Vibidia he could not repel, when, with a vehemently indignant appeal, she demanded that a wife should not be given up to death without a hearing. So Narcissus replied that the emperor would hear her, and that she should have an opportunity of disproving the charge. Meanwhile the holy virgin was to go and discharge her sacred duties.

35. All throughout, Claudius preserved a strange silence; Vitellius seemed unconscious. Everything was under the freedman's control. By his order, the paramour's house was thrown open and the emperor conducted thither. First, on the threshold, he pointed out the statue of Silius' father, which a decree of the Senate had directed to be destroyed; next, how the heirlooms of the Neros and the Drusi had been degraded into the price of infamy. Then he led the emperor, furious and bursting out in menace, into the camp, where the soldiers were purposely assembled. Claudius spoke to them a few words at the dictation of Narcissus. Shame indeed checked the utterance even of a righteous anger. Instantly there came a shout from the cohorts, demanding the names of the culprits and their punishment.

Brought before the tribunal, Silius sought neither defense nor delay, but begged that his death might be hastened. A like courage made several Roman knights of the first rank desirous of a speedy doom. Titius Proculus, who had been appointed to watch Messalina and was now offering his evidence, Vettius Valens, who confessed his guilt, together with Pompeius Urbicus and Saufellus Trogus from among her accomplices, were ordered to execution. Decius Calpurnianus too, commander of the watch, Sulpicius Rufus, who had the charge of the Games, and Juncus Virgilianus, a senator, were similarly punished.

36. Mnester alone occasioned a pause. Rending off his clothes, he insisted on Claudius looking at the scars of his stripes and remembering his words when he surrendered himself, without reserve, to Messalina's bidding. The guilt of others had been the result of presents or of large promises; his, of necessity. He must have been the first victim had Silius obtained empire.

Caesar was touched by his appeal and inclined to mercy, but his freedmen prevailed on him not to let any indulgence be shown to a player when so many illustrious citizens had fallen. "It mattered not whether he had sinned so greatly from choice or compulsion." Even the defense of Traulus Montanus, a Roman knight, was not admitted. A young man of pure life, yet of singular beauty, he had been summoned and dismissed within the space of one night by Messalina, who was equally capricious in her passions and dislikes. In the cases of Suilius Caesoninus and Plautius Lateranus, the extreme penalty was remitted. The latter was saved by the distinguished services of his uncle; the former by his very vices, having amid that abominable throng submitted to the worst degradation.

37. Messalina meanwhile, in the gardens of Lucullus, was struggling for life, and writing letters of entreaty, as she alternated between hope and fury. In her extremity, it was her pride alone which forsook her. Had not Narcissus hurried on her death, ruin would have recoiled on her accuser. Claudius had returned home to an early banquet; then, in softened mood, when the wine had warmed him, he bade some one go and tell the "poor creature" (this is the word which they say he used) to come the morrow and plead her cause. Hearing this, seeing too that his wrath was subsiding and his passion returning, and fearing, in the event of delay, the effect of approaching night and conjugal recollections, Narcissus rushed out, and ordered the centurions and the tribunes, who were on guard, to accomplish the deed of blood. Such, he said, was the emperor's bidding. Evodus, one of the freedmen, was appointed to watch and complete the affair. Hurrying on before with all speed to the gardens, he found Messalina stretched upon the ground, while by her side sat Lepida, her mother, who, though estranged from her daughter in prosperity, was now melted to pity by her inevitable doom, and urged her not to wait for the executioner. "Life," she said, "was over; all that could be

looked for was honor in death." But in that heart, utterly corrupted by profligacy, nothing noble remained. She still prolonged her tears and idle complaints, till the gates were forced open by the rush of the new comers, and there stood at her side the tribune, sternly silent, and the freedman, overwhelming her with the copious insults of a servile tongue.

38. Then for the first time she understood her fate and put her hand to a dagger. In her terror she was applying it ineffectually to her throat and breast, when a blow from the tribune drove it through her. Her body was given up to her mother. Claudius was still at the banquet when they told him that Messalina was dead, without mentioning whether it was by her own or another's hand. Nor did he ask the question, but called for the cup and finished his repast as usual. During the days which followed he showed no sign of hatred or joy or anger or sadness, in a word, of any human emotion, either when he looked on her triumphant accusers or on her weeping children. The Senate assisted his forgetfulness by decreeing that her name and her statues should be removed from all places, public or private. To Narcissus were voted the decorations of the quaestorship, a mere trifle to the pride of one who rose in the height of his power above Pallas and Callistus.

BOOK XII **65–69**

Claudius dies in 54 C.E. at the hands of his fourth wife Agrippina.

65. It was charged on Lepida that she had made attempts on the Emperor's consort by magical incantations, and was disturbing the peace of Italy by an imperfect control of her troops of slaves in Calabria. She was for this sentenced to death, notwithstanding the vehement opposition of Narcissus, who, as he more and more suspected Agrippina, was said to have plainly told his intimate friends that "his destruction was certain, whether Britannicus or Nero were to be emperor, but that he was under such obligations to Claudius that he would sacrifice life to his welfare. Messalina and Silius had been convicted, and now again there were similar grounds for accusation. If Nero were to rule, or Britannicus succeed to the throne, he would himself have no claim on the then reigning sovereign. Meanwhile, a stepmother's treacherous schemes were convulsing the whole imperial house, with far greater disgrace than would have resulted from his concealment of the profligacy of the emperor's former wife. Even as it was, there was shamelessness enough, seeing that Pallas was her paramour, so that no one could doubt that she held honor, modesty and her very person, everything, in short, cheaper than sovereignty."

This, and the like, he was always saying, and he would embrace Britannicus, expressing earnest wishes for his speedy arrival at a mature age, and would raise his hand, now to heaven, now to the young prince, with entreaty that as he grew up, he would drive out his father's enemies and also take vengeance on the murderers of his mother.

66. Under this great burden of anxiety, he had an attack of illness, and went to Sinuessa to recruit his strength with its balmy climate and salubrious waters. Thereupon, Agrippina, who had long decided on the crime and eagerly grasped at the opportunity thus offered, and did not lack instruments, deliberated on the nature of the poison to be used. The deed would be betrayed by one that was sudden and instantaneous, while if she chose a slow and lingering poison, there was a fear that Claudius, when near his end, might, on detecting the treachery, return to his love for his son. She decided on some rare compound which might derange his mind and delay death. A person skilled in such matters was selected, Locusta by name, who had lately been condemned for poisoning, and had long been retained as one of the tools of despotism. By this woman's art the poison was prepared, and it was to be administered by an eunuch, Halotus, who was accustomed to bring in and taste the dishes.

67. All the circumstances were subsequently so well known, that writers of the time have declared that the poison was infused into some mushrooms, a favorite delicacy, and its effect not at the instant perceived, from the emperor's lethargic, or intoxicated condition. His bowels too were relieved, and this seemed to have saved him. Agrippina was thoroughly dismayed. Fearing the worst, and defying the immediate obloquy of the deed, she availed herself of the complicity of Xenophon, the physician, which she had already secured. Under pretense of helping the emperor's efforts to vomit, this man, it is supposed, introduced into his throat a feather smeared with some rapid poison; for he knew that the greatest crimes are perilous in their inception, but well rewarded after their consummation.

68. Meanwhile the Senate was summoned, and prayers rehearsed by the consuls and priests for the emperor's recovery, though the lifeless body was being wrapped in blankets with warm applications, while all was being arranged to establish Nero on the throne. At first Agrippina, seemingly overwhelmed by grief and seeking comfort, clasped Britannicus in her embraces, called him the very image of his father, and hindered him by every possible device from leaving the chamber. She also detained his sisters, Antonia and Octavia, closed every approach to the palace with a military guard, and repeatedly gave out that the emperor's health was better, so that the soldiers might be encouraged to hope, and that the fortunate moment foretold by the astrologers might arrive.

69. At last, at noon on the 13th of October, the gates of the palace were suddenly thrown open, and Nero, accompanied by Burrus, went forth to the cohort which was on guard after military custom. There, at the suggestion of the commanding officer, he was hailed with joyful shouts, and set on a litter. Some, it is said, hesitated, and looked round and asked where Britannicus was; then, when there was no one to lead a resistance, they yielded to what was offered them. Nero was conveyed into the camp, and having first spoken suitably to the occasion and promised a donative after the example of his father's bounty, he was unanimously greeted as emperor. The decrees of the Senate followed the voice of the soldiers, and there was no hesitation in the provinces. Divine honors were decreed to Claudius, and his funeral rites were solemnized on the same scale as those of Augustus; for Agrippina strove to emulate the magnificence of her great-grandmother, Livia. But his will was not publicly read, as the preference of the stepson to the son might provoke a sense of wrong and angry feeling in the popular mind.

BOOK XIII 1–5

The accession of the emperor Nero (54–68 c.e.)

1. The first death under the new emperor, that of Junius Silanus, proconsul of Asia, was, without Nero's knowledge, planned by the treachery of Agrippina. Not that Silanus had provoked destruction by any violence of temper, apathetic as he was, and so utterly despised under former despotisms, that Gaius Caesar used to call him the golden sheep. The truth was that Agrippina, having contrived the murder of his brother Lucius Silanus, dreaded his vengeance; for it was the incessant popular talk that preference ought to be given over Nero, who was scarcely out of his boyhood and had gained the empire by crime, to a man of mature age, of blameless life, of noble birth, and, as a point then much regarded, of the line of the Caesars. Silanus in fact was the son of a great-grandson of Augustus. This was the cause of his destruction. The agents of the deed were Publius Celer, a Roman knight, and Helius, a freedman, men who had the charge of the emperor's domains in Asia. They gave the proconsul poison at a banquet, too openly to escape discovery.

With no less precipitation, Narcissus, Claudius' freedman, whose quarrels with Agrippina I have mentioned, was driven to suicide by his cruel imprisonment and hopeless plight, even against the wishes of Nero, with whose yet concealed vices he was wonderfully in sympathy from his rapacity and extravagance.

2. And now they had proceeded to further murders but for the opposition of Afranius Burrus and Annaeus Seneca. These two men guided the emperor's youth with an unity of purpose seldom found where authority is

shared, and though their accomplishments were wholly different, they had equal influence. Burrus, with his soldier's discipline and severe manners, Seneca, with lessons of eloquence and a dignified courtesy, strove alike to confine the frailty of the prince's youth, should he loathe virtue, within allowable indulgences. They had both alike to struggle against the domineering spirit of Agrippina, who inflamed with all the passions of an evil ascendancy had Pallas on her side, at whose suggestion Claudius had ruined himself by an incestuous marriage and a fatal adoption of a son. Nero's temper however was not one to submit to slaves, and Pallas, by a surly arrogance quite beyond a freedman, had provoked disgust. Still every honor was openly heaped on Agrippina, and to a tribune who according to military custom asked the watchword, Nero gave "the best of mothers." The Senate also decreed her two lictors, with the office of priestess to Claudius, and voted to the late emperor a censor's funeral, which was soon followed by deification.

3. On the day of the funeral the prince pronounced Claudius' panegyric, and while he dwelt on the antiquity of his family and on the consulships and triumphs of his ancestors, there was enthusiasm both in himself and his audience. The praise of his graceful accomplishments, and the remark that during his reign no disaster had befallen Rome from the foreigner, were heard with favor. When the speaker passed on to his foresight and wisdom, no one could refrain from laughter, though the speech, which was composed by Seneca, exhibited much elegance, as indeed that famous man had an attractive genius which suited the popular ear of the time. Elderly men who amuse their leisure with comparing the past and the present, observed that Nero was the first emperor who needed another man's eloquence. The dictator Caesar rivaled the greatest orators, and Augustus had an easy and fluent way of speaking, such as became a sovereign. Tiberius too thoroughly understood the art of balancing words, and was sometimes forcible in the expression of his thoughts, or else intentionally obscure. Even Gaius Caesar's disordered intellect did not wholly mar his faculty of speech. Nor did Claudius, when he spoke with preparation, lack elegance. Nero from early boyhood turned his lively genius in other directions; he carved, painted, sang, or practiced the management of horses, occasionally composing verses which showed that he had the rudiments of learning.

4. When he had done with his mimicries of sorrow he entered the Senate, and having first referred to the authority of the senators and the concurrence of the soldiery, he then dwelt on the counsels and examples which he had to guide him in the right administration of empire. "His boyhood," he said, "had not had the taint of civil wars or domestic feuds, and he brought with him no hatreds, no sense of wrong, no desire of vengeance." He then sketched the plan of his future government, carefully avoiding anything which had kindled recent odium. "He would not," he said, "be judge in all

cases, or, by confining the accuser and the accused within the same walls, let the power of a few favorites grow dangerously formidable. In his house there should be nothing venal, nothing open to intrigue; his private establishment and the State should be kept entirely distinct. The Senate should retain its ancient powers; Italy and the State-provinces should plead their causes before the tribunals of the consuls, who would give them a hearing from the senators. Of the armies he would himself take charge, as specially entrusted to him."

5. He was true to his word and several arrangements were made on the Senate's authority. No one was to receive a fee or a present for pleading a cause; the quaestors-elect were not to be under the necessity of exhibiting gladiatorial shows. This was opposed by Agrippina, as a reversal of the legislation of Claudius, but it was carried by the senators who used to be summoned to the palace, in order that she might stand close to a hidden door behind them, screened by a curtain which was enough to shut her out of sight, but not out of hearing. When envoys from Armenia were pleading their nation's cause before Nero, she actually was on the point of mounting the emperor's tribunal and of presiding with him; but Seneca, when everyone else was paralyzed with alarm, motioned to the prince to go and meet his mother. Thus, by an apparently dutiful act, a scandalous scene was prevented.

BOOK XIV I–II

In 59 C.E., Nero decides to rid himself of his mother Agrippina, whom he feels has blocked his marriage to Poppaea. The murder of Agrippina.

1. In the year of the consulship of Gaius Vipstanus and Gaius Fonteius, Nero deferred no more a long meditated crime. Length of power had matured his daring, and his passion for Poppaea daily grew more ardent. As the woman had no hope of marriage for herself or of Octavia's divorce while Agrippina lived, she would reproach the emperor with incessant vituperation and sometimes call him in jest a mere ward who was under the rule of others, and was so far from having empire that he had not even his liberty. "Why," she asked, "was her marriage put off? Was it her beauty and her ancestors, with their triumphal honors, that failed to please, or her being a mother, and her sincere heart? No; the fear was that as a wife at least she would divulge the wrongs of the Senate, and the wrath of the people at the arrogance and rapacity of his mother. If the only daughter-in-law Agrippina could bear was one who wished evil to her son, let her be restored to her union with Otho. She would go anywhere in the world, where she might hear of the insults heaped on the emperor, rather than witness them, and be also involved in his perils."

These and the like complaints, rendered impressive by tears and by the cunning of an adulteress, no one checked, as all longed to see the mother's power broken, while not a person believed that the son's hatred would steel his heart to her murder.

2. Cluvius relates that Agrippina in her eagerness to retain her influence went so far that more than once at midday, when Nero, even at that hour, was flushed with wine and feasting, she presented herself attractively attired to her half intoxicated son and offered him her person, and that when kinsfolk observed wanton kisses and caresses, portending infamy, it was Seneca who sought a female's aid against a woman's fascinations, and hurried in Acte, the freed-girl, who alarmed at her own peril and at Nero's disgrace, told him that the incest was notorious, as his mother boasted of it, and that the soldiers would never endure the rule of an impious sovereign. Fabius Rusticus tells us that it was not Agrippina, but Nero, who lusted for the crime, and that it was frustrated by the adroitness of that same freed-girl. Cluvius' account, however, is also that of all other authors, and popular belief inclines to it, whether it was that Agrippina really conceived such a monstrous wickedness in her heart, or perhaps because the thought of a strange passion seemed comparatively credible in a woman, who in her girlish years had allowed herself to be seduced by Lepidus in the hope of winning power, had stooped with a like ambition to the lust of Pallas, and had trained herself for every infamy by her marriage with her uncle.

3. Nero accordingly avoided secret interviews with her, and when she withdrew to her gardens or to her estates at Tusculum and Antium, he praised her for courting repose. At last, convinced that she would be too formidable, wherever she might dwell, he resolved to destroy her, merely deliberating whether it was to be accomplished by poison, or by the sword, or by any other violent means. Poison at first seemed best, but, were it to be administered at the imperial table, the result could not be referred to chance after the recent circumstances of the death of Britannicus. Again, to tamper with the servants of a woman who, from her familiarity with crime, was on her guard against treachery, appeared to be extremely difficult, and then, too, she had fortified her constitution by the use of antidotes. How again the dagger and its work were to be kept secret, no one could suggest, and it was feared too that whoever might be chosen to execute such a crime would spurn the order.

An ingenious suggestion was offered by Anicetus, a freedman, commander of the fleet at Misenum, who had been tutor to Nero in boyhood and had a hatred of Agrippina which she reciprocated. He explained that a vessel could be constructed, from which a part might by a contrivance be detached, when out at sea, so as to plunge her unawares into the water. "Nothing," he said, "allowed of accidents so much as the sea, and should she be overtaken by shipwreck, who would be so unfair as to impute to crime an offense committed by the winds and waves? The emperor would add the honor of a temple and of shrines to the deceased lady, with every other display of filial affection."

4. Nero liked the device, favored as it also was by the particular time, for he was celebrating Minerva's five days' festival at Baiae. Thither he enticed his mother by repeated assurances that children ought to bear with the irritability of parents and to soothe their tempers, wishing thus to spread a rumor of reconciliation and to secure Agrippina's acceptance through the feminine credulity, which easily believes what joy. As she approached, he went to the shore to meet her (she was coming from Antium), welcomed her with outstretched hand and embrace, and conducted her to Bauli. This was the name of a country house, washed by a bay of the sea, between the promontory of Misenum and the lake of Baiae. Here was a vessel distinguished from others by its equipment, seemingly meant, among other things, to do honor to his mother; for she had been accustomed to sail in a trireme, with a crew of marines. And now she was invited to a banquet, that night might serve to conceal the crime. It was well known that somebody had been found to betray it, that Agrippina had heard of the plot, and in doubt whether she was to believe it, was conveyed to Baiae in her litter. There some soothing words allayed her fear; she was graciously received, and seated at table above the emperor. Nero prolonged the banquet with various conversation, passing from a youth's playful familiarity to an air of constraint, which seemed to indicate serious thought, and then, after protracted festivity, escorted her on her departure, clinging with kisses to her eyes and bosom, either to crown his hypocrisy or because the last sight of a mother on the even of destruction caused a lingering even in that brutal heart.

5. A night of brilliant starlight with the calm of a tranquil sea was granted by heaven, seemingly, to convict the crime. The vessel had not gone far, Agrippina having with her two of her intimate attendants, one of whom, Crepereius Gallus, stood near the helm, while Acerronia, reclining at Agrippina's feet as she reposed herself, spoke joyfully of her son's repentance and of the recovery of the mother's influence, when at a given signal the ceiling of the place, which was loaded with a quantity of lead, fell in, and Crepereius was crushed and instantly killed. Agrippina and Acerronia were protected by the projecting sides of the couch, which happened to be too strong to yield under the weight. But this was not followed by the breaking up of the vessel; for all were bewildered, and those too, who were in the plot, were hindered by the unconscious majority. The crew then thought it best to throw the ves-

sel on one side and so sink it, but they could not themselves promptly unite to face the emergency, and others, by counteracting the attempt, gave an opportunity of a gentler fall into the sea. Acerronia, however, thoughtlessly exclaiming that she was Agrippina, and imploring help for the emperor's mother, was dispatched with poles and oars, and such naval implements as chance offered. Agrippina was silent and was thus the less recognized; still, she received a wound in her shoulder. She swam, then met with some small boats which conveyed her to the Lucrine lake, and so entered her house.

6. There she reflected how for this very purpose she had been invited by a lying letter and treated with conspicuous honor, how also it was near the shore, not from being driven by winds or dashed on rocks, that the vessel had in its upper part collapsed, like a mechanism anything but nautical. She pondered too the death of Acerronia; she looked at her own wound, and saw that her only safeguard against treachery was to ignore it. Then she sent her freedman Agerinus to tell her son how by heaven's favor and his good fortune she had escaped a terrible disaster; that she begged him, alarmed, as he might be, by his mother's peril, to put off the duty of a visit, as for the present she needed repose. Meanwhile, pretending that she felt secure, she applied remedies to her wound, and fomentations to her person. She then ordered search to be made for the will of Acerronia, and her property to be sealed, in this alone throwing off disguise.

7. Nero, meantime, as he waited for tidings of the consummation of the deed, received information that she had escaped with the injury of a slight wound, after having so far encountered the peril that there could be no question as to its author. Then, paralyzed with terror and protesting that she would show herself the next moment eager for vengeance, either arming the slaves or stirring up the soldiery, or hastening to the Senate and the people, to charge him with the wreck, with her wound, and with the destruction of her friends, he asked what resource he had against all this, unless something could be at once devised by Burrus and Seneca. He had instantly summoned both of them, and possibly they were already in the secret. There was a long silence on their part; they feared they might protest in vain, or believed the crisis to be such that Nero must perish, unless Agrippina were at once crushed. Thereupon Seneca was promptly glanced back on Burrus, as if to ask him whether the bloody deed must be required of the soldiers. Burrus replied "that the praetorians were attached to the whole family of the Caesars, and remembering Germanicus would not dare a savage deed on his offspring. It was for Anicetus to accomplish his promise."

Anicetus, without a pause, claimed for himself the consummation of the crime. At those words, Nero declared that that day gave him empire, and that a freedman was the author of this mighty boon. "Go," he said, "with all speed and take with you the men readiest to execute your orders." He himself, when he had heard of the arrival of Agrippina's messenger, Agerinus, contrived a theatrical mode of accusation, and, while the man was repeating his message, threw down a sword at his feet, then ordered him to be put in irons, as a detected criminal, so that he might invent a story how his mother had plotted the emperor's destruction and in the shame of discovered guilt had by her own choice sought death.

8. Meantime, Agrippina's peril being universally known and taken to be an accidental occurrence, everybody, the moment he heard of it, hurried down to the beach. Some climbed projecting piers; some the nearest vessels; others, as far as their stature allowed, went into the sea; some, again, stood with outstretched arms, while the whole shore rung with wailings, with prayers and cries, as different questions were asked and uncertain answers given. A vast multitude streamed to the spot with torches, and as soon as all knew that she was safe, they at once prepared to wish her joy, till the sight of an armed and threatening force scared them away. Anicetus then surrounded the house with a guard, and having burst open the gates, dragged off the slaves who met him, till he came to the door of her chamber, where a few still stood, after the rest had fled in terror at the attack. A small lamp was in the room, and one slave-girl with Agrippina, who grew more and more anxious, as no messenger came from her son, not even Agerinus, while the appearance of the shore was changed, a solitude one moment, then sudden bustle and tokens of the worst catastrophe. As the girl rose to depart, she exclaimed, "Do you too forsake me?" and looking round saw Anicetus, who had with him the captain of the trireme, Herculeius, and Obaritus, a centurion of marines. "If," said she, "you have come to see me, take back word that I have recovered, but if you are here to do a crime, I believe nothing about my son; he has not ordered his mother's murder."

The assassins closed in round her couch, and the captain of the trireme first struck her head violently with a club. Then, as the centurion bared his sword for the fatal deed, presenting her person, she exclaimed, "Smite my womb," and with many wounds she was slain.

9. So far our accounts agree. That Nero gazed on his mother after her death and praised her beauty, some have related, while others deny it. Her body was burnt that same night on a dining couch, with a mean funeral; nor, as long as Nero was in power, was the earth raised into a mound, or even decently closed. Subsequently, she received from the solicitude of her domestics, a humble sepulcher on the road to Misenum, near the country house of Caesar the Dictator, which from a great height commands a view of the bay beneath. As soon as the funeral pile was lighted, one of her freedmen, surnamed Mnester, ran himself through with a sword, either from love of his mistress or from the fear of destruction. Many years before Agrippina had anticipated this end for herself and had spurned the thought. For when she consulted the astrologers about Nero, they replied that he would be emperor and kill his mother. "Let him kill her," she said, "provided he is emperor."

10. But the emperor, when the crime was at last accomplished, realized its portentous guilt. The rest of the night, now silent and stupefied, now and still oftener starting up in terror, bereft of reason, he awaited the dawn as if it would bring with it his doom. He was first encouraged to hope by the flattery addressed to him, at the prompting of Burrus, by the centurions and tribunes, who again and again pressed his hand and congratulated him on his having escaped an unforeseen danger and his mother's daring crime. Then his friends went to the temples, and, an example having once been set, the neighboring towns of Campania testified their joy with sacrifices and deputations. He himself, with an opposite phase of hypocrisy, seemed sad, and almost angry at his own deliverance, and shed tears over his mother's death. But as the aspects of places change not, as do the looks of men, and as he had ever before his eyes the dreadful sight of that sea with its shores (some too believed that the notes of a funereal trumpet were heard from the surrounding heights, and wailings from the mother's grave), he retired to Neapolis and sent a letter to the Senate, the drift of which was that Agerinus, one of Agrippina's confidential freedmen, had been detected with the dagger of an assassin, and that in the consciousness of having planned the crime she had paid its penalty.

11. He even revived the charges of a period long past, how she had aimed at a share of empire, and at inducing the praetorian cohorts to swear obedience to a woman, to the disgrace of the Senate and people; how, when she was disappointed, in her fury with the soldiers, the Senate, and the populace, she opposed the usual donative and largess, and organized perilous prosecutions against distinguished citizens. What efforts had it cost him to hinder her from bursting into the senate-house and giving answers to foreign nations! He glanced too with indirect censure at the days of Claudius, and ascribed all the abominations of that reign to his mother, thus seeking to show that it was the State's good fortune which had destroyed her. For he actually told the story of the shipwreck; but who could be so stupid as to believe that it was accidental, or that a shipwrecked woman had sent one man with a weapon to break through an emperor's guards and fleets? So now it was not Nero, whose brutality was far beyond any remonstrance, but Seneca who was in ill repute, for having written a confession in such a style.

BOOK XV 37–44

The great fire of 64 C.E. destroyed much of Rome, and Nero builds a vast new palace called the "Golden House." He also blames the Christians for the arson.

37. Nero, to win credit for himself of enjoying nothing so much as the capital, prepared banquets in the public places, and used the whole city, so to say, as his private house. Of these entertainments the most famous for their notorious profligacy were those furnished by Tigellinus, which I will describe as an illustration, that I may not have again and again to narrate similar extravagance. He had a raft constructed on Agrippa's lake, put the guests on board and set it in motion by other vessels towing it. These vessels glittered with gold and ivory; the crews were arranged according to age and experience in vice. Birds and beasts had been procured from remote countries, and sea monsters from the ocean. On the margin of the lake were set up brothels crowded with noble ladies, and on the opposite bank were seen naked prostitutes with obscene gestures and movements. As darkness approached, all the adjacent grove and surrounding buildings resounded with song, and shone brilliantly with lights. Nero, who polluted himself by every lawful or lawless indulgence, had not omitted a single abomination which could heighten his depravity, till a few days afterwards he stooped to marry himself to one of that filthy herd, by name Pythagoras, with all the forms of regular wedlock. The bridal veil was put over the emperor; people saw the witnesses of the ceremony, the wedding dower, the couch and the nuptial torches; everything in a word was plainly visible, which, even when a woman weds darkness hides.

38. A disaster followed, whether accidental or treacherously contrived by the emperor, is uncertain, as authors have given both accounts, worse, however, and more dreadful than any which have ever happened to this city by the violence of fire. It had its beginning in that part of the circus which adjoins the Palatine and Caelian hills, where, amid the shops containing inflammable wares, the conflagration both broke out and instantly became so fierce and so rapid from the wind that it seized in its grasp the entire length of the circus. For here there were no houses fenced in by solid masonry, or temples surrounded by walls, or any other obstacle to interpose delay. The blaze in its fury ran first through the level portions of the city, then rising to the hills, while it again devastated every place below them, it outstripped all preventive measures; so rapid was the mischief and so completely at its mercy the city, with those narrow winding passages and irregular streets, which characterized old Rome. Added to this were the wailings of terror-stricken women, the feebleness of age, the helpless inexperience of childhood, the crowds who sought to save themselves or others, dragging out the infirm or waiting for them, and by their hurry in the one case, by their delay in the other, aggravating the confusion. Often, while they looked behind them, they were intercepted by flames on their side or in their face. Or if they reached a refuge close at hand, when this too was seized by the fire, they found that, even places, which they had imagined to be remote, were involved in the same calamity. At last, doubting what they should avoid or whither betake themselves, they crowded the streets or flung themselves down in the fields, while some who had lost their all, even their very daily bread, and others out of love for their kinsfolk, whom they had been unable to rescue, perished, though escape was open to them. And no one dared to stop the mischief, because of incessant menaces from a number of persons who forbade the extinguishing of the flames, because again others openly hurled brands, and kept shouting that there was one who gave them authority, either seeking to plunder more freely, or obeying orders.

39. Nero at this time was at Antium, and did not return to Rome until the fire approached his house, which he had built to connect the palace with the gardens of Maecenas. It could not, however, be stopped from devouring the palace, the house, and everything around it. However, to relieve the people, driven out homeless as they were, he threw open to them the Campus Martius and the public buildings of Agrippa, and even his own gardens, and raised temporary structures to receive the destitute multitude. Supplies of food were brought up from Ostia and the neighboring towns, and the price of corn was reduced to three sesterces a peck. These acts, though popular, produced no effect, since a rumor had gone forth everywhere that, at the very time when the city was in flames, the emperor appeared on a private stage and sang of the destruction of Troy, comparing present misfortunes with the calamities of antiquity.

40. At last, after five days, an end was put to the conflagration at the foot of the Esquiline hill, by the destruction of all buildings on a vast space, so that the violence of the fire was met by clear ground and an open sky. But before people had laid aside their fears, the flames returned, with no less fury this second time, and especially in the spacious districts of the city. Consequently, though there was less loss of life, the temples of the gods, and the porticoes which were devoted to enjoyment, fell in a yet more widespread ruin. And to this conflagration there attached the greater infamy because it broke out on the Aemilian property of Tigellinus, and it seemed that Nero was aiming at the glory of founding a new city and calling it by his name. Rome, indeed, is divided into fourteen districts, four of which remained uninjured, three were leveled to the ground, while in the other seven were left only a few shattered, half-burnt relics of houses.

41. It would not be easy to enter into a computation of the private mansions, the blocks of tenements, and of the temples, which were lost. Those with the oldest ceremonial, as that dedicated by Servius Tullius to Luna, the great altar and shrine raised by the Arcadian Evander to the visibly appearing Hercules, the temple of Jupiter the Stayer, which was vowed by Romulus, Numa's royal palace, and the sanctuary of Vesta, with the tutelary deities of the Roman people, were burnt. So too were the riches acquired by our many victories, various beauties of Greek art, then again the ancient and genuine historical monuments of men of genius, and, notwithstanding the striking splendor of the restored city, old men will remember many things which could not be replaced. Some persons observed that the beginning of this conflagration was on the 19th of July, the day on which the Senones captured and fired Rome. Others have pushed a curious inquiry so far as to reduce the interval between these two conflagrations into equal numbers of years, months, and days.

42. Nero meanwhile availed himself of his country's desolation, and erected a mansion in which the jewels and gold, long familiar objects, quite vulgarized by our extravagance, were not so marvelous as the fields and lakes, with woods on one side to resemble a wilderness, and, on the other, open spaces and extensive views. The directors and contrivers of the work were Severus and Celer, who had the genius and the audacity to attempt by art even what nature had refused, and to fool away an emperor's resources. They had actually undertaken to sink a navigable canal from the lake Avernus to the mouths of the Tiber along a barren shore or through the face of hills, where one meets with no moisture which could supply water, except the Pomptine marshes. The rest of the country is broken rock and perfectly dry. Even if it could be cut through, the labor would be intolerable, and there would be no adequate result. Nero, however, with his love of the impossible, endeavored to dig through the nearest hills to Avernus, and there still remain the traces of his disappointed hope.

43. Of Rome meanwhile, so much as was left unoccupied by his mansion, was not built up, as it had been after its burning by the Gauls, without any regularity or in any fashion, but with rows of streets according to measurement, with broad thoroughfares, with a restriction on the height of houses, with open spaces, and the further addition of colonnades, as a protection to the frontage of the blocks of tenements. These colonnades Nero promised to erect at his own expense, and to hand over the open spaces, when cleared of the debris, to the ground landlords. He also offered rewards proportioned to each person's position and property, and prescribed a period within which they were to obtain them on the completion of so many houses or blocks of building. He fixed on the marshes of Ostia for the reception of the rubbish, and arranged that the ships which had brought up corn by the Tiber, should sail down the river with cargoes of this rubbish. The buildings

themselves, to a certain height, were to be solidly constructed, without wooden beams, of stone from Gabii or Alba, that material being impervious to fire. And to provide that the water which individual license had illegally appropriated, might flow in greater abundance in several places for the public use, officers were appointed, and everyone was to have in the open court the means of stopping a fire. Every building, too, was to be enclosed by its own proper wall, not by one common to others. These changes which were liked for their utility, also added beauty to the new city. Some, however, thought that its old arrangement had been more conducive to health, inasmuch as the narrow streets with the elevation of the roofs were not equally penetrated by the sun's heat, while now the open space, unsheltered by any shade, was scorched by a fiercer glow.

44. Such indeed were the precautions of human wisdom. The next thing was to seek means of propitiating the gods, and recourse was had to the Sibylline books, by the direction of which prayers were offered to Vulcanus, Ceres, and Proserpina. Juno, too, was entreated by the matrons, first, in the Capitol, then on the nearest part of the coast, whence water was procured to sprinkle the temple and image of the goddess. And there were sacred banquets and nightly vigils celebrated by married women. But all human efforts, all the lavish gifts of the emperor, and the propitiations of the gods, did not banish the sinister belief that the conflagration was the result of an order. Consequently, to get rid of the report, Nero fastened the guilt and inflicted the most exquisite tortures on a class hated for their abominations, called Christians by the populace. Christus, from whom the name had its origin, suffered the extreme penalty during the reign of Tiberius at the hands of one of our procurators, Pontius Pilatus, and a most mischievous superstition, thus checked for the moment, again broke out not only in Judaea, the first source of the evil, but even in Rome, where all things hideous and shameful from every part of the world find their center and become popular. Accordingly, an arrest was first made of all who pleaded guilty; then, upon their information, an immense multitude was convicted, not so much of the crime of firing the city, as of hatred against mankind. Mockery of every sort was added to their deaths. Covered with the skins of beasts, they were torn by dogs and perished, or were nailed to crosses, or were doomed to the flames and burnt, to serve as a nightly illumination, when daylight had expired.

Nero offered his gardens for the spectacle, and was exhibiting a show in the circus, while he mingled with the people in the dress of a charioteer or stood aloft on a car. Hence, even for criminals who deserved extreme and exemplary punishment, there arose a feeling of compassion; for it was not, as it seemed, for the public good, but to glut one man's cruelty, that they were being destroyed.

BOOK XV **60–64**

The death of the philosopher Seneca, once Nero's tutor.

60. . . . .Then followed the destruction of Annaeus Seneca, a special joy to the emperor, not because he had convicted him of the conspiracy, but anxious to accomplish with the sword what poison had failed to do. It was, in fact, Natalis alone who divulged Seneca's name, to this extent, that he had been sent to Seneca when ailing, to see him and remonstrate with him for excluding Piso from his presence, when it would have been better to have kept up their friendship by familiar intercourse; that Seneca's reply was that mutual conversations and frequent interviews were to the advantage of neither, but still that his own life depended on Piso's safety. Gavius Silvanus, tribune of a praetorian cohort, was ordered to report this to Seneca and to ask him whether he acknowledged what Natalis said and his own answer. Either by chance or purposely Seneca had returned on that day from Campania, and had stopped at a country house four miles from Rome. Thither the tribune came next evening, surrounded the house with troops of soldiers, and then made known the emperor's message to Seneca as he was at dinner with his wife, Pompeia Paulina, and two friends.

61. Seneca replied that Natalis had been sent to him and had complained to him in Piso's name because of his refusal to see Piso, upon which he excused himself on the ground of failing health and the desire of rest. "He had no reason," he said, for "preferring the interest of any private citizen to his own safety, and he had no natural aptitude for flattery. No one knew this better than Nero, who had oftener experienced Seneca's freespokenness than his servility." When the tribune reported this answer in the presence of Poppaea and Tigellinus, the emperor's most confidential advisers in his moments of rage, he asked whether Seneca was meditating suicide. Upon this the tribune asserted that he saw no signs of fear, and perceived no sadness in his words or in his looks. He was accordingly ordered to go back and to announce sentence of death. Fabius Rusticus tells us that he did not return the way he came, but went out of his course to Faenius, the commander of the guard, and having explained to him the emperor's orders, and asked whether he was to obey them, was by him admonished to carry them out, for a fatal spell of cowardice was on them all. For this very Silvanus was one of the conspirators, and he was now abetting the crimes which he had united with them to avenge. But he spared himself the anguish of a word or of a look, and merely sent in to Seneca one of his centurions, who was to announce to him his last doom.

62. Seneca, quite unmoved, asked for tablets on which to inscribe his will, and, on the centurion's refusal, turned to his friends, protesting that as he was forbidden to requite them, he bequeathed to them the only, but still the noblest possession yet remaining to him, the pattern of his life, which, if they remembered, they would win a name for moral worth and steadfast friendship. At the same time he called them back from their tears to manly resolution, now with friendly talk, and now with the sterner language of rebuke. "Where," he asked again and again, "are your maxims of philosophy, or the preparation of so many years' study against evils to come? Who knew not Nero's cruelty? After a mother's and a brother's murder, nothing remains but to add the destruction of a guardian and a tutor."

63. Having spoken these and like words, meant, so to say, for all, he embraced his wife; then softening awhile from the stern resolution of the hour, he begged and implored her to spare herself the burden of perpetual sorrow, and, in the contemplation of a life virtuously spent, to endure a husband's loss with honorable consolations. She declared, in answer, that she too had decided to die, and claimed for herself the blow of the executioner. There upon Seneca, not to thwart her noble ambition, from an affection too which would not leave behind him for insult one whom he dearly loved, replied: "I have shown you ways of smoothing life; you prefer the glory of dying. I will not grudge you such a noble example. Let the fortitude of so courageous an end be alike in both of us, but let there be more in your decease to win fame."

Then by one and the same stroke they sundered with a dagger the arteries of their arms. Seneca, as his aged frame, attenuated by frugal diet, allowed the blood to escape but slowly, severed also the veins of his legs and knees. Worn out by cruel anguish, afraid too that his sufferings might break his wife's spirit, and that, as he looked on her tortures, he might himself sink into irresolution, he persuaded her to retire into another chamber. Even at the last moment his eloquence failed him not; he summoned his secretaries, and dictated much to them which, as it has been published for all readers in his own words, I forbear to paraphrase.

64. Nero meanwhile, having no personal hatred against Paulina and not wishing to heighten the odium of his cruelty, forbade her death. At the soldiers' prompting, her slaves and freedmen bound up her arms, and stanched the bleeding, whether with her knowledge is doubtful. For as the vulgar are ever ready to think the worst, there were persons who believed that, as long as she dreaded Nero's relentlessness, she sought the glory of sharing her husband's death, but that after a time, when a more soothing prospect presented itself, she yielded to the charms of life. To this she added a few subsequent years, with a most praiseworthy remembrance of her husband, and with a countenance and frame white to a degree of pallor which denoted a loss of much vital energy.

Seneca meantime, as the tedious process of death still lingered on,

begged Statius Annaeus, whom he had long esteemed for his faithful friendship and medical skill, to produce a poison with which he had some time
before provided himself, same drug which extinguished the life of those who
were condemned by a public sentence of the people of Athens. It was
brought to him and he drank it in vain, chilled as he was throughout his
limbs, and his frame closed against the efficacy of the poison. At last he
entered a pool of heated water, from which he sprinkled the nearest of his
slaves, adding the exclamation, "I offer this liquid as a libation to Jupiter the
Deliverer." He was then carried into a bath, with the steam of which he was
suffocated, and he was burnt without any of the usual funeral rites. So he
had directed in a codicil of his will, when even in the height of his wealth and
power he was thinking of his life's close.

BOOK XVI **18–19**

*The death of the courtier Petronius. Petronius, who wrote the famous
"Satyricon," faces his death with the ironic amusement of his life and
writings. His last hours mock the philosophical death of Seneca.*

18. With regard to Gaius Petronius, I ought to dwell a little on his
antecedents. His days he passed in sleep, his nights in the business and pleasures of life. Indolence had raised him to fame, as energy raises others, and
he was reckoned not a debauchee and spendthrift, like most of those who
squander their substance, but a man of refined luxury. And indeed his talk
and his doings, the freer they were and the more show of carelessness they
exhibited, were the better liked, for their look of natural simplicity. Yet as
proconsul of Bithynia and soon afterwards as consul, he showed himself a
man of vigor and equal to business. Then falling back into vice or affecting
vice, he was chosen by Nero to be one of his few intimate associates, as a
critic in matters of taste, while the emperor thought nothing charming or
elegant in luxury unless Petronius had expressed to him his approval of it.
Hence jealousy on the part of Tigellinus, who looked on him as a rival and
even his superior in the science of pleasure. And so he worked on the prince's
cruelty, which dominated every other passion, charging Petronius with having been the friend of Scaevinus, bribing a slave to become informer, robbing
him of the means of defense, and hurrying into prison most of his servants.

19. It happened at the time that the emperor was on his way to Campania
and that Petronius, after going as far as Cumae, was there detained. He bore
no longer the suspense of fear or of hope. Yet he did not fling away life with
precipitate haste, but having made an incision in his veins and then, according to his humor, bound them up, he again opened them, while he conversed

with his friends, not in a serious strain or on topics that might win for him the glory of courage. And he listened to them as they repeated, not thoughts on the immortality of the soul or on the theories of philosophers, but light poetry and playful verses. To some of his slaves he gave liberal presents, a flogging to others. He dined, indulged himself in sleep, that death, though forced on him, might have a natural appearance. Even in his will he did not, as did many in their last moments, flatter Nero or Tigellinus or any other of the men in power. On the contrary, he described fully the prince's shameful excesses, with the names of his male and female lovers and their novelties in debauchery, and sent the account under seal to Nero. Then he broke his signet-ring, that it might not be subsequently available for imperiling others.

HISTORIES

Tacitus' first narrative history covered the reigns of the Flavian emperors: Vespasian (69–79 C.E.), following by his sons Titus (79–81 C.E.) and Domitian (81–96 C.E.). This is the period of Tacitus' own boyhood and his political career, so it is particularly unfortunate that only four books and part of a fifth survive of the original twelve.

The books that survive treat the civil wars of 69 C.E.—the "Year of the Four Emperors." It is the most detailed treatment of any period in the whole of ancient historical writing. Here Tacitus displays his narrative skills in portraying battles and the burning of Rome.

BOOK I 1–16

After brief comments on the writing of history, Tacitus begins the account of the fateful year 69 C.E. which brought four emperors to the throne. The elderly and indecisive Galba was the first.

1. I begin my work with the time when Servius Galba was consul for the second time with Titus Vinius for his colleague. Of the former period, the 820 years dating from the founding of the city, many authors have treated; and while they had to record the transactions of the Roman people, they wrote with equal eloquence and freedom. After the conflict at Actium, and when it became essential to peace, that all power should be centered in one man, these intellects passed away. Then too the truthfulness of history was impaired in many ways; at first, through men's ignorance of public affairs,

which were now wholly strange to them, then, through their passion for flattery, or, on the other hand, their hatred of their masters. And so between the enmity of the one and the servility of the other, neither had any regard for posterity. But while we instinctively shrink from a writer's adulation, we lend a ready ear to detraction and spite, because flattery involves the shameful imputation of servility, whereas malignity wears the false appearance of honesty. I myself knew nothing of Galba, of Otho, or of Vitellius, either from benefits or from injuries. I would not deny that my elevation was begun by Vespasian, augmented by Titus, and still further advanced by Domitian; but those who profess inviolable truthfulness must speak of all without partiality and without hatred. I have reserved as an employment for my old age, should my life be long enough, a subject at once more fruitful and less anxious in the reign of the Divine Nerva and the empire of Trajan, enjoying the rare happiness of times, when we may think what we please, and express what we think.

2. I am entering on the history of a period rich in disasters, frightful in its wars, torn by civil strife, and even in peace full of horrors. Four emperors perished by the sword. There were three civil wars; there were more with foreign enemies; there were often wars that had both characters at once. There was success in the East, and disaster in the West. There were disturbances in Illyricum; Gaul wavered in its allegiance; Britain was thoroughly subdued and immediately abandoned; the tribes of the Suevi and the Sarmatae rose in concert against us; the Dacians had the glory of inflicting as well as suffering defeat; the armies of Parthia were all but set in motion by the cheat of a counterfeit Nero. Now too Italy was prostrated by disasters either entirely novel, or that recurred only after a long succession of ages; cities in Campania's richest plains were swallowed up and overwhelmed; Rome was wasted by conflagrations, its oldest temples consumed, and the Capitol itself fired by the hands of citizens. Sacred rites were profaned; there was profligacy in the highest ranks; the sea was crowded with exiles, and its rocks polluted with bloody deeds. In the capital there were yet worse horrors. Nobility, wealth, the refusal or the acceptance of office, were grounds for accusation, and virtue ensured destruction. The rewards of the informers were no less odious than their crimes; for while some seized on consulships and priestly offices, as their share of the spoil, others on procuratorships, and posts of more confidential authority, they robbed and ruined in every direction amid universal hatred and terror. Slaves were bribed to turn against their masters, and freedmen to betray their patrons; and those who had not an enemy were destroyed by friends.

3. Yet the age was not so barren in noble qualities, as not also to exhibit examples of virtue. Mothers accompanied the flight of their sons; wives followed their husbands into exile; there were brave kinsmen and faithful sons in law; there were slaves whose fidelity defied even torture; there were illustrious men driven to the last necessity, and enduring it with fortitude; there were closing scenes that equaled the famous deaths of antiquity. Besides the manifold vicissitudes of human affairs, there were prodigies in heaven and earth, the warning voices of the thunder, and other intimations of the future, auspicious or gloomy, doubtful or not to be mistaken. Never surely did more terrible calamities of the Roman People, or evidence more conclusive, prove that the Gods take no thought for our happiness, but only for our punishment.

4. I think it proper, however, before I commence my purposed work, to pass under review the condition of the capital, the temper of the armies, the attitude of the provinces, and the elements of weakness and strength which existed throughout the whole empire, that so we may become acquainted, not only with the vicissitudes and the issues of events, which are often matters of chance, but also with their relations and their causes. Welcome as the death of Nero had been in the first burst of joy, yet it had not only roused various emotions in Rome, among the Senators, the people, or the soldiery of the capital, it had also excited all the legions and their generals; for now had been divulged that secret of the empire, that emperors could be made elsewhere than at Rome. The Senators enjoyed the first exercise of freedom with the less restraint, because the Emperor was new to power, and absent from the capital. The leading men of the Equestrian order sympathized most closely with the joy of the Senators. The respectable portion of the people, which was connected with the great families, as well as the dependents and freedmen of condemned and banished persons, were high in hope. The degraded populace, frequenters of the arena and the theater, the most worthless of the slaves, and those who having wasted their property were supported by the infamous excesses of Nero, caught eagerly in their dejection at every rumor.

5. The soldiery of the capital, who were imbued with the spirit of an old allegiance to the Caesars, and who had been led to desert Nero by intrigues and influences from without rather than by their own feelings, were inclined for change, when they found that the donative promised in Galba's name was withheld, and reflected that for great services and great rewards there was not the same room in peace as in war, and that the favor of an emperor created by the legions must be already preoccupied. They were further excited by the treason of Nymphidius Sabinus, their prefect, who himself aimed at the throne. Nymphidius indeed perished in the attempt, but, though the head of the mutiny was thus removed, there yet remained in many of the soldiers the consciousness of guilt. There were even men who talked in angry terms of the feebleness and avarice of Galba. The strictness once so commended, and celebrated in the praises of the army, was galling to troops who

rebelled against the old discipline, and who had been accustomed by four-teen years' service under Nero to love the vices of their emperors, as much as they had once respected their virtues. To all this was added Galba's own expression, "I choose my soldiers, I do not buy them," noble words for the commonwealth, but fraught with peril for himself. His other acts were not after this pattern.

6. Titus Vinius and Cornelius Laco, one the most worthless, the other the most spiritless of mankind, were ruining the weak old Emperor, who had to bear the odium of such crimes and the scorn felt for such cowardice. Galba's progress had been slow and blood-stained. Cingonius Varro, consul-elect, and Petronius Turpilianus, a man of consular rank, were put to death; the former as an accomplice of Nymphidius, the latter as one of Nero's gen-erals. Both had perished without hearing or defense, like innocent men. His entry into the capital, made after the slaughter of thousands of unarmed sol-diers, was most ill-omened, and was terrible even to the executioners. As he brought into the city his Spanish legion, while that which Nero had levied from the fleet still remained, Rome was full of strange troops. There were also many detachments from Germany, Britain, and Illyria, selected by Nero, and sent on by him to the Caspian passes, for service in the expedition which he was preparing against the Albani, but afterwards recalled to crush the insurrection of Vindex. Here there were vast materials for a revolution, with-out indeed a decided bias towards any one man, but ready to a daring hand.

7. In this conjuncture it happened that tidings of the deaths of Fonteius Capito and Clodius Macer reached the capital. Macer was executed in Africa, where he was undoubtedly fomenting sedition, by Trebonius Garutianus the procurator, who acted on Galba's authority; Capito fell in Germany, while he was making similar attempts, by the hands of Cornelius Aquinus and Fabius Valens, legates of legions, who did not wait for an order. There were however some who believed that Capito, though foully stained with avarice and profl-igacy, had yet abstained from all thought of revolution, that this was a treach-erous accusation invented by the commanders themselves, who had urged him to take up arms, when they found themselves unable to prevail, and that Galba had approved of the deed, either from weakness of character, or to avoid investigation into the circumstances of acts which could not be altered. Both executions, however, were unfavorably regarded; indeed, when a ruler once becomes unpopular, all his acts, be they good or bad, tell against him. The freedmen in their excessive power were now putting up everything for sale; the slaves caught with greedy hands at immediate gain, and, reflecting on their master's age, hastened to be rich. The new court had the same abuses as the old, abuses as grievous as ever, but not so readily excused. Even the age of Galba caused ridicule and disgust among those whose associations were with the youth of Nero, and who were accustomed, as is the fashion of the vulgar, to value their emperors by the beauty and grace of their persons.

8. Such, as far as one can speak of so vast a multitude, was the state of feeling at Rome. Among the provinces, Spain was under the government of Cluvius Rufus, an eloquent man, who had all the accomplishments of civil life, but who was without experience in war. Gaul, besides remembering Vindex, was bound to Galba by the recently conceded privileges of citizenship, and by the diminution of its future tribute. Those Gallic states, however, which were nearest to the armies of Germany, had not been treated with the same respect, and had even in some cases been deprived of their territory; and these were reckoning the gains of others and their own losses with equal indignation. The armies of Germany were at once alarmed and angry, a most dangerous temper when allied with such strength; while elated by their recent victory, they feared because they might seem to have supported an unsuccessful party. They had been slow to revolt from Nero, and Verginius had not immediately declared for Galba; it was doubtful whether he had himself wished to be emperor, but all agreed that the empire had been offered to him by the soldiery. Again, the execution of Capito was a subject of indignation, even with those who could not complain of its injustice. They had no leader, for Verginius had been withdrawn on the pretext of his friendship with the Emperor. That he was not sent back, and that he was even impeached, they regarded as an accusation against themselves.

9. The army of Upper Germany despised their legate, Hordeonius Flaccus, who, disabled by age and lameness, had no strength of character and no authority; even when the soldiery were quiet, he could not control them, much more in their fits of frenzy were they irritated by the very feebleness of his restraint. The legions of Lower Germany had long been without any general of consular rank, until, by the appointment of Galba, Aulus Vitellius took the command. He was son of that Vitellius who was censor and three times consul; this was thought sufficient recommendation. In the army of Britain there was no angry feeling; indeed no troops behaved more blamelessly throughout all the troubles of these civil wars, either because they were far away and separated by the ocean from the rest of the empire, or because continual warfare had taught them to concentrate their hatred on the enemy. Illyricum too was quiet, though the legions drawn from that province by Nero had, while lingering in Italy, sent deputations to Verginius. But separated as these armies were by long distances, a thing of all others the most favorable for keeping troops to their duty, they could neither communicate their vices, nor combine their strength.

10. In the East there was as yet no movement. Syria and its four legions were under the command of Licinius Mucianus, a man whose good and bad fortune were equally famous. In his youth he had cultivated with many intrigues the friendship of the great. His resources soon failed, and his posi-

tion became precarious, and as he also suspected that Claudius had taken some offense, he withdrew into a retired part of Asia, and was as like an exile, as he was afterwards like an emperor. He was a compound of dissipation and energy, of arrogance and courtesy, of good and bad qualities. His self-indulgence was excessive, when he had leisure, yet whenever he had served, he had shown great qualities. In his public capacity he might be praised; his private life was in bad repute. Yet over subjects, friends, and colleagues, he exercised the influence of many fascinations. He was a man who would find it easier to transfer the imperial power to another, than to hold it for himself. Flavius Vespasian, a general of Nero's appointment, was carrying on the war in Judaea with three legions, and he had no wish or feeling adverse to Galba. He had in fact sent his son Titus to acknowledge his authority and bespeak his favor, as in its proper place I shall relate. As for the hidden decrees of fate, the omens and the oracles that marked out Vespasian and his sons for imperial power, we believed in them only after his success.

11. Ever since the time of the Divine Augustus Roman Knights have ruled Egypt as kings, and the forces by which it has to be kept in subjection. It has been thought expedient thus to keep under home control a province so difficult of access, so productive of corn, ever distracted, excitable, and restless through the superstition and licentiousness of its inhabitants, knowing nothing of laws, and unused to civil rule. Its governor was at this time Tiberius Alexander, a native of the country. Africa and its legions, now that Clodius Macer was dead, were disposed to be content with any emperor, after having experienced the rule of a smaller tyrant. The two divisions of Mauritania, Rhaetia, Noricum and Thrace and the other provinces governed by procurators, as they were near this or that army, were driven by the presence of such powerful neighbors into friendship or hostility. The unarmed provinces with Italy at their head were exposed to any kind of slavery, and were ready to become the prize of victory. Such was the state of the Roman world, when Servius Galba, consul for the second time, with T. Vinius for his colleague, entered upon a year, which was to be the last of their lives, and which well nigh brought the commonwealth to an end.

12. A few days after the 1st of January, there arrived from Belgica dispatches of Pompeius Propinquus, the Procurator, to this effect; that the legions of Upper Germany had broken through the obligation of their military oath, and were demanding another emperor, but conceded the power of choice to the Senate and people of Rome, in the hope that a more lenient view might be taken of their revolt. These tidings hastened the plans of Galba, who had been long debating the subject of adoption with himself and with his intimate friends. There was indeed no more frequent subject of conversation during these months, at first because men had liberty and inclination to talk of such matters, afterwards because the feebleness of Galba was notorious. Few had any discrimination or patriotism, many had foolish hopes for themselves, and spread interested reports, in which they named this or that person to whom they might be related as friend or dependent. They were also moved by hatred of T. Vinius, who grew daily more powerful, and in the same proportion more unpopular. The very easiness of Galba's temper stimulated the greedy cupidity which great advancement had excited in his friends, because with one so weak and so credulous wrong might be done with less risk and greater gain.

13. The real power of the Empire was divided between T. Vinius, the consul, and Cornelius Laco, prefect of the Praetorian Guard. Icelus, a freedman of Galba, was in equal favor; he had been presented with the rings of knighthood, and bore the Equestrian name of Martianus. These men, being at variance, and in smaller matters pursuing their own aims, were divided in the affair of choosing a successor, into two opposing factions. T. Vinius was for Marcus Otho, Laco and Icelus agreed, not indeed in supporting any particular individual, but in striving for someone else. Galba indeed was aware of the friendship between Vinius and Otho; the gossip of those who allow nothing to pass in silence had named them as father-in-law and son-in-law, for Vinius had a widowed daughter, and Otho was unmarried. I believe that he had also at heart some care for the commonwealth, in vain, he would think, rescued from Nero, if it was to be left with Otho. For Otho's had been a neglected boyhood and a riotous youth, and he had made himself agreeable to Nero by emulating his profligacy. For this reason the Emperor had entrusted to him, as being the confidant of his amours, Poppaea Sabina, the imperial favorite, until he could rid himself of his wife Octavia. Soon suspecting him with regard to this same Poppaea, he sent him out of the way to the province of Lusitania, ostensibly to be its governor. Otho ruled the province with mildness, and, as he was the first to join Galba's party, was not without energy, and, while the war lasted, was the most conspicuous of the Emperor's followers, he was led to cherish more and more passionately every day those hopes of adoption which he had entertained from the first. Many of the soldiers favored him, and the court was biased in his favor, because he resembled Nero.

14. When Galba heard of the mutiny in Germany, though nothing was as yet known about Vitellius, he felt anxious as to the direction which the violence of the legions might take, while he could not trust even the soldiery of the capital. He therefore resorted to what he supposed to be the only remedy, and held a council for the election of an emperor. To this he summoned, besides Vinius and Laco, Marius Celsus, consul elect, and Ducennius Geminus, prefect of the city. Having first said a few words about his advanced years, he ordered Piso Licinianus to be summoned. It is uncertain whether he acted on his own free choice, or, as believed by some, under the influence of

Laco, who through Rubellius Plautus had cultivated the friendship of Piso. But, cunningly enough, it was as a stranger that Laco supported him, and the high character of Piso gave weight to his advice. Piso, who was the son of M. Crassus and Scribonia, and thus of noble descent on both sides, was in look and manner a man of the old type. Rightly judged, he seemed a stern man, morose to those who estimated him less favorably. This point in his character pleased his adopted father in proportion as it raised the anxious suspicions of others.

15. We are told that Galba, taking hold of Piso's hand, spoke to this effect: "If I were a private man, and were now adopting you by the Act of the Curiae before the Pontiffs, as our custom is, it would be a high honor to me to introduce into my family a descendant of Cn. Pompeius and M. Crassus; it would be a distinction to you to add to the nobility of your race the honors of the Sulpician and Lutatian houses. As it is, I, who have been called to the throne by the unanimous consent of gods and men, am moved by your splendid endowments and by my own patriotism to offer to you, a man of peace, that power, for which our ancestors fought, and which I myself obtained by war. I am following the precedent of the Divine Augustus, who placed on an eminence next to his own, first his nephew Marcellus, then his son-in-law Agrippa, afterwards his grandsons, and finally Tiberius Nero, his stepson. But Augustus looked for a successor in his own family, I look for one in the state, not because I have no relatives or companions of my campaigns, but because it was not by any private favor that I myself received the imperial power. Let the principle of my choice be shown not only by my connections which I have set aside for you, but by your own. You have a brother, noble as yourself, and older, who would be well worthy of this dignity, were you not worthier. Your age is such as to be now free from the passions of youth, and such your life that in the past you have nothing to excuse. Hitherto, you have only borne adversity; prosperity tries the heart with keener temptations; for hardships may be endured, whereas we are spoiled by success. You indeed will cling with the same constancy to honor, freedom, friendship, the best possessions of the human spirit, but others will seek to weaken them with their servility. You will be fiercely assailed by adulation, by flattery, that worst poison of the true heart, and by the selfish interests of individuals. You and I speak together today with perfect frankness, but others will be more ready to address us as emperors than as men. For to urge his duty upon a prince is indeed a hard matter; to flatter him, whatever his character, is a mere routine gone through without any heart.

16. "Could the vast frame of this empire have stood and preserved its balance without a directing spirit, I was not unworthy of inaugurating a republic. As it is, we have been long reduced to a position, in which my age confers no greater boon on the Roman people than a good successor,

your youth no greater than a good emperor. Under Tiberius, Caius, and Claudius, we were, so to speak, the inheritance of a single family. The choice which begins with us will be a substitute for freedom. Now that the family of the Julii and the Claudii has come to an end, adoption will discover the worthiest successor. To be begotten and born of a princely race is a mere accident, and is only valued as such. In adoption there is nothing that need bias the judgment, and if you wish to make a choice, an unanimous opinion points out the man. Let Nero be ever before your eyes, swollen with the pride of a long line of Caesars; it was not Vindex with his unarmed province, it was not myself with my single legion, that shook his yoke from our necks. It was his own profligacy, his own brutality, and that, though there had been before no precedent of an emperor condemned by his own people. We, who have been called to power by the issues of war, and by the deliberate judgment of others, shall incur unpopularity, however illustrious our character. Do not however be alarmed, if, after a movement which has shaken the world, two legions are not yet quiet. I did not myself succeed to a throne without anxiety; and when men shall hear of your adoption I shall no longer be thought old, and this is the only objection which is now made against me. Nero will always be regretted by the thoroughly depraved; it is for you and me to take care, that he be not regretted also by the good. To prolong such advice, suits not this occasion, and all my purpose is fulfilled if I have made a good choice in you. The most practical and the shortest method of distinguishing between good and bad measures, is to think what you yourself would or would not like under another emperor. It is not here, as it is among nations despotically ruled, that there is a distinct governing family, while all the rest are slaves. You have to reign over men who cannot bear either absolute slavery or absolute freedom." This, with more to the same effect, was said by Galba; he spoke to Piso as if he were creating an emperor; the others addressed him as if he were an emperor already.

BOOK III 66–72

The troops of the emperor Vitellius attempt to hold Rome against the supporters of Vespasian, who would rule from 69 to 79 C.E. During the civil war, the temple of Jupiter on the Capitol was burned. The language of Tacitus here draws upon Virgil's depiction of the sack of Troy in his Aeneid.

66. Could Vitellius have swayed the feelings of his partisans as easily as he had himself yielded, the army of Vespasian might have entered the capital without bloodshed. But the more loyal his adherents, the more did they protest against peace and negotiation. They pointed out the danger and disgrace of a submission in which the caprice of the conqueror would be their sole guarantee. "And Vespasian," they said, "is not so arrogant as to tolerate such a subject as Vitellius. Even the vanquished would not endure it. Their pity would be dangerous to him. You certainly are an old man, and have had enough both of prosperity and of adversity, but think what a name, what a position, you will leave to your son Germanicus. Now indeed they promise you wealth, and a large establishment, and a luxurious retreat in Campania; but when Vespasian has once seized the throne, neither he, nor his friends, nor even his armies, will feel themselves secure till all rivalry has been extinguished. Fabius Valens, captive as he was, and reserved against the chance of disaster, was yet too formidable to them; and certainly Primus, Fuscus, and Mucianus, who exhibits the temper of his party, will not be allowed power over Vitellius except to put him to death. Caesar did not leave Pompey, Augustus did not leave Antony in safety, though, perhaps, Vespasian may show a more lofty spirit, Vespasian, who was a dependent of Vitellius, when Vitellius was the colleague of Claudius. If you would act as becomes the censorship, the thrice-repeated consulate of your father, and all the honors of your illustrious house, let despair at any rate arm you to courageous action. The troops are still firm, and among the people there is abundant zeal. Lastly, nothing can happen to us more terrible than that upon which we are voluntarily rushing. If we are conquered, we must die; we must die, if we capitulate. All that concerns us is this; shall we draw our last breath amidst scorn and insult, or in a valiant struggle?"

67. The ears of Vitellius were deaf to manly counsels. His whole soul was overwhelmed by a tender anxiety, lest by an obstinate resistance he might leave the conqueror less mercifully disposed to his wife and children. He had also a mother old and feeble, but she, expiring a few days before, escaped by her opportune death the ruin of her house, having gained from the Imperial dignity of her son nothing but sorrow and a good name. On the 18th of December, after hearing of the defection of the legion and the auxiliary infantry which had surrendered at Narnia, he left the palace, clad in mourning robes, and surrounded by his weeping household. With him went his little son, carried in a litter, as though in a funeral procession. The greetings of the people were flattering, but ill-suited to the time; the soldiers preserved an ominous silence.

68. There could hardly be a man so careless of human interests as not to be affected by this spectacle. There was the Roman Emperor, lord but a few days before of the whole human race, leaving the seat of his power, and passing through the midst of his people and his capital, to abdicate his throne. Men had never before seen or heard of such an event. Caesar, the Dictator, had fallen by sudden violence, Caligula by secret treason. The shades of

night and the obscurity of a rural hiding-place had veiled the flight of Nero. Piso and Galba had, it might be said, fallen in battle. In an assembly of his own people, and in the midst of his own soldiers, with the very women of his family looking on, Vitellius stood and spoke a few words suitable to the sad conjuncture. "He gave way," he said, "for the sake of peace, for the sake of his country; let them only remember him, and think with compassion of his brother, of his wife, of his young and innocent children." At the same time he held out his son, commending him first to individual bystanders, then to the whole assembly. At last, unable to speak for weeping, he unfastened the dagger from his side, and offered it to the Consul, Caecilius Simplex, who was standing by him, as if to indicate that he surrendered the power of life and death over the citizens. The Consul rejecting it, and those who were standing by in the assembly shouting remonstrance, he departed, as if with the intention of laying aside the emblems of Imperial power in the Temple of Concord, and of betaking himself to his brother's house. Louder shouts here met him from the crowd, which hindered him from entering a private house, and invited him to return to the palace. Every other route was closed, and the only one open was one which led into the Via Sacra. Then in utter perplexity he returned to the palace. The rumor that he had renounced the Imperial dignity had preceded him thither, and Flavius Sabinus had sent written orders to the tribunes of the cohorts to keep their soldiers under restraint.

69. Then, as if the whole State had passed into the hands of Vespasian, the leading men of the Senate, many of the Equestrian order, with all the city soldiery and the watch, thronged the dwelling of Sabinus. Intelligence was there brought to him of the enthusiasm of the populace and of the threatening attitude of the German cohorts. He had now gone too far to be able to retreat, and everyone, fearing for himself, should the Vitellianists come upon them while they were scattered and comparatively weak, urged him, in spite of his reluctance, to hostilities. As usually happens, however, in such cases, all gave the advice, but few shared the risk. The armed retinue which was escorting Sabinus was met, as it was coming down by the Lake Fundanus, by some of the most determined of the Vitellianists. From this unforeseen collision resulted an encounter slight indeed, but terminating favorably for the Vitellianists. In the hurry of the moment Sabinus adopted the safest course open to him, and occupied the Capitol with a miscellaneous body of soldiery, and some Senators and Knights. It is not easy to give the names of these persons, since after the triumph of Vespasian many pretended to have rendered this service to his party. There were even women who braved the dangers of the siege; the most conspicuous among them being Verulana Gratilla, who was taken thither, not by the love of children or kindred, but by the fascination of war. The Vitellianists kept but a careless watch over the besieged, and thus at the dead of night Sabinus was able to bring into the Capitol his own children

and Domitian his brother's son, and to send by an unguarded route a messenger to the generals of the Flavian party, with information that they were besieged, and that, unless succor arrived, they must be reduced to distress. The night passed so quietly that he might have quitted the place without loss; for, brave as were the soldiers of Vitellius in encountering danger, they were far from attentive to the laborious duties of watching. Besides this, the sudden fall of a winter storm baffled both sight and hearing.

70. At dawn of day, before either side commenced hostilities, Sabinus sent Cornelius Martialis, a centurion of the first rank, to Vitellius, with instructions to complain of the infraction of the stipulated terms. "There has evidently," he said, "been a mere show and pretense of abdicating the Empire, with the view of deceiving a number of distinguished men. If not, why, when leaving the Rostra, had he gone to the house of his brother, looking as it did over the Forum, and certain to provoke the gaze of the multitude, rather than to the Aventine, and the family house of his wife? This would have befitted a private individual anxious to shun all appearance of Imperial power. But on the contrary, Vitellius retraced his steps to the palace, the very stronghold of Empire; thence issued a band of armed men. One of the most frequented parts of the city was strewn with the corpses of innocent persons. The Capitol itself had not been spared. I," continued Sabinus, "was only a civilian and a member of the Senate, while the rivalry of Vitellius and Vespasian was being settled by conflicts between legions, by the capture of cities, by the capitulation of cohorts; with Spain, Germany, and Britain in revolt, the brother of Vespasian still remained firm to his allegiance, till actually invited to discuss terms of agreement. Peace and harmony bring advantage to the conquered, but only credit to the conqueror. If you repent of your compact, it is not against me, whom you treacherously deceived, that you must draw the sword, nor is it against the son of Vespasian, who is yet of tender age. What would be gained by the slaughter of one old man and one stripling? You should go and meet the legions, and fight there for Empire; everything else will follow the issue of that struggle." To these representations the embarrassed Vitellius answered a few words in his own exculpation, throwing all the blame upon the soldiers, with whose excessive zeal his moderation was, he said, unable to cope. He advised Martialis to depart unobserved through a concealed part of the palace, lest he should be killed by the soldiers, as the negotiator of this abhorred convention. Vitellius had not now the power either to command or to forbid. He was no longer Emperor, he was merely the cause of war.

71. Martialis had hardly returned to the Capitol, when the infuriated soldiery arrived, without any leader, every man acting on his own impulse. They hurried at quick march past the Forum and the temples which hang over it, and advanced their line up the opposite hill as far as the outer gates of

the Capitol. There were formerly certain colonnades on the right side of the slope as one went up; the defenders, issuing forth on the roof of these buildings, showered tiles and stones on the Vitellianists. The assailants were not armed with anything but swords, and it seemed too tedious to send for machines and missiles. They threw lighted brands on a projecting colonnade, and following the track of the fire would have burst through the half-burnt gates of the Capitol, had not Sabinus, tearing down on all sides the statues, the glories of former generations, formed them into a barricade across the opening. They then assailed the opposite approaches to the Capitol, near the grove of the Asylum, and where the Tarpeian rock is mounted by a hundred steps. Both these attacks were unexpected; the closer and fiercer of the two threatened the Asylum. The assailants could not be checked as they mounted the continuous line of buildings, which, as was natural in a time of profound peace, had grown up to such a height as to be on a level with the soil of the Capitol. A doubt arises at this point, whether it was the assailants who threw lighted brands on to the roofs, or whether, as the more general account has it, the besieged thus sought to repel the assailants, who were now making vigorous progress. From them the fire passed to the colonnades adjoining the temples; the eagles supporting the pediment, which were of old timber, caught the flames. And so the Capitol, with its gates shut, neither defended by friends, nor spoiled by a foe, was burnt to the ground.

72. This was the most deplorable and disgraceful event that had happened to the Commonwealth of Rome since the foundation of the city; for now, assailed by no foreign enemy, with Heaven ready to be propitious, had our vices only allowed, the seat of Jupiter Supremely Good and Great, founded by our ancestors with solemn auspices to be the pledge of Empire, the seat, which neither Porsenna, when the city was surrendered, nor the Gauls, when it was captured, had been able to violate, was destroyed by the madness of our Emperors. Once before indeed during civil war the Capitol had been consumed by fire, but then only through the crime of individuals; now it was openly besieged, and openly set on fire. And what were the motives of this conflict? what the compensation for so great a disaster? was it for our country we were fighting? King Tarquinius Priscus had vowed its erection in his war with the Sabines, and had laid the foundations on a scale which suited the hopes of future greatness rather than what the yet moderate resources of Rome could achieve. After him, Servius Tullius, heartily assisted by the allies, and Tarquinius Superbus, employing the spoils of war from the conquered Suessa Pometia, raised the superstructure. But the glory of its completion was reserved for the days of liberty. After the expulsion of the Kings, Horatius Pulvillus, in his second consulate, dedicated it, a building so magnificent, that the vast wealth afterwards acquired by the people of Rome served to embellish rather than increase it. It was rebuilt on the same

site, when, after an interval of 415 years, it was burnt to the ground in the consulate of Lucius Scipio and Caius Norbanus. Sulla, after his final triumph, undertook the charge of restoring it, but did not live to dedicate it, the one thing denied to his uniform good fortune. The name of Lutatius Catulus, the dedicator, remained among all the vast erections of the Emperors, down to the days of Vitellius. This was the building that was now on fire.

WRITERS OF AUGUSTAN HISTORY

(SCRIPTORES HISTORIAE AUGUSTAE)

Thirty biographies of emperors of the second and third centuries were gathered together in medieval manuscripts under the title "Writers of Augustan History." The lives are attributed to six different writers of the early fourth century, but scholars now believe that they are an ancient "forgery." The collection was probably written about 395 C.E. by a single author, who shows a bias toward paganism and the senatorial class.

The lives are modelled on Suetonius and likewise contain the texts of letters and decrees. One of the problems is that most of these documents are fraudulent, and the lives contain many imaginary names. Despite the dishonest aim of the author, he had access to much material which is now lost so that historians must use this material. The life of Hadrian, the first in the series, is thought to be among the most reliable.

LIFE OF HADRIAN*

Hadrian, who was born in Spain, ruled from 117 to 138 C.E.

1. The original home of the family of the Emperor Hadrian was Picenum, the later, Spain; for Hadrian himself relates in his autobiography that his forefathers came from Hadria, but settled at Italica in the time of the Scipios. The father of Hadrian was Aelius Hadrianus, surnamed Afer, a

---

*[Aelius Spartianus?]. 1922. *Scriptores Historiae Augustae*. Vol. 1. Translated by David Magie. Loeb Classical Library.

cousin of the Emperor Trajan; his mother was Domitia Paulina, a native of Cadiz; his sister was Paulina, the wife of Servianus, his wife was Sabina, and his great-grandfather's grandfather was Marullinus, the first of his family to be a Roman senator.

Hadrian was born in Rome on the eighth day before the Kalends of February in the seventh consulship of Vespasian and the fifth of Titus. Bereft of his father at the age of ten, he became the ward of Ulpius Trajanus (Trajan), his cousin, then of praetorian rank, but afterwards emperor, and of Caelius Attianus, a knight. He then grew rather deeply devoted to Greek studies, to which his natural tastes inclined so much that some called him "Greekling."

2. He returned to his native city in his fifteenth year and at once entered military service, but was so fond of hunting that he incurred criticism for it, and for this reason Trajan recalled him from Italica. Thenceforth he was treated by Trajan as his own son, and not long afterwards he was made one of the ten judges of the inheritance-court, and, later, tribune of the Second Legion, the Adjutrix. After this, when Domitian's principate was drawing to a close, he was transferred to the province of Lower Moesia. There, it is said, he heard from an astrologer the same prediction of his future power which had been made, as he already knew, by his great-uncle, Aelius Hadrianus, a master of astrology. When Trajan was adopted by Nerva, Hadrian was sent to convey to him the army's congratulations and was at once transferred to Upper Germany. When Nerva died, he wished to be the first to bring the news to Trajan, but as he was hastening to meet him he was detained by his brother-in-law, Servianus, the same man who had revealed Hadrian's extravagance and indebtedness and thus stirred Trajan's anger against him. He was further delayed by the fact that his traveling-carriage had been intentionally broken, but he nevertheless proceeded on foot and arrived before Servianus' personal messenger. And now he became a favorite of Trajan's, and yet, owing to the activity of the guardians of certain boys whom Trajan loved ardently, he was not free from. . . . Indeed, at this time he was even anxious about the Emperor's attitude towards him, and consulted the Vergilian oracle. This was the lot given out:

> But who is yonder man, by olive wreath
> Distinguished, who the sacred vessel bears?
> I see a hoary head and beard. Behold
> The Roman King whose laws shall establish Rome
> Anew, from tiny Cures' humble land
> Called to a mighty realm. Then shall arise

Others, however, declare that this prophecy came to him from the Sibylline Verses. Moreover, he received a further intimation of his subsequent power, in a response which issued from the temple of Jupiter at Nicephorium and has been quoted by Apollonius of Syria, the Platonist.

3. Finally, through the good offices of Sula, he was instantly restored to a friendship with Trajan that was closer than ever, and he took to wife the daughter of the Emperor's sister—a marriage advocated by the empress Plotina, but, according to Marius Maximus, little desired by Trajan himself. He held the quaestorship in the fourth consulship of Trajan and the first of Articuleius, and while holding this office he read a speech of the Emperor's to the senate and provoked a laugh by his somewhat provincial accent. He thereupon gave attention to the study of Latin until he attained the utmost proficiency and fluency. After his quaestorship he served as curator of the acts of the senate, and later accompanied Trajan in the Dacian war on terms of considerable intimacy, seeing that falling in with Trajan's habits, as he says himself, he partook freely of wine, and for this was very richly rewarded by the Emperor. He was made tribune of the plebs in the second consulship of Candidus and Quadratus, and he claimed that he received an omen of continuous tribunician power during this magistracy, because he lost the heavy cloak which is worn by the tribunes of the plebs in rainy weather, but never by the emperors. And down to this day the emperors do not wear cloaks when they appear in public before civilians. In the second Dacian war, Trajan appointed him to the command of the First Legion, the Minervia, and took him to the war; and in this campaign his many remarkable deeds won great renown. Because of this he was presented with a diamond which Trajan himself had received from Nerva, and by this gift he was encouraged in his hopes of succeeding to the throne. He held the praetorship in the second consulship of Suburanus and Scrivianus, and again received from Trajan two million sesterces with which to give games. Next he was sent as praetorian legate to Lower Pannonia, where he held the Sarmatians in check, maintained discipline among the soldiers, and restrained the procurators, who were overstepping too freely the bounds of their power. In return for these services he was made consul. While he was holding this office he learned from Sura that he was to be adopted by Trajan, and thereupon he ceased to be an object of contempt and neglect to Trajan's friends. Indeed, after Sura's death Trajan's friendship for him increased, principally on account of the speeches which he composed for the Emperor.

4. He enjoyed, too, the favor of Plotina, and it was due to her interest in him that later, at the time of the campaign against Parthia, he was appointed the legate of the Emperor. At this same time he enjoyed, besides, the friendship of Sosius Papus and Platorius Nepos, both of the senatorial order, and also of Attianus, his former guardian, of Livianus, and of Turbo, all of equestrian rank. And when Palma and Celsus, always his enemies, on whom he later took vengeance, fell under suspicion of aspiring to the throne, his adoption seemed assured; and it was taken wholly for granted when, through Plotina's favor, he was appointed consul for the second time. That he was bribing Trajan's freedmen and courting and corrupting his favorites all the while that he was in close attendance at court, was told and generally believed.

On the fifth day before the Ides of August, while he was governor of Syria, he learned of his adoption by Trajan, and he later gave orders to celebrate this day as the anniversary of his adoption. On the third day before the Ides of August he received the news of Trajan's death, and this day he appointed as the anniversary of his accession. There was, to be sure, a widely prevailing belief that Trajan, with the approval of many of his friends, had planned to appoint as his successor not Hadrian but Neratius Priscus, even to the extent of once saying to Priscus: "I entrust the provinces to your care in case anything happens to me." And, indeed, many say that Trajan had intended to follow the example of Alexander of Macedonia and die without naming a successor. Again, many others declare that he had meant to send an address to the senate, requesting this body, in case anything befell him, to appoint a ruler for the Roman empire, and merely appending the names of some from among whom the senate might choose the best. And the statement has even been made that it was not until after Trajan's death that Hadrian was declared adopted, and then only by means of a trick of Plotina; for she smuggled in someone who impersonated the Emperor and spoke in a feeble voice.

5. On taking possession of the imperial power Hadrian at once resumed the policy of the early emperors, and devoted his attention to maintaining peace throughout the world. For the nations which Trajan had conquered began to revolt; the Moors, moreover, began to make attacks, and the Sarmatians to wage war, the Britons could not be kept under Roman sway, Egypt was thrown into disorder by riots, and finally Libya and Palestine showed the spirit of rebellion. Whereupon he relinquished all the conquests east of the Euphrates and the Tigris, following, as he used to say, the example of Cato, who urged that the Macedonians, because they could not be held as subjects, should be declared free and independent. And Parthamasiris, appointed king of the Parthians by Trajan, he assigned as ruler to the neighboring tribes, because he saw that the man was held in little esteem by the Parthians.

Moreover, he showed at the outset such a wish to be lenient, that although Attianus advised him by letter in the first few days of his rule to put to death Baebius Macer, the prefect of the city, in case he opposed his elevation to power, also Laberius Maximus, then in exile on an island under suspicion of designs on the throne, and likewise Crassus Frugi, he nevertheless refused to harm them. Later on, however, his procurator, though without an order from Hadrian, had Crassus killed when he tried to leave the island, on the ground that he was planning a revolt. He gave a double donative to the soldiers in order to ensure a favorable beginning to his principate. He deprived Lusius Quietus of the command of the Moorish tribesmen, who were serving under him, and then dismissed him from the army, because he had fallen under the suspicion of having designs on the throne; and he appointed Marcius Turbo, after his reduction of Judaea, to quell the insurrection in Mauretania. After taking these measures he set out from Antioch to view the remains of Trajan, which were being escorted by Attianus, Plotina, and Matidia. He received them formally and sent them on to Rome by ship, and at once returned to Antioch; he appointed Catilius Severus governor of Syria, and proceeded to Rome by way of Illyricum.

6. Dispatching to the senate a carefully worded letter, he asked for divine honors for Trajan. This request he obtained by a unanimous vote; indeed, the senate voluntarily voted Trajan many more honors than Hadrian had requested. In this letter to the senate he apologized because he had not left it the right to decide regarding his accession, explaining that the unseemly haste of the troops in acclaiming him emperor was due to the belief that the state could not be without an emperor. Later, when the senate offered him the triumph which was to have been Trajan's, he refused it for himself, and caused the effigy of the dead Emperor to be carried in a triumphal chariot, in order that the best of emperors might not lose even after death the honor of a triumph. Also he refused for the present the title of Father of his Country, offered to him at the time of his accession and again later on, giving as his reason the fact that Augustus had not won it until late in life. Of the crown-money for his triumph he remitted Italy's contribution, and lessened that of the provinces, all the while setting forth grandiloquently and in great detail the straits of the public treasury.

Then, on hearing of the incursions of the Sarmatians and Roxolani, he sent the troops ahead and set out for Moesia. He conferred the insignia of a prefect on Marcius Turbo after his Mauretanian campaign and appointed him to the temporary command of Pannonia and Dacia. When the king of the Roxolani complained of the diminution of his subsidy, he investigated his case and made peace with him.

7. A plot to murder him while sacrificing was made by Nigrinus, with Lusius and a number of others as accomplices, even though Hadrian had destined Nigrinus for the succession; but Hadrian successfully evaded this plot. Because of this conspiracy Palma was put to death at Tarracina, Celsus at Baiae, Nigrinus at Faventia, and Lusius on his journey homeward, all by order of the senate, but contrary to the wish of Hadrian, as he says himself in his autobiography. Whereupon Hadrian entrusted the command in Dacia to Turbo, whom he dignified, in order to increase his authority, with a rank analogous to that of the prefect of Egypt. He then hastened to Rome in

order to win over public opinion, which was hostile to him because of the belief that on one single occasion he had suffered four men of consular rank to be put to death. In order to check the rumors about himself, he gave in person a double largess to the people, although in his absence three aurei had already been given to each of the citizens. In the senate, too, he cleared himself of blame for what had happened, and pledged himself never to inflict punishment on a senator until after a vote of the senate. He established a regular imperial post, in order to relieve the local officials of such a burden. Moreover, he used every means of gaining popularity. He remitted to private debtors in Rome and in Italy immense sums of money owed to the privy-purse, and in the provinces he remitted large amounts of arrears; and he ordered the promissory notes to be burned in the Forum of the Deified Trajan, in order that the general sense of security might thereby be increased. He gave orders that the property of condemned persons should not accrue to the privy-purse, and in each case deposited the whole amount in the public treasury. He made additional appropriations for the children to whom Trajan had allotted grants of money. He supplemented the property of senators impoverished through no fault of their own, making the allowance in each case proportionate to the number of children, so that it might be enough for a senatorial career, to many, indeed, he paid punctually on the date the amount allotted for their living. Sums of money sufficient to enable men to hold office he bestowed, not on his friends alone, but also on many far and wide, and by his donations he helped a number of women to sustain life. He gave gladiatorial combats for six days in succession, and on his birthday he put into the arena a thousand wild beasts.

8. The foremost members of the senate he admitted to close intimacy with the emperor's majesty. All circus-games decreed in his honor he refused, except those held to celebrate his birthday. Both in meetings of the people and in the senate he used to say that he would so administer the commonwealth that men would know that it was not his own but the people's. Having himself been consul three times, he reappointed many to the consulship for the third time and men without number to a second term; his own third consulship he held for only four months, and during his term he often administered justice. He always attended regular meetings of the senate if he was present in Rome or even in the neighborhood. In the appointment of senators he showed the utmost caution and thereby greatly increased the dignity of the senate, and when he removed Attianus from the post of prefect of the guard and created him a senator with consular honors, he made it clear that he had no greater honor which he could bestow upon him. Nor did he allow knights to try cases involving senators whether he was present at the trial or not. For at that time it was customary for the emperor, when he tried cases, to call to his council both senators and knights and give a verdict based on their joint decision. Finally, he denounced those emperors who had not shown this deference to the senators. On his brother-in-law Servianus, to whom he showed such respect that he would advance to meet him as he came from his chamber, he bestowed a third consulship, and that without any request or entreaty on Servianus' part; but nevertheless he did not appoint him as his own colleague, since Servianus had been consul twice before Hadrian, and the Emperor did not wish to have second place.

9. And yet, at the same time, Hadrian abandoned many provinces won by Trajan, and also destroyed, contrary to the entreaties of all, the theater which Trajan had built in the Campus Martius. These measures, unpopular enough in themselves, were still more displeasing to the public because of his pretense that all acts which he thought would be offensive had been secretly enjoined upon him by Trajan. Unable to endure the power of Attianus, his prefect and formerly his guardian, he was eager to murder him. He was restrained, however, by the knowledge that he already labored under the odium of murdering four men of consular rank, although, as a matter of fact, he always attributed their execution to the designs of Attianus. And as he could not appoint a successor for Attianus except at the latter's request, he contrived to make him request it, and at once transferred the power to Turbo; at the same time Similis also, the other prefect, received a successor, namely Septicius Clarus.

After Hadrian had removed from the prefecture the very men to whom he owed the imperial power, he departed for Campania, where he aided all the towns of the region by gifts and benefactions and attached all the foremost men to his train of friends. But when at Rome, he frequently attended the official functions of the praetors and consuls, appeared at the banquets of his friends, visited them twice or thrice a day when they were sick, even those who were merely knights and freedmen, cheered them by words of comfort, encouraged them by words of advice, and very often invited them to his own banquets. In short, everything that he did was in the manner of a private citizen. On his mother-in-law he bestowed especial honor by means of gladiatorial games and other ceremonies.

10. After this he traveled to the provinces of Gaul, and came to the relief of all the communities with various acts of generosity; and from there he went over into Germany. Though more desirous of peace than of war, he kept the soldiers in training just as if war were imminent, inspired them by proofs of his own powers of endurance, actually led a soldier's life among the maniples, and, after the example of Scipio Aemilianus, Metellus, and his own adoptive father Trajan, cheerfully ate out of doors such camp-fare as bacon, cheese and vinegar. And that the troops might submit more willingly to the increased harshness of his orders, he bestowed gifts on many and honors on a few. For he reestablished the discipline of the camp, which since the time of

Octavian had been growing slack through the laxity of his predecessors. He regulated, too, both the duties and the expenses of the soldiers, and now no one could get a leave of absence from camp by unfair means, for it was not popularity with the troops but just deserts that recommended a man for appointment as tribune. He incited others by the example of his own soldiery spirit; he would walk as much as twenty miles fully armed; he cleared the camp of banqueting-rooms, porticoes, grottos, and bowers, generally wore the commonest clothing, would have no gold ornaments on his sword-belt or jewels on the clasp, would scarcely consent to have his sword furnished with an ivory hilt, visited the sick soldiers in their quarters, selected the sites for camps, conferred the centurion's wand on those only who were hardy and of good repute, appointed as tribunes only men with full beards or of an age to give to the authority of the tribuneship the full measure of prudence and maturity, permitted no tribune to accept a present from a soldier, banished luxuries on every hand, and, lastly, improved the soldiers' arms and equipment. Furthermore, with regard to length of military service he issued an order that no one should violate ancient usage by being in the service at an earlier age than his strength warranted, or at a more advanced one than common humanity permitted. He made it a point to be acquainted with the soldiers and to know their numbers.

11. Besides this, he strove to have an accurate knowledge of the military stores, and the receipts from the provinces he examined with care in order to make good any deficit that might occur in any particular instance. But more than any other emperor he made it a point not to purchase or maintain anything that was not serviceable. And so, having reformed the army quite in the manner of a monarch, he set out for Britain and there he corrected many abuses and was the first to construct a wall, eighty miles in length, which was to separate the barbarians from the Romans.

He removed from office Septicius Clarus, the prefect of the guard, and Suetonius Tranquillus, the imperial secretary, and many others besides, because without his consent they had been conducting themselves toward his wife, Sabina, a more informal fashion than the etiquette of the court demanded. And, as he was himself wont to say, he would have sent away his wife too, on the ground of ill-temper and irritability, had he been merely a private citizen. Moreover, his vigilance was not confined to his own household but extended to those of his friends, and by means of his private agents he even pried into all their secrets, and so skillfully that they were never aware that the Emperor was acquainted with their private lives until he revealed it himself. In this connection, the insertion of an incident will not be unwelcome, showing that he found out much about his friends. The wife of a certain man wrote to her husband, complaining that he was so preoccupied by pleasures and baths that he would not return home to her, and Hadrian found this out through his private agents. And so, when the husband asked for a furlough, Hadrian reproached him with his fondness for his baths and his pleasures. Whereupon the man exclaimed: "What, did my wife write you just what she wrote to me?" And, indeed, as for this habit of Hadrian's, men regard it as a most grievous fault, and add to their criticism the statements which are current regarding the passion for males and the adulteries with married women to which he is said to have been addicted, adding also the charge that he did not even keep faith with his friends.

12. After arranging matters in Britain he crossed over to Gaul, for he was rendered anxious by the news of a riot in Alexandria, which arose on account of Apis; for Apis had been discovered again after an interval of many years, and was causing great dissension among the communities, each one earnestly asserting its claim as the place best fitted to be the seat of his worship. During this same time he reared a basilica of marvelous workmanship at Nimes in honor of Plotina. After this he traveled to Spain and spent the winter at Tarragona, and here he restored at his own expense the temple of Augustus. To this place, too, he called all the inhabitants of Spain for a general meeting, and when they refused to submit to a levy, the Italian settlers jestingly, to use the very words of Marius Maximus, and the others very vigorously, he took measures characterized by skill and discretion. At this same time he incurred grave danger and won great glory; for while he was walking about in a garden at Tarragona one of the slaves of the household rushed at him madly with a sword. But he merely laid hold on the man, and when the servants ran to the rescue handed him over to them. Afterwards, when it was found that the man was mad, he turned him over to the physicians for treatment, and all this time showed not the slightest sign of alarm.

During this period and on many other occasions also, in many regions where the barbarians are held back not by rivers but by artificial barriers, Hadrian shut them off by means of high stakes planted deep in the ground and fastened together in the manner of a palisade. He appointed a king for the Germans, suppressed revolts among the Moors, and won from the senate the usual ceremonies of thanksgiving. The war with the Parthians had not at that time advanced beyond the preparatory stage, and Hadrian checked it by a personal conference.

13. After this Hadrian traveled by way of Asia and the islands to Greece, and, following the example of Hercules and Philip, had himself initiated into the Eleusinian mysteries. He bestowed many favors on the Athenians and sat as president of the public games. And during this stay in Greece care was taken, they say, that when Hadrian was present, none should come to a sacrifice armed, whereas, as a rule, many carried knives. Afterwards he sailed to Sicily, and there he climbed Mount Etna to see the sunrise, which is many-hued, they say, like the rainbow. Thence he returned to Rome, and from

there he crossed over to Africa, where he showed many acts of kindness to the provinces. Hardly any emperor ever traveled with such speed over so much territory.

Finally, after his return to Rome from Africa, he immediately set out for the East, journeying by way of Athens. Here he dedicated the public works which he had begun in the city of the Athenians, such as the temple to Olympian Jupiter and an altar to himself; and in the same way, while traveling through Asia, he consecrated the temples called by his name. Next, he received slaves from the Cappadocians for service in the camps. To petty rulers and kings he made offers of friendship, and even to Osdroes, king of the Parthians. To him he also restored his daughter, who had been captured by Trajan, and promised to return the throne captured at the same time. And when some of the kings came to him, he treated them in such a way that those who had refused to come regretted it. He took this course especially on account of Pharasmanes, who had haughtily scorned his invitation. Furthermore, as he went about the provinces he punished procurators and governors as their actions demanded, and indeed with such severity that it was believed that he incited those who brought the accusations.

14. In the course of these travels he conceived such a hatred for the people of Antioch that he wished to separate Syria from Phoenicia, in order that Antioch might not be called the chief city of so many communities. At this time also the Jews began war, because they were forbidden to practice circumcision. As he was sacrificing on Mount Casius, which he had ascended by night in order to see the sunrise, a storm arose, and a flash of lightning descended and struck both the victim and the attendant. He then traveled through Arabia and finally came to Pelusium, where he rebuilt Pompey's tomb on a more magnificent scale. During a journey on the Nile he lost Antinous, his favorite, and for this youth he wept like a woman. Concerning this incident there are varying rumors; for some claim that he had devoted himself to death for Hadrian, and others—what both his beauty and Hadrian's sensuality suggest. But however this may be, the Greeks deified him at Hadrian's request, and declared that oracles were given through his agency, but these, it is commonly asserted, were composed by Hadrian himself.

In poetry and in letters Hadrian was greatly interested. In arithmetic, geometry, and painting he was very expert. Of his knowledge of flute-playing and singing he even boasted openly. He ran to excess in the gratification of his desires, and wrote much verse about the subjects of his passion. He composed love-poems too. He was also a connoisseur of arms, had a thorough knowledge of warfare, and knew how to use gladiatorial weapons. He was, in the same person, austere and genial, dignified and playful, dilatory and quick to act, niggardly and generous, deceitful and straightforward, cruel and merciful, and always in all things chargeable.

15. His friends he enriched greatly, even though they did not ask it, while to those who did ask, he refused nothing. And yet he was always ready to listen to whispers about his friends, and in the end he treated almost all of them as enemies, even the closest and even those whom he had raised to the highest of honors, such as Attainus and Nepos and Septicius Clarus. Budaemon, for example, who had been his accomplice in obtaining the imperial power, he reduced to poverty; Polaenus and Marcellus he drove to suicide; Heliodorus he assailed in a most slanderous pamphlet; Titianus he allowed to be accused as an accomplice in an attempt to seize the empire and even to be outlawed; Ummidius Quadratus, Catilius Severus, and Turbo he persecuted vigorously; and in order to prevent Servianus, his brother-in-law, from surviving him, he compelled him to commit suicide, although the man was then in his ninetieth year. And he even took vengeance on freedmen and sometimes on soldiers. And although he was very deft at prose and at verse and very accomplished in all the arts, yet he used to subject the teachers of these arts, as though more learned than they, to ridicule, scorn, and humiliation. With these very professors and philosophers he often debated by means of pamphlets or poems issued by both sides in turn. And once Favorinus, when he had yielded to Hadrian's criticism of a word which he had used, raised a merry laugh among his friends. For when they reproached him for having done wrong in yielding to Hadrian in the matter of a word used by reputable authors, he replied: "You are urging a wrong course, my friends, when you do not suffer me to regard as the most learned of men the one who has thirty legions."

16. So desirous of a wide-spread reputation was Hadrian that he even wrote his own biography; this he gave to his educated freedmen, with instructions to publish it under their own names. For indeed, Phlegon's writings, it is said, are Hadrian's in reality. He wrote *Catachannae*, a very obscure work in imitation of Antimachus. And when the poet Florus wrote to him:

> *"I don't want to be a Caesar,*
> *Stroll about among the Britons,*
> *Lurk about among the . . .*
> *And endure the Scythian winters,"*

he wrote back

> *"I don't want to be a Florus,*
> *Stroll about among the taverns,*
> *Lurk about among the cook-shops,*
> *And endure the round fat insects."*

Furthermore, he loved the archaic style of writing, and he used to take part in debates. He preferred Cato to Cicero, Ennius to Vergil, Caelius to Sallust; and with the same self-assurance he expressed opinions about Homer and Plato. In astrology he considered himself so proficient that on the Kalends of January he would actually write down all that might happen to him in the whole ensuing year, and in the year in which he died, indeed, he wrote down everything that he was going to do, down to the very hour of his death.

However ready Hadrian might have been to criticize musicians, tragedians, comedians, grammarians, and rhetoricians, he nevertheless bestowed both honors and riches upon all who professed these arts, though he always tormented them with his questions. And although he was himself responsible for the fact that many of them left his presence with their feelings hurt, to see anyone with hurt feelings, he used to say, he could hardly endure. He treated with the greatest friendship the philosophers Epictetus and Heliodorus, and various grammarians, rhetoricians, musicians, geometricians—not to mention all by name—painters and astrologers; and among them Favorinus, many claim, was conspicuous above all the rest. Teachers who seemed unfit for their profession he presented with riches and honors and then dismissed from the practice of their profession.

17. Many whom he had regarded as enemies when a private citizen, when emperor he merely ignored; for example, on becoming emperor, he said to one man whom he had regarded as a mortal foe, "You have escaped." When he himself called any to military service, he always supplied them with horses, mules, clothing, cost of maintenance, and indeed their whole equipment. At the Saturnalia and Sigillaria he often surprised his friends with presents, and he gladly received gifts from them and again gave others in return. In order to detect dishonesty in his caterers, when he gave banquets with several tables he gave orders that platters from the other tables, even the lowest, should be set before himself. He surpassed all monarchs in his gifts. He often bathed in the public baths, even with the common crowd. And a jest of his made in the bath became famous. For on a certain occasion, seeing a veteran, whom he had known in the service, rubbing his back and the rest of his body against the wall, he asked him why he had the marble rub him, and when the man replied that it was because he did not own a slave, he presented him with some slaves and the cost of their maintenance. But another time, when he saw a number of old men rubbing themselves against the wall for the purpose of arousing the generosity of the Emperor, he ordered them to be called out and then to rub one another in turn. His love for the common people he loudly expressed. So fond was he of travel, that he wished to inform himself in person about all that he had read concerning all parts of the world. Cold and bad weather he could bear with such endurance that he

never covered his head. He showed a multitude of favors to many kings, but from a number he even purchased peace, and by some he was treated with scorn; to many he gave huge gifts, but none greater than to the king of the Hiberi, for to him he gave an elephant and a band of fifty men, in addition to magnificent presents. And having himself received huge gifts from Pharasmanes, including some cloaks embroidered with gold, he sent into the arena three hundred condemned criminals dressed in gold-embroidered cloaks for the purpose of ridiculing the gifts of the king.

18. When he tried cases, he had in his council not only his friends and the members of his staff, but also jurists, in particular Juventius Celsus, Salvius Julianus, Neratius Priscus, and others, only those, however, whom the senate had unanimously approved. Among other decisions he ruled that in no community should any house be demolished for the purpose of transporting any building-materials to another city. To the child of an outlawed person he granted a twelfth of the property. Accusations for *lèse majesé* he did not admit. Legacies from persons unknown to him he refused, and even those left to him by acquaintances he would not accept if they had any children. In regard to treasure-trove, he ruled that if anyone made a find on his own property he might keep it, if on another's land, he should turn over half to the proprietor thereof, if on the state's, he should share the find equally with the privy-purse. He forbade masters to kill their slaves, and ordered that any who deserved it should be sentenced by the courts. He forbade anyone to sell a slave or a maidservant to a procurer or trainer of gladiators without giving a reason therefore. He ordered that those who had wasted their property, if legally responsible, should be flogged in the amphitheater and then let go. Houses of hard labor for slaves and free he abolished. He provided separate baths for the sexes. He issued an order that, if a slave-owner were murdered in his house, no slaves should be examined save those who were near enough to have had knowledge of the murder.

19. In Etruria he held a praetorship while emperor. In the Latin towns he was dictator and aedile and duumvir, in Naples demarch, in his native city duumvir with the powers of censor. This office he held at Hadria, too, his second native city, as it were, and at Athens he was archon. In almost every city he built some building and gave public games. At Athens he exhibited in the stadium a hunt of a thousand wild beasts, but he never called away from Rome a single wild-beasthunter or actor. In Rome, in addition to popular entertainments of unbounded extravagance, he gave spices to the people in honor of his mother-in-law, and in honor of Trajan he caused essences of balsam and saffron to be poured over the seats of the theater. And in the theater he presented plays of all kinds in the ancient manner and had the court-players appear before the public. In the Circus he had many wild beasts killed and often a whole hundred of lions. He often gave the people exhibitions of military Pyrrhic dances, and he frequently attended gladiatorial shows. He built public buildings in all places and without number, but he inscribed his own name on none of them except the temple of his father Trajan. At Rome he restored the Pantheon, the Voting-enclosure, the Basilica of Neptune, very many temples, the Forum of Augustus, the Baths of Agrippa, and dedicated all of them in the names of their original builders. Also he constructed the bridge named after himself, a tomb on the bank of the Tiber, and the temple of the Bona Dea. With the aid of the architect Decrianus he raised the Colossus and, keeping it in an upright position, moved it away from the place in which the Temple of Rome is now, though its weight was so vast that he had to furnish for the work as many as twenty-four elephants. This statue he then consecrated to the Sun, after removing the features of Nero, to whom it had previously been dedicated, and he also planned, with the assistance of the architect Apollodorus, to make a similar one for the Moon.

20. Most democratic in his conversations, even with the very humble, he denounced all who, in the belief that they were thereby maintaining the imperial dignity, begrudged him the pleasure of such friendliness. In the Museum at Alexandria he propounded many questions to the teachers and answered himself what he had propounded. Marius Maximus says that he was naturally cruel and performed so many kindnesses only because he feared that he might meet the fate which had befallen Domitian.

Though he cared nothing for inscriptions on his public works, he gave the name of Hadrianopolis to many cities, as, for example, even to Carthage and a section of Athens; and he also gave his name to aqueducts without number. He was the first to appoint a pleader for the privy-purse. Hadrian's memory was vast and his ability was unlimited; for instance, he personally dictated his speeches and gave opinions on all questions. He was also very witty, and of his jests many still survive. The following one has even become famous: When he had refused a request to a certain gray-haired man, and the man repeated the request but this time with dyed hair, Hadrian replied: "I have already refused this to your father." Even without the aid of a nomenclator he could call by name a great many people, whose names he had heard but once and then all in a crowd; indeed, he could correct the nomenclators when they made mistakes, as they not infrequently did, and he even knew the names of the veterans whom he had discharged at various times. He could repeat from memory, after a rapid reading, books which to most men were not known at all. He wrote, dictated, listened, and, incredible as it seems, conversed with his friends, all at one and the same time. He had as complete a knowledge of the state-budget in all its details as any careful householder has of his own household. His horses and dogs he loved so much that he provided burial-places for them, and in one locality he founded a town called

Hadrianotherae, because once he had hunted successfully there and killed a bear.

21. He always inquired into the actions of all his judges, and persisted in his inquiries until he satisfied himself of the truth about them. He would not allow his freedmen to be prominent in public affairs or to have any influence over himself, and he declared that all his predecessors were to blame for the faults of their freedmen; he also punished all his freedmen who boasted of their influence over him. With regard to his treatment of his slaves, the following incident, stern but almost humorous, is still related. Once when he saw one of his slaves walk away from his presence between two senators, he sent someone to give him a box on the ear and say to him: "Do not walk between those whose slave you may some day be." As an article of food he was singularly fond of tetrapharmacum, which consisted of pheasant, sow's udders, ham, and pastry.

During his reign there were famines, pestilence, and earthquakes. The distress caused by all these calamities he relieved to the best of his ability, and also he aided many communities which had been devastated by them. There was also an overflow of the Tiber. To many communities he gave Latin citizenship, and to many others he remitted their tribute. There were no campaigns of importance during his reign, and the wars that he did wage were brought to a close almost without arousing comment. The soldiers loved him much on account of his very great interest in the army and for his great liberality to them besides. The Parthians always regarded him as a friend because he took away the king whom Trajan had set over them. The Armenians were permitted to have their own king, whereas under Trajan they had had a governor, and the Mesopotamians were relieved of the tribute which Trajan had imposed. The Albanians and Hiberians he made his friends by lavishing gifts upon their kings, even though they had scorned to come to him. The kings of the Bactrians sent envoys to him to beg humbly for his friendship.

22. He very often assigned guardians. Discipline in civil life he maintained as rigorously as he did in military. He ordered senators and knights to wear the toga whenever they appeared in public except when they were returning from a banquet, and he himself, when in Italy, always appeared thus clad. At banquets, when senators came, he received them standing, and he always reclined at table dressed either in a Greek cloak or in a toga. The cost of a banquet he limited according to the nature of the occasion, all with the utmost care, and he reduced the sums that might be expended to the amounts prescribed by the ancient laws. He forbade the entry into Rome of heavily laden wagons, and did not permit riding on horseback in cities. None but invalids were allowed to bathe in the public baths before the eighth hour of the day. He was the first to put knights in charge of the imperial corre-spondence and of the petitions addressed to the emperor. Those men whom he saw to be poor and innocent he enriched of his own accord, but those who had become rich through sharp practice he actually regarded with hatred. He despised foreign cults, but native Roman ones he observed most scrupu-lously; moreover, he always performed the duties of pontifex maximus. He tried a great number of lawsuits himself both in Rome and in the provinces, and to his council he called consuls and praetors and the foremost of the sen-ators. He drained the Fucine Lake. He appointed four men of consular rank as judges for all Italy. When he went to Africa, it rained on his arrival for the first time in the space of five years, and for this he was beloved by the Africans.

23. After traversing, as he did, all parts of the world with bare head and often in severe storms and frosts, he contracted an illness which confined him to his bed. And becoming anxious about a successor he thought first of Ser-vianus. Afterwards, however, as I have said, he forced him to commit suicide; and Fuscus, too, he put to death on the ground that, being spurred on by prophecies and omens, he was hoping for the imperial power. Carried away by suspicion, he held in the greatest abhorrence Platorius Nepos, whom he had formerly so loved that, once, when he went to see him while ill and was refused admission, he nevertheless let him go unpunished. Also he hated Ter-entius Gentianus, but even more vehemently, because he saw that he was then beloved by the senate. At last, he came to hate all those of whom he had thought in connection with the imperial power, as though they were really about to be emperors. However, he controlled all the force of his innate cru-elty down to the time when in his Tiburtine Villa he almost met his death through a hemorrhage. Then he threw aside all restraint and compelled Ser-vianus to kill himself, on the ground that he aspired to the empire, merely because he gave a feast to the royal slaves, sat in a royal chair placed close to his bed, and, though an old man of ninety, used to arise and go forward to meet the guard of soldiers. He put many others to death, either openly or by treachery, and indeed, when his wife Sabina died, the rumor arose that the Emperor had given her poison.

Hadrian then determined to adopt Ceionius Commodus, son-in-law of Nigrinus, the former conspirator, and this in spite of the fact that his sole rec-ommendation was his beauty. Accordingly, despite the opposition of all, he adopted Ceionius Commodus Verus and called him Aelius Verus Caesar. On the occasion of the adoption he gave games in the Circus and bestowed largess upon the populace and soldiers. He dignified Commodus with the office of praetor and immediately placed him in command of the Pannonian provinces, and also conferred on him the consulship together with money enough to meet the expenses of the office. He also appointed Commodus to a second consulship. And when he saw that the man was diseased, he used often to say: "We have leaned against a tottering wall and have wasted the four hundred million sesterces which we gave to the populace and the soldiers on the adoption of Commodus." Moreover, because of his ill-health, Commodus could not even make a speech in the senate thanking Hadrian for his adoption. Finally, too large a quantity of medicine was administered to him, and thereupon his illness increased, and he died in his sleep on the very Kalends of January. Because of the date Hadrian forbade public mourning for him, in order that the vows for the state might be assumed as usual.

24. After the death of Aelius Verus Caesar, Hadrian was attacked by a very severe illness, and thereupon he adopted Arrius Antonius (who was afterwards called Pius), imposing on him the condition that he adopt two sons, Annius Verus and Marcus Antoninus. These were the two who afterwards ruled the empire together, the first joint Augusti. And as for Antoninus, he was called Pius, it is said, because he used to give his arm to his father-in-law when weakened by old age. However, others assert that this surname was given to him because, as Hadrian grew more cruel, he rescued many senators from the Emperor; others, again, that it was because he bestowed great honors upon Hadrian after his death. The adoption of Antoninus was lamented by many at that time, particularly by Catilius Severus, the prefect of the city, who was making plans to secure the throne for himself. When this fact became known, a successor was appointed for him and he was deprived of his office.

But Hadrian was now seized with the utmost disgust of life and ordered a servant to stab him with a sword. When this was disclosed and reached the ears of Antoninus, he came to the Emperor, together with the prefects, and begged him to endure with fortitude the hard necessity of illness, declaring furthermore that he himself would be no better than a parricide, were he, an adopted son, to permit Hadrian to be killed. The Emperor then became angry and ordered the betrayer of the secret to be put to death; however, the man was saved by Antoninus. Then Hadrian immediately drew up his will, though he did not lay aside the administration of the empire. Once more, however, after making his will, he attempted to kill himself, but the dagger was taken from him. He then became more violent, and he even demanded poison from his physician, who thereupon killed himself in order that he might not have to administer it.

25. About this time there came a certain woman, who said that she had been warned in a dream to coax Hadrian to refrain from killing himself, for he was destined to recover entirely, but that she had failed to do this and had become blind; she had nevertheless been ordered a second time to give the same message to Hadrian and to kiss his knees, and was assured of the recovery of her sight if she did so. The woman then carried out the command of the dream, and received her sight after she had bathed her eyes with the water in the temple from which she had come. Also a blind old man from Pannonia came to Hadrian when he was ill with fever, and touched him; whereupon the man received his sight, and the fever left Hadrian. All these things, however, Marius Maximus declares were done as a hoax.

After this Hadrian departed for Baiae, leaving Antoninus at Rome to carry on the government. But he received no benefit there, and he thereupon sent for Antoninus, and in his presence he died there at Baiae on the sixth day before the Ides of July. Hated by all, he was buried at Puteoli on an estate that had belonged to Cicero.

Just before his death, he compelled Servianus, then ninety years old, to kill himself, as has been said before, in order that Servianus might not outlive him, and, as he thought, become emperor. He likewise gave orders that very many others who were guilty of slight offenses should be put to death; these, however, were spared by Antoninus. And he is said, as he lay dying, to have composed the following lines:

> O blithe little soul, thou, flitting away,
> Guest and comrade of this my clay,
> Whither now goest thou, to what place
> Bare and ghastly and without grace?
> Nor, as thy wont was, joke and play.

Such verses as these did he compose, and not many that were better, and also some in Greek. He lived 62 years, 5 months, 17 days. He ruled 20 years, 11 months.

26. He was tall of stature and elegant in appearance; his hair was curled on a comb, and he wore a full beard to cover up the natural blemishes on his face; and he was very strongly built. He rode and walked a great deal and always kept himself in training by the use of arms and the javelin. He also hunted, and he used often to kill a lion with his own hand, but once in a hunt he broke his collar-bone and a rib; these hunts of his he always shared with his friends. At his banquets he always furnished, according to the occasion, tragedies, comedies, Atellan farces, players on the sambuca, readers, or poets. His villa at Tibur was marvelously constructed, and he actually gave to parts of it the names of provinces and places of the greatest renown, calling them, for instance, Lyceum, Academia, Prytaneum, Canopus, Poecile and Tempe. And in order not to omit anything, he even made a Hades.

The premonitions of his death were as follows: On his last birthday, when he was commending Antoninus to the gods, his bordered toga fell down without apparent cause and bared his head. His ring, on which his portrait was carved, slipped of its own accord from his finger. On the day before his birthday some one came into the senate wailing; by his presence Hadrian was as disturbed as if he were speaking about his own death, for no one could understand what he was saying. Again, in the senate, when he meant to say, "after my son's death," he said, "after mine." Besides, he dreamed that he had asked his father for a soporific; he also dreamed that he had been overcome by a lion.

27. Much was said against him after his death, and by many persons. The senate wished to annul his acts, and would have refrained from naming him "the Deified" had not Antoninus requested it. Antoninus, moreover, finally built a temple for him at Puteoli to take the place of a tomb, and he also established a quinquennial contest and flamens and *sodales* and many other institutions which appertain to the honor of one regarded as a god. It is for this reason, as has been said before, that many think that Antoninus received the surname Pius.

AMMIANUS MARCELLINUS*

Life

Ammianus (330–395 C.E.) was a native Greek, born in the great eastern metropolis of Antioch near the Syrian coast. He was well educated in both Greek and Latin literature before joining the Roman army. He served under Julian in Gaul, Germany, and on the emperor's final campaign against the Persians; Julian remained his hero. About 378 Ammianus settled in Rome to write a continuation of Tacitus from 96 to the disaster at Hadrianople in 378. He wrote thirty one books in Latin, but only the final eighteen survive (covering the years 353 to 378).

Ammianus was not only interested in political and diplomatic history, but he was interested in administration and bureaucracy as well. As an easterner, he had an interest in, and sympathy for, peoples throughout the empire.

Though he was a trained rhetorician, there is little of the rhetorical distortion of earlier historians. The breadth of Ammianus' reading was vast, and his history is filled with allusions to Greek and Latin literature. And this was not schoolbook learning. Ammianus was deeply imbued with the culture and values of an earlier time, and his scathing judgments on many of his contemporaries show his profound dissatisfaction with the philistine attitudes of the nobility of his own day.

*Ammianus Marcellinus. 1862. Translated by C.D. Yonge. Bohn Classical Library.

HISTORIES

BOOK XXV 1–4

The death of the emperor Julian (361–363 c.e.) while fighting the Persians. Julian attempted to restore the pagan gods, an effort which earned him the title "The Apostate."

1. The night was dark and starless, and passed by us as nights are passed in times of difficulty and perplexity; no one out of fear daring to sit down, or to close his eyes. But as soon as day broke, brilliant breastplates surrounded with steel fringes, and glittering cuirasses, were seen at a distance, and showed that the king's army was at hand. The soldiers were roused at this sight, and hastened to engage, since only a small stream separated them from the Persians, but were checked by the emperor; a sharp skirmish did indeed take place between our outposts and the Persians, close to the rampart of our camp, in which Machamaeus, the captain of one of our squadrons, was stricken down: his brother Maurus, afterwards Duke of Phoenicia, flew to his support, and slew the men who had killed Machamaeus, and crushed all who came in his way, till he himself was wounded in the shoulder by a javelin; but he still was able by great exertions to bring off his brother, who was now pale with approaching death.

Both sides were nearly exhausted with the intolerable violence of the heat and the repeated conflicts, but at last the hostile battalions were driven back in great disorder. Then while we fell back to a greater distance, the Saracens were also compelled to retreat from fear of our infantry, but presently afterwards joining themselves to the Persian host, they attacked us again, with more safety to themselves for the purpose of carrying off the Roman baggage. But when they saw the emperor they again retreated upon their reserve.

After leaving this district we reached a village called Hucumbra, where we rested two days, procuring all kinds of provisions and abundance of corn, so that we moved on again after being refreshed beyond our hopes; all that the time would not allow us to take away we burnt. The next day the army was advancing more quietly, when the Persians unexpectedly fell upon our last division, to whom that day the duty fell of bringing up the rear, and would easily have slain all the men, had not our cavalry which happened to be at hand, the moment that they heard what was going on, hastened up, though scattered over the wide valley, and repulsed this dangerous attack, wounding all who had thus surprised them. In this skirmish fell Adaces, a noble satrap, who had formerly been sent as ambassador to the emperor

Constantius, and had been kindly received by him. The soldier who slew him brought his arms to Julian, and received the reward he deserved.

The same day one of our corps of cavalry, known as the third legion, was accused of having gradually given way, so that when the legions were on the point of breaking the enemy's line, they nearly broke the spirit of the whole army. And Julian, being justly indignant at this, deprived them of their standards, broke their spears, and condemned all those who were convicted of having misbehaved of marching among the baggage and prisoners; while their captain, the only one of their number who had behaved well, was appointed to the command of another squadron, the tribune of which was convicted of having shamefully left the field. And four other tribunes of companies were also cashiered for similar misconduct; for the emperor was contented with this moderate degree of punishment out of consideration for his impending difficulties.

Accordingly, having advanced seventy furlongs with very scanty supplies, the herbage and the corn being all burnt, each man saved for himself just as much of the grain or forage as he could snatch from the flames and carry. And having left this spot, when the army had arrived at the district called Haranx, near daybreak an immense multitude of Persians appeared, with Herenes, the captain of their cavalry, and two sons of the king, and many nobles. All the troops were clothed in steel, in such a way that their bodies were covered with strong plates, so that the hard joints of the armor fitted every limb of their bodies; and on their heads were effigies of human faces so accurately fitted, that their whole persons being covered with metal, the only place where any missiles which fell upon them could stick, was either where there were minute openings to allow of the sight of the eyes penetrating, or where holes for breathing were left at the extremities of the nostrils.

Part of them who were prepared to fight with pikes stood immovable, so that you might have fancied they were held in their places by fastenings of brass; and next to them the archers (in which art that nation has always been most skillful from the cradle) bent their supple bows with widely extended arms, so that the strings touched their right breasts, while the arrows lay just upon their left hands; and the whistling arrows flew, let loose with great skill of finger, bearing deadly wounds. Behind them stood the glittering elephants in formidable array, whose grim looks our terrified men could hardly endure; while the horses were still more alarmed at their growl, odor, and unwonted aspect.

Their drivers rode on them, and bore knives with handles fastened to their right hands, remembering the disaster which they had experienced at Nisibis; and if the ferocious animal overpowered his overseer, they pierced the spine where the head is joined to the neck with a vigorous blow, that the beast might not recoil upon their own ranks, as had happened on that occasion, and trample down their own people; for it was found out by Hasdrubal, the brother of Hannibal, that in this way these animals might be very easily deprived of life.

The sight of these beasts caused great alarm, and so this most intrepid emperor, attended with a strong body of his armed cohorts and many of his chief officers, as the crisis and the superior numbers of the enemy required, marshaled his troops in the form of a crescent with the wings bending inwards to encounter the enemy. And to hinder the onset of the archers from disordering our columns, by advancing with great speed he baffled the aim of their arrows; and after he had given the formal signal for fighting, the Roman infantry, in close order, beat back the front of the enemy with a vigorous effort.

The struggle was fierce, and the clashing of the shields, the din of the men, and the doleful whistle of the javelins, which continued without intermission, covered the plains with blood and corpses, the Persians falling in every direction; and though they were often slack in fighting, being accustomed chiefly to combat at a distance by means of missiles, still now foot to foot they made a stout resistance; and when they found any of their divisions giving way, they retreated like rain before the wind, still with showers of arrows seeking to deter their foes from pursuing them. So the Parthians were defeated by prodigious efforts, till our soldiers, exhausted by the heat of the day, on the signal for retreat being sounded, returned to their camp, encouraged for the future to greater deeds of daring. In this battle, as I have said, the loss of the Persians was very great—ours was very slight. But the most important death in our ranks was that of Vetranio, a gallant soldier who commanded the legion of Zianni.

2. After this there was an armistice for three days, while the men attended to their own wounds or those of their friends, during which we were destitute of supplies, and distressed by intolerable hunger; and since, as all the corn and forage was burnt, both men and cattle were in extreme danger of starvation, a portion of the food which the horses of the tribunes and superior officers were carrying was distributed among the lower classes of the soldiers, who were in extreme want. And the emperor, who had no royal dainties prepared for himself, but who was intending to sup under the props of a small tent on a scanty portion of pulse, such as would often have been despised by a prosperous common soldier, indifferent to his own comfort, distributed what was prepared for him among the poorest of his comrades.

He gave a short time to anxious and troubled sleep; and when he awoke, and, as was his custom, began to write something in his tent, in imitation of

Julius Caesar, while the night was still dark, being occupied with the consideration of the writings of some philosophers, he saw, as he told his friends, in
mournful guise, the vision of the Genius of the Empire, whom, when he first
became emperor, he had seen in Gaul, sorrowfully departing through the
curtains of his tent with the cornucopia, which he bore in his hand veiled, as
well as his head. And although for a moment he stood stupefied, yet being
above all fear, he commended the future to the will of heaven; and leaving his
bed, which was made on the ground, he rose, while it was still but little past
midnight, and supplicating the deities with sacred rites to avert misfortune,
he thought he saw a bright torch, falling, cut a passage through the air and
vanish from his sight; and then he was horror-stricken, fearing that the star of
Mars had appeared openly threatening him.

For this brightness was of the kind which we call *diaissonta*, not falling
down or reaching the ground. Indeed, he who thinks that solid substances
can fall from heaven is rightly accounted profane and mad. But these occur-
rences take place in many ways, of which it will be enough to enumerate a
few. Some think that sparks falling off from the ethereal fire, as they are able
to proceed but a short distance, soon become extinguished; or, perhaps, that
rays of fire coming against the dense clouds, sparkle from the suddenness of
the contact; or that some light attaches itself to a cloud, and taking the form
of a star, runs on as long as it is supported by the power of the fire; but being
presently exhausted by the magnitude of the space which it traverses, it
becomes dissolved into air, passing into that substance from the excessive
attrition of which it originally derived its heat.

Therefore, without loss of time, before daybreak, he sent for the Etruscan soothsayers, and consulted them what this new kind of star portended:
who replied, that he must cautiously avoid attempting any new enterprise at
present, showing that it was laid down in the works of Tarquitius, *On Divine
Affairs*, that when a light of this kind is seen in heaven, no battle ought to be
engaged in, or any similar measure be undertaken.

But as he despised this and many other similar warnings, the diviners at
least entreated him to delay his march for some hours; but they could not
prevail even to this extent, as the emperor was always opposed to the whole
science of divination. So at break of day the camp was struck.

3. When we set forward, the Persians, who had learnt by their frequent
defeats to shun pitched battles, laid secret ambuscades on our road, and,
occupying the hills on each side, continually reconnoitered our battalions as
they marched, so that our soldiers, being kept all day on the watch, could neither find time to erect ramparts round their camp, or to fortify themselves
with palisades. And while our flanks were strongly guarded, and the army
proceeded onward in as good order as the nature of the ground would allow,

being formed in squares, though not quite closed up, suddenly news was brought to the emperor, who had gone on unarmed to reconnoiter the ground in front, that our rear was attacked.

He, roused to anger by this mishap, without stopping to put on his breastplate, snatched up his shield in a hurry, and while hastening to support his rear, was recalled by fresh news that the van which he had quitted was now exposed to a similar attack. Without a thought of personal danger, he now hastened to strengthen this division, and then, on another side, a troop of Persian cuirassiers attacked his center, and pouring down with vehemence on his left wing, which began to give way, as our men could hardly bear up against the foul smell and horrid cries of the elephants they pressed us hard with spears and clouds of arrows.

The emperor flew to every part of the field where the danger was hottest; and our light-armed troops dashing out wounded the backs of the Persians, and the hocks of the animals, which were turned the other way. Julian, disregarding all care for his own safety, made signs by waving his hands, and shouted out that the enemy were fleeing in consternation; and cheering on his men to the pursuit, threw himself eagerly into the conflict. His guards called out to him from all sides to beware of the mass of fugitives who were scattered in consternation, as he would beware of the fall of an ill-built roof, when suddenly a cavalry spear, grazing the skin of his arm, pierced his side, and fixed itself in the bottom of his liver. He tried to pull it out with his right hand, and cut the sinews of his fingers with the double-edged point of the weapon; and, falling from his horse, he was borne with speed by the men around him to his tent, and the physician tried to relieve him.

Presently, when his pain was somewhat mitigated, so that his apprehensions were relieved, contending against death with great energy, he asked for arms and a horse, in order that, by revisiting his troops, who were still engaged, he might restore their confidence, and appear so secure of his own recovery as to have room for anxiety for the safety of others; with the same energy, though with a different object, with which the celebrated leader, Epaminondas, when he was mortally wounded at Mantinea, and had been borne out of the battle, asked anxiously for his shield; and when he saw it he died of his wound cheerfully, having been in fear for the loss of his shield, while quite fearless about the loss of his life.

But as Julian's strength was inferior to his firmness, and as he was weakened by the loss of blood, he remained without moving: and presently he gave up all hope of life; because, on inquiry, he found that the place where he had fallen was called Phrygia; for he had been assured by an oracle that he was destined to die in Phrygia. When he was brought back to his tent, it was marvelous with what eagerness the soldiers flew to avenge him, agitated with anger and sorrow; and striking their spears against their shields, determined to die if Fate so willed it. And although vast clouds of dust obscured their sight, and the burning heat hindered the activity of their movements, still, as if they were released from all military discipline by the loss of their chief, they rushed unshrinkingly on the enemy's swords.

On the other hand the Persians, fighting with increased spirit, shot forth such clouds of arrows, that we could hardly see the shooters through them; while the elephants, slowly marching in front, by the vast size of their bodies, and the formidable appearance of their crests, terrified alike our horses and our men. And far off was heard the clashing of armed men, the groans of the dying, the snorting of the horses, and the clang of swords, till both sides were weary of inflicting wounds, and the darkness of night put an end to the contest.

Fifty nobles and satraps of the Persians, with a vast number of the common soldiers, were slain; and among them, two of their principal generals, Merena and Nohodares. Let the grandiloquence of antiquity marvel at the twenty battles fought by Marcellus in different places; let it add Sicinius Dentatus, adorned with his mass of military crowns, let it further extol Sergius, who is said to have received twenty-three wounds in his different battles among whose posterity was that last Catiline, who tarnished the glories of his distinguished family by everlasting infamy.

But sorrow now overpowered the joy at this success. While the conflict was thus carried on after the withdrawal of the emperor, the right wing of the army was exhausted by its exertions; and Anatolius, at that time the master of the offices, was killed; Sallust the prefect was in imminent danger, and was saved only by the exertions of his attendant, so that at last he escaped, while Sophorius his counselor was killed; and certain soldiers, who, after great danger, had thrown themselves into a neighboring fort, were unable to rejoin the main army till three days afterwards.

And while these events were taking place, Julian, lying in his tent, thus addressed those who stood around him sorrowing and mourning: "The seasonable moment for my surrendering this life, O comrades, has now arrived, and, like an honest debtor, I exult in preparing to restore what nature reclaims; not in affliction and sorrow, since I have learnt, from the general teaching of philosophers, how much more capable of happiness the mind is than the body; and considering that when the better part is separated from the worse, it is a subject of joy rather than of mourning. Reflecting, also, that there have been instances in which even the gods have given to some persons of extreme piety, death as the best of all rewards.

"And I well know that it is intended as a gift of kindness to me, to save me from yielding to arduous difficulties, and from forgetting or losing myself; knowing by experience that all sorrows, while they triumph over the weak, flee before those who endure them manfully. Nor have I to repent of any actions, nor am I oppressed by the recollection of any grave crime, either when I was kept in the shade, and, as it were, in a corner, or after I arrived at the empire, which, as an honor conferred on me by the gods, I have preserved, as I believe, unstained. In civil affairs I have ruled with moderation and, whether carrying on offensive or defensive war, have always been under the influence of deliberate reason. Prosperity, however, does not always correspond to the wisdom of man's counsels, since the powers above reserve to themselves the regulation of results.

"But always keeping in mind that the aim of a just sovereign is the advantage and safety of his subjects, I have been always, as you know, inclined to peace, eradicating all licentiousness—that great corruptness of things and manners—by every part of my own conduct; and I am glad to feel that in whatever instances the republic, like an imperious mother, has exposed me deliberately to danger, I have stood firm, inured to brave all fortuitous disturbing events. Nor am I ashamed to confess that I have long known, from prophecy, that I should fall by the sword. And therefore do I venerate the everlasting God that I now die, not by any secret treachery, nor by a long or severe disease, or like a condemned criminal, but I quit the world with honor, fairly earned, in the midst of a career of flourishing glory. For to any impartial judge, that man is base and cowardly who seeks to die when he ought not, or who avoids death when it is seasonable for him.

"This is enough for me to say, since my strength is failing me; but I designedly forbear to speak of creating a new emperor, lest I should unintentionally pass over some worthy man; or, on the other hand, if I should name one whom I think proper, I should expose him to danger in the event of some one else being preferred. But, as an honest child of the republic, I hope that a good sovereign will be found to succeed me."

After having spoken quietly to this effect, he, as it were with the last effort of his pen, distributed his private property among his dearest friends, asking for Anatolius, the master of the offices. And when the prefect Sallust replied that he was now happy, he understood that he was slain, and bitterly bewailed the death of his friend, though he had so proudly disregarded his own. And as all around were weeping, he reproved them with still undiminished authority, saying that it was a humiliating thing to mourn for an emperor who was just united to heaven and the stars.

And as they then became silent, he entered into an intricate discussion with the philosophers Maximus and Priscus on the sublime nature of the soul, while the wound of his pierced side was gaping wide. At last the swelling of his veins began to choke his breath, and having drank some cold water, which he had asked for, he expired quietly about midnight, in the thirty-first year of his age. He was born at Constantinople, and in his childhood lost his father, Constantius, who, after the death of his brother Constantine, perished amid the crowd of competitors for the vacant crown. And at the same early age he lost his mother, Basilina, a woman descended from a long line of noble ancestors.

4. Julian was a man to be classed with heroic characters, and conspicuous for the brilliancy of his exploits and his innate majesty. For since, as wise men lay it down, there are four cardinal virtues—temperance, prudence, justice, and fortitude—with corresponding external accessories, such as military skill, authority, prosperity, and liberality, he eagerly cultivated them all as if they had been but one. And in the first place, he was of a chastity so inviolate that, after the loss of his wife he never indulged in any sexual pleasures, recollecting what is told in Plato of Sophocles the tragedian, that being asked when he was a very old man whether he still had any commerce with women, he said "No," with this further addition that "he was glad to say that he had at all times avoided such indulgence as a tyrannous and cruel master."

And to strengthen this resolution he often called to mind the words of the lyric poet Bacchylides, whom he used to read with pleasure, and who said that as a fine painter makes a handsome face, so chastity adorns a life that aims at greatness. And even when in the prime of life he so carefully avoided this taint that there was never the least suspicion of his becoming enamored even of any of his household, as has often happened. And this kind of temperance increased in him, being strengthened by a sparing indulgence in eating and sleeping, to which he rigidly adhered whether abroad or at home. For in time of peace his frugal allowance of food was a marvel to all who knew him, as resembling that of a man always wishing to resume the philosopher's cloak. And in his various campaigns he used commonly only to take a little plain food while standing, as is the custom of soldiers.

And when after being fatigued by labor he had refreshed his body with a short rest, as soon as he awoke he would go by himself round all the sentries and outposts; after which he retired to his serious studies. And if any voice could bear witness to his use of the nocturnal lamp, by which he pursued his lucubrations, it would show that there was a vast difference between some emperors and him, who did not even indulge himself in those pleasures permitted by the necessities of human nature.

Of his prudence there were also many proofs, of which it will be sufficient to recount a few. He was profoundly skilled in war, and also in the arts of peace. He was very attentive to courtesy, claiming just so much respect as he considered sufficient to mark the difference between contempt and insolence. He was older in virtue than in years, being eager to acquire all kinds of knowledge. He was a most incorruptible judge, a rigid censor of morals and manners, mild, a despiser of riches, and indeed of all mortal things. Lastly, it was a common saying of his, "That it was beneath a wise man, since he had a soul, to aim at acquiring praise by his body."

Of his justice there are many conspicuous proofs: first, because, with all proper regard to circumstances and persons, he inspired awe without being cruel; secondly; because he repressed vice by making examples of a few and also because he threatened severe punishment more frequently than he employed it. Lastly, to pass over many circumstances, it is certain that he treated with extreme moderation some who were openly convicted of plotting against him, and mitigated the rigor of the punishment to which they were sentenced with genuine humanity.

His many battles and constant wars displayed his fortitude, as did his endurance of extreme cold and heat. From a common soldier we require the services of the body, from an emperor those of the mind. But having boldly thrown himself into battle, he would slay a ferocious foe at a single blow; and more than once he by himself checked the retreat of our men at his own personal risk. And when he was putting down the rule of the furious Germans, and also in the scorching sands of Persia, he encouraged his men by fighting in the front ranks of his army.

Many well-known facts attest his skill in all that concerns a camp; his storming of cities and castles amid the most formidable dangers; the variety of his tactics for battles, the skill he showed in choosing healthy spots for his camps, the safe principles on which his lines of defense and outposts were managed.

So great was his authority, that while he was feared he was also greatly loved as his men's comrade in their perils and dangers. And in the hottest struggles he took notice of cowards for punishment. And while he was yet only Caesar, he kept his soldiers in order while confronting the barbarians, and destitute of pay as I have mentioned before. And haranguing his discontented troops the threat which he used was that he would retire into private life if they continued mutinous. Lastly, this single instance will do as well as many, by haranguing the Gallic legions, who were accustomed to the frozen Rhine, in a simple address, he persuaded them to traverse vast regions and to march through the warm plains of Assyria to the borders of Media.

His good fortune was so conspicuous that, riding as it were on the shoulders of Fortune, who was long his faithful guide, he overcame enormous difficulties in his victorious career. And after he quitted the regions of the west, they all remained quiet during his life-time, as if under the influence of a wand powerful enough to tranquilize the world.

Of his liberality there are many and undoubted proofs. Among which are his light exactions of tribute, his remission of the tribute of crowns, and of debts long due, his putting the rights of individuals on an equal footing with those of the treasury, his restoration of their revenues and their lands to different cities, with the exception of such as had been lawfully sold by former princes; and also the fact that he was never covetous of money, which he thought was better kept by its owners, often quoting the saying, "that Alexander the Great, when he was asked where he kept his treasures, kindly answered 'Among my friends.'"

Having discussed those of his good qualities which have come within our knowledge, let us now proceed to unfold his faults, though they have been already slightly noticed. He was of an unsteady disposition; but this fault he corrected by an excellent plan, allowing people to set him right when guilty of indiscretion. He was a frequent talker, rarely silent. Too much devoted to divination, so much so as in this particular to equal the emperor Hadrian. He was rather a superstitious than a legitimate observer of sacred rites, sacrificing countless numbers of victims; so that it was reckoned that if he had returned from the Parthians there would have been a scarcity of cattle. Like the celebrated case of Marcus Caesar, about whom it was written, as it is said, "The white cattle to Marcus Caesar, greeting. If you conquer there is an end of us."

He was very fond of the applause of the common people, and an immoderate seeker after praise even in the most trifling matters; often, from a desire of popularity, indulging in conversation with unworthy persons. But in spite of all this he deserved, as he used to say himself, to have it thought that that ancient Justice, whom Aratus says fled to heaven from disgust with the vices of men, had in his reign returned again to the earth; only that sometimes he acted arbitrarily and inconsistently.

For he made some laws which, with but few exceptions, were not offensive, though they very positively enforced or forbade certain actions. Among the exceptions was that cruel one which forbade Christian masters of rhetoric and grammar to teach unless they came over to the worship of the heathen gods. And this other ordinance was equally intolerable, namely one which allowed some persons to be unjustly enrolled in the companies of the municipal guilds, though they were foreigners, or by privilege or birth wholly unconnected with such companies.

As to his personal appearance it was this. He was of moderate stature, with soft hair, as if he had carefully dressed it, with a rough beard ending in a point, with beautiful brilliant eyes, which displayed the subtlety of his mind, with handsome eyebrows and a straight nose, a rather large mouth, with a drooping lower lip, a thick and stooping neck, large and broad shoulders. From head to foot he was straight and well proportioned, which made him strong and a good runner.

And since his detractors have accused him of provoking new wars, to the injury of the commonwealth, let them know the unquestionable truth, that it was not Julian but Constantius who occasioned the hostility of the Parthians by greedily acquiescing in the falsehoods of Metrodorus, as we have already set forth. In consequence of this conduct our armies were slain, numbers of our soldiers were taken prisoners, cities were razed, fortresses were stormed and destroyed, provinces were exhausted by heavy expenses and in short the Persians, putting their threats into effect, were led to seek to become masters of everything up to Bithynia and the shores of the Propontis.

While the Gallic wars grew more and more violent, the Germans overrunning our territories, and being on the point of forcing the passes of the Alps in order to invade Italy, there was nothing to be seen but tears and consternation, the recollection of the past being bitter, the expectation of the future still more woeful. All these nurseries, this youth, being sent into the West with the rank of Caesar, put an end to with marvelous celerity, treating the kings of those countries as base-born slaves. Then in order to re-establish the prosperity of the east, with similar energy he attacked the Persians, and would have gained in that country both a triumph and a surname, if the will of heaven had been in accordance with his glorious plans and actions.

And as we know by experience that some men are so rash and hasty that if conquered they return to battle, if shipwrecked, to the sea, in short, each to the difficulties by which he had been frequently overcome, so some find fault with this emperor for returning to similar exploits after having been repeatedly victorious.

BOOK XXXI 12–14

At the battle of Hadrianople in northern Greece (378 C.E.), for the first time a barbarian army defeats Roman legions in fixed battle. The emperor Valens dies on the battlefield.

12. At this time Valens was disturbed by a twofold anxiety, having learned that the people of Lintz had been defeated, and also because Sebastian, in the letters which he sent from time to time, exaggerated what had taken place by his pompous language. Therefore he advanced from Melanthias, being eager by some glorious exploit to equal his youthful nephew, by whose virtue he was greatly excited. He was at the head of a numerous force, neither unwarlike nor contemptible, and had united with them many veteran bands, among whom were several officers of high rank, especially Trajan, who a little while before had been commander of the forces.

And as by means of spies and observation it was ascertained that the enemy were intending to blockade the different roads by which the necessary supplies must come, with strong divisions, he sent a sufficient force to prevent this, dispatching a body of the archers of the infantry and a squadron of cavalry, with all speed, to occupy the narrow passes in the neighborhood. Three days afterwards, when the barbarians, who were advancing slowly, because they feared an attack in the unfavorable ground which they were traversing, arrived within fifteen miles from the station of Nice, which was the aim of their march, the emperor, with wanton impetuosity, resolved on attacking them instantly, because those who had been sent forward to reconnoiter (what led to such a mistake is unknown) affirmed that their entire body did not exceed ten thousand men.

Marching on with his army in battle array, he came near the suburb of Hadrianople, where he pitched his camp, strengthening it with a rampart of palisades, and then impatiently waited for Gratian. While here, Richomeres, Count of the Domestici, arrived, who had been sent on by that emperor with letters announcing his immediate approach. And imploring Valens to wait a little while for him that he might share his danger, and not rashly face the danger before him single handed, he took counsel with his officers as to what was best to be done. Some, following the advice of Sebastian, recommended with urgency that he should at once go forth to battle; while Victor, master-general of the cavalry, a Sarmatian by birth, but a man of slow and cautious temper, recommended him to wait for his imperial colleague, and this advice was supported by several other officers, who suggested that the reinforcement of the Gallic army would be likely to awe the fiery arrogance of the barbarians. However, the fatal obstinacy of the emperor prevailed, fortified by the flattery of some of the princes, who advised him to hasten with all speed, so that Gratian might have no share in a victory which, as they fancied, was already almost gained.

And while all necessary preparations were being made for the battle, a presbyter of the Christian religion (as he called himself), having been sent by Fritigern as his ambassador, came, with some colleagues of low rank, to the emperor's camp; and having been received with courtesy, he presented a letter from that chieftain, openly requesting that the emperor would grant to him and to his followers, who were now exiles from their native homes, from which they had been driven by the rapid invasions of savage nations, Thrace, with all its flocks and all its crops, for a habitation. And if Valens would consent to this, Fritigern would agree to a perpetual peace.

In addition to this message, the same Christian, as one acquainted with his commander's secrets, and well trusted, produced other secret letters from his chieftain who, being full of craft and every resource of deceit, informed Valens, as one who was hereafter to be his friend and ally, that he had no other means to appease the ferocity of his countrymen, or to induce them to accept conditions advantageous to the Roman state, unless from time to time he showed them an army under arms close at hand, and by frightening them with the name of the emperor, recalled them from their mischievous eagerness for fighting. The ambassadors retired unsuccessful, having been looked on as suspicious characters by the emperor.

When the day broke which the annals mark as the fifth of the Ides of August, the Roman standards were advanced with haste, the baggage having been placed close to the walls of Hadrianople, under a sufficient guard of soldiers of the legions, the treasures and the chief insignia of the emperor's rank were within the walls with the prefect and the principal members of the council. Then, having traversed the broken ground which divided the two armies, as the burning day was progressing towards noon, at last, after marching eight miles, our men came in sight of the wagons of the enemy, which had been stated by the scouts to be all arranged in a circle. According to their custom, the barbarian host raised a fierce and hideous yell, while the Roman generals marshaled their line of battle. The right wing of the cavalry was placed in front; the chief portion of the infantry was kept in reserve. But the left wing of the cavalry, of which a considerable number were still straggling on the road, were advancing with speed, though with great difficulty; and while his wing was deploying, not as yet meeting with any obstacle, the barbarians being alarmed at the terrible clang of their arms and the threatening crash of their shields (since a large portion of their own army was still at a distance, under Alatheus and Saphrax, and, though bent for, had not yet arrived), again sent ambassadors to ask for peace.

The emperor was offended at the lowness of their rank, and replied, that if they wished to make a lasting treaty, they must send him nobles of sufficient dignity. They designedly delayed, in order by the fallacious truce which subsisted during the negotiation to give time to their cavalry to return, whom they looked upon as close at hand; and for our soldiers, already suffering from the summer heat, to become parched and exhausted by the conflagration of the vast plain; as the enemy had, with this object, set fire to the crops by means of burning faggots and fuel. To this evil another was added, that both men and cattle were suffering from extreme hunger.

In the meantime Fritigern, being skillful in divining the future, and fearing a doubtful struggle, of his own head sent one of his men as a herald, requesting that some nobles and picked men should at once be sent to him as hostages for his safety, when he himself would fearlessly bring us both military aid and supplies. The proposition of this formidable chief was received with praise and approbation, and the tribune Equitius, a relation of Valens, who was at that time high steward of the palace, was appointed, with general consent, to go with all speed to the barbarians as a hostage. But he refused, because he had once been taken prisoner by the enemy, and had escaped from Dibaltum, so that he feared their vengeful anger; upon this Richomeres voluntarily offered himself, and willingly undertook to go, thinking it a bold action, and one becoming a brave man; and so he set out, bearing vouchers of his rank and high birth. And as he was on his v ay towards the enemy's camp, the accompanying archers and Scutarii, who on that occasion were under the command of Bacurina, a native of Iberia, and of Cassio, yielded, while on their march, to an indiscreet impetuosity, and on approaching the enemy, first attacked them rashly, and then by a cowardly flight disgraced the beginning of the campaign.

This ill-timed attack frustrated the willing services of Richomeres, as he was not permitted to proceed; in the meantime the cavalry of the Goths had returned with Alatheus and Saphrax, and with them a battalion of Alani these descending from the mountains like a thunderbolt spread confusion and slaughter among all whom in their rapid charge they came across.

13. And while arms and missiles of all kinds were meeting in fierce conflict, and Bellona, blowing her mournful trumpet, was raging more fiercely than usual, to inflict disaster on the Romans, our men began to retreat; but presently, roused by the reproaches of their officers, they made a fresh stand, and the battle increased like a conflagration, terrifying our soldiers, numbers of whom were pierced by strokes from the javelins hurled at them, and from arrows. Then the two lines of battle dashed against each other, like the beaks (or rams) of ships, and thrusting with all their might, were tossed to and fro, like the waves of the sea. Our left wing had advanced actually up to the wagons, with the intent to push on still further if they were properly supported; but they were deserted by the rest of the cavalry, and so pressed upon by the superior numbers of the enemy, that they were overwhelmed and beaten down, like the ruin of a vast rampart. Presently our infantry also was left unsupported, while the different companies became so huddled together that a soldier could hardly draw his sword, or withdraw his hand after he had once stretched it out. And by this time such clouds of dust arose that it was scarcely possible to see the sky, which resounded with horrible cries; and in consequence, the darts, which were bearing death on every side, reached their mark, and fell with deadly effect, because no one could see them beforehand so as to guard against them.

But when the barbarians, rushing on with their enormous host, beat down our horses and men, and left no spot to which our ranks could fall back to deploy, while they were so closely packed that it was impossible to escape by forcing a way through them, our men at last began to despise death, and again took to their swords and slew all they encountered, while with mutual blows of battle-axes, helmets and breastplates were dashed in pieces. Then you might see the barbarian towering in his fierceness, hissing or shouting, fall with his legs pierced through, or his right hand cut off, sword and all, or his side transfixed, and still, in the last gasp of life, casting round him defiant glances. The plain was covered with carcasses, strewing the mutual ruin of the combatants; while the groans of the dying, or of men fearfully wounded, were intense, and caused great dismay all around.

Amidst all this great tumult and confusion our infantry were exhausted by toil and danger, till at last they had neither strength left to fight, nor spirits to plan anything; their spears were broken by the frequent collisions, so that they were forced to content themselves with their drawn swords, which they thrust into the dense battalions of the enemy, disregarding their own safety, and seeing that every possibility of escape was cut off from them. The ground, covered with streams of blood, made their feet slip so that all that they endeavored to do was to sell their lives as dearly as possible; and with such vehemence did they resist their enemies who pressed on them, that some were even killed by their own weapons. At last one black pool of blood disfigured everything, and wherever the eye turned, it could see nothing but piled-up heaps of dead, and lifeless corpses trampled on without mercy.

The sun being now high in the heavens, having traversed the sign of Leo, and reached the abode of the heavenly Virgo, scorched the Romans, who were emaciated by hunger, worn out with toil, and scarcely able to support even the weight of their armor. At last our columns were entirely beaten back by the overpowering weight of the barbarians, and so they took to disorderly flight, which is the only resource in extremity, each man trying to save himself as well as he could. While they were all flying and scattering themselves over roads with which they were unacquainted, the emperor, bewildered with terrible fear, made his way over heaps of dead, and fled to the battalions of the Lancearri and the Mattiarii, who, till the superior numbers of the enemy became wholly irresistible, stood firm and immovable. As soon as he saw him, Trajan exclaimed that all hope was lost, unless the emperor, thus deserted by his guards, could be protected by the aid of his foreign allies.

When this exclamation was heard, a count named Victor hastened to bring up with all speed the Batavians, who were placed in the reserve, and who ought to have been near at hand, to the emperor's assistance; but as none of them could be found, he too retreated, and in a similar manner Richomeres and Saturninus saved themselves from danger.

So now, with rage flashing in their eyes, the barbarians pursued our men, who were in a state of torpor, the warmth of their veins having deserted them. Many were slain without knowing who smote them; some were overwhelmed by the mere weight of the crowd which pressed upon them; and some were slain by wounds inflicted by their own comrades. The barbarians spared neither those who yielded nor those who resisted. Besides these, many half slain lay blocking up the roads, unable to endure the torture of their wounds; and heaps of dead horses were piled up and filled the plain with their carcasses. At last a dark moonless night put an end to the irremediable disaster which cost the Roman state so dear.

Just when it first became dark, the emperor being among a crowd of common soldiers, as it was believed—for no one said either that he had seen him, or been near him—was mortally wounded with an arrow, and, very shortly after, died, though his body was never found. For as some of the enemy loitered for a long time about the field in order to plunder the dead, none of the defeated army or of the inhabitants ventured to go to them. A similar fate befell the Caesar Decius, when fighting vigorously against the barbarians; for he was thrown by his horse falling, which he had been unable to hold, and was plunged into a swamp, out of which he could never emerge, nor could his body be found.

Others report that Valens did not die immediately, but that he was borne by a small body of picked soldiers and eunuchs to a cabin in the neighborhood, which was strongly built, with two stories; and that while these unskillful hands were tending his wounds, the cottage was surrounded by the enemy, though they did not know who was in it; still, however, he was saved from the disgrace of being made a prisoner. For when his pursuers, while vainly attempting to force the barred doors, were assailed with arrows from the roof, they, not to lose by so inconvenient a delay the opportunity of collecting plunder, gathered some faggots and stubble, and setting fire to them, burnt down the building, with those who were in it.

But one of the soldiers dropped from the windows, and, being taken prisoner by the barbarians, revealed to them what had taken place, which caused them great concern, because they looked upon themselves as defrauded of great glory in not having taken the ruler of the Roman state alive. This same young man afterwards secretly returned to our people, and gave this account of the affair.

When Spain had been recovered after a similar disaster, we are told that one of the Scipios was lost in a fire, the tower in which he had taken refuge having been burnt. At all events it is certain that neither Scipio nor Valens enjoyed that last honor of the dead—a regular funeral.

Many illustrious men fell in this disastrous defeat, and among them one of the most remarkable was Trajan, and another was Sebastian, there perished also thirty-five tribunes who had no particular command, many captains of battalions, and Valerianus and Equitius, one of whom was master of the horse and the other high steward. Potentius, too, tribune of the promoted officers, fell in the flower of his age, a man respected by all persons of virtue, and recommended by the merits of his father, Ursicinus, who had formerly been commander of the forces, as well as by his own. Scarcely one-third of the whole army escaped. Nor, except the battle of Cannae, is so destructive a slaughter recorded in our annals; though, even in the times of their prosperity, the Romans have more than once had to deplore the uncertainty of war, and have for a time succumbed to evil Fortune; while the well-known dirges of the Greeks have bewailed many disastrous battles.

14. Such was the death of Valens, when he was about fifty years old, and had reigned rather less than fourteen years. We will now describe his virtues, which were known to many, and his vices. He was a faithful and steady friend —a severe chastiser of ambition—a rigid upholder of both military and civil discipline—always careful that no one should assume importance on account of any relationship to himself; slow both in conferring office, and in taking it away; a very just ruler of the provinces, all of which he protected from injury, as if each had been his own house; devoting singular care to the lessening the burdens of the state, and never permitting any increase of taxation. He was very moderate in the exaction of debts due to the state, but a vehement and implacable foe to all thieves, and to everyone convicted of peculations; nor in affairs of this kind was the East, by its own confession, ever better treated under any other emperor.

Besides all this, he was liberal with due regard to moderation, of which quality there are many examples, one of which it will be sufficient to mention here: As in palaces there are always some persons covetous of the possessions of others, if any one petitioned for lapsed property, or anything else which it was usual to apply for, he made a proper distinction between just and unjust claims, and when he gave it to the petitioner, while reserving full liberty to any one to raise objections, he often associated the successful candidate with three or four partners, in order that those covetous suitors might conduct themselves with more moderation, when they saw the profits for which they were so eager diminished by this device.

Of the edifices, which in the different cities and towns he either repaired or built from their foundations, I will say nothing (to avoid prolixity), allowing those things to speak for themselves. These qualities, in my opinion, deserve the imitation of all good men.

Now let us enumerate his vices. He was an immoderate coveter of great wealth; impatient of labor, he affected an extreme severity, and was too much inclined to cruelty, his behavior was rude and rough, and he was little imbued with skill either in war or in the liberal arts. He willingly sought profit and advantage in the miseries of others, and was more than ever intolerable in straining ordinary offenses into sedition or treason; he cruelly encompassed the death or ruin of wealthy nobles. This also was unendurable, that while he wished to have it appear that all actions and suits were decided according to the law, and while the investigation of such affairs was delegated to judges especially selected as the most proper to decide them, he still would not allow any decision to be given which was contrary to his own pleasure. He was also insulting, passionate, and always willing to listen to all informers, without the least distinction as to whether the charges which they advanced were true or false. And this vice is one very much to be dreaded, even in private affairs of everyday occurrence. He was dilatory and sluggish; of a swarthy complexion; had a cast in one eye, a blemish, however, which was not visible at a distance; his limbs were well set; his figure was neither tall nor short; he was knock-kneed, and rather pot-bellied.

This is enough to say about Valens: and the recollection of his contemporaries will fully testify that this account is a true one. But we must not omit to mention that when he had learnt that the oracle of the tripod, which we have related to have been moved by Patricius and Hilanus, contained those three prophetic lines, the last of which is,

"Repelling murd'rous war in Mimas' plain;"

—he, being void of accomplishments and illiterate, despised them at first; but as his calamities increased, he became filled with abject fear, and, from a recollection of this same prophecy, began to dread the very name of Asia, where he had been informed by learned men that both Homer and Cicero had spoken of the Mountain of Mimas over the town of Erythrae.

Lastly, after his death, and the departure of the enemy, it is said that a monument was found near the spot where he is believed to have died, with a stone fixed into it inscribed with Greek characters, indicating that some ancient noble of the name of Mimas was buried there.

SELECT BIBLIOGRAPHY

For those interested in reading more extensively in the historians in this collection, one or more translations are listed in **boldface** for each author. The Loeb Classical Library, published by the Harvard University Press, contains volumes on all these authors with Latin (or Greek) text and English translation on facing pages. This select bibliography also includes important general books which might help in understanding the historians and their histories. Books marked with an * are currently available in paperback.

Roman Historiography - General

Dorey, T.A. (ed.) *Roman Historians* (London, 1966)
*Grant, M. *The Ancient Historians* (London, 1970)
*Laistner, M. *The Greater Roman Historians* (Berkeley, 1947)
*Mellor, R. *The Roman Historians* (New York, 1999)

Polybius

*Polybius *The Rise of the Roman Empire* (tr. I. Scott-Kilvert) Penguin Books
Sachs, K. *Polybius on the Writing of History* Classical Studies vol. 24 (Berkeley, 1981)
Walbank, F. *Polybius* (Berkeley, 1972)

Appian

*Appian *The Civil Wars* (tr. John Carter) Penguin Books
Gowing, A.M. *The Triumviral Narratives of Appian and Cassius Dio* (Ann Arbor, 1993)

Julius Caesar

*Caesar *The Conquest of Gaul* (tr. S.A. Hanford) Penguin Books
*Caesar *The Civil War* (tr. J. Gardner) Penguin Books
Adcock, F. *Julius Caesar as Man of Letters* (Cambridge, 1956)
Meier, C. *Caesar: A Biography* (New York, 1982)

Sallust

*Sallust *Jugurthine War & Conspiracy of Catiline* (tr. S.A. Hanford) Penguin Books
Earl, D.C. *The Political Thought of Sallust* (Cambridge, 1961)
Syme, R. *Sallust* (Berkeley, 1964)

Livy

*Livy *The Early History of Rome* (Books 1–5) (tr. A. de Selincourt) Penguin Books

*Livy *Rome and Italy* (Books 6–10) (tr. B. Radice) Penguin Books
*Livy *The War with Hannibal* (Books 21–30) (tr. A. de Selincourt) Penguin Books
*Livy *Rome and the Mediterranean* (Books 31–45) (tr. H. Bettenson) Penguin Books
Dorey, T. (ed.) *Livy* (London, 1970)
Luce, T.J. *Livy The Composition of his History* (Princeton, 1983)
Walsh, P.J. *Livy: His Historical Aims and Methods* (Cambridge, 1961)

Augustus

*Brunt, P. & Moore, J.M. (edd.) *Res Gestae Divi Augusti* (Oxford, 1967)
*Jones, A.H.M. *Augustus* (New York, 1970)
*Miller, F. & Segal, E. *Augustus: Seven Essays*

Suetonius

*Suetonius *The Twelve Caesars* (tr. R. Graves) Penguin Books
*Wallace-Hadrill, A. *Suetonius: The Scholar and His Caesars* (London, 1983)

Tacitus

*Tacitus *The Annals of Imperial Rome* (tr. M. Grant) Penguin Books
*Tacitus *The Histories* (tr. K. Wellesley) Penguin Books
*Tacitus *The Agricola* and *The Germania* (tr. H. Mattingly) Penguin Books
*Martin, R. *Tacitus* (London, 1981)
*Mellor, R. *Tacitus* (New York, 1993)
Mellor, R. *Tacitus: The Classical Heritage* (New York, 1995)
Syme, R. *Tacitus* (Oxford, 1958)

Augustan History

Lives of the Later Caesars (tr. A. Birley) Penguin Books
Syme, R. *Ammianus and the Historia Augusta* (Oxford, 1968)
Syme, R. *Emperors and Biography: Studies in the Historia Augusta* (Oxford, 1971)

Ammianus Marcellinus

*Ammianus Marcellinus *The Later Roman Empire* (tr. W. Hamilton) Penguin Books
Matthews, J. *The Roman Empire of Ammianus* (London, 1989)
Barbes, T.D. *Ammianus Marcellinus and the Representation of Historical Reality* (Cornell, 1998)